Symbols

Signs and their Meaning
and Uses in Design

Second Edition

ARNOLD WHITTICK

Charles T. Branford Company
Newton, Massachusetts 02159

First published by
Leonard Hill Books
A division of
International Textbook Company Ltd.
158 Buckingham Palace Road
London SW1

This edition published by
Charles T. Branford Company
Newton, Massachusetts 02159

First U.S. edition 1960
New U.S. edition 1971

SBN 8231–1019–2

Printed in Great Britain

*To the memory of my father John Whittick, 1863–1953,
who first stimulated my interest in many of the things
of which I have written in this book.*

Preface to the Second Edition

ADDITIONS to this second edition include Chapter XI on Postage Stamps, the enlargement of Chapter XVIII on Architecture, the inclusion in several chapters of designs of the sixties, and forty-three further symbols described in the Encyclopaedic Dictionary. Many of the additions are of architectural symbols, including oriental examples, and they make Part IV a little more comprehensive. A central, but not exclusive, theme in choosing these additions is visual symbolism that exists and could be used in the architectural and graphic arts.

In spite of the reasons given in the preface to the first edition for the arrangement of the parts, a change has been made in this second edition so that the former Part IV becomes Part III, and Part III becomes Part IV, thus with the more customary arrangement of the Encyclopaedia at the end.

I have to thank the Royal Mint, the British Post Office, the British Museum, the Victoria and Albert Museum, the Arts Council of Great Britain, the Postmaster General of the United States, the Department of the Air Force of the United States, the Government of India, the United Nations Office at Geneva, and Mr. Paul Vincze for their kindness in supplying photographs to illustrate the additional material.

Crawley   ARNOLD WHITTICK

September 1971

Preface to the First Edition

THIS work is designed partly to entertain the curiosity of the general reader, partly for the practical purpose of assisting designers and artists who use symbols in their work, and wish to use them correctly, and for those who are interested in various forms of symbolic expression.

A word of explanation is perhaps necessary of the arrangement of the parts. It was felt that Part II, which is devoted to the more precise and practical application of symbolism, should be followed by an encyclopaedic dictionary of traditional and familiar symbols; and that the part dealing with symbolism which is inherent in the forms of life and art, and that created by artists as a means of expression, should be separate as a more speculative aspect of the subject. To have placed the dictionary at the end would have been more customary, but would have had less the virtue of logical sequence.

The vastness of the subject has made it necessary to impose limitations on the scope of the book. I have, therefore, confined the study to visual symbols and symbolism and mainly to Western uses and examples, including only the better known Oriental examples. Sound symbolism, involving music and much of literature, is outside the scope of the work except in its closer associations with visual symbolism.

These studies have occupied much of my leisure time for many years. In 1935 some results of my earlier study were published in a small volume entitled *Symbols for Designers* which has been out of print since 1939. Some items from that work have been incorporated in Part III.

There are surprisingly few general books on visual symbolism, and much of the available information is scattered among numerous books on a wide variety of subjects. I must express my indebtedness to their authors, many of whom led me to original sources. They are mentioned in the references or in the bibliographical note. I must also express thanks to the many who have assisted me with information and illustrations: to the staffs of the various departments of the British Museum, of the Royal Mint, and of the Imperial War Museum; to the London Embassies of the U.S.A., France, Italy, Spain, Western Germany and the Scandinavian Countries; to the staffs of the High Commissioners of Australia, Canada, New Zealand and South Africa; and to the Secretaries of the states of the U.S.A. Finally, I am grateful to Mr. Wilfred Salter for many helpful suggestions.

Beckenham
January, 1960

ARNOLD WHITTICK

Table of Contents

PART I—INTRODUCTION

I The meaning and types of symbolism   3

PART II—SYMBOLISM IN ITS PRECISE AND
APPLIED FORMS, AND ITS PRACTICAL USES—
IDENTIFICATION, AUTHENTICATION, EXCHANGE,
GUARANTEE AND PROPAGANDA

II Totems, standards and flags   15
III Coats of arms and military badges   21
IV Seals   36
V Civic heraldry   60
VI Coins   74
VII Medals   81
VIII Trademarks   87
IX Shop and inn signs   96
X Pictorial advertising   104
XI Postage stamps   112

PART III—INDIVIDUAL AND COLLECTIVE
EXPRESSION—INSTINCTIVE, CREATIVE AND
IMAGINATIVE SYMBOLISM

XII Instinctive and unconscious symbolism   125
XIII Religious symbolism   130
XIV National and state symbolism   137
XV Symbolism in art   140
XVI The dance, gesture and the ceremonies of everyday life   149
XVII Dress   154
XVIII Architecture   166
XIX Sculpture   174

XX Painting 180

XXI Drama—the theatre and cinema 185

PART IV—ENCYCLOPAEDIC DICTIONARY

XXII Traditional and familiar symbols, their origin, meaning and history 193

Bibliographical note 355

Index 359

List of Plates

I Totem poles: (*a*) Totem pole from Haida, Queen Charlotte Island; (*b*) Totem pole from the village of Angyada, Nass river, British Columbia

II The Queen's Beasts: (*a*) The Lion of England; (*b*) The Unicorn of Scotland; (*c*) The White Horse of Hanover

III The Queen's Beasts: (*a*) The Greyhound of the Tudors; (*b*) The Dragon of the Tudors; (*c*) The Bull of Clarence

IV The Queen's Beasts: (*a*) The White Lion of Mortimer; (*b*) The Yale of the Beauforts; (*c*) The Falcon of the Plantagenets; (*d*) The Griffin of Edward III

V Seals of English sovereigns: (*a, b*) The first seal of Edward the Confessor; (*c, d*) The first seal of William I; (*e, f*) The first great seal of Henry III

VI Seals of English sovereigns: (*a*) The second seal of Richard I; (*b*) The second seal of Elizabeth I

VII (*a*) The second seal of the Commonwealth; (*b*) The fifth seal of George III; (*c*) The seal of George V

VIII The seal of Elizabeth II

IX Greek symbolic coins

X Coins showing representations of Britannia: (*a*) Nero; (*b*) Hadrian; (*c*) Antoninus Pius; (*d*) Charles II; (*e*) George IV; (*f*) George III

XI British coins: (*a*) Gold angel of Edward IV; (*b*) Gold George noble of Henry VIII; (*c*) Coins of George VI, 1951

XII (*a*) Elizabeth II coins, 1953; (*b*) Decimal coinage

XIII (*a*) Bahama Island coins, 1966; (*b*) Gambia coins, 1966; (*c*) Ghana coins, 1966

XIV (*a*) New Zealand coins, 1966; (*b*) Tanzania coins, 1966

XV (*a*) Irish Republic 10s., 1966; (*b*) Singapore coins, 1967; (*c*) Fiji coins, 1968

XVI Symbolic medals: (*a*) Cecilia Gonzaga; (*b*) Vittorina da Feltre; (*c*) Elizabeth I; (*d*) Charles I

XVII Coronation medals: (*a*) Edward VI; (*b*) Charles I; (*c*) Charles II

XVIII Coronation medals: (*a*) William and Mary; (*b*) George I; (*c*) Victoria

XIX   Symbolic medals: (*a*) International Fisheries Exhibition; (*b*) Johannes Gutenberg; (*c*) Andrew W. Mellon; (*d*) Mond Nickel Company

XX   Modern medals: (*a*) Ashanti 1901; (*b*) Second World War; (*c*) Observer Corps; (*d*) Korea; (*e*) Ministry of Housing

XXI   (*a*) Housing medal, 1962; (*b*) Mullard medal, 1967; (*c*) Royal Numismatic Society of New Zealand medal, 1966

XXII   Shop signs: (*a*) Shoemaker; (*b*) Three loaves; (*c*) Clothiers; (*d*) Bakers

XXIII   Bank, insurance and old adopted signs in the City of London: (*a*) Barclays Bank; (*b*) Martins Bank; (*c*) Scottish Widows Fund and Life Assurance Society; (*d*) Commercial Bank of Scotland; (*e*) Cornhill Insurance Co. Ltd.; (*f*) Lloyds Bank

XXIV   Modern inn signs: (*a*) Brewer's Delight, Canterbury; (*b*) Duke of York, Cranbrook; (*c*) Rose and Crown, East Grinstead; (*d*) The Queen's Head, Westminster

XXV   Modern inn signs: (*a*) The Ordinary Fellow, Chatham; (*b*) Clothworkers' Arms, Sutton Valance; (*c*) Sportsman's Inn, Barnsley; (*d*) Coach and Horses, Fenny Bentley

XXVI   Modern inn signs: (*a*) The North Pole, Wateringbury; (*b*) The Anchor, Stowting; (*c*) Nag's Head, St. Leonards; (*d*) Startled Saint, West Malling

XXVII   Four British Railway posters

XXVIII   London Transport posters: (*a*) and (*b*) Symbolism by association; (*c*) War-time poster; (*d*) Poster based on familiar saying

XXIX   *The Times*, British Railway and Capstan cigarette posters

XXX   Pictorial advertising. Two I.C.I. advertisements: (*a*) Shrink fit; (*b*) Cuckoo in the nest

XXXI   British postage stamps of George VI's reign up to 1948

XXXII   British commemorative stamps 1951–58

XXXIII   British commemorative stamps 1960–63

XXXIV   British commemorative stamps 1964–65

XXXV   British commemorative stamps 1966–69

XXXVI   U.S.A. symbolic postage stamps 1957–65

XXXVII   United Nations stamps

XXXVIII   United Nations stamps

XXXIX   American symbolic state flowers

XL   American symbolic state flowers

XLI   Symbolism in architecture—precise symbolism in which alpha and omega form the elevation of the campanile and the plan of the Lutheran church of the Holy Trinity at Hamburg. Architect: Reinhard Riemerschmid

XLII   Symbolism in architecture: (*a*) Interior of Amiens Cathedral; (*b*) The Parthenon, Athens

XLIII   Symbolism in architecture: (*a*) The spire of Salisbury Cathedral; (*b*) Interior of the dome of St. Paul's Cathedral

XLIV   Symbolism in architecture: (*a*) Ronchamp Chapel, 1954; Architect: Le Corbusier; (*b*) Pont du Gard; (*c*) Hornsey Town Hall, 1933 Architect: Reginald H. Uren

XLV Symbolism in architecture: (*a*) The Church of the Advent, Copenhagen, 1947; Architect: Erik Moller; (*b*) Liverpool Cathedral, 1967; Architect: Sir Frederic Gibberd

XLVI Symbolical sculpture: (*a*) Memorial which marks the spot where the armistice of the First World War was signed; (*b*) Memorial seat to Margaret MacDonald; (*c*) Sculpture in the grounds of the Shell building at The Hague

XLVII Symbolical sculpture: The Medici tombs by Michelangelo. (*a*) Tomb of Lorenzo de Medici with figures of 'Twilight' and 'Dawn'; (*b*) Tomb of Guiliano de Medici with figures of 'Night' and 'Day'

XLVIII Symbolical sculpture: (*a*) Mourning woman, Greek of the fourth century B.C.; (*b*) Warrior with shield by Henry Moore; (*c*) The sun-worshipper by Alex Ebbe

XLIX (*a*) and (*b*) Symbolic sculptures of 'Night' and 'Day' by Sir Jacob Epstein on the London Passenger Transport building

L Abstract sculpture of an organic character with symbolical expression

LI Abstract sculpture of an organic character with symbolical expression

LII Abstract sculpture of a geometric or mechanical character with symbolical expression

LIII Abstract sculpture of a geometric or mechanical character with symbolical expression

LIV Pictures in which the infant Christ and the birth of Christianity are seen against a background of classical ruins: (*a*) The Adoration of the Kings by Mabuse; (*b*) Adoration of the Magi by Veronese; (*c*) The Virgin and Child, attributed to Durer

LV Symbolism by expression of space in pictures: (*a*) The Resurrection by Piero della Francesca; (*b*) The Virgin and Child with angel by Perugino; (*c*) The Crucifixion by Raphael

LVI Symbolism by linear rhythms: (*a*) 'Pieta' by an unknown painter of Avignon; (*b*) 'Primavera' by Botticelli

LVII Symbolism in painting by abstracted shapes, emotional rhythms and dream objects: (*a*) Comedy by Paul Klee; (*b*) Girls on a bridge by Edward Munch; (*c*) Landscape from a dream by Paul Nash

LVIII Angels in pictorial art: The Palmieri altar-piece, Assumption of the Virgin by Botticini

LIX Symbolism of the apple and angels in pictorial art: (*a*) Sculpture in wood of the Madonna and child with the symbol of the apple; (*b*) Elijah in the Wilderness by Lord Leighton

LX (*a*) Christ of St. John of the Cross by Salvador Dali; (*b*) The Crucifixion by Velasquez

LXI (*a*) Axe shown on Cretan pot of about 2000 B.C.; (*b*) Palmette shown on Cretan pot of about 2000 B.C.; (*c*) War Memorial, Leicester

LXII Caduceus. Bronze entrance doors to the Bank of England designed by Sir Herbert Baker and A. T. Scott

LXIII Caduceus: (*a*) Bronze caduceus of the fifth century; (*b*) Bronze statue of Mercury by Giovanni da Bologna

LXIV   (*a*) The Cenotaph; (*b*)–(*e*) Some fountains of Rome; (*f*) American War Memorial Fountain

LXV   Columns: (*a*) Lion Gate, Mycenae; (*b*) Trajan's Column, Rome; (*c*) American Meuse Argonne Memorial at Montfaucon

LXVI   (*a*) Greek stele in the Dipylon cemetery at Athens with the handshake as symbol of farewell; (*b*) Griffins on the temple of Didyma; (*c*) Gorgon's head on the temple of Didyma

LXVII   (*a*) Mitre, Cardinal's hat; (*b*) Papal Tiara; (*c*) Turkish stelec surmounted by hats

LXVIII   Stained glass window in Newbiggen church, Newcastle, designed by S. M. Scott, showing a profusion of symbols

LXIX   (*a*) Obelisk: Washington Memorial; (*b*) Chinese pottery lion

LXX   (*a*) Gods of Olympus and their symbols and emblems; (*b*) Relief of Artemis; (*c*) Menorah

LXXI   (*a*) Sarcophagus of Theodore, Bishop of Ravenna, in the Basilica of St. Apollinare in Classe, Ravenna; (*b*) Mosaic of Christ enthroned with angels, in the Basilica of St. Apollinare Nuovo, Ravenna

LXXII   (*a*) Ring cross with sacred monogram, alpha and omega, pelican and its young and tree of life; (*b*) Virgin and Child by di Camaino; (*c*) Carving of pelican and its young

LXXIII   Statue of the Good Shepherd from the catacombs of St. Callistus

LXXIV   (*a*) Torch; (*b*) Aesculapius; (*c*) Rattlesnake

LXXV   (*a*) Twin Buddhist Stupas at Sanchi, India; (*b*) Buddhist Stupa inside a cave temple at Ajanta, India

LXXVI   (*a*) Malayan Nensan; (*b*) Three grave memorials in Malacca near a fig tree

LXXVII   (*a*) Stone memorial at Kirkcaldy, Fife, in which early Christian symbolism is freely used; (*b*) Roman cinerary urn to the memory of P. Octavius Secundus; (*c*) Wheel of the Doctrine with crouching deer; (*d*) Memorial headstone in Amberley churchyard

LXXVIII   (*a*) Signs of the zodiac forming decorative balcony fronts of modern building in Salzburg; (*b*) Signs of zodiac medals for American Numismatic Association

List of Figures

1 Early versions of the Royal Arms: (*a*) Richard I; (*b*) Edward III; (*c*) The second of Edward III; (*d*) Henry V   22

2 The Royal Arms: (*a*) Edward IV; (*b*) Henry VII   24

3 The Royal Arms of Queen Anne   24

4 Military Badges: (*a*) Queen's West Surrey Regiment; (*b*) The Buffs, The East Kent Regiment; (*c*) 3rd The King's Own Hussars; (*d*) The York and Lancaster Regiment; (*e*) The Gloucestershire Regiment; (*f*) The South Wales Borderers   26

5 Military Badges: (*a*) Royal Warwickshire Regiment; (*b*) The Royal Corps of Signals; (*c*) The Royal Army Medical Corps; (*d*) The Royal Army Veterinary Corps; (*e*) The Parachute Regiment   28

6 Divisional and formation signs: (*a*) Supreme Headquarters, Allied Expeditionary Force; (*b*) Allied Land Force, South East Asia; (*c*) Headquarters of the Supreme Allied Command, South East Asia; (*d*) Northern Home Command; (*e*) Third Army Corps; (*f*) Second Army Corps; (*g*) Ninth Army; (*h*) First Army   30

7 Divisional and formation signs: (*a*) Eleventh Armoured Division; (*b*) Second Armoured Division; (*c*) First Anti-Aircraft Command; (*d*) First Anti-Aircraft Corps; (*e*) First Anti-Aircraft Division (London); (*f*) Fifth Anti-Aircraft Division; (*g*) Second Anti-Aircraft Division; (*h*) Tenth Army   32

8 Divisional and formation signs: (*a*) Fifty-sixth (London) Division; (*b*) Forty-seventh (London) Division; (*c*) Forty-sixth (North Midland) Division; (*d*) Forty-ninth (West Riding) Division; (*e*) Airborne Division; (*f*) Seventy-seventh Division   33

9 Badges of the Sixth, Ninth, Fourteenth, Seventeenth, Eighteenth, Nineteenth, Twenty-first and Twenty-second American Air Forces   34

10 Great Seal of the U.S.A.: obverse and reverse   43

11 State Seals of the U.S.A.: Delaware, New Jersey, Pennsylvania— (obverse and reverse)   44

12 State Seals of the U.S.A.: Georgia (obverse and reverse), Connecticut, Massachusetts — 45

13 State Seals of the U.S.A.: Maryland (obverse and reverse), South Carolina, New Hampshire — 46

14 State Seals of the U.S.A.: Virginia (obverse and reverse), New York, North Carolina — 47

15 State Seals of the U.S.A.: Rhode Island, Vermont, Kentucky, Tennessee — 48

16 State Seals of the U.S.A.: Ohio, Louisiana, Indiana, Mississippi — 49

17 State Seals of the U.S.A: Illinois, Alabama, Maine, Missouri — 50

18 State Seals of the U.S.A.: Arkansas, Michigan, Florida, Texas — 51

19 State Seals of the U.S.A.: Iowa, Wisconsin, California, Minnesota — 52

20 State Seals of the U.S.A.: Oregon, Kansas, West Virginia (obverse and reverse) — 53

21 State Seals of the U.S.A.: Nevada, Nebraska, Colorado, North Dakota — 54

22 State Seals of the U.S.A.: South Dakota, Montana, Washington, Idaho — 55

23 State Seals of the U.S.A.: Wyoming, Utah, Oklahoma, New Mexico — 56

24 State Seals of the U.S.A.: Arizona, Alaska, Hawaii, District of Columbia — 57

25 Civic Heraldry—Coats of Arms of Boston, Droitwich, Leeds and Bristol — 62

26 Civic Heraldry—Coats of Arms of City of London and Liverpool — 63

27 Civic Heraldry—Coats of Arms of Barnsley, Bury, Leicestershire and Morley — 65

28 Civic Heraldry—Coats of Arms of Rawtenstall, Widnes, Swindon and Bromley — 67

29 Civic Heraldry—Coats of Arms of Cardiff, Stoke-on-Trent, Buxton and Beckenham — 68–9

30 Civic Heraldry—Coats of Arms of Stevenage, Crawley, Hemel Hempstead and Harlow — 70

31 Civic Heraldry—Coats of Arms of Basildon, Bracknell, Newton Aycliffe and Peterlee — 71

32 Civic Heraldry—Coats of Arms of East Kilbride, Glenrothes and Corby. Badge of Cwmbran — 72

33 Symbolic trade marks by means of a rebus: John Drummond and Sons Ltd., Littlewoods Mail Order Stores Ltd., Martineau's Ltd., Burman and Greenwood Ltd., Frank Starkey Ltd., Webster & Co. (Fernbank) Ltd. — 88

34 Trade mark symbols by association: Ford Motor Co. Ltd., Gillett and Johnston Ltd., J. A. Phillips & Co. Ltd., Old Roundhegions Association, Vine Products Ltd. — 89

35 Trade mark symbols by association: The British Lubricating Research Organization Ltd., Air Survey Co. Ltd., James Powell & Sons (Whitefriars) Ltd., O. Kavli Akheselshrap, Elliott Equipment Ltd. — 90

36 Trade mark symbols by analogy: Thermocontrol Installations Co. Ltd., Elastica Ltd., Ducksback Ltd., Albert V. Martin — 93

37 Trade mark symbols by analogy: Xavier Giralt Ltd., Cuprinol Ltd., Eldorado Ice Cream Co. Ltd., Thwaites Engineering Co. Ltd., H. L. Savory & Co. Ltd. — 94

38 Pictorial advertising by analogy: First time does it — 107

39 Analogous symbolism in advertising—rigid flexibility 110

40 (a) Ankh held in the hand of the Fire-goddess Sekhmet; (b) Modified copy of an 1829 model of an anchor; (c) Chalice and host derived from a fifteenth-century Italian specimen 205

41 Forms of the Cross: (a) Equilateral; (b) Equilateral diagonal; (c) Tau; (d) Latin; (e) Double Latin; (f) Cross Patée; (g) Maltese cross 225

42 (a) Winged disk from the Temple of Edfou; (b) Bas-reliefs of dolphins from the catacombs of St. Callistus 230

43 (a) English mediaeval use of the fish symbol; (b) Regular hexagram: Shield of David; (c) Symbolic eye from painted bedhead 242

44 (a) Fasces, from a stone relief of about A.D. 100 from Ephesus; (b) Four variations of the fleur-de-lis 244

45 (a) Hour glass with wings from a tomb in Père Lachaise, Paris; (b) Scythes with hour glass from a headstone dated 1763; (c) and (d) Two types of lyre common in ancient Greece 259

46 (a) Pascal Lamb from monstrance in Aix-le-Chapelle Cathedral; (b) Egyptian lotus water lilies 262

47 (a) White or Madonna Lily; (b) Lily of the Valley 266

48 (a) and (b) Terra cotta lamps from the San Giovanni catacombs at Syracuse; (c) Pottery lamp of the fifth century A.D. with representation of lion; (d) Palm and sacred monogram on lamp from San Giovanni catacombs at Syracuse 268

49 (a) Bay laurel; (b) Olive; (c) Myrtle 278

50 (a)–(e) Principal forms of the Constantinian monogram; (f) Sacred monogram with alpha and omega, circle of eternity and s, probably denoting Saviour 281

51 Passion flower 292

52 (a) Representation of the Phoenix from the design used by the Phoenix Assurance Co.; (b) Conventional rendering of the Pelican and its Young from the policy heading of the Old Pelican Assurance Co. 295

53 (a) Rosemary; (b) The dog rose 304

54 (a) Bas-relief of the figure of Time with the scythe, skull and hour glass; (b) Granite scarab of the sixteenth Egyptian dynasty; (c) Swastika; (d) The Nazi form of the swastika 308

55 (a) An old shop sign with representation of the sunflower; (b) Common marigold 312

56 (a) Wheel cross; (b) Ring cross; (d) Archbishop's cross in Addington churchyard showing Christ as the Good Shepherd with serpent 327

57 (a) and (b) Two mediaeval sepulchral slabs showing the association of the cross with the sacred tree; (c) Unicorn resting its head on a Virgin's lap 338

58 (a) Narcissus; (b) Dog violet 346

PART I

INTRODUCTION

I The Meaning and Types of Symbolism

THE process of man's development beyond mere animal existence has been achieved partly by his ability to use and invent symbols. Communication depends on the symbolism of language, and thus man becomes aware of another's thought by means of symbols. By language, combined with his propensity to dream, plan and speculate, man extends his thought beyond his own time and place, a detachment indispensable to the enlargement of his activities. 'By this act of detachment and abstraction,' says Lewis Mumford, 'man gained the power of dealing with the non-present, the unseen, the remote, and the internal: not merely his visible lair and his daily companions, but his ancestors and his descendants and the sun and the moon and the stars: eventually the concepts of eternity and infinity, of electron and universe: he reduced a thousand potential occasions in all their variety and flux to a single symbol that indicated what was common to them all.'[1] Carlyle felt the dependence of civilization on symbolism when he said in *Sartor Resartus* that 'it is in and through symbols that man, consciously or unconsciously, lives, works and has his being'.[2]

All social and economic activities are carried on by means of symbols; the various offshoots and adjuncts of language, like numbers and money, make this apparent. Religious worship and government, too, are dependent on them. A. N. Whitehead, in his valuable book on Symbolism, shows that society is held together by acceptance of, and reverence for, its symbols.[3] Knowledge, following perception, has a symbolic structure, and the vast realm of instinctive and unconscious symbolism investigated in modern psychology has further added to its importance in modern thought.

The concept of symbolism can be taken even further, for the whole of the external world can be thought of as symbolism, the meaning of which is unknown and matter for religious speculation. However, for more practical purposes it is desirable to restrict the sense to the symbols created by man, whether entirely conscious, partly conscious or largely unconscious, as in the case of dreams, and to the symbolism involved in perception.

'Symbol' is a generic term, and in the modern sense includes all that is meant by a sign, mark or token. In philosophy, psychology, sociology and art it is regarded as that which stands for something else. The Greek word σύμβολον from which the term symbol is derived, appears to have meant a bringing together, and this meaning is the logical antecedent of the modern meaning, for symbolism is a bringing together of ideas and objects, one of which expresses the other. The symbol is either an object that stands for another object, or an object that stands for an idea.

Dependence on symbols is most effectively demonstrated by language, both spoken and written, in which sounds, letters, and names are signs for things. Thought cannot progress far without its subjects being named. The name of an object creates an image of that object by remembered association of the name with the object, and it is impossible to think of many objects in relation to each other, or of objects acting on each other, without naming them. Max Müller[4] contended that without language, or signs that correspond to language, thought is impossible. This may be carrying the importance of symbolism a little too far. It is true that instinctive emotion and action can hardly be regarded as thought, at least in its logical and purposeful sense, but if we accept the theory of biological evolution, thought emerges from instinctive emotion, and in the stage between this and language there must have been conception of objects without naming them, for the need of naming them beyond instinctive sounds is evidence of the existence of thought before language. The birth of language would answer this need—a need that may be defined as the feeling that no great advance can be made in thinking about objects without naming them.

Language probably arose in the first place from instinctive sounds. Cries of grief, fright, joy, affection, anger, triumph are the most primitive. These sounds would be associated with the things that aroused such emotions, like wild animals, thunder and lightning, fighting, sexual excitement and maternal affection—the sounds varying in kind and intensity according to the emotions and the objects that excited them. Thus, these sounds became symbols of the emotions and objects, to be used as the vehicle of thought about them, and led the way to the naming of objects and ideas for the purpose of communication.

From the available evidence the symbolism of written language appears to have begun by the representation of objects, and then in the expression of abstract ideas by the combination of objects. The best examples of symbolism of this kind originating a written language are to be found in the early pictography of China. It is more helpful than ancient Egyptian script, for although in both the signs for concrete objects were conventional and summary representations of the objects, the development to the expression of abstract ideas in Chinese was by means of true picture symbolism, whereas in Egyptian it was by the association of sounds. If in Egyptian the sounds for a concrete object and an abstract idea were almost the same, then the abstract idea would be denoted by the same picture. The ankh or *crux ansata*, the hieroglyph for life, and thus the famous Egyptian symbol of life, is thought to owe its shape to the similarity between the sounds for life and for a sandal strap, of which it is a conventional drawing. A study of Egptian hieroglyphs will reveal numerous further examples.[5]

Most forms of what are known as traditional signs and symbols of a religious and social character expressing abstract ideas, like a crown, symbol of glory; an hour-glass symbol of time; pelican and young and phoenix, symbols of resurrection; peacock of pride; ring of marriage; serpent and owl, symbols of wisdom; swastika and triscele, symbols of revival; and most of the symbols included in Part IV of this book, are of a similar kind to this early picture writing of China.

4

Symbols may be conveniently divided into four classes:

(1) Symbolism of a concrete object or group of objects by approximate or conventional imitation, and of a part of an object to represent the whole.

(2) Symbolism of an idea, activity, occupation, or custom by an object associated with it.

(3) Symbolism of an idea by an object which by its nature, analogous character, function or purpose suggests the idea.

(4) Symbolism of an idea by the relationship of two or more objects.

There is a further type, exceedingly important in artistic expression, which may be added here to complete the list of types, and will be discussed in the chapters on the various arts:

(5) Symbolism of an idea or concrete object by shapes incorporated in the design which suggest or express the idea or object.

In ancient Chinese, concrete objects were denoted by conventional drawings (greatly summarized in modern Chinese). In expressing abstract ideas, the Egyptian method of using the sign of an object which in speech has a sound similar to that denoting the idea was, in a few instances, followed in Chinese. The sun, moon, fire and animals are all almost recognizable drawings. Water is shown as flowing, using a character which is similar to that denoting a stream or river. Rain is depicted by drops of water falling from heaven. Man, woman and child were also represented by conventional drawings.

As pictures of objects, Egyptian hieroglyphs are better, as they are nearer to the original picture-writing, whereas most of the ancient Chinese is the work of scholars after the burning of the books by the Emperor Ts'in Shihuang-ti in 213 B.C. These scholars wrote the script from memory. Probably the script had already been greatly conventionalized and, according to recent authorities, originated between 2500 and 2000 B.C.

In ancient Chinese, associational symbolism occurs when music is denoted by a drum and bells on a stand—which also denote joy. Food and drink are denoted by the vessels to contain them; work is denoted by a carpenter's square; and walking by a footpath. In the third class, in which the idea is symbolized by the nature of the object, 'beautiful' is denoted by a big sheep. 'Height' is symbolized by a tower. Chinese, however, is richest where modern symbolism is poorest; that is, in the symbolism by relationship of objects. These symbols are called compound characters, and some of them are very apt. 'Happy' is expressed by a woman and child; 'peace' or 'rest' by a house, heart and cup; 'anxious' by a heart in a window; and 'dangerous' by a man with one leg over a precipice.[6]

Today the types defined in the first four classes are used in objects connected with state and religious ceremonies; in the regalia of monarchs; in ecclesiastical furnishing; in advertising; for seals, badges, stamps, coins; and in objects of a more commemorative nature, like public and cemetery monuments, and medals and sports trophies, such as cups and shields.

The chief modern examples of the first type are the crucifix and all conventional, as distinct from realistically representational, religious figures.

All idealized religious figures are clearly symbolic, even the statues of the Greek gods, which, though made with a realistic intention, and becoming so real to the

Greek worshippers that the gods were actually thought of as dwelling within them, they were nevertheless the symbols of the Greeks' ideas of their gods. As most of the Greek gods represented the elements—Apollo the sun, Artemis the moon, Demeter the earth—the representations were in some degree symbolic of their functions.

How far can the distinction between reproduction, imitation and realistic representation, on the one hand, and approximate or conventional representation (which includes idealistic representation) on the other, be logically maintained? Nobody, for example, regards realistic portraiture as symbolism in the ordinary sense (although it may be in another aesthetic sense as I hope to show in the chapter on symbolism in art), yet when that portraiture becomes conventionalized it may become symbolism. In the Oxford Dictionary a symbol is defined as 'standing for, representing or denoting something else', but not, it is added, 'by exact resemblance, but by vague suggestion, or by some accidental or conventional relation'. A realistic painting of a fish would not commonly be regarded as symbolic, but four incised lines on a stone vase suggesting a fish might be so regarded. At what point does the representation cease to be a realistic rendering and become sufficiently conventional or vague to enter the class of symbolism? The answer would appear to be when the two objects have become sufficiently different to have little sense of visual identity and become dissimilar things having a common quality.

This characteristic of visual symbolism appears to have a deep instinctive origin. It is an expression of man's adaptation to his environment. When man migrates to unfamiliar surroundings, he desires, in answer to the instinct of self-preservation, to feel as much at his ease as possible. He is thus impelled to find in his unfamiliar surroundings likenesses to things familiar to him, and in unfamiliar objects he perceives qualities similar to remembered qualities of familiar objects. It is strongly apparent in a child's perception. A child perceives a particular quality in an object that interests him and he gives that quality a name. When perceiving the same quality in other objects it is *that* which interests him in those objects, and they therefore receive the same name. It is one expression of the initial mode of perception when qualities in objects, or, in Bertrand Russell's term, 'entities', are perceived, and by unconscious reference to the memory the object is constructed from those qualities. It might be suggested, therefore, that the origin of a common type of visual symbolism is a desire to find likenesses in dissimilar things, which may be the outcome of an instinctive craving for unity and order.

Many examples of the second and third types of symbols will readily occur on a little reflection; some of them will be found in the present work. The cross is perhaps the most widespread example of the second type. Objects with a particular commemorative purpose, like medals, provide numerous examples of this associative symbolism—a typical modern example being the aeroplane on the reverse of the Houston Mount Everest Flight Expedition medal, presented by *The Times*.

Trade marks, badges of societies, clubs, and insurance companies often have symbols of this kind. The badge of the 'Beefsteak Club', designed in 1810, has a gridiron in the centre of a circle. The badge of the Farming Society of Ireland, designed about 1806, has a handplough, and the old Farmers' Union Insurance Company had a wheatsheaf on its badge. Postage stamps commemorating important anniversaries provide excellent examples of this associative symbolism.

6

An example of associational symbolism of a type similar to the *crux ansata* as a symbol of life, is the choice of devices in heraldry because of the similarity between sounds for objects and family names. Obvious instances of puns of this character are trumpets on the coat of arms of the Trumpington family, and falcons for the Fauconer family, but many are less obvious, as when the gold dances (dancette) on blue represents the sparkling waves in the De la Ryver coat of arms.[7]

Of the third type, the lotus, phoenix and pelican are among the best traditional examples, and modern designs, often in advertising, present some original examples.

Examples of the fourth type are rare. The dragon or serpent among avens foliage in Gothic carving, and the many symbols of Christ's crucifixion are hardly good examples, certainly not comparable with the excellent examples of ancient Chinese script.

The fifth type, defined as the symbol of an idea or concrete object by shapes incorporated in design which suggest or express the idea or the object, exists widely in various forms of visual art. Human gestures which are used to express objects or ideas are of this kind, and may, consciously or unconsciously, promote this symbolic content in a design. It affects the general character of works of art, and is particularly conspicuous in the dance and architecture. Its presence in sculpture and painting, if less apparent, is often an important factor in design. It will be considered in the chapters on the arts.

The terms emblem and symbol are sometimes used in the same sense, but it is desirable to observe a distinction between them. The term emblem is derived from the Greek word ’εμβλημα meaning a thing put on, or ’εμβάλλειν meaning to throw in. The sense of a thing put on explains its use. It is a sign or symbol attached to something. Thus we speak of the emblems of the Saints, most of whom are represented with some object traditionally associated with them, which thus become their emblems. The eagle is both a symbol and an emblem of St. John: when it is represented with him it is as an emblem; alone, it stands for him as a symbol. The key is an emblem of St. Peter, and it is sometimes shown separately as his symbol.

In the common traditional forms of conscious symbolism the purpose of symbols is to enhance the value of what is symbolized. The other forms of symbolism briefly indicated at the beginning of this chapter are of a more obscure yet no less important kind.

Symbolism forms part of the theory of sense perception in the philosophy of organic unity associated mainly with A. N. Whitehead and his followers. The theory is of some significance in modern realist philosophy. The world as we perceive it consists of coloured shapes and sounds, which are for us the symbols of meanings that lie behind these appearances. They are the effects of causes. This perception of coloured shapes and sounds is a characteristic of high grade organisms, and is termed by Whitehead as 'presentational immediacy'.

The other mode of perception which informs the percipient of the nature of things, and which corresponds to the meanings behind appearances, is direct and gives cognizance of what Whitehead terms 'causal efficacy'. This direct perception is a characteristic of low grade organisms.

In our perception the appearance of objects is referred to experience and thus we become aware of their causal efficacy. The process is termed symbolic reference.

Simply stated: we look and perceive a coloured shape; we refer this coloured shape to a store of images in our mind, and we are then conscious of, say, a chair. This symbolic reference may be wrong, as it sometimes is when we are tired or the mind is fevered. In such conditions perceptions in a dim light might prompt all kinds of fantastic interpretations.

The problem that this theory seeks to solve is the old problem of causation. In the sceptic philosophy of Hume and his followers the perception of a coloured shape or a sound is all we really perceive. Hume was sceptical of the theory of causation, and contended that we cannot say that the impressions we have are produced, logically, by causes. At most we associate impressions and the thought or ideas about these impressions, but we cannot say that they are cause and effect. We cannot say that they are any more than an unrelated sequence. Whitehead seeks to refute this by his theory of conformation. Hume's idea of time as mere sequence or succession he regards as fallacious. Time is, he maintains, conformation of present to past and of future to present. This theory of conformation or causation, apart from direct perception, explains how we think by symbolic reference from presentational immediacy to causal efficacy—from the coloured shape to the import of the object.

Awareness of the external world is also produced by the perceiving individual being part of what is perceived and vice versa. This is stronger in low grade organisms than in high. In the latter the separation gradually occurs, but is never quite complete. The separation from environment is, for example, stronger in man than in insects and animals. Testimony of this is provided by animal reaction to changes in that environment, such as changes of weather. But it is possible that we have not wholly lost direct perception, and to an extent we experience the two modes of perception together, because we often act instinctively in response to external stimulus of which we have had apparently no previous experience, although it is difficult to obtain evidence of reaction of this kind to environment.

Presentational immediacy, which is the mode of perception belonging to high grade organisms, is largely an abstraction of qualities of objects. These qualities are the special interest of the artist and the aesthetic vision. They are symbols, and when used and created anew by the artist, they are also symbolic of the individual artist's character.

The importance of Whitehead's theory of symbolism for most practical matters is described in the final chapter of his thesis on the *Uses of Symbolism*.[3] Society expresses itself by symbols, which are manifest in the ceremonies attending national and local government, its institutions, rites, customs, and habits. The power of this symbolism varies with the society, and the gist of his argument is that while veneration for its symbolism plays an important part in the preservation of a society, a constant inquiry into the meanings of the symbolism and frequent revisions indicates progress. He concludes with the profound utterance that 'those societies which cannot combine reverence to their symbols with freedom of revision, must ultimately decay, either from anarchy, or from the slow atrophy of a life stifled by useless shadows'.

Whitehead maintains that the appearance of things are the symbols which convey us by means of our remembered experiences to the world of reality. To repeat the argument in Whitehead's terminology, we are taken by symbolic reference from presentational immediacy to causal efficacy, which corresponds to reality.

8

The thought of many modern physicists appears to lead to the position that the appearances are shadows or symbols, and that we cannot know the reality behind these symbols; that is, we know the symbols which make up the visual world, but we can never know their meanings. Sir Arthur Eddington speaks of the physicist's world as one of symbols, and contrasts it with the familiar world. The materials of the physicist—aether, electrons, quanta, potentials, Hamiltonian functions—are all symbols. 'In the world of physics', he says, 'we watch a shadowgraph performance of the drama of familiar life. The shadow of my elbow rests on the shadow table as the shadow ink flows over the shadow paper. It is all symbolic, and as a symbol the physicist leaves it. Then comes the alchemist Mind who transmutes the symbols. The sparsely spread nuclei of electric force become a tangible solid; their restless agitation becomes the warmth of summer; the octave of aethereal vibrations becomes a gorgeous rainbow. Nor does the alchemy stop here. In the transmuted world new significances arise which are scarcely to be traced in the world of symbols; so that it becomes a world of beauty and purpose—and, alas, suffering and evil.'[8] It will be noted that the symbols of physics are transmuted by the mind into the familiar world, and it may be presumed that they are just transmuted symbols existing also as symbols in the familiar world, although Eddington speaks of significances. But the significances are clearly in no sense the meaning of the symbols, or, in other words, the reality behind appearances, but rather the response of the human emotions. Wordsworth's:

> My heart leaps up when I behold
> A rainbow in the sky:

is the emotional response to the rainbow as an appearance in the familiar world and not to the scientific conception of the octave of aethereal vibrations. There are really two ways of regarding the same symbol, and mankind will probably never know whether the meaning can be reached by science or by the response of the human heart.

Sir James Jeans[9] follows a line of thought similar to that of Eddington, and he cites Plato's famous simile that begins the seventh book of the Republic. We are asked to imagine men living in an underground cave, which has a mouth open towards the light and reaching all along the cave; here they have been from their childhood, and have their legs and necks chained so that they cannot move, and can only see before them, being prevented by the chains from turning their heads. Above and behind them a fire is blazing at a distance, and between the fire and the prisoners there is a raised way, and a low wall built along the way. Men pass along this wall carrying all sorts of vessels, and statues and figures of animals made of wood and stone, and various materials, which appear over the wall. The chained men see only their own shadows, or the other shadows which the fire throws on the opposite wall of the cave.

According to Jeans the physical world to us is like the shadows on the wall to these chained men in the cave. 'We are', he says, 'still imprisoned in our cave, with our backs to the light, and can only watch the shadows on the wall.' He had said previously that 'the pictures which science now draws of nature, and which alone seem capable of according with observational fact, are mathematical pictures', and he adds that 'most scientists would agree that they are nothing more than pictures—fictions, if you like, if by fiction you mean that science is not yet in contact with ultimate reality'. These pictures are Eddington's symbols, and from such speculations we can only deduce that according to these modern physicists the physical world is but a symbol of reality, the nature of which we have no means of ascertaining. It is a view that is closely akin to that of the philosophical idealist.

As is well known, symbolism occupies a prominent place in psycho-analytic theory. Such symbolism is mainly unconscious, and its importance is such that it merits a brief account, which is given in Chapter XII.

The English writer who has perhaps devoted most study to the subject is Dr. Ernest Jones.[10] Dr. Jones would like to limit the term symbolism to unconscious symbolism. He proposes the term metaphor for the other general types of symbolism. The distinction between the two classes of symbols is that in general conscious symbolism the symbol is employed to enhance the value of what is symbolized, and in unconscious symbolism, revealed by psycho-analysis, the symbol comes into existence with the function of concealing the meaning, as a substitute for something repugnant.

Dr. J. C. Flügel[11] speaks of these two classes of symbolism as pre-conscious and unconscious. In the former, which is fairly precise, there is no difficulty in bringing the meaning to consciousness. The emotional elements in the two kinds of symbolism are also very different, for in unconscious symbolism the emotional value of what is symbolized is greater than that of the symbol, in conscious symbolism the emotional value of the symbol is greater. This is true of the unconscious symbolism, but only partly so, I think, of conscious symbolism.

Flügel gives the example of the serpent which in unconscious symbolism symbolizes the phallus, and in conscious symbolism, wisdom; and he suggests that the emotion engendered by phallus is stronger than that engendered by serpent, whereas the emotion engendered by serpent is stronger than that engendered by wisdom. In the case of a national flag, like the Union Jack, the symbol may not be of greater emotional value than what is symbolized, yet it serves to excite that emotion, which may partly be the same thing.

Referring to Ernest Jones's proposed restriction of the term to what he calls 'true symbolism' and the substitution of the term metaphor for other symbolism, Flügel remarks that it seems doubtful whether it will be possible or even desirable thus to narrow the meaning of symbol, and Flügel suggests the term 'crystophor' for unconscious symbolism.

It might be helpful to distinguish these two main kinds of symbolism by a special adjective in the case of unconscious symbolism, but whether they are conscious or unconscious, and whether the emotion aroused by the thing symbolized or by the symbol is greater, they are both essentially symbolism in conforming to the essential conditions that one thing, for the purpose of expression, stands for another.

The difficulty of using the term 'metaphor' is that it is mainly linguistic in its application. 'Simile' is really closer to symbol, because the complete image of one thing standing for another is clearly expressed, as in the famous lines of Shakespeare's sonnet:

> Like as the waves make toward the pebbled shore
> So do our minutes hasten to their end.

10

This is complete symbolism. When such imagery becomes metaphor half the simile is assumed in the compression, as in Shelley's string of metaphors in *Love's Philosophy*:

> See the mountains kiss high Heaven
> And the waves clasp one another;
> No sister-flower would be forgiven
> If it disdained its brother;
> And the sunlight clasps the earth
> And the moon beams kiss the sea.

Metaphors, when they have been used for many generations and become a current part of language, are apt to lose their vividness, and many have by various stages become so merged in common speech that they are no longer recognized as such. Ernest Jones refers to what philologists call the decay of the metaphor, and indicates the three stages of this decay, in the final stage of which the word has become so merged in language that we are no longer aware that it is a metaphor. The very linguistic motive of metaphor, and the circumstance that it is so interwoven in the texture of language, and not always discernible, rather precludes its substitution for the term 'symbol', especially since the latter is used in the visual arts. 'Simile' is better, but its meaning is too restricted to be used as a substitute for conscious symbolism. Simile means the selection of similitude in different things, whereas symbolism, although comprehending this, means other things as well such as symbolism by association. The cross is the chief symbol of Christianity, but it is hardly a simile, and although it can be used as a metaphor, its sense would be more restricted than the meaning that is given to it when it stands on the altar of a Christian church.

REFERENCES

1. LEWIS MUMFORD, *The Conduct of Life*, p. 41 (London, 1951).
2. THOMAS CARLYLE, *Sartor Resartus*. Chapter on 'Symbols' (London, 1836).
3. A. N. WHITEHEAD, *Symbolism: Its Meaning and Effect* (Cambridge, 1928).
4. MAX MÜLLER, *The Science of Thought*, pp. 51–60 (London, 1887).
5. A. H. GARDINER, *Egyptian Grammar* (Oxford, 1927).
6. These examples are taken from *Sound and Symbol in Chinese*, by BERNHARD KARLGREN (London, 1923). This interesting work is recommended to students of symbolism.
7. See: ANTHONY WAGNER, *Heraldry in England*, p. 12 (London, 1946).
8. SIR ARTHUR EDDINGTON, *The Nature of the Physical World*. Introduction (London, 1928).
9. SIR JAMES JEANS, *The Mysterious Universe*. Mainly the last chapter: 'Into the Deep Waters' (Cambridge, 1930).
10. DR. ERNEST JONES, 'The Theory of Symbolism' in *Papers on Psycho-analysis*, (1st edition, London, 1912; 5th edition, 1948).
11. DR. J. C. FLÜGEL, *An Introduction to Psycho-analysis*, pp. 61–2 (London, 1932).

PART II

SYMBOLISM IN ITS PRECISE AND APPLIED FORMS AND ITS PRACTICAL USES—IDENTIFICATION, AUTHENTICATION, EXCHANGE, GUARANTEE, AND PROPAGANDA

II   Totems, Standards and Flags

THE life of both primitive and civilized communities is divided into groups of various kinds. In modern Christian society the principal, though smallest, group is the family. There are the geographical groups of parish, village, town, county, nation, which are often held together by emotions as strong as those that bind the family. There are also the functional classifications for religious, educational, economic and recreational activities. In times of war, or in preparedness for defence, there are the further divisions for military purposes. All these different groups merge into each other, although for purposes of analysis they can be kept separate. They are characteristic of a modern state whether it be a democracy or a dictatorship, and have emerged from the social classifications of mediaeval feudalism, where the essential group beyond the family was that of serfs and tenants under a feudal lord. The tenants, in return for the land which they held and by which they derived their livelihood, owed allegiance to their feudal lord and served under him in times of war.

In primitive societies the groups are somewhat different. In these the clan is all-important, and family groups, if they exist as entities in the modern sense, are generally subservient to the clan. In many tribes the totem group, which has its own conditions, is the binding power and is fundamental.

These various groups, into which both primitive and civilized communities appear to be naturally and inevitably divided, employ marks, badges and signs, symbols, in short, by which they are identified and by which they are held together. These symbols are generally first employed for the utilitarian purpose of identification, but after a time they often evoke by association feelings of devotion and pride, like a nation's flags or military badges.

In the social and economic intercourse between individuals and groups, food, clothing and the other necessities and luxuries of life are obtained, basically, by means of exchange. One man produces clothes for his fellows, who in return produce for him the other necessities of life. As Plato says in the *Republic* (Book II) 'It was to produce this exchange that the community was formed and the town, city and State founded.' To effect this exchange in a community tokens or symbols came into being. Buying and selling, by which a society functions economically, is accomplished by means of these tokens or symbols of exchange. 'If a man come with his produce into the market,'

15

says Plato, 'at a time when none of those who wish to make an exchange with him is there, is he to leave his occupation and wait in the market place?' That is impossible if a community is to exist, expand and prosper, so tokens are given in exchange for goods, and these tokens purchase for, say, the producer of clothes, the other necessities of life. Thus these symbols of exchange are fundamental in the organization of a state. To authenticate the symbols, they are marked with signs or representations—further symbols in fact. It is necessary to go over this rather elementary ground in order to make quite clear the symbolism of money, and thus of coins.

The need to authenticate agreements and ownership of property brings into being other tokens or symbols. Among the oldest of these symbols of authentication are seals attached to documents, and although in modern communities authentication by signature largely replaces seals they are still used for State purposes, and for important documents.

In social, commercial and military activities we thus have—in addition to the fundamental symbolism of communication—three principal kinds of symbols: symbols of identification, of exchange and of authentication. To these might perhaps be added symbols of status, honour and achievement, but these could strictly be comprehended in a wide application of authentication.

Among the symbols of identification are totems among primitive peoples; flags; military badges; coats of arms and the modern heraldry of divisional signs and formation badges; shop and inn signs. The signs used in commerce, such as trade marks, are symbols, partly of identification and partly of authentication, while postage stamps are authenticated receipts affixed to a written message to indicate that payment for the service of transmission has been made. Seals are symbols of authentication, and in this category it is logical also to place badges and insignia of rank. Medals are symbols of honour and achievement, but also in a sense of authentication.

It is proposed firstly to consider some of the principal symbols of identification, such as the totems, flags, coats of arms and military badges; then, symbols of authentication and exchange, such as seals, coins and medals and postage stamps. Finally commercial symbols of identification and authentication, like shop and inn signs and trade marks, are considered, and the symbolism of propaganda, such as diagrammatic and pictorial advertising.

The Totem

The earliest and most primitive form of a group badge appears to be the totem. The origin of totemism is still a mystery. Various anthropologists have given explanations which are all conjectural. Some, among them Herbert Spencer[1] and Andrew Lang,[2] consider that totemism originates from the naming of individuals after animals, and that the name extended to the individual's family and to his descendants. A man might have been given the name of a lion or bear for qualities he possessed, or as a nickname, and the name passed to his family and descendants. Andrew Lang suggests that the reason for the totem was unknown to the people themselves, who finding that they had the name of an animal thought that they had some connection with it, either a secret bond or that they were descended from it. Other sociological and psychological theories have been put forward by Sir James Frazer,[3] E. Durkheim,[4] and others.

16

The theory of its origin which has been most widely considered is its connection with exogamous prohibition, that is the prohibition of sexual intercourse between members of the same totem. Sigmund Freud, who derived much of his knowledge of totemism and exogamy from Frazer's extensive researches, has given a psycho-analytical explanation based largely on the Oedipus complex.[5] In this theory the father of the family, or the father of the primal horde, keeps all the females to himself and prevents the growing sons from gratifying their sexual desires. The brothers thus suppressed band together and kill the father. But they all naturally share the ambivalent attitude to the father of loving and hating him, and once they have killed him the emotion of love is uppermost and he becomes an object of veneration. They discover a substitute for him in the totem animal whom they venerate as a symbol of their father. Although they killed the father to overcome the frustration of their sexual demands, they now no longer, in their veneration, remorse and sense of guilt, wish to satisfy their sexual desires within the group of former prohibition. Thus by their act they confirm the prohibition and seek marriage with members of other totems. Although this seems to be one of the most feasible explanations, it is not entirely satisfactory because the substitution of the totem animal for the dead father is not explained. There is also the further difficulty that the connection of totemism and exogamy is not universal.

Among the Aruntas, a tribe of Central Australia, for example, the totem clans are not exogamous, and one of the purposes of totemism in this tribe may be the provision of food. A clan could not eat its own totem because it would be like eating itself. Each totem clan, therefore, by identifying itself with a totem animal, ensured food for another totem group. Reference is made in Chapter XVI to the identification in the dance with the kangaroo totem. Although it has been suggested that the Aruntas are a particularly primitive race, and that their system of totemism is, therefore, likely to be close to its origin, Freud disputes this and expresses the view that the Aruntas are the most developed of the Australian tribes and represent totemism in its dissolution rather than in its beginning; and the wish that the Aruntas are free to eat the totem and marry within it are wish phantasies.

The various theories of totemism cannot, however, be pursued here. It is sufficient to add that totemism is widespread among a great variety of primitive peoples from North America and the Pacific Islands to Africa and Australia, and that in most tribes it is an extremely powerful social influence. To some it is an early form of religion. Of particular interest in symbolism is that the totem animal, or, more rarely, plant or inanimate object, was the symbol and badge of the clan or tribe and a powerful force in holding the tribe together. Members of many tribes paint or tattoo the picture of the totem upon themselves, decorate their weapons with images of the totem, carve the image of the totem on poles and don the skin of the totem animal. It is thus the sacred symbol of the tribe very much as a flag is the symbol of a nation.

STANDARDS AND FLAGS

It is an easy and logical stage from the totem to the flag, which has a long and ancient history. The flag appears to have originated as an appendage to the military standard or lance. In ancient Egyptian, Persian, Assyrian and Greek civilizations, military companies had their own standards, which consisted generally of a symbolic device carved at the top of a long pike or staff. The standard was the head or centre of the military company or group, and it may originally have been associated with the word 'stand' in the sense of being steadfast. There are several biblical references to standards. We read that 'the Lord spake unto Moses and unto Aaron, saying, Every man of the children of Israel shall pitch by his own standard, with the ensign of their father's house' (Numbers ii. 1 and 2).[6] This indicates that the standards were of a family character, marked with family devices, rather like the flags and coats of arms in mediaeval times.

Among ancient peoples the symbolic devices carved at the top of the standards were generally of an associative character, sometimes religious, sometimes derived from the family. Sacred animals were often employed in Egypt, while among the Persians the eagle was common, with a disk symbolizing the sun. The Greeks often used their national or regional symbols, thus the Athenian standards carried the olive and the owl, which were associated with Athena. Figures of animals frequently surmounted the standards of Rome—the wolf, horse, bear, and most importantly, the eagle. The dragon figures in the standards of many Eastern peoples, and was doubtless designed to strike awe into the hearts of the enemy.

The flag first appears as a streamer attached to the staff below the emblem in Egyptian and Assyrian standards. Later it becomes the banner and the larger flag, and is the field on which the symbolic devices are represented. Banners are referred to in the Psalms (xx. 5 and lx. 4). The combination of the carved symbol surmounting the staff with a decorated banner became common in ancient Rome, and this elaborate standard formed a pattern for those used in the ceremonies of the Christian Church. Gibbon transcribes the description of the Labarum, as adopted by Constantine, as 'a long pike intersected by a transversal beam. The silken veil which hung down from the beam was curiously enwraught with the images of the reigning monarch and his children. The summit of the pike supported a crown of gold which enclosed the mysterious monogram, at once expressive of the figure of the cross and the initial letters of the name of Christ.'[7] The use of the sacred monogram, which is an abbreviation of the Greek word for Christ, χριστός, being a combination of the two initial letters X (chi) and P (rho), dates from the time of Constantine's conversion to Christianity, which is connected in some accounts with the supposed vision of Constantine and his army of the cross, or monogram, above the mid-day sun inscribed with the words 'By this sign thou shalt conquer.'

Describing the emotional effect of this standard on the soldiers during the second civil war, Gibbon remarks that 'Licinius felt and dreaded the power of this consecrated banner, the sight of which, in the distress of battle, animated the soldiers of Constantine with an invincible enthusiasm, and scattered terror and dismay through the ranks of the adverse legions.' History provides numerous examples of the powerful effect of symbolism of this kind.

In mediaeval times several varieties of flag developed, the chief being the banner, a square flag hung from the cross bar of the pike, like the Roman labarum; another was the long flag attached to the staff at the side, while a smaller flag, called the pennon, was either pointed or swallow-tailed at the end. The latter was often a family ensign, and was carried on lances. Battles in the Middle Ages presented colourful arrays of hundreds of flags, banners and pennons. The devices on early mediaeval flags were mainly of a religious character, the cross being the commonest symbol, and then, with the progress of heraldry, family devices began to appear.

The oldest national flag still in use is that of Denmark. It is thought to have originated from a vision of King Waldemar in 1219 which recalls that of Constantine. During a critical moment when the Danish king was leading his troops against the Livonians, he saw a white cross in a red sky which he interpreted as a sign of celestial aid in answer to his prayers. King Waldemar later adopted this as the national flag. It is called 'Danneborg', signifying the strength of Denmark.

The British national flag similarly originated as a simple red cross on a white ground. It has been suggested that it was first adopted by Edward I after his visit to the Holy Land as Prince Edward. We know, however, that in the fourteenth century during the reign of Edward III this cross of St. George was firmly established as the national flag and that it was worn on the surcoats of English soldiers. The badge of the oldest Order, that of the Garter, founded by Edward III in 1350, is a representation of St. George slaying the dragon.

The flag of Scotland was a diagonal or saltire white cross on a blue ground, because, according to tradition, Scotland's patron saint was crucified on a cross of that shape. In 1606, after the union of England and Scotland upon the accession of James VI of Scotland as James I of Britain, the two flags were combined. During the Commonwealth the Irish harp was introduced in the centre of the flag, while Cromwell's own flag, which supplanted the Royal Standard, consisted of the cross of St. George in the first and fourth quarters, the cross of St. Andrew in the second quarter, the golden Irish harp on a blue ground in the third quarter, and Cromwell's escutcheon of a white lion rampant on a black shield. At the Restoration the former union flag of 1649 was restored, on which Ireland was not represented. In 1801 the red saltire cross of St. Patrick on a white ground was incorporated in the Union flag, resulting in the British national flag that everybody knows.

Several explanations have been given of why it is called Union Jack. It was first so called officially in a proclamation by Queen Anne in 1707. Some have suggested that the term Jack is derived from an English rendering of Jacques, French for James, but it is much more probable that it was so named from being hoisted on the Jack-staff in the bows of ships. The term Jack-staff was first employed at the time of the Restoration in 1660. Jack is a general name for any man, which may explain the derivation of Jack-staff.

Interesting symbolism is often incorporated in national flags,[8] and is generally, as would be expected, of an associational character. The blue ensign of Australia consists of the Union flag in the first quarter, with the constellation of the southern cross, four stars forming the cross with one large star beneath the Union flag, and one smaller star which appears (with other smaller stars) in the constellation. In the blue ensign of New Zealand only the four stars of the cross appear, red on a blue ground.

Among flags of the Commonwealth the usual symbols of cross, crown and shield, appear. In the flags of some of the Malay States, such as Selangor and Johore, are the crescent moon and star, while in that of Kelantan an addition to the crescent and star are two krises and two spears, white on a red ground, making an attractive design. The star and crescent also appear on the flags of Egypt and Turkey.

The flag of the United States was adopted in 1717 and consisted of a circle of thirteen white stars in a blue rectangle in the first quarter, with thirteen red and white stripes, both signifying the thirteen states. In 1818 it was decided by Congress that a star should be added for each new state, and that the stripes should represent the thirteen original states. There are now fifty stars corresponding with the number of states; but it is always possible that this number may be increased.

Interesting symbolism appears on many of the State flags of America. In several, fairly simple geometric designs are employed, similar in character to the majority of national flags. One of the most vivid is that of Arizona which has the copper-coloured star of Arizona in the centre rising from a blue field in the lower half, in the face of the setting sun represented by thirteen red and yellow rays in the upper half. A principal motif in about half of the state flags is an adaptation of the state seal.

Other symbols of interest are the sun on flags of China and Japan, the swastika on the Nazi flag of Germany and the hammer and sickle on the U.S.S.R. flag. One of the most decorative flags is that of Brazil, which consists of a blue globe on a yellow diamond in the centre of the green flag. On the blue globe is a constellation of white stars with a white equatorial band inscribed in green *Ordem e Progresso*.

Expressive symbolism often appears on flags of shipping lines, on departmental and municipal flags. Thus, on the flag of the Commissioners of Customs, the portcullis appears, and on that of the Port of London Authority, St. Paul rising from the Tower of London. The meanings of most of the symbols used in national and other flags are given in Part IV.

REFERENCES

1. HERBERT SPENCER, *Principles of Psychology*, Vol. 1 (London, 1903).
2. ANDREW LANG, *Social Origins* and *The Secret of the Totem* (London, 1905).
3. SIR JAMES FRAZER, *Totemism and Exogamy* (London, 1910).
4. E. DURKHEIM, *Les Formes Élémentaires de la Vie Religieuse; Le Système Totémique en Australia* (Paris, 1912).
5. SIGMUND FREUD, *Totem and Taboo*, especially the last chapter on 'The Infantile Recurrence of Totemism.' English translation by A. A. BRILL (London, 1919).
6. Other Biblical references to standards are: Numbers i. 52, ii. 10, x. 14; Psalms xx. 5, lx. 4; Isaiah v. 26, x. 18, lix. 19; Jeremiah iv. 21.
7. EDWARD GIBBON, *Decline and Fall of the Roman Empire*, Chapter XX.
8. If the reader wishes to pursue further the subject of symbolism in flags, there are numerous books on the subject, among which may be mentioned *A Manual of Flags*, incorporating *Flags of the World* by W. J. GORDON, revised by V. WHEELER-HOLSASHAN (London, 1933); and *British Flags, their Early History and their development at Sea*; with an account of the Origin of the Flag as a National Device, by W. G. PERRIN (Cambridge, 1922).

III   Coats of Arms and Military Badges

SATISFACTORY means of identification of troops has always been of fundamental importance in war, although as the character of war changes so does the method of identification. From the Middle Ages until the end of the nineteenth century identification in the open battle field was necessary to distinguish between friend and enemy, and also to distinguish the various military groups. In modern warfare such identification is equally important, but is attended with secrecy, so that often, although signs are used for identification, they are such that their significance shall not be conveyed to the enemy.

Under the feudal system men served under their feudal lord. It was important that in battle their leader should be easily identified. This was particularly so in the Crusades where armies of many nations fought together. Thus, in the first half of the twelfth century shields began to be painted in bright colours with some device, the pennons on lances were similarly coloured and surcoats worn over armour bore the device also. The group of men under the feudal lord wore badges taken from his device. Even more neccessary were the identifying devices worn on the shield and surcoat in the tournaments between knights that were common in those days. Football shirts are a modern parallel. Thus originated armorial bearings and coats of arms, and thus has evolved the science or art of heraldry with all its complicated technical terminology.

The devices quickly became a family possession, as wars were fought by groups of men under a family, the head of which was generally the leader. Upon the death of a feudal lord his device would be adopted by his heirs, and thus it became a symbol of the family and its tradition and pride.

While the feudal system lasted and military groups were formed of men serving under the lords and their families, the armorial bearings served the useful purpose of military identification. Armorial bearings were also used in standards. When, however, that military purpose ceased, their usefulness ceased also, and today they are merely interesting survivals of a past age. The study of family coats of arms is interesting and valuable mainly as throwing sidelights on history.

The true successors of heraldry in war are the divisional and formation signs of the two world wars. The heraldry of institutions and of local authorities is, however, still

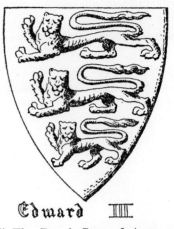

Richard I.

(a) The first authentic Royal Coat of Arms, from the reverse of the second seal of Richard I. *Circa* 1195.

Edward III

(b) The Royal Coat of Arms remained unchanged from Richard I to early in the reign of Edward III. This is the latter's first coat of arms from his first Great Seal.

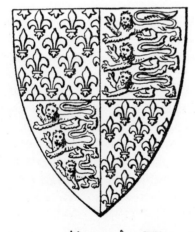

Edward III

(c) The second Coat of Arms of Edward III, from his tomb in Westminster Abbey. The fleur-de-lis symbol of the French Monarchy indicates Edward's claim to the throne of France.

Henry V.

(d) The Coat of Arms of Henry V. The drawings on this page are derived from Thomas Willement's *Regal Heraldry* (London, 1821).

Fig. 1. Early versions of the Royal Arms.

very much alive, as in the latter case it is the badge or emblem of a locality, carrying significant symbolism of that locality.

The symbolism of family armorial bearings was frequently of a crude associational or punning type based on the suggestion of the family name. A few examples, to add to those mentioned in Chapter I, are: shell fish used for Shelley, a doe between three bells for Dobell, ram's head for Ramsey, horse for Trotter, hedgehogs—French 'herisson'—for Herries, rooks for Rokeby, pelican for Pelham, fish for Fishawe, boar for Swinburne, horseshoes for Ferrers, mill-crosses for Miller, and wavy bars and shrimps for Atsea.[1] The more expressive symbolism by analogy rarely appears in old family coats of arms. As previously implied, in municipal coats of arms the symbolism is of a richer and more elaborate type, especially in some of the later examples where the aim has been to express something of the history and character of the locality. Examples are given in Chapter V.

THE ROYAL COAT OF ARMS

One of the most important examples of an ancient coat of arms is the Royal Arms, of which the origin is obscure. William the Conqueror is accredited with two golden leopards on a red shield, although there is little evidence for this. On the monument of Queen Elizabeth I in Westminster Abbey, erected in 1604, shields are shown on the entablature which illustrate Elizabeth's descent from former sovereigns. The first of these shields is of Edward the Confessor, and the second is that of William I, which is divided into the dexter side with two lions and the sinister side for his wife; but where the designer derived his information is unknown. The first authentic royal coat of arms is that of Richard I, knowledge of which is derived from the reverse of his second seal. The shield has three lions passant, guardant, and it remained so until the reign of Edward III, who, claiming the throne of France, added the fleur-de-lis. The shield was divided into four quarters, a close pattern of several golden fleur-de-lis on a blue ground in the first and fourth quarters, and three golden lions on a red ground in the second and third quarters. In the reign of Henry V the fleurs-de-lis were reduced to three in the first and fourth quarters.

At the accession of James I the arms of England occupied the first and fourth quarters of the new bearings, the arms of Scotland, consisting of a red lion and border on a gold ground, appeared in the second quarter, and the gold Irish harp on a blue ground in the third quarter. Except during the period of the Commonwealth this remained unchanged until the reign of Queen Anne, when it was redesigned, but the same symbols were retained. With the accession of George I the arms of Hanover appeared in the fourth quarter. In 1801 the fleur-de-lis disappeared, the three gold lions on a red ground appeared in the first and fourth quarters, the second and third quarters of the Stuart standard were reversed, and the shield of Hanover appeared in the centre, but the electoral bonnet was replaced by a crown. With the accession of Queen Victoria in 1837 the arms of Hanover were removed, and the Royal Coat of Arms has remained the same ever since. It is a combination of the arms of England, Scotland and Ireland. Some think that it should also include some symbolism of the Dominions and perhaps it may be time for some revision of the design to be considered. Scotland and Ireland could together occupy one quarter, England one quarter, which would leave the remaining two quarters for the Dominions (Figs. 1-3).

The supporters of the shield varied with the families that occupied the throne. They do not appear before the reign of Richard II, whose shield was supported by two angels. The shield of Henry IV was supported on the dexter side by a swan and on the sinister side by a yale. For the arms of Henry V the yale remained, but on the dexter side a lion was substituted for the swan. Henry VI had both yale supporters. The lion returns to the dexter side with the arms of Edward IV, but on the sinister side the supporter becomes sometimes a white hart and sometimes a bull. Both supporters of

(a) Arms of Edward IV. The dexter supporter is the lion, and the sinister is the white hart.

(b) Arms of Henry VII. The dexter supporter is the red dragon and the sinister is the white greyhound.

Fig. 2. Royal Coats of Arms
(see pp. 23–5).

Fig. 3. The Royal Arms of Queen Anne based on the Royal Arms of James I. The former arms of England occupy the first and fourth quarters, the arms of Scotland the second quarter and the Irish Harp the third quarter. In this design, derived from a contemporary print early in the reign of Anne the shield is encircled by the garter, the lion places his left foot on the rose of England, and the unicorn his right foot on the thistle of Scotland.

the shield of Richard III are boars. Henry VII, being of Welsh descent, chose the red dragon as the supporter on the dexter side, with a white greyhound on the sinister side. Henry VIII retained the red dragon, but changed it to the sinister side and returned the lion to the dexter side. Under Mary, the lion, rampant instead of guardant, was changed to the sinister side and the Imperial eagle of Spain was placed on the dexter side. Elizabeth changed the lion back to the dexter side, and returned the dragon to the sinister side, but changed its colour to gold. With the union of England and Scotland under James I, the lion remained on the dexter side, guardant with a gold crown, and on the sinister side the white unicorn of Scotland was introduced. They have continued the same under succeeding reigns (for symbolism, see Part IV).

These supporters, now known as the Queen's beasts, formed decorative sculptures to the Annexe to Westminster Abbey at the Coronation of Queen Elizabeth II in 1953, and were made by James Woodford, R.A., under the guidance of Sir George Bellew, Garter King of Arms. Following is the official description of these beasts. (Plates II–IV.) They now line the drawbridge of the main entrance to Hampton Court Palace.

(1) *Supporter.* The Lion of England dexter supporter of the Royal Arms, gold with the Royal Crown on its head, with red claws and tongue.
Shield. Present Royal Arms of England.

(2) *Supporter.* The silver unicorn of Scotland, sinister supporter of the Royal Arms, its mane, horn, hoofs, beard and the tufts of hair on its body and tail of gold. Round its neck is a coronet of gold composed of crosses patée and fleurs-de-lys, to which a golden chain is attached. The chain passes between the beast's forelegs and then is reflexed over its back.
Shield. The Royal Arms of Scotland.

(3) *Supporter.* The silver horse of Hanover.
Shield. Royal Arms as used 1714–1801.

(4) *Supporter.* The silver greyhound of the Tudors, a supporter of Royal Arms of Henry VII. The greyhound has a red collar around its neck. The collar is edged and studded with gold, and a golden ring is affixed to the front of it.
Shield. Crowned Tudor Rose on field of Tudor livery colours.

(5) *Supporter.* The red dragon of the Tudors, a supporter of Royal Arms of Henry VII. The red shades into a golden belly.
Shield. Arms of Llyewelyn ab Gruffydd. Now borne in pretence by Princes of Wales.

(6) *Supporter.* The black bull of Clarence, with golden hoofs and horns. A badge of Lionel Duke of Clarence, son of King Edward III, and an ancestor of the Yorkist and Tudor Sovereigns.
Shield. Royal Arms as used from King Henry IV until Queen Elizabeth I.

(7) *Supporter.* The silver lion of Mortimer with a blue tongue and blue claws. The Mortimers were descended from King Edward III and were ancestors of the Yorkist kings.
Shield. White Rose en Soleil on a field of the livery colours of the House of York. A Yorkist Badge.

(8) *Supporter.* The silver yale of the Beauforts, covered with golden spots, its hoofs, horns, tusks and the tufts of hair on its body and tail are of gold. Margaret Beaufort, mother of King Henry VII, was a descendant of King Edward III.
Shield. Crowned portcullis on a field of the Beaufort liveries. A badge of the Beauforts and of King Henry VII.

(9) *Supporter.* The silver falcon of the Plantagenets with its wings out-spread; its beak and legs are gold. A favourite badge of King Edward IV.
Shield. Falcon within a fetterlock. It is shown on a field of the livery colours of King Edward IV.

(10) *Supporter.* The golden griffin of Edward III from his Privy Seal. Its beak and claws are red.
Shield. Badge of the House of Windsor on a field of the present Royal livery colours.

(*a*) Paschal Lamb, badge of Queen's West Surrey Regiment.

(*b*) Dragon of the House of Tudor, badge of The Buffs, the East Kent Regiment. The dragon is also the badge of the Monmouthshire Regiment.

(*c*) The White Horse of Hanover, badge of the 3rd King's Own Hussars. It also forms the second badge of the Royal Scots Greys.

(*d*) Tiger beneath the Tudor Rose, the badge of the York and Lancaster Regiment. The tiger also appears in the Leicestershire Regiment.

(*e*) and (*f*) The sphinx, the badge of the Gloucestershire Regiment and the South Wales Borderers. It also appears on the badges of the Lincolnshire and East Lancashire Regiments, and of the Lancashire Fusiliers.

Fig. 4. Military Badges (*see* p. 27).

REGIMENTAL BADGES

THE purpose of identification by coats of arms in the Middle Ages is now served, with the added purpose of secrecy, by divisional and formation signs. During active service regimental badges awarded at various times since the seventeenth century were largely supplemented by the divisional signs, although they are still retained by the regiments. The badges were often changed in the course of a regiment's history. Originally for identification, they became symbols of honour and pride.

In some regimental badges the symbolism is interesting and expressive, in many it is of the usual associative type; and in some cases is derived from family coats of arms. For example, the Paschal Lamb of the Queen's West Surrey Regiment was the crest of Catherine of Braganza, wife of Charles II, after whom the regiment was named at its formation in 1661; and the dragon of the House of Tudor forms the badge of The Buffs, the East Kent Regiment formed in 1572 and also of the Monmouthshire regiment. The White Horse of Hanover appears in the second badge of the Royal Scots Greys, and in the badge of the 3rd King's Own Hussars.

Among the many symbols of the associative type are the sphinx on badges of the Lincolnshire Regiment, the Gloucestershire and East Lancashire Regiments, the Lancashire Fusiliers and the South Wales Borderers, employed in each case to signify service in Egypt. The Leicestershire Regiment has a tiger for its badge, signifying service in India and Afghanistan. A tiger also appears beneath the Tudor Rose on the badge of the York and Lancaster Regiment. On the badge of the Suffolk Regiment is the Castle of Gibraltar, signifying the siege of Gibraltar. Some of the badges have trophies, such as the antelope on the badge of the Royal Warwickshire Regiment, which commemorates the victory at Saragossa in 1710, when the regiment captured a Moorish flag, carrying the device of an antelope. Another trophy symbol is the eagle on the badge of the Royal Irish Fusiliers, which commemorates the capture of the first French eagle standard in the Peninsular War. (Several badges are illustrated, Figs. 4 and 5.)

The badges of the Scots, Irish and Welsh Guards carry the familiar national emblems of thistle, shamrock and leek.

Among the particularly expressive badges is that of the Royal Corps of Signals, which shows the figure of Mercury, messenger of the gods, with the caduceus, standing with one foot on a globe, thus symbolizing world-wide communication; the badge of the Royal Army Medical Corps which has the staff of Aesculapius, the Greek God of Medicine, with the serpent set in a laurel wreath (see Part IV); the Royal Army Veterinary Corps, which shows Chiron the centaur, who taught the art of healing to Aesculapius; and the badge of the Artists' Rifles, designed by Lord Leighton, the first colonel of the regiment, which consists of the heads of Minerva, the goddess of the arts, and Mars, the god of war, who is depicted with the helmet over his eyes and therefore blind.

DIVISIONAL AND FORMATION SIGNS

What might logically be called the new heraldry arose in the First World War as divisional and formation signs. On grounds of security it was important that the identity of troops and units should not be disclosed to the enemy. To ensure this in the field of operations all identity marks, like regimental badges and names, were

27

(a) Antelope, with crown and chain, the trophy badge of the Royal Warwickshire Regiment.

(b) Mercury, ancient messenger of the gods, carrying the caduceus, and standing on the globe, the badge of the Royal Corps of Signals.

(c) The staff of Aesculapius, with the serpent, set in a laurel wreath, the badge of the Royal Army Medical Corps.

(d) Cheron the centaur, who taught the art of healing to Aesculapius, the badge of the Royal Army Veterinary Corps.

(e) Badge of the Parachute Regiment.

Fig. 5. Military Badges (*see* p. 27).

removed from uniforms, equipment and vehicles. Yet at the same time it was necessary, in order to facilitate recognition of divisions and corps, that some distinguishing mark should be employed, and thus divisional signs were introduced. Divisional signs were mainly used in the First World War, because a division is the smallest unit in which all the branches—infantry, artillery, engineers—necessary for effective military operations are combined. These signs would at first be intelligible only to the initiated, although after a period it would hardly be possible to conceal the significance of them from the enemy's intelligence services. They served, however, an additional purpose similar to that served by regimental badges and colours; that of fostering *esprit de corps*, so that troops began to feel a pride in their divisional sign. Operating in self-contained units, divisions in the First World War became famous.

Divisional signs were again adopted early in the Second World War; and later, in 1941, they were called Formation Badges, and these were worn by all groups and all ranks. Some of the formation badges of headquarters staffs, both of the larger and smaller commands at home and overseas, of armies, and corps of armoured, infantry and airborne divisions, and of aircraft corps and divisions, have interesting symbolism, while each group often has a marked family character.

The badge of the Supreme Headquarters Allied Expeditionary Force consisted of a black shield, worn as a cloth patch on the left arm, which symbolized, according to the official description, the darkness of Nazi oppression. On the shield was a Crusaders' sword of liberation with the red flames of avenging justice leaping from its hilt. Above is a rainbow, symbol of hope, above which again is a band of blue indicative of peace and tranquillity. This is a good, effective design with interesting symbolism when explained, although not otherwise immediately apparent. More directly expressive was the badge of the Headquarters of the Supreme Allied Command, South-East Asia, which consisted of a blue phoenix on a white ground rising from red flames encircled by a blue border. The phoenix symbolizes Allied Power rising from the ashes of the countries occupied by Japan. The badge of the Allied Land Forces, South-East Asia, consisted of a white shield with the red cross of the Crusaders, behind which are the golden wings of victory and the Crusader's sword set on a pale blue ground with dark blue base. It is intended to suggest that the wings carry the sword and shield across the seas to liberation from the Japanese yoke.

Reminiscent in its source of the old coats of arms is the green apple on a dark blue diamond of the badge of the Northern Home Command. It was derived from the name of the Commander, Sir Ronald F. Adam—thus, Adam's apple. Previously Sir Ronald Adam commanded the 3rd Corps which had a green fig leaf on a white ground also chosen for its association with his name. Another example of a similar kind is the badge of the 2nd Corps which had a red leaping salmon and three dark blue wavy bands on a white ground, suggested apparently by the name of the Commander, Sir Alan Brooke (later Field-Marshal Viscount Alanbrooke). So with the motif of the Ninth Army badge; it consisted of a charging elephant with a castle on its back, above which is the Commando flag, the elephant being red on a black disk. The idea was apparently suggested by the nickname, Jumbo, of the Commander, Sir Henry Maitland Wilson.

In the early days of the War against Germany in 1939 the campaign was often spoken of as a crusade, and many of the formation badges expressed this idea, for

(a) Supreme Headquarters of the Allied Expeditionary Force.

(b) Allied Land Force, South East Asia.

(c) Headquarters of the Supreme Allied Command, South-East Asia.

(d) Northern Home Command.

(e) Third Army Corps.

(f) Second Army Corps.

(g) Ninth Army.

(h) First Army.

Fig. 6. Divisional and formation signs of the Second World War. The significance of these signs is given on pages 29 and 31.

example, those of the First, Second and Eighth armies. That of the First army was the red cross of St. George on a white shield with the Crusader's sword superimposed on the cross. That of the Second army was similar except that the cross was blue. That of the Eighth army was without the sword, being a golden Crusader's cross on a white shield set in a dark blue rectangle.

The armoured divisions had expressive symbols on their badges. The First armoured division had a charging rhinoceros in white on a black oval background, the Eleventh had a charging black bull on a yellow rectangular ground, the Second a knight's helmet, white on a red square, the Sixth a clenched mailed gauntlet, white in a black square. Legend says that the giant panda of the Ninth armoured division was a pun on the German 'Panzer' division.

The well-known badge of the anti-aircraft command, adopted for all anti-aircraft corps and divisions since 1943, consisted of a black bow and arrow pointing upwards on a scarlet square. Before 1943 there were several badges for the various anti-aircraft corps and divisions. An expressive badge of the analogous type was that of the First Anti-aircraft Corps (South of England), which consisted of a red eagle in flight with an arrow through its breast, set in a blue square. Similar was that of the Eleventh division which had a standing German eagle in black and yellow pierced by a scarlet arrow. The badge of the First anti-aircraft division (London) consisted of a bomber in black, pierced by a red sword on a light blue ground with a black border; that of the Fifth a falling bomber with five red flames, and that of the Eighth, a shell burst represented by a red eight-point star on a falling bomber in a sky-blue square. An amusing example is that of the Second division which had a red witch on a broomstick on a dark blue ground, expressive of the division's motto: 'We sweep the skies.'

The majority of the symbols used in the formation badges were of the associative type. A few of the more interesting examples might be cited. The Tenth army, which was raised and operated in Iraq, had for its badge a golden Assyrian winged lion with human head, derived from the sculptured lions flanking the entrances to ancient Assyrian palaces; the badge of the 56th (London) Division had a black cat on a red ground, suggested apparently by Dick Whittington's cat, and also the traditional luck that goes with a black cat; the badge of the 47th (London) Division had two red bells tied with a red bow on a dark blue background, symbolical of Bow bells; the badge of the 46th (North Midland) Division consisted of the Sherwood Forest oak, with brown trunk and green foliage, outlined with a white border and set in a black square; while the badge of the 49th (West Riding) Division had a polar bear in a black rectangle, which was adopted while the Division was on service in Iceland.

This is but a selection from the numerous formation badges adopted in the Second World War. Similar badges were adopted by the Dominion, Colonial and American Forces, several of which present interesting symbolism.[2] The tendency appears now to be to make the badges of lower formations more and more of a geometric character with bright colours that are easily seen and recognized, and to reserve the more elaborate symbolism for the badges of higher formations such as S.H.A.E.F. A selection of divisional and formation signs are illustrated, Figs. 6–9.

(a) Eleventh Armoured Division.

(b) Second Armoured Division.

(c) First Anti-Aircraft Command.

(d) First Anti-Aircraft Corps (South of England).

(e) First Anti-Aircraft Division (London).

(f) Fifth Anti-Aircraft Division.

(g) Second Anti-Aircraft Division.

(h) Tenth Army.

Fig. 7. Divisional and formation signs of the Second World War. The significance of these signs is given on p. 31.

(*a*) Fifty-sixth (London) Division.

(*b*) Forty-seventh (London) Division.

(*c*) Forty-sixth (North Midland) Division.

(*d*) Forty-ninth (West Riding) Division.

(*e*) Airborne Division.

(*f*) Seventy-seventh Division.

Fig. 8. Divisional and formation signs of the Second World War. The significance of these signs is given on p. 31.

6TH AIR FORCE

(a) Star and wings with ship.

9TH AIR FORCE

(b) Another design with star and wings, a motif which is also similarly used in the badges of the first, eighth, tenth, twelfth, thirteenth, fifteenth and 20th American air forces.

14TH AIR FORCE

(c) Star with tiger.

SEVENTEENTH AIR FORCE

(d) Star with Pegasus the Greek winged horse.

18TH AIR FORCE

(e) 3 parachutes with wings.

(*f*)　NINETEENTH AIR FORCE

(*g*)　21ST AIR DIVISION

(*f*) Sword with wing and globe.

(*g*) Stars, sword and olive branch.

(*h*) Dividers and globe.

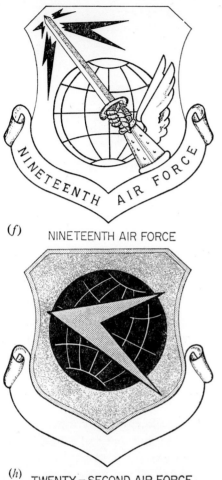

Fig. 9. Eight American Air Force Badges. The symbols give some indication of the function of the force.

(*h*)　TWENTY – SECOND AIR FORCE

Symbolism is also sometimes expressively used in American military badges, and as examples illustrations are shown (Fig. 9) of eight American Air Force badges. In all flight is symbolised and in addition an indication is given of the special function of the several air forces.

REFERENCES

1. Numerous examples can be obtained from any book of Heraldry. Good books on Heraldry are rare. Among them are J. R. PLANCHÈ's *The Pursuivant of Arms*, 3rd edition (London, 1873); SIR W. H. ST. JOHN HOPE's *Heraldry for Craftsmen and Designers* (London, 1913). A convenient text-book is A. C. FOX-DAVIES' *A Complete Guide to Heraldry*, revised edition (London, 1929). A valuable contribution to the subject is OSWALD BARRON's article on 'Heraldry' in the *Encyclopaedia Britannica*. A good and outspoken short essay on the subject is E. A. GREENING LAMBOURN's introduction to his *The Armorial Glass of the Oxford Diocese* 1250–1850 (Oxford, 1949), in which he pays tribute to the work of PLANCHÈ, J. H. ROUND, OSWALD BARRON and SIR W. H. ST. JOHN HOPE in rescuing Heraldry from the jargon of the Heralds' College. 'The reformed blazon' he says, 'which translates the original description word for word into simple English is used by all scholarly writers on the subject—except the members of the College of Arms.' A good book on the history of the Royal Arms up to George IV is THOMAS WILLEMENT's *Regal Heraldry, The Armorial Insignia of the Kings and Queens of England from Coeval Authorities* (London, 1821).
2. The most complete record of Formation Badges is given in *Heraldry in war—Formation Badges 1939–1945*, by LT.-COL. HOWARD H. COLE (Aldershot, 1st edition, 1946; 2nd, 1947; 3rd, 1949).

IV Seals

To authenticate ownership, contracts, agreements and documents, a distinctive mark, often of a complex character to render imitation difficult, is the obvious method to employ, and this has been done since remote antiquity by means of the seal, long before writing was a common accomplishment. It thus precedes the modern signature by which for most purposes it has been superseded, although for State enactments and particularly important contracts or agreements, and to protect the transit of important documents and valuable articles, it is still used. In China and among other Oriental countries the seal is still in common use.

Among the earliest seals of which there is record are the circular stamp and cylinder seals of the Uruk Period in Mesopotamia, which is well before 3000 B.C. Almost as early are cylinder seals in Elam and Syria. The impressions on clay made by the cylinders in these early seals were generally between one and one and a half inches wide and from two to five inches long. Cylinder seals were first used for sealing jars. A cloth was taken over the top of the jar, tied with string round the neck, the string was covered with clay which received the seal impression that was the mark of ownership. The use for documents and contracts was a later development. The representations on the seals, a very large number of which remain and are preserved in various museums, are often very elaborate. The subjects are associated with the early religion or mythology of Mesopotamia, with regeneration and fertility, and animal worship, or the worship of gods in animal form, as common themes. Thus plants are shown symbolically, and figures and animals, and fabulous creatures are represented engaged in performing various rites. Incidentally, Dr. H. Frankfort in his learned work on Cylinder Seals, in speaking of those of the Uruk Period, suggests that on several of the seals we have the origin of the caduceus. He is referring to the symbols of the Tammiz, the god of corn, and remarks that 'the snake emerging from Mother Earth with the sprouting corn was another of the god's symbols, sometimes elaborated (with an obvious reference to his generative aspect) into a pair of copulating vipers, the origin of the caduceus.'[1] Other seals, somewhat later in the early Dynastic period show this motif and suggest by its form the prototype of the caduceus.

These cylinder seals continued in use through the dynasties of Ur and Babylon and on to the Assyrian civilization. Many of the designs are famous for their decorative beauty.

36

Early Egyptian Seals

Cylinder seals appear in Egypt about 3000 B.C., during the early dynasties. The stamp seal was also in use in Egypt at this time. The earliest type was round like a button with a perforated ridge behind for holding. It has been suggested that this button seal was derived from the Aegean Islands. It was superseded in Egypt during the twelfth dynasty (about 2000 B.C.) by the scarab seal, which remained the commonest form until the twenty-sixth dynasty (about 650 to 560 B.C.). The scarab had existed as a gem in Egypt since the sixth dynasty, but it does not appear to have been used as a seal until the twelfth dynasty, when its base became a signet ring. Derived from it was the scaraboid with the flat underside engraved, but the round upperside was not cut like a beetle, but either left plain or carved in the shape of a head or an animal.

The scarab beetle was worshipped in ancient Egypt from a very early period and was a sacred symbol of life, and from this became a symbol of good luck and was worn as an amulet, either as a bead or as the bezel of a ring. (For explanation of its symbolism and sacred character see Part IV). The base of the scarab formed the die for the seal, the devices for which consisted of a variety of designs, among them being the lotus lily, symbol of life and regeneration, seen particularly in seals of the eighteenth dynasty; representations of the deities, common in the nineteenth and twenty-sixth dynasties; the king, often represented in his chariot, in the eighteenth dynasty, while symbols of royalty like the Sphinx often appear in the later dynasties. Inscriptions are common at all periods.

Ancient Greek Seals

Seals are among the interesting and often beautiful relics of ancient Greece and Rome, many taking the form of engraved gems.

In ancient Greece they appear at all periods from the Mycenaean age, the earliest forms being the lenticular and glandular intaglio gems, the former shaped like a broad bean, the latter like a sling bolt. Later, in the archaic period, scarabs and scaraboids appear, both also being used by the Etruscans. The gems of signet rings in the Classical and Hellenistic periods are mostly round or elliptical in shape.

The representations in these seal gems are exceedingly varied, and are often of a symbolic character. Up to the time when royal portraits were introduced in the late Greek period and in seals of the Roman Empire, the majority of subjects are religious. Among those from the Melian period (700–600 B.C.) are a dolphin and a head of tunnyfish on one seal, a heron holding an eel above a dolphin on another, and a centaur. The dolphin was a symbol of Apollo who took the form of a dolphin when he guided the Cretan ship to Crissa. Dolphins also appear in many gems of later periods. A not uncommon symbol in the archaic period (550–480 B.C.) is the ram or ram's head, expressive of Zeus and also of Apollo as god of flocks and herds. Among the symbols appearing on gems of the Classical period (480–300 B.C.) are the lion, bull, hare, wild goose, dolphin, and grasshopper, while figures of the gods, like Atlas, and Apollo riding on a man were common. Animals were generally used as symbols of the gods, because the gods had performed certain functions or rendered services to mankind in the shapes of such animals, as in the example of the dolphin cited. For their significance see Part IV.

Portraits appear on seals of the Roman Republic and of the early, middle and late Empire, many of these being of the Roman Emperors. Other subjects are agricultural such as shepherd with goat, a reaper, a man gathering dates, a mule cart, and themes connected with the theatre, like actors rehearsing, or comic and tragic masks.

ENGLISH SEALS OF STATE

With the Middle Ages a new kind of seal was adopted which appeared in England at the time of the Saxon Heptarchy. This was the two-sided seal with obverse and reverse, as with a coin. Cord was threaded through the document and sometimes fixed with wax and the two ends of the cord were held by a lead, silver or gold seal. The earliest example in England was the lead seal of Coenwulf, King of Mercia, dating from the early ninth century. This form was adopted by Edward the Confessor, except that his seal was of wax. This double pendant seal of Edward the Confessor was the first of the great seals of English kings. On the obverse Edward is seated in majesty, holding in his right hand the sceptre and in his left the orb. On the reverse he is similarly seated on his throne, but holding the sword, and the sceptre surmounted by the dove. The design of the seal of William the Conqueror is a little different; it is important as forming the prototype of most succeeding Great Seals of State. On the reverse is the king seated on his throne crowned, with sword and orb as in the seal of Edward the Confessor, but on the obverse the king is shown in his capacity as conqueror and warrior, in armour, mounted on a horse, thus giving most importance to this aspect of his character. With the Great Seal of William Rufus the king enthroned appears on the obverse and the equestrian portrait on the reverse side, and this formed the type for most of the succeeding Great Seals of England with a few exceptions, which will be noted. Many of the mediaeval royal seals are of much beauty, carrying interesting symbolism (see Plate V).

The obverse of the first seal of Richard I shows on either side of his head a crescent with a wavy star expressive of his Crusade in the Holy Land, and on either side of the throne a sprig of the plantagenista, or broom, expressive of the name Plantagenet. The second seal is similar (Plate VI).

The first seal of Henry III is, I think, one of the most beautiful of the state seals. The king is enthroned on a bench against a plain background. Above his crown is the star and crescent, in his right hand he holds the sword, in his left the orb, from which rises a foliated stem surmounted by a cross. A shorter foliated stem appears in the seals of Richard I and John, but it has grown to greater length in that of Henry III. This stem probably has a religious significance; may be Aaron's rod, or possibly a lily. Henry was a devout admirer of Edward the Confessor, on whose seal two sceptres are shown because he is depicted enthroned on both sides. It was difficult for Henry to show a dove in imitation of one of those sceptres, because of the difficulty of incorporating this with the cross. Henry, therefore, probably wished to introduce something of similar significance in the tall stem rising from the orb. Both the obverse of this seal and the equestrian group on the reverse have much decorative beauty and refinement, and the well arranged inscription round the circumference enhances the effect. The sword, stem and cross are held vertically, which gives effective emphasis to the symbolism (Plate V).

After the first and second seals of Henry III the designs became more elaborate.

Whereas in these he sits on a bench, in his third seal he is seated on a Gothic throne. Edward I is seated on a still more elaborate throne, and on the seal of Edward III this has become a throne with Gothic canopy, with the Royal Arms in niches on either side. In the seals of Henry VIII the greyhound is introduced, while in the two great seals of Elizabeth I a note of gaiety is apparent. On the reverse of the first seal of the latter, in the field above the horse's head, is a fleur-de-lis crowned; on the ground are plants and tufts of grass, and from it, rising in the background, spring two rose-trees in flower. The reverse of the larger second seal is similar, but there are additional symbols. In the field are a rose, fleur-de-lis and harp, each with crown, symbolizing the three kingdoms of England, France and Ireland, while overhead is a cloud from which emerges the rays of the sun (Plate VI).

With the two Commonwealth seals of 1648 and 1651 occurs the first departure from the customary type. On the obverse there is the map of Great Britain and Ireland, and on the reverse a representation of Parliament in session (Plate VII). The two seals of Oliver Cromwell show the arms of the United Kingdom on the obverse and an equestrian effigy of Cromwell on the reverse.

From the seals of Queen Anne the designs became more crowded with the frequent introduction of allegorical figures. The obverse of the second seal of Anne is loaded with symbolic devices. On the right side of the queen enthroned is a lion crowned, holding a shield charged with the cross of St. George, and on the left side is the unicorn holding a shield charged with the cross of St. Andrew. Above these, on the right is a figure of Piety holding a model of a church, on the left side is a figure of Justice holding a pair of scales in her right hand and a bundle of Roman fasces in her left. The Royal Arms on an oval shield encircled with the Garter appears on the front of the canopy supported by two angels each sounding a trumpet.

The obverse of the third seal of Anne is similar, but the reverse represents a second departure from the equestrian effigy and shows instead a figure of Britannia holding in her right hand a lance, and at her left side an oval shield with the Royal Arms as on the obverse. In the field are a five-petalled rose and thistle with crown.

The seal of George II and the second seal of George III are particularly elaborate and may be selected as examples of the crowding of figures into a restricted space. In the former George II is enthroned on the obverse in the midst of allegorical persons. To his right are Hercules with a club on his shoulder and a crowned lion couchant at his feet, a symbolic figure of Plenty with a cornucopia, and Minerva with spear and shield; on the king's left is a female figure in classic dress holding the sceptre and oval shield on which are the Arms of England and Scotland, and also a female figure with a lamb in her arms, probably denoting innocence. A figure of Envy overthrown and chained is under the throne. The design also includes two sceptres saltire, an oval shield with the Royal Arms ensigned with the crown between a palm branch and cornucopia.

In the second seal of George III six allegorical figures are represented, each depicted with their accessories and emblems: Justice is shown with broken sword and balance; Peace with palm branch; Learning in the guise of Minerva is shown with helmet and javelin; strength is depicted as Hercules with his club and lion's skin; Victory with javelin and shield over which she holds a laurel twig, while Plenty is shown as Ceres with cornucopia.

The third, fourth, fifth (Plate VII(*b*)) and sixth seals of George III, the seals of George IV and William IV were all on similar lines. The second seal of Victoria shows figures of Justice and Religion, the latter being shown with the cross and a book.[2]

The seal of Edward VII continues the trend of over-elaboration. The king wears his crown and is seated in the usual manner with the sceptre in his right hand and the orb in his left. Two figures stand on the pedestal of his throne, one a winged figure of St. Michael with sword, the other St. George with standard and the shield of England. On either side are two allegorical figures, one with a ship and globe symbolizing dominion of the seas, the other a blindfolded figure with sword and scales, symbolizing Justice. On the reverse is the equestrian statue of the king, behind him are the Royal Arms, and forming a border on either side of the upper part are the cinquefoil rose, thistle and shamrock. The British oak is also introduced. Forming a background to the legs of the horse is the sea with sailing ship and steam ship, and the trident beneath. The simple direct use of symbolism, employing few devices, as in the beautiful seal of Henry III is far more effective than the crowd of allegorical figures that appears on the seal of George III, or the conglomeration of symbols on the seal of Edward VII.

The obverse of the first great seal of George V appears to be derived in general character from that of Edward III, but the reverse shows another departure from the equestrian effigy; instead, the king is shown in naval uniform with sword, standing on the bridge of a battleship, part of which is shown in the background. On either side two lions are shown with the Royal Arms below. This design was no doubt prompted by the fact that George V was trained in the Royal Navy and it was felt, therefore, that a symbol of the Navy would be more appropriate than the equestrian group, which suggests army cavalry. However, in the reverse of the second seal of George V he is shown in the traditional equestrian manner.

With the second seal of George V and that of George VI, there is a complete reaction from the over-ornate seals of Anne to Edward VII. Instead, they are refreshingly simple, both the obverse and reverse having a plain field. This simplicity is accompanied by a somewhat stylish archaic treatment.

This simplification is continued in the seal of Elizabeth II. An interesting feature of this seal is that contrary to the tradition established by the seal of William II, the equestrian figure of Elizabeth II is shown on the obverse, while the monarch enthroned is on the reverse, thus being similar in this respect to the seal of William the Conqueror. The reason for this change appears to be that in Gilbert Ledward's design of the monarch enthroned the robe of the Queen encroached upon the border, which thus did not allow space for the full royal style and titles, which it is important to include on the obverse. It was therefore decided to use the equestrian figure. (Plate VIII.)

Seals of lords and knights in the Middle Ages often showed the mounted figure on one side and the coat of arms on the other. Sometimes the mounted figure carries a shield with the coat of arms corresponding to the coat of arms on the other side, an example being the seal of the Earl of Gloucester and Hereford of A.D. 1300. Seals of ladies often showed the coat of arms on one side with the standing figure of the lady on the other, sometimes flanked with the heraldic shields hanging from a tree.

Ecclesiastical Seals

Ecclesiastical and monastic seals and those of bishops are generally shaped like the mandorla or vesica piscis, which was used as an aureole surrounding figures of Christ in mediaeval representations. Whether this shape is employed because the fish, from which it is derived, is a symbol of Christ and of baptism, it is difficult to decide. It may be that it was adopted for seals as the result of the influence of Gothic architecture, but it is more probably derived from the aureole surrounding the figure of Christ. This was a convenient shape for bishops, who are shown enthroned under a Gothic canopy; but this Gothic architectural background is a later innovation. The earliest seals of bishops show them standing against a plain background with border inscription. An example is that of Richard FitzNeale, Bishop of London from 1189–1198. He stands in his vestments, a staff in his left hand, and right hand uplifted with two fingers pointing upwards. This form is similar to that of the seal of the Archbishop of Canterbury, and it was generally adhered to in successive seals of archbishops and bishops, with variations in details and elaborations.

Municipal Seals

Perhaps the types of seals which are most interesting symbolically are those of local authorities. The symbolism is generally of an associative character. Representations on some of the earliest local seals include the patron saint of the town; the coat of arms of a family associated with the town, such as the lord of the manor; a prominent building of the town or group of buildings; and devices suggested by names, such as the heraldic pun or rebus. A fine example of a local seal is that of the City of London of the thirteenth century, which shows on the obverse St. Paul the patron saint, holding a sword in his right hand and a banner with the Royal Arms in his left, standing above the city with its walls and river in the foreground. On the reverse is St. Thomas of Canterbury enthroned on an arch over the city, with clerics and merchants on either side.

The first common seal of Bristol of the fourteenth century shows a view of the castle with much detail. On one tower is a watchman blowing a long trumpet. On the other side is a ship with sail set heading towards a round-headed archway at the corner of a building on which a watchman points the way to the steersman. All this is expressive of a fortified port. In the foreground on the beach is a conger eel symbolic of the trade of the port.

Examples of the rebus are not uncommon. The thirteenth-century seal of Appleby in Westmorland has an apple-tree with seven fruitful branches. It bears a shield with the Royal Arms of Henry III. The fourteenth-century seal of Ashburton in Devon has a churchlike building with ash-tree on one side and a star and crescent. The seal of Lichfield of 1688 shows a battlefield with dead bodies, weapons, flag and crown, apparently because 'lich' was the Anglo-Saxon for corpse. The old seal of Hartlepool shows a hart in a pool.

With towns near the sea, or situated on navigable rivers, ships commonly figure on the seals, as in the case of Bristol. Thus Aldeburgh in Suffolk, formerly an important seaport, has on its early seal a three-masted ship at sea. On the obverse of the seal of Dover of 1305 is a detailed representation of a warship, and on the reverse the patron saint, St. Martin, on a horse, dividing his cloak with a beggar under the doorway of

Dover Castle. The thirteenth-century seal of East Looe in Cornwall has a single-masted ship with a castle. On the thirteenth century seal of the port of Lydd in Kent is a ship passing from behind a church with a spire, and included in the seal is a shield with four lions rampant in its four quarters. Maritime and religious symbolism are combined in the thirteenth-century seal of Lyme Regis. There is a single-masted ship with banners of the Royal Arms; over the ship is Christ on the cross, and the Archangel Michael, the patron saint of the town, with St. George and the Dragon on his shield; above are the star and crescent. As in the case of the Great Seals of State, the earliest of the local seals are generally the most artistically effective.[3]

STATE SEALS OF THE U.S.A.

The state seals of the U.S.A. are particularly rich in symbolism. Many of them indicate the industries of the states and provide significant glimpses of their history. 'Those who have never made a systematic study', says George Earlie Shankle, 'of the symbolic messages in the Great Seals of the various states have yet a store of information open to them which is almost as fascinating as the contents of the cave in the Arabian Nights.'[4] Many of these seals are of a pictorial character and thus different from those familiar in Great Britain.

The great seal of the U.S.A. was first employed in 1782, and was confirmed at the time of the adoption of the Constitution in 1789. The central device on the obverse is the American eagle. The adoption of the eagle as a principal symbol of America was probably partly due to its being a traditional symbol of victory, power and authority in Western Europe, derived from its association with Zeus, and partly because the native Indians used it as an emblem. On the eagle's breast is an unsupported shield, signifying self-reliance, and on the shield are thirteen red and white stripes denoting the thirteen original states, bound together in the upper part of the shield by a blue band signifying unity of the whole in Congress. (Fig. 10.)

Above the eagle's head are thirteen stars on a blue ground set on the centre of the sun's rays, or ring of light, breaking through a cloud which denotes a new nation taking its place among the sovereign powers. In the eagle's right talon is held an olive branch with thirteen leaves, symbolic of peace, and in its left talon thirteen arrows expressing defence. The idea of unity is further emphasized by the motto *E Pluribus Unam* (one out of many), on a scroll held in the eagle's beak. On the reverse of the seal, which, however, has never been cut, the principal device is a pyramid, expressing the firm and durable building of the new Union. The pyramid is unfinished at the top to suggest that the development of the nation is not complete and that there is room for other states. Above is an eye, set in a triangle, surrounded by a glory or sun's rays. It can be interpreted as the eye of providence, set in the symbol of the Trinity, surrounded by the light of the universe. Over the eye are the words *Annuit Coeptis* (God has favoured our undertakings), while below is the motto *Novis Ordo Sectorum* (a new order of the ages). The date at the base of the pyramid is 1776.

Most of the State seals are one-sided, only a few have designs on the reverses. Some consist principally of a landscape occupying the major area of the seal, sometimes with symbolic or other figures. Examples of these landscape seals are those of California, Florida, Indiana, Kansas, Minnesota, Montana, Nebraska, Nevada, North Dakota, Ohio, South Dakota and the reverses of Georgia and Virginia.

Sometimes the coat of arms forms the design of the seal, and in some of these a landscape appears on the shield, examples being Arizona, Idaho, Maine, New York, and Oregon. Almost half the landscapes mentioned show the rising sun—it actually appears on eleven state seals—which is employed as a symbol of life and regeneration. The seal of California, which is an interesting example of landscape symbolism, shows a sea with distant mountains, representing the Sierra Nevada, while ships indicate commercial prosperity. In the foreground is the figure of Minerva, who, having sprung full grown from the brain of Jupiter, symbolizes the political birth of California which was admitted as a state without the usual probationary period as a territory. In front of Minerva's shield is a grizzly bear, the state animal, common at one time

Fig. 10. Great Seal of the U.S.A., first adopted in 1782 and confirmed at the adoption of the Constitution in 1789. *Left:* obverse; *right:* reverse. The symbolism is described on page 42.

in the region but now extinct, while wheat and vine indicate principal items of agricultural produce. In the middle distance is a miner, indicating a leading industry, while above are 31 stars representing the number of states in the Union after the admission of California in 1850. The motto, *Eureka*, 'applies either to the principle involved in the admission of the state, or to the success of the miner at work.'

The seal of New York consists of the coat of arms adopted originally in 1777 and subsequently modified five times. A landscape with sun above distant mountains, with two ships approaching each other on a river with a grassy shore in the foreground, occupies the shield—a romantic landscape expressive of the local scene. The crest is an American eagle on a globe showing the North Atlantic, while the supporters are the figures of liberty (dexter) and of Justice, with *Excelsior* for motto. The landscape seal of Minnesota (1858) shows the falls of St. Anthony in the distance on the right, with the setting sun on the left, an Indian riding in the direction of the latter, while in the foreground is a white man ploughing eastward, the significance of which is at once apparent. In the seal of Kansas (1861) the sun rises above distant hills, in front of these is a river with a steamboat indicative of commerce, and in the middle distance is a train of ox wagons moving west, and beyond this a herd of buffalo pursued by two Indians on horseback, while in the foreground a man is ploughing.

(a) Delaware, 7th December, 1787. On the shield are a wheat sheaf and an ear of maize and below is a ruminating ox. The crest is a ship under full sail, and the supporters are a husbandman holding a hilling hoe and a rifleman with a musket. The motto is 'Liberty and Independence'. The seal was originally adopted in 1777 and revised occasionally, the last revision being in 1907.

(b) New Jersey, 18th December, 1787. Three ploughshares are shown on the shield, the head of a horse forms the crest, while the supporters are the female figures of Liberty on the dexter side and Ceres on the sinister side. Originally adopted in 1776 the seal has been modified from time to time, the present form being that of 1928.

(c) Pennsylvania, 12th December, 1787. At the top of the shield is a ship in full sail, a plough is in the centre and three golden sheaves at the bottom. The crest is an American eagle. On the dexter side of the shield is a stalk of Indian corn and on the sinister side an olive branch. The seal was adopted in 1778, and has been modified several times, the present version being that of 1893. The reverse of the seal shows the female figure of liberty trampling on the lion, symbol here of tyranny, with the words: 'Both can't survive'. It is obviously the British lion. *Note:* The seals are arranged in the historical order of admission to the Union, the date being given in each case. In the brief enumerations of the symbols it is assumed that in many cases the meanings are obvious, but some indication of significance is given where it is felt necessary.

Fig. 11. State Seals of the U.S.A.

(*a*) Georgia, 2nd January, 1788. Three columns support a lintol and arch, signifying the support of the constitution by the three departments of government, legislative (wisdom), judicial (justice) and executive (moderation). A man is shown between two of the columns with a drawn sword symbolizing defence. It was originally adopted in 1799, and the date was changed to 1776 in 1914. This is a pendant seal and thus has a reverse which depicts a ship being loaded with commodities produced by the State, a man ploughing, with a flock of sheep are in the background. It is inscribed 'agriculture and commerce'.

(*b*) Connecticut, 9th January 1788. Three grape vines with the motto 'Qui Transtulit Sustinet'—'He who transplanted continues to sustain'. According to tradition the vine symbolizes the colony planted in the wilderness in illustration of the 80th Psalm (ver. 8): 'Thou has brought a vine out of Egypt, thou has cast out the heathen, and planted it'. The seal dates from the middle of the seventeenth century, the present form having been adopted in 1931.

(*c*) Massachusetts, 6th February, 1788. On the shield is an Indian holding an arrow, and a five-pointed star. The crest is a right arm with the hand grasping a broad sword, and the motto, written about 1659 by the Englishman Algernon Sydney and adopted in 1775, is: 'Ense petit placidam sub libertate quietem'—'By the sword we seek peace, but peace only under liberty'. This seal was originally adopted in 1785 and was modified in design but not in subject to its present form in 1898.

Fig. 12. State Seals of the U.S.A.

(a) Maryland, 28th April, 1788. In the seal of Maryland the reverse only has been cut and thus used, the obverse being for decorative purposes. The obverse shows Lord Baltimore as a knight on a charger, Lord Baltimore having sent the Ark and Dove to Maryland. The reverse shows the coat of arms of the Calvert and Crossland families. The supporters are a farmer and fisherman, symbolizing Lord Baltimore's estates of Maryland and Avalon. The seal was originally used in 1648, discontinued in this form in 1776 and readopted in 1876.

(b) South Carolina, 23rd May, 1788. In the left oval referred to as the obverse is a palmetto tree, symbolic of the fort in Charleston Harbour which was constructed of palmetto logs. An uprooted oak tree lies at the foot, symbolizing the defeated British fleet. Twelve spears representing the first twelve States of the Union are bound crosswise to the trunk of the palmetto. The motto is 'Animis Opibusque Parati'—'Prepared with minds and resources'. In the right oval, or reverse, a woman walks on the sea shore over swords, expressing hope overcoming dangers which the rising sun will reveal, while she holds an olive branch. The motto is 'Dum Spiro Spero'—'While I breathe I hope'. The seal was originally adopted in 1776, the year the constitution of the State was adopted.

(c) New Hampshire, 21st June, 1788. The seal shows the frigate *Raleigh* on the stocks, the *Raleigh* being one of the first thirteen ships of the American Navy, built at Portsmouth in 1776. In the background is the rising sun, symbolical of a new era. The design is encircled by a wreath of olive and laurel. This seal was originally adopted in 1784.

Fig. 13. State Seals of the U.S.A.

(*a*) Virginia, 25th June, 1788. On the obverse is the female figure of Virtus, standing over the prostrate body of a man representing Tyranny. Virtus holds a spear in her right hand and a sheathed sword in her left. A crown has fallen from the head of Tyranny, while he has a broken chain in his left hand and a scourge in his right. He is obviously symbolical of the tyranny and fate of Britain. 'Sic Semper Tyrannis' — 'Thus ever to tyrants' is the motto. The three figures on the reverse are Acternitas with a globe and phoenix, Libertas with a wand and liberty cap, and Ceres with a cornucopia and ear of wheat. The subjects seem to have been prompted by the mythology of Republican Rome.

(*b*) New York, 26th July, 1788. The arms of the state are used for the seal. On the shield the sun rises above a range of three mountains, on the river are a ship and sloop with a grassy shore in the foreground. The crest is the American eagle rising from two-thirds of a globe, showing the North Atlantic. The dexter supporter is a figure of Liberty and the sinister supporter a figure of Justice. The motto is 'Excelsior'.

(*c*) North Carolina, 21st November, 1789. The two figures are Liberty and Plenty. Liberty stands with a staff and Liberty cap in her left hand, and a scroll with 'Constitution' written on it, in her right hand. The seated figure of Plenty holds three heads of wheat in her right hand, and in her left a horn from which the contents are rolling out. The motto is 'Esse Quam Videri'— 'To be rather than to seem'.

Fig. 14. State Seals of the U.S.A.

(*a*) Rhode Island, 29th May, 1790. The traditional use of the anchor symbol is indicated by the word hope, used here in the sense of hope for the future as it has been used since 1647. It also indicates faith in the future.

(*b*) Vermont, 4th March, 1791. The sheaves of wheat and the cow indicate agriculture, the pine tree and the young pines may suggest the Green Mountains, the spontoon on the left is probably expressive of Vermont's early struggles, while the wavy lines at the bottom probably express the lakes and rivers of the state. This seal was first used in 1779 and was revived in 1937. There does not appear to be a precise definition of its meaning, so the description is partly conjectural.

(*c*) Kentucky, 1st June, 1792. Originally adopted in 1792 the seal shows two friends with right hands clasped and left hands on shoulders. They are supposed to be on the edge of a precipice which gives point to the motto 'United we stand, divided we fall'.

(*d*) Tennessee, 1st June, 1796. The number XVI indicates the order of admission to the Union, the plough, wheat sheaf, and cotton plant express agriculture, while the boat expresses commerce. This design was originally used in 1866.

Fig. 15. State Seals of the U.S.A.

(*a*) Ohio, 19th February, 1803. The sun appears rising above the hills of Mount Logan, and was originally adopted in 1803 as signifying the birth of a new state. In the foreground is a sheaf of wheat, and a sheaf of seventeen arrows, indicating the seventeenth state. The seal was repealed in 1805 but readopted in 1868.

(*b*) Louisiana, 8th April, 1812. The pelican tearing its breast to feed its young is the traditional Christian symbol of sacrifice. The American brown pelican (*Pelecanus occidentalis*) is familiar in the state and breeds along the coast which obviously suggested its use as an emblem. Its association with the Christian symbol is an easy transition of thought and it can signify that Louisiana cares for its youth, and thus the future. It was adopted in 1902.

(*c*) Indiana, 11th December, 1816. A woodsman is shown felling a tree, a buffalo runs from the forest, and the sun sets behind the hills which indicates that the eyes of the country are turned towards the west, as the design is symbolic of westward expansion. It was in use on official papers in 1801 and was retained as the state seal when Indiana became a member of the Union.

(*d*) Mississippi, 10th December, 1817. The American eagle has a quiver of arrows in its right talon and olive branch in its left, although it is sometimes shown with an olive branch in the right and arrows in its left talon as in the Great Seal of the U.S.A. On its breast is a shield with stars and stripes. This seal was adopted at the time of the admission to the Union.

Fig. 16. State Seals of the U.S.A.

(*a*) Illinois, 3rd December 1818. The American eagle stands on a boulder in a prairie with the rising sun in the background. Below the eagle is the shield with the stars and stripes, and on the scroll held by the eagle are the words 'State Sovereignty National Union'. An olive branch lies beneath the shield. The seal was adopted in 1867. The previous seal was similar to that of the U.S.A.

(*b*) Alabama, 14th December 1819. A map is shown of the territory of Alabama with the rivers clearly defined. This seal was originally used in 1817, but was discontinued in 1868 for one with an American eagle and shield, but the original seal was revived in 1939.

(*c*) Maine, 15th March, 1820. On the shield a moose is shown beneath a white pine, both natives of Maine. The dexter supporter is a husbandman with a scythe and the sinister a seaman with an anchor together representing agriculture, fisheries and commerce. The star forming the crest is a guide to sailors with the motto 'Dirigo'—'I direct'. The seal was adopted in 1820.

(*d*) Missouri, 10th August, 1821. On the shield the new moon expresses a young State with a future, the American eagle is taken from the U.S.A. seal, above it is the Missouri star against a cloud indicating the difficulties of the State before its admission to the Union surrounded by twenty-three other States. The supporter bears express size and strength. Above the crest are twenty-four stars, with one bigger than the others, for Missouri was the twenty-fourth and the then largest State. The seal was adopted in 1822.

Fig. 17. State Seals of the U.S.A.

(a) Arkansas, 15th June, 1836. The American eagle with the olive branch and arrows in its claws, holds in its beak a scroll inscribed 'Regnat Populus'—'The people rule'. On the shield is a steamboat, a beehive, a plough, and a wheat sheaf. Above the eagle is the goddess of Liberty holding a wreath in one hand and a liberty pole and cap in the other, and surrounded by a wreath of stars. To the left of the eagle is the angel of mercy and on the right is the sword of justice. The seal was adopted in 1864 being based on the original seal of 1820.

(b) Michigan, 20th January, 1837. On the shield is a man on a peninsula by a lake with the rising sun. The motto is 'Tuebor' —'I will defend'. The supporters are a moose and elk, the crest is the American eagle with the same motto as on the U.S.A. seal, while the motto below is 'Si Quaeris Peninsulam Amoenam Circumspice'—'If you seek a pleasant peninsula look around'. The seal was adopted in 1835, and after several changes was readopted in its original form in 1911.

(c) Florida, 3rd March, 1845. A steamboat is seen against the rising sun, in the middle distance is a cocoa tree, and in the foreground is an Indian woman scattering flowers. The seal was originally adopted in 1868 and readopted in 1885.

(d) Texas, 29th December, 1845. An illustration of this seal is not shown because permission was not granted for the purpose of this book. The design, however, is very simple and consists of a five-pointed star encircled by a wreath of olive and oak. It was first adopted in 1836 and readopted with modifications in 1839.

Fig. 18. State Seals of the U.S.A.

(a) Iowa, 28th December, 1846. A citizen soldier holding the United States flag with a liberty cap in his right hand and a gun in his left stands in front of a plough. On the left are other farming implements, a sickle, rake, with a wheat sheaf and field of wheat. On the right is a pile of piglead and a lead furnace, while the steamer *Iowa* on the Mississippi is in the background. An eagle above holds the scroll with the motto. It was adopted in 1847.

(b) Wisconsin, 29th May, 1848. Consisting of the state coat of arms, the first quarter shows a plough, the second a pick and shovel for mining, the third an arm and hammer for manufacturing, and the fourth an anchor for navigation. The U.S.A. coat of arms in a garter with the motto appears in the centre, so placed to express the loyalty of Wisconsin to the Union. The dexter supporter is a sailor with a coil of rope, and the sinister a yeoman with a pick, the crest is a badger, while below the shield is a cornucopia and a pyramid of pig lead. The seal was adopted in 1851 and slightly modified in 1881.

(c) California, 9th September, 1850. The seated figure of Minerva, who was born full grown from the brain of Jupiter, indicates that California was admitted to the Union 'full grown' without the usual probationary period. The grizzly bear at her side, the wheat and the grapes are associative symbols, while the miner in the middle distance represents an important industry, and the ship expresses commerce. 'Eureka' applies to the principle involved in the admission of the State or to the success of the miner at work. The seal was adopted in 1849.

(d) Minnesota, 11th May, 1858. The Indian riding towards the setting sun is watched by the ploughman. It expresses the advance westward of white civilization. A gun rests on a tree trunk to the left, and a waterfall is in the middle distance to the right, a noted feature of the territory, 'L'Etoile du Nord', indicates Minnesota's geographical position and association with the French. The seal was adopted in 1858.

Fig. 19. State Seals of the U.S.A.

(*a*) Oregon, 14th February, 1859. A sea coast scene with the sun setting and a departing British man-of-war under full sail, while an American steamer moves towards the shore. Trees on the right indicate the timber industry, while mining and agriculture are indicated by a pick, plough and wheat sheaf. The American eagle with olive and arrows forms a crest for the shield. The covered wagon and oxen in the centre suggest the pioneer character of the settlers. The seal was adopted in 1859.

(*b*) Kansas, 29th January, 1861. The sun rising above distant hills is depicted with a steamboat on the river, suggesting commerce, a plough and horses, agriculture, while in the middle distance is a settlers' cabin, and ox waggons going west, while further in the distance is a herd of buffalo pursued by two Indians on horseback. The motto, 'Ad astra per aspera'—'Through hard ways to the stars', appears above the thirty-four stars. The seal was adopted in 1861.

(*c*) West Virginia, 20th June, 1863. A rock with ivy expressive of stability appears in the centre, on the right of the rock is a farmer, with his right hand resting on plough handles, and his left holding a woodman's axe. A cornstalk and wheat sheaf appear by his side. On the left of the rock is a miner with pickaxe and anvil and barrels. In front of the rock are two rifles and cap of liberty. 'Montani semper Liberi'—'Mountaineers are always free'— is the motto. On the reverse is a landscape with a factory in the centre and a shed and derrick indicative of the production of salt and petroleum. In the foreground cattle graze. In the middle distance a railway train crosses a viaduct. The sun is above the mountains emerging from clouds suggesting the emergence from early troubles and difficulties. The motto above is 'Libertas e Fidelitate'—'Freedom through Loyalty'. The seal was adopted in 1863.

Fig. 20. State Seals of the U.S.A.

a) Nevada, 31st October, 1864. At the base of two mountains in the middle distance is a quartz mill, and a tunnel, from which a miner runs out a carload of ore. Below is a team loaded with ore for the mill. In the foreground are a plough, sheaf and sickle, in the distance a railway over a bridge, and beyond a range of snowclad mountains with the sun rising. The seal was adopted in 1886.

b) Nebraska, 1st March 1867. In the foreground is a smith with hammer and anvil, symbolizing the mechanical arts, while sheaves of wheat and stalks of corn with the settler's cabin signify agriculture, in the middle distance a steamboat is seen on the Missouri river, while a railway train in front of the Rocky Mountains signifies transport which contributed much to the development of the State. The motto is 'Equality before the Law'. The seal was adopted in 1867.

c) Colorado, 1st August, 1876. At the top of the shield are snow-capped mountains, below is a miner's pick and hammer. Above are fasces which bear the words 'Union and Constitution' and above this is the eye of God in a triangle similar to that on the reverse of the great seal of the U.S.A. The motto, 'Nil Sine Numine'—'Nothing without Divine Providence', is derived from Virgil's *Aeneid*. The seal was adopted in 1877.

d) North Dakota, 3rd November, 1889. Grouped round a central tree are bundles of wheat, a plough, anvil and a bow crossed with arrows. In the distance is an Indian pursuing a buffalo in the direction of the setting sun. The motto is a quotation from Webster's speech in 1830 made in defence of the Union.

Fig. 21. State Seals of the U.S.A.

(*a*) South Dakota, 3rd November, 1889. In the foreground is a farmer with his plough, to the right cattle graze, a steamboat on the river signifies transport, on the left is a smelting furnace indicating mining. A range of mountains and a forest form the distance. It was adopted in 1889.

(*b*) **Montana**, 8th November, 1889. In the distance are the Great Falls of the Missouri with the Rocky Mountains to the left, while in the foreground is a plough, pick and shovel indicating agriculture and mining as the chief occupations of the State. 'Oro y Plata'—'Gold and Silver', indicate the mineral wealth. The seal was used by the territory in 1865 and adopted by the State in 1893.

(*c*) Washington, 11th November, 1889. The head of George Washington was adopted as the State seal in the year of its admission to the Union.

(*d*) Idaho, 3rd July, 1890. On the shield is the Great Snake river in the centre, a ploughman to the left, and a tree to the right, indicating agriculture and forestry, further expressed by the wheat sheaf and cornucopia beneath the shield. The crest is the elk's head. The dexter supporter is the female figure of justice and liberty, with scale and the liberty cap on a spear; the sinister supporter is a miner with pick and shovel; the supporters suggest the idea of equality of the sexes; the whole being designed by Emma Edwards, an advocate of woman suffrage. The motto is 'Esto Perpetua', which can be rendered 'It is forever'. The seal was adopted in 1891.

Fig. 22. State Seals of the U.S.A.

(*a*) Wyoming, 10th July, 1890. In the centre a female figure of victory stands on a pedestal, and in her right hand she holds a banner inscribed 'Equal Rights'. It represents the status that women have enjoyed in the State. Two columns on either side support lamps of knowledge, while the male figures represent agriculture (dexter) and mining and oil. The seal was adopted in 1893.

(*b*) Utah, 14th January, 1896. Utah was originally called 'Descret', meaning honey-bee, thus the beehive. The date 1847 indicates the founding of the community by a group of Mormons. Sego lilies, the State flower, are on either side of the beehive. The eagle, arrow and flag are U.S.A. motifs. The seal was adopted in 1896.

(*c*) Oklahoma, 16th November, 1907. The central five-pointed star is the forty-sixth State, the other forty-five stars are shown surrounding it. In the centre of the star stand the figures of the Frontiersman, the Indian, and Justice, with the motto above: 'Labor Omnia Vincit'—'Labour conquers all'. On the left ray of the star is a seven-pointed star with an oak wreath, symbol of the Cherokee nation. On the top ray is an Indian warrior, the ancient seal of the Chickasaw nation. On the right ray is a tomahawk, bow, and three crossed arrows, symbol of the Choctaw nation. In the lower right ray are houses, a factory, and lake with an Indian hunter in a canoe, representing the Seminole nation. In the lower left ray is a sheaf of wheat and a plough, symbol of the Creek nation. The seal was adopted in 1907.

(*d*) New Mexico, 5th January, 1912. Consisting of the State coat of arms, the Mexican eagle is depicted with a serpent in its beak and cactus in its talons and shielded by the larger, American eagle. The motto is, 'Crescit Eundo'—'We grow as we go', derived from the *De Rerum Natura*—'Concerning the Nature of Things', of Lucretius. The seal was first in use in the 1880's.

Fig. 23. State Seals of the U.S.A.

(*a*) Arizona, 14th February, 1912. On the shield the sun rises behind distant mountains, a little to the right is a dam and reservoir, and in the middle distance are irrigated fields and orchards, with cattle grazing in the right foreground. To the left a miner with pick and shovel stands in front of a quartz mill. 'Ditat Deus'—'God enriches', is the motto. The seal was adopted in 1912.

(*b*) Alaska, 3rd January, 1959. The sun rises behind the distant mountains and the representations in the landscape are of the industries of the state—agriculture, forestry, fisheries, and mining, while a railway and ships are shown expressing transport and commerce with four seal rookeries in the middle distance. The seal was first used in 1910.

(*c*) Hawaii, 21st August, 1959. This seal follows in principle that adopted at the establishment of the territory in 1900, which in turn followed that of the Republic. On the shield are the stripes of the United States flag in the first and fourth quarters, and a pierced ball on a staff in the second and third quarters, while a small superimposed shield bears a gold star. The dexter supporter is Kamehameka the first who united the islands in 1791. The sinister supporter is the Goddess of Liberty wearing a Phrygian cap and laurel wreath and holding the territorial flag. The crest is the rising sun, and below the shield is a phoenix rising from flames, expressing eternal life and on either side are eight taro leaves, banana foliage and tall maiden hair fern. The motto is generally interpreted as: 'The life of the land is preserved by righteousness'.

(*d*) District of Columbia. The statue on the pedestal is of George Washington. The female figure is of Justice blinded with a wreath in her right hand and a tablet in her left, on which is written 'Constitution'. To her right is an eagle, a sheaf of wheat, and agricultural produce. In the background is the Virginia shore with the Potomac river flowing between Virginia and the city of Washington. To the left is the rising sun and to the right the Capitol of the United States. The seal was adopted in 1871 as shown in the wreath with the motto 'Justitia Omnibus'—'Justice for all'.

Fig. 24. State Seals of the U.S.A.

In the landscapes of some of the state seals agriculture is combined with representations of other industries like mining, engineering and manufacture—those of Nevada (1866), Nebraska (1867), and the reverse of the seal of West Virginia (1863), and South Dakota (1889) being examples. That of Nebraska, to describe a typical example, shows in the foreground a smith with hammer and anvil, sheaves of wheat, growing corn and a settler's cabin; in the middle distance is a steamboat on the Missouri river, and in the distance a railway train crossing a bridge, with hills forming the background. The smith symbolizes the mechanical arts and the steamboat and train the significance of transport for the speedy development of the state.

Some of the seals have more formal or conventional representations, among them that of Connecticut with its grape vines set in an ellipse, the only seal of the forty-nine of this shape, all the remainder being circular. This seal, confirmed in 1931, follows the subject of the old colonial seal of about 1644. The seal of Rhode Island has an anchor; that of Texas a star encircled by a wreath of olive and oak; and that of Louisiana has the traditional Christian symbol of the pelican and its young. The seal of Colorado shows an heraldic shield with snow capped mountains above, and miner's pick and hammer below; above the shield fasces bear the words 'Union and Constitution', while over this is the eye of God set in a triangle with the sun's rays. The motto is *Nil sine Numine*, Nothing without Divine Providence. It is thus similar in idea to part of the reverse of the U.S.A. seal.

The design of the New Jersey shield, which is one of the oldest (1776), is perhaps closest to European heraldry. The charge on the shield consists of three ploughs, the crest is a sovereign's helmet supporting a wreath and horse's head and the supporters are the goddesses Liberty (dexter) and Ceres. The seals of Mississippi, Illinois and Utah have the American eagle, while New Mexico has the Mexican eagle with a serpent in its beak and a cactus in its talons, sheltered by the American eagle, symbolism which is certainly expressive. Alabama is the only state seal which has a map of its territory as its principal subject. This was first adopted in 1818.[5] It was changed in 1868 and re-adopted in 1939.

Some states have symbolic classical figures as the principal representations on their seals. That of Virginia (1788) shows (to quote from the official description) 'Virtus, the genius of the Commonwealth, dressed as an Amazon, resting on a spear in her right hand, point downward touching the earth, and holding in her left hand, a sheathed sword or parazonium, pointing upward, her head erect and face upturned, her left foot on the form of Tyranny represented by the prostrate body of a man, with his head to her left, his fallen crown nearby, a broken chain in his left hand, and a scourge in his right'. The motto is *Sic Semper Tyrannis*. Virtus, it should be mentioned was a Roman female personification of valour and there was a Roman temple of Virtus. The reverse of this seal shows 'Libertas holding a wand and a pileus in her right hand, on her right, Aeternitas, with a globe and phoenix in her right hand; on the left of Libertas, Ceres, with a cornucopia in her left hand, and an ear of wheat in her right.' At the top is the word 'Perseverando'. A similar theme to that of the obverse of this seal appears in the reverse of the seal of Pennsylvania, which shows Liberty trampling on a lion, the symbol of tyranny, and doubtless the British Lion. One of the simplest themes is that on the seal of Kentucky (1792), which depicts two friends embracing each other with the words 'United we stand, divided we fall.' (The seals are illustrated Figs. 11–24.)

REFERENCES
1. H. FRANKFORT, *Cylinder Seals* (London, 1939). See also C. LEONARD WOOLLEY, *The Development of Sumerian Art* (London, 1935).
2. Descriptions of British State and other seals up to Victoria are given in the catalogue of seals in the British Museum.
3. There are several excellent books on seals. Among them may be mentioned: A. WYON, *The Great Seals of England* (London, 1887); WALTER DE GRAY BIRCH, *Seals* (London, 1907); J. HARVEY BLOOM, *English Seals* (London, 1906); GALE PEDRICK, *Monastic Seals of the XIIIth Century* (London, 1902); and his *Borough Seals of the Gothic Period* (London, 1904).
4. GEORGE EARLIE SHANKLE, *State Names, Flags, Seals, Rings, Birds, Flowers and Other Symbols*, revised edition, 1938, p. 224 (New York, 1934).
5. See G. E. SHANKLE, *op. cit.*, p. 185. The seals of the U.S.A. are also described and illustrated by Elizabeth W. King: 'Seals of Our Nation, States and Territories', *The National Geographic Magazine*, Vol. XC—I (Washington D.C., July 1946).

V Civic Heraldry

THE symbolism of local seals is particularly interesting because it is so often the source of the devices of the coats of arms of cities and towns, which, with military formation signs, constitute the living heraldry of today. These coats of arms are not so much coats of arms in the original sense—in which identification, in battle and at the tournaments, was the main purpose—as symbols of cities and towns to enhance civic dignity, expressed within the framework of traditional heraldry. That this form of expression is still very much alive is demonstrated by the large number of armorial bearings granted to boroughs in the present century, which amount to more than for the whole of the previous period.

In the case of the majority of cities and towns a coat of arms has been granted by the College of Arms, although the granting has often come after a similar device has been used for many years. Supporters have sometimes been granted at the same time or later. In some cases the coat of arms has been designed by the borough architect, surveyor, engineer or other competent person; in others a badge or device is used which is often merely derived from the seal.

The examples to be described are selected mainly for their interest as symbolism. In the earlier examples the coats of arms often follow those of families connected with the locality, and the symbolism is sometimes based on punning allusions to names. As the main purpose of a military coat of arms was identification the early examples were generally fairly simple with strong colours so that they were easily recognized at a distance. Thus the early civic coats of arms have this simplicity, but modern coats of arms are generally more elaborate, with much greater variety of expressive symbolism.

Civic coats of arms have been used since the fourteenth century. Historically they may be grouped into those granted or adopted before about 1670 and those, a larger number, granted or adopted after 1840. Very few seem to have been granted between 1670 and 1840; indeed the only city or town of any size to which a coat of arms appears to have been granted during this period is Liverpool, in 1797.

EARLY MUNICIPAL COATS OF ARMS

The subjects adopted for the coats of arms up to about 1670 and after 1840 are broadly similar, although the extent to which the different subjects are used varies.

The principal subjects before 1670 were royal and family emblems or devices; religious symbols, which mainly took the form of patron saints; and ships and fish expressive of maritime associations. A few industrial symbols and rebuses were also employed.

After 1850 the royal emblems disappear, but the family emblems are even more numerous, the religious devices continue, but they have become of a more historical and less devotional character; maritime and river symbols appear; there are a few rebuses; and the symbolism of industry is more conspicuous than in coats of arms before 1670.

The royal emblems that were employed in the early coats of arms were the various crowns, coronets, and heraldic lions, the fleur-de-lis, the star and crescent derived from their use on the Great Seals of Richard I and Henry III, the rose, the dragon, and several other subjects which in the course of history have appeared in the seals of State or Royal arms (*see* Chapter III).

Some of the early rebus devices are derived from seals. Thus, the device on the shield of Oxford derived from the fourteenth century seal shows an ox fording water, represented by barry wavy. The crest is a Royal device and consists of a lion wearing a crown and holding a Tudor rose. The dexter supporter is an elephant ermined with collar and chain, and the sinister supporter is a beaver with coronet round its neck with gold chain.

Examples of the early use of symbols of industry are found on the coats of arms of Boston, Droitwich, and Leeds. The arms of Boston were granted in 1568. The shield consists of three gold crowns on a black ground supported by two mermaids wearing crowns, and the crest of a woolpack in which is represented a couchant ram. The woolpack appears on a fourteenth century seal and, with the ram, signifies the mediaeval woollen industry of Boston. The mermaids signify that Boston was a port, and their crowns are supposed to express the association with Boston of Anne Boleyn and Princess Mary, Duchess of Suffolk. The arms of Droitwich have two lions passant against a sword pointing downwards on the dexter side, from the arms of Prince John, with two wicker moulds for salt manufactured with chequered pattern in two quarters on the sinister side. The manufacture of salt was a jealously guarded monopoly in Droitwich during the Middle Ages. The arms of Leeds were granted in 1662, and the crest and supporters added in 1922. On the shield are three silver stars on a black ground, and below a golden fleece expressive of the woollen manufacturers of the city. The crest and supporters consist of owls, the latter crowned, the owl being the crest of the Saville family. (Fig. 25.)

One of the most interesting of the older coats of arms is that of Bristol. It is derived in some measure from the old seal previously described, and shows a ship sailing out of the portway of a castle. The crest consists of two arms, with forearms crossed, one hand holds a snake, symbolic of wisdom and the other a pair of scales, symbolic of justice. The supporters are two unicorns. (Fig. 25.)

The arms of the City of London are worthy of note. They consist of the red cross of St. George on a white ground with the sword of St. Paul in the first quarter. The crest is a dragon's wing charged with a red cross, and the supporters are dragons with red crosses on their wings. The arms are taken from a thirteenth century seal and, as G. W. Scott-Giles[1] points out, the crest is shown on the seal as a helmet with a

(a) Boston—Granted in 1568 but in use earlier. The three crowns are thought to denote the Dukes of Brittany, Richmond, and Suffolk. The mermaids represent Boston as a port, while the woolpack and ram represent the woollen industry in the town. The motto means 'By sea and by land'.

(b) Droitwich—fifteenth century. There is a legend that King John sold his rights to the burgesses of the town for an annuity which he disposed of to his brother William of the Long Sword, and the charge on the first half of the shield shows John's lions impaled on William's sword. The wicker moulds symbolize the salt industry which has existed in the town for five centuries, while the chequer tables indicate the accounts.

(c) Leeds—originally adopted in 1626. The fleece indicates the woollen manufacturers of the city, the three stars are from the arms of Thomas Danby, first Mayor of Leeds, and the owls are derived from the arms of the city's first alderman, Sir John Savile. The motto is: 'For king and the law'.

(d) Bristol—derived from a fourteenth-century seal. The prow of a ship emerging from a castle expresses the idea of a fortified port. The crest consists of two arms, one holding a snake, symbolizing wisdom, the other scales symbolizing justice. The unicorns symbolize virtue and express the motto: 'By virtue and industry'.

Fig. 25. Examples of civic heraldry.

(*a*) City of London—Cross of St. George with the sword of St. Paul, the city's patron. The crest, derived from a sixteenth-century Corporation seal, is a dragon's wing, and the two dragon supporters were added in the seventeenth century to accord with the crest. The seal, however, shows a fan above a helmet which seems to have been erroneously interpreted as a dragon's wing. The motto is: 'Lord direct us'.

(*b*) Liverpool—This coat of arms was used before the grant was obtained in 1797. A cormorant is the charge on the shield with a branch of seaweed called Laver in its beak, repeated for the crest but with elevated wings. The dexter supporter is Neptune, wreathed with Laver, the sinister supporter is a triton, similarly wreathed. The crest bird is commonly referred to as a liver. The motto is rendered 'God has given this leisure to us'.

Fig. 26. Examples of civic heraldry.

fan-shaped top marked with a cross, and the fan came to be mistaken for a dragon's wing. As the dragon supporters were added in the seventeenth century to match the crest, the present crest and supporters would appear to be due to a mistaken reading of the seal.

The arms of Liverpool, standing in isolation between the old and the recent are interesting symbolically. The shield is charged with the liver bird, which is a cormorant, with a branch of laver or seaweed in its beak. The crest is a repetition of this, but with wings spread. The dexter supporter is Neptune with a gold crown, sea-green mantle, and a loin band of laver, holding in his right hand a trident, and in his left a banner with the arms repeated. The sinister supporter is a Triton blowing his horn and holding a banner with a ship under sail. The use of the liver bird obviously originates as a heraldic pun. (Fig. 26.)

MODERN MUNICIPAL COATS OF ARMS

The modern coats of arms generally show a rich and expressive symbolism. It must suffice to select a few examples of these, in which the various types of symbolism, such as religious, family and other associative kinds, and especially industrial symbolism, are apparent. The last figures more prominently than in the older coats of arms.

Two interesting county coats of arms are those of the Isle of Ely and of Leicestershire. The former, granted in 1931, consists of a silver shield with three blue wavy bars, and a red pile charged with three golden crowns from the arms of St. Etheldreda, the foundress of the Cathedral. The crest consists of a human arm holding a gold trident entwined by an eel, from which, according to Bede, the district is supposed to have taken its name. Round the wrist is the knot of Hereward the Wake, who fought William I in the fen country. The arms of Leicestershire, granted in 1930, are charged in the four quarters with ermine cinquefoil, a double-tailed lion rampant, an upright ermine ostrich feather and a black sleeve. The first three are taken from the family of the Earldom of Leicester, the fourth is from the arms of Hastings, Baron Loughborough. The crest, a running fox together with the motto—'For'ard'—is symbolic of Leicestershire as a foxhunting county, while the supporters, a black bull with a ducal coronet round its neck on the dexter side and a ram on the sinister side, are symbolic of the cattle breeding and wool production of the county. (Fig. 27.)

The arms of many of the cities and towns in the industrial districts are noteworthy as including interesting symbols of industry, among them the county boroughs of Barnsley, Barrow-in-Furness, Blackburn, Bury, Manchester, Salford, Sheffield, Stoke-on-Trent and the Boroughs of Accrington, Bacup, Blyth, Hyde, Middleton, Morley, Rawtenstall, Swindon and Widnes.

Barnsley has a very elaborate coat of arms granted in 1869, with industrial symbols consisting of shuttles on the shield and in the crest, symbolic of weaving and the woollen industry; crossed pickaxes on the shield symbolic of mining; while the supporters granted later, in 1913, are, on the dexter side, a miner holding a pickaxe with a pit lamp round his neck, and on the sinister side a glass-blower with a blowpipe. The arms of Barrow-in-Furness, granted in 1867, have a bee, which is a common symbol of industry used on many coats of arms, and a paddle-steamship with sails, which denotes Barrow as a shipbuilding centre. The arms of Blackburn (1852) show three bees, and the Corporation regards these as symbolic of the ability and perseverance

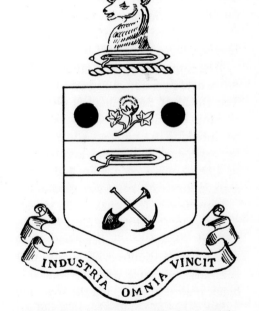

(*a*) Barnsley—granted in 1869. On the chevron is a falcon holding a padlock between two boars' heads, each holding a cross patée, derived from the arms of the two local families of Locke and Beckett. On the sable band is a crosspater between two covered covers derived from the arms of the Monk Bretton Priory, while the griffin is from the crest of the Wentworths of Wentworth Woodhouse. The shuttles on the shield symbolize the cotton industry and the pickaxes mining. The supporters were added in 1913 and are a miner on the dexter side and a glassblower on the sinister side. The motto is, 'Let us be judged by our works.'.

(*b*) Bury—granted in 1877. This is interesting as being entirely industrial in its symbolism—the anvil representing the iron industry, the fleece the woollen industry, the shuttle cotton and the papyrus plant paper-making. The bee of the crest symbolizing industry is between two flowers of the cotton tree. The motto is appropriately 'Industry overcomes all things'.

(*c*) Leicestershire—granted in 1930. The charges on the shield are derived from the arms of Leicestershire families. The supporters symbolize the industries of the country, the bull for grazing, and the ram for wool, while the fox and the motto (between a hazel leaf and martlet) symbolize the sport for which the county is famous.

(*d*) Morley—granted in 1887. An example of industrial symbolism, the sprig of cotton and the shuttle, the ram's head, and the pick-axe and spade symbolize the principal industries of the town: cotton, wool, and coal mining. The motto is the same as that of Bury.

Fig. 27. Examples of civic heraldry.

of the merchants who have raised the town to its present importance. The crest has a dove standing on a shuttle with an olive branch and a thread from the shuttle in its beak. The four charges on the shield of Bury, granted in 1877, are all industrial. The first quarter has a black anvil signifying the iron and steel industries; the second quarter has a golden fleece, signifying wool; the third has crossed shuttles signifying cotton weaving, and the fourth the papyrus plant, symbolizing paper making. A bee between cotton flowers forms the crest. These armorial bearings are entirely industrial. Its motto, *Vincit omnia industria*—industry overcomes all things—is certainly appropriate.

Another coat of arms which is entirely industrial is that of Morley, granted in 1887. In the chief (upper part of the shield) is a sprig of cotton between two black pellets; on a red fesse in the centre is a gold shuttle; below are a pickaxe and spade saltirewise. The crest is composed of a ram's head and shuttle. Thus the arms are expressive of the woollen, cotton and coal industries. The motto—*Industria omnia vincit*—is the same as for Bury. (Fig. 27.)

The arms of Swindon, granted in 1901, have very prominent industrial and some family and ecclesiastical symbols. The most prominent charge is, appropriately, a Great Western Railway steam engine, while in a fourth quarter below is a winged wheel expressive of the speed of railway transport. The crest is an arm, the hand holding two crossed golden hammers, symbolizing the mechanical engineering to which modern Swindon owes its life and prosperity. The latter is symbolized by the gold. The other symbols are three crescents, and three castles, both taken from the arms of families associated with Swindon, and in the third quarter a bishop's mitre denoting that the Manor of Swindon was granted by William the Conqueror to his half-brother, Odo, Bishop of Bayeux. (Fig. 28).

This same bishop is symbolized by a pastoral staff of silver enfiled by a bishop's mitre held by a lion guardant in the crest of the arms of Beckenham, granted in 1931. The shield of Beckenham is pleasingly expressive. It is green, with charges of two chestnut trees in full bloom, which symbolizes the verdant character of the district and the intention to keep it so, while the white wavy bars denote the river Beck from which the town derives its name, and below is the white horse of Kent. Supporters, granted in 1935, consist of a man and woman in Tudor costume, because of the Tudor associations with what was then a small village. (Fig. 29.)

Manchester (1842) has on its shield a ship in full sail which is clearly symbolic of overseas trade, while the crest has seven bees on a globe, suggesting world industry. Salford, Manchester's neighbour (1844), has also seven gold bees flying in a blue shield, with a shuttle in the centre with three wheat sheaves. Above, on a gold chief, is a bale, indicative with the shuttle of the cotton industry, while on either side are black millrinds signifying the iron industry.

The shield of Sheffield consists of arrows saltirewise, representing cutlery, and three wheat sheaves, with supporters added in 1893, Thor with his hammer on the dexter side, and Vulcan with pincers and anvil on the sinister side both expressing the steel industry. The pottery industry is represented, as would be expected, on the arms of Stoke-on-Trent (1912). The Portland vase appears in the first quarter, and the crest shows an ancient Egyptian potter throwing a pot on his wheel (Fig. 29).

Accrington (1879) has a shuttle, expressing cotton spinning, and printing cylinders,

(*a*) Widnes—granted in 1893. The red rose in the first and fourth quarters is a common emblem in the coats of arms of Lancashire and its towns, appearing in that of the county, in those of Oldham, Fleetwood, Mossley, Prestwich, Radcliffe, Stretford, Swinton, and Pendelbury, and several of the arms of the urban and rural district councils. The bees and hives in the second and third quarters are symbolical of industry and likewise common in the heraldry of the industrial areas of Lancashire. The alembic surmounting the furnace that forms the crest symbolizes the alkali and soap manufacture of the town. The motto can be read as 'Industry enriches'.

(*b*) Swindon—granted in 1901. The three crescents of the first quarter are from the arms of the Goddard family who held the manor of Swindon from 1560; the three castles are from the arms of the Vilett family who held the manor from the seventeenth century, the mitre represents Odo, Bishop of Bayeux, to whom William the Conqueror gave the manor and the land in 1066, while the winged wheel expresses swift travel which Swindon provides by means of locomotives. That at the top of the shield is the 'White Horse', a 4–2–2-class locomotive constructed in 1891. The strong arm and crossed hammers illustrates the motto 'Health and industry'.

(*c*) Rawtenstall—granted in 1891. The two stags, the wolf, and the squirrel symbolize the forest of Rossendale which once surrounded Rawtenstall, while the red hand, cut off at the wrist, represents the penalty for killing the royal deer. The cows represent agriculture and the cotton sprigs and wool-packs represent those industries. The motto is interpreted as 'He who works hard prospers'.

Fig. 28. Examples of civic heraldry.

(*d*) Bromley—granted in 1904. The broom in the first quarter, the sun in the second and the ravens on the wavy band are rebuses on the name of Bromley, the River Ravensbourne which runs through the town, and the Manor of Sundridge. The scallop shell is from the arms of the Bishop of Rochester, while the White Horse of Kent occupies the fourth quarter. The crest repeats the shell and broom. The motto can be rendered: 'While we grow we hope'.

with a piece of printed calico of Paisley pattern. Bees appear again in the shield of Bacup (1883) on either side of a black fleece, while above is a squirrel between two bales of cotton, below is a block of stone, and in the crest a stag stands beside a bale of cotton. The cotton, woollen and stone quarrying industries are thus obviously represented. Coal mining and shipbuilding are symbolized in the arms of Blyth (1923), the former in the crest which has three miners' picks on a crown, above which

(a) Cardiff—granted in 1906. On the shield a red dragon, emblem of Wales, holds a standard bearing three chevronels attributed to Iestin ap Gwrgrant, the last Prince of Glamorgan (eleventh century). From the mound springs a leek. A Tudor rose on three ostrich feathers issuing from a mural crown forms the crest. The dexter supporter is a Welsh goat, emblem of the mountains, and the sinister supporter is a hippocamp or sea-horse, representing the Severn and maritime trade. Suspended from the neck of each supporter is the Royal Badge of Wales, which was introduced in 1956 on the recognition of Cardiff as the capital of Wales. The motto is: 'The Red Dragon will lead the way', and the crest motto is 'Awake it is day'.

(b) Beckenham—granted in 1931. The chestnut trees in bloom symbolize the profusion of flowering trees and shrubs which are a treasured characteristic of the town. The wavy lines indicate the River Beck, while below is the White Horse of Kent. The lion of the crest is derived from the arms of the Cator family, the crozier and mitre symbolize Odo, Bishop of Bayeux, to whom William the Conqueror gave the manor and land. Odo was William's half-brother (see Swindon). The supporters, a lady and gentleman in Tudor dress, were added in 1935 after West Wickham with its Tudor associations had become part of the town of Beckenham. The motto is a Ciceronian principle: 'Not for ourselves alone'.

Fig. 29 Examples of civic heraldry.

is a lion holding a miner's lamp, while in the lower part of the shield is a ship. Hyde (1882) has a flake and a potter's bow, in the upper part of the shield on the dexter side a cogwheel, and on the sinister side miners' picks crossed saltirewise with lamp, while the crest consists of a bale of printed cotton, the cotton plant and a shuttle, thus expressing coal mining, cotton and hats. Sprigs of the cotton tree appear on the shield of Middleton (1887) together with the silkworm, which express the local industries, while the unusual device of a stork is said to be due to the desire for an increase in population. Rawtenstall has a very full shield; a red left hand between two deer in chief, a wolf between bales of wool on a red fesse, and two black cows grazing in the base. The crest is a squirrel between two sprigs of the cotton tree. The cotton, woollen and agricultural industries are thus represented; the deer, wolf and squirrel denote the Forest of Rossendale in the vicinity of Rawtenstall, and the hand cut off at the wrist is a reminder of the penalty for killing the Royal deer. Widnes is a further somewhat unusual example of industrial symbolism. The red Lancastrian roses appear in the first and fourth quarters, and four golden bees with a golden beehive in

(c) Buxton—granted in 1917. The shield expresses the healing properties of Buxton's eight thermal springs symbolized by the eight heraldic fountains and the rod of Aesculapius. The stag is derived from the arms of the Dukes of Devonshire, a patron of the town. The motto is appropriately, 'O all ye springs, bless ye the Lord'.

(b) Stoke-on-Trent—In 1912, when these arms were granted, the six towns were amalgamated under the City and County Borough. The boar's head is from the Stoke arms, the Stafford knot from those of Tunstall, the Portland vase from Burslem, the dromedary from Hanley, the eagle from Longton, the sneyd scythe from both Tunstall and Burslem, and the Fretty cross from the Fenton Arms. The Egyptian potter at his wheel represents the industry for which the city is famous throughout the world. The dromedary was originally from the arms of John Ridgeway, Mayor of Hanley, and was probably a rebus. The motto is 'United strength is stronger'. The motto of the old Stoke arms was particularly appropriate: 'E terris dare Artem'—'To produce beauty from the earth'.

Fig. 29. Examples of civic heraldry.

the second and third quarters. The crest consists of a gold furnace surmounted by a gold alembic, which symbolizes alkali and soap manufacturing, the gold denoting the prosperity confirmed in the motto: *Industria ditat*—Industry enriches. (Fig. 28.)

Arms of health and seaside resorts and ports often include similar or kindred symbols. Maritime symbols are generally ships, used in the arms of Lydd, Lytham St. Annes, Malden, Morecambe, Ramsgate, which has a lighthouse upon a pierhead for a crest, Redcar and Torquay. Fish, dolphins, shells, mermaids, sea-horses also appear

(a) Harlow—granted in 1948. The symbolism of the shield is of the religious associations of the district. The black cross represents Waltham Abbey, and the golden fleur-de-lis alludes to the Premonstratensians at Beeleigh. The arrow-pierced crowns represent the Abbey of Bury St. Edmunds. The griffin derives from the arms of Latton Priory, and the Saxon sword is derived from the Essex arms.

(b) Crawley—granted in 1951. The crows allude to Crawley, the interlaced chevrons to Three Bridges, and the surrounding martlets to the County of Sussex. The palisade represents the designated area of the new town, and the trowel indicates building. The dexter supporter refers to the coaching days, when Crawley was a stopping place on the Brighton road; and the other supporter alludes to the wooded areas of the district.

(c) Hemel Hempstead—granted 1948. The Tudor rose signifies that the town received its original charter from Henry VIII, while the surveyor's chain encircling it alludes to the foundation of the new town. The lodged hart of the crest is derived from the arms of Hertford, the dexter supporter is the greyhound of the Tudor royal arms, while the sinister supporter is the hart again derived from Hertfordshire. The motto is, 'Greater, more abundant, fairer things'.

(d) Stevenage—granted in 1950. The motto is: 'Consider thy purpose'. The oak tree and strong gate are symbolic of old and new Stevenage respectively, and the supporting harts stand for Hertfordshire. The indented chief represents the ancient monument of Six Hills and also refers to the family of Lytton of Knebworth.

Fig. 30. New Towns Heraldry.

pressing the oak forests which formerly covered the region, while the broken branch symbolizes the disappearance of the oak forests from the area. The crest is also a rebus on the name of the town, the Saxon name 'A cle' meaning oak leaf. The supporter lions are derived from the arms of the See of Durham. The motto is rendered 'Not the least but the greatest we seek'.

(*a*) Basildon—granted 1950. The embattled line represents the wall or boundary of the new town, the silver stars (mullets) are derived from the arms of the de Vere family who held the Manor of Botelers in Basildon in the fourteenth century. The fountain (roundle barry wavy) denotes the lost River Lyge, while the tree on the mount represents the woodlands, and the strength of the Development Corporation with roots firmly in the soil and the branches the parishes to be developed. The crest is a wyvern taken from Laindon church and the sword is that of St. Paul and indicates association with the See of London.

(*c*) Bracknell—granted 1951. The three rings linked together express the linking of the components of a new town: home, industry, and leisure in the setting of the green countryside. The stag's head indicates Windsor Forest, which once covered the area.

(*b*) Newton Aycliffe—granted 1956. The sheaves of corn are taken from the Eden family on whose estate the new town was built, the chevron represents the bridge over St. Cuthbert's Way which links the town with the Aycliffe Trading Estates, and the hand grenade the Ordnance Factory from which the trading estate was converted. The crest consists of an oak tree on a limestone cliff, the former ex-

(*d*) Peterlee—granted 1956. The Blazon contains three popinjays, a device used in the arms of the ancient Lords of Horden. The lion is that of the de Brus family, who after the Conquest were the Lords of Eden and from whose manorial residence the name of Castle Eden probably originated. The banner on the castellation is charged with the arms attributed to St. Cuthbert. The supporters are on the dexter side, a bishop, and on the sinister a miner. The bishop recalls the times when the whole of the area was in the hands of the Bishop of Durham, and the miner industry of the area today. The motto is rendered: 'I will find a way or make it'.

Fig. 31. New Towns Heraldry.

(*a*) East Kilbride—granted in 1952. The cogwheel on the black background represents industry and the sun on the green background agriculture or nature, the whole being intended to symbolize the attention paid to the importance of a balanced community, or to the town with its green belt which is not to be encroached upon. The blue and silver chequer is the Stuarts of Torrance and the black and silver the Maxwells of Calderwood. The cross represents St. Bryde. The motto is 'Forward'.

(*b*) Glenrothes—granted in 1950. The chevron bearing an otter's head is from the Balfour family arms, part of whose land is within the designated area. The wavy lines represent the River Leven which flows through the new town. The oak trees are symbolic of the old district name of the area, Fythkill, which means 'the wood above the slow flowing stream'. The wheel is emblematic of the new Rothes Colliery. The motto 'Out of the earth, power', refers to the local mining industry.

(*c*) Corby—granted in 1958. The cross is derived from the coat of arms of the Latymer family who were for long the Lords of Corby. The four crowned oak leaves represent the royal forest of Rockingham, on part of which the new town is sited. The crest is a crow being a rebus on the Latin name—corvus—of crow. It holds in its claw a gad of steel expressing the principal industry of the town.

(*d*) Badge of Cwmbran, which is a Welsh name meaning Valley of the Crow.

Fig. 32. New Towns Heraldry.

as maritime symbols; in the arms of Poole maritime significance is heavily emphasized by three scallop shells, a dolphin on wavy bars, and the crest a mermaid holding an anchor and ball. Health resorts have similar themes. Buxton (1917) has eight roundels barry wavy, which are heraldic fountains, representing Buxton's eight springs, surrounding the snake and rod of Aesculapius. These fountains also appear in the crest of Cheltenham, in the first and fourth quarters of the shield of Harrogate, and in the shield of Tunbridge Wells, where they are accompanied by drops of water. (Fig. 29.)

The snake and rod of Aesculapius also appear in the crest of Leamington (1876). Two snakes encircling a tree trunk on a tower surmounted by a black cock form the crest of Harrogate.

Other interesting symbols are the broom plant used as a heraldic pun in the arms of Bromley and indicative of the district of Bromley in the arms of Gillingham. The broom has an honoured history because from it—*Planta genista*—the Plantagenets are supposed to derive their name. Bromley has the further pun of three ravens for the river Ravensbourne that runs through the town, and the sun for the Manor of Sunbridge. The white horse of Kent, and the scallop shell, from the arms of the See of Rochester, complete its symbolism. (Fig. 28.)

One of the most modern symbols is that used in the crest of the arms of Hendon (1932), namely the winged propeller, signifying that the town is associated with aviation. Further notable examples of modern civic coats of arms are those of the new towns, eleven of which are illustrated, while the badge of another is shown.

These modern civic coats of arms in which symbolism is taken from the character, life and activities of the district can, after a little experience, be read as picture writing. It should not be difficult with the more expressive examples, to learn something of the town by looking at the coat of arms. Here, therefore, symbolism tells its story while giving a note of dignity.

REFERENCE

1. C. WILFRID SCOTT-GILES, *Civic Heraldry of England and Wales*, 2nd edition (London, 1948), p. 48. This is a valuable and systematic record of the Municipal Coats of Arms up to 1948, to which I must express my indebtedness for much useful information.

VI Coins

FOR buying and selling it has always been necessary for communities to have objects, goods or tokens which represent fixed values. Among the earlier media of exchange in ancient times were cattle, and to a less extent, agricultural implements and household utensils. This rough 'currency' was superseded by pieces or bars of metal valued by weight. To obviate the necessity for constantly re-weighing them, the pieces of metal were stamped with their weight and a guarantee by the authority using them, at first the private trader or banker and later the State. Eventually their value was fixed by the State. This was the origin of coins and money as we know them today.

It will be seen therefore that as society became too complex for direct barter, the exchange of goods of related value gradually gave way to indirect exchange by means of symbols. These were authenticated by a symbolic mark.

The Lydians of the eighth century B.C. were, according to Herodotus, the first to use coins. They appear almost simultaneously in China and Greece in the early seventh century, the earliest examples of the latter being in the Ionian territory west of Lydia, and a little later they appear in the island of Aegina and on the mainland of Greece. The earliest coins of Lydia and Iona were of electrum, a natural mixture of gold and silver, while those of the Greek mainland and islands were mainly of silver.

GREEK COINS

The guarantee stamp on early Greek coinage was of a religious character and was issued from the various religious sanctuaries. Thus common symbolism on early Greek coins were the heads or figures of gods and of animals associated with them. Among the earliest are the coins of Aegina from the seventh to the fifth century B.C., which have on one side an incuse square and on the other a tortoise, a symbol of Aphrodite. The coins of Athens in the sixth, fifth and fourth centuries consisted of the head of Athena on one side and the owl and olive branch on the other, which were both sacred to Athena, being symbols of wisdom and peace. The design of the coins varies with different periods; on the fifth century coinage, for example, a wreath of olive is placed round the helmet of Athena, to commemorate the victory at Marathon. The coins of Corinth have on one side the winged horse, Pegasus, because, according to the myth, he first alighted at Corinth. The earliest coins of Corinth, of about

600 B.C. have the swastika on the other side, but this was replaced in the later sixth, fifth and fourth centuries by the head of Athena. The coins of Thebes from the sixth to the fourth centuries have the shield on one side, probably as a symbol of Hêrakles, and this was adopted by the other cities of Boeotia, but they placed symbols of other gods and goddesses on the other side; thus there is the amphora or wine cup symbolical of Dionysus, the trident for Poseidon, the disk for Apollo and the crescent for Artemis. The coins of Delphi show the symbols of Apollo—such as the dolphin and the ram's head—as the god of flocks and herds.

The coins of Olympia varied, but most carried the devices sacred to Zeus, such as an eagle, often with the serpent in its beak, the thunderbolt and the figure of Nike. On one early coin of the late sixth century B.C. is the eagle in flight on one side, and thunderbolt on the other; another example of the early fifth century shows on one side a magnificent design of eagle and on the other a flying figure of Nike.

The coins of Sicily are particularly interesting and beautiful and in many, symbols indicative of some aspect of the locality are used. Thus a crab appears on sixth century coins of Akragas expressive of local produce; the wild parsley, from which the city of Selinus derives its name, appears on its coins of the sixth century, the coins of Zancle-Messina have a representation of a dolphin in a semi-circular form, indicative of the labour of the city. From Sicily came the lovely commemorative coins; one the famous Damareteion of Syracuse (480 B.C.) shows a laurel crowned head encircled with dolphins on one side and the Quadriga (see Encyclopedia p. 299) with the winged figure of victory and running lion; and the famous coin of Agrigentum (415 B.C.) with two eagles, one with head uplifted and the other with head bent and wings outstretched standing on the dead body of a hare, with the Quadriga on the other side of the coin. The meaning of the two eagles and hare is obscure. As suggested by Charles Seltman,[1] it may be a pun on the Greek name of the city—Akragas—which means harsh or stormy, a suitable appellation for an eagle. Barclay Head[2] suggested that it might be a reference to the *Agamemnon* of Aeschylus, in which he writes of birds devouring a hare. The eagles may be taken as symbols of victory, but there is obviously some dramatic emphasis of the victory commemorated here. (A selection of Greek coins is shown on Plate IX.)

Other symbols on Greek coins are the lyre of Calymna, sacred to Apollo (approximately 460 B.C.) the sphinx of Chios (approximately 375 B.C.), the eagle of Elis (390 B.C.) symbolic of Zeus, and the vine of Maronea, expressive of the produce of the district and of Dionysus.

At the time of Philip of Macedon and Alexander the Great a universal coinage was adopted for Greece. For the former the heads of Zeus and Apollo appear on the obverse with a boy driving a chariot on the reverse. The contemporary coins of Alexander show the head of Heracles with the seated figure of Zeus on the reverse. Those of a little later show the idealized head of the god with the seated Athena on the reverse.

It is widely thought that these heads are idealized portraits of Alexander, and if this is the case they constitute the first examples of portraits of an actual person appearing on coins. We know that the likeness of Alexander was recorded by the painter Apelles, the sculptor Lysippus and the gem-cutter Pyrgoteles, and it has been suggested that the head on the coins were derived from their portrayals of Alexander.

As gods had previously been exclusively represented on coins, this portrayal of Alexander was the beginning of the representations of the heads of sovereigns, which was the characteristic of most European coins since the beginning of the Roman Empire. The ancient tradition of representing only gods was, however, so strong that it still dominated the coins of Alexander, who was represented as a deified hero, almost as a god, and thus the image that we see on coins is so idealized as only remotely to resemble the probable subject. This point, however, is important symbolically. The subject of the god gave place to that of the idealized ruler, and this tradition has never died, for it lives in the coins of Elizabeth II. Although a portrayal of an individual, the head is also a symbol of sovereignty and it is presented with the impersonal dignity befitting the role. A symbolic portrait rather than a realistic one, it is a conception which derives from the religious coinage of Greece.

ROMAN COINS

Early Roman money follows the same course as that of Lydia and Ionian Greece. Pieces of metal were used which were exchanged on the basis of weight, being called *aes rude*. These later gave place to pieces of bronze marked with some device and significantly called *aes signatum*. One example has a trident marked on one side and an anchor on the other.

Early Republican coins, equivalent to the standard pound, called the *as*, have the head of Janus on the obverse. The obverse of other coins shows the head of Jupiter crowned with a laurel wreath, Minerva, Hercules with the lion's skin, and Mercury with winged cap. All the reverses have the prow of a warship, which continued on the reverses of some coins throughout the period of the Republic. Heads of deities continued to appear on the obverses. On one coin the head of Roma appears, with Castor and Pollux on the reverse.

The first portrait of a Roman to appear on coins is that of Flamininus in the early second century B.C. As the conqueror of Macedonia, he had the precedent of Alexander. This was later followed by the coins of Julius Caesar, Brutus, Antonius and other generals of the Republic, bearing their portraits. In one coin of Brutus the reverse shows a cap of liberty between the two daggers that had stabbed Caesar with the words *eid mar*—the Ides of March. The way was thus prepared for the first Roman Emperor to place his portrait on the obverse of coins and establish a tradition which has been followed in the monarchies of Europe ever since, and also in many of the republics, by using the head of the president, or the head of some symbolic figure of state, such as the woman's head of the French Republic. The heads of the emperors were generally shown in profile crowned with a laurel wreath, and encircled with an inscription of raised letters, and these details have been widely followed.

During the great days of the Roman Empire very large numbers of coins were struck in the various provinces, and the reverses exhibit a variety of symbolic devices. These symbols were sometimes directed to the glorification of the Emperor and the celebration of his virtues and exploits, or in commemoration of events connected with his reign, or were devices expressive of the well-being of the Empire. The common and similar themes of plenty, fertility and fecundity are symbolized by the cornucopia or horn of plenty, capricorn or sea goat, ears of corn, the modius or bushel measure filled with corn, and the goddess Ceres. Ideas of security, peace and health are expressed by a column or pillar, or the right hand raised, while hands joined suggest concord, and a hand holding a caduceus, concord and peace. Maritime associations are indicated by the prow of a ship, a dolphin, crab and several others. The rudder or helm of a ship is also used to express fortune.

Various parts of the Empire were often symbolized on coins by trees, plants and animals associated with the countries. Thus Egypt is indicated by a crocodile or lotus flower, Africa by a lion or elephant, Arabia by a camel or a branch of frankincense; while oriental towns, like Damascus, Judea, Sidon and Tyre, are symbolized by a palm tree. One of the most interesting symbols of countries is the triquetra or triscele as a symbol of Sicily, representing, it has been suggested, the three-sided shape of the island or its three promontories. It had been used on the Greek coins of Sicily, on the coins of Lycia and Melos and on the shield of Athena, so that it may be used as a sun symbol, and the association with the shape of Sicily may be subsequent to its use in coins there. On some of these coins the head of Medusa appears in the centre of the three legs, with ears of corn joined thereto. Some of the symbols of the gods are a bow, laurel or lyre for Apollo; a bow and club for Hercules; a bow and quiver for Diana; an owl for Pallas Athena; a peacock for Juno; vine or a panther or a thyrsus—a staff surmounted by a pine cone and sometimes entwined with ivy—for Bacchus. Other interesting symbols appearing on coins are a sow with litter representing the Roman people, while a man driving oxen to plough indicates the idea of Roman colonization. The fasces with axe is the well-known symbol of sovereign authority. Shortly after the conversion of Constantine to Christianity the chi rho monogram appears on the reverses of coins.

These are but a selection. For a more exhaustive discussion of the symbolism used on ancient coinage the reader is referred to the numerous works on the subject.[3]

British Coins

Coins commemorating conquests were issued as the Roman Empire expanded. Thus the reverse of the denarius of Claudius commemorating the invasion of Britain shows a triumphal arch surmounted by the Emperor riding a horse, flanked by trophies of captured arms. The reverse of coins of Hadrian (3rd consulship c. A.D. 119) show a seated woman with spear and shield by her side and inscribed with the word Britannia, a design which clearly leads to the modern penny. This is, apparently, the first personification of Britannia.

The British coins of Antoninus Pius (A.D. 154) depict Britannia seated on a rock in thoughtful mood with the shield and staff by her side. The British coins of Septimus Severus (A.D. 210) show on the reverse the winged figure of Victory holding a laurel wreath and palm branch encircled by the words Victoriae Brit.

As in this broad survey of symbolism on coins we can refer only to a few examples from selected fields, we will pass over the Anglo-Saxon and Danish periods and trace briefly the designs of coinage since William the Conqueror in so far as it shows symbolism of interest. The precedent of Roman coinage is followed with little variation by placing the head of the monarch on the obverse. In most of the coins from William I to Richard III the heads are shown full face, in the minority they are in profile. Sometimes the king is shown enthroned with sceptre and orb as in the representations on the great seals, examples being a gold penny of Henry III and a gold florin of Edward III. Some of the heads are shown with a sword or sceptre. Another variation for the obverse is the king standing on a ship with shield and sword, as appears on gold nobles of Edward III and Henry V, a half noble of Henry VI and a gold ryal of Edward IV. The reverses of most of the coins between William I and Richard III show the religious symbol of the cross variously decorated. This decoration is often of a Gothic character, as when the cross is set in a quaterfoil. One interesting coin, the design of which departs somewhat from the general run is the gold angel, first introduced in the reign of Edward IV. On the obverse appears the Archangel Michael slaying a dragon, hence the name of the coin, and on the reverse is a ship with the royal standard in the centre at the side of the ship, above which is a cross flanked by a rose and small sun, while above the cross is a larger sun. The angels of later reigns, like those of Mary I, Elizabeth and Charles I are in essentials similar, but with variations in the details of the designs.

The coins of the Tudors continue the tradition of showing the head of the Monarch either full face or in profile and sometimes enthroned, as in sovereigns of Henry VII and Henry VIII, while the equestrian portrait is sometimes introduced as in the silver crown of Edward VI. After the Tudors all heads of monarchs are shown in profile. The cross continues occasionally no the reverses, but often shown on the Royal Arms, the cross arms dividing the four quarters. The Tudor rose—the red rose of Lancaster placed on the white rose of York—with the Royal Arms in the centre, appears on the first sovereign of Henry VII. The Tudor rose is a common device on Tudor coins, often shown with the crown above it. Another symbol introduced into coins of Elizabeth is the portcullis. St. George and the Dragon appears on English coinage for the first time in the gold George noble of Henry VIII. The theme of St. George and the Dragon is, of course, similar to that of the Archangel Michael on the angel coins. St. George was to reappear later on the reverse of sovereigns and crowns from George III onwards, in Pestrucci's famous and beautiful design. This design lasted until the disappearance of the sovereign and half sovereign in the First World War. The crown continued to be issued mainly for commemorative purposes. The reverse of the George V Silver Jubilee crown of 1955 had St. George and the Dragon, but Pestrucci's design was replaced by a stiff angular representation by Percy Metcalf.

An interesting feature of the coinage of the Stuarts is the reappearance of Britannia. She appears on the reverse of the farthing of Charles II seated on a rock with the shield bearing the Union Jack by her side, with spear in her left hand and olive branch in her right hand (1672). There can be little doubt that this design was derived from Britannia on the coins of Hadrian and Antoninus Pius previously mentioned. It appears again on James II farthings with much the same posture, and later, on farthings of William III, Anne and George III, becoming quite maidenly in those of Anne. Britannia appears for the first time on a silver coin in the Bank of England dollar of George III of 1804. She still holds the olive branch, somewhat grown in size, with the spear, and the Union Jack shield is by her side, while the symbols of the beehive and cornucopia are added, expressive of industry and plenty. In the cartwheel penny of George III Britannia is given a maritime significance. The spear is changed for a trident, waves are at her feet, while a ship sails in the distance. The olive branch is still there. So far she has always faced to her right (the spectator's left); in the farthing of George IV she is turned round, the trident still, however, in her left hand and the olive branch in her right, but she wears a plumed helmet for the first time and an additional symbol appears in the form of a lion peeping from behind her. The sea and ship have gone. In the George IV penny Britannia loses the olive branch. In the pennies of Victoria, the maritime accessories of Britannia are reintroduced, but not the olive branch. In a penny first issued in 1860 she is shown with trident, Union Jack, shield, sea and ship with the addition of a lighthouse. For the pennies of Edward VII and George V both ship and lighthouse have disappeared, while in the Edward VII florin Britannia stands for the first time. The lighthouse returns without the ship on the pennies of George VI.

The history of the representation of Britannia on coins suggests that successive generations have joined in the game of changing, adding, subtracting symbols.[4] The spear with the olive branch signifies that by preparation for defence we have peace. This was changed to ruling and defending the sea, still with the symbol of peace. It is a pity that the olive branch departed in the reign of George IV, but it returned in 1969 with the 50 pence coin in the new decimal series, where the British lion is introduced by the side of Britannia.

The reverses of many coins since the Tudors have the Royal Arms, variously treated, the crown and the British lion. In modern coins some new symbols are occasionally introduced which always give a freshness and added interest to the coinage, and this is certainly preferable to repeating for ever the same traditional symbols. It is an indication that we give thought to making the devices on coinage of some significance. It was customary for the smaller copper or bronze coins before the reign of George VI to have reverses like that of Britannia on the penny, but with George VI some fresh symbols were introduced. Thus on the reverse of the threepenny piece a clump of thrift is shown: on the halfpenny a ship—Drake's *Golden Hind*—the first ship to sail round the world; and the wren on the smallest of coins, the farthing. On the threepenny piece of Elizabeth II the portcullis is introduced. This may be as a symbol of safety, but it was probably prompted by the use of the portcullis on some coins of Elizabeth I, as previously noted.

The decimal coinage, as previously mentioned, presents a new version of Britannia in the 50 pence coin. The 10 pence coin has the lion from the crest of the Royal Arms (see Fig. 3), the 5 pence piece has the Scottish thistle, royally crowned, the 2 pence coin has the three ostrich feathers enfiling a coronet of crosses patée and fleur-de-lis, the badge of the Prince of Wales. The 1 pence coin has the portcullis like the threepenny coin of Elizabeth II, while the $\frac{1}{2}$ penny coin has the royal crown.

Some of the most interesting associative symbolism on coins is seen in those of the British Commonwealth countries. In the series for the Bahama Islands, Gambia, Ghana, New Zealand, Tanzania and Singapore of 1966–67, the fauna and flora of the countries have provided the subjects for design. In the reverses of the coins for the Bahama Islands by Arnold Machin, flamingoes (2 dollar), a jumping blue martin (50 cents), a bone fish (10 cents), and star fish (1 cent) are chosen as representative fauna, and the hibiscus plant (15 cents) and pineapple (5 cents) represent the flora, while other associated objects are a conch shell and a native sloop. The reverses of the Gambia coins designed by Michael Rizzello show among the fauna a crocodile (4 shillings), a long-horned bull (2 shillings) and a bush fowl (3 pence). Oil-palm (1 shilling), ground nuts (3 pence) and a native cutter are the other symbols. Cocoa pods and a talking drum appear on the obverses of Ghana coins designed by Michael Rizzello.

The new decimal coinage for New Zealand introduced in 1967 has many interesting associative symbols. The dollar coin, designed by William Gardner, has the New Zealand shield of arms encircled by fern fronds. The other reverses designed by James Berry show Captain Cook's ship *Endeavour* off Mount Egmont (50 cents), two national emblems—the kiwi and fern bush—(20 cents), a traditional Maori head (10 cents), a tuatara on a rock (5 cents), kowhai flowers (2 cents) and a fern leaf (1 cent). The reverses on the coins of Tanzania of 1966 designed by Christopher Ironside show the torch of freedom (1 shilingi), a rabbit (50 senti), ostrich (20 senti) and a sail fish (5 senti). Those of Singapore show a lion flanked by sheaves of rice (1 dollar), and a selection from the fauna on the other coins. The 1 cent coin has a modern building and a fountain which is a change of theme.

In some cases the symbols chosen for the coins indicate some of the customs of the people. Thus in the 20 cents coin of Fiji of 1968, designed by J. K. Payne, a whale's tooth with plaited cord is depicted,which is expressive of the custom of presenting a sperm whale's tooth for a wide variety of ceremonial occasions from birth to death. The 1 cent coin shows a communal mixing and serving bowl used for the Kava drink at ceremonies commemorating special occasions. Other symbols used in the Fiji coinage of 1968 are a wooden throwing club (10 cents) a Fijian drum (5 cents) and a fan (2 cents). Coin symbols of this kind form a small index of a country's life.[5]

REFERENCES

1. CHARLES SELTMAN, *Masterpieces of Greek Coinage* (Oxford, 1949).
2. BARCLAY V. HEAD, 'Greek Coins' in *Coins and Medals* by the authors of the British Museum Official Catalogues (London, 1892).
3. Among works on ancient coinage may be mentioned: G. F. HILL, *A Handbook of Greek and Roman Coins* (London, 1899); CHARLES SELTMAN, *Masterpieces of Greek Coinage* (Oxford, 1949) and HAROLD MATTINGLY, *Coins of the Roman Empire in the British Museum*, 5 vol. (London, 1923–50).
4. For further study of symbolism in English coinage there are numerous works which are very helpful, among which may be mentioned: SIR CHARLES OMAN, *The Coinage of England* (Oxford, 1931); GEORGE C. BROOKE, *English Coins from the seventeenth century to the present day* (London, 1932) (3rd edition, revised, 1950); M. COMENCINA, *Coins of the Modern World*, 1870–1936 (London, 1937) and PETER SEABY, *The Story of the English Coinage* (London, 1952).
5. Royal Mint Annual Reports (London 1869–1970).

VII Medals

COINS for commemorative purposes, not intended to be used as currency, made occasionally in ancient Greece, and more frequently in ancient Rome, and usually referred to as medallions, lead naturally to modern medals. These are generally considered to begin with those of Pisanello, whose first, produced in 1438, was that of John VIII Palaeologus, the Byzantine Emperor, on the occasion of his visit to Italy in that year.

A medal may be defined as a coin-like object issued to commemorate a person or event, or achievement—either collective or individual. In the last case, especially when of the military type, it is used in modern times very much as the laurel, oak or olive crowns were used as rewards for achievement and valour in ancient Greece and Rome.

The medals of the Renaissance were generally made to commemorate some event connected with the ruling princes; or sometimes merely from a desire among the members of ruling families to have their portraits, as one would have a painted portrait or photograph today. Generally on the obverse is a portrait in profile, rarely full face as sometimes seen on coins. These portraits in the medals of Pisanello are fine renderings of character, with beautiful placing on the field, and the lettering round the circumference and sometimes across the field is felicitously spaced and arranged. It is tempting to dwell on the aesthetic qualities of Pisanello's medals, the most beautiful ever produced, but we must concern ourselves with the interesting symbolism often found in the reverses.

Pisanello made several medals for the Marquess Leonello d'Este, one of which commemorates the marriage of the Marquess with Maria of Aragon in 1444. The reverse of this medal is a pun on the name Leonello and shows a little cupid in front of a lion holding an unrolled scroll on which are the musical notes of the lion's marriage song. Pisanello's medal of Cecilia Gonzaga (1447), a lady who later became a nun, shows on the reverse a seated woman with her hand resting on a unicorn reclining by her side, the unicorn being a symbol of virginity (see Part IV). The inscription on the obverse reads: *Cecilia virgo filia Johannis Francisci primis marchionis Mantue*. The reverse of Pisanello's medal of the mathematician Vittorino de Feltre shows a pelican and its young, used to symbolize his great qualities as a teacher. One of his medals of Alfonso V of Aragon has on the reverse the eagle with its prey at its feet, part of which he spares for the lesser birds that surround him. The eagle, a mediaeval symbol of magnanimity, indicated that this quality was possessed by Alfonso.

The work of the Italian medallists who followed Pisanello, if not of such outstanding excellence, is still of considerable merit, with interesting symbolism. In the reverse of the fine medal of Giulia Astollea, probably by Pier Jacopo Alari Bonacolsi, appears the phoenix rising from the flames, which symbolizes the lady's fortitude and chastitity. A medal of Isabella d'Este, Marchesa of Mantua, made in 1498 by Geancristoforo Romano, expresses on the reverse her interest and belief in astrology and shows a winged female figure holding a wand with a serpent before her, and the sign of the archer over her head. Other symbols which appear in Italian Renaissance medals are the figure of justice with scales, in the medal of Leonardo Loredano the Doge of Venice (1501–21) by Vettor Gambello; a crowned eagle on a rock, symbol of kingly constancy, on the medal (1523) of Vincenzo Malipieri by Maffeo Olivieri; and on the reverse of the Florentine medals of Savonarola a hand emerging from the clouds holding a dagger and threatening the city of Florence, this illustrating his words; 'The sword of the Lord shall come upon the earth soon and speedily.' On the reverse of the medal of Francesco Taverna, Count of Sandriano, by Pier Paolo Galeotti is a hound, symbol of constancy, shown against a background of trees and classical architecture. The medal of Francesco Lomellini made in Padua by Lodovico Leoni shows on the reverse an anvil with two banners against a landscape background with the sun shining above, considered to symbolise firmness. It will be seen that the meanings given to the symbols are stretched a little to meet the occasions, while in some instances the symbolism is not intelligible, as in the case of the medal of Cardinal Francesco Gonzago by Sperandio, which shows a lynx or cat seated before a narrow pyramid, or that of Giuliano della Rovere which shows a woman with a dog, pelican and cock on a galley; or again the medal of the Papal Nuncio at Venice, Girolamo Veralli, which displays a griffin at the top of a palm tree, with, at the foot, a beast with the body of a dog and the neck and head of a dragon.

The symbolism employed on Italian Renaissance medals is not always very apt or expressive, and its occasional obscurity defeats its purpose. Symbols, with some assistance from traditional understanding, should tell their own story.

German, Dutch and French medals, often have interesting symbolism, but we shall limit our selection to the symbolism of English medals from the Renaissance to the present day.

English Medals

The earliest medals made for Englishmen were the work of foreign artists. The first appears to be that of John Kendal made by an Italian artist of the Florentine School in 1480 when Kendal was in Italy. The obverse shows a spirited portrait, and Kendal's coat of arms appears on the reverse.

Most of the medals of the reign of Henry VIII are foreign workmanship. An exception, commemorating Henry's proclamation of his supremacy over the Church in 1545, was a medal by the Englishman Henry Basse. There is however little of symbolic interest in the medals of this reign. The Italian Jacopo da Trezzo made some excellent portrait medals of Mary Tudor about the year 1554, and on the reverse of one is a design of the figure of Peace setting fire to military equipment. Behind her are the blind and distressed, and the implication of the motto is that vision and tranquillity come with peace.

Interesting symbolism appears on some of the many Elizabethan medals. Two celebrate Elizabeth's recovery from smallpox. The first one, struck in 1572, shows on the reverse the hand of St. Paul which is unharmed by the serpent that is shown fastened to it, as an analogy of Elizabeth being unmarked by the disease. The other medal, dated 1574, has on the reverse the phoenix, used as a symbol of Elizabeth's recovery, and also her personal badge. Several medals were made to commemorate the Armada. One shows on the reverse a bay-tree on a small island in the sea with lightning, from which the bay-tree was then supposed to be immune, thus symbolizing the safety of this island country. A similar theme appears on the reverse of another medal which shows the Ark floating on a rough sea, the Ark also signifying Britain. Other symbolism employed in connection with the Armada is the release of the globe from the bands that Philip of Spain had fastened round it, and young birds beating off birds of prey. Some of the Armada medals are vehicles of satire, especially those produced by the Dutch. One, of 1588, shows on the reverse the Pope with kings and others seated in conference, with eyes bandaged, while the floor is studded with spikes, the representation intending to indicate the blindness of the Papacy. The reverse shows the Armada being dashed on the rocks. The peace with Spain in 1604, in the reign of James I, is celebrated in a medal which shows James full-face, and on the reverse two female figures with palm branch and cornucopia, illustrating the prosperity that peace was to bring. A year later, in 1605, the Gun Powder Plot is symbolized on a Dutch medal by a snake among lilies and roses, the snake being Jesuit intrigue and the lilies and roses, presumably, Protestant England.

The first Coronation medal was that of Edward VI, in 1547, which shows on the obverse the king in profile with sword, orb and crown; Tudor rose, harp and portcullis are in the border with the inscription. The reverse merely repeats the inscription in Hebrew and Greek. There are no further Coronation medals until that of James I. Interesting symbolism for such medals begins with that of Charles I. It is rather belligerent in character, showing an arm with a sword on the reverse symbolizing the intention to prosecute war with vigour until peace is restored. Numerous medals of various kinds were produced in the reign of Charles I, but none is more interesting symbolically than the memorial medal made by Thomas Rawlins, which shows on the reverse a hammer striking a stone on a block, the king being compared to a diamond which damages the hammer that strikes it. There is truth in this symbolism, because at the moment of the execution of Charles the tide began to turn in favour of the monarchy. The memorial medal of Cromwell in 1658 by Thomas Simon also has an interesting item of symbolism, for on the reverse a young olive tree grows by a dead stump, expressing the hopes that were centred on Cromwell's son Richard.

There were two Coronation medals of Charles II, both by Thomas Simon. The reverse of one presents Charles seated with sceptre and orb being crowned by a winged figure; the reverse of the other shows the oak tree in full foliage, symbolizing renewal, with three crowns in the foliage and the sun shining overhead.

One of the most interesting, symbolically, of Coronation medals is that of William and Mary, struck in Holland in 1689, and designed by R. Arondeaux. On the obverse of this medal is the orange-tree and the rose encircling the portraits of William and Mary with the four sceptres of England, France, Scotland and Ireland united under one crown, and below the Bible and a book of the laws of England, while the eye of Providence looks on. This combination of symbols is intended to express that on the foundations of the monarchy, law and religion, the security and happiness of the kingdom depends. The design of the reverse is similar to that of the medal struck earlier in the year by John Smeltzing, which commemorates the offer of the crown to William. An oak-tree, symbol of James, is shown broken at the stem; in the Coronation medal the tree has been torn out by the roots and lies on the ground, a feat accomplished by the Coronation. Beside the fallen oak is the orange-tree, symbolic of William and Mary. Another Coronation medal of William and Mary by George Bower (of which there are similar examples by John Smeltzing) presents William as Perseus rescuing Andromeda representing England (Plate XVIII).

The Coronation medal of Anne in 1702, by John Croker, depicts the queen as Athene wielding the thunderbolts of Zeus, expressive of her determination to continue the policy of William in opposing the power of France.

The Coronation medals of the first three Georges represent on the reverses the theme of the king being crowned by Britannia. In those of George I by Ehrenreich Hannibal and John Croker, struck in 1714, the king is seen seated in profile, while the royal arms appear in Britannia's oval shield. Croker also made the Coronation medal of George II in 1727. In this medal Britannia holds a cornucopia and leans on the fasces, a Roman symbol of authority. (See Part IV).

In the Coronation medal of George IV, instead of the figure of Britannia a winged figure crowns the king, who is seated to the left on a dais, while three figures representing England, Scotland and Ireland advance towards him. In the reverse of Victoria's Coronation medal the figures of England, Scotland and Ireland unite to proffer the imperial crown. A lion with a thunderbolt is shown behind the queen. In the 'official' Coronation medals of William IV, Edward VII, George V and George VI, the obverse shows the crowned head of the king and the reverse the crowned head of the queen. The reverse of the Coronation medal of Elizabeth II merely gives the Royal Cypher and crown. These later Coronation medals are dull, and betray a lack of imaginative expression.

A fine design appears on a medal of 1691 made by Jan Luder commemorating the suppression of rebellion in Ireland, which shows Hêrakles killing the Hydra. Many medals were struck to commemorate the defeat of the French fleet at La Hogue in 1692. One by Jan Boskan depicts a naval battle in the distance and in the foreground a lion and unicorn chasing the French cock from the sea. The unicorn carries a trident rather clumsily with its foreleg, an elaboration which exemplifies the tendency prevalent at this time to overdo the symbolism.

Medals commemorating battles continued to be issued throughout the seventeenth and eighteenth centuries, generally showing the portrait of the monarch on the obverse and a representation of the battle on the reverse. Medals awarded for military service, gallantry, and valour did not become general until the nineteenth century, although a few instances occur before that time. The first was the medal issued to the officers and men who were victorious in the battle of Dunbar in 1650. This medal, designed by Thomas Simon, bears on the obverse the head of Cromwell and on the reverse

Parliament in session. Of other medals since the seventeenth century a few may be noted for their interesting symbolism. An example in the reign of George II is the medal awarded to officers who were present at the battle of Culloden in 1746. Designed by Richard Yeo, it shows on the obverse a head of the Duke of Cumberland and on the reverse Apollo standing by a dragon killed by his arrow, with the words, 'Tis done and ended, he lies dead', referring to the Jacobite ambitions.

In 1784 a medal was awarded by the Calcutta Government for services in the Maratha and Second Mysore which shows a figure of Britannia offering a wreath with a fortress in the background. Another medal was awarded in 1793 for service in the Mysore campaign, depicting a Sepoy holding the British flag with the enemy flag reversed. Several medals were awarded at the end of the eighteenth century and early nineteenth for various campaigns, generally to the commanders and higher officers, or those favourably mentioned. An interesting medal is that awarded for the storming of Seringapatam and the second war with Tipu Sahib. On the obverse the Tiger of Tipu succumbs to the onslaught of the British lion, who is typified in the inscription as the Lion of God, the Conqueror.

A medal was awarded in 1816 to all officers and men who had taken part in the Battle of Waterloo (1815). It was designed by Thomas Wyon with the head of the Prince Regent on the obverse and on the reverse the seated winged figure of Victory, a design derived from a Greek fifth century coin. Those who fought in the Peninsular War (1793–1814) received a medal for their services if they lived until 1847, for it was issued in that year. Designed by W. Wyon, the obverse has Queen Victoria's head, and the reverse the queen crowning the kneeling Duke of Wellington with a laurel wreath, while a tiny British lion couchant is shown against the dais on which the queen stands.

In most medals from the middle of the nineteenth century it can be assumed, unless otherwise stated, that the head of the monarch appears on the obverses, the reverses generally containing the symbolic expression. The Indian General Service Medal shows the winged figure of Victory placing a wreath of laurel on the head of a seated warrior, while below is a lotus flower and leaves, symbol of the Orient. The Crimean medal issued in 1854, depicts the standing figure of a Roman soldier armed with shield and sword being crowned, somewhat awkwardly, with a laurel wreath by the figure of winged victory. The British lion is one of the commonest symbols on British military medals. He appears in the East and Central Africa and Africa General Service medals issued in 1899 and 1902, and in other African medals, standing beside the figure of Britannia with a trident in his right paw and a scroll and palm branch in his left, which is extended towards the rising sun. In the Ashanti medal, issued in 1901, the British lion looks towards the rising sun, while a native shield and two spears appear at his feet. Both representations suggest the idea that by British endeavour the bright day of Africa is dawning. (Plate XX).

The symbolism on the British war medal for the First World War of 1914–18 is somewhat elaborate. The design of W. McMillan has St. George on a horse trampling on the eagle shield of Germany with the skull and crossbones symbols of death. Above the horse's head is the risen sun of victory. The symbolism of horse and rider has been extended to suggest the control of greater physical forces by smaller. The horse also signifies the mechanical appliances which contributed so much to victory.

The war medal of the Second World War (1939–45) presents the British lion standing triumphant over a two-headed dragon, signifying the occidental and oriental enemies. The defence medal displays the crown surmounting an oak-tree with two lion supporters. The Observer Corps Medal is expressive. It shows an Elizabethan helmeted figure standing by a signal fire and looking out to sea, holding aloft a fire-brand. It is inscribed 'Forewarned is forearmed'. The King's medal for service in the cause of freedom issued in 1948 depicts a woman giving succour to a warrior in armour (Plate XX.)

The last British war medal to be issued is that for Korea. (Plate XXd.) On the reverse Hêrakles is shown killing the Hydra, and the prow of a ship is introduced into the design. The theme of Hêrakles killing the Hydra was also employed, it will be remembered, on the medal by Jan Luder commemorating the suppression of the Irish rebellion in 1691. The latter design is more spirited and better composed than that on the Korean medal.

Medals issued by institutions and companies to commemorate anniversaries, or on the occasion of exhibitions, or as rewards for meritorious work such as scientific discovery and invention, sometimes show excellent examples of associative or analogous symbolism, in which the subject matter is composed into effective design. It is simple enough to think of suitable and expressive objects associated with the purpose of a medal but it is not so simple to arrange such objects into effective designs. The merit of the medal of the International Fisheries Exhibition of 1883, (Plate XIXa), is not so much in the subjects, various kinds of fish and a fishing net, but in the arrangement of them in so beautiful a design. Another good example is the medal commemorating the five-hundredth anniversary of the birth of Johannes Gutenberg, the inventor of printing in Europe, in which is shown the earliest printing-press, two books and palm symbolizing victorious achievement. The medal, designed by Percy Metcalf and issued in connection with the British Empire Exhibition of 1925, is an effective example of associative symbolism in which agriculture, industry and the home are symbolized by three figures, one with a sheaf of wheat, another with hammer and wheel, and the third a woman holding the model of a house.

A particularly interesting example of symbolism appears in the twenty-fifth anniversary medal of the Mond Nickel Company, designed by Percy Metcalf. On the obverse a demon is represented springing from flames, which express the refining of nickel by volatilization, a discovery of Dr. Ludwig Mond and Dr. Large. The explanation of the demon is that the word 'nickel' originally meant rascal or mischievous demon, and the name was given to kupfernickel, from which nickel was separated by Cronstead in 1751, because, contrary to the expectation prompted by its appearance, it yielded no copper. On the reverse of the medal are shown maple leaves representing Canada, where nickel is found, and daffodils representing Wales where it is refined. (Plate XIXd.)

Among more recent medals in which objects associated with the purpose are employed in an effective design, is the housing medal first issued in 1950, and awarded by the Ministry of Housing and Local Government for excellence in the planning and design of housing. On the reverse of the medal is shown a terrace block of houses, a wreath and the tools of the draughtsman: dividers, set square, plumb line and scrolls. (Plate XXe.)

VIII   Trademarks

SIGNS and devices have been used in all periods to identify and authenticate goods of a particular producer or manufacturer. Many early seals were possibly trademarks. The marks on the lumps of clay used for sealing jars in Mesopotamia are generally regarded as seals of ownership, but if jars were delivered sealed with a mark from the producer, this would be a very early trademark. Certainly in ancient Greece and Rome there are the marks of the producer or manufacturer on pottery, masonry and bricks. Later, during the Middle Ages, it was common for craftsmen to employ their signatures, signs or devices as authentication of their work. These all took the form of letters, monograms or symbolic devices of various kinds, and they led naturally to the modern trademark.

To appreciate the purpose and full significance of the modern trademark as it is used by the producers of goods, it is helpful to consider in the first instance the authentication, by a signature or device, of the work of craftsmen and artists. Most, although not all, artists have inscribed their pictures with their signature or with a decorative monogram or symbolic device. Van Dyck, Tiepolo, Franz Hals, Perugino, Jan Van der Lys and John Millais were a few of the painters who signed their works with decorative monograms. Some used more elaborate devices. Correggio used a heart with 'regio' over it. Henri de Bless, called Ciretta, used an owl in a window, Jonathan Richardson, the English painter, used a palette and brushes with R scrawled on the palette, Lucas Cranach used a very elaborate device consisting of three shields placed round a centre space in which his monogram is placed. On one shield are crossed swords, on another a dragon and on the third, part of a crown on bars. Albrecht Dürer depicted a roofed structure on a shield, with his monogram in the centre, while the French engraver Isabella Quatrepomme amusingly signs herself with a 4 on an apple with stem and leaves. Now the signature or device of an artist or craftsman identifies and authenticates his work, and if the artist acquires a reputation for work of high excellence this signature or device confirms the value of the work, like the hall-mark on gold or silver.

In the same way the quality of certain goods may become well known, and it is of value that these goods be identified or authenticated by a mark and distinguished from

(a) John Drummond & Sons Ltd. of Greenock, Scotland, manufacturers of Drummond wood-ware—containers, barrels, factory cases.

(b) Littlewoods Mail Order Stores Ltd., Liverpool. Spinney is a little wood. The company also uses the name Golden Spinney to denote goods of the highest quality.

(c) Martineau's Ltd. of London—sugar refiners.

(d) Burman and Greenwood Ltd., Darwen, Lancashire.

(e) Frank Starkey Ltd., of Birmingham, bakers and confectioners.

(f) Webster & Co. (Fernbank) Ltd., manufacturers of cotton and rayon. The trademark derived from the name has a spider's web, complete with spider, and the completion 'Sterco'.

Fig. 33. Symbolic trademarks by means of a rebus.

(a) Ford Motor Co. Ltd., manufacturers of farming machinery expressed in the trademark by wheat in association with a cog wheel.

(b) Old Roundhegians Association, Leeds. Trademark for articles of clothing for men and boys. The stars and golden fleece are derived from the coat of arms of Leeds.

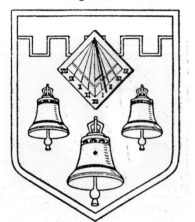

(c) Gillett and Johnston Ltd., of Croydon, manufacturers of bells for clocks, expressed in the trademark by bells and a sundial.

(d) J. A. Phillips & Co. Ltd., of Birmingham, manufacturers of bicycles and parts thereof. The trademark was designed for use on bicycles in the 'New World' and the use of the Drake ship was thought to be appropriate. Ideas suggested by it are English tradition and adventure.

(e) Vine Products Ltd., a simple but effective example of association.

Fig. 34. Trademark symbols by association.

(*a*) The British Lubricating Research Organization Ltd. The oilcan, cogwheel, and eye, for research, make an expressive trademark.

(*b*) Air Survey Co. Ltd., aerial photographers. A trademark which expresses by representation the purpose of the company.

(*c*) James Powell & Sons (Whitefriars) Ltd. manufacturers of glass. This use of the friar device is an example of historical association with early location of the firm. The old works of the company stood between Fleet Street and the Thames within the area once occupied by the church house and grounds of the White or Carmelite Friars.

(*d*) O. Kavli Akheselshrap, manufacturers of crisp-bread and biscuit.

(*e*) Elliott Equipment Ltd., of Rhondda, South Wales, manufacturers of inflatable equipment, boats, rafts, and parachutes. A good example of association for in front of the anchor is the lifebelt within which is the safety-first sign, while the wings express the parachute.

Fig. 35. Trademark symbols by association.

other goods of the same class. This is the essential function of a trademark; but it does more. It often performs an advertising function, indicating by its character, by analogy, for example, the excellence of the goods with which it is associated; or it can by its design attract attention to the goods. Thus a trademark conforms to Whitehead's suggestion mentioned in the first chapter that one of the objects of symbolism is to enhance the importance of what is symbolized. This particular purpose of symbolism is well exemplified by trademarks.

The well known definitions of trademarks should confirm what has been said of their origin and function. The definition in the Trade Marks Act 1938 (Section 38) may be abbreviated as 'a mark used in relation to goods so as to indicate a connexion between the goods and some person having the right to use the mark,' while 'mark' is defined as 'including a device, brand, heading, label, ticket, name, signature, word, letter, numeral, or any combination thereof'. The definitions given in Kerly's *Law of Trade Marks and Trade Names*[1] and in the *Encyclopaedia Britannica* both refer to trademark as a symbol applied or attached to goods so as to distinguish them from similar goods and to identify them with a particular trader. Another recent definition is given by the American designer Egbert Jacobson in *Seven Designers look at Trademark Design*,[2] who also gives the American legal definition. They are essentially the same as the definitions cited.

Forms of Trademark

Following largely the ancient and mediaeval marks on various goods and works of art, the modern trademark can take a variety of forms. A requirement of a trademark is that is shall be remembered, and this is probably achieved as much, or more, by sound as visually, the appeal to the ear rather than to the eye. As this book is concerned with visual rather than sound symbolism, more attention is given to the visual aspects of trademarks, which means chiefly those with pictorial design, but those which depend mainly on sound cannot be ignored because of their importance. It is probably more because of the sound than the appearance of the name that words like Kodak, Mum, Bovril, Mazawattee, Lux, Oxo are so successful as trademarks, and it is from an advertising standpoint—although this is not the legal purpose of a trademark—that a good sounding word is important.

According to the Trade Marks Act 1938 (Section 9) a trademark to be registrable must contain or consist of at least one of the following particulars:

(a) the name of a company, individual or firm, represented in a special or particular manner;
(b) the signature of the applicant for registration or some predecessor in his business;
(c) an invented word or invented words;
(d) a word or words having no direct reference to the character or quality of the goods, and not being according to its ordinary signification a geographical name or a surname;
(e) any other distinctive mark, but a name, signature, or word or words other than such as fall within the descriptions in the foregoing paragraphs (a), (b), (c) and (d), shall not be registrable under the provisions of this paragraph except upon evidence of its distinctiveness.

A classification of trademarks from the standpoint of their interest as symbols would be a little different, but this statutory enumeration of requirements does indicate a good classification to adopt.

From the symbolic standpoint trademarks may be classified as follows:

(1) The name of the proprietor of the goods represented, or his signature, or an abbreviation or other modification of the name. Famous examples are Cadbury, Rowntree, Fry, Ford, Firestone, Coty, Heinz, Player.

(2) Ordinary non-descriptive words without any particular association with the product or the firm, such as Swan, North Star, Capstan.

(3) Ordinary words partly or indirectly descriptive or suggestive of the product. Such words as 'Speedway' for roller skates; 'Slumberland' for mattresses, 'Penguin' for swimming sandals and caps, but best of all the names given to aircraft, like Hurricane, Spitfire, Mosquito, Comet, Meteor jet, Whirlwind, Thunderbolt.

(4) Invented or coined words or adaptations of Latin or foreign or obsolete words which are not descriptive or associative. Examples are Kodak, Drene, Lux, Mum, Iodent.

(5) Invented words as in (4), but which are indirectly descriptive or expressive of the product. Such words are derivations from Latin, like 'Aquascutum', meaning water shield, 'Bovril' from bovinus, and Innoxa, implying that the cosmetics are harmless. Some invented words suggest by their character the kind of product, such as 'Flannath' for clothing; 'Tumble-Togs' for children's clothes; 'Flexwelt' for women's shoes; 'Excaveyor' for combined excavating and conveying machines; 'Dri-Brite' for floor-polish and 'Quink' for writing ink.

(6) Invented words as in (4) and (5), but mainly associative, like 'Nordral', a combination of Norwich and Cathedral for the furniture sold by Wallace King Limited of Norwich; 'Copknit' for knitted articles of clothing for the Scottish Cooperative Wholesale Society.

(7) A pictorial design with or without words that represents the place of manufacture, or is a pun on the manufacturer's name, or some other association. Examples of pictorial trademarks which are puns on the proprietor's name are the willow-tree in the trademark of Willows Francis Pharmaceutical Products Limited; the playing-card of the King in that of George W. King, manufacturer of milking stools; a flying duck or goose for P. C. Drake Limited, manufacturer of detergents; a flying martin in an O for Martineaus Limited, producers of refined sugar and syrup; while a pun on a place name is the trademark of Hazlewood and Company (Products) Limited of Rowditch, Derby, which shows a jockey on a racehorse. These punning representations show that the designers of trademarks are moved by an impulse similar to that of the originators of numerous coats of arms. Numerous associations with places are used, dissimilar examples being a representation of a monk or friar for James Powell and Sons (Whitefriars) Limited, the manufacturers of decorative glass, and the representation of the famous Saltash bridge in Cornwall for O. H. Ingram and Son Limited of Saltash, manufacturers of leather goods. An association with an historical person is sometimes used, as the figure of Sir Walter Raleigh in the trademark of 1876 for Samuel Goode's, tobacco manufacturer.

(b) Elastica Ltd., manufacturers of women's underclothing. The idea of the balanced figure or posture is emphasized by the scales.

(a) Thermocontrol Installations Co. Ltd., manufacturers of temperature control equipment. The trademark expresses control of heat by means of the flame in the hand, while the cog wheel expresses engineering.

(c) Ducksback Ltd., manufacturers of waterproofing oils. The trademark was probably prompted by the saying 'Water off a duck's back', which is thus a symbol of the waterproofing oil.

(d) Albert V. Martin of Nottingham, manufacturers of hosiery, slumberwear, and underwear. The Emprex silver net trademark could express the idea of the fineness or delicacy of the materials.

Fig. 36. Trademark symbols by analogy.

(b) Cuprinol Ltd., manufacturers of cuprinol timber impregnation to combat pests. The snake here represents the pests and the sword piercing the snake symbolizes Cuprinol as destructive of pests.

(a) Xavier Giralt Ltd., of Glasgow, merchant for face powder, skin perfume, skin lotions, etc. The hour glass and shield imply a shield against time which the firm's preparations provide. The shield is held by a wise man of the East. The motto, 'elan de vie' is translated 'ardour of life'. It is one of the best examples of symbolism in trademarks.

(c) Eldorado Ice Cream Co. Ltd. The Jaunty polar bear expresses cold associated with joie de vive—an excellent symbol for ice cream.

(d) Thwaites Engineering Co. Ltd., manufacturers of earthmoving machines. Although this was partly derived from the family coat of arms, the elephant fully expresses the idea of powerful movement expressive of earthmoving equipment.

(e) H. L. Savory & Co. Ltd. The name given to this tobacco and the words 'nothing smoother than baby's bottom' express clearly the quality in the tobacco it is wished to recommend. It is simple yet direct symbolism.

Fig. 37. Trademark symbols by analogy.

(8) A pictorial design which expresses by analogy the nature of the product, or suggests its character by partial representation. These are certainly the most interesting of trademarks symbolically, and although they may not be so successful as some of the words like Bovril and Kodak, they are among the most ingenious and expressive. Such is one of 1899 for Simpson and Bodman, motor-car manufacturers, which shows three horse's legs in the form of a triscele with squibs spurting fire from the hoofs, and S.B.M. in the spaces. Marley Tiles Limited has a cock as a trademark, with the words 'cock o' the walk', indicating the supremacy of the tiles. This, and the bison for Bison floors, indicating great strength, clearly contain an advertising purpose. Among expressive pictorial trademarks are the night-light with the word 'Dormy' for the bed blankets of Wormalds and Walker Limited; the cog wheel and lightning sign in the bottom of a triangle with H.S. for electrically-propelled mail vehicles of Hindle Smart and Company Limited; while the aeroplane over an island with the grid of a map on the island is very expressive of the photographs, maps and prints of Air Survey Company Limited. (A selection of symbolic trademarks is shown in Figs. 33–37.)

Trademarks are a kind of heraldry of trade, designed primarily for recognition and identity, employed sometimes with an advertising purpose and sometimes becoming a badge of pride and honour.

REFERENCES
1. KERLY's *Law of Trade Marks and Trade Names*, 7th edition (London, 1951).
2. *Seven Designers look at Trademark Designs* (Chicago, 1952). The seven designers are BERNARD RUDOFSKY, HERBERT BAYER, ALVIN LUSTIG, PAUL RAND, WILL BURTIN, H. CRESTON DONER and EGBERT JACOBSON.

IX   Shop and Inn Signs

AMONG the most picturesque means of identification in trade are shop signs, which have been used since the most ancient civilizations. There is evidence of their use in ancient Egypt, and Greek writers have referred to them, but the earliest actual remains are from the buried cities of Pompeii and Herculaneum. Here we find painted signs as well as signs in terracotta and stone relief. The general subjects of these signs are of typical goods for sale, or some suggestion of these goods by allusion. Thus, a goat is for a dairy, shoe for a shoemaker, chisel and adze for carpenter, a mule drawing a mill for a baker, and Bacchus pressing a bunch of grapes for a wine-merchant. A common tavern sign in Rome was a clump of ivy and vine leaves—symbol of Bacchus. This was called a bush, and hence the proverb 'Good wine needs no bush'. Later writers refer to other tavern signs such as the Cock, and the Shepherd and Staff, while one tavern sign in Pompeii depicts two slaves carrying an amphora. Another sign found at Pompeii which has persisted until modern times, and is one of the aristocrats of inn signs, is The Chequers. It was probably used as a sign because it was the mechanical help to cast up the reckoning—a money changer's abacus. Alternatively, it may be that as games of draughts and backgammon were commonly played in the inns, the sign was derived from this circumstance.

The subject of the shop sign was an object indicative by representation, or association of the commodity sold. In the case of the shoe for shoemaker it is simple representation, in the cases of the goat for dairy, or chisel and adze for carpenter, Bacchus pressing a bunch of grapes for wine-merchant, it is association with means of production. These were the principal types of signs when they were revived in the Middle Ages, and they continued as the essential basic types until the end of the eighteenth century, although by that time signs had become very complicated, and in many cases their origins are difficult to discern.

It should be remembered that until the nineteenth century the production of most goods involved handicraftmanship, and that the craftsman usually worked in the shop itself or in a room at the back or in adjoining premises. Norman Wymer points out that in Lincoln as late as in 1856, when the decline of hand-work had already begun, the manufacture of goods was carried on in the shops in a large number of trades, which he enumerates.[1]

In the eighteenth century when signs reached their greatest profusion some of the simple types representative of goods sold were: golden boot and last for shoemakers; cabinet, chair, looking glass and walnut tree for cabinet makers; four coffins for carpenters; haunch of venison, golden pheasant and pineapple for confectioners; peacock, rainbow and dove together for dyers; fig tree and three sugar loaves for grocers; anchor and key (together), dust-pan, frying-pan, three keys, lock and hinge, stove, grate and padlock for ironmongers; blue bodice, hood and scarf and lamb for milliners; blue curtain, royal bed, crown and cushion and three tents for upholsterers; and for booksellers, in addition to Bible, or Bible with crown, it was common to have the head of a famous writer like Homer, Virgil, Horace, Shakespeare or Pope.[2]

Signs became more elaborate and complicated when it was necessary to differentiate between the same class of shops in one district. With the closer concentration of trade in big cities, this became more amd more necessary. It was not uncommon to have ten shops of the same kind in one street in London in the eighteenth century, and thus other symbols were introduced on the signboards to secure differentiation and distinctiveness, for the majority of people up to the beginning of the nineteenth century could not read, and the numbering of premises was not general until the latter part of the eighteenth century. A shop was known, therefore, by its sign. 'At the sign of . . .'. 'I will meet you at the sign of . . .' were common phrases of the time.

With differentiation and the introduction of distinctive symbols it meant that many lost their function of symbolizing the goods sold. In 1710 Addison in his essay on the subject complains of this. He refers to the streets being 'filled with blue boars, black swans and red lions; not to mention flying pigs and hogs in armour with many other creatures more extraordinary than any in the deserts of Africa.' Addison is petitioning in a fictional, satirical, epistolary form for the position of officer to regulate the signs. He says that his first task would be to clear the city of monsters. 'In the second place, I would forbid that creatures of jarring, incongruous natures should be joined together in the same sign; such as the bell and the neat's tongue, the dog and the gridiron. The fox and the goose may be supposed to have met, but what has the fox and the seven stars to do together? And when did the lamb and dolphin ever meet, except upon a sign-post?' He says later, that he 'would enjoin every shop to make use of a sign which bears some affinity to the wares in which it deals. What can be more inconsistent than to see a bawd at the sign of The Angel, or a tailor at The Lion? A cook should not live at The Boot, nor a shoemaker at the Roasted Pig; and yet, for want of this regulation, I have seen a goat set up before the door of a perfumer, and the French king's head at a sword-cutler's'.[3]

Some explanation, however, can be given of some of the signs. Addison himself gives one reason when he says that 'it is usual for a young tradesman, at his first setting up, to add to his own sign that of the master whom he served; as the husband, after marriage, gives a place to his mistress' arms on his own coat'. Another reason suggested by Jacob Larwood and John Camden Hotten is that when a trader removed from one shop to another it was customary, presumably for the sake of tradition, good will and perhaps a degree of sentiment to combine the signs of the old shop and the new. This is probably one reason for the curious combination of objects, especially in tavern signs, of which Larwood and Hotten give many examples.[4] The bank signs in Lombard Street provide some interesting examples of the retention of existing signs by a new tenant or owner of a site or building. The sign of the black spread eagle which hangs outside Barclays Bank (Plate XXIIIa) was there as the sign of the house of the eagle when the bank moved to the house in 1728 from another part of the street. In 1937 the black spread eagle, in combination with three crowns, another old Lombard Street sign, was adopted as the coat of arms of the bank. Another Lombard Street sign is that of the black horse, 1677, which hangs outside Lloyds Bank. At that date the sign was over a shop at No. 53, occupied by Humphrey Stocks as one of the 'Keepers of Running Cashes'. It passed with new owners to No. 62 as the sign of Bland and Barnett one of the predecessors of Lloyds Bank. It was then adopted by the bank, and when it moved from 62 to 71 it took the sign to the new premises (Plate XXIIIf.)

Hanging outside the Commercial Bank of Scotland at 60 and 62 Lombard Street are two signs: the 'King's Head' and the 'Cat-a-Fiddling'. In 1677, according to Samuel Lee's London Directory, issued in that year, Thomas Kilborne and Capill were at the 'King's Head', and the sign has remained since. The Cat-a-Fiddling was in 1672 the sign of Anthony Dansie haberdasher hanging outside 63 with the black horse, as previously mentioned, outside 62. When Lloyds Bank moved to 71, the Commercial Bank of Scotland moved the Cat-a-Fiddling sign from 63 and hung it outside its building at 62, partly because the bank wished to hang out a sign on the occasion of the coronation festivities in 1902 (Plate XXIIId).

Many signs had a partly heraldic character—which was to become very marked later in inn signs—and this was due to the introduction of the coat of arms, or crest, or part thereof, or badge, of an aristocratic patron; or the coat of arms of the city or town. Heraldic lions, unicorns, griffins, crowns, roses, and lambs were very common. A sign of a seventeenth-century bookseller, John Allen near St. Paul's, has the sun rising on a landscape, a marigold in the bottom right-hand corner, the city coat of arms top right and a lion in a panel above,[5] and many other examples could be given of the introduction of coats of arms. These heraldic signs, or signs other than those representative of goods, such as puns on the names of the shopowners, were used either independently, or in addition to objects representing or signifying in some way the goods sold. Thus, a pair of breeches was a usual sign of a breeches-maker, but in that of Martha Holmes of Piccadilly (1760) a bell is introduced in addition. A civet cat was a common sign for an apothecary, but in the sign of Stephen Brearcliffe of West Smithfield (1760) three herrings are added. As the herrings have crowned heads, this is probably an heraldic introduction. A case of knives was a common sign for a cutler, but in that of Alexander Burges of Leadenhall Street (1720) a red bull is added. The introduction of a rose and crown to two fustian rolls for the linen draper, Jeremiah Hemsworth of Drury Lane (1750) and of the white hart to coffin and skull and crossbones for the undertaker, William Boyce of Newgate, are further examples.

As Addison contended, the best shop signs are those which bear some affinity to the goods sold; these are the most expressive and the most interesting symbolically. Among them may be mentioned three carved chairs, two mirrors and a walnut tree for the cabinet maker, John Brown, St. Paul's Churchyard (1728); four coffins and heart for John King, carpenter (1720); and an elephant, hand and comb for Thomas Hedges, comb maker of St. Martin's-le-Grand (1730), where the suggestion is that the combs are made of ivory.

Good expressive signs that were used by several of the same trade were the rainbow and the dove with olive branch for dyers, hat and beaver for hatters, peacock alone or with star or turks head for lacemen, and globe and sun for scientific instrument makers.[6]

With the spread of literacy at the end of the eighteenth century, and the street numbering of premises, shop signs gradually ceased to perform the function of identification, although they continued in some instances to serve an advertising and even decorative function. They declined considerably in number during the nineteenth century. Some, however, survive to this day. In addition to shop signs those for banks and insurance companies are not uncommon. These often take the form of the coat of arms or the badge of the bank or the company. Two examples interesting as symbolism are in Cornhill, London. One is that of the Cornhill Insurance Company (Plate XXIIIe) which is taken from the company's coat of arms, being a rebus on corn hill, the word corn being shown by two sheaves of corn on either side of the hill which is represented by the heraldic pile. The shield is set in a wreath of corn. The other example is that of the Scottish Widow's Fund and Life Assurance Society. It is based on a design by Walter Crane made in 1888 and contains some elaborate symbolism. Time is symbolized both by a scythe and a winged horse, and a man is depicted grasping the forelock of the horse while the inscription reads: 'Take time by the forelock—Fronte Capillata est Post est occasio calva' from the moral apophthegms of Dionysius Cato. The design originally had the signs of the zodiac on the scythe with the exception of Leo whose four stars were shown on the right with the Scottish thistle, but these were omitted as it would have made the sign somewhat too elaborate. Two common signs which have persisted, although in decreasing numbers, are the three golden balls of the pawnbroker, and the barber's pole.

The origin of the sign of the three golden balls for pawnbrokers is obscure. A common notion is that the sign was derived from the Medici coat of arms, because the early bankers were in the Medici States and from Lombardy. But, as Sir Ambrose Heal has pointed out, the Medici coat bore roundels, which are discs and not spheres, they varied in number from eleven to six, but were never three: nor was the metal gold.[7] The earlier sign of pawnbrokers was three bowls, which, by the eighteenth century were generally blue, and at that time changed to balls. In the late eighteenth century they gradually changed to gold. Sir Ambrose Heal suggests that possibly their origin was connected with the legend of St. Nicholas in which he gives three bag-shaped purses to three nobleman's daughters.

The origin of the barber's pole is similarly uncertain. One tradition is that it dates from the time when the function of barber and surgeon were combined, when in the operation of blood letting a pole was held tightly to make the blood flow freely. The pole was painted red so as less to show the blood stains, and barbers often hung it, when not in use, outside the shop with bandages twisted round it; thus the red and white spiral of the barber's pole today.

CLASSIFICATION OF INN SIGNS

Although, as mentioned, the use of pictorial shop signs has declined considerably since the end of the eighteenth century, only a comparatively few remaining today, the tavern or inn sign is still used as much as ever. There are such a large number, and they are so varied that it is desirable, if we are to appreciate their expressiveness and symbolism, to attempt some sort of classification. There are those which are directly expressive and obvious in meaning, and those which are apparently inexplicable, but which in some cases admit of possible or probable historical explanation.

A rough classification of inn signs according to type is: (1) signs that express directly or by association what is obtainable at the inn, either liquor or food; (2) signs with a religious origin; (3) signs of heraldic derivation; (4) signs of a national or historic character; (5) signs showing historical, mythological or fictional characters; (6) trade signs; (7) military and sporting signs; (8) transport signs; (9) geographical signs; (10) signs with marine symbols; (11) signs suggested by puns or rebuses; (12) signs suggested by local landmarks; (13) combinations of objects; (14) humorous signs. (A selection of modern inn signs is illustrated in Plates XXIV–XXVI.)

(1) Signs Indicative of Drink or Food

Examples of these are the already mentioned bush of ivy and vine, symbol of Bacchus, Bunch of Grapes, or Grapes, Barley Mow, The Hop-pole, The Hop and Barleycorn; while signs of utensils associated with drinking are The Leather Bottle, The Bottle and Glass, The Brown Jug, The Pitcher and Glass, The Pewter Pot and the Cork and Bottle, The Cock on the Hoop, cock being the word for the spigot of a cask, and used in association with beer. Grapes were perhaps the commonest of this type of sign. Larwood gives sixty-four in his list of London signs in 1864.

Some interesting signs for food are Baron of Beef, Round of Beef, Ribs of Beef, Dog and Bacon, Shoulder of Mutton, and Leg of Mutton and Cauliflower. In the signs of inns near the sea, fish and edible marine animals were often introduced; thus, The Cod and Lobster, The Crawfish, The Oyster, The Crab, The Crab and Lobster. The Cheshire Cheese in Fleet Street is perhaps the most famous of all signs of food. Others from the past are, The Pickled Egg, Pigeon Pie, and Cask and Pie.

(2) Signs of a Religious Character

Probably some of these originated from the period of the Middle Ages, when inns were only drinking houses, and lodgings of travellers were either in the nobleman's castle or manor house, in the case of the more well-to-do travellers, or in the hostels attached either to the castle or to a monastery for others. Such a hostel may have had a sign as well as the drinking house. When, later, the hostel and inn were combined, the tradition of the hostel attached to a monastery would have some religious character, with the signs expressing that. Thus, we have signs like The Angel, Angel and Crown, The Virgin, The Baptist's Head, The Good Samaritan, The Prodigal's Return, The Fatted Calf, King David, David and Harp, various forms of Cross, and the popular Adam and Eve. Signs of Saints were not uncommon before the Reformation and were employed because a saint was patron of a trade or craft, the members of which met at the inn. Among such signs were those of St. Crispin, the patron saint of shoemakers, of St. Blaize, the patron saint of woolcombers, while the patron saints of travellers St. Julian and St. Christopher naturally had their signs. The commonest sign of this kind is, of course, St. George, often with the Dragon, probably more often chosen for national and patriotic reasons. Similarly, we find St. Patrick in Ireland and St. Andrew in Scotland, while patron saints of cities and towns, like St. Paul for London, often appear on inn signs. St. Peter is responsible for the cross keys sign.

(3) Signs of Heraldic Character

These are perhaps the commonest of all types, and the numerous animals, natural and fabulous, are usually heraldic derivations. A very large number are obviously taken from the supporters of the Royal arms, which are given in Chapter III, and include: swan, antelope, lion, white hart, bull, boar, dragon, greyhound, eagle and unicorn; the white horse appeared in the arms of Hanover, and the griffin on the seal of Edward III. The King's Arms, one of the commonest of all signs, was often a representation of the royal coat of arms with supporters and crest. Both the rose and crown are heraldic derivations, and many signs are derived from the arms of the landowning family of the district. Sometimes the arms of the borough or county are used.

(4) Signs of a National or Patriotic Character

The commonest of these, which are, of course, very close to those of an heraldic type, are the King's Head, or Queen's Head. In giving the number of inn signs of various kinds in London in 1864 Larwood records eighty-nine King's Arms as the most, seventy-three Red Lions next, and sixty-three for both King's Head and White Hart. Queen's Head is a little way down with forty-nine. The King's Head generally took the form of a selected historical king like Edward I, Henry VIII, Charles I, Charles II, or one of the Georges, the head following well-known representations.

(5) Signs of an Historical, Mythological, or Fictional Character

Allied to the signs of national or patriotic character are those showing historical characters, especially famous military leaders, like Lord Nelson, Duke of Wellington, Sir Francis Drake, Lord Roberts and General Gordon, the first two being very popular signs at one time. Political leaders, like William Pitt and Lord Beaconsfield have also appeared on signboards, as well as literary figures such as Shakespeare, Marvell and Ben Jonson, the first named being common at all times. Other historical characters with a fictional tradition are Robin Hood, Sir John Falstaff, Don Juan, Whittington and his cat, while more purely fictional characters are Robinson Crusoe, and the Vicar of Wakefield. Some mythological characters that have appeared on inn signs are Bacchus, Apollo, Minerva, Mercury, Cupid and Bow, Hercules' Pillars, Neptune for inns near the sea, and Vulcan.

(6) Trade Signs

Trade symbols for inns were probably derived partly from shop signs and were used because of the trade in the district. The Anvil, The Blacksmith, the Bag of Nails, The Windmill or The Mill, The Plough, The Woodman have all been popular signs at various times. They were probably sometimes adopted because the inn was the headquarters of a tradesmen's or craftsmen's club, or similar institution. That is partly the explanation of names like The Bricklayers' Arms, The Bootmakers' Arms, The Gravediggers' Arms, The Platelayers' Arms and several others.

(7) *Military and Sporting Signs*

These have taken the form of weapons, names of military personnel, and instruments in military hands. Among the first are Crossed Swords, Crossed Lances, Crossed Pistols, Sword and Buckler, Dagger, or Sword and Dagger and others of a similar kind. The personnel are represented by A Grenadier, The Rifle Volunteer, Light Dragoon and several others similar, while favourite band instruments were The Trumpet and The Drum. The portraits of famous military leaders classified under (4) could also be regarded as military signs.

Sporting signs are classed with military signs because they are so often both concerned with combat; the mild form of combativeness seen in modern sport is rarely a subject of signs—the only one which has become popular is The Cricketers, or the Cricketers' Arms. A favourite sign representing a sport was that of The Fighting Cocks. Another sport is celebrated in the Fox and Hounds, and the Fox's Tail. There is scope for celebration of sport in modern signs. The Footballers has rarely been used, and I am not aware of The Tennis Ace or The Boatrace Arms, although The Boat, the Boatman and the Boatman's Call have all appeared at one time or another.

(8) *Transport Signs*

Transport has inevitably provided many subjects for the inn sign. It begins with the earliest form, The Horse, with its many variations, like the Pack Horse, The Coach and Horses, The Wagon and Horses, and later the railways provided subjects, like The Steam Engine and The South Eastern, while air transport is represented in inns near areas of aircraft manufacture as The Comet at Hatfield, The Canopus at Rochester and Happy Landings near Bristol. Motor transport does not seem to have inspired the sign artist, for I cannot recall The Limousine, or The Pirate Bus.

(9–12) *Geographical, Marine, Punning and Local Signs*

Among geographical signs we find The Globe, The North Pole, The Jamaica Tavern, The North Britain and several others. Common signs with marine symbols are The Ship, Anchor, these two combined, names of various ships, like The Golden Hind, The Arethusa, The Shannon and Chesapeake. There are endless combinations with Ship, such as Ship and Bell, Rainbow, Star and Castle. Other signs are The Packet Boat, The Pilot Boat, The Fishing Smack, The Mariner, and The Three Mariners.

Signs suggested by puns are similar to those found in heraldry. Examples of signs suggested by local landmarks are those with names of trees such as The Chestnut Tree, The Yew Tree and The Oak.

(13) *Combinations of Objects*

The curious combinations of objects in many signs appear to be due to a variety of causes, some of which are the same as in the curious combinations in shop signs. They may have been due to a publican changing premises and liking to retain the old name and combine it with the new. Some combinations were also probably due to the objects painted on an old sign being unrecognizable, so that in repainting a likely but erroneous interpretation was put on them. Also, names were mispronounced and after a time meant something else. Larwood cites many of these strangely coupled objects, like Naked Boy and Mitre, The Hog in Armour, The Razor and Hen, and The Pig and Checkers.

(14) *Humorous Signs*

The humorous signs are in a class by themselves, because, though some could be placed in other classifications, in all considered here humour has been the main prompting. Such is obviously the case with the famous sign of A Man with a Load of Mischief, one such in Oxford Street, reputed to have been painted by Hogarth, shows a man with a woman, and a monkey on his shoulder, the woman holding a glass of gin. The Good Woman sign shows a female without a head. An elaborate sign with humorous intent is The Five Alls, which had many variations, one showing the clergyman, lawyer, farmer and soldier, who pray, plead, maintain, and fight for all, while lastly the devil takes all. The best humorous modern sign that I have seen, which, although it might quite justifiably be claimed as a religious sign is, I think, more fittingly in this section, is the sign called The Startled Saint at West Malling. It shows him with five aircraft round his head, appropriately startled, as St. Leonard, who is associated with the district, would certainly be, if he had returned after long absence and found the airfield there. (Plate XXVId.)

Is the art of the inn sign dying at last, as the shop sign has almost died, and with it some interesting art and symbolism? There have been numerous attempts to keep it alive, in the form of exhibitions, which have met with some success; but too often one finds the mere name of the inn on the signboard. How dull this is compared with the lively representations like The Man with a Load of Mischief or The Cricketers in action, or the bright colours of The Ship or The Red Lion, or the picturesque effect of The Wagon and Horses; or the beautiful sculptured sign of The Comet. Looking at the astonishingly varied inn signs of England one sees in them a colourful expression of ordinary contemporary life, and England would be the poorer if they were to disappear.

REFERENCES

1. NORMAN WYMER, *English Town Crafts* (London, 1949), p. 10.
2. A list of the signs characteristic of trades is given in SIR AMBROSE HEAL's *The Signboards of Old London* (London, 1949) which is a review of the shop signs employed by the London tradesmen during the seventeenth and eighteenth centuries. The major portion of the book is devoted to an abridged directory of the shop signs of London tradesmen taken from the author's collection of trade-cards, and billheads, a selection of which are illustrated.
3. JOSEPH ADDISON, *The Spectator*, Monday, 2nd April, 1711.
4. JACOB LARWOOD and JOHN CAMDEN HOTTEN, *History of Signboards*, 1st edition (London, 1866), 12th edition (London, 1907). In 1951 a revised and modernized version of the book was published under the title of *English Inn Signs*. This is the most exhaustive and comprehensive book on the subject. Other books are that by SIR AMBROSE HEAL previously mentioned; C. J. MONSON-FITZJOHN, *Quaint Signs of Olde Inns* (London, 1926); F. G. H. PRICE, *The Signs of old Lombard Street* (London, 1887); REGINALD TURNER, *The Spotted Dog* (London, 1948) and BRIAN HILL, *Inn-Signia* (London, 1948).
5. Illustrated in SIR AMBROSE HEAL's book, *op. cit.*, p. 30.
6. The examples cited are taken from billheads with London shop signs in the collection of SIR AMBROSE HEAL and reproduced in his *The Signboards of Old London Shops*.
7. SIR AMBROSE HEAL, *The London Goldsmiths 1200–1800* (Cambridge, 1935).

X Pictorial Advertising

THERE can be little doubt that advertising, particularly during the present century, has contributed much to material progress simply by the process of making things known. New inventions, new modes of transport, developments in household equipment and furnishing of all kinds have been furthered by the dissemination of information by means of advertising, because the more rapidly they become known the quicker the sales, and the more money for further developments. It is true that some forms of advertising have been very much open to criticism, and unscrupulous advertisers have imposed on the credulity of the public, but, if one believes in material progress—speed in communications, more efficient equipment, greater comfort, improved standards of cleanliness—then on the balance advertising has much benefited mankind. It has certainly contributed to improving the general standard of living. And not only has it contributed to material progress, for awareness of cultural activities—books, exhibitions, drama, music—has been fostered by advertising. A function that it performs then is the spread of information, which is often, although not always, coloured with propaganda; for the purpose is, after all, to sell. That it is done generally with a certain ethical code indicates that in the long run this pays.

The earliest forms of advertising of which we have record are public criers and shop and tavern signs discussed in the previous chapter, some ancient examples of which were mentioned. In ancient Rome occurred the first known examples of public notices of theatrical performances, games, sports, taverns and of other places of entertainment, which were generally painted on the walls in conspicuous places in the cities and towns, and were the ancestors of the modern poster. Remains of some of these posters were found at Pompeii. In the Middle Ages a conspicuous form of advertiser was the public crier, or barker, as he was called, and a common employment for criers was to call the price of wines for various taverns. Posting of notices was revived with the advent of printing in the fifteenth century; periodical advertising began in the early seventeenth century, and handbills a little later, becoming very common in the eighteenth century.

The Committee of Definitions of the American Marketing Association defined advertising as 'any paid form of non-personal presentation and promotion of ideas, goods, or services by an identified sponsor. It involves the use of such media as the following: magazine and newspaper space, motion pictures, outdoor (poster, signs, skywriting, etc.), direct mail, store signs, novelties (calendars, blotters, etc.) radio, cards (car, bus, etc.) catalogues, directories and references, programmes and menus and circulars.'[1] This is a comprehensive definition, if a little clumsy. A convenient grouping of advertising media, which would accord roughly with this definition, is (a) newspapers and periodicals of all kinds; (b) handbills, catalogues and circulars; (c) posters; and (d) radio, television and the cinema. The last two groups are in some measure developments of the older forms of advertising, as the poster derived partly from wall-writing and the shop sign, the radio from the public crier, while television and the cinema are to some extent a combination of the public crier and the animated poster.

Pictorial advertising, other than the signboard, began to appear in a small way in periodical advertisements in the middle of the seventeenth century, and blossomed into a very attractive illustrative art in eighteenth century handbills. There was little development of either in the first half of the nineteenth century, and it was not until the later years of the century that pictorial advertising, both in periodicals and posters, began to show any marked artistic merit. The contribution of France was outstanding with posters by Jules Chéret and Toulouse-Lautrec.

The use of Millais's 'Bubbles' as a poster for Pears soap in 1887 set the example for the use of famous pictures for advertisements. It was followed by the use of Frith's 'The New Frock' as an advertisement for Sunlight soap, with the title changed to 'so clean'; and many other pictures by well-known artists were used in a similar way. These adaptations of Academy pictures may not have resulted in pictorial advertising at its best, as for this to be achieved a picture must have been designed as an advertisement, but it served to bring about a more complete marriage of art and advertising, and to show that the best contemporary artistic talent might find worthy employment in this field.

Although the purpose of advertising can be simply stated as that of selling goods, services or entertainment, methods of achieving the purpose are often very complicated. The character of the advertising is determined by the nature of the particular goods, services or entertainment and by the kind of public to which the appeal is made. Various classifications of goods and services have been made for advertising purposes, but none is entirely satisfactory. One classification, seemingly clever, but of doubtful validity, is (a) goods that people need but do not want; (b) goods that people want but do not need and (c) goods that people both need and want. Unfortunately for this classification, wants and needs vary so much with time, place and mental and physical conditions, that it is difficult to apply it even roughly.

The distinction between goods and services for the general or lay public and those for the specialist public must necessarily control the technique of advertising. The specialist public is often looking for the advertisement because it wants information about goods or services in its particular field, whereas the attention of the general public has more often to be arrested. Advertising addressed to the specialist public can therefore be practical and detailed, but that to the general public must attract attention quickly and convey its message almost immediately. It has been aptly said that the poster is a quick firing weapon aimed at a moving target. The target is not quite so rapid in its movement with newspaper and periodical advertising, and still less so with technical and trade advertising. But generally one of the fundamental aims, which has largely created pictorial advertising, is to arrest attention, and then to hold it until the message has been delivered. To what extent does symbolism assist in this purpose?

In advertising such things as activities of a cultural nature all that is necessary is to make them known. The bare announcement of a Beethoven symphony concert conducted by Klemperer is enough, but it is essential for it to be widely known for the hall to be full. Little more than a reminder is necessary of certain very well known quality products, such as Wedgwood bone china, or Waterford glass.

Generally, however, when advertising goods which do not evoke associations by their names, it is necessary to recommend them in some way and to create these associations. Thus, as a general rule, with the exceptions already noted, it is not so much the goods and services which are advertised as ideas about them. This is at once apparent if some famous advertisements are considered. An early advertisement for Coleman's mustard, in about 1900, by John Hassall, shows a tramp on his way to Klondike sitting in the snow and warming his hands by a tin of mustard set on a bundle of faggots; thus the idea of heat. A Pears soap advertisement manager once remarked at a meeting of the Publicity Club in London that the Palmolive soap advertisement 'Keep that schoolgirl complexion' was the best of all soap advertisements. It was a splendid idea by which to sell soap. In one of the Palmolive advertisements an elderly man says affectionately as he bends over an elderly woman, 'Still that schoolgirl complexion'. An advertisement of Saxone of Scotland by André Amstuts shows a Scottish lad asleep in a shoe with the words 'Cosiest comfort in Saxone'. The association of comfort with Saxone shoes will remain. Similarly, a picture of a man and an armchair on a wheel, with 'Travel in rail comfort; it's worth it in the long run', emphasize the idea of comfort. Another example on this theme of comfort is a rail passenger, snug in a compartment, incorporated in an umbrella design, while strings of rain are shown with the words 'Travel in rail comfort'. (Plate XXVII.)

A further noteworthy example of advertising an idea is the series of advertisements of 'Guinness for Strength'. These foster the idea that Guinness keeps up one's strength, and attention is attracted to the posters by humorous and exaggerated expression of the idea. One shows a workman negligently leaning against a massive column whilst drinking a glass of Guinness, whereupon the column collapses, to the amazement of his fellow workmen. Another shows a workman, having drunk a glass of Guinness, carrying a massive steel girder on his head. A war-time poster related to the 'dig for victory' campaign shows a man pushing a wheelbarrow greatly overloaded with vegetables. Such advertisements provided a degree of entertainment for casual spectators.

Another outstanding series of advertisements (1956–57), resulting from an excellent idea appealing to the urge for self-advancement, was that of *The Times*, under the general heading of 'Top people take *The Times*', with illustrations of various professional people in positions of authority—an architect, scientist, headmaster, woman M.P., ship-builder. Most of the advertisements carried further comments such as 'Maybe that's how they got there', 'Maybe it helped them to get there' and 'And those on the way to the top'. This is a classic example of the use in advertising of an idea

First time does it!

First time does it!

First time does it!

At one stroke Saladin, renowned for his chivalric

Fig. 38. Pictorial advertising by analogy.

A series of four advertisements of I.C.I. (Pharmaceuticals Division) Ltd., the purpose of which is to emphasize that the first injection of 'Sulphamezathine' sodium 33⅓% is adequate and effective in curing certain cattle diseases like actinobacillosis and interdigital necrosis. For the skittles player the point of the advertisement is prefaced by the caption 'One well-aimed shot is always the quickest way of winning the game—the same principle often applies in the treatment of disease'. For the cricketer: 'Out first ball'. Every bowler knows that he stands his best chance against a new batsman before he is properly 'settled in'. Likewise, etc. For the circus rider the picture is left to be self-explanatory, and for Saladin: 'At one stroke Saladin, renowned for his chivalric courage and honour, could cut a cushion in two with one stroke of his sword'.

107

which has the virtue of being true in relation to what is advertised, while appealing to a powerful human urge.

These expressions of ideas about goods and services are mainly by representation, but the expression is often effectively done by symbolism, either of an associated kind or by analogy.[2] (See (2) and (3) in classification in Chapter I). Some excellent passenger transport advertising is of the former kind. A common form is a group of objects associated with, for example, a seaside holiday, like the pail, spade, ball, starfish and the railway line in the British Railways Poster (1950), or the sunshade, seahorse, golf clubs, cricket and tennis racket and fishing net, with the suggestion that Lytham St. Annes caters for all; or the deer in the London Transport poster of Richmond Park. More eloquent than the advertisements of special places by things associated with them are the symbols of ideas of a more general character, and here objects suggestive of the whole are often more effective than a representational picture, like a landscape. Thus a British Railways poster conveys the message 'Enjoy the country-side' by means of a pattern of naturalistically rendered leaves of forest trees, corn-fields and hedge plants, which gives a refreshing sense of the leafy countryside in contrast to the dry, hard masonry of the city. The London Transport poster 'Leisure days in the Parks' just shows knitting on the grass, but it conjures up a vision of peace among trees and lawns on summer afternoons. (Plate XXVIII.)

Potentially the most powerful and effective pictorial advertising is by means of analogous symbolism, and there is scope for much further development and experiment on these lines. The war-time poster showing a chain with a missing link, with the words, 'Don't be an absentee; absentees help the Axis', speaks volumes. Apt, although less effective, is the London Transport poster showing a tin of sardines, with the words 'Staggered working hours reduce crowding'. The columns of *The Times* arranged like the façade of a Greek temple, with the words, 'The most famous columns in the world', is effective advertising because the picture is arresting and the symbolism applicable. The same can be said of the British Railways 'Feeling caged, get out with a cheap day ticket', depicting a City man struggling in a birdcage. (Plate XXIX.)

This introduces the very important question of the symbolic appropriateness of the pictorial representation. Much pictorial advertising fails because the picture has not sufficient connection with the idea to be expressed for the reason that too much is sacrificed to the picture designed to arrest attention. Although it must be acknowledged that the first thing in general advertising is to attract attention, if the picture fails because of far-fetched or strained analogy to convey its message, then attention has been attracted to little purpose.

Certain subjects attract attention well, such as pretty or sex-appealing girls in various stages of undress, appealing animals like wistful dogs and pretty cats, grotesque or comical animals in fantastic attitudes, grotesque and funny men, and so on. These are the symbols of the ideas the advertiser wishes to express. Sometimes the symbols are first chosen, and then efforts are made to connect them with the idea. Pretty girls are associated with machinery, and wistful or comical animals with beer.

However entertaining the picture may be, unless the symbolism is apt, there is the risk that the picture will be remembered without association with the idea or message it is intended to convey. In discussing this matter of relevancy in advertising illustration H. W. Hepner mentions that experiments show that the memory value for the brand, name or article is much greater for relevant than for irrelevant illustration and that 'as a result, the trick method of catching attention even to the use of illustrations of only slightly remote relevance—is decreasing in advertising'.

Good pictorial advertising is where the association is at once apparent, or the idea is expressed by analogy. In other words, the associative or analogous symbolism impresses by its aptness. A supreme example of associative symbolism which struck at once powerfully and dramatically was the picture of a grief-stricken woman wearing widows' weeds, with the words: 'Keep death off the road, carelessness kills.' This poster was in fact too powerful and apt, and was withdrawn.

The completely symbolic pictorial advertisement is by analogy, where an object or incident symbolizes by its character the message or idea to be expressed. The missing link symbolizing the absentee war worker, already mentioned (Plate XXVIII), is a good, simple, effective example, because it suggests by a break in a vital chain the possible extent of damage resulting from absenteeism. The use of animals to symbolize qualities of machinery and other products are common forms of this advertising by analogy. A famous example is the Jaguar symbolizing the car of that name, which suggests that the car has the qualities of speed or toughness associated with the animal. Chatwood Steel Partitioning in advertising the apparently contradictory qualities of rigidity and flexibility in its partitioning gives the excellent analogy of the cobra, a drawing of which also serves to arrest attention.

A few further examples of pictorial symbolism by analogy should demonstrate also that it is a method that could be used to a greater extent with profit to the advertiser.

In a Government poster advocating the protection of children from diphtheria by immunization the black hand of death is used as a symbol for diphtheria and is shown about to clutch the head of a crying baby. Pleasanter subjects are the pictures of spring and the countryside, with appropriate poetry, offered as wayside refreshment by Whitbreads—spiritual or mental refreshment symbolizing the refreshment of Whitbread's beer. The excellence of this series is that it conveys the idea of refreshment of the very best kind, such as a glimpse of the beauties of spring and the country in the centre of a big city.

Some of the best pictorial advertising by symbolic analogy is of a specialist scientific character, and it has been used to a considerable extent by Imperial Chemical Industries Ltd. in advertising their products. It has not always been equally apt—that is too much to expect—but the many advertisements of this kind by the I.C.I. demonstrates the value of this method. A series which showed varying excellence, but which reached a good standard, was that advertising 'Sulphamezathine' for the injection of cattle in cases of interdigital necrosis. The point that it was desired to make in the advertisements was that a single injection of 'Sulphamezathine' Sodium $33\frac{1}{3}$ per cent would effect a cure. Thus the theme was 'First time does it', and one advertisement showed a man knocking down all nine skittles with the first ball, another a batsman bowled first ball, another a rugby-footballer putting the ball over the bar in one kick, another a circus performer going through the hoop the first time, and yet another, Saladin cutting a cushion with one stroke of his sword. (Fig. 38.)

'Scopel' Cream, a skin protective against water-soluble irritants, is advertised by a picture of rain falling on a duck, with the words 'Like water off a duck's back'. On

RIGID FLEXIBILITY

A contradiction in terms, you say. But Chatwood Steel Partitioning is certainly rigid. Its deep section ensures freedom from "drumming", as well as giving great fire-resistance.

And because Chatwood Partitioning is manufactured in convenient sizes, it is indeed flexible and easy to install or move . . . in every architectural surrounding. Add the fact that it offers exceptional sound resistance to assure your privacy, and you will know Chatwood Partitioning is the answer to *your* office problem.

THE FINEST YOU CAN BUY

Chatwood
STEEL PARTITIONING

Fig. 39. The idea of flexibility combined with rigidity which it is wished to convey is excellently expressed by the analogy of the cobra, which serves also to arrest attention.

110

the same lines, but a little strained, is the advertisement for 'Shrink fit' in effecting repairs to machinery by applying extreme cold to the part to be fitted so that when the temperature rises to normal again a tight fit is ensured (Plate XXX). In the advertisement a fashionable lady of the eighteenth century is shown undergoing tight lacing by her maid. It serves to attract attention, because the picture has a touch of the dramatic with effective chiaroscuro. By contraction, it is presumed, the lady's waist shrinks to its minimum, under the efforts of the maid, and then relaxes again within the tight lacing. Another in the series refers to the use of chloride of lime, as a principal raw material, in the manufacture of chloroform which caused excessive frothing in the distillation process. The difficulty was overcome by the substitution of chlorine and hydrated lime instead of chloride of lime. The advertisement explaining this shows a picture by C. F. Tunnicliffe of a cuckoo in the nest, confronting with open beak the nest's owner. The cuckoo symbolizes, of course, the disturbing action of the chloride of lime. The advertisement serves to attract attention in the first place, and by interesting analogy drives home the point, and if it is not completely apt it is sufficiently good to demonstrate the value of such advertising. Analogies of this kind are not easy to conceive, but they generally succeed in making an advertisement which has point, and is remembered. In a lighter vein is the advertisement for Truman's beer which shows an old pirate of the seventeenth century with a wooden leg dancing, with the words 'More hops in Ben Truman'. Another is 'Let Capstan take the strain' (Plate XXIX). The apt and telling analogy that is also original is necessarily rare, but when it is achieved it usually effects notable conquests.

REFERENCES
1. Quoted in *Modern Advertising Practices and Principles* by HARRY WALKER HEPNER (New York, 1956), p. 21.
2. Representation in a broad sense is symbolism, and this is discussed in Part III, Chapters XV and XX on Art and Painting, but here it can for practical purposes be distinguished from symbolism as it is more generally understood.

XI   Postage Stamps

POSTAL services have evolved to make possible speedy communication firstly for state purposes and later between individuals. They existed in ancient civilizations, in Persia, Egypt and Greece, and in the Roman Empire they were brought to some degree of efficiency. Most of such services seem to have disappeared during the Middle Ages, but began to be revived in the fourteenth century.

Organized state postal services were first established in modern Britain in 1635, and the Post Office was founded in 1657. Postmarks indicating the date of posting appear to have been first used in Italy in the fifteenth century. Letters were marked on the addressed side by small hand stamps which showed in some cases the symbol or emblem of the town of origin. In Britain a date-stamp was first used in 1661, being introduced by Henry Bishop, then Postmaster-General. It showed the date within a small circle. In 1680 this was elaborated for a period by William Dockwra with the addition of MOR (morning) and AF (afternoon) and the hour of the day. The first receipt or paid stamp was also introduced in Britain in 1680—the first in the world. It consisted of a triangular stamp inscribed 'Penny Post Paid'.

Although the adhesive stamp for the pre-payment of letters was proposed by Rowland Hill and James Chalmers in 1837, it was not until 6th May, 1840, that it was first used. This, known as the penny black, consisted of the crowned head of Queen Victoria on a black ground. The head was based on that on a medal designed by William Wyon in 1837 to commemorate the Queen's first visit to the City of London in that year. Britain was the first country in the world to use adhesive stamps for letters. Other countries followed rapidly. In the U.S.A. the New York City Despatch Post introduced adhesive stamps in February, 1842. This service was taken over by the Government in the August of that year, but adhesive stamps were not issued by the United States Post Office until 1847. In Europe the first country to follow Britain in issuing adhesive stamps was Switzerland in 1843, and by the eighteen-fifties most European countries had adopted them. Outside Europe, apart from the private enterprise in New York, Brazil was the first country to do so, shortly after Switzerland, in 1843. By 1860 almost every country in the world had adopted them.

During the nineteenth century most postage stamps with a few exceptions were designed with the conventional state symbols. In the case of monarchies the head of the reigning monarch was usually shown, sometimes crowned, sometimes not. The coat of arms of the royal family was occasionally used as in an Italian stamp of 1889 which showed the arms of Savoy. In the case of a Republic the head of a President either past or present was often shown, or a symbolic head or figure, as in the head of Ceres in the early French stamps of 1849 onwards, or the figure of Peace and Commerce of 1876, or the figure of the Sower of 1903 onwards.

As would be expected the Crown is the most persistent symbol in postage stamps of monarchical countries. The head of Victoria is almost always crowned, the only exception, as far as I am aware, to her wearing a regal crown is in the stamp of Jamaica of 1860 in which she wears a crown of laurel. Wyon's head of Queen Victoria persisted on postage stamps of Great Britain throughout her reign, the principal variations in design being in the framing and the manner of stating the value. In this framing small royal or national symbols, or symbols of peace or achievement were introduced. In the stamps of 1887, the $1\frac{1}{2}d$. stamp has laurel on a banner forming the frame, and the 2d., $2\frac{1}{2}d$. and 3d. all have laurel (or olive) to different designs. The 5d. has the royal coat of arms below the Queen's head and the 6d. has the Tudor rose. In the stamps of Edward VIII the King is not crowned, but the crown is shown above his head outside the oval frame, and the same principle of design was followed for the stamps of George V. Oak and laurel were used on the Edward penny stamp, and in the stamps of George V the lion and dolphin, familiar national symbols, were introduced. In the larger 2s. 6d., 5s., 10s. and £1 stamps of 1912, Britannia is shown in a chariot drawn by three horses riding the waves, a trident in one hand and Union Jack on a shield held in the other. This is the first elaborate pictorial postage stamp of Great Britain although by this year they were fairly common in many other countries. The British Empire Exhibition stamp of 1924 was the first of the British commemorative stamps and these, often rich in symbolism, will be considered later after glancing at a few stamps of other countries.

The crown continued to appear in the stamps of Edward VIII and George VI, a small representation in the top right corner in the former, and above, not on, the head in the latter. In the stamps of India, George V and VI are almost always shown crowned. With the British stamps of Elizabeth II there is a return to the design of Victoria's stamps with the monarch actually wearing the crown, suggesting the crown rests more becomingly perhaps on a woman's head. The crowned head continued in all stamps of Elizabeth II until 1966. With the issue of four landscape stamps on 2nd May of that year a British postage stamp of the Queen's head appears without the crown but with the fillet of laurel similar to the head on coins from the sculptured relief by Mary Gillick, and this is the case in most commemorative stamps since. In the new series of definitive stamps designed by Arnold Machin she is shown crowned, and the head is similar in character to the Wyon stamps, both being reproductions of sculptured reliefs.

The earliest postage stamps of the U.S.A., those of 1847 to 1861, showed heads of Benjamin Franklin and of past presidents Washington, Jefferson and Andrew Jackson, and were thus commemorative. In 1869 pictorial stamps were introduced. Three depicted the transport of letters: one of a post-rider (2 cents), one of a locomotive (3 cents) and one of a ship, the s.s. *Adriatic* (12 cents). There were also in this year pictorial commemorative issues of the Landing of Columbus (15 cents) and of the Declaration of Independence (24 cents). In this same year two symbolic designs were employed, one an eagle surmounting a shield (10 cents), the other similar but with the addition of flags (30 cents).

It could be claimed that these early U.S.A. stamps, both the heads and the two pictorial stamps celebrating historical events are the earliest commemorative stamps, and the prelude to the commemoratives that became so plentiful throughout the world in the mid-twentieth century. The earliest commemoratives in the British Commonwealth are those of New South Wales, which were issued in 1888 to commemorate the hundredth anniversary of the colony. Several were issued and in the series was a view of Sydney (1*d*.), an emu (3*d*.), Capt. Cook (4*d*.), kangaroo (1*s*.), map of Australia (5*s*.) and portrait of Lord Carrington then the Governor together with Capt. Arthur Phillip the first Governor (20*s*.).

Commemorative stamps and those issued to mark particular occasions began to appear in Europe about the beginning of the century. Among the earliest were some German stamps of 1899; one depicted pictorially an allegorical union of north and south Germany, another the unveiling of the Kaiser Wilhelm I memorial and another Wilhelm II delivering a speech. Switzerland issued a stamp in 1900 commemorating the twenty-fifth anniversary of the founding of the Universal Postal Union which showed a globe, a woman holding the Swiss flag, and the words Jubile de L'Union Postale Universelle. Italy celebrated the jubilee of its unity in stamps of 1911, and the re-erection of the campanile of St. Mark's, Venice, in a stamp of 1912. The earliest French commemoratives were during the first world war in a series issued in 1917, one showing a war widow, another the replacement of man by woman in agricultural work, and another a bombed hospital and the sinking of a hospital ship, using postage stamps, to some extent, as war propaganda.

In the first British commemorative stamp, celebrating the British Empire Exhibition of 1924, the lion figures prominently. Then after a gap of five years special stamps were issued in the summer of 1929 to mark the Postal Union Congress. They were simple designs, except the large £1 black stamp which showed a magnificent design of St. George and the Dragon by Harold Nelson. Another long gap followed until May 1935 when George V silver jubilee stamps were issued, in a rather simple conventional design showing on the right of the head a laurel wreath with a sprig of oak. In 1937 the coronation of George VI was marked with several stamps, some having for the first time emblems of the countries of the United Kingdom, the rose, thistle, daffodil and shamrock. The most interesting of this series was the large 1½*d*. which depicts George and Elizabeth with the crown between and other symbols of royal authority, the orb and cross, and the eagle-shaped ampula. The centenary of the first adhesive postage stamps was celebrated by one in 1940 which depicts the heads of Queen Victoria and George VI side by side. Much more interesting was the Peace or Victory stamp of 1946 with its theme of reconstruction, showing in the 2½*d*. blue summary line drawings of a tractor, house, power station and ship, and in the 3*d*. violet the flying dove with olive branch, bricklayer's trowel, dividers and square. (For illustrations of British commemorative stamps, plates XXXI to XXXV.)

Three special issues were made in 1948, one celebrating George VI's and Elizabeth's silver wedding, both designs presenting them together in profile; one celebrating the liberation of the Channel Islands, and four stamps marking the Olympic games held in London in that year. The 2½*d.* blue shows the globe encircled by laurel wreath, the 3*d.* violet a ball moving through space with the Olympic symbol of five rings suggesting speed, the 6*d.* purple with the five rings, and the 1*s.* brown with the figure of winged victory striding the globe carrying a laurel wreath. In 1949 four stamps were issued to celebrate the seventy-fifth anniversary of the Universal Postal Union; the 2½*d.* blue showing the two hemispheres, the 3*d.* violet an impressive design showing the U.P.U. monument in Berne, the 6*d.* purple, another good and ingenious design, depicting the Goddess Concordia holding letters in her out-stretched hands, with globe and points of compass, and the 1*s.* brown showing globe encircled by posthorn. In 1951 there were two special issues, one commemorating Nelson's *Victory* with four stamps, and two for the Festival of Britain. The four *Victory* stamps are rather ordinary in design, the 2*s.* 6*d.* green showing the *Victory* in an oval, the 5*s.* red similarly depicting the cliffs of Dover, the 10*s.* blue St. George and the Dragon, and the £1 brown the royal coat of arms. The two Festival of Britain stamps are a little more ingenious, the 2½*d.* red displaying the head of Minerva with the caduceus and cornucopia in a diagonal cross design, and the 4*d.* blue with the festival emblem of Minerva's head and the points of the compass.

In 1953, four Coronation stamps were issued. In the 2½*d.* carmine-red are the symbol of the Coronation, the two crowns (the Imperial State Crown and St. Edward's crown), the orb, ampula, rod and sceptre; the 4*d.* blue has the emblems of the four countries, rose, thistle, daffodil and shamrock, with the crown, orb and ampula, the 1*s.* 3*d.* yellow-green represents the Queen in her Coronation robes holding sceptre and orb.

With the reign of Elizabeth II, commemorative stamps and those to mark special occasions became more frequent, and during the nineteen-sixties several were issued each year. Subjects for stamp designs thus became more varied and stimulated the ingenuity of designers. This can be said of stamps in most countries since about 1955. Up to that time stamp designs in Great Britain were rarely very distinctive, conventional state symbols were too often repeated without much originality or inventiveness in their treatment. There were a few notable exceptions among those mentioned such as Harold Nelson's £1 Postal Union Congress stamp of 1929, with St. George and the Dragon, the two Peace stamps of 1946, the 2½*d.* designed by H. L. Palmer and the 3*d.* by Reynolds Stone, the 3*d.* U.P.U. stamp with the Berne Monument of 1949 designed by Percy Metcalfe and the 6*d.*, with the goddess Concordia designed by H. Fleury.

Themes of special stamp issues could be broadly classified as:

1. Those which represent interesting features and life of a country or locality such as landscapes, fauna and flora, industry and technology, buildings and city scenes.

2. Stamps commemorating a particular person. This has been a frequent subject for stamps in numerous countries, but not often in Great Britain. Among the few who have been thus commemorated in British stamps are Shakespeare (1963), Churchill (1965), Joseph Lister (1965) and Robert Burns (1966). In the case of Churchill and Burns mainly their heads are shown, but in the case of Shakespeare stamps, famous characters in his plays are represented in addition to his head; while in the case of one

115

of the Lister stamps the carbolic spray which he used when he introduced his antiseptic technique is illustrated.

3. Stamps celebrating historical events like Christopher Columbus' discovery of America, a common theme in U.S.A. stamps, and among modern British stamps, the series of the Battle of Hastings (1966) taken from the Bayeux tapestry, the nine-hundredth anniversary of the founding of the Royal Church of Westminster Abbey (1966), seven-hundredth anniversary of Simon de Montfort's Parliament (1965), the hundredth anniversary of the Salvation Army, and the series celebrating the twenty-fifth anniversary of the Battle of Britain are examples.

4. Stamps to mark national or international occasions like those in Britain marking the seventh Commonwealth Parliamentary Conference (1961), the ninth international life-boat conference (1963), the International Botanical Congress (1964), the twentieth Geographical Congress (1964), the opening of the Forth Bridge (1964) and several others of a similar character.

5. The celebration of scientific discoveries like the series of four of British discoveries.

6. Stamp designs expressing ideas like peace, rebuilding, freedom, human rights, education, unity and security. In stamp designs with such themes ingenious symbolism is often used and thus we find some of the best stamps of this kind are those of the United Nations.

Recalling the classification of types of symbols given in the first chapter and applying it to the designs of postage stamps, it could be said that the classes most commonly used in minuscule design are the: (1) symbolism of objects by approximate or conventional imitation, and of a part of an object to represent the whole, (2) the expression of an idea, activity or event by an object or objects associated with it, and (3) symbolism of an idea by analogy. Because of the subjects expressed and commemorated, in national stamps the first and second types are most commonly used, although the third is occasionally found, but where the expression is mainly of ideas as with United Nations stamps then the third type is more often employed.

The 1957 British stamps of the World Scout Jubilee Jamboree show associative and analogous symbolism. The 2½d. magenta red designed by Mary Adshead depicts the Scout badge and a rope illustrating a knot, the 4d. blue designed by Pat Keely shows birds (swallows) on either side of the Queen's head, flying inwards symbolizing Scouts coming to Britain, while the 1s. 3d. green designed by W. H. Brown depicts the globe and compass. In 1958 the British Empire and Commonwealth Games were held in Cardiff and this event was celebrated by three stamps all depicting in different ways the Welsh Dragon, the rich pattern of the 1s. 3d. green designed by Pat Keely being the most impressive.

Two very interesting stamps were issued in 1960 commemorating the tercentenary of the Act of 1660 establishing the General Letter Office. The 3d. violet designed by R. Stone shows a postboy riding a horse, blowing a horn, with the post-bag at his back, an attractive simple design. The other stamp for this event was a 1s. 3d. green which has the crown and horn among oak sprays. Another postal event commemorated by stamps in this year was the first anniversary of the Conference of European Postal and Telecommunications Administration which had two stamps, the 6d. purple and brown and the 1s. 6d. steel blue and green of identical simple design with a central wheel. Incidentally, this was the first time that two colours were used in Great Britain.

Three special stamps belong to 1961 and one to 1962. For the second anniversary of the Conference of European Postal and Telecommunications Administration there were were three stamps, all designed by T. Kurpershock and M. Goaman, showing flights of doves, or carrier pigeons. The two stamps, celebrating the seventh Commonwealth Parliamentary Conference, 1961, designed by Miss P. Jacques, depict (6d.) the roof of Westminster Hall and (1s. 3d.) the Parliament building both with the rod and sceptre. Three stamps marked the centenary of the Post Office Savings Bank. The 3d.—the first three colour issue—a felicitous design by M. Goaman employing analogous and associative symbolism with a squirrel in the branches of a tree, and an owl in the top right hand corner, attractively suggesting the wisdom of saving. The 1s. 6d. echoes the thrift plant on the three-penny piece. To 1962 belong the three stamps of National Productivity Year.

With 1963 there is a blossoming of special colourful stamps, no less than twelve being issued commemorating six events. The two issued for the Freedom from Hunger campaign were designed by M. Goaman and show conventionalized renderings of wheat ($2\frac{1}{2}d$.), and for the 1s. 3d. stamp three children and a globe. In May, the Paris Postal Conference Centenary was celebrated by two very attractive stamps in the same month for National Nature Week. One designed by S. D. Scott (3d.) shows flowers and a bee, and the other by M. Goaman a delightful design of plants, animals and birds. It was, of course, a subject which lent itself to effective patterning.

The International Lifeboat Conference had three stamps, all designed by David Gentleman. The $2\frac{1}{2}d$. which is the most interesting, shows a helicopter engaged in rescue operations with the lifeboat. The three stamps for the Red Cross Centenary Congress are not particularly notable.

The 1s. 6d. for the Commonwealth Trans-Pacific Cable designed by Peter Gauld shows a globe, the conventional electrical signs and a simulation of waves all appropriately in various shades of blue.

In 1964 four events were commemorated with five stamps for the four-hundredth anniversary of the birth of Shakespeare. Four of the Shakespeare stamps of 1964 were designed by David Gentleman each with a portrait and scenes from his plays, while the fifth designed by C. and R. Ironside depicts the grave scene from Hamlet.

Four stamps were issued for the International Geographical Congress all ingenious designs by D. Bailey depicting in summarized form various scenes of Britain; the $2\frac{1}{2}d$. depicting flats in Richmond Park, the 4d. shipbuilding yards in Belfast, the 8d. Beddgelert Forest Park, Snowdonia, and the 1s. 6d. the nuclear reactor, Dounreay, thus symbolizing various aspects of life in Britain. Another four, this year, marked the 10th International Botanical Congress—all designed by M. Goaman. The subject is an attractive one and four very decorative, colourful designs of wild flowers emerged: the 3d. with gentian, the 6d. with wild rose, the 9d. with honeysuckle and the 1s. 3d. with convolvulus. This year two stamps celebrated the completion of the Forth Bridge, both designed by Andrew Restall, the 3d. which shows a view of the bridge, and the 6d. depicts in addition to the new road bridge a glimpse of the old railway bridge.

At the end of 1964 the Postmaster-General stated the aims in the choice of subjects for special postage stamps. These were:

1. To celebrate events of national and international importance.
2. To commemorate important anniversaries.
3. To reflect the British contribution to world affairs, including the arts and sciences.
4. To extend public patronage to the arts by encouraging the development of minuscule art.

Subsequent issues of special stamps reflect to some extent these aims.

Two stamps were issued in 1965 to mark the Centenary of the International Tele-communication Union, both designed by Andrew Restall. The 9d. stamp shows a design symbolic of world telecommunication stations, while the 1s. 6d. stamp suggests a radio or sound wave with a symbolic representation of a switchboard. These were followed by the 4d. and 1s. 3d. Churchill stamps of identical design, with a slight variation of scale and colour, designed by David Gentleman and his wife, Rosalind Dease. These were followed by the 6d. and 2s. 6d. stamps commemorating the seven-hundredth anniversary of Simon de Montfort's Parliament. Both are interesting designs: the 6d. displaying the seal of Simon de Montfort, and in the 2s. 6d., unusually long, is a view from the river of the Parliament building as it was in the thirteenth century. A little later still, in 1965, the centenary of the Salvation Army was celebrated in two colourful stamps. Some reference has already been made to the 4d. Lister stamp and to the carbolic spray included in the design by Peter Gauld.

The 1s. stamp, designed by Frank Ariss, incorporates a portrait of Lister and a hexagon with the letters OH—the whole representing the chemical symbol for carbolic acid [Phenol—C_6H_5 (OH)]—the fluid used by Lister. Both these elements are placed within a third, the white square. This represents a square of lint and the black outer border over-lapping the white square a sheet of lead or thin block tin, the whole a symbolic representation of Lister's initial experiments.

In 1965 two special stamps served to mark the Commonwealth Arts Festival, a 6d. showing three dancing figures from the famous Trinidad Shrove Monday Carnival, and a 1s. 6d. stamp depicting folk-dancing by three members of Les Feux Follets, a Canadian dance company. Both were designed by David Gentleman and Rosalind Dease. They also designed seven of the eight stamps issued to commemorate the twenty-fifth anniversary in 1965 of the Battle of Britain. These stamps represent an innovation. There are six different designs for the 4d. value, the first time there had been more than one design for one value in a special issue. They are examples of associative symbolism and from the fighter and bombing planes a series of excellent designs were evolved. The six are: (1) flight of Supermarine Spitfire fighters; (2) pilot silhouetted in the cockpit of a Hawker Hurricane fighter; (3) wing-tips of a German Messerschmitt and a Spitfire showing the markings of the two opposing fighter planes; (4) a pair of Spitfires attacking a Heinkel bomber; (5) Hurricanes attacking a Junkers dive bomber; and (6) a flight of Hurricanes returning to base over the wreckage of a ditched Dornier bomber. The 1s. 3d. stamp is more pictorial and the aim was to show the battle as the people of London remember it, with the white vapour trails in a blue sky, with the dome of St. Paul's surrounded by bombed buildings. The 9d. stamp designed by Andrew Restall shows an anti-aircraft gun battery in action.

Other special stamps issued in 1965 and 1966 celebrated the opening of the Post Office Tower, and the nine-hundredth anniversary of the foundation of Westminster Abbey, but neither is remarkable in design or has any symbolic interest. Other stamps of 1966 of pictorial and design interest were four landscape subjects, three for the World Cup Football event, four of British birds and two rather silly Christmas stamp designs by children.

A series of four illustrating British technology are of some symbolic interest. The 4d. stamp illustrates the Jodrell Bank telescope, the 6d. symbolizes British motor engineering, with an E-type Jaguar car and a background of mini-minors, both designed by David and Ann Gillespie. The 1s. 3d. stamp depicts a Hovercraft, and the 1s. 6d. illustrates nuclear power with the advance gas-cooled reactor at Windscale, both designed by Andrew Restall. Together these four symbolize British technology. Similar in theme are the four expressive of British discovery issued in 1967. As with the Technology series, parts are selected to symbolize the whole. The 4d. stamp depicts a radar screen, the 1s. stamp illustrates a penicillin mould, the 1s. 6d. twin jets of a V.C.10 are shown, and in the 1s. 9d. stamp a television camera. The two last mentioned are excellent designs by Negus Sharland, but it is questionable whether the two discs of the radar screen and pencillin mould make good designs or are particularly expressive. A design that is intelligible in itself without the label is generally more eloquent than one that has to be interpreted by a label. Expressive in this respect are the two stamps issued in 1967 for the European Free Trade Association, one (9d.) depicting a freight ship, the other (1s. 6d.) showing a freight plane being loaded or unloaded, with the flags of member nations in a line below.

An attractive theme for design was the nine-hundredth anniversary of the Battle of Hastings in October 1966, a series of eight stamps designed by David Gentleman and derived from the Bayeux Tapestry. With a variety of colours the designs make decorative patterns. Another way of treating the theme would have been to try to indicate symbolically the historical significance of the Norman conquest of England, but this is a difficult subject. British flora, and famous paintings were other subjects in 1967, while British bridges and anniversaries of the T.U.C., votes for women, Royal Air Force and First Voyage of Discovery are commemorative stamps in 1968, but none of these displays any very distinctive symbolic design.

The subjects of the stamps of the United Nations are to a large extent abstract ideas, and therefore lend themselves to expression by analogous symbolism. Writing of these stamps in *Commemorative Art* (October 1966), A. G. K. Leonard remarks that U.N. stamps 'serve as postal messengers of peace—miniature advertising posters exemplifying the aims and achievements of the United Nations and its specialized agencies. Since 1951, there have been issued altogether 172 different U.N. stamps, ordinary and commemorative, publicising a wide range of United Nations themes, activities and occasions with an attractive variety of designs, the work of leading graphic artists and specialist printers from more than a dozen countries.' Among the early notable United Nations stamps is a design exemplifying U.N.I.C.E.F., showing an adult hand reaching down to hold that of a child. Another early stamp (1952) is one designed by H. Woyty-Wimmer for Human Rights day which shows a flame surrounded by a white circle between two hemispheres. The designer is recorded as saying (*Commemorative Art*, October 1966) that he chose 'two hemispheres to represent the whole of mankind', and 'since Human Rights are the assumption of human happiness as expressed in the soul and spirit, I symbolized those with a flame surrounded by a white circle—also a symbol of infinity—and this bears the inscription.' This encircled flame symbol gained international currency. Sometimes in United Nations stamps it was varied with the torch.

United Nations stamps sometimes set the theme for stamps in the various countries of the world. One such is the staff of Aesculapius with snake in conjunction with the globe and some other symbol, such as the mosquito for malaria, to symbolize world health and medical care. Another theme was that for World Refugee Year, a design by Olav Mathieson, showing the silhouette of protecting hands around a figure, with an encircling laurel wreath.

The U.N. Economic Commission for Asia and the Far East is symbolized in a design of 1960 by Woyty-Wimmer depicting an immense suspended girder against the map of Asia, with a small laurel-encircled globe in the corner. Similar is the International Bank theme, in a design by A. M. Medina, of a block and tackle symbolizing reconstruction and development, a good example of a small part signifying much. The Economic Commission for Latin America stamp of 1961 designed by Robert Perrot, has a cogwheel encircling a map of South America. In 1961, also, is a design by Minoro Hisano for the United Nations Children's Fund of a bird with a worm in its beak, feeding three young ones in the nest. In 1946 one of the stamps issued to publicize the Geneva Conference on Trade and Development designed by H. Sanborn and Ole Hamann, shows a globe, a packing crate and six dark and light diverse arrows, three each pointing in reverse directions, suggesting goods and movement round the world. Another ingenious design shows a globe from which the light of wisdom radiates, and in front two hands, dark against the light, holding the letters U.N., together with a tiny map of the world representing equilibrium and union, a design by Renato Ferrini of Italy. (See plates XXXVII and XXXVIII.)

In conclusion a few stamps are selected from various countries as examples of interesting and original symbolical design in minuscule art. Some themes have international currency like human rights, World or European co-operation or unity, health and campaigns against disease, Freedom from Hunger, Olympic Games, welfare of children and old people, and several countries have for their stamps taken the same or similar designs or given variations of these themes.

Among the notable stamps marking the fifteenth anniversary in 1963 of the Declaration of Human Rights, was a Russian stamp which showed a flame, against a faint suggestion of a globe and a very prominent rainbow. A particularly ingenious design marking the same anniversary is a stamp of Tunisia, called Miss World, which depicts a human face in outline made as an oval with balanced scales forming eyes and nose, and latitudes and poles to associate the face with a globe.

Common symbols illustrating the world campaign against disease are the staff and snake of Aesculapius in association with the globe. In the case of the campaign against malaria a mosquito is also introduced. In an Indian stamp of 1955 in connection with the India Five Year Plan, the caduceus is shown with the mosquito, a possible mistake. The symbol of Aesculapius, however, is correctly shown in the Indian stamp with a similar theme issued in 1962. It is a variant of an international design. The symbol of Aesculapius is variously treated in the stamps of nations. The Israeli Medical Association World Congress stamp of 1964 shows the snake encircling the globe in which is drawn the menora (the seven-branched candlestick). An original treatment is in a Finnish stamp of the same year to mark the World Medical Association eighteenth general assembly, which depicts the snake with rod against the globe. Campaigns against cancer are sometimes illustrated by combat with a monster. A dramatic example is a French stamp of 1940 issued in connection with the anti-cancer fund depicting a woman with a sword in combat with a many headed monster.

Freedom from Hunger is an international theme for stamps variously treated. Two totally different but good designs are on Indian and Israeli stamps both of 1963. In the former the design depicts many hands stretched upwards towards the F.A.O. symbol of wheat growing from the globe. In the Israeli stamp the theme is symbolized by a bird in the hand, summarily but effectively rendered.

The dove of peace with olive branch figures frequently in various international themes. A German stamp of 1947 shows hands stretched upwards towards the flying dove. The hands are chained together at the wrists, but a link is broken. In an Italian stamp for Holy Year 1933, the dove with an olive branch flies against a night sky from the dome of St. Peter's to the Church of the Holy Sepulchre.

Treaties or collaborations between nations are often celebrated by postage stamps. The U.S.A.–Japan Treaty was celebrated in 1960 by a stamp depicting cherry blossom seen against the Washington Monument, a rather felicitous design. The opening of the St. Lawrence seaway in 1959 was celebrated by U.S.A. and Canadian stamps of identical design displaying the maple leaf of Canada linked with the American eagle. (For American symbolic stamps see plate XXXVI.)

European unity is simply expressed in two Swiss stamps, one of 1957 illustrates strands wound together into a strong cable, while another of 1959 consists of a geometric design of four rings and four squares linked together forming a cross.

The Olympic Games have been celebrated in a large number of stamps in every country taking part since their revival in 1896. In several stamps subjects have been selected from Ancient Greece. The first were held in Athens and several Greek stamps were then issued to celebrate the occasion, expressing their origin by associative symbolism. One depicts the 'Discobolus', the sculpture of the discus thrower by Myron, the Greek sculptor of the early fifth century B.C. The figure is flanked by sprigs of laurel and framed by Ionic columns and entablature. Another stamp shows a black figured ancient Greek vase with a representation of Athena, and a shield flanked by cocks on pedestals. The vase is in a niche with Corinthian pilasters and a festoon of laurel above. Most Olympic stamps since these original ones have concentrated on the global extent of the games and on picturing various athletes, generally accompanied by the Olympic symbol of the five linked rings. Occasionally association with ancient Greece is expressed again. A design in a German stamp of 1956 makes an ingenious pattern of a Greek key ornament and an outline of a running track overlaid by the five Olympic rings. In the same year a Netherlands stamp shows a black figured amphora decorated with runners.

Industry, production and international trade have been represented in a considerable number of designs. One very effective pattern is that of an Australian stamp of 1963 devoted to the export theme. Rays of light shine from the map of Australia and encircle the globe, and a ship, aeroplane, crane and crate are effectively placed to complete the composition. Very different, but more summarily expressed is a Finnish design of 1962 on the theme of home production which displays the Finnish labour emblem related to the abstract of a conveyor belt.

Some stamps are eloquent by means of symbolism. Simple but effective is a Russian stamp of 1917—the year of the revolution—with an illustration of the chain being cut and the sun in the background. Dramatic and moving is the French stamp of 1958 marking the fortieth anniversary of the First World War armistice. It depicts a grave in Flanders with a soldier's helmet on a tombstone seen behind growing wheat, which could be taken to symbolize the sustenance of life—life for which the soldier died.

Lastly, the design by Harry Teale to celebrate the maiden flight of the Concorde supersonic air liner, awarded first prize in the *Sun* competition, is an exceptionally succinct statement and is picture-writing at its best, showing two hands, with the French and British flags as wristlets, together lifting the plane. Such is the nature of postage stamps design: trying to say much in a small area, most effective when it is like expressive ancient picture writing, such as the Chinese hieroglyph that signifies 'anxious' by a heart at a window.

PART III

INDIVIDUAL AND COLLECTIVE EXPRESSION—INSTINCTIVE, CREATIVE AND IMAGINATIVE SYMBOLISM

XII Instinctive and Unconscious Symbolism

SYMBOLISM which comes into being as unconscious expression of instinctive urges occupies a prominent place in psychoanalysis, of which it is a fundamental part. If it is too much to say that unconscious symbolism is a discovery of Freud, yet it is he and his followers who have formed a fairly precise and logical theory of unconscious symbolism. Such symbolism among primitive peoples has often been recognized by anthropologists, but it was Freud who first recognized it as a means whereby we may penetrate into the obscure workings of the human mind.

To appreciate fully the character and significance of instinctive and unconscious symbolism as understood in modern thought, it is necessary to have a fairly clear notion of the theory of psychoanalysis. The theory is widely familiar, yet in discussing one aspect it is useful to state as precisely as possible the main principles of the theory, especially as inaccuracies and misleading interpretations often creep into popular expositions.

Many psychologists believe that the constitution of our beings, our thoughts, actions and behaviour are determined by instinctive urges. This theory depends much on the Darwinian theory of evolution in which the view is maintained that man's desires and behaviour, in common with those of animals, are determined by instincts which are blind in their operation. Instinct has been variously defined, but there is wide agreement on its main characteristic, that it is an innate propensity or impulse, that it is directed to certain ends, and that there is no conscious or purposeful adaptation of means to ends.[1]

Many theories of instincts have been developed, among the most famous being the apparently very different theories of McDougall and Freud. McDougall's is closely based on the biological theory, and is particularly serviceable as providing a classification of eleven major instincts[2] with three further less well defined instincts. Each instinct is accompanied by what is termed a primary emotion.

By the very nature of his work as a psychoanalyst Freud approaches the subject of instinct somewhat differently. In his earlier work he classifies two groups of instincts, the ego instincts, which include self-preservation, and the sexual, love or libidinal instincts. The former correspond very largely to the assertive or aggressive instincts, which are so conspicuous a feature of Adler's Individual Psychology.

Whereas instincts are classified by McDougall under such heads as flight (or self-preservation), sex (or reproduction), gregariousness, curiosity, self-assertion and self-abasement, pugnacity, repulsion, acquisition, construction, and the parental instinct, which are operative throughout life in varying stages of intensity, Freud's theory of the libidinal instincts is an account of the natural craving for pleasurable acts (called the pleasure principle) associated with the various organs of the body, from infancy. The first of these is associated with the mouth, which first manifests as the sucking of the infant, the second is the anal stage, the third is associated with the organs and processes of micturition, the fourth with the genital organs, the fifth with vision, and so on. These component instincts are all of an auto-erotic character: a further stage is when pleasure or love is directed towards an object. This begins as narcissism, and then this self-love is projected to an external object, generally the mother. In loving the mother the child develops hostility to the father who is feared as a force which might prevent gratification of the love for the mother, and this involves the mental state known as the Oedipus complex.

It will be seen that the ego and libidinal instincts are separately grouped and are distinct in this conception. However Freud later modified this view. Instead of separating these groups, he associated them, and introduced another class of instincts which he termed the destructive or death instincts. One group of instincts, the ego and libidinal group, aims at the perpetuation and maintenance of life, the other aims at its destruction. It is worth quoting Freud's definition.

'We have' [he says] 'to distinguish two classes of instincts, one of which, Eros or the sexual instincts, is by far the more conspicuous and accessible to study. It comprises not merely the uninhibited sexual instinct proper and the impulses of a sublimated or aim-inhibited nature derived from it, but also the self-preservative instinct, which must be assigned to the ego and which at the beginning of our analytic work we had good reason for setting in opposition to the sexual object instinct. The second class of instincts was not so easy to define; in the end we came to recognize sadism as its representative. As a result of theoretical considerations supported by biology, we assumed the existence of a death-instinct, the task of which is to lead organic matter back into the inorganic state; on the other hand we supposed that Eros aims at complicating life by bringing about a more and more far-reaching coalescence of the particles into which living matter has been dispersed, thus, of course, aiming at the maintenance of life.'[3]

The reasoning by which this interesting but debatable conclusion was reached was that the ego instincts, especially in the form of the super-ego, to which reference will be made later, is the repressive force which seeks to destroy the repugnant libidinal instincts. If their destructive repressive force is redirected outward, then it can be appreciated that it becomes a destructive instinct. It is a parallel, in a reverse direction, of sadism, becoming masochism. Sadism, which is one of the stages of the libido, is the hurting of a loved object for sexual gratification. This impulse when directed to the self, as it often is in women, becomes masochism. Many of Freud's most brilliant and ardent followers find this later development of his theory regarding an instinct of destruction difficult to follow and accept. The very existence of an instinct of assertion and aggression has been questioned, because it is argued that it never seems to exist on its own, and only comes into being when aroused by sex feelings or created by frustration.[4]

Different as are the approaches of McDougall and Freud to the subject of instincts, their theories have yet much in common, and there is much real correspondence on

126

fundamentals. The differences are chiefly in the terms employed rather than in the meanings. Neither system seems to be entirely comprehensive, which would be asking too much of a science still very much in its infancy. For example, in McDougall's system insufficient account is taken of the love of the young child for its mother, while it might be suggested that in Freud's system not enough account is taken of the affection of the mother for the young child, and the effect of this on the child. But whatever differences exist they agree in the fundamental that instinctive urges are the determining forces of our beings.

Psychoanalysis owes its existence to the circumstance that many of these instinctive urges are repugnant to the conscious self, and are therefore driven into the unconscious mind, which is thus the repository of all those urges which are too repellent to be acknowledged. However, these instinctive urges are often so powerful that their repression results in disturbing conflict, and a neurotic condition is produced in the individual. The instinctive urges which are repugnant to consciousness are naturally those which are not in accord with whatever ethical and social codes provide the moral standards for consciousness. It can readily be appreciated that in a modern society many of these repressed urges are of a sexual character. Other instinctive forces which suffer repression in varying degrees are the aggressive or assertive instincts, in which is included self-preservation.

In psychoanalytic theory the human mind is divided into three main parts; the id, which is the unconscious part; the ego, which is the conscious individual fashioned by the current standards of ethical thought and conduct; and the super-ego, which is an ego formed in early childhood and which has largely become unconscious. The real conflict, producing neurosis, is between the id and the super-ego, which it is necessary to define more closely.

The super-ego is constructed after the fashion of the first love object, which is generally the mother. It is largely a derivative of the Oedipus complex. As previously indicated, the child, loving the mother, desires to possess her completely and develops hostility to the father as a rival. The hopelessness of these wishes prompts a renunciation provided that the child incorporates something of the parents within himself, and thus is formed the super-ego. Thus moral ideas are derived from the parents at a very early age (possibly before five), and are inextricably interwoven into the personality. It will be seen therefore that the super-ego is deeply embedded, while the ego is comparatively superficial. Conscience and the ego-ideal are parts of the super-ego which occasionally rise to the surface.

The super-ego differs in character from the ego as the moral code of one generation differs from that of another. For example, a child is born in the late Victorian era of a father and mother with a stern religious and moral code of conduct which produces a highly artificial mode of life. The child grows up, and on becoming a man likes to keep abreast of modern movements. His ego in 1925 is based on the contemporary ideas of social life, but the super-ego is the product of the stern, artificial religious morality of a Victorian. In this case that ego is more in harmony with the animal instincts than the super-ego, but far less powerful. The real conflict of the mind is that between the animal instincts and the super-ego.

Powerful instinctive urges of a sexual and perhaps aggressive character are clamouring to determine and control the thought and action of the individual, yet they are sternly repressed by the super-ego. So powerful are they, however, that they cannot be completely repressed, and they emerge in consciousness in a sublimated form and as symbolism. With the latter this emergence takes place when the mind is relaxed as in sleep or in day-dreaming, or in supposed linguistic accidents like slips of the tongue. It is in dreams that we get the clearest instinctive and unconscious symbolism. The theory is that the super-ego is unable to keep the repugnant instinctive urges constantly submerged, and the unconscious compromises by allowing them to emerge in a changed character, thus as symbolism. The super-ego employs an agent termed the censor for this purpose. Thus a young woman dreams of a burglar pointing a revolver at her, or of a snake approaching her, both of which are phallic symbols. It is the constant endeavour of the super-ego to prevent the meanings of the symbols being known, and the dreams from remaining in consciousness, which is the reason why people so often find it difficult to remember some dreams which were quite vivid.

The clearly remembered dream is called the manifest content, the forgotten dream is the latent and important content.

The number of symbols employed in this way are exceedingly numerous. People often dream of things seen or experienced during the day, but these are merely selected as symbols because they are readily apparent to consciousness. The number of things symbolized is very small, the principal of which seems to be (1) the human body, especially the sexual organs, (2) bodily excretions, (3) members of the family, especially the father and mother, (4) and certain processes like birth and death.[5] A very large number of symbols expresses these things. They have been broadly and roughly classified.

In the first category the objects selected to symbolize bodily organs are generally those which have similar physical characteristics. Thus phallic symbols, probably the commonest of all, are long pointed round objects, while female symbols are hollow round objects. In the second category physical similarity or suggestiveness similarly obtains. In the third category the father and mother are often symbolized by exalted personages, while in the fourth category physical similitude in the case of birth seems to be a strong determinant in the selection of the symbols, and in the case of death departure on a journey or wandering is often thought to be symbolical. Works on psychoanalysis and dreams by psychoanalysts give some idea of the great variety of symbols used.[6]

The question we have to ask is: are these genuine symbols that, according to the theory, are selected by the censor on behalf of the super-ego and are disguised expressions of unconscious and instinctive urges? What means have we of determining? An exhaustive examination cannot be attempted here. It must suffice to say that from the experience of qualified psychoanalysts the interpretations of these dream symbols have been of great service in unravelling the hidden sources of conflicts which have caused neurosis, and that they have been useful in effecting cures. This seems to be evidence of the genuine character of the symbols. There is also the simple evidence of probability, because there is nothing more natural in choosing symbols than that the choice should be governed by the simple principle of like qualities in dissimilar objects.

This theory of dream symbolism could be accepted only on the basis of causation, the symbol being the effect of a cause which is a repressed instinct. As the cause is hidden and it is the purpose of the super-ego to keep it hidden, its discovery and the substantiation of the cause by the evidence of neurosis would seem to provide additional valuable evidence for the theory of causation. It would appear to provide refutation of Hume's scepticism regarding causation additional to that advanced by Whitehead, to which reference was made in the first chapter.

The theory is held by Jung that the material of dreams, in which we subsconsciously think as children, is similar to that of the primitive thoughts of mankind among the earliest races, when thought was more often of a dreamy associative type than of a purposeful logical type. If we would really let ourselves go in day-dreaming, releasing ourselves from the current ethical code, we might begin to experience remotely the kind of associative thinking that was probably common to primitive man. The very nature of this associative thinking is that the string of images is really threaded on a series of like qualities, one quality leading to another. As we have previously observed, children often call dissimilar things by the same name because of like qualities.

Jung says that 'the state of infantile thinking in the child's psychic life, as well as in dreams, is nothing but a re-echo of the prehistoric and the ancient',[7] and Jung commends a passage from Nietzsche (*Human, All too Human*)—'in our sleep and in our dreams we pass through the whole thought of earlier humanity'. Nietszche says that in the same way that man reasons in his dreams, he reasoned when in the waking state many thousands of years ago, and that the dream carries us back into earlier states of human culture, and affords us a means of understanding them better. This is the theme of much of Jung's writing. Its interest in the study of symbolism is that it links the symbolism of dreams with the symbolism of primitive peoples, their beliefs and religions; and from primitive religions emerge the doctrinal religions of civilization, each with its cargo of symbolism. Thus it may be that the rich symbolism of Christianity is more closely connected with the symbolism of our dreams than is often imagined. This symbolism of religion figures prominently in the arts, for it was in the service of religion that art in its many forms has developed so profoundly and extensively. Thus it is logical to think of symbolism in religion and then in the various arts.

REFERENCES

1. Compare for example the definitions of instinct given by the Oxford Dictionary, WILLIAM McDOUGALL (*Outline of Social Psychology*), and EDWARD GLOVER (*Social Aspects of Psycho-Analysis*).
2. WILLIAM McDOUGALL, *Outline of Social Psychology*, Chap. III, 29th edition (London, 1931).
3. SIGMUND FREUD, *The Ego and the Id*, English translation, p. 55 (London, 1927).
4. See Paper on 'Psycho-Analysis and the Instincts' (1935) by ERNEST JONES. This appears in his collected papers, 5th edition (London, 1948).
5. This classification is based on J. C. FLÜGEL's *Introduction to Psycho-analysis*, p. 59 (London, 1932).
6. SIGMUND FREUD's *The Interpretation of Dreams* (English translation by A. A. BRILL, 1913; revised edition, 1915) is one of the most exhaustive. ERNEST JONES in his paper on 'The Theory of Symbolism' gives a list of books on the subject. *Papers on Psycho-Analysis*, 5th edition (1948), p. 102.
7. C. C. JUNG, *Psychology of the Unconscious*, English translation, p. 14 (New York, 1927; there is also a London edition, 1933).

XIII   Religious Symbolism

As THE subject matter of religion is of a mysterious and abstract character much of its expression flows naturally into various forms of symbolism. There is also the desire in religious teaching to enhance the importance of religious devotion, beliefs, creeds and doctrines, and this can often be accomplished by symbolic expression. As Whitehead reminded us, the purpose of symbolism is to enhance the importance of what is symbolized, and it can be appreciated that symbolic expression has proved to be of great assistance in religious teaching.

For the purpose of the study of religious symbolism, religious activity can be broadly classified under two heads: propitiation and worship of a spirit or deity, and expression or teaching. Propitiation and worship are forms of expression, but the expression is to the spirit or deity, whereas the expression that accompanies teaching is to one's fellow-men. To appreciate the symbolism in propitiation and worship it is useful to glance briefly at early forms of religion and consider how they have evolved to the more complex doctrinal religions of civilization.

Various definitions have been given of religion, many of which have been coloured by the ethics and thought of the period from which they emerged. E. B. Tylor's minimum definition of religion as the belief in spiritual beings is broad, and simple,[1] and is good in an evolutionary sense; but in a more highly evolved state the sense of unity in all things would correspond more closely to some conceptions of religion.

Tylor amplifies his definition considerably. He uses the term animism for his investigation of the doctrine of spiritual beings, primarily among primitive races, and states that 'the theory of animism divides into two great dogmas, forming parts of one consistent doctrine; first, concerning souls of individual creatures capable of continual existence after the death or destruction of the body; second, concerning other spirits, upward to the rank of powerful deities. Spiritual beings are held to affect or control the events of the material world, and man's life here and hereafter; and it being considered that they hold intercourse with men, and receive pleasure or displeasure from human actions, the belief in their existence leads naturally, and it might almost be said inevitably, sooner or later, to active reverence and propitiation. Thus animism, in its full development, includes the belief in souls and in a future state, in controlling deities and subordinate spirits, these doctrines practically resulting in some kind of active worship'.[2]

Other definitions are too restrictive or too much influenced by an ethical code. Thus attempts have been made to distinguish between primitive propitiation of spirits merely for the sake of material welfare, and worship with some moral purpose, where it has been suggested that the former is rather a superstition than a religion. But such a distinction can hardly be logically maintained. Primitive man praying for rain to make crops grow, and the English boy praying to God to help him to be good may appear to have the difference that the latter has a moral intention which the former has not. The 'being good' may, however, be no more than a matter of policy. It raises the question whether people are good for virtue's own sake, or whether they are good because it is more likely to result in happiness than being bad. Is this, therefore, fundamentally different in intention from primitive man praying for rain so that his crops will grow?

Sir James Frazer defines religion as a 'propitiation or conciliation of powers superior to man which are believed to direct and control the course of nature and of human life'.[3] This definition would accord with Tylor's minimum definition and its amplification. In Frazer's elucidation of his own definition 'religion consists of two elements, a theoretical and a practical', or in other words, belief and propitiation, and he adds that 'unless the belief leads to a corresponding practice it is not a religion, but merely theology'. It is difficult to accept this denial of the term religion to belief without practice. A man may believe ardently in a deity who directs and controls the course of life, yet he may not be moved to any religious practice, and this attitude may be a part of belief. It is not impossible, for example, for a man to be deeply religious, yet have no belief in the efficacy of prayer.

In Tylor's theory of animism human personality and life are imparted to spirits, whether of the dead, animals, inanimate objects like trees and stones, or the forces of nature. It is an anthropomorphizing tendency which Tylor regards as natural to a primitive mind. Tylor is clearly influenced by Hume's great work on the *Natural History of Religion* and he quotes from it in support of his view. Hume says that 'there is a universal tendency among mankind to conceive all beings as like themselves, and to transfer to every object those qualities with which they are familiarly acquainted, and of which they are intimately conscious'.

Tylor's theory of animism has not met with complete acceptance in all its details. R. R. Marett,[4] for example, thinks that the endowment of inanimate objects with spirits based on the human personality represents a higher stage of thought than is likely to occur in the most primitive races, and that instead the conception did not go beyond the imparting of life and will in a more vague sense than Tylor implied. This was a pre-animistic stage to which Marett gave the term 'animatism'. It is questionable, however, whether the most primitive mind is not most likely to conceive life and will on the human pattern. There is a certain parallel here with the thought of very young children, who habitually project their human personalities to inanimate objects. Life, it seems, exists largely in terms of themselves.

To answer the question of why primitive man animates the world with spirits which have power over him for good or evil is to indicate the origin of religion. From the evidence collected by travellers and anthropologists primitive worship appears to be of two principal kinds, the worship of nature and the worship of the dead. The worship of nature includes all the natural forces and elements, like the sun, wind and rain, thunder and lightning, which affect, or appear to affect, the welfare of man. We see the survival of such worship in a highly developed civilization like that of ancient Greece, where some of the gods are personifications of the elements. The worship of the dead depends on the belief that the dead survive and acquire power to influence the fortunes of the living, and numerous customs in most races of mankind testify to its wide prevalence. Herbert Spencer attributed the root of religion to the worship of the dead, and he adduced much evidence in support of this view.[5] The indications here given of the origin of religion are broadly accepted with differing emphasis on different factors by most impartial students of the subject, and are sufficient to assist in forming an idea of the purpose of symbolism employed in acts of worship.

The many forms of propitiation, worship and devotion common to primitive and civilized religions are attended by ceremonies and rites, but only some of these give rise to any marked degree of symbolism. These forms may be classified as prayer; offerings; sacrifices; the inducement by various methods like fasting and drugs of religious ecstasy and mysticism; orientation and lustration. All these begin as practical acts and may, like prayer, remain so in the religions of civilizations, but others survive mainly as symbolism. Offerings and sacrifices are examples. When offerings are made by primitive peoples to their spirits or gods, they are given as presents to please the spirit or god, as a propitiatory act. Offerings of food were common, and it was thought that the spirit liked such offerings and consumed the food. To the objection that the food did not disappear it was generally replied that the spirit consumed the essential part. Often it was the blood, and with some tribes the blood was extracted for the offering.[6] A common form of sacrifice in many religions is the burnt offering. It is based on the belief that the offering can be conveyed in a vaporous form to the spirit or god who resides above, and in the religions of Greece and Rome and in Christianity is symbolized in the burning of incense, thus becoming a symbol of prayer.

Of a higher ethical character is the central idea of sacrifice in Christianity. The sacrifice of Christ for mankind and His martyrdom on the cross is symbolized in a variety of ways, and it is thus symbolism which plays an important part in the ceremonies of Christian devotion. The cross is by association a symbol of Christ's sacrifice, and has become the universal sign of Christianity. The ceremony of the Eucharist is symbolic of this sacrifice. When 'Jesus took bread and blessed it and brake it and gave it to the disciples and said, Take, eat, this is My body', and when 'He took the cup and gave thanks, and gave it to them saying, Drink ye all of it; for this is My blood',[7] He was, it seems, thinking of the bread and wine as symbols. The Roman Catholic Church, however, makes the interpretation that Christ miraculously transformed the bread and wine into His body and blood, and in the ceremony of the Eucharist the priest effects the same miraculous transformation. To believers this would make it reality and not symbolism. In the Protestant Church the interpretation is that Christ was using the bread and wine symbolically, and the ceremony of Communion is conducted in that belief.

Several kinds of religious symbolism have evolved, naturally and inevitably, from our physical environment. Among these the most important are light and darkness, and the main directions of space like height and east and west.

132

Light is perhaps the most important of religious symbols. It has constantly been used as a symbol of the deity, and in some religions God is identified with light, as in the case of Ra in ancient Egypt, and in Christianity when John came to bear witness to the Light (John I, 4–9). By this association of light with God it has become symbolic of such qualities as knowledge, wisdom, truth and goodness, while darkness is associated with the opposites of these qualities, folly, ignorance and evil. (*See* Part IV, Lamp, Sun and Torch.)

The association of light with the deity or special deities was common in many ancient religions. In ancient Greece Zeus and Apollo were gods of light. The sun as the source of light was either identified with God or was the instrument of God. Zeus and, in the Latin religion, Janus and Jupiter, were originally identified with the sky and light and then, with the elaboration to a hierarchy of gods, Apollo, to take the example of Greece, became god of light and Helios of the sun, the former becoming later also the sun-god. In much Greek thought light is used as a symbol of the deity and of qualities associated with the deity, as knowledge and goodness. Philo, the exponent of Graeco-Judaic philosophy, also thinks of light as a symbol of God in that, as the sun is the source of its own illumination, so God is the source of his own light.[8] Strictly, however, this is not symbolism, as it does not involve one thing standing for or expressing another. Here light is a quality of God.

In the Bible there are numerous associations of light with God, and although, as in the case previously cited, this would appear to be identification in the minds of some writers, the fair interpretation would be that in the mind of most of the Old and New Testament writers, light is used in a figurative sense, and the sun and light are regarded as part of God's world. The implication of Genesis is that God had being before light 'when the earth was without form and void; and darkness was upon the face of the earth', and then God said 'Let there be light'. The subsequent allusions to the light of God is as one of His gifts, and the allusion to God as light is a figurative or symbolic one, as one would say that the teachings of Christ are as light. In this sense the inspired teachers of the religion are conceived of as being gifted with light, and thus they are represented in art surrounded by light, or glory conventionalized into the nimbus. (*See* Part IV, Nimbus.)

The extensive symbolism of height which impregnates our language and thought probably arises with the conception, common in most ancient religions, of God and heaven in or above the sky. In Greek religion this originated with the vague belief that the vast sky was the principal agency of man's destiny, as it held the sun, and the source of life, gave the rain, and was often angry with thunder and lightning. A. B. Cook adduces evidence to show that the primitive Greeks probably identified the sky with God, that is, the sky was God, and that anthropomorphization, when a personal god dwelt in the sky, was a second stage, and heaven peopled by an hierarchy of gods was a later stage still.[9] A further variation in Greek religion which appears in Homer is the conception of the summit of Mount Olympus, which pierced the sky, as the abode of the gods.

In Hebrew religion and Christianity the abode of God and heaven is also conceived of as being in or above the sky, but there is no evidence of an identification of God with the sky as in Greek religion. In the Hebrew conception God existed before heaven, for in the first sentence of the Bible God creates 'the heaven and the earth', heaven in this sense being synonymous with sky. God then divided the waters above and under the firmament, and 'God called the firmament heaven'. It is thus that God and heaven are above and it became a habit of thought, which was particularly strong in the Middle Ages, that the higher one reached the nearer one came to God and heaven, and much religious architecture, especially of the Gothic period, seems to have been governed by this thought.

Ancient philosophies that invoked a conception of deity all seem to regard God as above. Edwyn Bevan remarks that 'the three greatest schools of philosophy which shaped the thoughts of men in the ancient world from Alexander to the last days of paganism, Platonic, Peripatetic, Stoic, co-operated to make them think that the sky itself to which they looked up was divine—was God Himself in the Stoic view, was the home of gods made of the matter nearest to soul in the Platonic and Aristotelian view.[10] The conception of God as above in the sky seems almost universal amongst mankind, as Bevan remarks,[11] and it is little wonder that height, and that which is above, has thus become a symbol of the movement towards God and towards qualities associated with Him, goodness, nobility, power, glory; indeed it would be impossible to express these qualities fully without use of the words which are themselves derived from the symbolism, and express the idea, of height: words like lofty, supreme, exalted, sublime. Language is impregnated with this symbolism—as when we say movement to higher things, aspiration, and when in official and business jargon we speak of things being done at various levels. It also permeates the visual world, which is led by religious architecture and ceremony. Everything leads up to the altar, placed high above the level of the floor of the church and approached by steps; and the lofty arches aspire towards heaven, symbolizing the religious aspiration of man to reach to God.

This religious symbolism spreads to the symbolism of the State. The throne of the monarch is also raised up and approached by steps; and other thrones and important seats—of the Lord Chancellor, the Speaker, of Mayors and others—are placed on a higher level. The levels of society ascend in stages to the monarch—the highest in the land. This may be obvious, but we rarely reflect that it all originated with the primitive belief that God was above in the sky.

The symbolism of the horizontal directions of space is mainly determined by the sun's course in the heavens, and is very important in religious devotion.

The association of the east with ideas of life and renewal, light and warmth, and the west with darkness and cold, death and decay is present in many religions. It determines the siting of temples and churches and the orientation of graves. Christian churches are built with the altar towards the east, and worshippers thus face the east in their devotions. The sun may here be regarded as symbolic of light and life, but the ritual is partly a survival of sun worship. Tertullian remarked that many pagans thought that the sun was the Christian God because of the Christian habit of praying towards the east. Although in some primitive religions, for example those of the Samoans and Fijians, the head of a deceased person is placed at the east end of a grave, in Christianity the head is placed at the west end, because Christ is thought to have been buried in that manner with His face looking eastward.

This orientation plays a part in the rite of baptism. The west, where the sun disappears, is the place of darkness and evil; the east, where the sun rises, is the place of dawning light and righteousness. Thus, one of the common rites of baptism in the Christian Church is for the catechumen first to turn towards the west, renounce the darkness and evil, and then turn towards the east and the light and righteousness of the Christian faith. The significance of this rite is described by Jerome, Augustine, Tertullian and other early Christian teachers, and it is still retained in the Greek Church.

The rite of purification, common in primitive religions, begins as actual cleansing, and survives in Christianity mainly as symbolism, as the washing away of sins in the rite of baptism. It takes many forms, from the literal imitation of the baptism of Christ by John the Baptist to the priest dipping his finger in water and making the sign of the cross on the forehead. The priest touching the forehead with his lips is a further purification by means of the priest's spittle. Purification by means of holy water when the worshipper enters the holy precincts obtained in the ancient religions of Greece and Rome and survives in the Catholic Church (*see* Part IV, Water).

Primitive religious rites yield a further example of symbolism in the primitive dances. These take the form of suggesting to the god or spirit by bodily actions what is desired. When sun or rain is wanted to make crops grow, when success in the hunt or war is desired, the prayer to the god takes the form of a dance expressive of the growing crops, of the activities of the hunt and of war. This will be considered in dealing with the symbolism of the dance (Chapter XVI.)

The employment of symbolism in religious teaching is rich and varied, and is often of a precise and definite character. Much of it arises from the figurative method of explanation adopted by religious teachers, the supreme example of which is found in the parables of Christ. Examples of well-known Christian symbols derived in some measure from Christ's parables are the Vine[12] and Shepherd and sheep.[13] Incidents in the Bible, such as the return of the dove with the olive branch to the ark, became familiar religious symbols, and in the two thousand years of Christianity many more symbols have been accumulated as signs of the faith, and as illustrations of doctrine and teaching, many of which are described in Part IV. These are found in the various arts employed by the Church expressing Christian worship and teaching—the arts of architecture, sculpture, mosaics, painting, stained glass windows, ivories, gold, silver and glass vessels, embroideries and much else that has contributed to church furnishing and Christian ceremonial. No activity is richer in symbolism, and a large number of the symbols in Part IV have arisen as expressions of Christian worship and teaching.

Many of the ceremonies of the Church are of a symbolic character even when they serve to effect a contract in social life, as in the case of the marriage ceremony. In this ceremony in the Church of England the priest speaks of holy matrimony, 'which is an honourable estate, instituted of God in the time of man's innocency, signifying unto us the mystical union that is betwixt Christ and His Church'.

In marriage, signifying the union of Christ and His Church, the relation of bridegroom to bride has sometimes been interpreted as that of Christ to the Church. Believing this, many priests have, for this reason, refused to agree to the omission of the bride's promise to obey.

In all religious doctrine and history the border-line between fact, or actual happening or recording of events, and symbolism has never been easy to place, and the confusion between the two has led to much controversy and strife. Who can say, for example, how much of the accounts of miracles was written as a record of actual happenings, and how much as symbolism?

REFERENCES
1. E. B. TYLOR, *Primitive Culture*, 5th edition, p. 424 (London, 1913).
2. E. B. TYLOR, *op. cit.*, Vol. I, p. 427.
3. SIR JAMES FRAZER, *The Golden Bough*, 3rd edition, Vol. I (London, 1936).
4. *Hastings Encyclopaedia of Religion and Ethics*.
5. HERBERT SPENCER, *Principles of Sociology*, 3rd edition, Vol. I, p. 249 *et seq.*, and p. 411 (London, 1885).
6. E. B. TYLOR gives many instances of primitive sacrifices. *Op. cit.*, Vol. II, pp. 375–410.
7. ST. MATTHEW xxvi. 26–28.
8. EDWYN BEVAN, *Symbolism and Belief*, pp. 133–4 (London, 1938).
9. A. B. COOK, *Zeus: A Study in Ancient Religion*, Vol. 1 (Cambridge, 1914).
10. EDWYN BEVAN, *Symbolism and Belief*, p. 42 (London, 1938).
11. *Ibid.*, p. 46.
12. ST. JOHN xv. 1–8.
13. ST. JOHN x. 11–16, also St. Luke xv, 4, 5.

XIV   National and State Symbolism

THE objects which have formed national and State symbols, flags, coats of arms, flowers and animals; and the tokens on which these symbols have been employed, such as seals, coins and medals, have been considered in the chapters and sections of Parts II and IV. In the United States almost every State has an officially adopted symbolic flower, many have symbolic trees and birds, and a few have adopted animals. As was noted in Chapter IV, the State seals are rich in symbolism, and from them it is possible to learn much of the history of the country.

Yet these forms of national and State symbolism are the expression of a general and fundamental symbolism which is inherent in the structure of societies, and which is a powerful force in holding them together. There is a natural tendency for societies to hold together, as instinctive forces, like self-preservation and gregariousness—the latter serving the former instinct—breed habits which are unifying agencies.

In the evolution of the human species, however, perception has been evolved which enables man to distinguish between what he sees and its meaning, as described in Chapter I. With this there emerges a consequent freedom of action. In the low grade organism, guided wholly by instinct, the sense of environment and corresponding action are one; but man has evolved to a state where he is able to separate the shape perceived and its meaning, which gives a degree of individual freedom in determining the course of action to be pursued. It may be a small degree, for in many situations man also is guided by instinctive responses common to the species, but the degree of freedom is sufficient to be an important factor in evolution and progress and, at the same time, to be a disruptive force in society. Thus, in the place of completely instinctive cohesion, there is expression and action by means of symbols and their meanings. This may, of course, also be instinctive but, if so, it is instinctive behaviour accompanied by greater illusion of freedom of action. It contributes to the unity of societies, while giving a degree of freedom to its individual members.

The unifying symbols evolved are generally in the form of leaders of tribes, kings and their hierarchies, and their trappings, some of which have been described. The veneration of these symbols is a strong factor in binding a society together.

In modern civilized communities the symbols are of various kinds, they permeate every branch of society and are ever present. In Britain the monarchy is perhaps the principal symbol, and it is explained and justified as a unifying force. At times, there has been almost blind worship of the occupant of the throne, and response to the symbol has become virtually a reflex action. The satellites of the throne, generally other members of the royal family, have also been objects of veneration. Great men, particularly those of a heroic character, have also been the objects of worship, and have often been viewed as symbols of the greatness of the country.

The teaching of history in schools was, until recently, often a recital of the deeds of the country's heroes, intended to foster a sense of the greatness of the country. As Whitehead so well says, 'When we examine how a society bends its individual members to function in conformity with its needs, we discover that one important operative agency is our vast system of inherited symbolism'.[1] So powerful is this symbolism that frequently it has an hypnotic effect on the populace. Much of the ceremonial of a State appears to be designed to increase veneration. The elaborate ceremonial and symbolism of the Coronation, inaugurating a new sovereign, is designed to enhance the importance both of the head of the State and of the State itself. It should not be thought, however, that this results from conscious deliberation on the part of governments or a ruling class. It is probably an instinctive urge which acts as a unifying agency, and which, after all, appears to be concerned with the preservation of the species. This elaborate ceremony, enhancing both the importance of the State and its head, is a characteristic of all societies based on whatever creeds, from the Republic of Russia to the Republic of U.S.A. and the monarchies of Britain and Scandinavia.

Sir Ivor Jennings in his book *The British Constitution* says that the British monarch has only one function of primary importance—that is to appoint a Prime Minister.[2] This is true in the governmental sense, but as an active working symbol of the nation and the commonwealth, by which all parts are united under a common head, his function is far more important. This Jennings recognizes, for he says later that 'more important than the king's governmental functions are what Bagehot calls his "dignified functions". Government', he says, 'is not just a matter of giving orders and enforcing obedience. It requires the willing collaboration of all sections of the people'; and it may be said that a central symbol such as the monarchy, to which all can look as a unifying force, is effective in helping to secure this collaboration.[3]

If there is not a monarchy there must be a head of a State to which people can look, and it is a logical supposition that this is more likely to be an effective symbol if it is non-party, non-sectarian, and represents the whole of the State.

With large sections of the population who have not enquired into the meaning of the symbol of the monarchy, it is blindly venerated, although this is less so with more widespread education. There is, moreover, a growing section of the population which does so enquire, if not completely, at least partially. This is brought about by more free and individual thinking, which is not necessarily the result of education, as such thinking often comes with very little knowledge.

This enquiry into the meaning of the symbolic functions of monarchy, with the discovery that it is essentially a unifying force representing the nation as a whole—so that one can damn the Government, yet be loyal to the throne and to the country— makes it of first importance that the symbol in the person of the reigning monarch and his family shall be truly expressive and representative. As a unifying agent the symbol must be representative of all strata of society, and not merely of one, as has

138

been the case in some reigns. The monarch must know not only the aristocracy and the wealthy, but all conditions of men, if the symbol is to be effective. The monarch who knows only the top strata, who associates only with wealthy people or who indulges too much his own pleasures, especially if they are of a rather frivolous kind, would tend to weaken the symbol, because it is not fully expressive or representative. It is important, too, that State symbolism should be realistic; that it should belong to its time and not be remote or mediaeval. 'In the Commonwealth Declaration of 1949,' says Sir Ivor Jennings,[4] 'the King was "recognized" as "the symbol of the free association" of the independent member nations of the Commonwealth "and as such the Head of the Commonwealth". How to make that symbol effective as a symbol is one of the problems which the British Constitution as well as the Commonwealth has to face.' The answer to this question is contained in the two concluding sentences of Whitehead's book on Symbolism. 'The art of free society', he says, 'consists first in the maintenance of the symbolic code; and secondly in fearlessness of revision to secure that the code serves those purposes which satisfy an enlightened reason. Those societies which cannot combine reverence to their symbols with freedom of revision, must ultimately decay either from anarchy, or from the slow atrophy of a life stifled by useless shadows.'[5]

The expression, the symbol, should therefore change as the life of the State changes, and outmoded forms expressive of different kinds of life should constantly be examined.

Carlyle, in the chapter on Symbols in *Sartor Resartus*, referring to creative symbolism and the shaping of new symbols, says 'we account him Legislator and wise who can so much as tell when a Symbol has grown old, and gently remove it'.

Many of the State ceremonies which surround the monarch are derived from religious symbolism, the principal of which, perhaps inevitably, is that of height. The head of the State is the apex of the pyramid; the monarch is the highest in the land, and in most State ceremonies this symbolism of height plays a part, as a little reflection will demonstrate. The sense of mystery and remoteness which is for most people associated with the monarchy derives partly from religious worship, and is in some measure designed to enhance the value and importance of that which is venerated; but it is obvious that this must also be reconciled with the monarchy as a living, vital symbol. The teachings and symbols of religion remain very much the same over two thousand years, but society and social life constantly change. The head of a State, and especially of a State closely linked with religious teaching, must combine expression of both. The monarchy or other head of a State is one of the most complex of symbols, existing constantly in a blaze of light.

REFERENCES
1. A. N. WHITEHEAD, *Symbolism, its Meaning and Effect*, p. 86 (Cambridge, 1928).
2. SIR IVOR JENNINGS, *The British Constitution*, 3rd edition, p. 108 (Cambridge, 1954).
3. *Ibid.*, p. 115.
4. Jennings, *op. cit.*, p. 118.
5. Whitehead, *op. cit.*, p. 103.

XV   Symbolism in Art

IF WE think of art as expression in which some degree of beauty is attained, then symbolism of the more conscious expressional type, as defined in the first four classes in Chapter I, is not a direct contributory factor in the creation of a work of art, although there is nonetheless unconscious symbolism. Conscious symbolism is a subject of expression, and whether that expression becomes beautiful depends on the artist's disposition of the parts, and on his feeling for aesthetic qualities. It is not silver birch trees dominating a landscape which make a picture of this subject a work of art, but what the artist does with the silver birch trees; it is the colour, the light and shadow, the rhythmical cohesion of forms and the design seen in the abstract which give the picture its aesthetic qualities. Yet the artist is dependent for his creations on the suggestions of his subject, and some subjects are more richly suggestive than others. It is true that some great artists could make the simplest and apparently most unpromising subjects into beautiful pictures, like Rembrandt with the carcase of an ox, and Cézanne with a group of bottles, or a heating-stove revealing unsuspected qualities of form and colour. But these are the exceptions rather than the rule. Roger Fry,[1] on the other hand, held that the subject is unimportant in the consideration of aesthetic qualities. This point of view is considered later in the chapter.

Great works of art have often come into the world on the wings of great subjects, and it is no accident that a very large number of the greatest works of art are of a religious character. In the record of Italian art of the Renaissance the development of both painting and sculpture were greatly assisted by subjects which were richly suggestive of many of the qualities that contribute to the creation of works of art. Much of the material that finds expression in works of art is of a symbolic character. What is that material?

It is perhaps necessary in the first place to enlarge upon this distinction between aesthetic qualities and what may be termed expressional symbolism, to distinguish it from unconscious or partly conscious symbolism. Mere expression is not art unless it is accompanied by certain qualities, and these qualities are not directly related to symbolic expression, although symbolic expression may contribute to their production. Much surrealist art is symbolic of repressed impulses, but such pictures or sculptures exist as works of art on their aesthetic merits like other pictures and sculptures, and not because of interesting symbolism present. Symbolism is important as subject for expression which contributes to the character of works of art as distinct from their aesthetic qualities, and in the psychology of expression; it is also important in an aesthetic sense, but this, as previously implied, is more vague and indefinite, and is often largely unconscious.

Symbolism in most forms of visual art, that is, the dance, dress, architecture, sculpture and painting may be broadly classified as symbolism which is inherent in the form or structure and that which is attached. The former may be sub-divided into that which is largely impersonal and that which is personal.

Symbolism which is inherent in the form and structure, and which is of an impersonal and general character, is found to a considerable extent both in the dance and in architecture, especially religious architecture. Among many primitive tribes dances are a form of prayer. When speech is not highly developed it is natural that people desiring to make their wishes and intentions apparent to a deity or spirit should do so by bodily movement, and much of this bodily movement is retained in religious ceremony today. When a primitive people prayed that the crops should grow, that the hunt or wars should be attended with success, this prayer often took the form of a dance imitative of their wish. Thus bodily movements imitated the crops growing, or the motions and activities of the hunt or of battle, and as these were performed by groups they were done in some rhythmic unison, with drums to give time, and later to more elaborate music. Sir James Frazer observes that 'in many parts of Europe dancing or leaping high in the air are approved homeopathic modes of making the crops grow high. Thus in Franche-Comté they say that you should dance at the Carnival in order to make the hemp grow tall'.[2] Frazer gives several other instances of the imitative dance formalized into a ceremony designed to make crops grow. He mentions for example, the people of Central Angoniland, who take branches of trees and dance and sing for rain, dipping the branches in a vessel of water and scattering the drops. There is clearly here no fundamental distinction between the dance and ceremony. The essential point for consideration is that the movements that form the dance are expressive of, and arise from, certain desired occurrences in the natural world and are therefore symbolic. Some amplification of this will be given in the next chapter.

In architecture a similar impulse operates. Because to the mediaeval mind, God and heaven are conceived as above, beyond the blue sky, religious aspiration was naturally and often expressed by a movement upwards. This is powerfully symbolized in the long vertical piers culminating in the lofty vaulted roofs of a Gothic cathedral. In other types of architecture bodily characteristics are transmuted to the forms of a building and express various ideas. Thus the grand and massive qualities of the head office building of an important institution like a bank, or some important national professional body, symbolize a dignity and stability associated with these institutions. Further examples and further consideration of why these architectural forms are symbolic of such feelings are given in Chapter XVIII.

Impersonal and general symbolism inherent in the form and structure of the work of art exists in the other arts, as in the dance and architecture, and really derives in character from these two arts. The dance and architecture are the parent arts. This is a confirmation of the view expressed by Havelock Ellis that 'dancing and building are the two primary and essential arts'. He adds that 'the art of dancing stands at the source of all these arts that express themselves first in the human form. The art of building, or architecture, is the beginning of all the arts that lie outside the person; and in the end they unite. Music, acting, poetry proceed in the one mighty stream; sculpture, painting, all the arts of design in the other. There is no primary art outside these two arts, for their origin is far earlier than Man himself; and dancing came first'.[3] It is clear that in this matter of symbolism in the general form of the work the dance precedes all the other arts and really determines the nature of that symbolism. It is because bodily feeling and bodily movement are the very materials of the art of dancing, and because we project these bodily movements and feelings into works of art, that the dance is the primary art. The idea has been developed by Lipps in the theory of Einfühlung.[4]

In sculpture, symbolism of ideas pervading the whole conception, figure, or group arises as the frozen dance or frozen ceremony, and much the same can be said of painting.

Personal symbolism that pervades the whole work of art is more complex. It can be said that every work of art or expression in an artistic medium—architecture, painting, sculpture, dress—is inevitably personal symbolism because it is personal expression; it is symbolic of the personality of the author of the work. This may be the case even when the artist is merely concerned to represent his subject with exactitude. Two painters, both technically competent, may aim at faithfully imitating a scene, yet there are differences in their pictures; not because of differences in technical competence, but because they cannot help having human emotions and feelings about what they are painting and because no two human beings are exactly alike. When, however, one considers the work of artists of strong individuality and with deep emotions about their subjects, then the differences in the renderings of a subject become more marked. In these differences lie the expressions or symbolism of the artist's personality.

This may however be carrying the application of the term symbolism a little too far. As previously observed, the accepted definition of symbolism as one thing standing for another is often tacitly understood also to mean not by exact resemblance. Thus, if this reservation is accepted, a painting of the Surrey Hills which gives a vivid and realistic impression of them is not symbolism, but a poster in which there is a suggestion of their character by a geometrical reminiscence would be symbolic. One would be an impression of the Surrey Hills, the other a symbol. Similarly, when Sargent painted a portrait it was regarded as a realistic rendering of character, but when Picasso paints a portrait in his Cubist phase, it is no longer a realistic rendering but an abstract of the subject, and could legitimately be regarded as a symbol of that subject, and also expressive or symbolic of Picasso's feelings and emotions. This latter personal symbolism is akin to the impersonal, which is really the collective personal, symbolism of religious architecture. But this personal symbolism of artistic expression is more complex than religious symbolism. There is here a great field for investigation. A certain amount of work is being done by psychologists, but the task is difficult because it requires not only a knowledge of the various psychological theories, but a considerable knowledge of art and an appreciation of what are essential aesthetic qualities, so that the extent to which the purely formal aesthetic aim modifies personal psychological expression can be apprehended.

The symbolism or expression of the artist's personality or feeling—some would say soul—in a work of art is what to many people makes such works of interest and value. It is an emotional tone that suffuses the whole, which gives a poetry and tenderness alike to the religious pictures of Fra Filippo Lippi, to the massive figures of Michelangelo, to the portraits of Moretto, Giorgione and Titian, to the Fêtes Galantes of Watteau and the Impressionist landscapes of Pissarro. Even in prosaic secular architecture this emotional tone is apparent. Sir Reginald Blomfield, Sir Herbert Baker and Sir Edwin Lutyens all designed buildings in the Renaissance style, and yet there is a character about their buildings which distinguishes them from each other, so that one can say: that building is by Lutyens, it couldn't be by anybody else—and the same with Blomfield and Baker. There are details and features which each of these architects liked and which he incorporated in his work and put together in a particular way. It is these which produce the emotional tone.

The expression of personality is of varying degrees of consciousness, sometimes, although rarely, it is almost completely conscious, as possibly in very robust and vigorous artists like Rubens; and sometimes it is completely unconscious. Mostly it is probably partly conscious and partly unconscious, and in the latter case the spectator may perceive in a work of art elements which were wholly unsuspected by the artist. An apt example of unconscious symbolism in art is provided by D. H. Lawrence in his *Twilight in Italy*. The Bavarian peasant, in carving his crucifixes, carves an image of Christ suffering on the cross, which to the Bavarian peasant becomes a symbol of that supreme act of sacrifice which meant the salvation of his soul. But D. H. Lawrence saw that 'the Christ was a peasant at the foot of the Alps. He had broad cheek-bones, and sturdy limbs. His plain rudimentary face stared fixedly at the hills, his neck was stiffened, as if in resistance to the fact of the nails and the cross, which he could not escape. It was a man nailed down in spirit, but set stubbornly against the bondage and disgrace. He was a man of middle age, plain, crude, with some of the meanness of the peasant, but also with a kind of dogged nobility that does not yield its soul to the circumstance. Plain, almost blank in his soul, the middle-aged peasant of the crucifix resisted unmoving the misery of his position. He did not yield. His soul was set, his will was fixed. He was himself, let his circumstances be what they would, his life fixed down'. Even allowing for Lawrence's subjectivity, the peasant here symbolizes far more than he is conscious of. This, and its numerous parallels in modern art, is a concrete thing standing for ideas, states of mind, emotions, which is the essence of one important type of symbolism. The concrete thing is the symbol by which the re-creation is enacted.

Symbolism which is attached as a feature in a work of art is of a more obvious kind. The badges or devices fixed to dress, to accoutrements, equipages, to furniture and buildings, of which heraldry is a conspicuous example, the carved symbols decorating a church, like the lamb or pelican and young, symbols of Christ, the mortality and life symbols on memorials, are all of this type. Many are described in the chapters on the various arts and in Part IV.

Before examining in subsequent chapters the presence and use of symbolism in the different arts it is important, I think, to discuss some of the objections that have been expressed to the notion that symbolism has any connection with the aesthetic qualities of a work of art. It was suggested at the beginning of the chapter that symbolism is not a direct contributory factor in the creation of a work of art, and the distinction between aesthetic qualities and symbolism was emphasized; but as material for expression symbolism is important, and by its suggestiveness often brings aesthetic qualities into being. Some writers have, however, denied even this, and refuse to admit any connection whatsoever between symbolism and aesthetic qualities. It is proposed to consider briefly the objections of Roger Fry, as he is probably the most influential of these writers. It is also significant that Fry denies the connection of art with the instinctive life. These opinions of Fry are expressed in a paper on *The Artist and Psycho-Analysis*.

Art is, according to Fry, an activity concerned with formal relations, and is distinct from the conception of art entertained by many psychologists as the creation of a phantasy-world. Art that is concerned with formal relations is an activity 'as much detached from the instinctive life as any human activity that we know; to be in that respect on a par with science'. Throughout the paper Fry insists on the complete detachment of art from the instinctive life.

Art that is the creation of a phantasy-world, that is wish-fulfilment; art which depends for its appeal on ideas associated with objects represented, may be the art of psychologists, but is to Roger Fry irrelevant to aesthetic qualities which make a work of art. Thus the dream, the phantasy, because they depend for their appeal on ideas associated with objects are contrary to the aesthetic faculty. The objects are but symbols of ideas. 'In a world of symbolists', he says, 'only two kinds of people are entirely opposed to symbolism, and they are the man of science and the artist, since they alone are seeking to make constructions which are completely self-consistent, self-supporting and self-contained—constructions which do not stand for something else, but appear to have ultimate value and in that sense to be real.' The lengthy quotation that follows makes clear Fry's position with regard to symbolism.

'It is', he says, 'of course, perfectly natural that people should always be looking for symbolism in works of art. Since most people are unable to perceive the meaning of purely formal relations, are unable to derive from them the profound satisfaction that the creator and those that understand him feel, they always look for some meaning that can be attached to the values of actual life, they always hope to translate a work of art into terms of *ideas* with which they are familiar. None the less in proportion as an artist is pure he is opposed to all symbolism.

'You will have noticed that in all these psycho-analytical enquiries into pictorial art the attention of the investigator is fixed on the nature of the images, on what choice the painter has made of the objects he represents. Now I venture to say that no one who has a real understanding of the art of painting attaches any importance to what we call the subject of a picture—what is represented. To one who feels the language of pictorial form all depends on *how* it is presented, *nothing* on what. Rembrandt expressed his profoundest feelings just as well when he painted a carcass hanging up in a butcher's shop as when he painted the Crucifixion or his mistress. Cézanne, who most of us believe to be the greatest artist of modern times, expressed some of his grandest conceptions in pictures of fruit and crockery on a common kitchen table.

'I remember when this fact became clear to me, and the instance may help to show what I mean. In a loan exhibition I came upon a picture by Chardin. It was a sign-board painted to hang outside a druggist's shop. It represented a number of glass retorts, a still, and various glass bottles, the furniture of a chemist's laboratory of that time. You will admit that there was not much material for wish-fulfilment (unless the still suggested remote possibilities of alcohol). Well, it gave me a very intense and vivid sensation. Just the shapes of those bottles and their mutual relations gave me the feeling of something immensely grand and impressive and the phrase that came into my mind was "This is just how I felt when I first saw Michelangelo's frescoes in the Sistine Chapel." Those represented the whole history of creation with the tremendous images of Sybils and Prophets, but aesthetically it meant something very similar to Chardin's glass bottles.'

In saying that the subject is of no importance, that everything depends on 'how' and nothing on 'what' Fry goes altogether too far, for it is impossible to separate subject and expression as Fry does. An artist has a better chance of painting a picture rich with aesthetic qualities if the subject is rich in such material. Some subjects provide far better opportunities than others. Rembrandt's carcass is a picture of some beauty, and the general feeling is that he made much of such a subject, but it is claiming far too much to say that this picture has an aesthetic interest equal to his 'Night Watch' or the 'Crucifixion' or many of his portraits.

Rubens revelled in subjects in which his powers as a vigorous designer of linear rhythms in three dimensional space would have full play. He revels in a subject like the 'Rape of the Sabine Women' which gives him full opportunity to express vigorous action by means of his design of linear rhythms. The varied muscular forms of the human being in action are rich in suggestion for linear design, and it is because of the material provided by such forms that Rubens was able to create some of the finest designs of their kind in the whole history of art.

Even so-called abstract designs of Picasso, Paul Klee, Braque and many others have a starting point in natural or external form and the character of that form influences very much the aesthetic qualities of the design. But in trying to separate the 'how' and 'what', and in not acknowledging the influence of the subject on expression, Fry is trying to separate the inseparable, and he is characteristic of that rather barren scientific mode of criticism that would like everything in water-tight compartments. Walter Pater was far nearer to the truth when he said that in art there should be perfect identification of matter and form, which is realized in music more than in the other arts.[5] In most great works of art the subject as shown in the picture or sculpture has no imagined existence outside that work of art.

How is it possible to determine which ideas associated with the forms are aesthetic and which are not aesthetic? For example, in looking at the pictures of Perugino one has a sense of space. It is not the mere two dimensional pattern of colour seen in the abstract that tells one this, but the illusion of depth, the representation of distance and the appreciation of it as representation. One of the motives which prompted this suggestion of space was religious feeling. All these factors contribute to the appreciation of the picture as a work of art. It is somewhat arbitrary to say where aesthetic qualities end and non-aesthetic associated ideas begin. Some would say they end with the two dimensional colour pattern, others would extend them to the representation of space, the figures set against the distant landscape and blue sky—and others would even include the associated religious feelings.

Later in the paper Roger Fry really expresses doubts about his own theory. He asks

'What is the source of the affective quality of certain systems of formal design . . . Why are we moved deeply by certain dispositions of space in architecture which refer, so far as we can tell, to no other experience?' He remarks the 'pleasure in the recognition of order, of inevitability in relations' and adds 'What the source of that satisfaction is would be a problem for psychology.' If Fry had not dissociated art from instinctive activity he might have found the answer to that himself. It might be suggested that the pleasure in order arises from the satisfaction of the instincts of self-preservation and of construction. It can be appreciated that it is natural to feel more secure and content in the presence of order, and uneasy in the presence of disorder. When order is preserved in a work of art there is a feeling of rest; when disorder is present, the feeling is rather of restlessness and uneasiness. The instinct to construct, present in many animals, also contributes to the sense of order.

But the affective quality is more than a recognition of order, it is the feeling of an emotional tone in the work of art, to which I have already referred, as constituting for many people its chief value. In defining this emotional tone Fry speaks of the 'substratum of all the emotional colours of life, something which underlies all the particular and specialized emotions of actual life.' This emotional tone that suffuses so many great works of art is precisely that symbolism of the artist's personality or feeling to which I have referred. I am fortified in this view and in the use of this terminology because Sir Herbert Read also regards this emotional tone of Roger Fry as 'the perfect adumbration of the abstract kind of symbolism for which we are seeking'.[6] Read speaks of it as subconscious or instinctive symbolism, representing a vague yet vast field of subjectivity. It is precisely that emotional tone to which Roger Fry refers; that emotional tone which is born of an artist's communion with a fragment of the external world and which could have no existence but for that. And the creation which is born with it is, among other things, a symbol, of which the meaning is sometimes apparent and sometimes hidden.

Sir Herbert Read discusses a slightly different kind of symbolism, that of representative and symbolic form, in the earlier part of *Art Now*, a symbolism of which Fry would certainly have denied the existence, but which Read restricts to modern art. It can surely be applied in varying degrees to art of all periods, and is essentially that impersonal symbolism inherent in the structure or character of a work of art which I have tried to describe.

Read deals with the change from traditional European painting that obeyed the condition of conformity to the appearance of the actual world, either by the scientific method of the Florentine artists or the empirical method of the Flemish artists, to the symbolism suggested to Paul Sérusier by the work of Gauguin. Read remarks that 'it is only because the contemporary literary movement in France usurped this name that painting since Gauguin has not been labelled Symbolist'.[7] Read cites the example of oriental art which, as is well known, had a considerable influence on French painting in the latter part of the nineteenth century, and which never conformed to the conditions of the reproduction of natural appearances. 'The aim of five centuries of European efforts', says Read, 'is openly abandoned. The actual appearance of the visible world is no longer of primary importance. The artist seeks something underneath appearances, some plastic symbol which shall be more significant of reality than any exact reproduction can be. Perhaps this theory, so quietly formulated in the seclusion of a French village, did not seem to be revolutionary at the time. But it opened the door to every development of modern art, to all the complexities which face us now. There is no kind of contemporary art which is not justified by that phrase of Cézanne's: "I have not tried to reproduce Nature: I have represented it." '

Read does not really establish this difference between European traditional art and modern symbolist art since Cézanne and Gauguin, which would include the work of artists like Matisse, Picasso, Braque, Kandinsky and many others, especially those whose work has been given the appellation 'abstract'. Although this modern art is symbolist, and the artist is seeking something underneath appearance, some plastic symbol which shall be more significant than reproduction, this is not the prerogative of modern art, but belongs equally to much of traditional European Art. All artistic expression is an abstraction by the artist's personal feeling, and the only difference between traditional and modern art with an unrecognizable subject is the degree of abstraction or conversion. As Lewis Mumford says 'even in the most realistic convention every work of art is an abstraction'.[8] In the Florentine search for scientific principles underlying appearances, and in their desire to express these principles, the Florentine artists were seeking for an inner reality, no less than Cézanne, Matisse and Picasso. Are the abstract patterns of modern artists more symbols of inner reality or of the artist's personality than the chiaroscuro of Leonardo da Vinci or Rembrandt or the rhythms of Rubens or El Greco? The best works of these masters have generally a higher abstract value than the works of modern artists.

In giving his account of the main tradition of European Painting Herbert Read simplifies too much. 'We may say', he says, 'without too much fear of contradiction that it [the main tradition of European Painting] begins [in the fourteenth century] with the desire to reproduce in some way exactly what the eye sees.' But does it begin like that? It emerges in Italy from mosaic painting as an architectural decoration with a subject in which the aim is very far from an exact reproduction of natural appearance. When the media changes to fresco and tempera this essential decorative purpose with a religious subject continues in Siena throughout the fourteenth and fifteenth centuries. In Florence Giotto aims with a high measure of success at giving greater realism to figures, but only to figures; the landscape and architecture are still mainly symbolic in the conventional sense.

This realistic aim becomes a scientific investigation of the laws underlying appearances in the work of Masaccio, Piero della Francesca, Paolo Uccello, Antonio Pollajuolo, Leonardo da Vinci, and many others, but the decorative aim still persists, and carries with it its own symbolism. In Flanders painting again begins as decoration, emerging from the illuminated manuscript, and although the empirical method of reproduction is followed as opposed to the scientific, the decorative purpose is still fundamental. It should be emphasized that there is nothing fundamentally new in modern art since Cézanne. The differences found in painting in the course of history are, in this matter, the degree of abstraction which is variously conscious and unconscious on the part of the artist. The aesthetic value or significance of a work does not depend on its interest as a reproduction of natural appearance, but on precisely the same qualities that give value to the best painting since Cézanne.

A more extensive application of symbolism, and one more in accord with its true place and meaning in life is made by Lewis Mumford. He emphasizes that it is language which is the chief symbolic instrument, the invention above all others which distinguishes man from the animals and has secured his progress. He also emphasizes the importance of the dream, and extends the function of symbolism beyond language to the whole of cultural life and to the whole of art.[9] 'The arts', he says, 'represent a specifically human need, and they rest on a trait quite unique in man: the capacity for symbolism. Unlike animals, man not merely can respond to visible or audible signals; he is also able to abstract and represent parts of his environment, parts of his experience, parts of himself, in the detachable and durable form of symbols.'[10]

Seeing the whole of art as a symbolic activity so that art in its entirety is a symbol of mankind, and the various manifestations of the various arts as symbols of man's instinctive urges, activities, dreams and aspirations, brings us back to the distinction implied at the beginning of this chapter, between conscious symbolism related to the subject and material and its expression on the one hand, and the more vague and unconscious symbolism related to the aesthetic qualities of a work of art. Purposeful symbolism is involved in the subject and expression, the aesthetic qualities are related to the beauty of the work, whether it affords delight or pleasure to disinterested contemplation. The work of art stands for something else outside itself and is thus a symbol of its subject, the beauty is apparently more of the work of art itself as an independent object. But it is not the beauty of the object in an objective sense, that is, as a quality of the object, for the quality of beauty is conferred by the percipient and is thus subjective. It is an embodiment of the dreams and desires of our beings, the sense of order, of serenity in a world of chaos, of delightful variety within that order and a thousand other values. The work of art is thus also in the purely aesthetic sense a symbol.

REFERENCES
1. ROGER FRY, *The Artist and Psycho-Analysis* (London, 1924).
2. SIR JAMES FRAZER, *The Golden Bough*, Part 1, 'The Magic Art and the Evolution of Kings', 3rd edition (London, 1936).
3. HAVELOCK ELLIS, *The Dance of Life*, p. 33 (London, 1923).
4. THEODOR LIPPS, *Archiv für die gesamte Psychologie* (Hamburg and Leipzig, 1903).
5. WALTER PATER, Essay on 'The School of Giorgione' in *The Renaissance* (1877).
6. HERBERT READ, *Art Now*, p. 135 (London, 1933).
7. HERBERT READ, *Art Now*, p. 67.
8. LEWIS MUMFORD, *Art and Technics*, p. 17 (London, 1952).
9. LEWIS MUMFORD develops this theory in *The Conduct of Life*, pp. 39–57 (London, 1951).
10. LEWIS MUMFORD, *Arts and Technics*, p. 21.

XVI   The Dance, Gesture and the Ceremonies of Everyday Life

ONE of the most natural forms of expression is by bodily movement and gesture. When speech was in its infancy among primitive peoples, expression and communication depended more on bodily movement than it did in later societies where language had developed considerably. When this bodily movement is prolonged with repetitive elements and thus conforms to a definite rhythm, as is the case at social, ceremonial or religious gatherings with a definite purpose, the dance results. As previously observed, the dance is an early form of prayer, or is closely related to prayer, and many primitive religious ceremonies have the character of the dance. The ceremonies of most primitive religions are organized with the utilitarian purpose of receiving from the spirit or deity what is desired for the welfare of the people.

From the evidence afforded by observation of primitive cultures, and the investigations of anthropologists, agricultural dances and dances forming part of the worship of Nature appear to be the most common. These dances, often propitiatory in character, generally occur at set seasons of the year. There are the dances which accompany the sowing of seed, the dances to encourage the growth of crops and to increase fertility, dances at harvest time and dances to bring rain.[1] They often take the form, as indicated in the previous chapter, of imitation by bodily gesture of the desired occurrence. If it is a dance expressing the desire for crops to grow, then this is made clear to the deity by an imitation of crops growing, as by leaping in the air to make hemp grow tall.[2] Rain is imitated in a similar way. Rites to make Nature as fertile as possible take many forms. With some, sexual activity of human beings expresses the desired fecundity of Nature, and this sometimes forms the theme of the religious dance. The carrying of phallic images in processions in the Egyptian festivals of Osiris and in those of many Asiatic peoples probably had a similar purpose.

Other desires and hopes, success in war and the hunt, form the themes of religious dances. All the solemn occasions of life: birth, marriage, death, are attended with ceremonies which often take the form of dances. Prayers are for the welfare of those born, who are married and who die, and when—speech is inadequate—bodily movement organized into the ceremony and the dance tells the god what is desired. Propitiation of the god so that he should grant the behests of the suppliants is the essence

149

of this prayer. Thus bodily prostration expressing submission, derived from the habitual gestures of propitiation, is generally a feature of ceremony or dances where there is no subject for imitation. Then there are the totem dances in which the dancers imitate the movements of their totems, and the dances associated with the more generalized acts of worship of natural phenomena, of the sun, moon and stars and great trees. Thus the dance drama evolves as a form of worship, which ultimately leads to the drama of Aeschylus. The subject of the Egyptian and Greek astronomical drama is really the movement of the heavenly bodies, and it is easy to see that this drama is the precursor of the modern ballet.

The complete identity of the dancers with the purpose of the dance is emphasized on good evidence by many writers. The war dance is often a preliminary of battle, and the warriors—by means of the dance worked themselves into a frenzy so that they would thereby fight more effectively; and, as already indicated, when imitating the growth of crops the dance is often so intense that the dancers are for the time identified with the growing crops. In the totem dances the participants imagine themselves to be the animals or other subjects. Jane Harrison suggests that in the dance of the tribe of the Kangaroo totem 'the men kangaroos did it, not to *imitate* kangaroos—you cannot imitate yourself—but just for natural joy of heart because they were kangaroos; . . . and delighted to assert their tribal unity. What they felt was not mimesis but "participation", unity and community'.[3] There may be some connection here with Frazer's theory of the origin of totemism derived from the Australian tribe the Aruntas.

The Aruntas appeared to be unable to connect the sexual act with conception. When a woman first felt herself to be pregnant the object, either animal or plant, which occupied her thoughts or fancy at the time was believed by her to have implanted itself into her, and would be born through her in human form. The tribe would venerate that animal or other totem and would not eat it because to do so would be like eating themselves.[4] Thus in the totem dance the members of the tribe quite simply thought they were the animal, and would move with the same spirit. There is much evidence of the great capacity of the primitive religious dancers for identifying themselves completely with the subject of the dance.

It will be apparent that in these primitive religious dances of an imitative character there is no conscious symbolism, but it is symbolism for the observer. This distinction is paralleled by another distinction in the evolution of ceremony. Herbert Spencer pointed out that most ceremonies originate by evolution, as natural actions with an interested purpose, but he rejected the hypothesis that ceremonies originate in conscious symbolization[5] and he adduces convincing evidence to support his view. Havelock Ellis, who thought of dancing as an instinctive activity, refers to the dance of courtship in both animals and man and speaks of the 'primitive love-dance of insects and birds that seems to reappear among human savages in various parts of the world, notably in Africa'. 'In a conventionalized and symbolized form', he adds, 'it is still danced in civilization today.'[6]

In the history of mankind the dance begins as expression with a practical, propitiatory or religious purpose. This practical purpose of the dance or ceremony in primitive life is gradually lost in civilization, and it survives as form. The dances at the sowing of seed, dances to make the crops grow, to bring rain and increase fertility exist in a more sophisticated culture mainly as local country dances or folk dances, and are enjoyed as recreation and for aesthetic reasons.

The symbols remain, but the meanings are either lost or at most are vague and are no longer the purpose of the dance. The modern ballet has much of the expressional purpose of the ancient religious dance, but without its seriousness and intensity, as it is acting and not life at first hand.

There is more reality in the ceremonies of daily life and social intercourse because we all attach some meanings to them, although we are for the most part unconscious of their origins. We think of kissing as expressing love and affection; shaking hands as symbolic of friendship and goodwill; and obeisance, from bodily prostration and kneeling to the bow, nod and uncovering of the head, as expressive of devotion, worship, reverence and respect. All these are everyday social ceremonies or symbols, the meanings of which are still very close to the meanings of the forms and ceremonies from which they are derived.

Kissing as an expression of affection obviously derives from the instinctive satisfaction that the act affords. The licking of animals—the cow licking its calf, the cat licking itself and its kittens, the dog licking the hands and face of its master, are expressions of animal affection closely akin to kissing. With mammals, as sucking is the earliest means by which food is received, it is the first pleasurable act, and it is not difficult to appreciate that both licking and sucking became formalized into the kiss. The kissing of lovers may be directly instinctive, but the more formal kiss in civilized society, like the kiss of greeting, or kissing the hand, is a symbol of affection and devotion derived from the instinctive impulse.

Complete prostration denotes entire submission and takes the form of lying on the face or back. It has been a practice among many primitive peoples, both in submission to a ruler or victorious enemy and in many religions. From this complete prostration there are many stages: kneeling on both knees with head and arms touching the ground, kneeling with hands together, which is a common attitude of Christian prayer, kneeling on one knee, and the many variations of the bow and nod.[7] All these forms of prostration derive from acts of submission to a victorious or more powerful enemy, or to a social superior. It is a gesture of physical surrender expressing consent that the person to whom the obeisance is made may do what he wishes with the person making the obeisance. From surrender and submission it becomes, in civilized society, expressive of service, and when you bow low to a social superior it is as if to say, 'I am your humble servant at your service.' When the bow is mutual between social equals and not merely an acknowledgement by one of the other, then it is as if to say, 'I respect you, I am at your service.' Propitiation is a guiding motive throughout. The bow, when it becomes a nod, has lost all this symbolism and merely becomes a sign of recognition, but even here the element of propitiation is not entirely absent.

The uncovering of the head as a mark of respect appears to derive from the custom in many primitive societies of removing dress or parts of dress as an act of submission. In military surrender it was usual for weapons to be delivered to the victor, and often with them several articles of dress, and this expression of submission has survived in various forms in many societies. The parts of dress usually discarded were those which gave dignity to the wearer. In France in 1467 when a town surrendered, three hundred citizens were brought to the camp of the victorious commander in their shirts, bareheaded and barelegged, and delivered the keys of the city and themselves to his mercy.[8] A similar procedure was followed on the surrender of Calais to Edward III.

Often the customs of military and civil life became part of religious ceremony, and the uncovering of parts of the body as an expression of subjection became a custom of religious worship. One survival of this is the removal of the hat by men only when entering a Christian church.

Holding the hands palm to palm in the attitude of prayer is symbolic of submission because it is in this attitude that hands are bound. Binding the hands of prisoners in this way is an ancient custom; it can be seen in the bas reliefs of Assyrian palaces, while hand-cuffing in this way still obtains. What more natural than that worshippers should adopt this submissive attitude of the hands in prostration before God?

The origin of the custom of shaking hands is more obscure. It is a very ancient gesture of greeting and farewell, of friendship, and sometimes of equality. It appears in numerous Greek sepulchral stelae from the fifth century before Christ, but the origin of this form seems to be lost in the mists of antiquity. Herbert Spencer makes an interesting speculation on how the act of shaking hands evolved. He quotes from M. Niebuhr[9] who says that 'two Arabs of the desert meeting, shake hands more than ten times. Each kisses his own hand, and still repeats the question, "How art thou?" . . . In Yemen, each does as if he wished the other's hand and draws back his own to avoid receiving the same honour. At length, to end the contest, the elder of the two suffers the other to kiss his fingers'. 'Have we not here', asks Spencer, 'the origin of shaking hands? If of two persons each wishes to make an obeisance to the other by kissing his hand, and each out of compliment refuses to have his own hand kissed, what will happen?' Spencer answers:

> 'If each of two tries to kiss the other's hand, and refuses to have his own kissed, this will result in a raising of the hand of each by the other towards his own lips, and by the other a drawing of it down again, and so on alternately. Though at first such an action will be irregular, yet as fast as the usage spreads, and the failure of either to kiss the other's hand becomes a recognized issue, the motions may be expected to grow regular and rhythmical. Clearly the difference between the simple squeeze, to which this salute is now often abridged, and the old-fashioned hearty shake, exceeds the difference between the hearty shake and the movement that would result from the effort of each to kiss the hand of the other.'[10]

There is no doubt that, as Spencer remarks, the hand-shake had a natural origin and that it was not fixed on as a symbolic observance; but whether his speculation as to its origin is the correct one it would be difficult to say in the absence of further evidence. If this be the true explanation then the original hand-shake was essentially a symbol of equality. Another line of thought suggests that the hand-shake of today may have been derived from touching and clasping hands. The attitude of the figures depicted in the ancient Greek sepulchral stelae of the fifth and fourth centuries B.C. suggests the more passive placing of one hand in another. We know that it is an instinctive gesture of affection for a person to place his (or her) hand on that of another, and it is likely that in more formal greeting this gesture is given the accent of a shake. It is a matter on which further knowledge would be interesting and illuminating.

Handshaking, like kissing, seems also to be symbolic of a desire to join oneself to another person, to be expressive of a sense of community or oneness with him.

It will be seen that these common ceremonies of everyday life almost certainly have an instinctive origin, and have evolved with changes in social life. There is nothing to suggest that they were deliberately chosen by any society as symbolic observances; although, having instinctive origins, they have become customary observances in most civilized communities, and illustrate how deeply rooted in community life such ceremonies are. Although they survive as symbols, they belong to the essential pattern of instinctive life.

REFERENCES
1. A very large number of instances of these agricultural dances among various primitive peoples are given in SIR JAMES FRAZER'S *Golden Bough*, 12 vols, 3rd edition, 1936.
2. SIR JAMES FRAZER, *op. cit.*, Vol. IX, 315.
3. JANE E. HARRISON, *Ancient Art and Ritual* (London, 1913).
4. SIR JAMES FRAZER, *Totemism and Exogamy*, Vol. II, p. 89, IV, p. 59.
5. HERBERT SPENCER, *The Principles of Sociology*, Vol. II, Part IV, 'Ceremonial Institutions', para. 346 (London, 1879).
6. HAVELOCK ELLIS, *The Dance of Life*, p. 42 (London, 1923).
7. HERBERT SPENCER in his chapter on 'Obeisances' in *Ceremonial Institutions* (*op. cit.*, IV, 383–391) collected numerous examples of all forms of prostration.
8. P. DE COMINES, *History of Louis XI*, English translation, 1614.
9. M. NIEBUHR, *Travels through Arabia*, English translation, 1792.
10. HERBERT SPENCER, *op. cit.*, para. 390.

XVII Dress

A STUDY of the origin and evolution of clothing suggests that symbolism may legitimately be regarded as constituting one of its many purposes, and that dress is naturally symbolic of many things in the course of its developments. A garment, ornament or badge is often worn, both in primitive and civilized societies, to signify the status or social function of an individual, or as a mark of honour. Such purposes of dress figure strongly in primitive societies, and they appear to derive in large measure from trophies. The wearing of trophies captured in war or the hunt signifies that the wearer is brave, powerful and to be respected, and a man often obtained tribal rank by such prowess. These trophies are clearly symbols largely by association and constitute one of the origins of dress.

Although dress originates partially as symbolism, in some societies, such as that of ancient Greece, this aspect is entirely lost. However, symbolism comes into being again by the conservative retention of some forms of dress for a particular purpose. Many forms which were once common everyday clothes of a particular period are retained by institutions, while the everyday clothes change and evolve. Examples are provided by ecclesiastical vestments, academic robes and robes of state.

There are further the social tendencies which dress symbolizes and which are found in every stage of its evolution.

To appreciate the part played by symbolism in dress it is helpful to examine briefly the impulses which prompt the various forms of clothing. To do this a glimpse at the probable origins of clothing will be illuminating.

From the researches of anthropologists and the evidence afforded by the primitive aboriginal peoples of the world, it would appear that the original reasons for the wearing of clothing, and the main influences in its evolution, may be roughly classified as follows: (1) as protection either from cold, from the sun, or from nuisances of various kinds, like insects; (2) as decoration for the purpose of sexual attraction; (3) as decoration for self-elation and to be admired, which is closely akin to decoration prompted by vanity; (4) modesty and the feeling of shame and (5) wearing of trophies, badges and other symbolic indications of the character and status of the wearer. We shall see that there is a very close connection between two, three and five which, together, probably provide the chief reasons why we wear clothes.

(1) *Clothing Worn as Protection*

According to Darwin[1] man became denuded of hair by sexual selection, but being a tropical or sub-tropical animal the evidence afforded by aboriginal peoples suggests that in consequence he merely suffered some inconvenience from the sun and from occasional cold winds. Migration to colder climates suggests the need of protection from cold, but evidence indicates that this probably depends on the speed of migration. If it is slow, as it probably was in the early history of man, then there is every reason to suppose that man can become accustomed to the rigours of a cold climate. The Fuegians, for example, who inhabit a climate colder and less pleasant than that of the north of Scotland, live practically naked. Darwin when exploring the islands of Tierra del Fuego with Captain FitzRoy, says that the only garment of the natives in the eastern part 'consists of a mantle made of quanaco skin, with the wool outside; this they wear just thrown over the shoulders, leaving their persons as often exposed as covered', and of the much more wretched and savage natives of Wollaston Island he says that 'the men have an otter-skin, or some small scrap about as large as a pocket handkerchief, which is barely sufficient to cover their backs as low down as their loins. It is laced across the breast by strings, and according as the wind blows, it is shifted from side to side'.[2] Darwin further records that while sitting round a blazing fire one night their party was joined by a small family of Fuegians. He says, 'We were well clothed, and though sitting close to the fire were far from too warm; yet these naked savages though further off were observed, to our great surprise, to be streaming with perspiration at undergoing such a roasting.' Commenting on this, Darwin remarks that 'Nature, by making habit omnipotent, and its effect hereditary, has fitted the Fuegian to the climate and the productions of his miserable country.' Further examples could be given of primitive people living in cold climates without clothing, or very little. It might be suggested that clothes as a protection from cold were only necessary if the speed of the migration was such that it did not permit bodies to become acclimatized, and the original nakedness or merely decorated condition to continue as customary. Man, therefore, took the readiest means of protection. He had already preyed upon animals for food; he now did so for clothing and wrapped himself in their warm skins.

With regard to protection of the body in sub-tropical and tropical climates, it would seem that painting the body was the method more frequently employed, as it was regarded as the most effective. David Livingstone recorded that the Griquas and Bechuanas of South Africa 'to assist in protecting the pores of the skin from the influence of the sun by day and of the cold by night, all smeared themselves with a mixture of fat and ochre'.[3] Dr. Ernst Grosse testifies that the Hottentots 'rub themselves with ashes and fat for defence against the cold, and the Shillocks smear their black bodies with a reddish mixture of cow-dung and ashes for protection against mosquito bites. In all these cases the painting, in correspondence with its purpose, is as uninterrupted as possible over the whole body'.[4] Herbert Spencer[5] cites evidence from various travellers of the custom of painting the body for protection against insects; and numerous other examples could be given. This painting and smearing, beginning as a protective measure, develops with some primitive peoples into expression or symbolism of rank.

155

Clothes were never, apparently, worn among primitive peoples as a protection against rain. Indeed, clothes would appear to have the opposite effect. Dr. Charles Pickering remarks that during his visit to Tahiti in 1850 they 'were exposed for some days to frequent and heavy rains', and they 'soon began to envy the naked condition of the natives, who became dry in a few minutes', whereas their clothing once wet remained so for hours. He also mentions that the Polynesians 'never had colds until they began wearing clothes'.[6]

Some primitive peoples wear a covering round the loins. As many of these are not decorative it is probable, as Fehlinger[7] suggests, that they were worn as protection against various forest and sea dangers and nuisances. Examples are the models of two Bushmen and a Bechuana in the British Museum made under the direction of Dr. Emil Holub, which show in one instance a covering of hide fastened round the pubic region, and in the other instance aprons of skins. The degree of protection afforded by the latter does not appear to be very great.

There is little evidence to suggest that man began wearing clothes in tropical or subtropical countries for protection, as this appears generally to be accomplished effectively by painting or smearing the body. With regard to colder climates there is again insufficient evidence to show that man could not have become acclimatized in a naked condition, although it must be admitted that rapidity of migration might be one small contributory factor.

(2) *Clothing Worn as Decoration for the Purpose of Sexual Attraction.*

Decoration for various purposes seems, from the evidence, to be the main origin of clothes. This evidence is voluminous and it is not necessary to cite it specifically; it can be found in the works of numerous authors.[8]

The purpose of the decoration is, however, the important factor. Much evidence has been adduced to show that one of the major purposes is sexual allurement. Darwin, Westermark, Fehlinger, Ernst Grosse, Havelock Ellis and many others have shown that ornament is used by primitive races to make themselves sexually attractive. The decoration of the body for this purpose would appear to be largely instinctive if Darwin's famous theory of sexual selection is accepted, because in this theory the rich plumage of male birds and other decorative characteristics of animals have gradually developed through sexual selection.

As we have seen, painting and smearing the body were done for protection, but the decorative purpose is apparent with bright colours and patterns, which has been widely observed by travellers. Tattooing was a further form of decoration. Natural elaborations of this painting were the use of ornaments attached to and suspended from the body. With some tribes head-dresses of feathers became common and a strange variety of ornaments were collected, such as shells, bones, teeth, fur and horns. Some means had to be devised to attach these objects to the body. Man was able to string them together by means of the hair of animals, and the most convenient places to receive such strings of ornaments are the neck, hips, wrists and ankles. The testimonies of travellers show that such ornaments are the earliest forms of decorative attachments, because they are seen when no other attachments are worn. Loading the body with ornaments was not an uncommon practice, resulting obviously from over-elaboration.[9] It is easy to appreciate, therefore, that the insatiable desire for ornament can develop into clothing. The early development suggests that one important purpose was sexual attraction.

The loins and head are the most richly ornamented parts of the body in almost all aboriginal peoples, but the development of clothes spreads principally from the girdle. We often find that the region of the sexual organs is covered with aprons of various decorative devices which afford little concealment and are discarded at pleasure. Australian aboriginal women whilst performing lascivious dances wore an apron of feathers.[10] The native females of Botany Bay wore a short apron of opossum or kangaroo skin cut into strips to form a sort of decorative fringe.[11] The fashionable young women of Wintum, a Californian tribe, wore a girdle of deerskin, with the lower edges slit into a long fringe, and at the end of each strand was a polished pine-nut, while the rest was studded with brilliant bits of shells.[12] The Bushwomen of South Africa wore an apron of springboks' skins cut into strips and ornamented with beads and egg-shells; the strips were so small and narrow that they did not serve as a covering at all. These instances could be multiplied many times. That decorative devices are worn mainly for sexual attraction there can be little doubt, and they are the prelude to the many fashions throughout the history of clothes which betray a similar purpose.

(3) *Clothing Worn for Self-elation and Admiration*

How far the body is decorated for reasons of self-elation, of vanity, for the desire to be admired and to 'swank' it is more difficult to assess. It is not easy to separate these feelings from the impulse to attract sexually, but all who have concerned themselves with good clothes, with looking their best (and who have not at some time of their lives?) will acknowledge that all these feelings can exist without the sexual purpose, although they probably more often exist when related to it in some degree. The peacock does not only strut with tail spread when the female is in attendance—it is exhilarating to feel a fine fellow.

Vanity appears to be just as strong among primitive belles as among their more civilized sisters. Captain FitzRoy took four natives of Tierra del Fuego to England, one of whom died here, and was returning them to their native country on the occasion of the Beagle's voyage. Darwin says of one of them, Jemmy Button, that he was 'short, thick and fat, but vain of his personal appearance; he used always to wear gloves, his hair was neatly cut, and he was distressed if his well polished shoes were dirtied. He was fond of admiring himself in a looking-glass'. Stanley, speaking of the chief of Manyeman says: 'Mwana Ngoy, I suppose, is one of the vainest of vain men. I fancy I can see him now strutting about his village with his sceptral staff, an amplitude of grass cloth about him, which, when measured, gives exactly twenty-four yards, drawn in double folds about his waist, all tags, tassels and fringes and painted in various colours, bronze and black and white and yellow, and on his head a plumy head-dress.'

Vanity and the desire to be admired are certainly contributory factors in prompting self-decoration and are clearly allied to the motive of sexual attraction, while having some relation to symbolism, as indicated later.

(4) *Clothing Worn from Modesty and a Feeling of Shame*

The extent to which modesty and a feeling of shame are factors in originating clothes is problematical. They are not quite the same. Clothing resulting from the latter would be prompted by a desire to conceal sexual excitement because of a feeling of shame, but there is not a great deal of reliable evidence that this was ever common among primitive peoples. The suggestion that it is so emanates largely from religious sources, and St. Augustine claimed that this explains the Biblical narrative of Adam and Eve. The account given in the Talmud of Adam and Eve clearly indicates that the forbidden knowledge was the manner of obtaining offspring. Directly they had sinned, their passions were inflamed, and they were occasionally conscious of sexual excitement. This from a feeling of shame they desired to conceal, so they 'sewed fig leaves together and made themselves aprons'.

Anthropologists and travellers mostly dispute that this is true to natural tendency. Westermarck marshalled much evidence to show that the most primitive peoples have no feelings of shame in nakedness.[13] Indeed, some testimonies indicate that clothes are more likely to prompt such feelings. Humboldt records, for example, that when missionaries offered clothes to the Indians on the Orinoco they threw them into the river; and when told to cover themselves they refused because they said it made them feel ashamed.[14] Fehlinger was a spirited antagonist of the belief that clothes were ever worn because of a feeling of shame, and many others have brought evidence to refute the theory.

Modesty is not quite the same, for it has an instinctive basis which a mere feeling of shame lacks. Modesty is, after all, very closely allied to feminine coyness with which Nature has endowed women for the purpose of sexual allurement. Modesty and coyness prompt concealment for the very purpose of attracting, and this modesty is probably a contributory factor in originating decorative clothing. Modesty is also a natural accompaniment of love, especially on the part of the woman, which prompts a natural desire to conceal anything that might offend. Love has a refining influence, and among its refinements is a fear of offending the sense of modesty. Dugas says that 'when love is really felt, and not vainly imagined, modesty is the requirement of an ideal of dignity, conceived as the very condition of that love'.[15] In the volume of the *Psychology of Sex* dealing with the 'Evolution of Modesty'[16] Havelock Ellis says that 'the social fear of arousing disgust combines easily and perfectly with any new development in the invention of ornament on clothing as sexual lures. Even among the most civilized races it has been noted that the fashion of feminine garments (as also the use of scents) has the double object of concealing and attracting'.

It frequently happens that the greater the concealment of the body by clothes and the more care spent in ornamentation, the greater the sexual attraction. The late Victorian dress hiding women from neck to feet yet accentuating feminine curves was probably more sexually alluring than the mini skirt of the late 1960's. Coquetry and coyness are woman's legitimate means of attraction, and can be quite in harmony with modesty.

(5) *Clothing as Trophies and Badges*

That the wearing of trophies, badges and other symbolic indications of the character and status of the wearer forms one of the main contributory factors in originating clothes has not been sufficiently credited. That is why it has been necessary to consider the other reasons for wearing clothes, so that the symbolic factor can be put in its proper relation with the other factors.

Trophies are expressive of achievement and conquest. In primitive war or the hunt trophies signify that the owner has triumphed over an enemy or wild animal, and is for this reason to be honoured and respected. This gives him some kind of authority, so that trophies became symbols of authority. Thus, the sword is a symbol of power. The sceptre is a symbol of authority which has developed from the sword or spear; and the mace, another symbol of authority, was originally a military weapon. In modern times the chief forms of trophy are for sport and for cultural and social contests, and are generally in the form of cups and shields.

Among primitive races trophies of war and the hunt took many forms. Of the latter, the skin of a wild and ferocious animal was one of the principal, and thus we see here one origin of clothing. The classical example is, of course, Hercules wearing the skin of the Nemean lion that he had slain. In some African races the wearing of a lion's skin or leopard's skin is symbolic of rank or royal blood.

Trophies of war take the form of captured weapons and parts of the bodies of slain enemies. Common are heads, skulls, hands, feet, jaw-bones, teeth, human skins, scalps. These are often worn on the body or hung on the dwelling. So we find often that ornaments worn by primitive races are of a character that indicates trophies. Strings of bones and teeth, both human and animal, are often hung round the waist or neck,[17] and sometimes the objects form a strange collection. Stanley refers to the hideous and queer appendages that the natives of Uhumbo wear round their waists; 'tags of monkey skin and bits of gorilla bone, goat horns' and around their necks 'skin of viper, adders' fork and blind worms' stings'. It is recorded of the Snake Indians of America that a collar worn round the neck consisting of the claws of the brown bear is regarded as highly honourable because to kill such an animal was an achievement.[18] It has been suggested that many of the ornaments worn are substituted for trophies and were originally representations of them. For example the people of Ashantee made small models in gold of jaw-bones.

The wearing of the skin of a ferocious animal, or of strings of jaw-bones, teeth, and scalps of enemies that the wearer had killed symbolized his power and bravery, and in primitive tribes, where worth is measured by physical prowess, he is thus a man of authority, and these trophies are the symbols of his authority. This is really the origin of many well-known symbols of authority, carried and worn in most civilized societies. These badges can so multiply and load the body that some clothing is required for their support.

Herbert Spencer observes that the habits of American Indians who wear, as marks of honour, the skins of formidable animals they have killed, 'suggest that the badge and the dress have a common root, and that the dress is, at any rate in some cases, a collateral development of the badge'. Spencer finds support for this inference in the remarks of Guhl and Koner in their *Life of the Greeks and Romans* that the covering of the head and the upper part of the body as protection from the weather and the enemy's weapon originally consisted of the hides of wild animals. 'Thus the hunters' trophy became the warriors' armour.'

In the most primitive societies the strongest and bravest man was the best; he gathered the trophies and enjoyed the highest status. In the course of evolution from primitive to more civilized states, while symbols of social and class distinction would be derived from and closely related to trophies, other factors contributed to the indication of class distinctions, and to the development of clothes. One is wealth, procuring greater elaboration of apparel, which in the early developments meant the transition from few clothes to many. An early stage of this occurs in painting the body. Smearing the body, as we have noted, was a common form of protection against insects, and the double purpose was sometimes served of protection and decoration. Some of the pigments, oils or fats used were costlier and rarer than others, and they thus became indicative of wealth; and a liberal use of costly pigment, oils or fats gradually became expressive of social status. Ample evidence of this exists in the observed customs of primitive peoples. Thus, as Herbert Spencer remarks,[19] 'the putting on of a protective covering to the skin, grows into a ceremony indicating supremacy', and anointing with costly oils or fats became a mark of distinction. From this, it is suggested, the religious rite of anointing was derived. Both with the ancient Egyptians and Jews the investiture to any high or sacred office was accompanied by the ceremony of anointing, and the custom survives in Christian ceremonies, including the coronation of a monarch.

In a similar way, it can be appreciated, the wealthier members of a tribe or society would tend to adorn themselves with more ornament and wear more clothes than the poorer members. The costliness of certain materials would emphasize these distinctions. Thus, finely textured fabrics and bright colours made possible by the more costly dyes would mark the clothes of the rich. It is probably in this way that purple, as the most costly dye of all, became an emblem of monarchy. This process of emphasizing social distinction would therefore be a factor in the evolution of clothing. Social distinctions and ranks call for ceremonies, and ceremonies call for more and more ornament and dress, developing to the gorgeous robes of civilized societies. Such ceremonial dress is the essence of symbolism.

Some primitive peoples wear dress only on ceremonial occasions, and at other times live naked.

Dress which is mainly ceremonial in character, like ecclesiastical vestments and robes of office, retains its basic forms, while everyday dress changes every few years with the cycles of fashion. The ecclesiastical vestments of the Roman Catholic and Greek churches have changed but very gradually in the history of Christianity, and the changes in many of the Protestant churches have also been extremely slow. The ecclesiastical vestments of the early Church were originally derived from everyday dress, but whereas the latter changed, the clergy retained the old forms of Greek and Roman costume. As the Church grew and ecclesiastical offices multiplied, elaborations in dress and religious appurtenances marked the various ecclesiastical ranks. The changes that do occur in the vestments in the course of the centuries are generally in the length of the garments and in their colour.

Thus, the most familiar of these garments—the cassock and surplice—have varied a little in length and colour since the eleventh century, but not in essential character. The cassock, originally a long-sleeved tunic worn by the Gauls in pre-Christian times and known as the caracalla, was assumed by clerics in the fifth century. By the eleventh century it had extended to reach the ankles, and has remained that length ever since. Coloured cassocks are worn by the higher dignitaries of the Church, but plain black cassocks are worn by priests, minor clergy and the choir. Derived from the tunica alb in the eleventh century, the surplice was first worn to the feet over the cassock, and remained so for about three centuries, after which it became the shorter length that is familiar today. The symbolism of these vestments is, therefore, something acquired from the ceremonies and offices for which they are worn, and they became significant of the purpose of these ceremonies.

In like manner we find that most ceremonial robes derive from everyday dress; the essential forms are retained and elaborated to mark differences of rank and status. This we find in the robes of peers and in judicial, academic and municipal robes. The first two mentioned have been worn since the fourteenth century, and their derivation from the civilian dress of that time is apparent in their form. Academic dress begins as the ordinary dress of the people of the fourteenth century; it is retained with little change, and certain of its forms became academic marks, badges or symbols. An example is the hood. Originally this was solely a utilitarian garment covering the head, and it was thrown back over the shoulders when not in use. (This form has recently been revived and has been a common garment since the Second World War for both men and women.) Being retained as part of the university academic dress, various kinds came to be worn, and it ultimately became a badge indicative of university degrees.

We find the same process in the retention of old forms of dress in various localities, and especially in country districts where conservatism and resistance to changes of fashion have created national and local costumes. Remoteness from the main currents of life has probably been in great measure the cause of this. These national and local costumes survive in modern societies mainly as curiosities, and it seems in some cases that they are artificially perpetuated for the sake of tourists. Individuals wearing these traditional native costumes, such as those of Holland, Brittany, Bavaria, the Tyrol, and several other places, are commonly used as symbols of these countries and districts.

Most writers on the history of costume have agreed that dress can be symbolic of the manners, social life and even the aspirations of an age. The historian of dress, so fully occupied with the subject, may be a little extravagant in his claims of its significance, as when James Laver says, 'the student of clothes and the accessories that go with them, from the broken handle of a fan, from a camera or a shoe-buckle, can build up a convincing picture of a bygone age. Josephine's Egyptian brooches enshrine the Oriental ambitions of Napoleon; the enamelled surface of a rococo snuff-box reflects the entire age of Louis XV; the pointed umbrella of an early Victorian lady implies a complete attitude to life. These things are more than relics— they are symbols, and the crinoline is as much a monument as the Albert Memorial.'[20] If this appears to exaggerate the significance of dress and its accessories, few students of the subject would deny that it is basically true. Laver indicates many ways in which feminine modes are expressive of the deeper movements of social life. He says, for example, that 'a hundred years hence grave historians will illustrate their account of the gradual subsidence of post-war hysteria by pointing to the more feminine modes which prevailed in the early nineteen thirties'.

In women's dress immediately after the First World War the elements of feminine allurement were accentuated, as if, following the war, woman was anxious to empha-size her strictly feminine role. Then came a change. From about 1923 the skirt began to get shorter, the dress simpler and straighter, so that by 1927 it was little more than a tube which reached to the knees; the waist had disappeared, and the hair was cut short. Was this an expression of women's newly-won emancipation? For they had acquired equal franchise with men. Was this expressed by an attempt to look less like a woman and more like a boy, with the straight slim figure and short hair? The thirties saw a return to the longer skirt and more graceful and seductive attire. But later, skirts again began to rise and towards the end of the Second World War again terminated at the knees, and dress generally had become utilitarian and drab. The years following the war very quickly saw a return to more feminine modes, called the 'new look' which was one of the earliest and most welcome gifts of peace. It was again an expression of an impulse, after years of denial, for woman to assert her femininity, and to emphasize that she was a woman with numerous sexual attractions. Trends of fashion up to 1959 suggest variations on the theme of the new look, but these have been followed by a stark and ugly simplicity comparable to the cloth tubes of the late twenties, followed in turn by a severe abbreviation culminating in the mini skirt. As no fashion lasts for more than a few years the next stage would either be a complete disappearance of the skirt for a period, or its lengthening which by 1970 had begun. The maxi coat down to or below the ankles had already appeared in 1969, and who can say that, in spite of women's emancipation, they will not again wear skirts trailing on the ground.

Numerous motifs, often of a character less personal to women, expressive of the age, are manifest in feminine modes. To quote Laver again: 'Woman is the mould into which the spirit of the age pours itself, and to those with any sense of history no detail of the resulting symbolic status is without importance.'[21]

It will be noted that reference has been made only to women's dress as symbolic of social movements. Until the early nineteenth century men's dress also could be said to symbolize social change. Since that period, however, until the early 1960's men's clothes have not fulfilled that rôle. Man, in western civilization, for over a century wore what was very little better than a uniform which changes comparatively slowly. J. C. Flügel describes this as the great masculine renunciation which occurred in consequence of the French Revolution. In the eighteenth century the highly decorated masculine dress of the aristocracy and wealthier classes seemed to emphasize differ-ences of social status. The new social order consequent upon the French Revolution with its doctrine of equality aimed at eradicating these social distinctions and the expression of them. 'The new social order', says Flügel, 'demanded something that expressed rather the common humanity of all men. This could only be done by means of a greater uniformity of dress.'[22] This was a less sudden change than Flügel appears to imply because the dress of men in the early nineteenth century, particularly of the wealthier strata of society, was still of a highly decorative character, with a movement, it is true, rather away from colour and towards the contrasting effects of black and white, while distinctions of the wealthy and less wealthy were still strongly apparent, if in a more subtle manner.

Another factor which contributed towards a standard dress in men was a changing attitude to work, with a comparative decrease in the size of the leisured classes and a greater proportion engaging in trades and professions. By the second half of the nineteenth century the standard male dress was established, and the changes since have been few and slow. Those that have occurred are in the direction of a general relaxation of the rather rigid uniform of the late Victorians, towards greater freedom and comfort, accompanied by more adaptability to various activities and to the changes of summer and winter, in part determined more by utilitarian considerations. Tentative efforts have been made to introduce more colour, but not with any marked success, until the sixties. These utilitarian modifications of the uniform serve to confirm the completeness of the renunciation, and to emphasize that one finds sartorial expression and symbolism of social movements, aspirations and morals mainly in feminine fashions.

During the sixties, however, a considerable change took place in dress. A much greater variety in the clothes of both sexes occurred, more colour was introduced into men's dress accompanied by long hair with the result that it was not always easy to distinguish at first glance the sex of a young person. This greater variety and freedom in dress is clearly an expression of the greater democratic freedom that came in the sixties. As Barbara Castle said, 'Democracy is breaking out. It's a new situation. Everybody—students, teachers, trade union members—is demanding a greater say in what happens to him. It's as though people are taking democracy into their own hands, and it's an international phenomenon.'[23] This is the reverse of regimentation, and the greater variety of clothing, as if half the population were in fancy dress, is an expression or symbol of this individual participation in democracy.

One other aspect of the subject calls for brief consideration: it is that certain forms of clothing are sexual symbols. This has emanated mainly from psychoanalysts. Professor Flügel expresses their viewpoint when he says:

'Clothes not only serve to assure sexual interest, but may themselves actually symbolize the sexual organs. Here again psycho-analysis has added considerably to our knowledge, and has shown that in the domain of clothes phallic symbolism is scarcely less important than, for instance, in the domain of religion. Indeed, we are still almost certainly as yet ignorant concerning the full extent of this symbolism in the case of clothes and of the exact nature of the role this symbolism plays in the history of the individual and the race. We know, however, that a great many articles of dress, such as the shoe, the tie, the hat, the collar, and even larger and more voluminous garments, such as the coat, the trousers, and the mantle may be phallic symbols, while the shoe, the girdle and the garter (as well as most jewels) may be corresponding female symbols.'

A common criticism of the theories of psychoanalysts is that they tend to give a sexual significance to manifestations which is not warranted, and this attribution of sexual symbolism to many articles of dress might legitimately be regarded as an example. But in the present state of psychological knowledge it is extremely difficult to prove one way or the other. The symbolism of repressed impulses with which psychoanalysts are concerned is generally of an unconscious or partially conscious type and the denial of sexual exhibitionism resulting from the standard uniform clothing that men have worn for the last hundred and twenty years may have unconsciously prompted a recourse to sexual symbolism in many of the forms of garments. It is easier to perceive this sexual symbolism in women's dress, because women's fashions are consciously guided by the motif of sexual allurement. The suggestion of phallic symbolism may seem extravagant when applied to masculine dress

—that, for example, the top hat, the pointed shoe, the tie are phallic symbols, but that they were determined unconsciously or sub-consciously make it difficult to prove or disprove.

It should, however, be pointed out that generally there is a tendency to underrate the part played by sexual impulses in social life, because they are submerged by the force of the current moral code; but in primitive societies, where such a repressive force was much weaker, sexual impulses are not camouflaged to anything like the same extent. This greater consciousness and acknowledgement of the power of the sexual instinct might reduce the tendency to employ phallic and other sexual symbols in dress, but if they were employed their significance would obviously not prompt the same denial as if they were unconscious symbolism. This reasoning is not advanced in support of this external sexual symbolism of articles of dress, but rather to show the possibilities of the truth of such symbolism to an inevitably incredulous world. That there is much to be said for the view-point, however, must surely be apparent from the circumstance that history demonstrates that probably the strongest factor in the origin and manifold developments of clothing is sexual allurement. This is still strongly apparent in feminine attire, and although it has been comparatively submerged in masculine attire, it manifests itself, as a parallel to the process of repressed impulses, in the sexual symbolism of various articles of dress.

REFERENCES

1. CHARLES DARWIN, *Descent of Man* (London, 1871).
2. CHARLES DARWIN, *Journal of Researches: Voyage of the Beagle*, 2nd edition, 1845, pp. 213 *et seq.* (London, 1st edition, 1839).
3. DAVID LIVINGSTONE, *Missionary Travels and Researches in South Africa*, p. 97 (London, 1857).
4. ERNST GROSSE, *Die Anfange der Kunst* (Freiberg, 1894). *The Beginnings of Art*, p. 60, English translation (London, 1897).
5. HERBERT SPENCER, *The Principles of Sociology*, Part IV, Vol. II, pp. 195–6 (London, 1879).
6. CHARLES PICKERING, *The Races of Man*, p. 64 (London, 1851).
7. H. FEHLINGER, *Sexual Life of Primitive People*, English translation, pp. 8 *et seq.* (London, 1921).
8. DARWIN, *Voyage of the Beagle* (London, 2nd edition, 1845).
   EDWARD WESTERMARCK, *History of Human Marriage*, Vol. I (London, 1921).
   CHARLES PICKERING, *The Races of Man* (London, 1851).
   ERNST GROSSE, *The Beginnings of Art* (London, 1897).
   DAVID LIVINGSTONE, *Missionary Travels and Researches in South Africa* (London, 1857).
   LORD AVEBURY, *Origin of Civilisation* (London, 1912).
   SIR H. M. STANLEY, *Through the Dark Continent* (London, 1890).
   DR. WILHELM JUNKER, *Travels in Africa during the Years 1879–1883*, English translation (London, 1891).
   A. VON HUMBOLDT and A. BONPLAND. *Personal Narrative of Travels to the Equinoctial Regions of the New Continent during the years 1799–1804*. 7 vols. Written in French, English translation (London, 1814–29).
   H. FEHLINGER, *Sexual Life of Primitive People*, English translation (London, 1921).
   GEORGE BARRINGTON, *History of New South Wales* (London, 1802).
   SIR HARRY H. JOHNSTONE, *The River Congo* (London, 1st edition, 1884, 4th edition revised, 1895).
9. Much evidence can be given to support this. *See*, for example, SIR H. M. STANLEY, *Through the Dark Continent* (London, 1890), and DR. WILHELM JUNKER, *Travels in Africa* (London, 1891).
10. ERNST GROSSE, *The Beginnings of Art*, English translation, p. 98 (London, 1897).
11. GEORGE BARRINGTON, *History of New South Wales* (London, 1802).
12. EDWARD WESTERMARCK, *History of Human Marriage*, Vol. I, p. 548 (London, 1921).

13. EDWARD WESTERMARCK, *op. cit.*, Vol. I, Chapters 15 and 16.
14. A. VON HUMBOLDT and A. BONPLAND, *Personal Narrative*, Vol. 3, p. 230.
15. DUGAS, *La Pudeur, Revue Philosophique*, November, 1930.
16. HAVELOCK ELLIS, *Evolution of Modesty*, p. 59 (London, 1919).
17. HERBERT SPENCER collected evidence of this from various travellers. *The Principles of Sociology*, Vol. II, pp. 184, 185 (London, 1879).
18. M. LEWIS and W. CLARKE, *Travels to the Source of the Missouri*, p. 315 (London, 1814).
19. HERBERT SPENCER, *op. cit.*, p. 196.
20. JAMES LAVER, *Taste and Fashion from the French Revolution to the Present Day*, pp. 197 *et seq.* (London, 1945).
21. JAMES LAVER. *Op. cit.*
22. J. C. FLÜGEL, *The Psychology of Clothes*, p. 112. (London, 1930). The whole question is discussed in Chapter 7.
23. BARBARA CASTLE quoted by Adam Fergusson, 'Harnessing the energy of unrest', *The Times*, 20th May, 1970.

XVIII Architecture

SYMBOLIC devices as part of the decorative embellishment of a building, and symbolism incorporated or inherent in the form or structure, are apparent in most periods of architectural history. Much of the attached symbolism existing in the ornament, carvings, mosaics and mural decoration is logically considered as sculpture and painting. In one of the main traditions of art from ancient Greece and Rome to the Middle Ages and early Renaissance in Italy sculpture and painting were integral parts of architecture and had little existence apart. Although such painting and sculpture were often powerfully expressive and symbolical, considered from the formal standpoint of design they were decorative details in an architectural scheme. Since the easel picture and the exhibition statue there has been some separation of the visual arts, although much sculpture and painting is still fortunately comprehended in architectural design. Whether, however, it is an elaborate sculptured group in a pediment symbolizing peace and commerce, or a simple cross on a ball, or a heraldic shield, or a symbolic mosaic floor or wall fresco, all are attached architectural symbolism, because they are all incorporated to symbolize and express the purpose of the building or some association with it.

The more fundamental type of architectural symbolism is that which determines or pervades the entire form and structure. This is of two main kinds; that in which the basic form is a symbol beginning as a representation according to the first type in the classification given in chapter one (p. 5) of symbolism of an object by approximate or conventional imitation; and secondly where ideas and emotions associated with a building are symbolized in its forms. In the case of the former there is evidence that many of the well-known traditional architectural forms originated as symbols of the imitative or representational type. To appreciate the representational and symbolic origin of many architectural forms some preliminary cognizance of the evolution of architectural thought will be helpful.

Architectural thought in the West from the early sixteenth to the early twentieth century has largely been conditioned by Vitruvius, and architectural precepts are given in the terms of Vitruvius, who rationalized architectural design when he said buildings must be built with due reference to firmitas, utilitas and venustas, which Morgan renders as durability, convenience and beauty, and Granger as strength,

166

utility and grace.[1] Wotton's paraphrase as 'Wellbuilding hath three conditions: Commodity, Firmness and Delight' is the most often quoted version.

The three conditions are often thought of today as suitability for purpose or fulfilment of function, structural efficiency and aesthetic pleasure. But are they sufficiently comprehensive? It depends entirely on the interpretation one puts on purpose or function.

For twenty years, between the two world wars, functionalism was the prevailing architectural theory with the dictum of appropriateness of form to function. Its adequacy as a third part in fulfilling the conditions of wellbuilding in the sense of architectural completeness required by modern western societies depends on the interpretation given to functionalism. If it were the restricted interpretation given by many architects and theorists then it is not adequate and something more is required for architecture. The restricted interpretation would involve merely material fitness for purpose; if it is a town hall with offices it would mean a building so designed that the best accommodation is provided for the most convenient and efficient use and that is all; or if it is a church, the most convenient and useful setting provided for devotion, ceremony and teaching. A comprehensive interpretation would involve in addition to physical fitness for purpose some symbolic and spiritual expression, some expression in the architectural form of the town hall building of civic dignity and pride, and some expression in the forms of the church of religious devotion, aspiration and perhaps some suggestion of mystery. If this comprehensive definition of functionalism is allowed and it stands for the utilitas (convenience or utility) of Vitruvius, the commodity (which means convenience) of Wotton, then it is adequate. But more often it is regarded as meaning merely utilitarian, and if that is accepted a fourth condition should be added to the three of Vitruvius. I think expression or symbolism might be the term.

The rationalizing legacy of Vitruvius and the restricted view of functionalism has meant that architectural developments are often explained in histories in a much too limited manner.

Professor E. Baldwin Smith complains of this limited view by architectural historians. He speaks of the prevailing tendency in describing buildings of the Middle Ages 'to disregard the political issues involved in the symbolism and to minimise the spiritual connotations as mystic, vague, and non-essential to appreciation' and he deplores the assumption 'that the motivating forces of architectural creation were always, as they are today, only structural necessity, utility, decorative desire, and a particular kind of taste'.[2] So often developments are described from the standpoint of structure and aesthetic effect.

What are the principal architectural forms and how have they evolved? There is (1) the room or hall—the enclosed space—from the cave and tent to the modern domestic room, cathedral and market hall, (2) the column, (3) the lintel arch, dome and vault, (4) the Ziggurat, pyramid, tower and their variations. Those four classifications hold the essential forms.

The impulse to rationalize obscures for us the extent to which religion and the supernatural dominated the lives of primitive men. How did primitive man think of the universe? There is plenty of evidence that he thought of the sky as a great dome above the flat earth, with the stars patterning the dome and the sun sliding over it during the day and the moon by night, and heaven just beyond the dome, which is very different from our knowledge of it. Eddington put it aptly when he said that 'instead of standing on a firm immovable earth proudly rearing our heads towards the vault of heaven, we are hanging by our feet from a globe careering through space at a great many miles a second'.[3] There were variations of this primitive conception of the universe. Some thought of it as a flat sky supported at four corners by columns, others thought of the sky as supported on a mountain (the Greek Gods dwelt on Mount Olympus), others thought of it as being supported by a great tree in the centre.

An early structure in honour of the very ancient sky god Janus was this very arch of the sky supported on columns. It seems to have originated the many triumphal arches of ancient Rome. One of the earliest remaining is the equilateral Arch of Janus. Among its legacies is the baldachino—the small dome or vault supported on four columns over the oriental throne and the altar of the Christian church. One may find in the exhaustive researches of A. B. Cook voluminous evidence to show that the triumphal arches of Rome originated as copies of man's idea of the universe with the sky supported on columns.[4] It is a form still used. Three of the most magnificent of modern war memorials are Lutyens' three great arches at Leicester, Delhi and on the Somme. They are symbols of the universe deriving from primitive man's image of it.

Springing also from man's early idea of the universe is the domed structure which existed in ancient Babylon, Persia and Etruria, which has been a prominent feature of religious buildings ever since. The dome of the mosque is still covered with stars.

In many early religions and worship the mountain figures prominently. The Gods of the Sumerians and the Greeks dwelt at the summits of lofty mountains, and God communicated with Moses on the top of Mount Sinai (Exodus xix, 20). Thus the mountain was important in early religions, and for the purpose of worship where he had not a mountain man constructed one, and these constructions resulted in the ziggurats of the Sumerians, Babylonians and Assyrians, the pyramids of the Egyptians and the topes and stupas and towers of Asian religions. Lethaby says that 'the Ziggurat is an artificial hill. The type apparently originated with the Sumerians, who, coming from a hill country into the plains, found themselves at a loss how to worship, after the manner of their forefathers, the mountain deities. It was almost inevitable that the idea of a hill with which the building originated should soon be complicated by a symbolical idea. The artificial hill is a god's hill, the seat and throne of the city's god. Since the earthly temple that crowns the Ziggurat is the reflection of his celestial house, the mound itself becomes a symbol of the heavens.'[5] Thus a temple, the abode of the god, is built on the top of the mountain which is a feature of Ziggurats. And do we not find a parallel in ancient Greece, where the Gods dwelt on Olympus, in the building of the artificial hill, the Acropolis, on which is built the temple, the abode of the God. Did not the orthodox Athenians of the fifth century believe that Athena actually dwelt in the Parthenon? The great tomb of Mausolus was possibly surmounted by a hill, certainly those of Augustus and Hadrian were, and trees were planted on them.

The similitude of numerous architectural forms and ornament to natural forms suggests their derivation. A column as a supporting form is obvious, but only to our sophisticated perceptions, and the suggestion of its derivation from a tree seems childlike to such sophistication. Yet much of the naturalism was sometimes carried over to the structure. The column of the ancient temple of Ur of the Chaldees is very like a palm tree, with the texture imitated, and Professor Bruce Allsopp thinks that the downward tapering form of the Minoan column is taken from the cypress tree out of which it was made.[6] Probably all early columns were tree trunks, and even the columns at the entrances of cave dwellings, temples and tombs were cut in imitation of them.

How far can this suggestion of imitation or representation of natural and other forms in architecture be taken? A form may be imitated for the purpose of structure or for a symbolic purpose, as the cross plan in a Christian Church. Sometimes it is the principle of the organic structure that is adopted. When Frank Lloyd Wright built the research laboratory of the Johnson building in Racine in 1947 it was built like a cedar tree with a central poll deeply rooted in the earth with the floors cantilevered out like tree branches from this central stem. The thought may have been prompted by the structure of the pagoda with its central column. When he built a house for his son in the Arizona desert in 1952 he built it in the form of a coiled rattlesnake. The forms of the Einstein observatory tower at Potsdam built by Mendelsohn in 1919 are reminiscent of optical instruments. Here are three kinds of representation, the first for purposes of structure, the second for associational reasons and the third as symbolism, because Mendelsohn used these forms also to suggest a degree of mystery.

How far the adoption of organic structural principles—those of a tree for example applied to a building—can be called representation is debatable. Worringer would not accept the adoption of organic structural principles or forms as imitation of natural phenomenon.[7] The question arises how can one separate representation from the adoption of a structural principle which necessarily carries with it many of the organic forms? To say that they are abstractions of these forms does not make it an abstract geometric conception.

The Greek cross and the Latin cross both determined the forms of churches, and they were less convenient and functional than the earlier Basilican form, but in modern ecclesiastical architecture there has been some departure from this, partly because of modern liturgical ideas and requirements. The cross plan is not the most suitable one for the congregation to group round a central altar, and this has therefore been changed to square, circular, octagonal, triangular, elliptical plans—all of which can be regarded as religious symbols. A structure that seems to pervade the semi-consciousness of designers is the representation of the tent for the Christian church. It has the sanctity of being the abode of the prophets of the Old Testament, and in Isaiah (xl. 22) we read of the figurative allusion to the tent of the heavens being stretched out as a curtain 'spreadeth out as a tent to dwell in'. The crusaders' tents give strength to the idea.

Sir Basil Spence saw his Chapel of Unity at Coventry as a star, others have seen it as a tent and such it is to many people when the idea is suggested to them. Also strongly reminiscent of the tent is the new Roman Catholic Cathedral at Liverpool designed by Sir Frederick Gibberd. In his description of the design there is no mention of a tent but an emphasis on its structural qualities—'a structure' he says, 'primarily in pure compression, utilizing the least possible amount of material and the least possible money. Some two hundred feet of tapering tower subject to high wind load is placed over the middle of a free and considerable volume of space by structural members which diminish to a few square feet when they enter the ground— a system not possible in any other stage in history, not even possible twenty years ago.' Yet looking at this cathedral I think mainly of a bell tent such as the British Army used. A similar shape can be seen in ancient Assyrian reliefs and it is probable that the Israelites had such tents. In Liverpool Cathedral the likeness is very marked with a slope similar to that of the tent, and the projecting concrete ribs anchored to the ground following the guy ropes of the tent fixed to their pegs. The architect may have been unconscious of all this, but even in artistic creation there is more of the iceberg in the deep waters of the unconscious.

The emotional, aesthetic and spiritual values of functionalism provide the symbolic aspects of architecture. Lewis Mumford expressed this view in *Art and Technics*. It is a question of balancing the functional and symbolic claims of architecture. If the former is stressed, without due regard to the latter, as in much modern work, then architecture becomes expressionless and meaningless. If the symbolic element is over-done at the expense of the functional, buildings which might be perfectly suited to their purposes are sacrificed to emotional expression, as happened, of course, in much religious architecture. But we would not willingly sacrifice any of the fine symbolic Gothic architecture for a little more functional convenience, although with industrial and office buildings, the values are necessarily different.

The accent on functionalism in modern architecture, on the other hand, has meant a sacrifice of symbolic expression, and since the Second World War some reaction has occurred against functionalism because of the paucity of architectural expression. Lewis Mumford adversely criticized the United Nations headquarters building because it fails as a symbol. He quotes the architect as saying, when the plans were presented to the Committee, 'the world hopes for a symbol of peace; we have given them a workshop of peace'. 'As if', says Mumford, 'the symbolic part of architecture, the impression it makes on the mind and the senses, is of minor importance.'[8]

The Greek temple, which is a composition mainly of verticals and horizontals, is often regarded as expressing in its forms the spirit of quiescence, of peace and resignation. This has been fancifully carried further to suggest that it expressed the feeling of resignation of the Greeks to the thought of death as final and irrevocable, without hope of a future life. That is perhaps carrying the suggestion of architectural forms too far, but it is a widely shared experience that the Greek temples and Greek architecture as a whole express very strongly feelings of serenity and repose and a suggestion of peace.

The Gothic cathedral and the Greek temple are often regarded as the two greatest architectural creations of history. Yet the Gothic cathedral in its expression is the exact reverse of the Greek temple. Instead of peace and quiescence there is constant aspiration, a daring reaching upwards expressed by vertical piers of the interior culmination in lofty vaults, and the towers and steeples outside. This is seen most eloquently in some of the great French cathedrals like Le Mans, Beauvais, Chartres and Amiens. In the mediaeval mind God and heaven were conceived as dwelling above, beyond the ethereal blue, and the architectural forms of these cathedrals seem to express a fervent reaching towards heaven, combined with a feeling of mystery expressed by the vertical movement of the piers and ribs passing into the shadows of the lofty vaults, and with this, by the very loftiness of the building, there is the stimulation of the sense of space. The whole building thus appears as an act of worship. Here is symbolism of a very real kind. With the Renaissance cathedral, like St. Peter's or St. Paul's, in which the dome is a central feature, the sense of space as a religious emotion is stimulated in a different yet powerful manner. (Plates XLII and XLIII.)

Partly from such traditions and partly from instinctive bodily feelings in response to the physical world, certain forms and effects have become appropriate to certain types of buildings. Where dignity is to be expressed, as in the offices of important institutions, or in town halls, or in the head offices of large banks, the monumental grandeur that we feel in classical architecture has often been employed; the mystery and aspiration of religion finds expression in the vertical forms and lights and shadows of Gothic architecture; or in the spaciousness of Renaissance; gaiety associated with buildings of pleasure can be expressed by a Baroque style or other lively architectural design. In some of the modern architecture of steel and concrete, symbolism has been employed to give formal emphasis to the purpose of a building. This is found particularly in the work of Eric Mendelsohn, a conspicuous example being the Potsdam Observatory built for Einstein's researches in 1920. This building is a composition of circular forms, and the curved windows in the circular tapering tower are reminiscent of optical instruments, while the deep recesses create shadows giving a sense of mystery. Thus the form of this building appears to symbolize its purpose of scientific investigation into the nature of the universe. This is not merely the subjective interpretation of a percipient; Mendelsohn himself acknowledged that some such thoughts were in his mind when he designed the building. Similar symbolic expression is found in many of Mendelsohn's sketch projects, such as a design for an optical factory where again the shapes of optical instruments influence the forms. It is also seen in his De La Warr Pavilion at Bexhill, which might be called typical marine architecture and which appears to be partially influenced in its shapes by the long lines and character of the modern liner.

It has been assumed that certain forms express certain emotions and ideas: vertical forms express aspiration, a balance of horizontal and vertical forms with slight emphasis on the former express repose; and it might be added that flowing curves express movement; swag-like forms give notes of gaiety, and diagonals restlessness. It is important to ask why these forms suggest or express these ideas. In answering this we return to the instinctive basis of art, to the origin of all art which, as Havelock Ellis said, is in the dance.[9] The association of architectural forms with certain ideas and emotions emanates from our bodily feelings and impulses which are first artistically expressed in the dance. Bodily feelings and bodily movements, as mentioned in Chapter XVI are the materials of the dance, and these feelings and movements are projected into architectural forms.

The sense of repose is expressed by horizontal forms with subordinate vertical forms. The idea of the horizontal expressing repose is obviously derived from the human body in the habitual recumbent position of rest. A man reaching upwards with his arms towards the light or towards heaven suggests aspiration, and movement generally involves some departure from the horizontal or vertical position, and the more rapid the movement the more diagonal the forms become. This may be a rather geometrical way of expressing it, but the sense is apparent. Thus there is the projection of the emotional feelings accompanying the bodily postures into the inanimate forms of buildings, as defined in the theory of *Einfühlung*, and these forms become symbols of the human emotions, and in this way architecture is a powerful vehicle of expression.[10]

The expression is necessarily, by its very nature, somewhat vague, and for this reason it has been most effective in religious buildings where a sense of mystery imparted by light and shadows and a feeling of space have greatly contributed.

This architectural symbolism is a widely shared experience. The creation of the architecture that produced these effects was largely collective action, and the experience of it, though, of course, individual, is also collective, and it is thus to a degree impersonal. There are, however, more personal kinds of symbolism in architecture, such as were mentioned in Chapter XV, or, in other words, the expression of the Architect's personality. Several architects may design in the Renaissance tradition, or in the new forms of steel and concrete, yet each gives to his design a distinctive character which emanates from his personality. Examples of architects in the Renaissance tradition have already been cited, but the same can be said of such exponents of the new architecture as Le Corbusier, Gropius, Mendelsohn and Mies van der Rohe. Although they all use modern methods and materials fully and expressively, there are fundamental differences in the work of each. In the language of symbolism this individual style means that here are personal symbols in the form of insistent curves or particular shapes, the meaning of which lie in the artist's personality.

Again, a percipient of a building may read a symbolism which is of his own creation, but which by reason of its aptness is conferred on the building for others. Henry James, looking at the Pont du Gard on a splendid afternoon of autumn, felt its quality of greatness, yet at the time he discovered in it 'a certain stupidity, a vague brutality'. 'That element', he says, 'is rarely absent from great Roman work, which is wanting in the nice adaptation of means to the end. The means are always exaggerated; the end is so much more than attained. The Roman rigidity was apt to overshoot the mark, and I suppose a race which could do nothing small is as defective as a race that can do nothing great.'[11] And thus for Henry James the Pont du Gard is not only magnificent and beautiful, but it is in some respcts a symbol of Roman power. (Plate XLIV.)

Architecture probably most successfully satisfies human needs when there is a happy balance, depending on the type of building, between function and symbol, and this must necessarily be a primary aim of architects. The extremes are an industrial building where function is all-important, but where the introduction of the symbolic element might also have a place, and the religious building where the symbol is fundamental. In the buildings between these extremes the balance must be carefully adjusted. The humanist in his fulfilment of function is more likely to comprehend the symbolic element than the architect who is primarily a technician. Narrow functionalism and exclusive preoccupation with the solution of technical problems often results in uninteresting and aesthetically negligible buildings. Modern architecture shows vividly that the mid-twentieth century is an age of technicians; more artists are necessary if the essential spiritual values of civilization are to be preserved and enhanced.

REFERENCES

1. VITRUVIUS, 1–3–2, English translations by Morris Hicky Morgan (Harvard, 1914) and by Granger (London, 1931).
2. E. BALDWIN SMITH, *Architectural Symbolism of Imperial Rome and the Middle Ages* (Princeton, 1956).
3. ARTHUR EDDINGTON, *The Nature of the Physical World*, Chapter XII (London, 1928).
4. A. B. COOK, *Zeus—A Study in Ancient Religion*, 2 vols. (Cambridge, 1911 and 1925).
5. W. R. LETHABY, *Architecture, Nature and Magic*, p. 42 (London, 1956). Lethaby is condensing a description by C. Leonard Woolley.
6. BRUCE ALLSOPP, *A History of Classical Architecture*, p. 9 (London, 1965).
7. WILHELM WORRINGER, *Abstraction and Empathy*—a contribution to the Psychology of Style. Chapter on Ornament in Practical Section. First published in Munich in 1908. There have been several editions since. English translation by Michael Bullock (1963).
8. LEWIS MUMFORD, *From the Ground Up*, p. 32. Mumford deals with 'Architecture as Symbol', also in *Culture of Cities*, pp. 402–15 (London, 1938).
9. HAVELOCK ELLIS, *The Dance of Life* (London, 1923).
10. The theory of *Einfühlung* was developed by THEODOR LIPPS in *Archiv für die gesamte Psychologie* (Hamburg and Leipzig, 1903), and later by J. VOLKELT in *System der Asthetik* (Munich, 1927). It is rendered in English as *empathy*. Many English and American writers have further developed and applied the theory, among whom may be mentioned VERNON LEE, *Beauty and Ugliness and Other Studies in Psychological Aesthetics*, (London, 1912); BERNHARD BERENSEN, who applies the idea chiefly to the painting of Florence and Central Italy, *The Italian Painters of the Renaissance* (London, 1930); LORD LISTOWEL, survey and analysis, in *A Critical History of Modern Aesthetics* (London, 1933), pp. 51–82 and 169–92. Application to architecture: GEOFFREY SCOTT, *The Architecture of Humanism* (London, 1914), particularly Chapter VIII, 'Humanist Values'; ARNOLD WHITTICK, *Eric Mendelsohm* (London, 1956), Chapter 9; also *European Architecture in the Twentieth Century*, 2 vols. (London, 1950–53), particularly Vol. II, Chapters LIV and LVI.
11. HENRY JAMES, *A Little Tour in France* (London, 1885).

XIX   Sculpture

IN symbolic sculpture, as in all art, there is the important distinction between a subject which is a symbol, and vague symbolism of ideas and emotions expressed by means of the forms of the work. The former type comprises representations in sculpture of known symbols like the Egyptian sphinx, the winged lion and bull of ancient Assyria, the lion and eagle with their numerous symbolic meanings, St. George and the dragon as symbolic of the triumph of good over evil, all of which exist as symbols apart from any particular sculptures of them. Included in this type are traditional representations of Christian saints and other religious figures, who are generally shown with their emblems, like St. Peter with a key and St. Paul with a sword, although the emblems vary somewhat with different periods and countries. Thus St. Peter is sometimes shown with two keys, sometimes with a key and model of a church, sometimes with keys and closed book.[1]

In addition, certain ideas have often been embodied in sculpture, so that conventional figures with appropriate emblems have been developed, like the figure of Time, usually shown as an old man with a scythe, and the figure of Justice usually shown as a woman with scales and a sword. These have become conventional recognizable types, and the symbolism resides in the subject. These representations of known symbols are covered in Part IV.

Sometimes these traditional symbols are combined in a design in a particularly expressive manner, and memorial art provides some good examples, In the memorial in the Compiègne Forest near Paris, which marks the spot where the Armistice of 11th November, 1918 was signed, a sword forms a cross in an arch and a German eagle pierced by the sword lies at its foot. The Madonna and Child, in addition to being a representation of the Virgin and the Christ Child, can also be taken as symbolic of the care for and importance of future generations. It was probably a thought of this kind which prompted the war memorial by Antoine Bourdelle at Niederbruck, which shows a great figure of the Virgin holding aloft for all to see the infant figure of Jesus, the symbolism implicit in it being that men sacrificed their lives that future generations should enjoy the benefits of Christian civilization. A similar symbolic theme is found in the memorial to Margaret MacDonald (wife of Ramsay MacDonald) in Lincoln's Inn Fields, consisting of a seat surmounted by a woman extending protecting arms to a group of children.[2] (Plate XLVI (*a*) and (*b*).)

In the grounds of the Shell building in The Hague is a sculpture of a child taking a sheaf of wheat out of a shell. This was erected in gratitude by the employees of the Shell Company, because during the German occupation the Shell Company rendered much valuable service in supplying Dutch children with food; the sculpture symbolizes that service. (Plate XLVI (c).)

Essentially symbolic sculpture, however, is that in which ideas and emotions are expressed by the sculptured forms occurring in figures and designs which express ideas like peace, mourning, victory, or the seasons of the year, or twilight and dawn. The symbolism is not dependent on any conventional or recognizable type of figure or object, but is suggested by the shapes and rhythms, which by their nature cannot be precise, but are rather vague like music in its suggestiveness, yet often far more powerful and effectual than the more precise types of symbolism.

Symbolic figures of this kind occur only very occasionally in ancient Greece and Rome. Originally the sculptures of some of the gods were of this kind, because they were human symbols or personifications of the elements—Apollo the Sun, Artemis the Moon, Demeter the Earth, Persephone the Spring—but, like the traditional figures of Time and Justice, they became conventionalized to definite types, while, being gods, they were idealized to transcend the merely human. More strictly of the type where the forms express the ideas and emotions is such a classical Greek figure as that of a mourning woman, which is now in the British Museum. This work possibly belongs to the fourth century B.C. The full drapery of the figure covers both arms and hands and is carried over the head. The slightly bent head, the pensive expression of the face, the limp posture convincingly convey the feelings of sorrow.[3] (Plate XLVIII (a).)

In Greece and Rome the principal subjects for sculpture were the gods and goddesses and mythological themes, such as the birth of Athena, and the contest of Athena and Poseidon on the pediments of the Parthenon. In Rome portraiture was later a common subject. In Gothic sculpture, Christ and the Virgin, the saints and angels, carvings of incidents of Biblical history and Christian symbols, were the principal themes. The only other subjects that occur to any extent are the recumbent effigies for tombs and memorials, which often involve a degree of portraiture. These religious themes and memorials continued to be the principal subjects during the Renaissance until the latter part of the fifteenth century, when classical and other secular subjects were increasingly apparent, and we find some interesting and impressive examples of symbolic sculpture.

The most moving and impressive of all are Michelangelo's famous figures on the tombs of Guiliano and Lorenzo de Medici in the New Sacristy of San Lorenzo in Florence. Reclining on the sarcophagus, beneath the alert figure of Duke Guiliano seated in the niche, are the figures of 'Night' and 'Day'; the former is depicted as a woman seemingly in deep but restless sleep, the latter as a powerful male figure in a defiant attitude of awakening. The figures on the sarcophagus beneath the pensive and thoughtful figure of Duke Lorenzo are 'Dawn' and 'Twilight', the former a massive female figure awakening from sleep, and the latter the powerful male figure sinking to rest. (Plate XLVII.)

It was apparently Michelangelo's intention to show by means of these figures, and others never executed, the elemental powers of earth and heaven mourning over the death of the Dukes; the idea was probably derived from the symbolization of the elements by gods in human shape in classical mythology. However, the powerful symbolism of these figures expresses far more than sorrow and grief for the death of Florentine princes; here we have, rather, a mournful comment on the burden and tragedy of life. The two restless figures on the tomb of Guiliano seem to be a powerful and rebellious protest against the iniquities, difficulties and troubles of life. On the tomb of Lorenzo the figure of Dawn awakes with sadness, weariness and foreboding, and it is with no sense of peace and content but rather of melancholy recollection of the troubled day that the figure of Twilight sinks to rest. And the expression of these thoughts and emotions does not exist only in the faces (that of Day is but roughly sketched in the marble) but in the dynamic character of the figures and the rhythms of their forms. Here the symbolism exists in the complete figures, enhancing their grandeur and power; and it is doubtful whether in the whole history of art the symbolic power of sculpture is so movingly demonstrated.

In such work, where the ideas and emotions of the artist, partly conscious and partly unconscious, are expressed, everything depends on their re-creation by the spectator by means of the symbolic forms. The symbolism is necessarily somewhat vague, the creation of the artist and the re-creation of the spectator are subjective, thus it may mean that there is some variation between the two, the spectator may receive much of the unconscious emotion of the artist consciously. The interpretation of all art is subjective, but the sculptures of these Medici tombs generate by their nature a wider subjectivity than most works of art. Thus interpretations are varied, an example of a particularly speculative one being that of Walter Pater, who thought that the titles of the four symbolic figures—'Night' and 'Day', 'The Twilight' and 'The Dawn' far too definite for them. 'They concentrate and express', he says, 'less by way of definite conceptions than by the touches, the promptings of a piece of music, all those vague fancies, misgivings, presentiments, which shift and mix and are defined and fade again, whenever the thoughts try to fix themselves with sincerity on the conditions and surroundings of the disembodied spirit.' And from these figures, together with the most significant of Michelangelo's other work, Pater suggests Michelangelo's whole attitude to spiritual life.[4]

Among the most powerfully impressive symbolic sculptures are Michelangelo's of slaves or prisoners now in the gallery of the Academy in Florence. They were originally intended for the tomb of Pope Julius II and they are generally considered to be unfinished but this is doubtful. The struggles of these powerful figures half buried in the rock from which, it seems, they labour to be released, symbolizes the fierce struggles of humanity from bondage.

Two of the most impressive symbolic sculptures in modern art are the two figures of 'Night' and 'Day', over the entrances of the London Transport Executive Building at St. James's. The influence of ancient Egypt is apparent in these monumental figures. 'Night' is shown as a massive draped seated figure, holding across her knees the sleeping figure of a child. With the right hand she holds the head of the child, while the left arm is held almost horizontal above the child's recumbent form. Here, it seems, is the brooding spirit of night. It symbolizes in a monumental manner a great city asleep, and the forms are clearly designed to give this feeling. Whereas in 'Night' the prevailing form is horizontal, in 'Day' it is vertical, for between the legs of the seated figure a child stands upright and stretches upwards with his arms to the neck of the seated figure. Both figures are alert, in contrast to the massive restful figure of 'Night'.[5] The symbolism is more precise and definite than in the figures of the same names by Michelangelo, but the Medici figures, in admitting a wide range of speculation, seem thus to gain in power. (Plate XLIX.)

It has been suggested that some of the developments of modern sculpture towards more abstract form, like the work of C. Brancusi, Barbara Hepworth, and some of the work of Henry Moore, carry with them a degree of symbolism. Important purposes of these developments appear to be a more exclusive concentration on form and an expression of the materials in which the form is embodied. They probably carry a degree of personal symbolism, partly conscious and partly unconscious. Surrealism, which is, of course, essentially symbolic expression, has exerted some influence on modern sculpture, but as it has manifested far more strongly in painting it can fittingly be considered in the next chapter.

In the international sculpture competition sponsored by the Institute of Contemporary Arts in 1951, the subject was the theme of 'The Unknown Political Prisoner', which was selected (in the words of the President of the Institute, Sir Herbert Read)

> 'to pay tribute to those individuals who, in many countries and in diverse political situations, had dared to offer their liberty and their lives for the cause of human freedom. Our complex civilization has found its crisis in the contradiction that exists between individual concepts of truth and duty and totalitarian concepts of uniformity and blind obedience. Everywhere the human conscience has been in revolt against inhuman tyrannies. In that conflict lies the unique tragedy of our age, and the sculptors of the world, of the whole world, were asked to accept the challenge of such a theme and to express its significance in a monumental style. They responded in their thousands.'[6]

Here was an opportunity for powerful symbolic expression, yet judging from the prize winning entries and others, some one hundred and forty, which were exhibited at the International Exhibition at the Tate Gallery in 1953, the result was disappointing and the competitors showed little creative imagination.

The designs had generally a symbolic sameness. Most of the sculptors used the prison, or cage, as a motif expressed by various designs of metal structures. Mirko Basoldella of Italy, a principal prizewinner, showed a tall network mounted on a stepped pedestal with a figure gazing into it, and another standing at attention a little away.

A similar design was that of the American sculptor, Richard Lippold, whose network composed into a tall pyramid, with a solitary figure, tiny by comparison, at the base. The brothers Antoine Pevsner and Naum Gabo, both second-prize winners, showed abstract patterns, that of the former being a complicated design of nets composed largely of geometric radiating and circular forms, while the latter's design was more formal, somewhat like two delicate upright fins with a tall pole between them. The design of Luciano Minquizza of Italy was a little like strange animal forms caught in barbed wire entanglements. The best design, which had an element of grandeur, was that of the first-prize winner, Reg Butler. It was an immense (judging by the two solitary figures) steel structure on a rock expressive of prison and gallows and perhaps a pulpit. Few sculptors seemed to get away from the theme of the prison or cage expressed in terms of the steel structure and patterns of modern building; and it was a case where contemporary architecture has had a very strong influence on sculpture, as the designs would have been different had the competition been held, say, forty years earlier. One design, that of Nehmet Sadi Calik, was just a composition of steel stanchions suggesting the structural skeleton of a prison.

Here was a case where the use of rather stereotyped symbolism did not result in any powerfully expressive works. The reason for the failure was that the subject was not a good one. It is really too remote and intellectual, whereas if a sculptor is asked to symbolize in plastic form the elemental things of life which belong to his own instinctive being there is bound to be a readier imaginative response. The subjects of the figures of Michelangelo's Medici tombs—night and day and twilight and dawn— spring from the emotional lives of all men.

Since the break away from the classical tradition in modern sculpture there is perhaps more symbolic expression than ever. It is more successful when the subject emanates from the sculptor than when he has to work to a given subject. Most sculptors of any merit have something to say in their own medium, and the freedom to choose the subject and the most appropriate means of expression are the conditions which seem to be conducive to some of the most vital modern work. Several interesting examples of good symbolic expression have appeared at the open-air international exhibitions arranged by the London County Council, at Battersea Park in 1948, 1951, 1960, 1963, and 1966, and in Holland Park in 1954 and 1957. Two works from the last mentioned afford interesting examples. One is a figure entitled 'Man 1957' by Siegfried Charoux in cemented iron. It shows a strong man wearing a helmet and standing erect, with legs astride a heavy machine, firmly holding two handles. It is a symbol of our industrial age. The sculptor said of it that he had set himself 'the task of finding a theme peculiar to our time and shaping it in a material and technique also peculiar to our time, and the result is Man 1957'.

The other work is 'Warrior with Shield' in bronze by Henry Moore. It is a seated figure of a man holding a shield in his right arm, with the left arm and left leg amputated, and the right leg cut off at the foot. This finely modelled figure though maimed shows defiance and strength and the stubborn power to resist, a stubbornness expressed in what might be called an abstract of the human face. The sculptor himself says:

'The idea came from a pebble which reminded me of the stump of an amputated leg. The figure is perhaps emotionally connected with experiences and feeling about England during the crucial part of the last war. The sculpture is intended to express a battered but heroic resistance to physical misfortune. The head has a blunted and bull-like power, but also a sort of dumb animal acceptance and forbearance of pain.'

This fine delineation of vigorous form succeeds in being a powerful symbolic expression. (Plate XLVIII (b).)

The tendency of many modern sculptors is towards what is generally called abstract sculpture, although much of it has a starting point in representation. The aesthetic value of such sculpture depends chiefly on formal relations, as does architecture, but it often also has an expressional content which is necessarily symbolic. Abstract sculpture can be broadly divided into organic and geometric. Much of the latter where the medium is often metal, is symbolic of modern engineering and modern construction and it is essentially sculpture of an industrial and technological civilization. Sculpture that derives from organic forms is generally more profound and significant. It can be expressive of that organic interdependence which is symbolical of the natural integration of all forms of life.

REFERENCES

1. Numerous works deal with the emblems of the saints, among which may be mentioned, S. BARING GOULD, *Lives of the Saints* (London, 1897); MRS. ANNA JAMESON, *Sacred and Legendary Art*, 3rd edition (London, 1857) and P. H. DITCHFIELD, *Symbolism of the Saints* (London, 1910).
2. ARNOLD WHITTICK, *War Memorials* (London, 1946). The three memorials mentioned are reproduced in this book.
3. A good general book on Greek sculpture is that of E. A. GARDNER, *Handbook of Greek Sculpture* (London, 1911), and on Roman sculpture, MRS. EUGENIE STRONG, *Roman Sculpture* (London, 1907).
4. WALTER PATER. Essay on the Poetry of Michelangelo in *The Renaissance, Studies in Art and Poetry* (London, 1873).
5. JACOB EPSTEIN, autobiography, *Let there be Sculpture* (London, 1942).
6. SIR HERBERT READ. Foreword to the catalogue of the International Exhibition of Grand Prize Winner and other Prize-winning Entries and Runners-up. Tate Gallery, March–April, 1953.

XX Painting

IN painting, as in architecture and sculpture, symbolism is of two main kinds: that which is contained in the subject, and that which resides in the design. In the latter, ideas and emotions are expressed by the abstract forms of the picture.

The birth of western painting in the modern world is generally ascribed to the early Florentine and Sienese painters of the late thirteenth and early fourteenth centuries and coincides with the change from mosaic to fresco and tempera painting. Then began the long and arduous journey towards more realistic and vivid representations of the external world. Florentine painters especially, in the two hundred and fifty years from the works of Giotto to those of Leonardo da Vinci and Michelangelo, grappled with problems of representation so that the external world could be vividly revealed, not only as the eye perceived it, but as knowledge conceived it to be. It would seem that here was a movement away from an art which depends on symbolic expression. Instead of expressing the Christian religion by means of symbols, or by formal and conventional types, the purpose was to present realistic and vivid images of Christ, of the Saints and the significant incidents of Biblical and Christian history. Symbols of the attached kind were employed as significant details, like the lily in the hand of the angel in pictures of the Annunciation, the nimbus surrounding or over the heads of Christ, the Virgin and Saints, and the Dove signifying the Holy Ghost, while Saints are often shown with their emblems. Symbolism of a broader, less precise type is introduced into some pictures; a good and common example is the introduction of classical ruins as a background to pictures of the Virgin and Child, and the Adoration of the Kings or Shepherds. This was intended to symbolize the rise of Christianity and the ruin or end of the pagan world. An early example is the picture of the 'Nativity' at Siena by Francesco di Giorgio, which shows the Virgin and Saints kneeling round the infant Christ, with part of a ruin in the background. The setting of the 'Adoration of the Magi' by Paolo Veronese consists of the ruins of Roman classical architecture. The 'Adoration of the Kings' by the Flemish artist Mabuse is set in the midst of magnificent classical ruins. The very beautiful 'Virgin and Child' ascribed to Dürer, which, like the two pictures previously mentioned, is in the National Gallery, carries a similar symbolism. Immediately behind the Virgin, in her flowing red dress, are flowers and foliage, among them the iris and vine, and beyond are classical ruins and the sea. (Plate LIV.)

The symbolism that resides in the forms and design of a picture, as in the forms of Gothic architecture, was apparent in varying degrees in the early European religious paintings of the fourteenth and fifteenth centuries. The linear rhythms which are found in the religious pictures of Duccio, Simone Martini, Fra Filippo Lippi, Botticelli and El Greco are often eloquent of the religious emotions that their paintings express. In the picture of the Pietà by an unknown painter of Avignon (Plate LVI (a)), the bent form of the woman in unison with the limp figure of Christ reinforces and intensifies the feelings of pity and grief so movingly conveyed by the picture. The linear rhythms of Botticelli are charged with meaning so that the forms are symbols of ideas and emotions. The three figures on the right of the Primavera (Plate LVI (b)) are symbolic of the months changing from the cold and strong winds of winter to the gay and sprightly figure of spring with the transitional figure between. And rarely is religious fervour more powerfully expressed than in Botticelli's 'Nativity', in the National Gallery, where figures clasp one another, and the angels of heaven dance through the air in ecstasy. The symbolic element in Botticelli's use of line is educed in Brown and Rankin's description of Botticelli's drawings for Dante's *Divine Comedy*. 'The line sings, as it were, now in a tense springing, now in lyric-like spontaneity, now in rich flowing measures, ever one, yet ever changing, with modulating accents and intervals like a fine poem, suggesting life, yet disembodied and free, like early Japanese painting.'[1] And the strong expression of religious passion in the work of El Greco owes much to the value of the linear forms seen in the abstract. These combined with the use of colour and light and shadow, give the strong emotional tone to the pictures.

Reference was made in Chapter XV to the stimulation of religious feeling by the creation in a picture of a sense of space. When this is associated with a religious subject the feeling is intensified. It is found in the pictures of Piero della Francesca, and developed by Perugino and Raphael. The sense of space so often given by their pictures—an impressive example being Perugino's 'Crucifixion' seen through three arches in Santa Maria Maddalen Pazzi, Florence—is akin to the feeling of space created by the interior of large Gothic and Renaissance churches, like the Duomo at Florence or St. Paul's Cathedral in London. This again is a type of vague symbolism.[2] (Plate LV.)

The kind of symbolism that we find in the religious painting of the early Renaissance was revived with some intensity in the work of the Pre-Raphaelites, Rossetti, Holman Hunt and Millais. Many of their pictures, as for example Rossetti's 'Dante's Dream,' at Liverpool, are full of symbolic details, while in some cases the whole expression of the picture is of a symbolic character, as Holman Hunt's 'The Scapegoat' and 'The Light of the World', which both carry with them a strong moral purpose.

Symbolism as a vehicle of moral teaching is employed even more definitely in the paintings of G. F. Watts: indeed it would appear that this moral teaching was one of the main purposes of his painting, and he achieved it largely by means of symbolism. The pictures called 'Life's Illusion', 'Love and Life', 'Love and Death', 'The Angel of Death', 'Time, Death and Judgment' and 'Hope' all bear symbolic meanings with a moral purpose. As the symbols are not traditional and recognizable, but are of Watt's own invention, the meanings are not always apparent, and require explanation for their understanding; this is a serious disadvantage if they are to serve the purpose Watts intended. Thus, the picture of 'Love and Life' shows a powerful winged figure, with a weak female figure. The former is intended to represent 'Love' and the latter 'Life', and Love is depicted assisting the weak figure of Life up the difficult and rocky mountain path. It is obvious that without some such explanation the meaning would not be apparent. Even more obscure is the picture 'Hope', which shows a figure seated on the world listening, with bent head, to the sound of the lyre that she is playing. She plays only one string as the others are broken, and strives to get all the music possible from the one remaining. The music is apparently a symbol of the good in the world. Watts has explained his meanings, but to make the art of painting dependent for its expression on a literary explanation is hardly to use the medium well.

The pictures of both the Pre-Raphaelites and Watts demonstrate, however, the divorce between this kind of subject symbolism and aesthetic values. The colour and design of much of the work of the Pre-Raphaelites is of high excellence, but it does not depend on the conscious symbolic expression. Yet it should be observed that the very intensity of spirit that employed the symbolic expression was probably in part responsible for the interest of the designs.

With the twentieth century and the many modern movements in art, the place of symbolism in painting became a little more complex. The suggestion made by Sir Herbert Read in *Art Now* that in modern painting there is the complete change from the desire 'to reproduce in some way exactly what the eye sees', which is the main tradition of European painting, to symbolic expression, 'which shall be more significant of reality than any reproduction can be', was discussed in Chapter XV. It was questioned whether it is possible to make this distinction between traditional and modern painting, and it was suggested that this symbolism, which is more significant of reality than reproduction is not the prerogative of modern art, but belongs equally to much traditional art, especially Florentine paintings of the Renaissance. A hint of this is given in the quotation previously cited from Brown and Rankin's comments on the drawings of Botticelli when they say that 'the line sings . . . suggesting life yet disembodied and free like early Japanese painting'. It is not possible to make a clear differentiation between traditional and modern art by saying that in one the appearances of the actual world are reproduced and that in the other expression is by means of a symbolism of the realities underlying appearance. It is rather a matter of varying degrees of abstraction and emphasis for the purposes of expression which are found in all periods of art, although particularly marked in modern painting.

Sir Herbert Read reasserts this attitude in a later book on *The Philosophy of Modern Art* when he speaks of 'the distinction between image and symbol, which is fundamental to an understanding of the modern movement in art' and he suggests that the 'co-existence of the image and the symbol, as norms of art, explains the apparent complexity and disunity of the modern movement'.[3] It is the greater degree of abstraction which has presented difficulties in the understanding of modern art. Abstraction can be defined as distortion, or better still, conversion, of natural forms for the purpose of expressional design; and by this means it becomes symbolism. The expression of essential structure underlying appearance, which was such a pre-occupation with the Florentines of the Renaissance and which is a strong influence in some modern painting since Cézanne, could also be regarded as a kind of symbolism.

The symbolism by means of abstraction can be of various kinds. It can be in a precise conscious form, as in many pictures painted by Picasso, between 1925 and 1935, and which he called merely 'Abstractions'. There is evidence however to indicate that when Picasso painted some of these pictures he 'let himself go' without any definite intention or control, somewhat in the manner of doodling. Here, apparently, the intention is to give freedom to the untrammelled aesthetic impulse in the hope that some of the underlying urges and realities may emerge. It might be suggested that this method gives freedom to what Roger Fry calls emotional tone, which he amplifies as 'the residual traces left on the spirit by the different emotions of life without the limitation and particular direction it had in experience'.

In the more precise and conscious abstractions of Paul Klee the shapes and colours suggestive of his subject form the design; as when he paints a picture of 'Spring', the shapes and colours that make his pattern are strongly evocative of spring, and some of the shapes are recognizable representations. This is seen in pictures like 'Gay breakfast table' and 'Gay mountain landscape' where the recognizable objects like wine-glass, bottle, fork are arranged as a pattern somewhat as a child would arrange them. The more successful pictures of Paul Klee, however, are those in which the abstraction is more complete, so that recognition of objects suggests the feeling of the subject less than the colours and shapes, which thereby become the finer symbols. (Plate LVII.)

Symbolism is a fundamental part of the modern movement in art known as Surrealism, a movement which arrested much attention and prompted much controversy in the nineteen thirties. The symbolism here is of the unconscious type revealed in psychoanalysis. In form and essence it is really of the simple direct traditional type.

Surrealism in art, although it emerges from the irrationalism of Dadaism and is influenced by the earlier movement Expressionism, is made possible by, and is indeed based on the theories of psychoanalysis of Freud and the theories of analytical psychology of Jung. As was said in Chapter XII on Instinctive and Unconscious Symbolism, powerful instinctive urges of a kind repugnant to consciousness are repressed by the super-ego. So powerful are these urges that they cannot be completely repressed, so they emerge in consciousness transformed to more acceptable forms as symbolism by the censoring agent of the super-ego. The emergence takes place in the dreams of sleep, or in the relaxed state of uncontrolled thought, as in day-dreaming. Thus the instinctive urges are symbolized in dreams. Such urges are often sexual in character, because it is these which, by reason of the influences of social and ethical standards, are sometimes repugnant to consciousness.

The censorship, which is the symbolizing agent, selects symbols from the familiar world, but as these relations are determined by the repressed impulse a curious jumble usually results, and thus we get the strong and irrational character of most dreams. Or it may be, as Nietzsche and Jung[4] assert, that as these symbols represent the basic and primitive urges of our beings they are essentially the same as the symbolism and images of primitive peoples; that our dreams reveal our links with the primitive beliefs and desires, and that the symbolism of our personal unconsciousness is but a repetition of the symbolism of a universal unconsciousness, when man existed in a far more childlike and primitive state.

This symbolism is the subject of surrealist art. The meaning of the term—super realism—indicates that by means of the symbolism of dreams the submerged essential realities of life are expressed. If, therefore, a person with a gift for painting has a strange dream in which objects are curiously related, as probably in many previous dreams, and he paints as clearly as possible the vision of his dream, then he paints a surrealist picture. The strange assemblage of objects in many of the pictures by Max Ernst, Giorgio De Chirico, Picasso, Paul Nash and Salvador Dali, are a collection of symbols expressing submerged realities, which can be wholly or partly read by the psychologist. They are therefore psychological documents. The pictures of each artist have characteristics in common, and each artist seems to express dreams of certain recurring types. Thus the not uncommon dreams of deserted cities find expression in Chirico's pictures, although he places strange objects in the cities that seem more personal to himself. Strange monsters emerge in Max Ernst's pictures, as if he were preoccupied with primitive animal forms. Thus we may say that the essential subject of surrealist art is the symbolism of dreams and the irrational yet natural characters of life which are expressive of inner realities.[5]

A surrealist painting is a psychological document to be read by an interpreter, and the more faithfully it reproduces a dream the more valuable it is as a psychological document. Any changes of arrangement or details of subject made for purposes of design must lessen its value as a document. They may however be desired from aesthetic considerations, since a surrealist picture, like any other, succeeds as a work of art primarily by reason of its design, its relation of forms and colour. Its purposeful symbolism is artistically valuable as providing fresh subjects for the artist, and thereby increasing the variety of designs and pictures that can be provided for aesthetic delight.

It should be emphasized in conclusion that symbolism, which is used as a vehicle of conscious expression to enforce meaning and to make the emotional content of the subject more vivid and intense, as in some of the pictures of Paul Klee, is an important additional value to the essentials of design, form and colour.

REFERENCES
1. A. V. V. BROWN and W. RANKIN, *A Short History of Italian Painting*, p. 133 (London, 1914).
2. BERNARD BERENSEN, *The Central Italian Painters of the Renaissance* (London, 1909).
3. HERBERT READ, *The Philosophy of Modern Art*, pp. 19–26 (London, 1952).
4. C. G. JUNG, *Psychology of the Unconscious*. English translation, p. 14 (New York, 1921).
5. See ANDRÉ BRETON. *What is Surrealism*. English translation by David Gascoyne (London, 1936). Also HERBERT READ, *Art and Society* (London, 1936, 2nd edition, revised 1945); and *Surrealism* (London, 1936) to which Herbert Read writes an introduction.

XXI Drama—the Theatre and Cinema

LANGUAGE, by means of symbols, presents images and ideas to the mind—by sounds in speech, by visual signs in written language. By simile or analogy or association there is the additional symbolism of an idea or image standing for or suggesting another, and this is often a powerful means of expression.

By this symbolism in the theatre or cinema a tremendous amount of meaning can be concentrated into a moment. It can in a brief form epitomize the meaning or point of a whole play; or it can indicate by simple means, by an apparent trifle often, the emotional drift or trend. It will be found generally that this symbolism is employed in the second and third classifications given in Chapter I, that is, by association, by means of visual signs which lead to the meaning, or by analogy where the meaning of the whole play or part of a play is signified in miniature. Where symbolism of this kind has been aptly employed in the drama or on the screen, it will be found that it has generally given added power and lucidity to the work; although sometimes symbolism of an obscure and ambiguous character has been the main vehicle of expression and has resulted in drama which has done little more than provide a subject of controversy.

In the work of many famous dramatists, symbolism, as distinct from direct un-adorned representation, has been employed with great effect. Dramatists such as Ibsen, Chekhov, Barrie and many others, made full use of it. With the two first named the symbols sometimes form the titles of the plays, as in 'A Doll's House', 'The Wild Duck' and the 'Seagull'. In these plays the symbolism employed does much to enforce the meaning.

In Chekhov's 'The Seagull' a bird is shot and killed for sport, and forms the symbol of the young girl, Nina Zarietchnaya, who falls in love with a famous author, Boris Tregorin. He rather wantonly responds to her persistent attentions. In the second act, Constantine Treplieff, who is in love with Nina, shoots the seagull and lays it at her feet, remarking, as she picks it up, 'So shall I soon end my own life.' At the end of the second act Tregorin notices the dead seagull, and then, in reply to Nina's question 'What are you writing?' says

'Nothing much, only an idea that occurred to me. An idea for a short story. A young girl grows up on the shores of a lake as you have. She loves the lake, as the gulls do, and is as happy and free as they. But a man sees her who chances to come that way, and he destroys her out of idleness, as this gull here has been destroyed.'

185

That is a prophecy of Nina's own future. After two years Tregorin tires of her, and she is desolate and miserable. She has a child which dies.

In telling Eugene Dom, the doctor, of her fate, Treplieff says in the fourth act that in her letters 'she never complains but I can tell that she is profoundly unhappy; not a line but speaks to me of an aching, breaking nerve. She has one strange fancy: she always signs herself "The Seagull".' And when she secretly returns to Sorin's house and tells Treplieff of her life, she twice refers to herself as a seagull, and remarks 'Do you remember how you shot a seagull once? A man chanced to pass that way and destroyed it out of idleness.' Towards the end of the play, just before Treplieff shoots himself, Shamraeff, the manager of Sorin's estate, says to Tregorin 'Here is the stuffed seagull I was telling you about. You told me to have it done,' and Tregorin very expressively replies 'I don't remember a thing about it, not a thing.' Nina was not the only casualty of Tregorin's wanton sport with the seagull, as Treplieff killed himself because of his failure in his work and in winning Nina's love. The symbolism adds poignancy to the play.

In Ibsen's 'The Wild Duck' the symbolism is not quite so direct. There is the sense that both the young girl Hedvig and the duck that symbolizes her are the victims of selfishness, blindness and stupidity. The wild duck was shot under the wing so that she couldn't fly; she fell into the water and dived to the bottom; but a dog fetched her up, and she was given to Ekdal, who kept her in a garret with his rabbits. Gregers Werle asks, 'She thrives as well as possible in the garret there?' And Hialmar Ekdal replies, 'Yes, wonderfully well. She has got fat. You see, she has lived in there so long now that she has forgotten her natural wild life; and it all depends on that.' Gregers says in reply, 'You are right there, Hialmar. Be sure you never let her get a glimpse of the sky and the sea——'

The theme of the play is that a young girl, Hedvig, very fond of her father, Hialmar Ekdal, shoots herself because she thinks that her father has ceased to love her. Actually, the father, who is stupid and self-centred, has learnt of his wife's affairs with Werle, Gregers' father, in whose house she was a servant before her marriage, and begins to have doubts whether he is the father of Hedvig. He thus indulges in masochistic behaviour—thinks he cannot live under the same roof as his wife, thinks he has no right to his daughter's love, begins to doubt his daughter's love for him, and repulses her gestures of affection—behaviour which results in her suicide. She is a victim of selfish, stupid behaviour on the part of the father, aggravated by the interfering idealism of the so-called friend, Gregers Werle. She is a victim, just as the wounded wild duck is a victim, of a lack of imagination and understanding. The symbolism is interesting, but it has not the clarity of that of 'The Seagull'.

In the Australian play 'Summer of the Seventeenth Doll' by Ray Lawler, which was produced in London in the summer of 1957, the doll of the title acts as a symbolic focal point. It is the story of two men, Barney Ibbot and Roo Webber, who work on a sugar plantation in Queensland for seven months of each year, and then go south to live for the lay-off, the five summer months, with two women in a cottage in Carlton, Victoria, which belongs to the mother of one of them, Mrs. Leech. This habit of life has lasted unchanged for sixteen years. The play opens in the seventeenth year with the return of the men: but this year one of the women, Nancy, has married, and is not there for Barney. The men always bring presents for their women, and one special present that Roo brings for Olive Leech each year is a doll. These dolls she treasures above the other presents, as they are to her symbols of the return of her man each year, and the five months of happiness.

A widow, Pearl Cunningham, is on a visit to the house when the men arrive. There is perhaps a prospect of her taking Nancy's place, but it does not work out like that.

Roo Webber, a big strong man, is the leader of his gang—a position which in this last year seems, at least to him, to be in danger of being challenged by a sturdy young man named Johnnie Dowd. Owing to an upset, Roo had left the gang and returned to the cottage without money. He gets a job in the city, and his changed position is the cause of rows with Barney, and of tension with the women. Barney tries to reconcile Roo with Johnnie Dowd, but this merely intensifies the rows between Barney and Roo, which become violent, and have a bad effect on the women. Everything seems to go wrong, and these unhappy occurrences are very different from the previous sixteen lay-offs. Roo asks Olive's mother what is wrong with him, and she replies that they are getting old and these things do not go on for ever. Further friction with Olive reduces her to violent tears. He then tells her that he will keep his job in the city and not return to the plantation, and he asks her to marry him. That is not her idea of happiness, which is the five months of each year with her fine strong man who had been working in the sun in the Queensland plantation for the other seven months. So she just walks out. In grief he smashes the doll, symbol of his return each year for seventeen years, and symbol of their happiness for sixteen summers. For that their life was spent.

The meaning would have been clear without the doll, but the symbol gives it poignancy, enhances its significance, and adds to the expressional power.

Clear, simple symbolism has been used with great effect in films. An excellent example occurred in the late Sir Alexander Korda's film 'Rembrandt', produced in 1935. Some little time after the death of his first wife, Saskia, Rembrandt goes mournfully up into a disused room where the dust lies thick. He writes with his finger the name Saskia in the dust on the table. At that moment his housekeeper passes and climbs the stairs to an upper room, and Rembrandt follows her with his eyes. The wind from the open window scatters the dust on the table and obliterates the name of Saskia. By this simple symbolism a tremendous amount is conveyed, and the film continues to show what the symbol has foretold. This is symbolism by analogy. An example of simple and effective symbolism by association appears in the film 'Josephine and Men' (about 1953). A young woman is engaged to be married to a rich young business man. Her uncle, talking of his niece to a barman, explains one of her peculiar characteristics: her great care and tenderness for the weak and those in distress, and glimpses of this tendency are given in scenes of her childhood. She and her fiancé visit a friend of the latter who is a penniless author and playwright living untidily alone, and he stirs the tenderness of the young woman. This is expressed by the significant gesture of picking up his socks from the floor, folding them neatly and placing them on the back of a chair. Both men notice this. She falls in love with the penniless author, because, as she says, he needs her, and breaking with her fiancé, she marries him. He afterwards becomes successful.

Later in the film, when husband and wife are living in a comfortable country house, the woman's first fiancé, the business man, is being pursued by the police owing to the

187

action of his partner. He comes to the country house for asylum, tells them of his predicament and that he is ruined. This immediately stirs the tenderness of the wife. He is wet and cold, is given a bath and change of clothing; the wife takes his socks, folds them neatly and places them on the back of a chair precisely as she had those of the penniless author. The two men watch, and by that simple symbolic act much of what follows has been told. The wife goes away with her former fiancé, but when his business difficulties disappear and he is prosperous once more she returns to her husband.

Symbolism is often employed by means of a sign which, by its association, sheds a good deal of light on the theme of the film. An example is provided by Orson Welles' magnificent film 'Citizen Kane' (1939). The theme is the life of a very rich and successful newspaper proprietor. The film opens with his death, and as he dies he utters many times the word 'Rosebud'. A journalist sets out to learn the significance of this utterance, and reconstructs the man's life, which is revealed to the audience. The great newspaper proprietor, although he was so successful, seems rarely to have been happy, although he appears to have searched for happiness. The journalist was not successful in his quest. But at the end of the film, a glimpse is given of some of the old junk and rubbish of the deceased man being consigned to the flames, and among the objects is a boy's sledge with the name 'Rosebud'. In the picture of his life he is shown as a boy with a sledge in the snow. It is a legitimate interpretation that he was only really happy when, as a child, he enjoyed himself in this way, and that that highlight of happiness came to him when he was dying and he uttered the word 'Rosebud'. The greatness of 'Citizen Kane' as a film depends much on the dramatic power of the photography and the consummate use of chiaroscuro, but the effective use of the symbolic motif was no small contributory factor to its all-round excellence.

A further example of good symbolism in the cinema is afforded by the French film 'La Ronde' (1950). The theme of the endless chain of love is symbolized by a roundabout, and the film consists of a series of love affairs, A with B is the first episode, then B with C, then C with D and so on. The symbolism becomes particularly expressive and amusing when a young man in process of making love to a married woman breaks off to reflect on the basis of Stendal's account of the amours of several officers. Thus the works go wrong in the roundabout, and the master of ceremonies has to mend it. When the young man concludes his philosophic reflections and renews his lovemaking, and he and the woman embrace, the roundabout is repaired and continues to revolve.

The symbolism so far considered is introduced to emphasize meaning or to reveal it more fully, and it is shown as a valuable vehicle of expression, which could perhaps be employed more often. Some plays are almost wholly symbolic, as for example Karel and Josef Căpek's 'Insect Play' (1921). Here the meaning is clear enough, but in others the expression is ineffectual because of obscurity or ambiguity in the symbolism. This is not to argue that the meaning of symbols should be at once apparent; the exercise of some little thought in apprehending the significance of the symbols is often an advantage in registering the play in a person's mind, but the meaning should not be so obscure or ambiguous as merely to provoke controversy with very little ultimate agreement. Such a play is 'Waiting for Godot' by Samuel Beckett, which was produced in Paris in 1952 and in London in 1955.

No very definite interpretation of the play seems to be feasible. The many interpretations which have been given have been made with some uncertainty and with
awareness that others are possible. One interpretation makes it a play on the nature
of human life from the Christian standpoint. One writer[1] speaks of it as 'a modern
morality play, on permanent Christian themes. But even if the Christian basis of the
structure were not obvious, Mr. Beckett is constantly underlining it for us in the
incidental symbolism and the dialogue.' Another writer[2] sees in it straightforward
existentialism. The point is that it is equally possible to see the play as an expression
of modern Christian thought giving life meaning, and to see it as the atheistic variation of existentialism as expounded by Jean-Paul Sartre. Some may see in it a sense
of Christian purpose, as when Vladimir says 'What are we doing here, that is the
question. And we are blessed in this, that we happen to know the answer. Yes, in this
immense confusion, one thing alone is clear. We are waiting for Godot to come'—
and he continues 'Or for night to fall (Pause). We have kept our appointment, and
that's an end to that. We are not saints, but we have kept our appointment. How many
people can boast as much?' And yet the dialogue of the two tramps has an aimless
character throughout the play, which is illustrated by the closing dialogue.

VLADIMIR. We'll hang ourselves tomorrow. (Pause) Unless Godot comes.
ESTRAGON. And if he comes?
VLADIMIR. We'll be saved.
  Vladimir takes off his hat (Lucky's) peers inside it, feels about inside it, shakes it, knocks
  in the crown, puts it on again.
ESTRAGON. Well? Shall we go?
VLADIMIR. Pull on your trousers.
ESTRAGON. What?
VLADIMIR: Pull on your trousers.
ESTRAGON. You want me to pull off my trousers?
VLADIMIR. Pull on your trousers.
ESTRAGON (realizing his trousers are down). True.
  He pulls up his trousers. Silence.
VLADIMIR. Well? Shall we go?
ESTRAGON. Yes, let's go.
  They do not move.
Curtain.

In this apparently aimless dialogue one might see an expression of Sartre's species
of existentialism, which insists that human life is vain, absurd and meaningless; that
there are no absolute values, and that man is completely free and responsible for his
life. But other theories of existentialism, while agreeing on the matter of individual
freedom and choice, involve a belief in God. It is claimed that the Danish philosopher
and theologian Söven Kierkegaard expresses in his writings a kind of existentialism
in which worship of God is an individual and not a collective concern, while the
Catholic existentialist view is expressed by Gabriel Marcel. It is possible that there is
little real difference of interpretation in the two opinions cited, and that it may be a
Christian Existentialist play, but this is vague speculation, and the play does not
permit anything more definite. Many other interpretations have been given. Pozzo
symbolizes the oppressing ruling class, and leads by a rope which is fixed round his
neck the dumb Lucky, symbol of the oppressed working class (for he always carries
Pozzo's luggage). Once, Lucky's silence is broken with a long mechanical speech in
which he pours out a series of disjointed phrases of current jargon about life,

189

illustrating that he pours out what has been pumped into him. Both Lucky and Pozzo express ineptness and dependence on each other. The two tramps Vladimir and Estragon are the lookers-on who see all the fun—which is not much fun, and life seems a futile affair. A boy is a messenger from another unseen world where Godot dwells, but the boy knows very little of Godot, his replies to Vladimir's significant questions being 'I don't know, sir'. The tramps wait, but Godot does not come and the sense of the futility of life continues. It will always continue if Godot does not come. This is another interpretation of the play, which illustrates by negation that symbolism, if it is to be an effective and powerful means of expression, must be without ambiguity.

That may not be the view of the author because in Sartre's system ambiguity seems almost to be regarded as a virtue. This is expressed by a follower of Sartre, Simone de Beauvoir, in her essay *Pour une Morale de l'Ambiguité* in which ambiguity is given a moral quality. To follow the argument would take us too far from the theme of symbolism,[3] but it would seem that to pursue ambiguity as Samuel Beckett has done in his existentialist play, is to use symbolism as a vehicle for obscurity rather than for expression. It thus has a kinship with much instinctive and unconscious symbolism where the purpose is to suppress the meaning. In this intellectualism run-to-seed of much Existentialist thought is there an intellectual attempt to return to the instinctive life?

The value of symbolic expression in the arts is demonstrated by the examples cited from architecture, painting, sculpture, the drama, and the cinema, and the examples, like 'Waiting for Godot' indicate by negation the conditions which must be observed if symbolic expression is to be effective. By concentrating much in an associative touch or by apt analogy, it can be vital, powerful and memorable, and by promoting thought as it so often does, as in the case of 'The Seagull', or 'Summer of the Seventeenth Doll', or 'Citizen Kane', it can epitomize the significance of a play.

REFERENCES
1. *Times Literary Supplement*, 10th February, 1956, p. 84. This article by an anonymous writer, entitled 'They also Serve', was followed by a correspondence in the issues of 2nd, 9th, 23rd and 30th March.
2. *Times Literary Supplement*, 2nd March, 1956.
3. See the discussion by H. B. ACTON in *Philosophy*, Vol. XXIX, pp. 80, 81 (London, 1949).

PART IV

ENCYCLOPAEDIC DICTIONARY

XXII   Traditional and Familiar Symbols, their Origin, Meaning and History

ACACIA (*Acacia seyal*)—Ancient Egyptian symbol of immortality. The origin of the meaning is obscure, but it appears to be responsible for the custom of casting a sprig of acacia into the grave at burial. The tree is one of the largest in the Near East, and it figures in legends of ancient Egypt, one being the story of the Two Brothers of the D'Orbiney Papyrus, now in the British Museum.

The Hebrew name for acacia is shittah, plural shittim, and the tabernacle and ark were made of shittim wood (Exodus xxv. 10; xxxv. 7; xxxvi. 20; Deuteronomy x. 3). It is hard and durable which would explain the choice.

ACANTHUS—A familiar Greek and Roman architectural decoration which has occasionally been used in design as an associative symbol of ancient Greece and of classicism. The species from which Greek decoration is derived is the Acanthus spinosus. Vitruvius (IV, 1.) tells a story about its first use for the capital of a column which is traditionally thought to be the origin of the Corinthian order. After the death of a young girl her nurse collected in a basket a few things which had given the girl pleasure, and placed it on her grave above an acanthus root, covering the basket with a roof tile. In the Spring the acanthus grew round the basket and curled underneath the tile forming volutes. Callimachus, a noted artist in bronze, on seeing this conceived the design of the Corinthian capital.

ACROPOLIS—A sacred hill symbolical of Olympus and the celestial regions.

In many ancient Greek cities the acropolis was the sacred hill, generally partly natural and partly artificial, surmounted by sacred buildings, the principal of which was a large temple, the abode of the enthroned god. The Parthenon, occupied by the enthroned Athena, on the acropolis at Athens is the most famous example.

The enthroned god, in the temple surmounting a hill, was an imitation of the throne of Zeus and of the other gods on the summits of Olympus, which figured in early Greek religion. That the acropolis was originally a fortified hill, or fortress, as some writers have suggested, is hardly confirmed by the evidence of its summit being always devoted to religious purposes. In addition to the principal temple, there were generally smaller temples, sanctuaries and altars. That the acropolis may have been used for defensive purposes, and as a sanctuary for the population in time of war is probable, but this is not inconsistent with its fundamentally religious purpose.

ALMOND (*Amygdalus communis*)—The almond tree has sometimes been regarded as a symbol of spring, and of the idea of wakefulness, as its beautiful blossom is among the first to appear, as early as January in Palestine and generally late March in England. Its Hebrew name 'skeked' means to waken or to watch. There are Biblical references to almonds (Genesis xliii. 11; Exodus xxxvii. 20) and the almond tree (Ecclesiastes xii. 5) and the rod of Aaron (Numbers xvii. 8) was a branch of the almond tree.

ALPHA—The first letter of the Greek alphabet and used as a symbol of the beginning. In Christian symbolism it often appears with omega, the last letter of the Greek alphabet, as a symbol of the beginning and the end—or the first and the last, both expressions being used in Revelation (i. 8 and i. 11).

Alpha was originally derived from the first letter of the Hebrew and Phoenician alphabets áleph which was formed from the hieroglyph of an ox's head representing the ox at the head of the team of oxen.

ALTAR—Symbol of sacrifice, of worship, of thanksgiving and remembrance.

The altar is traditionally understood to be a surface, usually, but not always, raised, on which sacrifices and offerings are made to a god. It existed in most primitive and ancient religions. Sacrifices varied from human and animal victims to the more humane and harmless sacrifice of wine and food.

There is some reason to believe that the altar had a sepulchral origin. Herbert Spencer collected much evidence to show that among many primitive peoples, when a person died it was customary for the body to be left in the house, and for the family to live elsewhere.[1] The house thus became the sepulchre of the dead and the family came to make offerings at the house and to worship. Sir James Frazer collected similar evidence.[2] Many tombs among ancient peoples are like houses, such as those found in Lycia and Etruria. From much evidence Spencer developed his famous theory that temples and churches are derived from the ceremonies and structures surrounding tombs, and that ancestor worship is the main root of religion. The grave in the house to which propitiatory offerings were made thus became the altar in the temple. In a later development in Greece, the people did not enter the temple which housed the statue of the god, and the altar was placed in front. Often the external altar was for offerings by the people, while there was another altar inside in front of the statue of the god, for sacrifices made by the priest.

Much other evidence could be adduced to show that the altar was originally a tomb on which offerings for the welfare of the deceased were placed. When doctrinal religions evolved with set ritual and with a personal god or hierarchy of gods, offerings and sacrifices of all kinds were made which are too well known to need enumeration. In the later centuries of Rome when the senators were sworn on the altar of the god to observe the laws of the emperor and the empire, the offerings took the form of wine and incense. In the Protestant service today after the priest has blessed the monetary offering, he places it on the altar. It can be appreciated, however, that when an altar was erected, not only as a table for offerings or for a sacrifice, but for a commemorative purpose, it was as a symbol of sacrifice and of worship at which prayers can be offered.

The Christian altar derives from the older forms, and is a mingling of ancient traditions with the table of the Last Supper. That table has become the altar of the Christian church, and it is sacred as a symbol of Christ's sacrifice, for at this table Christ gave bread to his disciples, saying, 'This is My body which is given for you' and 'This cup is the new testament in My blood, which is shed for you'. (Luke xxii. 19, 20.)[3] These are prognostications of His sacrifice for mankind, and thus the Christian altar and the cross are pre-eminently symbols of Christ's sacrifice for mankind. Closely connected with this is its association with worship.

In the Catholic doctrine of transubstantiation the bread and wine are transformed into the body and blood of Christ in the ceremony of the Eucharist. In the Protestant ceremony of communion the taking of bread and wine is a symbolic act done (Luke xxii. 20) 'In remembrance' of Christ. The altar is thus also a symbol of remembrance of Christ. Each war cemetery of the Imperial War Graves Commission has a cross and altar-like stone, the former being called the cross of sacrifice and the latter the stone of remembrance.

At one time in Christian tradition, every altar should contain a sacred relic, in order to give it a sacred character. The bodies of many early Christian saints and martyrs were moved from the Roman catacombs in the fifth and sixth centuries A.D., after the incursions of the Vandals and Goths, to the churches within the walls, partly for safety and partly in order to use the tomb as the altar. The altar thus became a shrine for sacred relics, a custom that was general until the Reformation. In this we see a close connection with the tomb as the origin of the altar.

1. HERBERT SPENCER. *Principles of Sociology*, 3rd edition, Vol. 1, pp. 249 *et seq.* and p. 411 (London, 1885).
2. *The Belief in Immortality and the Worship of the Dead*. Vol. II, pp. 99 *et seq.* (London, 1922).
3. Also Matthew xxvi. 26–8; Mark xvi. 22–4.

AMARANTH—Principally symbol of immortality, but also of love. It has become the symbol of immortality because its bloom does not soon fade, its name ἀμάραντος meaning 'not fading'. Prince's feather and love-lies-bleeding are well-known species of the genus amaranthus, although the flower commonly known as everlasting, and for this reason equally suitable as a symbol of immortality, is quite different, belonging to the genus helichrysum.

It was anciently regarded as a symbol of immortality, and was used as decoration on tombs and images in ancient Greece. In modern times it has more literary than visual associations. It has become very popular with poets, doubtless because of the meaning and attractiveness of its name. Numerous allusions to it as the flower of immortality occur in poems of all ages. Milton's is one of the most richly significant:[1]

> Immortal amaranth, a flower which once
>   In Paradise, fast by the tree of life,
> Began to bloom; but soon for man's offence
>   To heaven removed, where first it grew, there grows
> And flowers aloft, shading the fount of life,
>   But where the river of bliss through midst of heaven
> Rolls o'er Elysian flowers her amber stream.

Coleridge, in his beautiful verses *Work without Hope*, bemoans that immortality is not for him:

> Yet well I ken the banks where amaranths blow,
>   Have traced the fount whence streams of nectar flow.
> Bloom, O ye amaranths! bloom for whom ye may,
>   For me ye bloom not!

It has occasionally been regarded as the flower of love because of a not unnatural confusion of Amar with amor, but this is not very common.

By a fanciful association of its meanings it might be regarded as typifying immortal love, a meaning that would make it appropriate as a decoration for ecclesiastical furnishings. The amaranth is a fresh and interesting subject for the designer, for the long pendant-like forms of some species and the shape of the everlasting flower could effectively be utilized.

1. *Paradise Lost*, Book III.

AMPULA—The vessel holding the consecrated oil used for anointing in certain religious ceremonies such as the investiture to a high or sacred office like the consecration of bishops and the coronation of kings. It is an ancient practice and there are numerous references to the anointing of priests, kings and prophets in the Old Testament. When a representation of the ampula is used in design it symbolizes the particular religious ceremony in which it was employed and its significance in the ceremony. An example is its use on the postage stamps commemorating the coronations of George VI and Elizabeth II, where it is shown with other items of the regalia.

The significance of anointing a priest or king is partly purification and partly the infusion of spiritual and beneficent qualities, and it is really a preliminary to and preparation for the assumption of the high office.

The ampula used in the coronation of British monarchs is a vessel of gold in the form of an eagle. The monarch is anointed with oil and balm which is poured through the beak of the ampula into the anointing spoon, and the Sovereign is touched on the head, breast and hands. In earlier mediaeval days the anointing was more thorough.[1]

The eagle shape is used as symbolical of Christianity, for the eagle signifies ascension, and is the symbol of St. John the Evangelist and of his mission of Christian teaching.

1. See PHILIP LINDSAY, *Crowned King of England—The Coronation of King George VI in History and Tradition* (London, 1937), Chapter IX, The Anointing.

ANCHOR—A Christian symbol of hope. Also a common marine symbol. It probably has its origin as a Christian symbol in St. Paul's typification of the hope resulting from God's promises to the faithful 'as an anchor of the soul, both sure and stedfast'.

It was a favourite symbol in early and mediaeval Christian times, and is often met with on the loculi slabs in the catacombs. As an illustration of early Christian thought associated with this symbol, Louise Twining[1] quotes a beautiful passage from an early Christian writer: 'As an anchor cast into the sand will keep the ship in safety, so Hope, even amidst poverty and tribulation, remains firm, and is sufficient to sustain

the soul, though in the eyes of the world it may seem but a weak and faint support.'
Poets have frequently alluded to this symbol. For instance, Tennyson, in *Enoch Arden*, says: 'Cast all your cares on God; that anchor holds.'

The principal sentiment prompting its use for religious purposes may be summarized as an anchoring of the soul in faith—faith being the ground of hope.

When used for secular purposes this symbol more usually has a marine significance. For example, on the arms of the Chartered Insurance Institute three anchors symbolize marine insurance.

The anchor is the emblem of Pope Clement I of the first century A.D., because of the popular legend, for which there is little evidence, that, while undergoing a sentence of hard labour in the Crimea, Clement was lashed to an anchor and thrown into the sea.

1. *Symbols and Emblems of Early and Medieval Christian Art*, 2nd edition, p. 199 (London, 1885).

ANEMONE—When Adonis was killed by a boar, Aphrodite in her grief made the anemone grow from his blood. From this the flower is sometimes thought to be symbolic of Adonis and of early death, or brief blossoming. The anemone coronaria is a common wild flower of Palestine and colours the landscape with bright purple, and it has been suggested that it was these flowers that were the lilies of the field referred to in Matthew (vii. 28, 29) and Luke (xii. 27).

ANGEL—Symbol of spiritual or divine communications.

The word 'angel' is derived from the Greek ἄγγελος meaning messenger, bearer of tidings. The messengers of the Lord who are alluded to in the Old Testament[1] indicate that a similar association with the term 'angel' existed in Hebrew as existed in Greek. The term in Christian theology has been enlarged in application to include numerous other meanings, most of which are familiar.

There is no reference in the Old or New Testaments to the origin or creation of angels; their existence, like the existence of God, being presupposed. A. B. Davidson puts forward two possible explanations for their origin in the Hebrew mind, the more feasible of the two being that they might be traced to the 'spirits' of the old Shemitic religion, who abode in natural phenomena, in rocks, trees and fountains, and who gradually 'came to be regarded as possessing a certain unity of will and action, and by a further concentration became the servants of one supreme will and formed the host of heaven'.[2] It is more probable, however, that the idea of heavenly messengers was received complete from other religions.

It is a simple deduction that, if in religious thought (where God is conceived as dwelling beyond the regions of space) communication between God and man is either to be symbolized or physically realized, a supernatural being should be represented with the figure of God and man, and with the means of travelling through space, which immediately suggests the wings of a bird. The study of the winged figures in various religions demonstrates that their origin is as simple as that. Such were the winged genii of ancient Assyria; Hermes, the messenger of the Greek gods; the Christian angels; and Horus, the messenger of Ra, with the exception that he usually took the form of a winged disk.[3] Numerous spiritual duties have developed in various religions as elaborations of their duties of communication which will be noted later, especially with regard to the Christian angel.

In many ancient countries fabulous creatures were often winged. Examples are the later Egyptian and the Assyrian and Greek sphinxes. In Assyrian sculpture there occurs also the winged human-headed bull and winged human figure with the head of an eagle. The later addition of wings to the Egyptian sphinx was probably an added expression of power, for the sphinx, which had the body of a lion and the head of the reigning king, seems to have been an attempt to express the utmost physical and mental power. The same seems to have been the case with the Assyrian winged bulls. These fabulous winged creatures of the Assyrian religion were probably the prototypes of the symbols of the Evangelists.

In the earlier pages of the Old Testament angels are constantly spoken of as men,[4] apparently with human dispositions. It was not until later, after the Babylonian captivity, that angels apart from their appearance as artistic representations, were described as of supernatural appearance, and were conceived in those forms which are now distinctive of them. Cherubim[5] are mentioned as being 'placed at the east of the garden of Eden' after the expulsion, but without any description of their form.[6] It is only in representations of cherubim as decoration for the mercy-seat and curtains of the Tabernacle[7] and for Solomon's Temple[8] that forms are indicated; the first description of cherubim appearing when they were employed as decorations of the Tabernacle, the building of which occurs shortly after the departure of the Israelites from Egypt. Angels, therefore, appear in the Old Testament as artistic representations before they appear as visions, and this fact throws some light on the probable origin of their forms.

It was from the Egyptians that the Assyrians probably first derived their employment of wings for images of their deities, an evolution which is partially responsible for their winged genii and animals. In turn these Assyrian winged beings, according to Layard and Tylor, and many who have followed them, are, in all probability, the prototype of the genii and winged gods of Greece and Rome, and of the Hebrew and Christian angels. Layard has pointed out that the four winged creatures of Ezekiel's vision (i. 5 et seq.) each with faces of a man, lion, ox, and eagle can be traced to the winged animals of Assyrian art.[9] He says: 'Those co-incidences are too marked not to deserve notice'; and do certainly lead to the inference that the symbols chosen by the prophet were derived from the Assyrian sculptures.[10] Tylor goes still further and notes the similarity of the description of the hands of a man under four wings[11] to the Assyrian representations of winged deities employed in artificially fertilizing the date palm; and he says that 'the types from which the visionary living creatures modelled themselves in the prophet's mind in his vision on the banks of the River Chebar, stand thus almost completely open to the modern student'.[12] These Assyrian forms being the predecessors of the genii in Greek and Roman art, and the influence of the latter being apparent in the angels of early Christian monuments, it will be seen, therefore, that the forms of Christian angels descend from Assyrian art through two channels: Hebrew theology, and Greek and Roman art. The former influence is, of course, immeasurably stronger, carrying with it a religious authority, while the latter was eschewed as pagan. The latter may be viewed more in the light of the technical assistance that was thereby afforded to artists.

198

According to existing knowledge then, the evolution of angelic forms may be summarized: the cherubim decorating the Tabernacle were derived from Egypt; those decorating Solomon's Temple came to Palestine by the same source, or from Assyria by means of the Phoenicians; while the rest, seraphim, archangels and winged animals, that appear so largely in early and mediaeval Christian art, may be traced to the influence of Assyrian sculptures, when Assyria ruled the world and when Israel dwelt in Babylon.

Angels are depicted in the Bible as acting as a manifestation of God;[13] as forming the host of heaven and surrounding the throne of God;[14] as messengers from God to man[15]—as a means of communicating God's will to man; as instruments of God in executing his divine will: they thus console, encourage, guide, or reprove, and chastise, in which last sense, instruments of divine punishment are often mistaken for evil angels.[16] Two biblical allusions to angels indicate that some act as guardians of individuals,[17] an idea that was enlarged upon by early Christians, so that, according to them, each individual is attended by a good angel who guides, corrects, and consoles him in life, and carries him through death to the eternal presence and to eternal life.[18]

The conception of the angelic hierarchy, which has been, to a large extent, the guide to early Christian theologians, poets and artists, is that which was for a long time attributed to Dionysius the Areopagite, who probably lived in the first century A.D., and who is mentioned in Acts xvii. 34, but which is now known to be the work of a pseudo-Dionysius of about four centuries later, who gave the name of the real Dionysius to his work. The 'Celestial Hierarchy' of the pseudo-Dionysius nevertheless became the textbook on angels for later theologians, and was valuable to artists, probably because information was conveniently systematized.

The pseudo-Dionysius conceived the Celestial Hierarchy as composed of three orders of angels surrounding, at different degrees, the throne of God. Each order is composed of three ranks or choirs. The first order nearest to God comprises the seraphim, cherubim, and thrones. The second and middle order comprises the dominations, virtues and powers.[19] The last order comprises principalities, archangels, and angels. Biblical authority would seem to exist for most of these ranks, though it is by no means clear that angelic forms are meant by them. Seraphim[20] and cherubim have Old Testament authority, while the rest can be traced in the New Testament.[21] It is probable, however, that the Slavonic Book of Enoch contributed to their formation, a book familiar to early Christian theologians, and probably to the writers of the New Testament. In chapter xx. 1. of the Slavonic Enoch, we read: 'And these men took me thence and brought me to the seventh heaven, and I saw there a very great light and all the fiery hosts of great archangels, and incorporeal powers, and lordships, and principalities and powers; cherubim and seraphim, thrones and the watchfulness of many eyes.'[22]

The three orders of the pseudo-Dionysius intervene between God and man, and it is through them that God guides, directs and reveals the light of His goodness and glory to man. The first order receives the divine illumination directly from God Himself, transmitting it to the middle order, from whom the third order receives it, and so carries the divine illumination to man. The will of God and instruction in the deifying sciences is similarly transmitted. Apparently the communication acts inversely from man to God, beginning with the guardian angel of the individual. An interesting parallel to this may be found in Jewish theology where, in the Midrash, the body of a man during his sleep tells the doings of the day to his soul, the soul tells them to his spirit, his spirit tells the angel, the angel reports to the cherub, and the cherub reports to the seraph, who brings them before God.[23]

The pseudo-Dionysius explains a special significance and function of each rank in the three orders, which will be found under the headings of seraphim, cherubim, thrones, dominations, virtues, powers, principalities and archangels.

Dismissing the winged genii that sometimes appeared on early Christian sarcophagi merely as ornaments, borrowed from classic art, we may say that angels do not appear in Christian art before the fourth century. Objections to their representation were held by the early fathers of the Church owing to the tendency to worship these supernatural beings, which was regarded as detrimental to the central and essential worship of Christianity. These objections evidently gradually weakened, for we find angels represented in all their glory in the mosaics in the church of Santa Agata at Ravenna, which probably date from about A.D. 400; and in the Second Council of Nice, A.D. 787, John of Thessalonica suggested that angels might be represented, and that they should have human form.[24]

From that time onward angels have constantly appeared in sacred art: in Byzantine mosaics; as ornamental sculpture in Byzantine, Gothic, and Renaissance churches; in Italian painting of the Middle Ages and Renaissance, beginning with Duccio and Giotto, and culminating in Raphael, Michelangelo, Correggio and Titian; in the mediaeval painting of Flanders, beginning with Van Eyck; in the great ages of painting in Spain and the north represented by Velasquez, Murillo, Dürer, Rubens, Van Dyck, Rembrandt, and a host of lesser painters, down to our own times in the works of the Pre-Raphaelites and some of their contemporaries. Though the pseudo-Dionysius was the main guide for mediaeval painters in their depiction of the heavenly regions, his conception is rarely followed with exactitude. Giotto, Duccio, and Fra Angelico usually show feminine angels suitably gowned, with wings; while painters of a little later sometimes show red seraphim and blue cherubim with their six wings, interspersed with the full figure angels, as, for example, in Matteo di Giovanni's Madonna of the Girdle in the National Gallery. The most complete pictorial conception of the heavenly hierarchy according to the description of the pseudo-Dionysius that, as far as I know, exists, is Botticini's Assumption of the Virgin in the National Gallery. Here the three triads are arranged in circles around the throne of God. First are the red seraphim, each with head and six wings, then appear the blue cherubim of similar form, then the thrones, who are painted blue and shown with head and shoulders, and body, emerging into wings at the waist, completing the first order. A space separates each order. The other six ranks are depicted as full human figures with wings. The powers apparently carry spears, the principalities and angels rods which may be sceptres, while some of the archangels carry caskets. Saints are intermingled with the angels in these circles.

The pseudo-Dionysius speaks of the clothes of angels as the wisdom of God that clothes the naked.[25] He speaks of a glowing raiment, a sacerdotal robe, and a girdle. Angels are mostly represented by painters as robed in white according to biblical testimony.[26] The most becoming dress, of which there are numerous examples in early Italian painting, is one of the greatest simplicity. The drapery of an angel in sculpture would obviously gain in effect by being of such a nebulous character as to be lost occasionally in the form. Embroidery or lace at the neck, flounces, or sleeves, are superfluous, and the nightdress effect they so often create hardly enhances the majesty and grandeur associated with the 'angel of the Lord'.

Methods of representing the wings may be broadly distinguished as the method which aims at so proportioning the wings to the figure that they shall appear adequate to lift the body in flight, the maximum of *natural* effect being accorded to a supernatural being; and the method which uses the wings merely as a symbol of an angel or an indication that an angel is intended. The latter method is less logical, for an attribute of what is a symbol of an idea is used to symbolize the symbol. The figure of the angel is no less a symbol than the wings. One is borrowed from man, the other from birds,[27] so that wholly to represent one and only half the other is incongruous. The former method aims at a vivid and life-like expression of a religious function—the meaning of which is the idea symbolized; while the other is merely an indication that such is meant. To show an angel capable, by reason of its wings and form, of carrying messages rapidly through vast spaces is to suggest divine grandeur and power. If the angel is robbed physically of that power, the feeling of the significance conveyed by that form is largely destroyed. The illusion of life conveyed by powerful wings, capable of carrying a human form in rapid flight, makes the idea and its representation as convincing as it possibly can be, while the alternative is little better than saying: 'Here is an angel.' Modern sculpture affords a few examples, such as F. V. Blunstone's angels for the Prudential Assurance Company's war memorial and Richard Goulden's 'Michael' for the St. Michael's, Cornhill, war memorial, where the wings are so proportioned to the figure as to give the exhilarating feeling that the body can be lifted in flight. An example in painting is Leighton's 'Elijah in the Wilderness' (Plate LIX (*b*)).

In the early pages of the Bible angels are spoken of as men[28] and referred to in the masculine gender.[29] When the angel of the Lord is mentioned in the Bible we instinctively visualize, by reason of description and association, a grand and powerful personage, more masculine than feminine, whereas, in art they are often represented as gentle docile women. It may be objected that the mention of angels as men is simply the use of the term 'men' as we use the term 'mankind', and includes women. This may or may not be, but the allusions certainly do not refer to womanlike beings, but essentially to beings of a masculine character, and therefore do not receive a true interpretation in most artistic representations.

The early Italian painters nearly all made women of their angels. The tendency seems to have been to emphasize the kind, pure, and gentle qualities of the angel at the expense of the more masculine qualities of strength and firmness, and thus angels became women. This is particularly noticeable in Fra Angelico's conceptions, where angels are some of the gentlest and most tender creatures ever conceived.

It is one of the greatest tributes ever paid to the character of womanhood that angels, in the evolution of art and colloquial use of words, have left to a great degree their original masculine character and become woman. It seems that a woman can embody better than a man all that is meant by angel. Yet this feminizing of angels, tribute as it is to woman, falls from an ideal religious conception. Strength and power

201

are so often associated with anything but an angelic character that artists have concentrated on qualities, like kindness and gentleness. Yet the ideal conception is surely that which blends the two, and strength and power, in spite of their human abuses, must exist in the 'angel of the Lord'. Madame de Staël erroneously says that angels are always supposed to be masculine, but very suggestively adds as the reason, because the union of power with purity constitutes all that we mortals can imagine of perfection.[30] But the ideal would eliminate thought of sex, and present an individual of grand, noble, and powerful aspect, yet expressing by his demeanour and facial expression the signs of habitual kindness and gentleness.

To summarize: the significance of Angel may be regarded as essentially a divine messenger whose duty is communication between God and man; and in this capacity is thus also a guardian and protector of both the living and the dead. A representation of an angel is thus a symbol of spiritual or divine communication.

1. Numbers xxi. 21; Deuteronomy, ii. 26; Joshua vi. 17.
2. A. B. DAVIDSON, article on 'Angels', in Hastings's *Dictionary of the Bible*, vol. i, p. 95 (1900).
3. *See* Winged disk.
4. Genesis xviii. 2 *et seq.*; xix. 1 *et seq.*; xxxii. 24 *et seq.*
5. Cherubim are not included among the angels by the modern Jews; see article on the subject of the Jewish Encyclopaedia, 1925.
6. Genesis iii. 24.
7. Exodus xxv. 18–22; xxvi. 1; xxvii. 7–9; xxxvi. 8.
8. I Kings vi. 23 *et seq*: II Chronicles iii. 11 *et seq*.
9. DELITIZCH, in considering the etymology of cherubim, connected the word with the Assyrian name *shedu*, meaning 'winged bull'. He subsequently, however, connected it with '*karubu*', which, he says, meant 'Great and Mighty', a meaning disputed by MUSS-ARNOLT (Jewish Encyclopaedia: *Cherubim*), who gives its meaning as 'Propitious'.
10. SIR A. H. LAYARD, *Nineveh*, vol. ii, p. 465.
11. Ezekiel i. 8; also x. 8.
12. E. B. TYLOR, 'The Winged Figures of the Assyrian and other Ancient Monuments', *Proceedings of the Society of Biblical Archaeology*, p. 391, June, 1890.
13. Genesis xxxi. 11–13; xxi. 17; xlviii. 16; Exodus iii. 2–6. A. B. DAVIDSON (*op. cit.*, vol. i, p. 94) refutes the suggestion that these manifestations indicate distinctions in the Godhead. He says that 'the only distinction implied is that between Jehovah and Jehovah in manifestation'.
14. I Kings xxii. 19; Psalm ciii. 21; Isaiah vi. 2.
15. Deuteronomy ii. 26.
16. Psalm lxviii. 49.
17. Matthew xviii. 10; Acts xii. 15.
18. *See* MRS. JAMESON, *Sacred and Legendary Art*, vol. i, p. 60 (1857).
19. J. PARKER translates these as 'authorities, lordships, and powers', vol. ii, pp. 23, 31 (1897).
20. Isaiah vi. 2.
21. Romans viii. 38; Ephesians i. 21; Colossians i. 16; ii. 10; Jude 9.
22. W. R. MORFILL's translation, 1896.
23. See article by LOUIS GINIZBURG on 'Cherubim' in *Jewish Encyclopaedia*, 1925.
24. See MRS. JAMESON, *op. cit.*, vol. i, p. 74.
25. Chapter xv.
26. John xx. 12.
27. MRS. JAMESON (*op. cit.*, vol. i, p. 55) thought it a mistake on the part of painters to make the wings like birds' wings, suggesting that the nondescript wings of the early painters, being more in harmony with a spiritual atmosphere, are preferable. Yet wings for angels were, after all, derived from birds.
28. Genesis xxxii. 2; Numbers xxi. 21; Deuteronomy ii. 26.
29. Genesis xvi. 7–13.
30. Quoted by MRS. JAMESON, *op. cit.*, vol. i, p. 51.

ANIMALS—Many animals in ancient times have been worshipped because of their qualities and attributes, and a large number of animals, birds and insects that were at all familiar became the subject of myths, legends and superstitions in different parts of the world, and they have, in some cases, become symbolic of certain ideas. It is probable, as Wallis Budge has remarked, that primitive man worshipped animals because they possessed strength and power greater than his own, and that fear and propitiation formed the foundation of the worship.[1] Many of the Egyptian gods were identified with certain animals and conceived in their forms or represented with heads of animals or birds, because the gods were conceived as having the qualities of such animals. The same symbolic ideas persist in mediaeval and modern times. In mediaeval times animals were often used in heraldry and taken as badges because they personified qualities thought to be possessed by a person or community. The lion of England, and the other Queen's beasts are examples, while the association of the bulldog with Sir Winston Churchill is an example from modern life. In the representations the qualities associated with the animal which it is desired to express are often exaggerated, like the heraldic representation of the lion. 'Thus a lion', says Sir George Bellew, Garter King of Arms, 'which in nature is not a very distinctive object, was portrayed, for greater distinction, with its leonine attributes, its fierce expression, frightful claws, lithe and lissom body all vastly exaggerated, so that indeed it looked more like a lion than did ever any lion of nature.'[2] Sometimes primitive people, not finding all the qualities they wanted in one animal, mixed them, and thus were created fabulous beasts like the dragon, griffin and basilisk.

Most animals that in ancient or modern times acquired a definite traditional symbolic meaning which survives in modern thought, are included in this book. It would be difficult, however, to cite an animal whose habits have prompted interest and excited imagination, which has not at some time been the subject of a myth, legend or superstition and so acquired some kind of symbolic significance. But in many cases the symbolic meanings which animals, birds and insects have at some time carried have become too remote and obscure to find a place in current thought. Among those which are not separately described here are the buffalo, crow, cuckoo, dog, eel, elephant, fly, leopard, lizard, magpie, mouse, shark, spider, swallow, tiger, tortoise, turtle, whale, and wren, and the curious reader must be referred to anthropological sources of information.[3]

1. E. A. WALLIS BUDGE. *The Gods of the Egyptians*, p. 22 (London, 1904).
2. Foreword to *The Queen's Beasts*, p. 11 (London, 1953).
3. A brief account of the myths and legends associated with these animals is given in the article on animals by N. W. THOMAS in Hastings's *Encyclopaedia of Religion and Ethics* (Edinburgh, 1925).

ANKH—(Also known as Key of Life and *Crux Ansata*.) Ancient Egyptian symbol of life, especially in the sense of revival and immortality.

This figure, like a tau cross with a loop at the top, was the Egyptian hieroglyph for life, and from that it became a general symbol of life. Many Egyptian gods and goddesses are shown holding the ankh. Sekhmet, the fire-goddess, is always so represented. Sometimes on stelae a god is represented holding the ankh to the nostrils of a dead king so as to give him everlasting life; or it may be thrown by the god towards the king.

The origin of its form is uncertain. The circumstance, however, that the hieroglyph for sandal strap is the same has suggested the most likely theory. The ankh is conceivably a representation of the sandal strap, and it is a reasonable deduction that the hieroglyph for life was derived from this because of the likeness of the sounds by which sandal strap and life were rendered. It is known that most of the Egyptian hieroglyphs for ideas evolved by the accidental likeness of sounds given to objects and ideas, rather than by relationship of suitable objects to express an idea, as in Chinese. In the case of the ankh it would seem that a sandal strap by this accident of sound has formed the important symbol of life. (Fig. 40.)

ANT—Symbol of industry, derived from the habits of the insect of the Hymenopterous order. The idea is fortified by the reference in Proverbs vi. 6–8 which says: 'Go to the ant, thou sluggard; consider her ways and be wise: which having no guide, overseer, or ruler, provideth her meat in the summer, and gathereth her food in the harvest.' From this proverb it might also fittingly be regarded as a symbol of resourcefulness.

ANTELOPE—*See* Yale.

APHRODITE—*See* Gods, Goddesses and Heroes of Antiquity.

APOLLO—*See* Gods, Goddesses and Heroes of Antiquity.

APPLE—In the Middle Ages the fruit of the tree of knowledge was commonly regarded as an apple, and it was sometimes used as a symbol of the fall of man. In the hand of Christ it signified redemption from sin. It is sometimes shown held by the Virgin Mary in representations of the Madonna and Child. In one example of wood, of about 1430, from the church of Seeon in Southern Bavaria, a large apple appears very prominently in the right hand of the Virgin. It similarly appears in the group by Jacob Kaschaur from the altar of Fresing Cathedral of about the same period.[1] The apple used in this way is clearly intended to symbolize that Christ's mission on earth is the redemption of man from sin. (Plate LIX.)

1. Both these works are now in the Bavarian National Museum at München.

APPLE-BLOSSOM—The symbolic flower of Michigan and Arkansas, and officially adopted by the former as its floral emblem in 1897 and by the latter in 1901. Every State of the U.S.A. has a symbolic flower, the particular flower adopted being usually determined by its familiarity in the landscape, so that it can be regarded as typical of the country. The particular apple blossom of Michigan is Pyrus Cornaria, and the reason given for its adoption is that the 'blossoming apple trees add much to the beauty of the landscape'. The flower is one of the most beautiful of apple blossoms, and the apples are world famous.[1] The species for Arkansas is Pyrus malus.

1. See GEORGE EARLIE SHANKLE, *State Names, Flags, Seals, Songs, Birds, Flowers and other Symbols*, p. 340 (New York, 1941).

ARCH, CEREMONIAL, TRIUMPHAL—Ancient Roman symbol of the sky, the heavens, and of the sky-gods Janus and Jupiter. It was a representation in miniature of the arch of the sky or the arch of heaven, the sky or the god of the sky being the all-powerful

deity. The arch was thus an important religious symbol, and for that reason monumental arches were erected in thanksgiving to god for military victories. That is the
probable origin of the triumphal arch and not the gateway detached from the city
wall as is sometimes thought.

Zeus was originally the sky, and was anthropomorphized into the god of the sky in
human shape with human passions.[1] The oldest of the Latin gods appears to have been

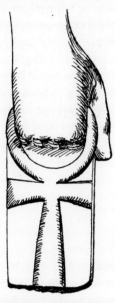

(b) Modified copy of an 1829 model of an
anchor in the Royal Naval Museum,
Greenwich—a common type (metal with
wooden stocks) during the last century,
and near in shape to symbolic anchors
generally used in design.

(a) Ankh held in the hand of the fire
goddess Sekhmet. From an eighteenth-
dynasty granite statue of the goddess, from
Thebes, and now in the British Museum.

(c) Chalice and Host. The shape of this
chalice is derived from a fifteenth-century
Italian specimen, of engraved copper gilt
with silver bowl. It is a typical example.

Fig. 40.

Janus who was similarly identified with the sky and similarly personified in a later
period. Jupiter is a parallel but later god. 'Janus and Jupiter', says A. B. Cook, 'were
the sky-gods worshipped by two successive strata in the population of Italy. Janus, it
would appear, belonged to the older stock,which, for want of a better name, I should

term Illyrian—and was retained by the incoming Latins, despite the fact that their own Jupiter was a god of essentially similar character.'[2] Among the attributes given to Janus the sky-god was that of time-god, and he logically became god of the months, seasons of the year and of eternity. Thus he was represented as looking to the past and to the future, and gave his name to the first month of the year.

Sir Herbert Baker, the famous architect of the Bank of England, was an enthusiastic student of symbolism and a reader and admirer of A. B. Cook.[3] Among the beautiful mosaic floors he designed for the Bank of England (laid by that master craftsman Boris Anrep) is one showing heads back to back on a pedestal beneath the arch of the sky, the whole supported on a cloud. Stars forming the constellations of the two bears are above these heads, an allusion to Janus controlling the two bears, while on either side of the arch are the names: Jupiter and Janus. At the front of the column are the eagle and the owl. This mosaic represents admirably the mythical story by which the arch became a religious symbol of the sky-god.

A large number of commemorative or triumphal arches were erected in the Roman Empire from about the middle of the first century B.C. to about the middle of the fourth century A.D. The German writer P. Graef enumerates 125, of which 54 have been traced in Africa, 30 in Italy, 20 in Asia and the East, 14 in France, 6 in Spain and one in Germany, but most have perished.

The four principal forms are the single, double and triple arch and the Janus arch which is three dimensional and square on plan and which expresses more completely the idea of the arch of heaven. A. B. Cook cites the opinion of A. L. Frothinghaim 'who after a wide survey of the facts concluded that the true parent of the triumphal arch was the old Roman ianus'. 'Frothinghaim argues', says Cook, '(a) that in early days, when Rome consisted of a group of neighbouring tribes, each tribe had its separate ianus on the line of its own pomverium (ianus Curiatius, ianus Carmentales, ianus Quivenius) such iani being, not gates in a fortified wall, but arches built outside to commemorate events of communal importance and placed under the protection of the communal god Janus; (b) that the unified Servian state similarly had its ianus, the porta triumphalis, on the enlarged palmovial line of the via Flaminia; and (c) that the famous portal was copied and re-copied by communal arches far and wide through the dominions of imperial Rome.' Cook himself conjectures that the triumphal arch 'represented the heavenly vault, and that the triumphing general whose statue stood upon it was viewed as an embodiment of the sky-god uplifted on his mimic sky.' This suggestion is corroborated by a 'first brass' of Trajan, which displays a fine triumphal arch supporting the emperor's chariot and explicitly dedicated I.O.M. 'to Jupiter best and Greatest'. Bearing in mind the religious origin of so many monumental forms, and the perpetual custom of dedicating memorials to God, this seems to be the probable origin of the triumphal arch.

Among the best known examples are the Arch of Titus, erected in A.D. 70 to commemorate the capture of Jerusalem; the Arch of Septimus Severus, erected in A.D. 204 to commemorate the Parthian victories of Severus and his two sons; and the arch of Constantine, erected in A.D. 312, to commemorate Constantine's victory over Maxentius. Two well known examples in Italy, other than Rome, are two Arches of Trajan, one at Ancona, erected in A.D. 113 in honour of the Emperor who had made the harbour, and the other at Beneventum, erected in A.D. 114, and also dedicated to

Trajan. The finest example in France is perhaps the Arch of Tiberius at Orange, and among other good examples are those at Palmyra, in Asia Minor, and Timgad and Tebessa, in Africa. The last named, the Arch of Caracalla, erected in A.D. 214, is of a square character with arches of the same width on four sides, because it stood at the meeting of the four main roads in the centre of the town, and it is thus a Janus arch. Another arch of similar character is that of Janus Quadrifrons in Rome, erected in the fourth century A.D.

The triumphal arch was revived during the late Renaissance in France. The Porte Saint Denis and the Porte Saint Martin in Paris were erected in 1672 and 1674 respectively to celebrate the victories of Louis XIV, and the Porte du Peyron at Montpelier was built at the close of the seventeenth century to commemorate the revocation of the Edict of Nantes of Louis XIV. Later the great Arc de Triomphe de l'Etoile was erected in the early nineteenth century to celebrate the victories of Napoleon.

The two best known commemorative arches in England are the arch at the top of Constitution Hill and the war memorial at Leicester. The former was designed by Decimus Burton and was originally erected at the entrance of Hyde Park in 1828. In 1846 an equestrian statue of the Duke of Wellington, whose victories it commemorated, was placed on its summit. In 1883 it was removed to its present position, when the equestrian statue was taken away, to be replaced in 1912 by the quadriga. The Leicester Memorial was designed by Sir Edwin Lutyens, and, like his great Somme Memorial Arch at Thiepval, has a three-dimensional effect which links it with the Janus arch. They are among the most impressive ever erected and recapture in some measure that religious feeling of the arch of the sky, of which it is a symbol.

1. The evolutions and numerous manifestations of Zeus, god of the Bright Sky, and Zeus, god of the Dark Sky, are traced by A. B. Cook with a wealth of illustration, in his work on *Zeus* (Cambridge, 1914–25).
2. A. B. Cook, *op. cit.*, pp. 340–1.
3. Baker acknowledged the value of A. B. Cook's study of the symbolism in ancient myths in a lecture he gave on 'Symbolism in Art' at the Royal Institution in 1933.

ARCHANGELS—These are, as the name implies, angels of the highest rank, who have been individualized and given special functions. Their number is generally thought to be seven, allusions in Revelation (viii. 2 and 6; xv. 1; xvi. 1) being thus interpreted. Their functions may be summed up as guardianship, communication and revelation of God to man, and the accounts of their functions make more explicit the general significance of angels.

Only Michael and Gabriel are mentioned in the Bible,[1] while Raphael and Uriel are mentioned in the Apocrypha.[2] These four are sometimes spoken of as the four angels that support the throne of God. Michael is conceived as a guardian of peoples and was chosen as prince of Israel.[3] In mediaeval legends he is represented as captain of the host of heaven who overthrew the forces of hell, and is conductor and guardian of the spirit of the dead. But these accord him an importance that is obviously contradicted by other legends and theories of theologians. Michael is usually represented as a warrior with a sword, sometimes with armour, sometimes with a pair of scales symbolic of justice, and sometimes with the dragon of Revelation (xii. 7) at his feet.

Gabriel in the Bible has no other function than that of messenger, but as messenger on supremely important occasions. He informs Daniel of the future happenings to his people;[4] he announces to Zacharias that Elizabeth shall bear him a son;[5] and to Mary that she is to conceive in her womb the Son of God.[6] Because of this last message to a virgin, Gabriel is represented with lilies in his hand.

Raphael is usually conceived as the prince of guardian angels, thus the guardian angel of humanity, but especially of pilgrims, and of the young and innocent, an idea derived from his guardianship of Tobias.[7] He is usually represented in the dress of a traveller, with a pilgrim's staff and a gourd of water.

Uriel, as his name implies, is the angel who shows to man the light of divine wisdom. This tradition arose mainly from Uriel demonstrating to Esdras his ignorance, revealing the significance of God's creations, and declaring the divine will.[8] Uriel is usually represented with a roll and a book.

The other three archangels are not named in Christian theology, but in Jewish theology all seven are named. There is no doubt of the four chief: Michael, Gabriel, Raphael, and Uriel, but accounts of the other three vary. According to the Ethiopic Book of Enoch, the other three are Raguel, Saraqâêl, and Remiel. Mrs. Jameson gives the three as Chamuel, Jophiel and Zadkiel.[9] The function of each angel is indicated in the passage in Enoch: 'Uriel . . . who is over the world and over Tartarus. Raphael . . . who is over the spirits of men. Raguel . . . who takes vengeance on the world of the luminaries. Michael . . . he that is set over the best part of mankind and over chaos. Saraqâêl . . . who is set over the spirits, who sin in the spirit. Gabriel . . . who is over Paradise and the serpents and the cherubim. Remiel . . . whom God set over those who rise.'[10] In every case, it will be observed, the name ends with 'el', signifying God. The meanings of the names are, therefore, all in reference to God; Michael: the likeness of God; Gabriel: the strength of God; Raphael: the medicine of God; Uriel: the light of God; Raguel: the terror of God; Saraqâêl: the turning of God; Remiel: the mercy of God; Chamuel: the seeing of God; Jophiel: the beauty of God; and Zadkiel; the righteousness of God.

In the angelic hierarchy of the pseudo-Dionysius archangels occupy the second rank in the third order. Together with the lowest rank of angels they are the messengers that directly reveal God to man, and make aware the troubles and prayers of man to God. These are the only ranks that are not hidden from man, these alone manifest God by visions and secret intimations. It is possible to regard this as a very profound symbolism.

1. Michael in Daniel xii. 1; x. 13; Jude 9; Revelation xii. 7.
2. Raphael in Tobit xii. 15; iii. 17; Uriel in II Esdras iv. 1.
3. Daniel xii. 1.
4. Daniel ix. 21 *et seq.*
5. Luke i. 26 *et seq.*
6. Luke i. 26 *et seq.*
7. Tobit xii. 15 *et seq.*; iii. 17, and iv. *et seq.*
8. Esdras, chaps. iv and v.
9. *Op. cit.*, vol. i, p. 88. Unfortunately MRS. JAMESON does not give the source of her information.
10. Chap. xx. Translated by R. H. CHARLES. 2nd edition, completely revised, 1912.

ARK—The term ark as used in the Old Testament is a translation of two different Hebrew words: 'têbah', meaning box of considerable dimensions and used for the

Plate I. Totem Poles.

(a) (*left*) Totem pole, 38 feet high, from Haida, Queen Charlotte Island, and now in the British Museum. This is an example of the totem poles erected before the dwellings of Tlingit, Haida and Tsimshian carved with the family crests of the owner. The carvings in this example are of ancestors and totem animals.

(b) (*right*) Totem pole of red cedar, 37 feet high, from the village of Angyada, Nass River, British Columbia, and now in the National Museum of Scotland, Edinburgh. It was erected in the nineteenth century in commemoration of Tsawit, a chief of the Niska, who had been killed by Tshimshian raiders. The carvings from the top are: ringed hat (Nikwaroet); human figure (family ancestor Towedstsatukt); raven, figuring as hlkuwilksegem Kaq, Prince of Ravens; human figure of an ancestor; fish, probably the white bullhead (Masrayait); and the Prince of Ravens again.

(a)

(b)

(c)

Plate II. The Queen's Beasts (*Crown copyright reserved*). These and the illustrations on the two following pages are of the sculptures of the Queen's Beasts made by James Woodford, R.A., and set in front of the Annexe of Westminster Abbey on the occasion of the Coronation of Elizabeth II (see p. 25). They now line the moat bridge at the entrance to Hampton Court Palace.

(*a*) The Lion of England. Dexter supporter of the present Royal Arms. A lion of gold with the royal crown on its head. *Shield:* present royal arms of England, the arms of Queen Elizabeth II.

(*b*) The Unicorn of Scotland. The sinister supporter of the royal arms. Round its neck is a coronet of gold composed of crosses patée and fleur-de-lis, to which a gold chain is attached. *Shield:* the royal arms of Scotland.

(*c*) The White Horse of Hanover. From arms borne by the kings of the Hanoverian dynasty. *Shield:* the royal arms as used by the Hanoverian kings of Britain from 1714 to c. 1801 (George I, II and III).

(a)

(b)

(c)

Plate III. The Queen's Beasts (*Crown copyright reserved*).

(*a*) The Greyhound of the Tudors. Supporter of the royal arms of Henry VII. A silver greyhound with a red collar round its neck. *Shield:* crowned Tudor rose on a field of the Tudor livery colours.

(*b*) The Dragon of the Tudors. Supporter of the royal arms of Henry VII. *Shield:* the arms of Wales. Heraldically the arms of Llywelyn ab Gruffydd, now borne in pretence by Princes of Wales.

(*c*) The Bull of Clarence. The black bull was a badge of Lionel, Duke of Clarence, son of Edward III and an ancestor of the Yorkist and Tudor sovereigns. *Shield:* Royal arms as used from Henry IV until Elizabeth I.

(*a*) The White Lion of Mortimer. A badge of the Mortimer family who were descended from Edward III and were ancestors of the Yorkist kings. *Shield:* white rose on soleil on a field of the livery colours of the House of York.

(*b*) The Yale of the Beauforts. *Shield:* Crowned portcullis on a field of the Beaufort liveries.

(*c*) The Falcon of the Plantagenets. A badge of Henry IV. *Shield:* A falcon within a fetterlock.

(*d*) The Griffin of Edward III, from his Privy Seal. *Shield:* badge of the House of Windsor on a field of the present royal livery colours.

Plate IV. The Queen's Beasts (*Crown copyright reserved*).

(*a*) and (*b*) Obverse and reverse of the first seal of Edward the Confessor (1042–66). In the obverse the sceptre held in the hand is surmounted by a fleur-de-lis. In the reverse the sceptre is surmounted by a bird while a sword is held in the left hand.

(*c*) and (*d*) Obverse and reverse of the first seal of William I (1066–87). This is the only example until the seal of Elizabeth II in which the obverse is an equestrian portrait of the monarch, and the reverse is the monarch enthroned, in all other seals the latter forms the obverse. It is thought that William I wished to be shown on the great seal of state firstly in his capacity of a warrior. In his left hand is a kite-shaped shield, held by a strap showing the inside.

(*e*) and (*f*) Obverse and reverse of the first great seal of Henry III. The obverse shows the king enthroned, the reverse the king mounted and carrying a shield of arms of England. (*Courtesy Trustees of the British Museum*).

Plate V. Seals of English Sovereigns.

(*a*) and (*b*) Obverse and reverse of the second seal of Richard I. The first seal showed on the obverse a crescent and wavy star on either side of the king's head and this second seal shows the crescent and sun both symbolical of Richard's crusade in the Holy Land.

(*c*) and (*d*) Obverse and reverse of the second seal of Elizabeth I. In the field above the horse on the reverse are the rose, fleur-de-lis and harp each with a crown above symbolizing the three kingdoms of England, France and Ireland.

Plate VI. Seals of English Sovereigns.

(a)

(b)

(c)

Plate VII.

(*a*) Reverse of the second seal of the Commonwealth, showing the interior of the House of Commons with the words 'In the third year of freedom by God's blessing restored', rule by the House of Commons being symbolical of that freedom. The first Commonwealth seal is similar.

(*b*) Obverse of the fifth seal of George III. The enthroned monarch holding sceptre and orb surmounted by cross is shown with three allegorical figures on his right: Justice with sword and scales, Minerva symbolizing learning, and Hercules expressive of power; on the monarch's left are Piety with church in her hand and Britannia with palm branch and the British Lion. This is typical of the other seals of the Georges with their allegorical figures.

(*c*) Reverse of the seal of George V which is unique among the royal seals, because instead of the usual equestrian effigy of the monarch King George is shown on the bridge of a battleship expressive of his naval training.

Plate VIII. Obverse and reverse of the seal of Elizabeth II. This design by Gilbert Ledward, R.A., continues the simpler treatment of the seal of George VI as a reaction to the ornate seals of Anne to Edward VII. An unusual feature of this seal is that the equestrian portrait forms the obverse, the only other example in English history being the seal of William the Conqueror. (*Reproduced by permission of the Lord Chancellor*)

(a)

(b)

(c)

(d)

(e)

(f)

(g)

(h)

Plate IX. Greek Symbolic Coins.

(*a*) Triscele, Syracuse, 357–317 B.C.
(*b*) Swastika, Syracuse, 357–317 B.C.
(*c*) Eagle, Capua, about 215 B.C.
(*d*) Serpent-staff of Aesculapius, Pergamum, 133–67 B.C.
(*e*) Sphinx, Gergis (Troas), 350–241 B.C.
(*f*) Vine, Soli (Cicilia), 385–333 B.C.
(*g*) Tripod, Croton, 550–510 B.C.
(*h*) Ear of corn, Metapontum, 550–510 B.C.

(a) Nero, A.D. 54–68. On the reverse is the figure of the goddess Roma with helmet which may have influenced representations of Britannia.

(b) Hadrian, A.D. 119. The reverse shows the figure o Britannia, one of the earliest representations of the subject.

(c) Antoninus Pius, A.D. 154. The representation of Britannia is a prototype of modern representations.

(d) At the time of the Stuarts the Roman use of Britannia was revived on the reverse of coins. In this farthing of Charles II she is shown with the shield bearing the Union Jack, spear and olive branch.

(e) Farthing of George IV with Britannia turned to the right with trident and Union Jack on the shield.

(f) Bank of England dollar of George III. Britannia is shown with olive branch, spear, Union Jack on shield with beehive and cornucopia, symbols of industry and plenty.

Plate X. Coins Showing Representations of Britannia.

(*a*) Gold angel of Edward IV, about 1470. Obverse shows Archangel Michael slaying a dragon, and reverse a ship with mast in the form of a cross and shield with royal arms. On one side of the mast is E and on the other a rose. A similar coin was issued in the latter part of the reign of Henry VI but with H and fleur-de-lis beside the mast.

(*b*) Gold George noble of Henry VIII. Obverse shows ship with Tudor rose and H and K (Henry and Katherine of Aragon). The reverse shows the earliest representation on coins of St. George and the Dragon.

(*c*) Coins of George VI, 1951. The sixpence, shilling and half-crown show the royal motifs of arms, crown and cypher, the florin has the floral emblems of England, Scotland and Ireland, the threepenny piece has appropriately the thrift plant, the five shilling piece perpetuates Pestrucci's famous design of St. George and the Dragon, the halfpenny shows the ship the *Golden Hind*, the wren—the smallest bird—appropriately occupies the farthing, while the penny shows the latest version of Britannia.

Plate XI. British Coins.

(*a*) Elizabeth II coins (see p. 79).

(*b*) Decimal coinage. Reverses designed by Christopher Ironside. The 50p coin shows Britannia with lion, shield, trident and olive branch, the first time since the coins of George III that Britannia is depicted holding an olive branch. The 10p coin shows part of the crest of England depicting the crowned lion, and the 5p coin shows the thistle, symbol of Scotland, crowned. On the 2p coin are three ostrich feathers in a coronet with crosses pattée and fleurs-de-lis with motto 'Ich Dien', emblem of the Prince of Wales. The 1p coin has a crowned portcullis which was originally a badge of the Beauforts and of Henry VII. It is used on the 1p coin, however, because of its long association with Parliament. On the $\frac{1}{2}$p coin is the Royal Crown.

Plate XII. British Coins.

(*a*) Bahama Island coins, 1966 (see p. 79).

(*b*) Gambia coins, 1966 (see p. 79).

(*c*) Ghana coins, 1966 (see pp. 79, 80).

Plate XIII.

(*a*) New Zealand coins, 1966 (see p. 80).

(*b*) Tanzania coins, 1966 (see p. 80).

Plate XIV.

(*a*) Irish Republic 10/– piece, 1966, commemorating the 50th anniversary of the rebellion at Easter 1916, symbolized on the reverse by the figure of Prometheus. Designed by T. H. Paget.

(*b*) Singapore coins, 1967 (see p. 80).

(*c*) Fiji coins, 1968 (see p. 80).

Plate XV.

(*a*) Reverse of medal of Cecilia Gonzaga (1447) by Pisanello, with the unicorn, symbol of virginity, reclining by the side of a seated woman.

(*b*) Obverse and reverse of medal of Vittorina da Feltre the mathematician. On the reverse is the pelican and its young.

(*c*) Obverse and reverse of one of the medals of Elizabeth commemorating the victory over the Spanish Armada. On the reverse is a bay-tree on a small island with lightning from which the bay-tree is immune, thus symbolizing the safety of England the island country.

(*d*) Obverse and reverse of memorial medal of Charles I. The reverse shows a diamond on an anvil which splits the hammer that strikes it.

Plate XVI. Symbolic Medals.

(a) The first coronation medal was this of Edward VI, which shows the crowned Tudor rose, harp, portcullis and fleur-de-lis on the border.

(b) Coronation medal of Charles I. The sword on the reverse expresses the intention to proceed vigorously with the war.

(c) Coronation medal of Charles II. The reverse shows the oak tree in full foliage, symbolizing renewal, with three crowns, and the sun shining overhead.

Plate XVII. Coronation Medals.

(*a*) One of the coronation medals of William and Mary by George Bower. The reverse shows Perseus and Andromeda symbolizing William's rescue of England.

(*b*) Coronation medal of George I by Ehrenreich Hannibal. On the reverse the king is represented being crowned by Britannia.

(*c*) One of the coronation medals of Victoria.

Plate XVIII. Coronation Medals.

(a) International Fisheries Exhibition, 1883; note-worthy for the beautiful design of fishes in a circle.

(b) Five-hundredth anniversary of the birth of Johannes Gutenberg, the inventor of printing in Europe. The earliest printing press is shown, with palm symbolizing victorious achievement.

(c) Andrew W. Mellon, Secretary of the United States Treasury, 1921. The American eagle stands on olive and oak branches, symbols of peace and strength. On the scroll are scales for justice, stars on a stripe, and a key.

(d) Twenty-fifth anniversary medal of the Mond Nickel Company. The word 'nickel' originally signified rascal or mischievous demon, the name given to kupfernickel, from which nickel was separated by Cronsted in 1751, because, contrary to the expectation prompted by its appearance, it yielded no copper. The demon is shown on the obverse springing from flames, which expresses the refining of nickel by volatilization, a discovery of Dr. Ludwig Mond and Dr. Langer. On the reverse are maple leaves symbolizing Canada, where nickel is found, and daffodils symbolizing Wales, where it is refined. Designed and modelled by Percy Metcalf.

Plate XIX. Symbolic Medals (reverses).

(a) Reverse of the Ashanti medal of 1901. The British Lion looks at the rising sun while a native shield and two spears lie at his feet.

(b) Reverse of the Second World War medal 1939–45. The British lion stands triumphant over a two-headed dragon signifying the enemies of the occident and the orient.

(c) Reverse of the Observer Corps medal. An Elizabethan helmeted figure stands by a signal-fire and looks out to sea holding aloft a fire brand.

(d) Reverse of Korea medal showing Hêraklês killing the Hydra.

(e) Ministry of Housing medal awarded for merit in the design and planning of housing 1950—this is a fairly direct expression with a block of houses and objects associated with their design like dividers, rolls of paper and a lamp.

Plate XX. Modern Medals.

(*a*) Housing medal, 1962, a close adaptation by Christopher Ironside of Leonardo da Vinci's drawing of a man in a circle illustrating Vitruvius's system of human proportions, thus symbolising that architectural excellence is based on proportion which is based in turn on the human figure. (See Vitruvius 3.1.)

(*b*) Obverse of the Royal Society, Mullard medal, 1967. The design shows a geometrical wave motif modelled by Abram Games. The medal is awarded for outstanding scientific or technological work. There does not appear to be any precise motif in the design, but, the designer being aware of the purpose of the medal, the symbolism is probably partly subconscious.

(*c*) Royal Numismatic Society of New Zealand medal, 1966, commemorating the introduction of decimal coinage, July 1967. The obverse shows six decimal coins overlapping, and the reverse a map of New Zealand with stars of the Southern Cross and fern. Modelled by James Berry.

Plate XXI. Modern Medals.

(a) In the Getreidegasse, Salzburg, are many decorative signs. In the foreground is the sign of a shoemaker and in the distance is the sign of a glazier which shows a stained glass disk with a key.

(b) Sign of crown with three loaves in Creechurch Lane, City of London. Below the sign is a tablet on the wall inscribed 'Hanging above this tablet is the ancient sign of Davison, Newman & Co. the oldest Teamen in the world—Established A.D. 1650.'

(c) Sign of a clothier's shop in the Getreidegasse, Salzburg.

(d) Brezel sign of Bakers' guild in the Getreidegasse, Salzburg. A café sign can also be seen.

Plate XXII. Shop Signs.

(a) Spreadeagle, Barclays Bank, Lombard Street.

(b) Grasshopper, Martin's Bank, Lombard Street.

(c) Sign of the Scottish Widows' Fund and Life Assurance Society, Cornhill.

(d) King's Head and Cat-a-Fiddling signs, Commercial Bank of Scotland, Lombard Street.

(e) Sign of the Cornhill Insurance Co. Ltd., Cornhill.

(f) Black Horse, Lloyd's Bank, Lombard Street.

Plate XXIII. Bank, Insurance and Old Adopted Signs (see p. 98) in the City of London.

(a) Brewer's Delight, Canterbury. A design of barley and hops by K. M. Doyle (1948) which suggests what can be obtained at the inn.

(b) Duke of York, Cranbrook (also a Whitbread sign). An heraldic sign expressing local association. These a the royal arms of Edward III. His son Langley Duke York introduced the original Flemish weaves Cranbrook, and from this sprang Britain's gre woollen industry. Design by Kathleen M. Claxton, 19.

(c) Rose and Crown at East Grinstead (an Ind Coope and Allsopp sign), sign of heraldic derivation. Design by Francis Coudrill.

(d) The Queen's Head, Westminster. Elizabeth I w usually the model for the Queen's Head, and this a the King's Head are very popular signs. Design by Stocks May.

Plate XXIV. Modern Inn Signs.

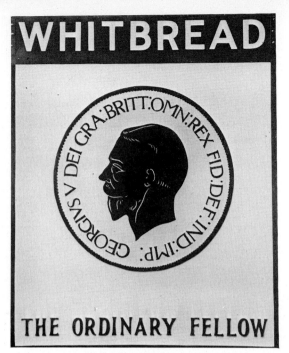

(a) The Ordinary Fellow, Chatham, from a remark of George V, 'I like to think of myself as just an ordinary sort of fellow.' Design by Violet Rutter, 1944.

(b) Clothworkers Arms, Sutton Valance. A trade sign design by Vena Chalker, 1946.

(d) Coach and Horses on the old London to Manchester road at Fenny Bentley, Derbyshire. Another design by F. Stocks May for Ind Coope and Allsopp.

(c) Sportsman Inn in Smithies, Barnsley. A sporting sign of Ind Coope and Allsopp. Design by F. Stocks May.

Plate XXV. Modern Inn Signs.

(*a*) The North Pole, Wateringbury. Design by Kathleen M. Claxton, 1939.

(*b*) The Anchor, Stowting. 'It is well to moor your boat with two anchors', Publius Syrus. Design by Kathleen M. Claxton, 1948.

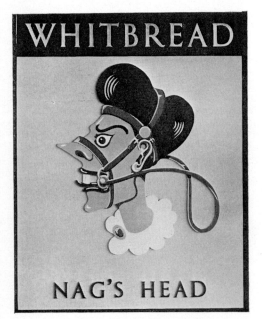

(*c*) Nag's Head, St. Leonards. 'It is better to dwell in the wilderness than with a contentious and an angry woman', Proverbs. Design by Violet Rutter, 1946. All the signs on this page are Whitbread's.

(*d*) Startled Saint, West Malling. The crusader St. Leonard is said to have rested at West Malling during his miraculous flight from a saracen prison to prevent his wife's second marriage. An aerodrome is now situated near West Malling and the sign is a speculation on St. Leonard's reaction should he return today. Design by Violet Rutter, 1940.

Plate XXVI. Modern Inn Signs.

Plate XXVII. Four British Railway posters. Effective examples of symbolism by association in which a vision of the delights of holidays and recreation and the comforts of travel are conveyed by objects and circumstances associated with them.

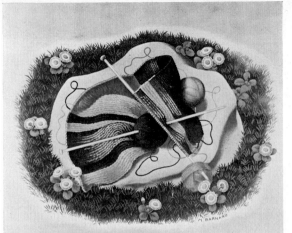

(*a*) and (*b*) suggest the value of symbolism by association.

(*c*) War-time poster simple and direct in its appeal.

(*d*) Poster based on a familiar saying.

Plate XXVIII. London Transport Posters.

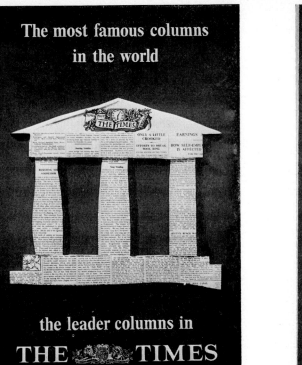

Plate XXIX. *The Times*, British Railway and Capstan cigarette posters. The symbolism of these posters is self-explanatory, apt and eloquent.

(*a*) Shrink Fit. This I.C.I. advertisement 'for Drikold' showing the tight lacing of a fashionable woman of the eighteenth century is an apt analogy of the shrink-fit process in engineering. A 2,000-ton hydraulic forging press had to be overhauled because of wear, and it was decided to 'shrink fit' new parts in place of worn ones. A metal part to be fitted by this process is deliberately made a precise amount too large. When extreme cold is applied the part shrinks and can be fitted into another. The metal expands as the temperature rises to normal and a very tight fit is thus ensured. 'Drikold' is a solid refrigerant which, with a temperature of minus 110° F., is a convenient means of producing extreme cold.

(*b*) Cuckoo in the Nest. The cuckoo is used in this I.C.I. advertisement as a symbol of the undesirable presence of excessive frothing in the distillation process in the production of chloroform, with the disadvantage that the stills could not be filled to capacity. The I.C.I. proposed the use of chlorine and hydrated lime instead of chloride of lime which eliminated the frothing with beneficial effects on output.

Plate XXX. Pictorial Advertising.

Plate XXXI. British postage stamps of George VI's reign up to 1948. The stamps at the top and bottom left corners are the peace stamps with the theme of reconstruction. The first use on stamps of the emblems of England, Scotland, Wales and Ireland is shown in the Coronation stamps of 1937. The stamp in the centre ($2\frac{1}{2}$d) celebrates the silver wedding of George VI and Elizabeth in 1948. Several stamps are shown commemorating the Olympic Games held in London in 1948. (*Courtesy of the Post Office*)

Plate XXXII. British commemorative stamps, 1951–1958. The two top stamps mark the Festival of Britain 1951 with appropriate symbols. The next four mark the Coronation of 1953, in which the regalia of the ceremony appear together with the national emblem. The three lower left celebrate the World Scout Jubilee Jamboree 1957, and the three lower right the Commonwealth Games held in Cardiff in 1958, as indicated by the Welsh dragon. (*Courtesy of the Post Office*)

Plate XXXIII. British commemorative stamps, 1960–1963. Top left (3d.) and right (1s. 3d.) celebrate the tercentenary of the General Letter Post 1960. One stamp (of an issue of two) marks the seventh Parliamentary Conference, one (of an issue of three) the Conference of European Telecommunications Administration; two (of an issue of three) mark the centenary of the Post Office Savings Bank, and two the Freedom from Hunger campaign 1963. (*Courtesy of the Post Office*)

Plate XXXIV. British commemorative stamps 1964–1965. Four stamps celebrated the International Geographical Congress, 1st July, 1964, two the opening of the Forth Bridge 1964, two the seven hundredth anniversary of Simon de Montfort's Parliament, two the Joseph Lister Centenary 1965, and two the Commonwealth Arts Festival. (*Courtesy of the Post Office*)

Plate XXXV. British commemorative stamps 1966-69. Two stamps celebrated the European Free Trade Association, 20th February, 1967; four commemorated British Technology, 19th September, 1966, and four British Discovery. Two of four commemorate Post Office Technology. The 9*d*., symbolizes International Subscriber Dialling by a hemisphere of the globe with a segment of a telephone dial in each corner. The 1/– stamp symbolizes Pulse Code Modulation which makes possible up to 24 telephone conversations to be made over one circuit simultaneously. The design shows the wave patterns of two voices travelling interleaved in one circuit. (*Courtesy of the Post Office*)

Plate XXXVI. U.S.A. symbolic postage stamps 1957–65. From left to right: 1957—Centenary of American Institute of Architects, with representation of an ancient Corinthian capital and modern mushroom capital. 1957—International Geophysical Year 1957–58, illustrating Michelangelo's 'Creation of Adam' above the sun. 1959—Commemorating the opening of the St. Lawrence seaway showing the Canadian maple linked with the American eagle. 1960—World Refugee Year showing a family looking towards the light. 1957—Centenary of American steel industry showing the eagle and ladle pouring molten steel. 1960—U.S.A.–Japan Treaty showing cherry blossom in front of Washington monument. 1961—Anniversary of Workman's Compensation; the symbol suggests that the interests of industry and family life are equally balanced. 1962—Anniversary of National Apprenticeship symbolizing the transfer or passing on of skill. 1963—Centenary of Emancipation Proclamation symbolized by the broken chain. 1965—Seven hundred and fiftieth anniversary of Magna Carta; King John's crown significantly suggests an ink-well with quills. (*Courtesy of the Postmaster-General of the United States*)

Plate XXXVII. United Nations Stamps (see pp. 119–20).

Plate XXXVIII. United Nations Stamps (see pp. 119–20).

Plate XXXIX. American Symbolic State Flowers.
1   Apple Blossom—Arkansas, Michigan
2   Hawthorn—Missouri
3   Indian Paint Brush—Wyoming
4   Sego Lily—Utah
5   Syringa (Lewis Mock orange)—Idaho
6   Bitter Root—Montana
7   Magnolia—Mississippi, Louisiana
8   Zinnia—Indiana
9   Purple Lilac—New Hampshire
10 American Dogwood—Virginia, North Carolina
11 Wild Rose—Iowa, North Dakota
12 Pine Cone and Tassel—Maine
13 Red Clover—Vermont
14 Bluebonnet—Texas
15 Golden Poppy—California
16 Yellow Jasmine—South Carolina
17 Moccasin Flower—Minnesota
18 Mayflower (Trailing arbutus)—Massachusetts

Plate XL. American Symbolic State Flowers.

1   Ox-eye Daisy—no longer a state flower
2   Peach Blossom—Delaware
3   Mountain Laurel—Connecticut, Pennsylvania
4   Passion Flower—formerly of Tennessee
5   Violet—Illinois, New Jersey, Rhode Island, Wisconsin
6   Black-eyed Susan—Maryland
7   Orange Blossom—Florida
8   Goldenrod—Alabama, Kentucky, Nebraska
9   Sunflower—Kansas
10 Columbine—Colorado
11 Yucca—New Mexico
12 Scarlet Carnation—Ohio
13 Cherokee Rose—Georgia
14 Forget-me-not—Alaska
15 Rose—District of Columbia, New York
16 Sagebrush—Nevada
17 Pasqueflower—South Dakota
18 Mistletoe—Oklahoma
19 Rhododendron—Washington, West Virginia
20 Oregon Grape—Oregon
21 Sanguaro (giant cactus)—Arizona

Plate XLI. Modern Lutheran church of the Trinity at Hamburg, completed in 1958. In this design alpha and omega have been taken as the symbolic motifs, alpha forming the elevation of the campanile, and omega the plan of the church. It is a precise form of symbolism like the cross plan. The architect, Reinhard Riemerschmid, states that the idea was based on the interior design. He intended to design a long central space, rising towards the altar, and symbolizing adoration. This concept has been realized. But even an instinctive feeling for statics called for the provision of a counter-arch which gave rise to the shielding walls on either side of the main entrance. This arch suited the architect also for town planning reasons, as it appears to spread out like two welcoming arms towards the road which runs up to the church at an oblique angle. The architectural idea of the belfry dates back much longer. When the architect found that the church nave and the alpha belfry were in a fortunate juxtaposition, he finally adopted this design for this church. It was only when seeing the design on a sketch that he discovered in the plan the omega of the church and the alpha of the belfry. The architect is inclined to see a parallel to this coincidence in the development of the cruciform design of the Roman Basilica which emerged from the use of the transept traditionally used in the ancient Basilicas, and probably assumed symbolic importance at a much later date.

(*a*) Interior of Amiens Cathedral (thirteenth century), one of the superb examples of Gothic architecture in which the idea of aspiration is expressed by the long columns terminating in the shadowy vault. It is one of the loftiest of Gothic vaults, being 140 feet from the floor. (*Courtesy Mansell Collection*)

(*b*) The Parthenon, Athens (fifth century B.C.), one of the perfect examples of the Greek temple in which the ideas of grandeur, repose and resignation are impressively expressed.

Plate XLII. Symbolism in Architecture.

(a) Goethe said in his autobiography that the steeple aspires to heaven without and the dome encloses heaven within. The loftiest spire in England, that of Salisbury (404 feet high), floodlit and reflected in the river and the dome of St. Paul's are selected as examples of this symbolism. (*Courtesy The Times*)

(b) The dome of St. Paul's is reproduced from an engraving by E. Challis from a drawing by R. W. Billings which appeared in Godwin's *Churches of London* (London, 1838).

Plate XLIII. Symbolism in Architecture.

(a) Notre-Dame du Haut pilgrim chapel at Ronchamp (aerial view) France, designed by Le Corbusier and completed in 1955. This is an interesting attempt to create religious character and atmosphere with the medium of mass concrete based on the nature of the building and its site. Here the symbolism is not precise, but emerges from the essential forms and the chiaroscuro of the interior, the latter achieved by small irregular windows in the thick concrete walls. (*Courtesy Editions Sofer*)

(b) Pont du Gard—Roman aqueduct near Nîmes in the south of France. In a famous passage in *A Little Town in France* Henry James saw in this a symbol of many aspects of ancient Roman civilization.

(c) Hornsey Town Hall (1933). Architect: Reginald H. Uren. The belfry which in the medieval town hall served the purpose of summoning citizens to a meeting survives in the modern town hall as a symbol of a building type. Other famous modern examples are the city or town halls of Stockholm (1914–24), Hilversum (1928–31), Swansea (1930) and Cachan on the Seine (1934).

Plate XLIV. Symbolism in Architecture.

(*a*) The Church of the Advent, Copenhagen (1947). Architect: Erik Møller. Although modern and belonging essentially to the mid-twentieth century, a religious feeling akin both to the Greek and Medieval is suggested in its forms.

(*b*) Liverpool Cathedral (Roman Catholic) completed in 1967. Architect: Sir Frederick Gibberd, A.R.A. (see pp. 169–70).

Plate XLV. Symbolism in Architecture.

(*a*) (*left*) Memorial in the Compiègne forest near Paris which marks the spot where the armistice of the First World War was signed on 11th November, 1918. The sword forms the cross, and the German eagle pierced by the sword lies on the base.

(*b*) (*below left*) Memorial seat to Margaret MacDonald in Lincoln's Inn Fields which shows a woman extending protecting arms to children.

(*c*) (*below*) Child taking a sheaf of wheat out of a shell in the grounds of the Shell building at The Hague. This sculpture was placed there by the employees of the Shell Company in gratitude for the food supplied to Dutch children by the Company during the German occupation.

Plate XLVI. Symbolical Sculpture.

(*a*) Tomb of Lorenzo de Medici with the reclining figures of 'Twilight' and 'Dawn'. (*Courtesy W. F. Mansell*)

(*b*) Tomb of Guiliano de Medici with the reclining figures of 'Night' and 'Day'. (*Courtesy W. F. Mansell*)

Plate XLVII. Symbolical Sculpture—the Medici Tombs in the New Sacristy of San Lorenzo in Florence, by Michelangelo.

(*a*) (*right*) Mourning woman, a Greek work of the fourth century B.C. in which the forms express the idea of sorrow.

(*b*) (*above*) Warrior with Shield by Henry Moore. This battered warrior symbolizes in the mind of the sculptor his feelings about England during the crucial part of the war. It expresses 'a heroic resistance to physical misfortune' with a 'blunted and bull-like power' (see p. 178). (*c*) (*left*) The Sun Worshipper, by Alex Ebbe, in the gardens at Malmo, Sweden.

Plate XLVIII. Symbolical Sculpture.

Plate XLIX. (*a*) and (*b*) Symbolic sculptures of 'Night' and 'Day' by Sir Jacob Epstein on the London Transport Executive Building at St. James's, London (see p. 176). (*Courtesy London Transport Executive*)

(*a*) 'Pointing Figure—with Child' 1966, bronze by Bernard Meadows. G.L.C. Sculpture Exhibition, Battersea Park, 1966.

(*b*) 'Maquette for Confluence' 1966, in cast aluminium by Ralph Brown. G.L.C. Sculpture Exhibition, Battersea Park, 1966.

(*c*) 'Booz' 1955, bronze by Martin Etienne. L.C.C. Sculpture Exhibition, Battersea Park, 1960.

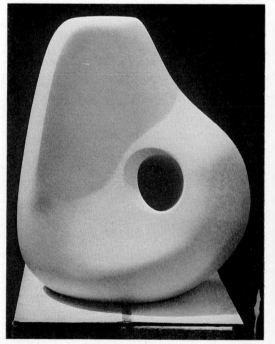

(*d*) 'Talisman II' 1960, white marble, by Barbara Hepworth.

Plate L. Abstract Sculpture of an Organic Character with Symbolical Expression.

Plate XLIX. (*a*) and (*b*) Symbolic sculptures of 'Night' and 'Day' by Sir Jacob Epstein on the London Transport Executive Building at St. James's, London (see p. 176). (*Courtesy London Transport Executive*)

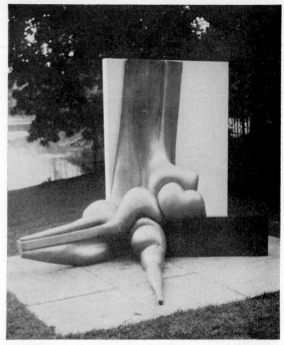

(a) 'Pointing Figure—with Child' 1966, bronze by Bernard Meadows. G.L.C. Sculpture Exhibition, Battersea Park, 1966.

(b) 'Maguette for Confluence' 1966, in cast aluminium by Ralph Brown. G.L.C. Sculpture Exhibition, Battersea Park, 1966.

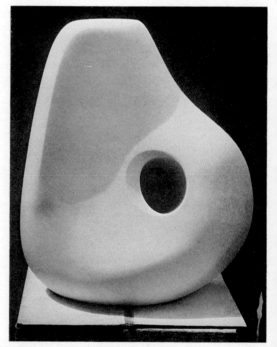

(c) 'Booz' 1955, bronze by Martin Etienne. L.C.C. Sculpture Exhibition, Battersea Park, 1960.

(d) 'Talisman II' 1960, white marble, by Barbara Hepworth.

Plate L. Abstract Sculpture of an Organic Character with Symbolical Expression.

(*a*) and (*b*) Two works in bronze by Henry Moore both called 'Two Piece Reclining Figures'. (*b*) is a smaller version of that in the Lincoln Centre, New York. The appeal of these works is both formal and symbolic. L.C.C. Sculpture Exhibition, Battersea Park, 1960.

(*c*) 'Serpent de Feu' (Serpent of Fire) 1956, bronze by François Stahly. L.C.C. Sculpture Exhibition, Battersea Park, 1960.

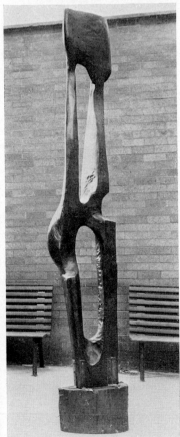

(*d*) (*left*) Joined upright formed in ciment fondu by Ronn Smith. Bone structure probably prompted this work and it could be regarded as symbolic of essential life forms.

(*e*) (*below*) 'Berger des Nuages' (Shepherd of the Clouds) 1953, bronze by Jean Arp. L.C.C. Sculpture Exhibition, Battersea Park, 1960.

Plate LI. Abstract Sculpture of an Organic Character with Symbolical Expression.

(*a*) (*above left*) 'O and A' 1965, steel, by Bryan Knealy. G.L.C. Sculpture Exhibition, Battersea Park, 1966.
(*b*) (*below left*) 'Isomet' 1966, welded steel painted by David Hall. G.L.C. Sculpture Exhibition, Battersea Park, 1966.
(*c*) (*right*) Sculpture in iron and steel, 1961, by Richard Stankiewicz. L.C.C. Exhibition, Battersea Park, 1963.

(*d*) 'Month of May' 1963, in aluminium and steel by Anthony Caro. G.L.C. Sculpture Exhibition, Battersea Park, 1966.

Plate LII. Abstract Sculpture of a Geometric or Mechanical Character with Symbolical Expression.

(a) (left) 'Signal' 1959, bronze by André Bloc. L.C.C. Sculpture Exhibition, Battersea Park, 1960.
(b) (right) 'Linear no. 3 with red' 1953, construction in plastic and stainless steel springs with aluminium base by Naum Gabo. In such sculpture or constructions one important purpose is the expression or symbolism of space, and of rhythms in relation to space.

Plate LIII. Abstract Sculpture of a Geometric or Mechanical Character with Symbolical Expression.

(*a*) (*above left*) The Adoration of the Kings by Mabuse (1478–1535).
(*b*) (*above*) Adoration of the Magi by Veronese (1528–1588).
(*c*) (*left*) The Virgin and Child, attributed to Dürer (1471–1528).

Plate LIV. Pictures in which the infant Christ, signifying the birth of Christianity, is seen against a background of classical ruins, symbolizing the end of the Pagan world. All are in the National Gallery, London, and are reproduced by courtesy of the Trustees.

(a) The Resurrection by Piero della Francesca, in Borgo San Sepolcro, Arezzo.

(b) Virgin and Child with an Angel by Perugino. Centre panel of a triptych in the National Gallery London.

(c) The Crucifixion by Raphael. National Gallery, London. This and the picture by Perugino are reproduced by courtesy of the Trustees.

Plate LV. Symbolism of Religious Emotion by Representation of Space.

(*a*) 'Pietà' by an unknown painter of Avignon—Louvre.
(*Courtesy Mansell Collection*)

(*b*) 'Primavera' by Botticelli in the Accademia, Florence.
The three figures on the right symbolize the change
from the cold and strong winds of winter to the
sprightly figure of spring. (*Courtesy Mansell Collection*)

Plate LVI. Symbolism by Linear Rhythms.

(*a*) (*above*) 'Comedy' by Paul Klee (1879–1940), Tate
Gallery, London. Copyright by S.P.A.D.E.M., Paris.
This and the picture by Paul Nash are reproduced by
courtesy of the Trustees.
(*b*) (*right*) 'Girls on the Bridge' by Edward Munch
(1863–1944). Norwegian National Gallery, Oslo.
(*c*) (*below*) 'Landscape from a Dream' by Paul Nash
(1889–1946), Tate Gallery, London.

Plate LVII. Symbolism in Painting by Abstracted
Shapes, Emotional Rhythms and Dream Objects.

The Palmieri altarpiece, Assumption of the Virgin, by Botticini (1446–98) in the National Gallery, London, and reproduced by courtesy of the Trustees. This picture of the angelic hierarchy shows the three orders of angels, each with three ranks, as given by the Pseudo-Dionysius the Areopagite. (See pp. 199–200)

Plate LVIII. Angels in Pictorial Art.

(*a*) Sculpture in wood of the Madonna and Child with the symbol of the apple. A work of the fifteenth century, from the church of Leen in Germany and now in the Bavarian National Museum at Munich.

(*b*) 'Elijah in the Wilderness' by Lord Leighton, in the Walker Art Gallery, Liverpool.

Plate LIX. Symbolism of the Apple and of Angels in Pictorial Art.

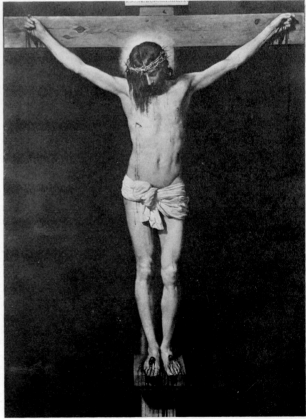

(a) 'Christ of St. John of the Cross' by Salvador Dali, in the Glasgow Art Gallery. In addition to depicting the central symbol of Christianity this picture gives an impression of vast space which itself stimulates the religious emotion and is a form of symbolism. This suggestion of space in association with religious feeling is apparent also in the pictures of Piero della Francesca, Perugino and Raphael (see Plate LV and Chapter XX).

(b) The Crucifixion, by Velasquez, in the Gallery of the Prado, Madrid. This famous painting is, in the opinion of many, one of the most moving conceptions of the subject. The legs of Christ being brought straight down makes a more impressive and dignified arrangement than crossed legs. The latter, however, is more familiar.

Plate LX. Crucifix.

Two Cretan pots of about 2000 B.C. in the museum at Herakleion, with, *left*, double headed axe and, *right*, palmette.

War Memorial (1914–18 war), Leicester, designed by Sir Edwin Lutyens, P.R.A. It will be seen that this beautifully proportional arch is three-dimensional in character, which, like the Somme Memorial, links it with the ancient Janus arch symbol of the sky and the heavens.

Plate LXI.

Bronze entrance doors to the Bank of England (*c.* 1930) on which caducei are represented. (See description, p. 217). Architects: Sir Herbert Baker, R.A., and A. T. Scott. (*Courtesy The Governor and Company of the Bank of England*)

Plate LXII. Caduceus.

(*a*) (*left*) Bronze caduceus of the fifth century B.C. discovered in a tomb in Sicily and now in the British Museum. It bears the inscription 'I belong to the people of Longene' (a Sicilian town). It was probably the staff of the herald of that town.

(*b*) (*right*) Bronze statue of Mercury, carrying the caduceus, made in 1567 by Giovanni da Bologna. Now in the Bargello gallery, Florence.

Plate LXIII. Caduceus.

(a)

(b)

(c)

(d)

(e)

(f)

(*a*) The Cenotaph, London. (*Courtesy The Times*)
(*b*) Pine Cone Fountain.
(*c*) Triton fountain by Bernini in the Piazza Barbarini.
(*d*) Shell fountain, Piazza Barbarini.
(*e*) Fountain in Museum of Capitol.
(*f*) American War Memorial Fountain.

Plate LXIV. Fountains and Cenotaph.

(a) Lion Gate, Mycenae, about 900 B.C.
(b) Trajan's Column, in the Forum of Trajan, Rome. (*Courtesy W. F. Mansell*)
(c) American Meuse Argonne Memorial at Montfaucon, battle memorial of the First World War. (*Courtesy American Battle Monuments Commission*)

Plate LXV. Columns.

(a) (left) Greek stele of the fourth century B.C., still in situ in the Dipylon Cemetery at Athens. It is typical of numerous other fourth century stelae showing family groups, in which the deceased either bids farewell to friends and relatives on earth or greets them in Hades. The symbol of farewell or greeting is, as will be seen, the handshake, which is the prototype of the clasped hands on the modern memorial.

(b) (below left) Griffins. Temple of Didyma, Miletus. 3rd–1st century B.C.

(c) (below right) Gorgon's Head. Temple of Didyma, Miletus. 3rd–1st century B.C.

Plate LXVI.

(b) Papal Tiara.

(c) Medieval Turkish tombstones surmounted by hats which indicate the social rank or status of the deceased.

(a) Cardinal Cristoforo Della Rovere. Sculptor: Mino da Fiesole. (*Courtesy W. F. Mansell*)

Plate LXVII. Mitre, Cardinal's Hat, Papal Tiara and Turkish Stelec.

Plate LXVIII. Stained glass window in Newbiggin church, Newcastle, designed by S. M. Scott, of Millican, Baguley and Atkinson Ltd. A profusion of Christian symbolism is shown in this window which is simply and effectively treated. At the top of the centre light is the Pascal Lamb, while the symbols of the four evangelists appear at the tops of the other lights. The figures are Christ and the four archangels; from left to right, Uriel, the light of God holding a book as the interpreter of the prophecies; Gabriel, the angel of the annunciation, holding a lily, symbol of purity; Michael, conqueror of evil, symbolized by the serpent; and Raphael, guardian of travellers with staff, scrip, and the pilgrim's scallop shell. At the feet of Christ is alpha and omega, and below are three fishes and coal symbolizing the industries of the district. The coats of arms are of the sees of Durham and Newcastle (second and fifth lights) and of the Province of York with the keys of St. Peter. The patron of the church, St. Bartholomew, was martyred by flaying and is represented by the three knives on the left shield.

(*a*) Washington obelisk monument, as seen from the Lincoln Memorial, with a tripod in the foreground.

(*b*) The lion as guardian. A pottery lion from China, Taang Dynasty (A.D. 618–906).

Plate LXIX. Obelisk and Lion.

Plate LXX. Gods of Olympus, Relief of Artemis, and Menorah.

(a) (above left) Gods of Olympus and their symbols and emblems. Marble relief over a chimney piece in the eighteenth-century house at 4 St. James's Square, London, now occupied by the Arts Council. Rupert Guinnis ascribes the work to M. Rysbrack. The relief depicts various gods before Zeus and Hera. Each is depicted with his emblem, thus Zeus with the eagle, Hera with the peacock, Poseidon with the trident, and Hermes with the caduceus. The ram, a common animal for sacrifice in Greece and Rome, is brought apparently by the only mortal in the scene.

(b) (left) Relief of Artemis from Helleuistre temple at Antalya now in museum. Behind her head is the sun and crescent moon, while she holds in her hand a bow indicating her capacity as a huntress.

(c) (above) Menorah—on the obverse of a medal by Paul Vincze to commemorate the three hundredth anniversary of the resettlement of the Jews in Great Britain—1965. The menorah (seven-branched candlestick) is similar to that shown on the Arch of Titus. In the panel at the top of the medal is shown the Tabernacle.

(*a*) Sarcophagus of Theodore, Bishop of Ravenna, in the
Basilica of St. Apollinare in Classe, Ravenna. Of the
fifth century, this sarcophagus is typical of many early
Christian sarcophagi. It is particularly rich in symbolism, showing representations of the sacred monogram
with alpha and omega, peacocks, vine and doves.

(*b*) Mosaic of Christ enthroned with angels, in the
Basilica of S. Apollinare Nuovo, Ravenna. Sixth
century A.D. The nimbus is treated with a brilliance that
suggests a sun round the head.

Plate LXXI. Sarcophagus and Nimbus.

(*a*) (*left*) The words on the ring of the cross: 'Jesus said I am the resurrection and the life', are illustrated by the symbolism. At the top is the chi-rho monogram symbol of Christ, on the arms are alpha and omega, and in the centre is the pelican and its young, symbol of resurrection. They are carved on a background of the tree of life which is a laurel, symbol of victory and achievement.

(*b*) (*below left*) Virgin and Child. Marble, by Tino di Camaino, Italian (Siennese), second quarter of the fourteenth century. (*Courtesy Victoria and Albert Museum*)

(*c*) (*below*) Stone memorial in a Zurich cemetery, 1962. Carving of a pelican and its young.

ANNA REICHLE
BOHNENBLVST
1894   1961

Plate LXXII.

Plate LXXIII. Statue of the Good Shepherd, from the catacombs of St. Callistus, and now in the Lateran Museum, Rome. It is probably a work of the third century, and is one of the finest Roman examples of the symbol.

Plate LXXIV. Torch and Snake.
(*a*) (*above left*) Monument in the Protestant Cemetery
in Rome, in which symbols of the pine cone and inverted
torch are employed.
(*b*) (*right*) Roman statue of Aesculapius in the Vatican
Museum, Rome.
(*c*) (*below left*) Aztec sculpture in stone of a rattlesnake
showing the thirteen rattles of the snake. (*Courtesy
British Museum. Crown copyright*)

(a) Twin Buddhist stupas at Sanchi, India. That on the right is the largest remaining example. It is 106 feet in diameter and 54 feet high. (*Courtesy Information Service of India*)

(b) Buddhist stupa inside a cave temple at Ajanta, India. (*Courtesy Press Information Bureau, Govt. of India*)

Plate LXXV. Buddhist Stupas.

(a) (above) Nensan made for Malay by the Italian Marble Co. Ltd. of Carrara. Nensans are male and female. On plan the male are circular, the female two flat arcs joined together. Their forms and Malayan tree-worship suggest tree symbolism, but male and female Nensans may denote a sexual significance. It is probably mixed symbolism—the fusing of tree and phallic worship. (b) (left) Three grave memorials, called Nensans, in Malacca (Malaya), near a fig-tree (round a host-tree) which, being venerated in Malacca as an abode of spirits, the graves are placed near to propitiate the spirits. It is thus a survival of a common form of tree-worship.

Plate LXXVI. Sacred Tree.

(a) Stone memorial at Kirkcaldy, Fife, in which early Christian symbolism is freely used. The peacocks on either side of the cross symbolize the Resurrection, the eagle the Ascension, the vine Christ and His followers and the Eucharist, while the vine and the oak on the pillasters suggest the symbolization of the Tree of Life. Miss Phyllis M. Bone, sculptor.

(b) Roman cinerary urn or sepulchral vase to the memory of P. Octavius Secundus. Urns of this type were probably placed in houses or on monuments, and they form the prototypes of modern symbolic urns.

(c) Wheel of the Doctrine, with crouching deer. Stone, Dvaravati style, 7th–8th century. From the National Museum, Bangkok.

(d) Memorial headstone in Portland stone with a carved symbol of a lawyer consisting of wig, quill and scroll. (Amberley churchyard). Designed by John Skelton, sculptor, and cut by his assistant Jack Trowbridge.

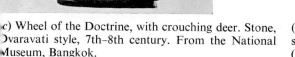

Plate LXXVII.

Plate LXXVIII. Signs of the Zodiac.

(*a*) (*left*) Signs of the Zodiac forming decorative balcony fronts of a modern building in Salzburg. The signs of the Zodiac are a common decorative motif in buildings and on a wide variety of objects.

(*b*) (*right*) Signs of Zodiac medals for the American Numismatic Association. Designed by Paul Vincze.

ark in which Noah survived the flood (Genesis vi. 14–17), and 'aron', meaning chest and used to denote the ark variously described, as the ark of the covenant, the ark of the testimony, or the ark of the law. (Exodus xxv. 10–22; xxvi. 31–3 and numerous other references.) That these are very different is indicated by their size. The ark of Noah was 300 cubits long by 50 cubits wide and 30 cubits high, which, translated into English measures was probably approximately 450 feet long by 75 feet wide by 45 feet high. The ark of the covenant was a small chest $2\frac{1}{2}$ cubits long, $1\frac{1}{2}$ cubits wide and $1\frac{1}{2}$ cubits high (3 feet 9 inches long by 2 feet 3 inches wide and high). It contained the tables of the law and was enshrined in the tabernacle—the tent of the Israelites. Both Noah's ark and the ark of the covenant have been used symbolically.

Noah's Ark was used by the early Christians as the symbol of the Church of Christ by which the faithful are saved in the midst of the wickedness of the world. Tertullian refers to the church as prefigured by the ark,[1] and Bede speaks of the ark signifying the church, which survives through the waves of the world. Bas-reliefs of this subject appear in the catacombs. They show Noah standing in a box floating on the waves with arms outstretched, with the returning dove with olive branch above. The ship, however, which has a similar significance as a symbol of the Church, occurs more frequently.

The ark of the covenant containing the Torah scrolls occupies the central place in the sanctuary of the synagogue, corresponding to the altar in the Christian church. Containing the words and laws of God it has an especially sacred character, and from this it is sometimes thought of as the divine dwelling, and when in the presence of the ark a person is in the presence of God. It has thus become a symbol of the divine presence. As St. Thomas Aquinas indicated, the Catholic Church regards it, by association, as the symbol of the divine law, and thus of Christ Himself.

1. TERTULLIAN, *De Baptismo*, c. 200 A.D.

ARROW—The arrow has been referred to as a symbol of authority in ancient times but the tradition is not very strong. It is possible that, like the sword, it became so as a military trophy, in which case a sheaf of arrows would serve as the symbol. It was certainly a very important weapon in ancient Greece. It will be remembered that Ulysses slaughtered the suitors of his wife with the bow and arrow and from such demonstrations it may have acquired a significance, like so many military weapons, of power and the authority that power confers. Many Gods and Goddesses are represented with arrows. Apollo, Artemis and Eros carry them as weapons of the hunt, Eros in the symbolical sense of hunting for victims of love. The arrow was also associated with the Persian sun-god Mithras, and is shown on Roman coins as a symbol of Mithras. It would seem that as it was associated with both Apollo and Mithras there may have been some symbolic connection of the arrow with the sun, as perhaps suggesting the sun's rays, or shafts of light, but this is not very apt.

The use of the broad arrow as a mark of Government property may have been derived from the slender tradition of its being significant of authority, but it is more probable that, as A. C. Fox-Davies says, it is because one of the Sydney family, when Master of Ordnance, marked everything with his private badge of the broad arrow so as to prevent disputes about the stores for which he was responsible.[1] This appears to have been in the late seventeenth century. The charge on the first and fourth quarters of the arms of the Sydney family (Baron D'Lisle and Dudley) is pheon azure which is a spear or arrow.

1. A. C. Fox-Davies, *Heraldic Badges*, pp. 20–1 (London, 1907).

ASPHODEL—An ancient Greek symbol of death. The asphodel became a symbol of death because in Greek mythology it was conceived as the flower that grew in Hades. This association of the flower with Hades was probably due either to its sombre colouring—its grey leaves and small flowers which are either dull yellow, dull pink or soft white, according to the species—or to the circumstance that it flowers throughout the winter and spring, often on bleak hillsides, which was, no doubt, the reason for its association with Persephone, who is sometimes represented wearing a garland of asphodels.

The earliest known mention of asphodels occurs in the *Odyssey*. Ulysses, when he descends to Hades and discourses with the ghosts of departed heroes, speaks of the spirit or soul of Achilles passing with great strides along the mead of asphodel;[1] and later he sees the mighty Orion driving wild beasts over the mead of asphodel.[2] In the earliest conceptions Hades was regarded merely as the abode of the dead, without any thought of reward or punishment, and asphodels flowering there would signify just death unmingled with any sentiment. It was not until later times, with the growth of moral ideas, that a moral conception of reward and punishment divided Hades into the lands of the blessed and the damned. And thus some writers have thought of the asphodel as growing in the Elysian Fields, and have regarded it as the flower of immortality. It is often imagined growing on the banks of the River Styx that surrounded Hades. Oliver Wendell Holmes, in *The Autocrat of the Breakfast Table*, refers to 'the banks of asphodel that border the river of life', but the Styx would more accurately be regarded as the river of death.

When Maurice Baring speaks of it in his novel *Cat's Cradle* as the flower of forgetfulness, he doubtless thinks of asphodels growing on the banks of Lethe, the stream of forgetfulness that flows through Hades, from which all drink before passing to the Elysian Fields in order to forget their earthly sorrows.

The asphodel is thus a symbol of death by association, expressing no sentiment about death unless it be conceived as growing on the banks of Lethe, when it would express forgetfulness of earthly sorrows. The literary interest in the flower is probably due partly to the sweet bell-like reverberations of its name.

1. *Odyssey*, xi. 539.
2. *Ibid.*, xi. 573.

AUREOLA—See Nimbus.

AXE—Ancient Cretan and Greek symbol of thunder and lightning, and one form of thunderbolt. It came to be habitually regarded as a religious symbol. The form was most commonly the double-headed axe.

In ancient Greece lightning was often thought of as a flash from the eye of Zeus; and destruction during a storm, which was regarded as the anger of the god, was by means of an axe, which was thus a form of thunderbolt. Support for these beliefs came from the occasional finding of a stone axe which was an early war weapon, while trees were often felled by lightning which was thus regarded as a weapon in the form of an axe.

The symbolism of the double axe appears to have originated in Crete as the sign of the sky-god. A. B. Cook, who deals at length with the Greek symbolism of the axe, remarks that 'as various nations of antiquity worshipped axe or spear or sword, meaning thereby to extol the power that wielded them, so the Minoans paid divine honours to the double axe qua sign and symbol of an anthropomorphic sky-god'.[1] This sky-god was known as Kraus and, with the passing of the Minoan civilization, became identified with the sky-god Zeus,[2] and from these early traditions the double axe became an accepted religious symbol which persisted into Roman times. The conjecture has been made, supported by some evidence, that the X (chi) P (rho) monogram of Constantine was originally a conventional sign of the double-headed axe, and Constantine used it as a sign that would appeal to both pagans and Christians.[3]

As destruction by the sky-god was by means of an axe, so the tradition grew that defence against thunder and lightning should be by means of a similar weapon, and this gave rise to many superstitions, some of which have persisted to modern times.

1. A. B. COOK, *Zeus: A Study in Ancient Religion*, Vol. II, pp. 544–8 (Cambridge, 1925).
2. *Ibid.*, p. 601.
3. *Ibid.*, p. 613.

BALDACHINO—Symbol of the sky, the heavens and the universe.

The baldachino is a canopy generally supported on four columns (less frequently suspended from the roof) and used in modern times above an altar, three famous examples being those over the main altars of St. Peter's, Rome (1633), of Westminster Cathedral (1922), and of St. Paul's Cathedral, London, (1955), the last mentioned having been incorporated in the replacement of the altar destroyed during the Second World War. This was in conformity with Wren's original design.

The name is derived from the embroidered woven material which formed the canopy of the throne of ancient Eastern kings and dignitaries, later followed in Rome and Byzantium. Coins of Domitian, Antoninus Pius and Commodus show statues of the Emperor under a domed baldachino. It possibly originated with the state and ceremonial tent of the monarch on the field of battle.

In the canopy of the enthroned monarch the domical structure expressed dominion over the world and association with divine power.[1] Its use over the Christian altar similarly expresses the spiritual dominion over the world, the universe and the celestial regions.

See also arch, canopy, ciborium and dome.

1. E. BALDWIN SMITH traces in some detail the evolution of the ciborium and baldachino in *Architectural Symbolism of Imperial Rome and the Middle Ages* (Princeton, 1956) particularly Chapter IV on 'The Imperial Ciborium'.

BAY LEAVES—See Laurel.

BEAR—In ancient Greece the bear was sacred to Artemis, especially in Arcadia where she was more particularly the huntress. Bears were sacrificed to Artemis, and in one cult young girls dressed as bears at religious rites, the dress later becoming a saffron robe. This was a kind of initiation ceremony before marriage. No very definite symbolism, however, emerges from these ancient Greek cults of the bear.

The California Grizzly bear (*Ursus Horribilis Californicus*) is the state animal of California, having been officially adopted in 1953. In the early years of the state it was a formidable and impressive animal, but is now extinct.

The bear is traditionally regarded as a heavy, rough creature, hence the typification of a rough, uncouth, bad-tempered person as a bear, although latterly the typification is not unmixed with affection, possibly because of a natural liking for the animal, especially as a cub.

A Bear in the Stock Exchange is the action of depressing the price of stocks in order to buy, and is supposed to have originated with the proverb 'to sell the bear's skin before one has caught the bear'.

The bear was widely used during the nineteenth century as a symbol of Russia, but less so since the First World War. Its selection as a Russian symbol is obviously due to the bear being one of the typical and imposing animals of the country. It was frequently used in political cartoons, famous examples being those of Sir John Tenniel in *Punch*. One that appeared in the issue for 16th February, 1878, shows the Russian bear, with arm in a sling, head bandaged and sword in hand, standing triumphant over the figure of Turkey, and facing the advancing figures of the two-headed eagle of Austria-Hungary, the British lion, the German and Italian eagles and the French cock. They are not labelled, and the only title is, 'On the Way to Peace'. Another, of 13th April, 1878, shows the Russian bear and British lion meeting on a mountain ledge, with the title, 'Which goes back?' Another, on 29th June, 1878, gives a rosier picture of 'A Happy Family in Berlin' which shows Disraeli as the showman with the British lion and Russian bear about to embrace, and the French cock, German eagle, and the double-headed eagle and turkey in the background.

The bear appears in heraldry mainly as a pun on names.

BEAVER—Formerly, in the eighteenth and early nineteenth centuries, a national symbol of Canada, but now largely superseded by the maple leaf.

It was regarded as a symbol of Canada because one of the first trading activities in that country was the trapping of the animal for its fur, and the pursuit of it in the wilder regions helped to open the country for permanent settlers. It remained the chief symbol of Canada until the amalgamation of the Hudson's Bay Company with the North West Company in 1821, causing the diversion of the fur trade from the St. Lawrence Valley to Hudson Bay and the loss of the trade to Canada, which meant that the beaver was a less appropriate symbol.

BEE—Symbol of industry. It is so used in many coats of arms. In the crest of the Manchester arms seven bees are represented on a globe. In the arms of Barrow-in-Furness, Blackburn, Burnley, Aylesbury, and Bacup it appears as a charge on the shield. In the case of Blackburn, three bees are shown, which are regarded by the town as symbolic, not only of industry, but of the ability and perseverance of the merchants who have been responsible for the growth and prosperity of the town.[1]

The bee also appears as a charge or crest in the arms of many families, and was adopted as a badge by Napoleon.

1. C. WILFRED SCOTT-GILES. *Civic Heraldry of England and Wales*, p. 100 (London 1933).

BEEHIVE—Emblem of St. Bernard (1090–1153) one of the three founders of the Cistercian order, who was renowned for his eloquence and its emotional appeal. He was called Doctor Mellifluus—the honeysweet preacher and thus was given the emblem of a beehive.

BIRCH—The white birch (*Betula papyreifera*) is the State tree of New Hampshire, having been adopted in 1947.

BITTERROOT (*Lewisia rediviva*)—State flower of Montana, adopted in 1895. Its vivid pink blossom near the ground is familiar in the country districts of the state where it has become one of the most popular of the wild flowers.

BLACK—Symbol of mourning. It is one of the five liturgical colours of the Roman and Anglican churches laid down by Pope Innocent III in 1200 to mark the seasons of the ecclesiastical year by the vestments of the priests in the ceremonies. Black is worn for funeral ceremonies, at Masses for the dead and at the Mass of the presanctified on Good Friday. In heraldry black is termed sable.

BLUE—Sometimes regarded in Christianity as a symbol of heaven. Cherubim, who are regarded in the angelic hierarchy as being engaged in devout contemplation, are represented as blue. Being the colour of the sky-god Zeus, who was the king of the Greek gods, it also became a symbol of monarchy. Although originally a liturgical colour it is now rarely used as such except in some dioceses of Spain for the Mass and the Immaculate Conception, the latter probably because the Virgin is so often represented in blue, being conceived of as the Queen of Heaven.

In heraldry blue is termed azure.

BLUEBIRD (*Sialia sialis*)—State bird of Missouri, officially adopted in 1927. It is also regarded, although not officially adopted, as the emblematic bird of New York. The mountain bluebird (*Sialia arcticia*) is the State bird of Idaho, officially adopted in 1931. It was also selected by popular vote in 1930–31 as the State bird of Nevada, although not officially adopted.

BOBWHITE (*Colinus virginianus*)—This bird was selected by popular vote as the state bird of Oklahoma and Rhode Island, the former in 1932 and by the latter in 1931. In neither was it adopted, as other birds were officially chosen. *See* Scissor-tailed Flycatcher and Hen.

BOOK—Representation of a book in a design has often been employed as a symbol of learning or of an author, and it has sometimes appeared on the memorial of a writer, scholar or book lover.

Books or scrolls have been used as symbols of the Evangelists, and four books appear in this sense in a mosaic in the fifth century mausoleum of Galla Placidia in Ravenna. Figures of the Evangelists are sometimes depicted with each holding a book, as in a fifth century mosaic of St. John Lateran in Rome, or the symbols of the Evangelists—the winged man, lion, ox and the eagle—are shown each holding a book as in a ninth century representation in S. Praxede, Rome. In the Durham Book of St. Cuthbert's Gospels a manuscript of the seventh century from the Monastery of Lindisfarne, and now in the British Museum, a page showing the evangelists is placed at the beginning of each gospel. St. Matthew is shown writing in a book, St. Mark on a tablet, and St. Luke and St. John on scrolls, and above the head of each is the angel, flying lion and ox, and eagle each holding a book.[1]

1. See also LOUISA TWINING, *Symbols and Emblems of Early and Mediaeval Christian Art* (London, 1852, second edition, 1885), Notes and Illustrations of the Symbols of the Four Evangelists, pp. 96–115.

BROWN THRASHER—This bird (*Toxustoma rufum*) is a state emblem of Georgia. It was selected by the school-children in 1928 and later officially adopted. The bird is brown with white breast splashed and striped, and is a native of the eastern part of the United States of America.

BUCKEYE—The nickname of Ohio as the Buckeye state is thought to have been derived from the tree of that name (*Aesulus Ohioensis* or *Gobra*) which is indigenous to the State and which was officially adopted as the state tree in 1953. The Indians called the tree 'Hetuck', meaning the 'eye of the buck', owing to the resemblance of the seed both in colour and shape to the eye of a buck. A second derivation of origin is that[1] at the opening of the first court in the Northwest Territory in September 1788, an imposing procession was formed which marched to Campus Martius Hall at Marietta, headed by the high sheriff, Col. Ebenezer Sproat, with drawn sword, all of which considerably impressed the Indians. Sprout was over six feet tall and well-proportioned and altogether made a very commanding figure. The Indians dubbed him 'Hetuck', or 'Big Buckeye', not in derision but in admiration. The sobriquet stuck, and Sproat became familiarly known to his associates as 'Big Buckeye'. Later the name was passed on to other Ohioans.

The sobriquet, whatever its source, was not crystallized until the presidential campaign of 1840 when General William Henry Harrison was a candidate for the presidency. In that campaign, buckeye cabins and buckeye walking sticks became emblems of Ohio's first citizen to try for the highest office in the land. It was this which forever labelled Ohioans as 'buckeyes'.

1. *Ohio Historical Publications*, Vol. XXIX, p. 275, and *Howe's Collections*, Vol. I, p. 201.

BUFFALO—The American buffalo (*Bos* or *Bison americanus*) was officially adopted as the emblematic animal of Kansas in 1955. The reasons given in the Act for its adoption are that buffaloes ranged over the Kansas territory in countless thousands in the early days of the state, and that it seemed appropriate to give recognition to the fact. The first line of the Kansas state song mentions 'a home where the buffaloes roam'.

BULL—Ancient symbol of power, fertility and strength.

The bull as a symbol of strength was of early origin in ancient Egypt and in this capacity was associated with early kings, who liked to be typified thus. It was worshipped in the earlier Egyptian dynasties at Memphis and Heliopolis, at the former as Mnevis, sacred to the sun, and at the latter as Apis, sacred to the moon. It was also associated with Osiris whose incarnation in the upper world was in the form of the black bull Apis. In ancient Crete the bull was a very important symbol of the sun (because both were generative forces), and in Greece it was associated with Zeus (and to a lesser extent with other gods), who often took the form of a bull. A. B. Cook, who made an exhaustive study of the cult of the bull in ancient Greece, says that 'the ultimate reason why both ram and bull were associated with sky-gods in general and with Zeus in particular, lay in the fact that these animals possessed to an exceptional degree Zeugungskraft or fertilizing force' and 'bulls and rams were sacrificed to Zeus because, according to the belief of early days, the gift of so much virility increased his power to fertilize and bless'.[1]

The black bull is one of the Queen's beasts, inherited from the Duke of Clarence, the third son of Edward III, who may have acquired it from his wife Elizabeth de Burgh. It possibly descended from Elizabeth de Clare; it was thought to have pertained to the 'Honour' or great estate of Clare of Clarence.[2] It may be conjectured that it was originally selected because it suggested the qualities of strength and power, which the person who selected it thought he possessed, very much as it was selected as a sign by the ancient Egyptian kings.

1. A. B. COOK, *Zeus*, Vol. I, p. 717 (Cambridge, 1914).
2. *See* H. STANFORD LONDON, *The Queen's Beasts*, p. 30 (London, 1953).

CACTUS—The Hepal cactus is the national flower of Mexico. The Saguaro cactus is the State flower of Arizona, officially adopted in 1931. The Act referred to 'the pure white waxy flower of the *Cereus Giganticus* (Giant Cactus).[1]

1. See GEORGE EARLIE SHANKLE, *op. cit.*, p. 331.

CADUCEUS—Symbol of Peace and Commerce.

The familiar representation of the caduceus as the wand of Hermes or Mercury consists of two serpents twined round a rod, at the top of which are two wings. This form is the result of a series of elaborations of earlier forms.

In ancient Greece the caduceus was carried by messengers and heralds, and its purpose appears to have been to protect the bearer and to indicate that he was engaged in a peaceful mission, in the same way as in war a white flag protects the envoy from the enemy. The caduceus may have been originally an olive branch, with two or three leaves, which was an important Greek symbol of peace. Homer refers to it as a flowered rod with three leaves.

As the wand of Hermes, the messenger of the gods, it had additional significance. It awakened men from sleep, it led them to Hades, and brought them back to earth. Hermes so rescued Alcestis from Thanatos (death) and brought her back to Admetus.[1] On the famous sculptured drum from the temple of Artemis at Ephesus in the British Museum, the scene depicted appears to be that of Alcestis standing by the winged figure of Thanatos, while Hermes advances and touches her with the caduceus and so brings her back to earth.

The form of caduceus common in the sixth, fifth, and fourth centuries B.C., which is like a rod surmounted by a circle and crescent, sometimes in the form of serpents, has been variously explained. The serpents are explained in myth by the association of the caduceus with Hermes, the messenger of the gods. The fable recounts how Hermes, finding two serpents entwined while fighting, separated them with his wand. The caduceus was thenceforth crowned with serpents, and became symbolic of the settlement of quarrels. The wings which later appeared at the top of the wand were supposed to indicate the speed of Hermes as messenger of the gods.

This pretty story, however, has probably little to do with the evolution of the forms of the caduceus, and we must look to more probable and scientific sources.

Earlier caducei than those of classical Greece, and of a similar shape, appear to have existed among the Assyrians, Hittites and Phoenicians. The form of the caduceus represented on Phoenician monuments, that is the crescent surmounting the circle, is especially like that of Greece. Count Goblet D'Alviella states that at Carthage the caduceus is associated on stelae with the sacred cone and dedicated to Baal Hamman, the Phoenician sun-god.[2] Or it may be that the connection is with the earthly representative and messenger of Baal Hamman, Malac Baal, who would thus correspond with Hermes in Greek religion. The Greeks, trading with the Phoenicians, doubtless knew of the Phoenician caduceus and of its association with the Phoenician gods, parallel to the association of the Greek caduceus with Hermes.

If these conjectures are correct, the Greeks, attracted by the design of the Phoenician caduceus, modified their own forms to something like it.

The question then arises: how did the Phoenician or Assyrian or Hittite form of caduceus evolve? Various theories have been advanced, one that it probably developed from a military weapon, but the main points of interest would appear to be how the circle and crescent became serpents, and how wings became attached to the wand.

A possible explanation is to be found in the migrations of the Egyptian winged disk, and its influence on other ornamental forms. D'Alviella has shown[3] how the winged disk spread throughout Asia Minor as far as Mesopotamia, influencing ornamental and symbolic forms, or, often, employed in its original Egyptian form, and sometimes placed at the top of a staff. The Greeks could hardly have been unaware of this so widely diffused ornament and symbol, and a feasible explanation of the later types of caducei is that they evolved under the influence of the winged disk. The caduceus in its latest form bears most of the features of the winged disk at the end of a staff. Whether the uraeus serpents suggested the transformation of the circle and crescent it is difficult to say, but where, in the latest form, these serpents have slipped down the wand, at or near the top is a small disk to which wings are attached. The serpents may first have appeared, however, because the reviving power of Hermes' wand was associated with serpents as a symbol of healing, and as sacred to Asklêpius, god of medicine.[4]

The adoption of the Phoenician form of caduceus by the Greeks would suggest to them its association with commerce. But as the attribute of a messenger engaged in a peaceful mission it can, by analogy, symbolize commerce, for traders are in a sense messengers, and are dependent on peace. Thus Hermes is the god and protector of commerce.

It is, therefore, as a symbol of commerce that the caduceus is a well-known ornament in modern commercial buildings, especially banks. It appears on the main entrance doors to the Bank of England, prompted by its extensive use as ornament in the old building of the Bank. A caduceus appears on each door, and the wings of each are given a special and original significance. Those of the left caduceus are of a long-distance flying bird, with rippling feathers, and express the dependence of bankers for much of their business upon ships, which, in the early type of sailing vessel, were dependent in turn on favourable winds. The wings of the right caduceus are those of the swift, with the feathers straight and stiff, capable of great speed, and represent, in association with the lightning held by Zeus, rapid means of communication by electricity, such as wireless, cable, telegraph, and telephone. (Plate LXII).

1. In Euripides' play it is Hêrakles who does this.
2. *Migration of Symbols*, English translation, pp. 226–37 (London, 1896).
3. *Ibid.*, pp. 204–20.
4. *See* Serpent.

CAMEL—Used occasionally as a symbol of the countries it inhabits, especially Egypt and Arabia. It appeared on Roman coins as a symbol of Arabia, and in the coat of arms of Lord Kitchener because of his association with Egypt.

CANOPY—Sometimes given in ecclesiastical use the significance of a symbol of the sky and thus of the celestial regions. Symbolically it is identified with structures, like the baldachino, the ciborium and the triumphal arch with this symbolic purpose. In figurative language such phrases as the canopy of heaven are common.

CARDINAL BIRD (*Cardinalis cardinalis*)—Well known in the United States, it is the emblematic bird of four states: having been officially adopted by Kentucky in 1926, by Illinois in 1929, and by Indiana and Ohio in 1933. Its song is heard in these states throughout the year. It is obviously named cardinal because it is red with a red crest.

CARNATION—The scarlet carnation is the state flower of Ohio, adopted in 1904 in memory of William McKinley, with whom it was associated because of his love for it.

CARP—An ancient Chinese and Japanese symbol of endurance, perseverance and fortitude, used to symbolize these qualities in boys and young men.

The symbolism derives from the habits of the carp, which is a native of China. The traditional account is that the ancient Chinese had observed that in the third month of each year the carp, which inhabited the Yellow River, leapt cataracts and swam rapids in order to reach the head-waters of the stream to spawn, and that the Chinese so admired this display of courage and perseverance against the currents and obstacles of the river that they chose it as a symbol of these qualities. Chinese youth was taught that as the carp overcame all obstacles to reach its goal, so they must likewise surmount all difficulties in obtaining their goal in life, and only in this way would they become human dragons.

The symbol was adopted by Japan in the tenth century A.D. It is used in a similar way as expressive of persevering youth, and figures prominently in the Boys' Festivals held on the fifth day of the fifth month, known as the Feast of the Flags. The flags were of brightly coloured paper or cloth, shaped like carp, and attached to high bamboo poles. They were contrived with a hole at each end, so that the wind blowing through them produced a movement which simulated that of the struggling carp swimming against the current.[1]

1. *See* KATHERINE M. BALL, *Decorative Motives of Oriental Art*, pp. 189 *et seq.* (London, 1927).

CAT—Although the cat was a sacred animal in Egypt, was often mummified, and was associated with the goddess Bastet of the eastern region of Egypt, no very definite symbolic tradition is typified by it. Bastet was a sun-goddess, expressing the beneficent powers of the sun, and was usually represented as a human figure with the head of a cat, as Sekhovet, expressing the destructive power of the sun, was represented with the head of a lioness. The origin of the association of the cat with the sun-goddess is obscure.

CATERPILLAR—The caterpillar badge was awarded by the caterpillar club—formed in the Second World War—to those whose life was saved by a parachute. It is obviously derived from the silk worm from which the material of the parachute was made.

CENOTAPH—A symbolic monument expressing mourning. The Greek word κενοτάφος means 'an empty tomb', erected to commemorate a person or persons buried elsewhere.

Cenotaphs were erected in Greece and Rome, although in Greece none remain. Surviving examples of the Roman cenotaphs are the Julia, S. Remy monument near Arles, the Igel monument near Treves and the Wadi-Tagite monument in North Africa.

The cenotaph was revived for memorials of the First World War, owing largely to the example of Sir Edwin Lutyens' design of the Cenotaph to form the National Memorial in Whitehall. Here the Cenotaph is an impressive and eloquent symbol of a nation's mourning.

CERES—*See* Gods, Goddesses and Heroes of Antiquity.

CHALICE AND HOST—A representation of these signifies faith in Christ's work of redemption.

The difference of significance between the Holy Sacrament of the Eucharist and the Protestant Holy Communion is that in the former, according to the doctrine of transubstantiation, the whole substance of the bread and wine are converted into the body and blood of Christ. In the Protestant ceremony there is no such conversion: it is commemorative and is, therefore, symbolic. The communion cup (which is larger than the chalice, because the laity also drink the wine) and bread are seldom used as symbols in design, whereas representations of the chalice and host (from the Latin hostia, meaning a victim for sacrifice, the name traditionally assigned to the consecrated wafer) are common.

A representation of the chalice and host typifying the converted bread and wine at the Holy Sacrament of the Eucharist would express a similar idea as participation in the ceremony, and would be an expression of faith in the efficacy of Christ's sacrifice. It is the appropriate symbol for a design commemorating a priest, and figures largely in Church embroidery.

CHERUB (pl. Cherubim)—A cherub is generally represented as a head with two, four or six wings. Cherubim occupy the second rank of the first order in the angelic hierarchy of the pseudo-Dionysius the Areopagite (seraphim occupying the first rank). According to the pseudo-Dionysius their name denotes their knowledge and vision of God, and they are engaged in divine contemplation. (*See* Angel.)

CHICKADEE—The chickadee (*Penthestes artricapillus*) is the state bird of Maine, officially adopted in 1927, and also of Massachusetts, officially adopted in 1941. One of the commonest of American birds, it is familiar throughout the year, and is very friendly.

The Carolina chickadee (*Parus carolinensis*) is the state bird of North Carolina and was officially adopted in 1931.

CHRISTMAS TREE—*See* Sacred Tree.

CHRYSANTHEMUM—National flower of Japan. The chrysanthemum originated in China, but it spread in ancient times to surrounding countries, among them Japan, where it has been cultivated for over two thousand years. Its popularity in Japan is due to the early interest of successive Emperors, who instituted chrysanthemum displays. The Emperor Ouda held annual chrysanthemum shows in the tenth century A.D., and ever since they have been a common feature in Japanese life. Being favoured above all other flowers, the chrysanthemum naturally became the national flower. At the Festival of Happiness, in which Japanese from all walks of life take part, it is displayed in the temples, houses and streets. The Order of the Chrysanthemum was founded in 1877. The flower appears on numerous objects in both Japan and China. In postage stamps of Japan it is usually a severely conventionalized representation, but in a recent stamp of China it is represented naturalistically.

CIBORIUM—Originally a drinking cup made of the seed vessel of the Egyptian water-lily. The term is used to describe cups of a similar shape. In the Roman Catholic church the cup called the ciborium holds the host kept in the tabernacle. In the seventh sacrament of extreme unction, the priest takes a host from the ciborium and places it in a small vessel known as the pyx and carries it to the dying person. Like the chalice the ciborium can be used as an associative symbol.

The name was given in ancient Rome and Byzantium to the domed canopy over the throne of a monarch and later over the Christian altar, for the ciborium inverted and suspended denoted this shape. Being domed like the vault of the sky, it expressed, in the case of the ciborium over the throne, dominion over the world, and over the altar the ciborium symbolized heaven and the universe. In modern times the term baldachino is more generally used. It has the same meaning.

CIRCLE—The circle, being without end, has from ancient days been a symbol of eternity.

In early Christian remains it frequently appears as a serpent with its tail in its mouth. This idea has often been associated with Moses' serpent of brass that the Lord commanded to be set 'upon a pole': 'and it shall come to pass, that every one that is bitten, when he looketh upon it, shall live.'[1]

A circle arranged between the arms of the cross has formed one of the commonest types of memorial throughout the Christian era, and is a characteristic of Celtic crosses.

1. Numbers xxi. 8 and 9. The probable significance of this serpent of brass is mentioned in the note on the symbolism of the serpent.

CLOVER—The red clover (*Tritolium pratense*) is the state flower of Vermont. It was adopted in 1894 because of its value to the farming industry of the state.

COCK—As a Christian symbol it has been used to signify vigilance. It is one of the emblems of the Passion, and in association with St. Peter it expresses repentance.

It was also in ancient Greece associated with Athene and was symbolic of Persephone's rising in the spring.

In the catacombs the cock is represented in a bas-relief, with Christ and St. Peter, as a symbol of repentance. In the Middle Ages it was often placed at the summits of towers and steeples to express the idea of vigilance, but partly as symbolizing St. Peter.

In a secular sense the cock is a symbol of supremacy in a particular sphere, and is sometimes associated with bragging and crowing.

As a symbol of supremacy it is used to some extent in commerce. An example is the trade mark of the Marley Tile Company, which shows a strutting cock with the words 'Cock-o'-the-Walk'. The *Coq gaulois* (Gaelic Cock) is a national symbol of France since the revolution when it appeared on French Flags. It often so figured in nineteenth century political cartoons. It was probably adopted in the sense of supremacy and vigilance.

COLOUR SYMBOLISM—See under the names of the various colours: black, blue, green, red, purple or violet and white.

COLUMBINE—The long-spurred blue columbine (*Aquilegia caerulea*), sometimes known as the Rocky Mountains columbine, is the state flower of Colorado, officially adopted in 1899. It was adopted, according to Albert B. Sanford, 'because the blue signifies the hue of the skies, the white represents the snowy ranges of the mountains and the yellow the gold that first attracted people here in 1858'.[1]

1. Quoted by G. E. SHANKLE, *State Names, Flags, Seals, Songs, Birds, Flowers and other Symbols* (New York, 1941).

COLUMN—A free-standing column was originally a symbol of the sky-god, became a symbol of deity, then of monarchical apotheosis, and finally a secular symbol of glory, achievement and honour.

Evidence of early Greek memorial columns exists mainly in coins and in paintings on vases. They show tall columns surmounted by figures of gods, heroes, and symbolic birds and sphinxes. Most of the early columns were erected in honour of Zeus as the sky-god. A. B. Cook[1] refers to the cult of Zeus who was conceived of as residing in or on a pillar at Tarentum in Italy. There are records of tall columns surmounted by gilded statues of Jupiter, which were destroyed in the second and first centuries B.C.; and in Germany there yet remain several Jupiter columns of a later time, which seem to belong to the same tradition. From the evidence of coins, memorial columns were erected to prominent Roman citizens as early as the fifth century B.C., but it is not easy to decide whether they were always surmounted by a figure.

The Jupiter columns in Germany (a famous example being that at Mayence), which belong to the period from the late second to the middle of the third century A.D., appear to perpetuate the character of the earliest Greek columns of Zeus, due, as A. B. Cook suggests, to an identification of Zeus as the sky-god with the Germanic sky-god and thus with the Latin Jupiter. The Saxons worshipped a high pillar named Irminsul as a sign and symbol of the sky-god.

Memorial columns were erected in the early period of the Roman Empire to Julius Caesar, and to Tiberius, Trajan, Antoninus Pius and Marcus Aurelius. Those to Trajan and Marcus Aurelius still remain. Both are decorated with spiral bands illustrating the campaigns of the emperors.

Among memorial columns of later Roman Emperors are those of Alexander Severus at Antinoe, of Diocletian in Alexandria, of Constantine in the Forum of Constantinople (now Istanbul), of Valentinian at Antioch, and of Justinian also in Constantinople. Tall memorial columns were revived during the Renaissance. The earliest example in England is The Monument, built in 1671 by Wren to commemorate the Great Fire of London. The first spectacular example in the Roman manner is the Colônne Vendôme in Paris, erected by Napoleon to celebrate the victory of Austerlitz. This is a fairly close copy of Trajan's column. The shaft is decorated with a spiral band of bronze reliefs of the exploits of the campaign, and at the top of the column is a statue of Napoleon. Another famous example in Paris is the Colonne de Juillet in the Place de la Bastille, erected in 1833–40. The Column of Victory in Königsplat in Berlin was erected in 1869–73; it is surmounted by a figure of Victory instead of the monarch or conqueror. Perhaps the most famous memorial column in England is Nelson's column in Trafalgar Square. Other examples are the Duke of York's column in Waterloo Place, the Nelson column at Yarmouth, the Wellington Column at Liverpool, and the Grey Column at Newcastle. In all these, the person commemorated stands at the top. One of the most recent examples is the large Doric column surmounted by a figure of Liberty, which forms the American Meuse-Argonne Battle Memorial of the First World War at Montfalcon. A memorial column also forms the central feature of the Indian National Memorial of the First World War at Neuve-Chapelle. This is surmounted by a lotus and crown, and flanked by seated tigers reminiscent of the lions of the gate at Mycenae.

The original purpose of the tall memorial column is found in the primitive religion of early Greece and other communities, and is akin to the origin of the triumphal arch. The primitive mind thinks of the sky as needing support, and without this

221

support there is constant fear that it will fall. It is not easy for the modern mind to enter into these primitive notions. A. B. Cook says that the Germanic 'Irminsul or universeprop implies the primitive notion that the sky stands in need of visible support. Early man was in fact haunted by a very definite dread that it might collapse on the top of him'.[2] There is a variety of evidence to indicate that this dread was widespread among primitive peoples. It is particularly understandable among dwellers in forests of tall trees, who feel on emerging into open country that the supports of the sky have gone.

The transition of thought from the conception of the column supporting the sky to supporting the anthropomorphized sky was an inevitable one in Greek religion, and thus the pillar supports the sky-god Zeus, the Germanic Irminsul and the Latin Jupiter. Ideas of the path of the soul to heaven are expressed by the decoration on the column, suggesting an upward movement.

The further transition from the god surmounting the pillar to the Emperor or military victor is a natural one. If a system of ancestor worship figures so prominently in many religions, then the apotheosis of Emperors is not a difficult stage of thought, and it seemed to be habitual in the first two hundred years of the Empire. Thus Zeus or Jupiter became Trajan, Antoninus Pius, Marcus Aurelius and their successors. The idea of deification doubtless appealed to Napoleon when he erected the Colonne Vendôme to his own glorification, and the idea is not entirely remote when we put Nelson on the top of a tall column, for we sometimes almost make gods of our heroes.

The interpretation of the spiral on these great columns, in accord with their religious origin, is that it is the path to heaven, and not, as Sir Banister Fletcher suggests,[3] the unwinding of a parchment scroll.

1. A. B. COOK, *Zeus: A Study in Ancient Religion*, Vol. II, pp. 52 *et seq.* (Cambridge, 1925).
2. *Op. cit.*, p. 54.
3. SIR BANISTER FLETCHER. *History of Architecture on the Comparative Method*, 15th edition, p. 187 (London, 1950).

COLUMN, BROKEN—Symbol of death, signified by the support of life being broken.

The employment of a broken column to symbolize death not unnaturally arose during the Renaissance when the impulse to emulate the achievements of classic art was accompanied by the less intelligent imitation of classic remains, even to the extent of imitating ruins. The broken columns that were such common features of the ruins of ancient Greece and Rome were eloquent of the pathos that seems, to the romantic view, to attend the fall of great civilizations. A broken column thus became the pathetic symbol of death, and was used as a gravestone.

COMPASSES OR DIVIDERS—Often used as an associative symbol of an architect or surveyor or of building and constructional work. Dividers appear with a building, wreath, rolls of paper and a lamp in the Ministry of Housing's medal design in 1950 (Plate XX (e)).

Compasses and dividers signify in ecclesiastical art the divine measuring and dividing of the world described in Genesis (i. 1–7) while in Proverbs (viii. 27) reference is made to the Lord setting 'a compass on the face of the depth'. In a French 'Bible moralisée' manuscript, probably of the thirteenth century, Christ is shown with dividers measuring the world.[1]

1. ALAN W. WATTS, *Myth and Ritual in Christianity* (London, 1954) p. 48 and plate I.

CONE—*See* Pine Cone.

CORNFLOWER—National flower of Germany. It is a common flower of the German landscape, growing plentifully in the cornfields. It appears to have been adopted in 1871, because it was a favourite with Kaiser Wilhelm I.

CORNUCOPIA, or HORN OF PLENTY—Symbol of fruitfulness. This horn is usually represented as filled to over-flowing with fruits, but it is also thought of as containing wine, anointing oil, medicines, charms and incantations. It probably became a symbol of fruitfulness because the horn itself was derived from the horns of an animal—a bull or goat—which were known as symbols of fertility and of power. (*See* Horns.)

COTTONWOOD TREE—The state tree of Kansas, officially adopted in 1937. The reason given in the enactment is that 'the successful growth of the cotton wood grove on the homestead was often the determining factor in the decision of the homesteader' 'to stick it out until he could prove up on his claim'.

COW—Symbol of procreation. In ancient Egypt the cow was sacred to and symbol of the goddess Hathor (or Isis), wife and sister of Osiris, and the mother of Horus. Hathor, who was thought of as the goddess of procreation and mother of the race, was usually represented with a cow's horns on her head, depicted on either side of the moon. A similar meaning attaches to the association of the cow with Hêrê, the wife of Zeus, in ancient Greece. It is a symbolism which has not entirely died.

CRESCENT—Ancient symbol of the moon, and symbol of the Ottoman Turks. The crescent moon symbolized Iô who was changed by Hêrê into a white cow. (The Egyptian goddess Hathor also took the form of a cow, and when represented in human form wore a crown with disk and horns.) Iô was possibly a priestess of Hêrê and by the association of the two Hêrê became a moon-goddess with the horns on the crescent as her symbol. A temple was erected to Hêrê on the site of Byzantium and for that reason the crescent became the symbol of Byzantium. The Ottoman Turks probably inherited the crescent from Byzantium. It was adopted in the thirteenth century by Seljuk Sultan of Iconium, and since that time has appeared on military standards, and, with the star, appears on the Turkish flag. It was probably originally adopted as a representation of the new moon, which in Turkey is a period of religious devotion. The suggestion that it was significant of a growing brightness and thus of Muslim religious belief may have been partly responsible for its use. G. Puttenham, the Elizabethan writer, in his *Arte of English Poesie*, says that it was introduced into Turkey early in the sixteenth century to signify increase and brightness.

CROOK—*See* Crozier.

CROSS—Symbol of Christ's redemption of mankind from sin.

Christ's death on the cross-shaped gibbet was the culmination of His mission of atonement, and this cross has become the chief symbol of Christianity.

The cross symbol, however, is much older than Christianity. The equilateral cross[1] was widely distributed in remote times, being employed with a similar significance by peoples who were, as far as we can judge, unconnected with each other. This is explained by a similarity in the independent processes of reasoning among widely separated peoples, not uncommon in the history of thought, and prompting, in this instance, similar symbolic forms for similar ideas. In each case, the equilateral cross seems to have symbolized something akin to the four main directions of space. It has been shown that the cross of pre-Columbian America denotes 'a kind of compass card, that represents the four quarters whence comes the rain',[2] and it thus symbolized the native weather god Thaloc.

Likewise the vajra, an equilateral diagonal cross in stone of the Hindu god Indra, is mentioned in the Veda as the stone with four points which brings the rain. Similarly the Assyrians symbolized their god of the sky Anu; but here, as the centre of the cross, which is in the form of a disk, would suggest, the god may be identical with the sun, while the arms signify the four main directions in which the sun shines. It was likewise employed by the Babylonians, Persians and Greeks.[3]

The Tau cross, named after the Greek letter by reason of similarity in shape, is sometimes called the gibbet cross owing to its likeness to one form of ancient gibbet. Like the equilateral cross it is found with similar meanings in all the countries in which it is distributed: in Egypt, Palestine, Gaul, ancient Germany, and probably from Semitic authority, in the catacombs. It signified life, fecundity, and similar ideas, and the tree of life is sometimes given the tau form. The cross formed of tree branches, sometimes seen in modern cemeteries, could be traced to this identification of the tau with the tree of life. In Christianity it is associated with St. Anthony.

The Christian symbol is the particular form of gibbet on which Christ met his death. Some contend that the tau most accurately reproduces the form, but this has not received unanimous support. It is generally understood that this gibbet, which was widely used as a particularly cruel method of putting criminals to death, was formed of a long upright stake with a transverse bar placed a short distance from the top, forming roughly the shape of what is now known as the Latin cross. The equiateral or Greek cross was also used by the early Church, but these two forms gradually became separated in their use to the Western and Eastern churches, when they received the names Latin and Greek by which they are known today.

After Constantine's conversion to Christianity the cross was used for the first time publicly, but it was not until some time later, in about the ninth century, that it was regarded as the universal symbol of Christianity. The Constantinian monogram, which appeared on the Labarum and the Roman military standards until the eighth century, is sometimes alluded to as the cross, and thus the mistake has occasionally been made that the cross became the most important symbol of Christianity on Constantine's conversion. Gibbon puts the matter more accurately when he speaks of the monogram as 'at once expressive of the figure of the cross and the initial letters of the name of Christ'.[4] But the cross alone, without the association with XP, did not become the chief symbol of Christianity until the use of the monogram had, to a large extent, died out. Since the cross in the ninth century became widely used, numerous variations were introduced, some of which were designed for particular application.

The idea of the double Latin cross arose from the form made by the superscription placed above the transverse beam. This form became the plan of many churches in which we see four transepts instead of the customary two, Salisbury and Canterbury

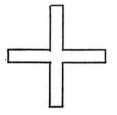

(a) Equilateral cross adopted by the Eastern Church.

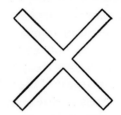

(b) Equilateral diagonal cross associated with St. Andrew.

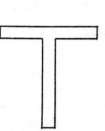

(c) Tau cross.

(d) Latin cross

(e) Double Latin cross.

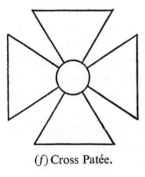

(f) Cross Patée.

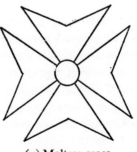

(g) Maltese cross.

Fig. 41. Forms of the Cross.

Cathedrals being two examples. The equilateral diagonal or saltire cross owes its association with Christianity mainly to the tradition that St. Andrew was crucified on a structure of that shape. The cross patée of formée has arms of equal length widening from a central disk and almost forming a square. This is often erroneously called the Maltese cross—the symbol of the mediaeval religious order of the knights of Malta—which differs from the patée by the ends of the arms being cut with a V, thus forming eight finer points. The quatrefoil, a common Gothic ornament, is a cross of four clover leaves. Since the Middle Ages the cross has been widely employed in ecclesiastical architecture in a number of fanciful and often elaborate varieties. The Crusaders wore the cross as a badge which was varied in form and colour to distinguish each army. Additional varieties were employed to distinguish important individuals, so that a considerable number evolved to result in the numerous varieties in heraldry. W. A. Copinger[5] gives two hundred and eighty-five, but many of these vary only slightly, and the number includes some that would hardly be called crosses outside heraldry. Many of them are anything but beautiful and would not compare with the generally beautiful architectural varieties.

The cross was not used by Protestants until about the middle of the nineteenth century, as a strong feeling had existed amongst ardent Protestants that its use was inimical to the spirit of the reformers, who considered that the symbol was abused by Roman Catholics. However, these objections have passed, and it has become, in its many varieties, the most popular symbol for all Christian communities. (Fig. 41).

1. This must not be confused with the swastika, as is often done, which is dealt with under that heading.
2. GOBLET D'ALVIELLA, *The Migration of Symbols*, English translation, p. 13 (1894).
3. GOBLET D'ALVIELLA, *op. cit.*, p. 14.
4. EDWARD GIBBON, *Decline and Fall of the Roman Empire*, Chap. xx.
5. W. A. COPINGER, *Heraldry Simplified* (Manchester, 1910).

CROWN—(Wreath is included in this term.) Symbol of sovereignty, honour, glory or victory; and in Christianity principally of the victory that martyrdom implies.

The earliest records of crowns as symbols of sovereignty are of the pre-dynastic crowns in Upper and Lower Egypt, which were combined into the double crown when the two kingdoms were united, either at the time of the first dynasty, by the legendary Menes, or by Narmer, who reigned a little before the first dynasty. The crown as a symbol of sovereignty is, therefore, at least five thousand years old, and possibly older.

On a pre-dynastic green slate pallet, Narmer is shown on the obverse wearing the red crown of Lower Egypt and on the reverse the white crown of Upper Egypt. From this it would seem that it was Narmer who united the two kingdoms. Both the crowns are tall hats, which would greatly increase the height of the wearer. No earlier representations of the individual crowns of Lower and Upper Egypt are known but it can be assumed by inference that earlier crowns existed.

Why did a tall hat become a symbol of sovereignty in Ancient Egypt? There is no evidence from the early history of Egypt to answer this question. The answer is probably that the authority of a ruler is expressed among other means by physical symbols; authority implies superiority, and one physical expression of superiority is by height, to which a tall hat contributed.

The crown of ancient Greece and Rome was of a different kind. It was composed of leaves and berries. Originally, as mentioned in the *Iliad* (xiii. 736) it was awarded only to the gods, or to an entire army, but later it was awarded as a prize at the sacred Greek athletic and musical festivals. Among the plants chosen for crowns were the laurel, parsley and olive. In Rome warriors were crowned with wreaths for distinguished service. The soldier who saved the life of a Roman citizen was crowned with a wreath of oak leaves and acorns (*see* Oak), and the soldier who saved an army in extreme crisis was awarded the crown of grass (*see* Grass) by the acclamation of the army itself.[1]

The early Christians took the Roman crown symbolizing honour, victory, glory, and adopted it for martyrs as symbolizing victory for the Christian faith over the temptations, sins and persecutions of the world. It had slight differences of meaning according to the individual with whom it was associated. It was often represented on the grave-stone of a nun—the bride of Christ—whose virginity and withdrawal from the world meant a victory over the flesh. The custom of placing a crown on the nun's head at the moment of consecration is no doubt derived from the wearing of crowns as adornments by Jewish brides in ancient times.[2]

Because of the constant Christian use of the regal crown to signify martyrdom and other victories for the Christian faith, it is understood to have this significance in modern ecclesiastical art. The wreath signifies honour and glory in the sense of the pagan crown.

In Roman times the attribute of sovereignty was the diadem. This was composed of an embroidered fillet of linen or silk, and was of oriental origin. The modern regal crown developed from the diadem combined with the helmet of the Middle Ages, so that the royal crowns of Britain today are diadems with two arches at right angles. This modern royal crown gives a height and dignity to the wearer which connects it symbolically with the royal crowns of ancient Egypt.

The two principal English crowns, St. Edward's Crown, with which the monarch is crowned, and the Imperial State Crown, worn after the ceremony of crowning, are both decorated with symbols—principally fleur-de-lis and cross patée above the diadem, and cross patée and orb surmounting the crossing of the two arches. The arches of the Imperial State Crown are decorated with oak leaves and acorns.

1. PLINY, *Natural History*, XVI. 4 and 5; XXII. 4 and 5.
2. ANNA JAMESON, *Sacred and Legendary Art*, 3rd edition, vol. i, p. 29 (1857).

CROZIER—Symbol of Christian guidance, ministration and correction.

Crozier is now generally understood to be a pastoral staff carried by a bishop. The idea obviously arose from the analogy of the priest, as the minister of Christ, caring for his congregation, or the pastor for his parish, as the shepherd cares for his flock, derived from many biblical allusions (*see* Shepherd and Sheep). The name crozier means cross, and is also applied to one who bears a cross in front of an archbishop. The name has gradually become associated with the staff with a shepherd's crook at the end, the crook being devised to hook the hind legs of straying sheep.

It is possible, as A. B. Cook has suggested, that the Christian pastoral staff was derived from the Roman lituus, which was a crooked stick which may have originally been a sceptre (*see* Sceptre). This however is largely conjectural; what is certain is that the shepherd's crook or crozier has been used as a symbol of Christian guidance by bishops since the fifth century. Several early croziers of various design remain, some simple and others ornate, decorated with acanthus, vine and other traditional ornaments. A well-known example of the tenth century is the crozier of Kells in the British Museum. Later examples became very elaborate, one being the crozier of William of Wykeham, Bishop of Winchester, in the late fourteenth century, now in the chapel of New College, Oxford. This crozier of silver gilt is decorated with tiers of niches, saints under canopies and angels in panels in the crook.[1]

The crozier is often used as a symbol on the memorial of a bishop.

1. An abridgement of W. H. St. John Hope's description (*Archaeologia*, Vol. ix) is given by HERBERT NORRIS in *Church Vestments, their Origin and Development*, pp. 126-7 (London, 1949).

CRUCIFIX—Generally a symbol by conventional representation. A picture or sculpture however, in which an attempt is made to conceive the physical realities of the crucifixion is hardly a symbol of that event. Both the conventional crucifix and the realistic picture of the crucifixion have a significance similar to that of the cross.

One point regarding its representation may be mentioned. The question has arisen whether three or four nails were used at the crucifixion. In the earliest representations four were used, then later the legs were crossed, which arrangement required only three. During the Renaissance the matter seemed to be left to artistic preference, but now, according to one authority,[1] there seems to be a general acceptance of four, though this is at variance with the majority of modern representations. The use of four where the legs are brought straight down is more impressive and dignified. This is splendidly demonstrated in Velasquez's picture of the Crucifixion in the Prado, Madrid, which is one of the most moving conceptions of the subject. (Plate LX.)

1. F. M. FALLOW on 'Cross' in the *Encyclopaedia Britannica*, 11th edition, 1911.

CUPID—*See* Gods, Goddesses and Heroes of Antiquity.

CUPOLA—*See* Dome.

CYPRESS—Symbol of mourning and death.

It has been universally so regarded from ancient times because of its vivid dark hue and because after it is once cut down it never grows again.[1] The Greeks and Romans placed branches of it in the houses of their departed friends.

It has been planted in most cemeteries in southern Europe. Its association with cemeteries has no doubt vividly preserved its significance and caused a poet to describe it as 'the only constant mourner o'er the dead'.

The cypress twig when united with a palm branch means victory in death, but this representation is rare.

1. This is, of course, true of many other trees, but it was apparently once thought that the cypress was exceptional in this respect.

DAFFODIL—A Welsh national emblem, and thus a symbol of Wales.

Up to the First World War the leek was more frequently used, but in the last thirty years the daffodil has been equally evident. It was used in the postage stamps of George VI and Elizabeth II, and in the Coronation decorations of the latter, generally in preference to the leek. This may be due to the daffodil being a more adaptable subject for design.

The use of both daffodil and leek as symbols of Wales is due to the similarity of their names in Welsh. Spurrell's Welsh-English Dictionary gives Cennin and Cenhinen as meaning leeks, and Cennin y gwinwydd cennin Pedr as meaning daffodil. (*See* Leek.)

DAVID'S SHIELD—*See* Hexagram.

DIADEM—*See* Crown.

DISK—A widely distributed ancient symbol of the sun; found in Egypt, Asia Minor, India, China, Greece and various parts of the Roman Empire on coins, pottery, and in stone carvings, from the thirteenth century before Christ. It was often used in association with other solar symbols like the swastika, triscele, trisula, crescent, thunderbolt and trident, and the way in which it was represented was generally determined by these associations.[1] Thus it is shown as a centre piece with swastikas or other disks revolving round it, or a swastika is represented on it; or it forms the centre of a swastika or triscele. Its common association with these provided evidence of their use as sun symbols. The representation of three or four disks, or swastikas, placed round a central disk was probably intended to suggest the sun's motion round the earth, when the central disk would represent the earth. The five bosses on several Irish Celtic crosses of the ninth century—one central boss and four on the limbs of the cross, placed at the points of intersection with the ring, or, to put it more expressively, in the path of the circle—were possibly representations of the sun's revolution round the earth. Two examples are the north and south crosses at Ahenny in Tipperary, both of the ninth century.[2]

Other common representations of the disk were as a series of rings, with radiating lines inside the disk, or with petals, in which case it was associated with the lotus, as in its incorporation in the trisula in India. Sometimes it is shown as a face, as in some Indian cave carvings.[3] As a Buddist symbol the disk was often shown with radiating lines, and this symbol afterwards became the Buddist 'Wheel of the Law'.[3]

1. D'ALVIELLA in *The Migration of Symbols*, *op. cit.*, gives numerous examples of the association of the disk with other symbols.
2. These are illustrated in ARNOLD WHITTICK's *History of Cemetery Sculpture*, Vol. 1, figs. 85 and 86 (London, 1938).
3. EDWARD THOMAS, *Numismatic Chronicle*, Vol. xx, fig. 40.

DISK, WINGED—Ancient Egyptian symbol of the protection of life; and, when used sepulchrally, of the protection of the dead from evil. It was also regarded as a symbol of the sun and, by a natural sequence of thought from this, a symbol of eternal life.

The symbol originated with the myth that tells of the war waged by Horus against the enemies of Ra, god of the sun and king of the gods, who dwelt on earth sailing the Nile. When he grew old his foes conspired against him, so he commanded his son Horus to wage war against them. So Horus, who was identified with a falcon or sparrow-hawk,[1] took the form of a great disk and, with his own falcon's wings, flew up to the sun. Horus pursued the enemies of Ra, flew down upon them and destroyed them. Apparently he then rejoined Ra in the barque on the Nile, and continued to wage war on Ra's enemies, who now attacked in the form of crocodiles and hippopotami. On a later occasion, when Horus again changed into a winged disk to war against Ra's enemies, he took with him Nekhebit, the goddess of the South, and Uazit, the goddess of the North, in the form of two serpents. After numerous battles all the foes of Ra were vanquished by Horus, chiefly when in the form of the winged disk. After the final victory Ra commanded Thoth to place an image of the winged disk in the sanctuaries of the gods so that it might banish evil from the vicinity.[2] Thus it is that during the middle kingdom throughout Egypt the winged disk appears over the entrances of temples, tombs, and other doorways and at the top of stelae. Appearing on tombs and stelae it doubtless signified protection of the dead from harm, and

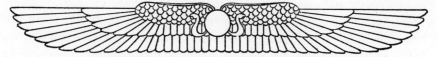

(a) Winged disk from the Temple of Edfou, Egypt.

(b) Fragment of bas-relief of dolphins from a small sarcophagus in the catacombs of St. Callistus, Rome.

Fig. 42.

probably also the survival of life by its symbolism of the sun which is life-giving. Sometimes simply the winged disk was employed, and sometimes the two serpents were placed on either side of the disk, occasionally crowned with the diadems of northern and southern Egypt.

It has been suggested that the winged disk was a symbol of thunder, lightning, and rain, as destructive powers of the gods.[3] It would thus be a symbol of destruction, but it was apparently thus interpreted as destructive only of the enemies of Ra, and in defence of his people. It is much more probable, however, that it was yet another expression of the eternal conflict of light and darkness[4]—good and evil.

It will be seen, then, that in using this feature of Egyptian architecture over the doorways of a mausoleum, a symbol denoting protection of the dead from evil and continuance of life was employed.

The symbol is remote, and appears only because the derivation of the style of a building from the Egyptian prompts the introduction of such a typical decorative feature. Attempts have been made to adopt the form of the symbol for modern purposes as is admirably done in the case of the entrances to the Mersey tunnel at Liverpool. Here the monolithic character and decorative effect obviously derive from Egyptian architecture, and the architect, Herbert J. Rowse, has used the same Egyptian decorative device over the entrances, but he has transposed the winged disk, symbol of the protection of life, to the winged arrow, symbol of speed.

1. Horus's name Horbehudti designates the god as a sparrow-hawk, though he is more generally associated with the falcon.
2. This account of the myth of the winged disk is taken from A. WIEDEMANN's *Religion of the*

230

Ancient Egyptians, pp. 69–78 (London, 1897), in which the author gives for the most part a literal translation of the text given by NAVILLE in *Textes relatifs au Mythe d'Horus recueillis dans le Temple d'Edfou*, 1870. *See also* SIR E. A. WALLIS BUDGE, *The Gods of the Egyptians*, Vol. i, pp. 483 *et seq.* (London, 1904), and SIR JAMES FRAZER, *The Worship of Nature*, pp. 594 *et seq.* (London, 1926).
3. G. ELLIOT SMITH, *The Evolution of the Dragon*, p. 124 (Manchester, 1919).
4. SIR E. A. WALLIS BUDGE, *op. cit.*, Vol. i, p. 483.

DOGWOOD—The American dogwood (*Cornus florida*) is the state flower of Virginia. It was adopted in 1918 because of its prevalence and because it gives beauty to the Virginian landscape. It is also for similar reasons the state flower of North Carolina, having been adopted in 1941. The flowering dogwood (*Cornus nuttalli*) is the emblem of British Columbia.

DOLPHIN—An ancient Greek symbol of the sea giving a maritime significance to that with which it is represented. In Christian symbolism it is uncertain whether it had a different significance from that of the fish, though in early representations it appears to have been recognized as distinct. The fish was used earlier and it may have been that the early Christians, influenced, as their art developed, by classic forms, gave in later work (fourth century onwards) the form of the dolphin to the fish. If, however, the dolphin had a distinct significance, it has not been discovered with certainty what that significance was, though numerous meanings have been given in later times to the Christian use of the dolphin.

Poseidon (identified with Neptune from 399 B.C.), the Greek god of the sea, was usually represented in Greek art with a trident sitting in a chariot made of shells drawn by sea-horses or dolphins. It was by means of a dolphin that Poseidon won the favours of Amphitrite, and the dolphin (delphinus) was henceforth placed amongst the constellations. The Nereids (nymphs of the sea) were represented riding on dolphins, and sometimes, as with Cyme, were depicted single, sitting on a rock holding a trident, with a dolphin at their feet.

Though the special Christian significance of the dolphin has not yet been discovered, the statement of F. E. Hulme[1] that 'the dolphin is often introduced in art as a symbol of maritime power, but finds no place in Christian art', is certainly incorrect. Evidence of its use as a Christian symbol is given in a letter of Paulinus, Bishop of Nola (353–431), to Bishop Delphinus, 'I remember that I am made the son of the dolphin (Delphinus) that I might become one of the fishes which pass through the paths of the sea.' Commenting on this E. R. Barker observes that there is here 'an identification in the writer's mind between Bishop Delphinus, the dolphin (as a symbol of Christ) and Peter, as pre-eminently the "fisher of men".'[2] The passage is, of course, in reference to the rite of baptism. As we may observe from the passage, the Early Christians regarded this cetacean mammal as a fish, and as a Christian symbol there is certainly strong reason to think that it was identical with the fish, to which heading the reader is referred.

Of the meanings given by modern writers to the dolphin as a Christian symbol, one is that 'the dolphin stands for the religious life and a symbol of the Resurrection, for, legend says, the dolphin on dying turned swiftly from one beautiful colour to another'.[3] The idea was probably derived from the circumstance that the richly coloured dorado, which is often popularly called the dolphin, when dying or when removed from the water, rapidly changes colour. This is a poor analogy of the resurrection, and there is no evidence that the connection existed in the minds of the early Christians. Another writer says that 'dolphins swimming on the surface of the water were by no means uncommon as symbols of happy souls swimming to the isles of the blest'.[4] And from another source[5] we learn that the 'dolphin was used as an emblem of love, diligence, or swiftness'—a significance that was doubtless derived from the supposed nature of the dolphin. But the origins and occasions of its employment with these meanings, and the sources of information, are in no case given.

The dolphin appears in the catacombs and on early Christian sarcophagi and ornaments, but it would be unwise to use it as a Christian symbol until its significance is more accurately known. It is most readily understood as symbolic of the sea and of maritime interests.

1. *The History, Principles, and Practice of Symbolism in Christian Art*, p. 206 (London, 1891).
2. E. R. BARKER, *Burlington Magazine*, October, 1913.
3. G. G. ROTHERY, *Decorators' Symbols, Emblems and Devices*, p. 95 (London, 1907).
4. NORTHCOTE AND BROWNLOW, *Roma Sottervanea*, p. 80 (London, 1879).
5. Oxford Dictionary.

DOME—Being shaped like the early conception of the sky its use in religious structures has been regarded as a symbol of the heavens, of the celestial regions and of the universe.

The term 'cupola', with which in architectural language it is occasionally inter-changeable, is descriptively more appropriate, being derived from the Latin word 'cupa' meaning cup, the cupola being an inverted cup. A further meaning of 'cupa' is small cask which has possibly led to the tradition in the minds of some architectural writers that cupola means small dome and is not used of larger domes. This, however, is not general.

The Latin term 'domus' means a house, and the Italian 'duomo' derived from it is applied to cathedral, the house of God, and because the cupola was a common feature of the duomo, it acquired that name, which anglicised becomes 'dome'.

Probably the earliest existing approximation to a dome in architecture is the Mycenean subterranean tomb chamber known as the 'Treasury of Atreus', or Tomb of Agamemnon constructed about 1325 B.C. It is 48 feet in diameter and 44 feet high shaped like a beehive. There is no reliable evidence to indicate whether there was any symbolic or religious purpose in this shape. The tomb is one of several similar and its shape was apparently fairly common not only for tombs but for the roofs of circular houses and huts among the Greek and Western Asiatic peoples, which may have evolved from the circular tents of nomad peoples.[1] Assyrian bas-reliefs of the seventh and eighth centuries B.C. show domed structures of a similar character.

The Romans adopted the dome for their circular temples of which the Pantheon built in the second century A.D. is the most impressive remaining example. With its span of $142\frac{1}{2}$ feet it remained the largest true dome in the world, until the construction in 1932 of the shell concrete dome of the Market Hall at Algeciras in Spain with its span of 156 feet. The fairly flat Pantheon dome is very different in shape from the early beehive domes. The Romans possibly gave domical roofs to their circular temples because they symbolized the celestial regions. Dio Cassius in his Roman

History says that the Pantheon was so named, perhaps, because it received among the images which decorated it the statues of many gods; 'but', he adds, 'my own opinion of the name is that because of its vaulted roof, it resembles the heavens', and there are several early references to this symbolic tradition[2] in connection with early Christian, Byzantine and Islamic domes.

The early Christian examples in Italy such as the mausoleum of S. Costanza in Rome, with its span of 74 feet, a work of the fourth century A.D., is erected on a circular structure, like the Roman domes. With the mausoleum of Galla Placidia at Ravenna (fifth century A.D.), however, the dome is placed for the first time on the cross plan, although this was obviously difficult to do. Thus there was the double symbolism of the cross and dome suggesting the divine authority or the universality of Christianity. This was followed a century later by the Church of Santa Sophia in Constantinople with its vast central dome buttressed by two semi-domes. Placing a large dome on a square base presented many structural problems, and although this was done on a small scale in the mausoleum of Galla Placidia it was rather crudely constructed. It had also been accomplished, prior to Santa Croce, in two Sassanian palaces—that of Feruzabad of the third century A.D. and that of Sarvistan of the fourth century A.D., both in the vicinity of Persepolis. These were higher domes, but were erected on square bases, and Heathcote Stathan[3] thinks that these were the logical precursors to the domes in Byzantine architecture.

The dome on the cross plan was a distinctive feature of a large number of Byzantine churches. The dome also became a feature of the Mohammedan mosque and it is probable that Muslim architects borrowed it from Byzantine architecture. The symbolism of the dome over the cross in Byzantine churches is strengthened by the decorative themes of the heavenly hierarchy which became common in Renaissance and Baroque churches. Similarly the frequent decoration of the domes of mosques with stars suggests its symbolism of the celestial regions.

This symbolism is fully apparent during the Renaissance. Leon Battista Alberti[4] refers to it and many other writers allude to this significance of the dome. Professor Rudolf Wittkower says that 'a cosmic interpretation of the dome was common from antiquity onwards and was kept alive, above all, in the Eastern Church', and he adduces considerable evidence to support this.[5] Among the famous domes of the Renaissance, all on Latin cross plans, are the octagonal dome of Florence Cathedral (span 138½ feet) built by Brunelleschi in 1420–34, the true dome of St. Peter's at Rome (span 137½ feet) built by Michelangelo in the early seventeenth century, which although 5 feet less than the Pantheon dome is yet much higher and nearer to a hemisphere; the dome of St. Paul's, London (span 112 feet), built by Wren in the early eighteenth century; and the dome of the Invalides in Paris (span 91 feet) built by Mansart in the late seventeenth century.

In modern architecture domes have become features of theatres, libraries, market halls and sports arenas, and they are, of course, the principal features of planetaria, which, with their patterns of stars, have similarities to the domes of mosques. Construction in steel and concrete, particularly shell-concrete, have made possible very big spans. One of the most notable of modern ecclesiastical domes is that of the temple of the synagogue at Cleveland, Ohio, with its hemisphere of 100 feet span, built by Eric Mendelsohn in 1946–52.[6]

1. WILLIAM BELL DINSMOOR, *The Architecture of Ancient Greece*, 3rd edition (London 1950) p. 5.
2. DIO CASSIUS, *History of Rome*, LIII, 27, English translation by E. Cary, on the basis of the version by H. B. Foster, Vol. 6, p. 263 (London, 1912).
3. H. HEATHCOTE STATHAN, *A History of Architecture*, 3rd edition revised by Hugh Braun (London 1950), Chapter III, Domed Styles and the Byzantine Type.
4. LEON BATTISTA ALBERTI, *Ten Books on Architecture*, English translation by James Leoni (London, 1755)
5. RUDOLF WITTKOWER, *Architectural Principles in the Age of Humanism*, 2nd edition (London, 1952), pp. 8 *et seq.*
6. ARNOLD WHITTICK, *Eric Mendelsohn*, 2nd edition (London, 1956), p. 162.

DOMINATIONS—The first rank of the second order of angels in the angelic hierarchy of the pseudo-Dionysius. (*See* Angel.) Their particular angelic function is the exercise of authority and the preservation of order and discipline in divine receptions. They are the highest rank of angels to be represented with full figures and wings.

DOVE—In its religious significance: symbol of the Holy Ghost. In a general sense: symbol of innocence, gentleness, conjugal affection and constancy.

As a symbol of the Holy Ghost it originates with the incident attending Christ's baptism, when, according to St. Luke, 'It came to pass, that Jesus also being baptized, and praying, the heaven was opened, and the Holy Ghost descended in a bodily shape like a dove upon Him, and a voice came from heaven, which said, "Thou art My beloved Son; in Thee I am well pleased".'[1] The symbol was employed in early Christian times, in the catacombs and in mosaics, and it was occasionally represented with the nimbus. During the eleventh century a human figure with a book or scroll took its place; but in the sixteenth century the older symbol was revived, and now the dove, as in early Christian times, is universally recognized as symbolizing the Holy Ghost.

The dove as a symbol of innocence and gentleness is derived from the habits of the bird, which prompted Christ to advise His disciples, when sending them out to teach His gospel to be 'harmless as doves'.[2] And the peacefulness of such a gentle bird's life receives tribute from David when, in the midst of the pain and troubles of his old age, he cries: 'Oh that I had wings like a dove! For then would I fly away, and be at rest.'[3]

From pagan times it has been widely understood as a symbol of conjugal affection and constancy, because of the affectionate mating habits and constancy of the species popularly known as turtle doves. The chariot of Venus, goddess of beauty and love, was drawn by turtle doves. On ancient monuments, gems, and coins of Assyria, Libya, Mycenae, and Phoenicia representations of two doves have been recognized which, according to Goblet D'Alviella, probably had some religious significance 'in the symbolism of the worship paid in Asia Minor to the great goddess of nature, venerated by the Phoenician populations under the name of Astarte'.[4] Similar representations can be seen in the catacombs, a particularly good example being where two doves with olive branches stand on either side of a vessel over which is placed the sacred monogram.[5]

1. St. Luke iii. 21 and 22. Also Matthew iii. 16; Mark i. 10; and John i. 32.
2. Matthew x. 16.
3. Psalm lv. 6.
4. *The Migration of Symbols*, p. 91.
5. Illustrated in LOUISA TWINING's *Symbols of Early Christian Art*, p. 183.

DOVE WITH OLIVE BRANCH IN ITS BEAK—Symbol of peace and good tidings.

The dove, which is a species of pigeon, has been employed as a messenger from the earliest civilizations to the present day. It was trained in that capacity by the Greeks and Romans, and in all ages of the Christian era, and was so used in the First World War. Its use as a Christian symbol of peace and good tidings originates from the return of the dove to the ark with the olive leaf, which, as a confirmation of the abatement of the flood, delivered Noah from anxiety—'And the dove came in to him in the evening; and, lo, in her mouth was an olive leaf pluckt off; so Noah knew that the waters were abated from off the earth.'[1]

It is a popular symbol, and in religious art obviously conveys the idea that after the troubles of this life death ends anxiety, bringing peace and security in the mercy of God and the future life.

1. Genesis viii. 11.

DRAGON—An ancient oriental symbol of life-giving powers through the agency of water; in western culture a symbol of evil, in which it is associated with the serpent. The latter meaning is that generally given to it in Christianity. It is a national symbol of China and of Japan.

As an ancient beneficent life-giving monster, the dragon symbol was widespread, being found in the ancient civilizations of Babylonia, Assyria, India, China and America. From researches made by anthropologists, the dragon does not appear to have arisen independently in various civilizations, but to have a common origin, probably in ancient Sumerian civilization, which may have derived ideas for its conception from Egypt.[1]

In most ancient conceptions of the dragon its principal function was control of water, either on the earth in the form of rivers, streams, seas, pools and wells, or in the sky in the form of clouds, and it was thus associated with thunder and lightning. As it was identified with the life-giving power of water, and worshipped as such, it was essentially a beneficent and all-powerful deity, that had its angry and menacing moods in storms, which in tropical and sub-tropical countries could be devastating and terrifying. It was thus composed of the most powerful and forbidding parts of many animals.

One of the earliest representations of dragons is on an archaic cylinder-seal from Susa, and consists of a lion or lioness combined with an eagle or falcon.[2] The ancient Chinese dragon, which is often represented among the clouds, is a complicated assemblage of features of many different animals. A description that has become traditional, derived from Wang Fu, a philosopher of the Han Dynasty (206 B.C.–A.D. 220), represents the dragon with the head of a camel, the horns of a deer, ears of an ox, the tusks of an elephant, the body of a serpent with the scales of a fish, a ridge-shaped horny spine, a long serpentine tail, and four legs with the feet of a tiger and the claws of an eagle.[3] The numerous ancient representations of the dragon show many other such curious combinations, and it is frequently shown with wings.

As the beneficent deity that controlled the life-giving element of water, and thus generally as a symbol of fertility and life, the dragon became the national symbol of China and the emblem of the Imperial Emperor of Japan.

It probably has the same significance in one of its penetrations to the West. The Romans adopted the dragon for their standard, and it also appeared on those of the Romanized Britons who were driven west by the Anglo-Saxon invasion to what is now Wales. Henry VII, being of Welsh descent, adopted the red dragon as a supporter on the dexter side of the Royal Arms. It was retained by Heny VIII, but placed on the sinister side, and also by Elizabeth, by whom it was changed to gold. With James I it disappeared from the royal arms. The red dragon was adopted as the royal badge of Wales in the late eighteenth century. In March 1953 it was augmented by a scroll inscribed with the words 'Y ddraig goch ddyry cychwyn', from a Welsh poem of the fifteenth century, and which, translated, reads 'The red dragon gives impetus'.

The dragon was adopted by the West Saxons for their standard, probably to signify their conquest of the Roman Britons, and thus it appears on the coat of arms of the Somerset County Council, where it is represented holding a mace. However, the dragon supporters and the dragon wing crest of the City of London coat of arms are probably due to an erroneous interpretation of the sixteenth century Corporation seal.[4]

The dragon is further represented in mythology as a guardian of treasure, a function he shares with several other fabulous monsters. The golden apples in the garden of the Hesperides were guarded by Ladon, the hundred-headed dragon.

As previously mentioned, the dragon as a symbol of evil is usually associated or identified with the serpent, to which heading the reader is referred.

1. See the discussion of this in G. ELLIOT-SMITH's *The Evolution of the Dragon* (London, 1919), mainly Chap. II, entitled 'Dragons and Rain Gods', and particularly the section dealing with 'The Evolution of the Monster', pp. 104 *et seq.*
2. G. ELLIOT SMITH, *op. cit.*, p. 79.
3. See G. ELLIOT SMITH, *op. cit.*, p. 81, also KATHERINE M. BALL, *Decorative Motives of Oriental Art* (London, 1927).
4. See C. WILFRID SCOTT-GILES, *Civic Heraldry of England and Wales*, p. 48 (London, 1933).

EAGLE—In ancient Greece and Rome the eagle was a symbol of victory; in modern civilization the eagle is a common national and imperial symbol. It is a Christian symbol of ascension and of St. John the Evangelist.

The eagle was sacred to Zeus the sky-god, and with its talons in a serpent it represented the triumph over evil and thus of victory. It also sometimes holds a thunderbolt, the instrument of Zeus, in its claws. Its association with Zeus, the king of gods, established the tradition whereby it became a symbol of authority and power.

In Rome, being sacred to Jupiter and a symbol of victory, it was adopted as the standard of the Roman legions. It appeared with spread wings, first as a silver eagle under the Republic, and later as a golden eagle under the Empire. It inevitably became the special emblem of the Roman Emperors in their identification with Jupiter.

In the Middle Ages it became the emblem of Germany, and Germanic States, and an important heraldic device. As a German national symbol it is shown with wings and feet spread, sometimes crowned, with a sceptre in one foot and an orb in the other.[1]

The eagle was adopted by Napoleon because he seemed anxious to imitate the Romans down to the smallest detail. The eagle is a symbol of the U.S.A. It was chosen as a principal feature of the design of the state seal adopted in 1782, and it appears on many of the seals of the various states. It is also the national emblem of Poland, depicted in white on a red background.

The double-headed eagle became the emblem of Germany, Austria, Russia and several Balkan states. The origin of this form can be traced to remote antiquity. The Prototype may have been the representation of two eagles leaning against each other, with heads facing in opposite directions, in some golden fibulae dug up among the ancient tombs of Mycene. It is suggested by D'Alviella that this was copied by artists of Asia Minor, but instead of representing it as two eagles the copyist, mistakenly perhaps, rendered it as one eagle with two heads. This appears in a relief carving in Pteria in Asia Minor which dates back to the civilization of the Hittites, when it appears also in Persia and in India. The Turkomans who occupied most of Asia Minor during the time of the Crusades used the device of the double-headed eagle on their coins and standards and there is a strong probability that many of the Crusaders adopted the device from the Turkomans army. It is unlikely, as D'Alviella says, that the double-headed eagle was the result of independent thought in the Middle Ages; it is much more likely that it came with the Crusaders' return, like so many other strange devices and legends.

The eagle was regarded as a Christian symbol of the ascension because of its powerful upward flight, with its gaze fixed on the sun. It appears with this significance in a sculpture in Bitton Church, Gloucestershire, and also in a window in Lyons Cathedral, where the parent bird is teaching its young to soar upwards towards the sun. It is not sufficiently current as a symbol of the ascension for that significance to be readily apprehended, though an eagle in a panel soaring towards the sun—the departed soul ascending to God—is good symbolism.

In Christian iconography, the eagle is best known as a symbol of St. John, but this may properly be understood only by a study of the symbolism of the Evangelists.

1. Various forms of decorative, symbolic and heraldic eagles are illustrated in FRANZ SALES MEYER'S *A Handbook of Ornament*, pp. 82–4, English translation (London, 1894), and in A. C. FOX-DAVIES *A Complete Guide to Heraldry*, pp. 233–40 (London, 1909).

EGG—Symbol of creation. The Easter egg in the Christian Church signified re-creation as typified by the resurrection. The present of an Easter egg signified rejoicing at the resurrection and also the end of fasting.

The egg was a symbol of creation among many ancient peoples. In Egyptian mythology Ptah was a god of creation and new birth, and with Tanen, a god of living but inert matter with whom Ptah was sometimes associated, the cosmic egg was created from which sprang the world. There are variations of the myth, and the creation of the cosmic egg is sometimes through the agency of a divine bird, and sometimes conceived as springing from the lotus bud. In another myth Ra the god of light, is conceived as springing from the cosmic egg.

Among the ancient peoples of Asia Minor and Persia the egg was regarded as a symbol of creation, and as eggs are particularly plentiful in the Spring, which is the time of renewal and revival, the creation of the world was thought of as being in the Spring. Thus later the egg was associated with Easter.

There is probably no more obvious symbol of creation than the egg, for the seemingly remarkable spectacle to the primitive mind of a live creature emerging from an inanimate object must have promoted a sense of wonder. The Egyptians, when they beheld the scarab beetle roll its ball of earth into a hole, and then later saw a young beetle emerge, wondered so much that they worshipped the scarab as a creator of life.

Among Christians it was perhaps inevitable that the egg as a symbol of creation should be taken as a symbol of new life given to mankind by Christ's Sacrifice, and as a symbol of the resurrection. It has sometimes been likened to the rock tomb from which Christ emerged. The Easter egg is often painted red, indicative of the Blood of Christ, and sometimes in gay colours to express the gladness of rebirth. That is probably the principal reason for the gifts of Easter eggs. These gifts, often in recent times something else than an egg, are thus a celebration of the joy in the resurrection. Roman ritual has a special prayer which asks the Lord for benign blessings upon the eggs which are partaken in honour of the resurrection of the Lord Jesus Christ.

The other sense in which eggs are associated with Easter is that they have been among the articles of food prohibited during Lent. St. Gregory in a communication to St. Augustine in England said that during Lent there is abstinence from meat, and from all things that come from flesh like milk, cheese and eggs, and it became a general rule to abstain during Lent from all foods of animal origin. Thus the eating of eggs on Easter Tuesday is the joyful celebration of the end of fasting, and because of their other symbolism of creation and resurrection they are chosen in preference to other foods to mark the occasion.

ELM—The American Elm (*Ulmus Americana*) is the state tree of Nebraska, adopted 1937, of Massachusetts, adopted 1941, and of North Dakota, adopted 1947. The impressive appearance of this stately tree, common in these three states, no doubt prompted its adoption. Many beautiful specimens line the streets of the older towns.

EMU—The species of emu, *Dromaeus novae—hollandiae*, inhabiting south eastern Australia is often used as a symbol of Australia. It is a very large bird second only in size to the ostrich. It appears as the sinister supporter on the Australian coat of arms granted by George V in 1912.

The emu is often used as a badge, sign or name for Australian products, Emu wool and Emu wine being examples.

EROS—*See* Gods, Goddesses and Heroes of Antiquity.

EYE—The representation of an eye has been a symbol of the deity and providence since the days of ancient Egypt. The Utchat, which was the name given to the representation of the eye in Egypt, symbolized the eye of Horus or the eye of the sun-god or moon-god which were often shown together, an early example being those at the head of the sepulchral stele of Antef-àger-Ankh-khu, a priestly official of the 13th dynasty. Amulets were often made in the shape of an eye or Utchat, conferring on the wearer the qualities of the god, such as strength and vigour, while they enjoyed his protection.

In mediaeval Christianity the eye is used in a similar symbolical way and has survived in use until the present day, but whether it was derived from its ancient Egyptian use it is impossible to say. Austria provides numerous examples of its use in Renaissance architecture. As symbolical of God it is usually shown in the centre of an equilateral triangle, symbolical of the Trinity, surrounded by the rays of the sun. It is often placed high above the altar as in the Pfarrkirche at Grmunden am Traunsee (1626) and the Fisherman's church at Traunkirchen, while it appears over the door-way of the church of the monastery of St. Florian near Linz. It is often used in furniture, examples being a wardrobe dated 1748 and the headboard of a bed dated 1843, both in the Kasererbräu Hotel at Salzburg. An interesting example of its use in America is in the reverse of the Great Seal of the U.S.A. where it appears set in a triangle, surrounded by the sun's rays, above the unfinished pyramid, with the motto 'Annuit Coeptis': God has favoured our undertakings. (Fig. 43 (c).)

FABULOUS BEASTS—Many animals of a fabulous character have acquired a symbolic significance. Some, which in ancient times were thought actually to exist, have emerged into modern life merely as symbols, while others have always been known to be of an imaginary character sometimes with a symbolic purpose.

Fabulous beasts seem to have originated in ancient times in several ways. One was by the mistakes of writers recording the exaggerated descriptions given by travellers, possibly received at second or third hand. Another was by the confusion of two animals in a description. Pliny in his *Natural History* refers to the existence of several fabulous animals and birds, such as the unicorn[1] and sphinx.[2] He refers also to the dragon, but from his descriptions he obviously meant a large serpent or snake.

Animals were sometimes employed in ancient times as symbols of the elements: of the sun, moon and stars and the wind. Animals, like the horse, were sometimes given wings to symbolize the wind. The constellation Pegasus was named after the winged horse because of a supposed similarity of shape. The process of thought which identifies animals with the elements and the heavenly bodies is akin to the anthropomorphizing of the elements. For example, Zeus, Janus or Jupiter was first the sky, and then the god of the sky in human shape.

There was, thirdly, the conscious putting together of parts of different animals, or of man or woman and an animal, in order to express, better and more fully than was possible by means of a known animal, particular attributes, such as power, strength and fearsomeness, as in the combination of lion, eagle and snake to form the dragon.

The combination of a man with an animal was common in representations of the Egyptian gods. Khnemu, Khensu and Anubis each with a man's body and the head of a ram, hawk and jackal respectively, and Sekhmet with a woman's body and the head of a lioness, were examples. A reversed example is the Egyptian sphinx, with the head of a man and the body of a lion.

Only the more important fabulous creatures, which have acquired a definite traditional symbolism, are included in this book. They are the dragon, griffin, phoenix, sphinx and unicorn. Only vague symbolism has emerged from others, such as the basilisk, centaur, harpy and satyr, and the mermaid. The chimera, a curious combination of lion, goat and dragon, has given a word to the language meaning all that is fanciful and unreal.

---

1. PLINY, *Natural History*, VIII, 3.
2. *Ibid.*, VIII, 30.
3. *Ibid.*, VIII, 11–13.

FALCON—The falcon is one of the Queen's beasts. It was adopted by Edward III as a badge because of his liking for the sport of hawking or falconry. He also gave the name falcon to one of his Kings of Arms.

In ancient Egypt the falcon or hawk was sacred to Horus and thus a symbol of the sun. (*See* Hawk.)

FEATHERS—Three ostrich feathers, the emblem of the Black Prince, form the well-known badge of the Prince of Wales, and are thus, a symbol of Wales.

Like so many heraldic emblems, the ostrich feathers were probably derived from a pun on a name: that of Countess Ostrevant, an hereditary title of the Black Prince's mother, Queen Philippa. In his will the Black Prince expressed the wish that on his monument in Canterbury Cathedral should be deployed his two shields, one for war, charged with his quartered arms of France and England, and one for peace consisting of a black shield charged with three white feathers, their quills passing through scrolls inscribed with the motto 'ich diene'.[1] The three ostrich feathers might also be taken as a symbol of peace. The Black Prince may have called it the badge of peace because it was derived from his mother and the sense of home. The ancient Chinese hieroglyph for peace was the representation of a woman under a roof. This, however, may be only a pleasant fancy.

1. *See* BOUTELL'S *English Heraldry*.

FASCES—An ancient Roman symbol of authority. It originated the name of Fascism, of which it was the principal symbol.

Fasces were bundles of elm or birch rods bound together with red thongs, each bundle containing an axe in the centre, the iron of which projected. They were carried by the lictors, the officers who attended the higher Roman magistrates. The lictors carried the fasces in the left hand and on the left shoulder in procession before the magistrates, and at the funeral of a magistrate fasces were carried behind the bier. The rods represent the power to scourge, and the axe to behead malefactors, and thus in a sense they are symbols of the administration of punishment.

The stone relief of fasces from which the illustration is taken was probably part of a sepulchral monument of a Roman magistrate. (Fig. 44 (*a*).)

The fasces on a tricolour shield was adopted by Mussolini as a symbol of his Italian nationalist movement because it symbolizes a holding together, and was significant of the close union of the followers of the movement.

FERN—Symbol of New Zealand. The variety of fern that forms the symbol is the *Cyanthea dealbata* (often known as 'ponga' or 'silver king') which is a tree fern ten to thirty feet high with fronds up to twelve feet long. It appears to have become a national symbol by gradual and spontaneous adoption because it is particularly common in the country and is an outstanding feature of its vegetation. An early example of its use as a badge was that worn by a New Zealand football team which visited Britain in the eighteen-eighties.

The invitation card for the Coronation of Elizabeth II was decorated with the flowers and plants of the Commonwealth on each side of the Royal Arms, and twining round the two sceptres, thus forming a border. The fern was used for New Zealand.

FIRE—This has inevitably many symbolical meanings because it is for man one of the most valuable of natural phenomena. It is both a great creative and destructive agency; it provides warmth and therefore makes possible the spread of peoples over the earth, it provides light in darkness, it is the main source of mechanical energy and is one of the main contributory factors in the making of civilization. In literature its significance is most powerfully expressed in the version of the Prometheus legend by Aeschylus in which Prometheus steals fire from the fire-god, Hephaestus, and brings it to mankind whereby it is the means to man's mastery over nature.

Many ancient religions include a degree of fire-worship and some have fire-gods like the Greek Hephaestus and the Roman Vulcan. In the numerous ancient religions where sacrifices were performed by burning the offering on an altar fire is the means of transmitting the sacrifice to heaven. In the Hebrew religion God is sometimes manifested by means of fire (Exodus iii. 2; Deuteronomy iv. 36). In many Eastern religions it is regarded as a purifying agent which led to the practice of cremation. It is also associated with sun worship and symbolism.

The main traditional meanings of the symbolism of fire are life, eternity and light, generally appearing in design as a flame or flames, torch and lamp. In a United Nations postage stamp of 1952 for Human Rights Day a flame surrounded by a white circle between two hemispheres was used to express, in the words of the designer: 'human happiness of the soul and spirit' (*see* Chapter XI). A similar design of a flame in a wreath was used as the United Nations symbol for International Year for Human Rights 1968.

Fire has contributed to figurative language—in such expressions as the fire of love, of passion, of ambition, while fiery has numerous applications. Landor's, 'I warmed both hands by the fire of life' with its symbolical suggestiveness is illustrated in a relief carving by John Skelton in a memorial in West Dene Churchyard, Sussex.

FISH—Early symbol of Christ and of baptism.

In the first five centuries of Christianity the fish was, judging by remains, one of the commonest of the early symbols of the Christian faith. It is found on the sarcophagi and loculi slabs in the catacombs, on rings and lamps, and as an architectural ornament. That its representation, in some examples, very nearly resembles the dolphin, is probably because the latter was a pagan symbol, and pagan forms in art influenced early Christian artists.

There is some uncertainty as to the circumstances of its adoption as a general symbol of Christian Faith. Documentary evidence suggests that it was widely understood as a symbol of baptism. Clement of Alexandria, in his hymn to Christ, for example, regards Christ as the Fisher who gives spiritual sustenance to the baptized: 'Fisher of men who are saved; Who does feed with sweet life the holy fishes from the perilous wave of the sea of life.'

Beyond signifying baptism, it is generally understood to symbolize the Christian faith because the initial letters of Jesus Christ, God's Son, Saviour, in Greek— Ἰησοῦς Χριστός, Θεόῦ Ὑιός, Σωτήρ—spelt the Greek word for fish: ἰχθύς. This is

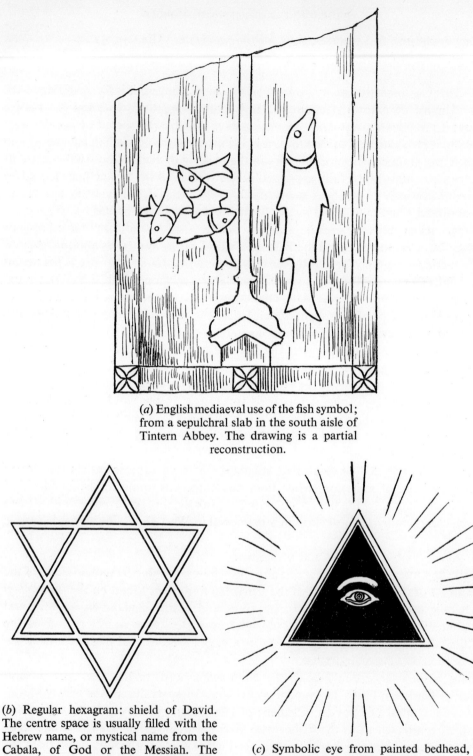

(a) English mediaeval use of the fish symbol; from a sepulchral slab in the south aisle of Tintern Abbey. The drawing is a partial reconstruction.

(b) Regular hexagram: shield of David. The centre space is usually filled with the Hebrew name, or mystical name from the Cabala, of God or the Messiah. The corner spaces are sometimes filled with appropriate quotations from the Hebrew scriptures, or with appropriate prayers.

(c) Symbolic eye from painted bedhead, 1843; also on wardrobe, 1748, in the Kasererbrau Hotel, Salzburg. The eye set in a triangle with the sun's rays is a common symbol in Renaissance churches in Austria.

Fig. 43. Fish, Hexagram and Eye.

regarded by some[1] as the origin of the fish as a symbol of Christianity, the connection with baptism being only subsidiary. But it is more probable, as Ethel Ross Barker thinks,[2] that 'the presence of the divine name in the word' was discovered subsequently to its adoption as a symbol of baptism, and being an additional consecration it brought the fish into current use as a general symbol of the faith. Some of the early Christian writers cleverly alluded to the symbol in both connections, thus making it an important object of religious veneration. Tertullian says: 'But we, little fishes, are born in water according to our Fish ($'I\chi\theta\acute{v}\varsigma$), Jesus Christ.' Three fishes were often represented together, forming roughly an equilateral triangle, an attempt to associate the symbol with the Trinity. (Fig. 43 (*a*).)

The fish symbol is responsible for the sacred figure of the mandorla (Italian for almond), also known as the vesica piscis, common on ecclesiastical seals, and frequently determining in paintings the shape of the aureolas surrounding the figures of the Trinity. The mandorla is often found serving as a panel for the sacred monogram and other symbolic devices.

1. *See* HULME, *Symbolism in Christian Art*, p. 204.
2. *Burlington Magazine*, p. 49, October 1913.

FLAME—*See* Fire.

FLAX—This has sometimes been regarded as a symbol by association of Northern Ireland by reason of flax being used as a raw material for the country's linen industry which constitutes its most important contribution to the world's textiles. The flax plant appears on the 1*s*. 3*d*. Northern Ireland stamp issued in 1958.

FLEECE—In ancient Greece the golden fleece came to be regarded as a symbol of treasure. In modern civic heraldry, it is used as a symbol of wool. In the familiar Greek myth, after the ram, which had carried Helle and Phrixus, was sacrificed by the latter, its golden fleece was placed by King Æetes in a consecrated grove guarded by a dragon until it was recovered by Jason as the result of his famous quest for it, accompanied by the Argonauts. It can be appreciated that it thus became a symbol of treasure. It was for this reason that it provided the subject of the famous Spanish Order of the Golden Fleece, instituted in 1430 by Philip the Good, Duke of Burgundy. It is represented in the badge of the Order and in modern civic heraldry as a dead ram suspended. It appears in the coats of arms of Nelson (Lancashire), Stourbridge (Worcestershire), Leeds, Batley, Barldon and Skipton (Yorkshire) and New South Wales.

FLEUR-DE-LIS—A common form of ornament, best known as an emblem of the French monarchy. A similar figure, from which the fleur-de-lis may be derived, was in ancient times symbolic of life.

Some regard the fleur-de-lis as a conventionalized rendering of three white lilies, or of the white iris, tracing it to ancient Egypt and India as originally a symbol of life, in common with many other flowers and trees. Others regard it as a development of the heads of ancient battle-axes, spears, sceptres, and such-like.

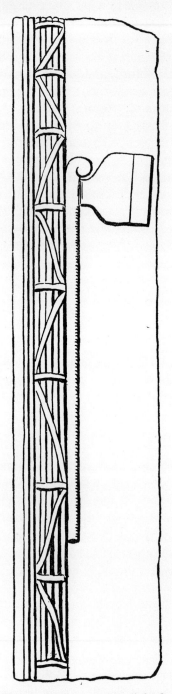

(a) Fasces, from a stone relief of about A.D. 100, from Ephesus, and now in the British Museum.

(b) Four of the many variations of fleur-de-lis. The first appeared in the Middle Ages, the second in the late fifteenth century, the third in the early seventeenth century, and the fourth in the time of the late Bourbon kings.

Fig. 44. Fasces and Fleur-de-lis.

The symbolic use of the fleur-de-lis form possibly originated in the myths of Egypt. Hathor, the mother of Horus, was often identified with the lotus, because the lotus was regarded as a typification of the very essence of life, for the reasons given under that heading, and Horus was sometimes represented as being born of the lotus. In the course of time fancy extended the symbolism of the lotus to other flowers, like the lily and iris, which were thus occasionally identified with Hathor, and associated with the instruments employed by Horus in destroying the enemies of Ra.

As thunder and lightning were destructive powers of the gods, the thunder weapon, which, like the winged disk, was employed by Horus, came to be associated with the iris or lily; the thunder weapon, consequently, was sometimes represented by a conventional rendering of the iris or lily; and as the thunder weapon, in being employed to destroy the enemies of Ra, was employed for the protection of the life of the Egyptian people, this representation by the iris or lily became symbolic of the maintenance and protection of life. It thus became a symbol of life in two senses, for it was already symbolic, in common with the lotus, of the essence and eternal renewal of life. The ancient prevalence and definite meaning of the symbol make it probable that it was the prototype of the fleur-de-lis.[1]

The fleur-de-lis was first definitely connected with France as emblematic of the monarchy by an 'ordonnance' of Louis le Jeune in 1147. The reason for this adoption is not known. Legend says that the fleur-de-lis originated with Clovis, because the white lily was given to him by an angel at his baptism; but the fleur-de-lis is far older than the kingdom of France. As an emblem of France it passed with the passing of the French monarchy; but is it not a fitting symbol to appear in designs associated with the few remaining French who believe a monarchy to be the best form of government?

The fleur-de-lis is now a common ornament. It figures, for example, as a pleasing terminal to the limbs of the cross where its symbolism is appropriate since it can, with some show of evidence, be regarded as an ancient symbol of life.

1. *See* discussion of this in G. ELLIOT SMITH's *The Evolution of the Dragon*, pp. 120 *et seq.* (Manchester, 1919).

FLYCATCHER—The scissor-tailed flycatcher (*Muscivora Forficata*) was adopted as the state bird of Oklahoma in 1951, having been selected by the people of the state. With its very long scissor tail and beautiful plumage it is a familiar and graceful spectacle in the country.

FOUNTAIN—Symbol of life and of its source.

An element so important to life as water has inevitably been the subject of much symbolism, particularly in tropical, sub-tropical and desert countries where an oasis with its shady trees and gushing water must often have seemed like heaven to the tired traveller (*see* Water). Running water of which the spring or fountain is the typification is particularly valuable for its refreshing, cleansing and purifying properties, and thus logically became a symbol not only of the source but of the maintenance of life.

In Greek mythology springs were often regarded as possessing healing and inspiring properties, and were thus held to be sacred, with Naiads and other nymphs as the deities. Naiads were the goddesses of marriage, and sprinkling the bride with spring water was one of the wedding ceremonies. The muses were originally fountain nymphs personifying the source of inspiration and of artistic creation.

Since the earliest times it has been the custom to facilitate the supply of water by building a structure round the spring, and the remains of fountain structures have been found in ancient Babylon and Assyria. In ancient Greece the structures built round the sacred springs of nymphs were known as nymphaea, which developed in Roman times to large buildings where marriages were celebrated. It can be appreciated that marriages and the muses have the kinship of being the sources of creation, physical and mental.

From ancient times through the middle ages to the Renaissance and modern times, fountains have been conspicuous, decorative features of cities and gardens especially in warmer countries round the Mediterranean, although in modern times they are also notable features of Scandinavian cities.

The symbolism of fountains and the beauty possible with such a structural and decorative theme has made them favourite motifs for memorials. A famous modern example in London is the Shaftesbury memorial fountain in Piccadilly Circus. Fountains have frequently formed war memorials, a particularly expressive and appropriate example of the First World War being the Memorial Fountain at Tours to the American Services of Supply.

GEOMETRIC FIGURES—In the alchemy and astrology of the Middle Ages the elements, planets and metals were commonly denoted by geometrical figures, which were mostly either representational, or suggestive of the character or properties of the subject. The elements, water, fire, earth and air, were represented by equilateral triangles, water and earth suggesting gravity and descent were shown with the point downwards, thus: water $\triangledown$ and earth $\triangledown$, and fire and air, suggesting ascent were represented thus: fire $\triangle$ and air $\triangle$. The combination of the signs for water and fire— the hexagram—$\maltese$ was the sign for alcohol—'burnt water' or 'fire water', which became the shield of David. (*See* Hexagram.) This incidentally may be an example of the purpose of many alchemists to use chemical combinations and transmutations as symbols of moral and spiritual life.

In astrology the sun, moon and planets were associated with metals which were often thus represented by the geometric sign for the planet. Thus, gold for the sun was shown by a disk $\bigcirc$, silver for the moon by a crescent $\leftmoon$. Copper was the metal for Venus, possibly because in ancient times mirrors were of polished copper, and the sign for copper $\female$ was a representation of a mirror, which, of course, was particularly appropriate for the goddess of love and beauty. Iron was the metal for Mars the god of war, as iron was the material of his weapons and the sign $\male$ may have been derived from his shield and spear. These signs are of the same family as the Egyptian hieroglyphics.

GODS, GODDESSES AND HEROES OF ANTIQUITY—Ancient deities and heroes are occasionally employed as symbols of ideas, emotions, qualities or attributes generally derived from their particular functions as gods. Those mainly so employed in modern English culture are the Greek deities or their Roman counterparts. Many of the

Greek deities, like Hermes, for example, were originally worshipped in a wide variety of functions, and only in later times was Hermes regarded in the particular capacity of messenger now traditionally assigned to him.

Many of the Greek and Roman gods first had separate existences and were later identified with each other, although their original functions were somewhat different. An example is the Greek Arês and the Roman Mars. The former was from the beginning god of war, but the latter originally had several functions, and was particularly a god of fertility. It was only later that he became god of war and was identified with Arês. It must suffice here to give a few examples of deities that have been, and still are, used as symbols. For more detailed information the reader is referred to the many classical dictionaries.

Perhaps the god most commonly used as a symbol is the Greek Eros, or the Roman equivalent, Cupid, as expressive of love. In the original conception of Eros by Hesiod he is not only the god of sensual love, but of universal love which unites the world by the inner union of different elements. Eros, or Cupid, is generally represented as a boy with wings and a bow and arrow, often shooting at a young man's or a young woman's heart. He is used in a wide variety of decorative symbolism, from valentines to theatre decorations. A famous use is in the memorial fountain of Lord Shaftesbury in Piccadilly Circus. Here Eros is chosen to symbolize Shaftesbury's wide love of humanity, thus conforming to one of the ancient meanings.

Poseidon, or the Roman equivalent, Neptune, god of the sea, is sometimes used as a symbol of the sea or of maritime associations. He is generally represented as a powerful oldish man with a beard, holding a trident, by which he is generally recognized, and sometimes with a dolphin or tunnyfish and the hull of a ship. The horse and pine tree were also sacred to him.

Hermes, although originally a god with various functions, is traditionally regarded as the messenger and herald of the gods. When later he was identified with the Roman Mercury, they together became a symbol of commerce and communication. He is usually represented as a young man with wings on his feet and carrying the caduceus.

Dionysus, or his Roman counterpart Bacchus, is often used as a symbol of wine and conviviality. Dionysus was originally a god of fertility, more particularly in the vegetable world, and especially of a luxuriant kind, and he thus became associated with the vine. He has been variously represented; sometimes as a man in full maturity, robust and bearded, sometimes as a young man of feminine character crowned with a fillet of vine or ivy, nude or clothed in a panther's skin, carrying a thyrsus, which is a staff surmounted by a pine cone and wreathed in ivy and vine leaves. Often he is depicted dancing with satyrs, nymphs, muses, and centaurs. Animals associated with him are the lion, panther, lynx, ox, goat and dolphin.

Arês, or his Roman counterpart, Mars, god of war, is sometimes used as a symbol of war. He is usually represented as a young man of powerful frame, sometimes in armour, sometimes with a helmet.

Athênê, but more especially her Roman equivalent, Minerva, (goddesses of the arts, wisdom and peace) is occasionally used symbolically in these capacities, a famous example being on the Great Seals of George II and George III. Another well-known example is on the state seal of California made in 1850. The reason for the use of Minerva was the analogy of her birth with that of the state. Minerva was born full grown from the brain of Jupiter, and California was admitted to the Union as a state without the usual probationary period. She is usually represented wearing a helmet, with aegis on her heart (the shield with the Gorgon's head), sometimes holding an olive branch, and sometimes a spear. The owl is sacred to her.

Asklêpius, or the Roman Aesculapius, god of healing has often been employed as a symbol of medicine. He is usually represented as an oldish, wise, bearded man, with a staff and a snake. (*See* snake.)

Of the heroes of antiquity the only one who has been used to any extent as a symbol in modern times is Hêraklês (Latin: Hercules), who is frequently used as a symbol of strength, often in an ideal sense, and of the unconquerable spirit. He is usually represented as a powerful, muscular figure of impressive proportions emphasized by a small head, with club and lion's skin. He was traditionally regarded as the founder of the Olympic games. In the seal of George II and the second seal of George III Hêraklês stands near the enthroned king as a symbol of unconquerable strength.

Other gods and goddesses are less frequently used as symbols. Although Apollo was god of many things at different periods and in different localities, he was chiefly god of the sun, of light and of music and the arts, but a figure of Apollo is only very occasionally used to symbolize any of these. The same is the case with Artemis (Roman Diana), Aphroditê (Venus), Dêmêtêr (Ceres), Hêphaestus (Vulcan) and Zeus (Jupiter) and Hêrê (Juno). Adonis is sometimes alluded to as a typification of youthful male beauty, but he has never become a traditional symbol in the visual arts. The true symbolism derived from his legends would be of early death, or brief blossoming and of change.

GOLD—Being the most precious metal and the most important medium of exchange, gold has become a familiar symbol of all that is precious, of value, and of perfection and wealth. It was also in ancient days a symbol of the sun, and in alchemy gold was indicated by the disk, the sign for the sun.

Gold has supplied the symbolic adjective for a very large number of states, conditions and objects in which it is intended to denote perfection, value or preciousness, such as golden age, golden mean, golden rule, golden section, and many others. For the various meanings the reader is referred to the larger dictionaries. The first and last mentioned should, however, be considered here.

The Golden Age was originally a conception of the earliest period of mankind, when man and woman lived in innocence and bliss and in the harmless enjoyment of pleasures, and all, animals included, were at peace with one another. It is a conception which seems to have belonged to most nations, and it is possible that the Greeks obtained it from the Egyptians. Such a period ended with guilt. It is, of course, similar to the conception of the enjoyment of the Garden of Eden, which ended with the fall of man, and its return has been a common conception of Paradise.

The term Golden Age subsequently came to be applied to those periods of plenty which seem to have been blessed with a high degree of achievement and happiness. Thus, among the ancient nations it has been applied to Egypt during the eighteenth and nineteenth dynasties (approx. 1600–1350 B.C.); to Assyria of the seventh century B.C.; to the Chaldee-Babylonian Empire from 606 to 538 B.C.; to the age of Pericles in Athens during the fifth century B.C. and to the Tang dynasty in China (A.D. 618–907). In modern times the reigns of Charles V of Germany (1519–58); of Elizabeth I (1558–1603); of Louis XIV and XV (1640–1740); of Peter the Great, of Russia (1672–1725); and of Frederick the Great of Prussia (1740–86), have often been referred to as golden ages in their respective countries.

The Golden Section is a formula which, according to an old tradition, produces the perfect geometric proportion. It has had great influence on architectural design, especially that of the Renaissance and of the modern classical school, in determining the proportions of rectangles such as window openings.

The Golden Section is covered by two propositions of Euclid: Book II proposition XI and Book VI proposition XXX, but it can be succinctly stated as the division of a straight line into two parts, so that the relation of the shorter to the longer is as the longer to the whole. The division, if the line is 1, is 0·381965 to 0·618035 or approximately 19 to 31, but not exactly, which has given a mystical significance to it. The theory is that the relation of these two parts makes the perfect rectangle and a large number of architects and artists of the classical school have introduced divisions and rectangles into their designs which correspond to the golden section. Le Corbusier has been much influenced by geometric principles and the golden section in his designs, a conspicuous example being his application of it to the large block of flats at Marseilles, built in 1946–49.

GOLDENROD (*Genus Solidago*)—The goldenrod is the state flower of three states of the U.S.A.: Alabama, Kentucky, and Nebraska.

The first state to adopt the flower officially was Nebraska which adopted the late goldenrod (*Solidago serotina*) in 1895. Kentucky officially adopted another species (*Solidago patula*) in 1926, and Alabama in 1927. In North Carolina the goldenrod was customarily regarded as the state flower before the official adoption of the dogwood in 1941.

The reason for its popularity as a state flower is that it is one of the commonest and most widespread wild flowers in America.

GOLDEN SECTION—*See* Gold.

GOLDFINCH—The eastern goldfinch (*Spinies trestis trestia*) is the state bird of Iowa and was officially adopted in 1933. The goldfinch is a well-known bird in the eastern areas of the United States north of the Carolinas.

GRASS—In ancient times grass was a symbol of victory and of the acquisition of territory by conquest. Pliny mentions that it was usual for the vanquished to present to the conqueror a handful of grass signifying the surrender of their native soil.

From this the crown of grass (*corona graminea*) became the highest military award in the Roman Army. It was awarded to a soldier who saved an army, which would otherwise have been beleaguered, from destruction, and was usually given on the acclamation of the whole army as a grateful acknowledgement of its deliverance.

The crown was rarely awarded. Pliny mentions only seven recipients, one of whom, P. Decius Mus, received it twice.[1]

The ancient custom of presenting a handful of grass, signifying the surrender of native soil, probably originated the English custom of delivering seisin in the form of a turf as a token of the freehold sale of land.

1. PLINY, *Natural History*, Book XXII, Chapter 4.

GRASSHOPPER—The grasshopper has long been associated with the Gresham family and the Royal Exchange, which was founded by Sir Thomas Gresham in 1566. It formed the crest of the Gresham coat of arms, which can be seen on the tomb of Sir Thomas in St. Helen's Church, Bishopsgate. It also appears at the termination of the tower or turret of the Royal Exchange, on the coat of arms of Martin's Bank, and as a sign outside the bank in Lombard Street. It was customary in the sixteenth century, before streets were numbered, for houses of the gentry to be distinguished by signs taken from their coats of arms. Sir Thomas Gresham's house in Lombard Street, where Martin's Bank now stands, was denoted by his sign of the Grasshopper, and next door was the Unicorn. (Plate XXIII (*b*).)

It has been suggested that the grasshopper is the sign of a grocer, and was adopted by Sir Thomas Gresham because he was a merchant grocer.[1] This does not appear to be correct. The grasshopper was an emblem of the Gresham family long before it was used by Sir Thomas. His great grandfather, James Gresham, used the grasshopper on his seal, and it so appears in letters written between 1443 and 1464 in a volume of Sir William Paston's letters.[2]

The adoption of the grasshopper by the Gresham family is clearly as a rebus. In the fifteenth century a common form of the word was Greshop, obviously sufficiently close to Gresham for the adoption.

Guillim makes some mention of the ancient symbolism of the grasshopper which is not very familiar in recent times. He says that 'among the Athenians the grasshopper was holden for a special note of nobility; and therefore they used to wear golden grasshoppers in their hair (as Pierius noteth) to signify thereby that they were descended of noble race and homebred. For such is the natural property of the grasshopper, that in what soil he is bred, in the same he will live and die; for they change not their place, nor hunt after new habitations.'[3] It may be that the Greshams of the fifteenth century or earlier knew of this Greek symbolism, and this provided an additional prompting for the adoption of the grasshopper for their seal.

1. *See* for example the note on grasshopper in Brewer's *Dictionary of Phrase and Fable*.
2. *See* J. W. BURGON, *The Life and Times of Sir Thomas Gresham*, p. 7 (London, 1839).
3. JOHN GUILLIM, *Display of Heraldry*, 6th Edition, p. 202 (London, 1724). The five previous editions are dated 1610, 1632, 1638, 1660 and 1666.

GREEN—In religious symbolism the colour green was sometimes regarded as symbolic of hope as it betokens the coming of spring. It is one of the liturgical colours, being assigned to the periods from the octave to Epiphany to Septuagesima and between Trinity and Advent, except on Ember-days and festivals and their octaves.

In language green is often used in the sense of permanence, or even of immortality, as when reference is made to keeping a person's memory green. Green, or greenhorn, is also commonly used in reference to one who is raw and inexperienced, and easily imposed upon. In this sense it obviously derives from much unripe fruit being green.

GRIDIRON—The gridiron is an attribute of St. Lawrence, who was roasted alive in A.D. 258. It is sometimes used separately as a symbol of St. Lawrence.

GRIFFIN (griffon or gryphon)—A fabulous beast usually represented with the body of a lion and the head and wings of an eagle, which was thus, like the dragon, a combination of two of the most powerful of beasts. Its function appears to have been that of a guardian of treasure, and it was thus regarded as a symbol of watchfulness. Pliny[1] refers to the conflicts of griffins with one-eyed Avimaspi for the gold which the former guarded and which they were supposed to dig out of the mines. There are numerous representations of the griffin in the art of ancient Assyria and that of Greece, the most famous example being on the helmet of Athena Parthenos.

The griffin is the insignia of the Society of Grays Inn, being first employed as its device in the second half of the sixteenth century. The griffin is also the sinister supporter of the arms of the Verulam family, and as Francis Bacon was Treasurer of Grays Inn, the Society may have derived the Griffin from Francis Bacon, or vice-versa.

1. PLINY, *Natural History*, Book VII, Chapter 2.

GROUSE—The ruffed grouse (*Bonasa umbellus*) is the symbolic state bird of Pennsylvania, having been officially adopted in 1931.

HAND (emerging from clouds)—Symbol of God the Father.

In early Christian art before the twelfth century this was the only symbol of God the Father. After that time a head and then the whole figure were shown, though the hand also continued to be used alone until the seventeenth century; since then it has appeared only very occasionally.

It is usually represented in the act of blessing, sometimes with a cross nimbus, and in some instances with rays of light radiating from the fingers. It received support as a symbol from the many allusions to the 'Hand of the Lord' in the Old Testament; though it is doubtful whether that explains its origin. Being Semitic in association it is more probably derived, as D'Alviella suggests, from such representations as that on an Assyrian obelisk, 'where two hands are shown to issue from a solar disk, the right open and exhibiting the palm, the left closed and holding a bow.'[1]

When the hand was changed to the figure, it ceased to be a symbol and became an image, and the mysterious suggestiveness was gone. The idea of the Creator and God of All just being represented by the hand, while His mighty and mysterious presence is veiled in cloud, has the elements of grandeur. And the tips of the fingers transmitting rays of light suggest that in God is the source of light both physical and spiritual.

Sometimes the hand is shown with the third and fourth fingers bent and the thumb, first and second fingers extended. This is a customary position in the act of blessing in the Western church, and is shown in numerous representations of God the Father and of Christ since the ninth century. The Pope blesses with fingers in this position. It is a sign much older than Christianity, and was employed with many curious attributes in ancient art.[2] For the blessing in the Eastern church the middle finger is bent and the thumb is crossed on the third finger, forming the initial letter of the Greek name of Christ.

1. GOBLET D'ALVIELLA, *The Migration of Symbols*, p. 26, in which it is illustrated.
2. *See* F. T. ELWORTHY, *Horns of Honour*, Chap. IV, 'The Manu Panten or Symbolic Hand' (London, 1900).

HANDS CLASPED—A common symbol of union, friendship, or affection. On the sepulchral monument this, in accordance with ancient tradition, may either mean farewell or reunion in the next life. A subsequent meaning may be that affection, love, friendship, is not severed by death.

The sepulchral idea is derived from scenes depicted on Greek stelae, mainly of the fourth century B.C., where the individual clasps the hand of a friend or relative who is sometimes accompanied by others of similar relationship to the departed. It is uncertain, as Percy Gardner[1] says, whether this indicates farewell to a person's friends in this life, or his reception in Hades by those friends who have gone before. Judging from the nature of the scenes and of contemporary Greek thought it is more likely that the former is meant. It is a common, natural, and perhaps instinctive practice to hold the hand of a dying person, thus imparting to him the physical assurance that he is not alone.

There is most support, from recent experience, for thinking that the idea vaguely existing in the minds of those who choose this subject is that friendship or love is stronger than death. The orthodox Christian, having enjoyed felicitous relationship with the departed, sees in death no spiritual separation, but a temporary physical separation, and that inseparability of spirit sometimes finds sepulchral expression by means of clasped hands.

1. *Sculptured Tombs of Hellas* (London, 1896).

HART—Sometimes regarded as signifying religious aspiration, from the Passage in Psalm xlii.1: 'As the hart panteth after the water brooks, so panteth my soul after thee, O God.'

Both Mrs. Jameson[1] and F. E. Hulme[2] state that the hart typified solitude and purity of life, but neither gives the origin of that significance, nor an example of its use in this capacity. Presumably it had such a meaning because of the habits of the animal.

This symbol, though it can be effectively used as a literary analogy, is hardly adequate when used solely as a pictorial representation, fully to express the thought.

1. *Sacred and Legendary Art*, Vol. i, p. 28.
2. *Symbolism in Christian Art*, p. 176.

HAT—Distinguishing the hat from other forms of headdress as a hemispherical, cylindrical or conical covering for the head surrounded by an approximately flat horizontal brim it was possibly, in its early uses, a symbol of the sky like the dome, umbrella and baldachino. Greek and Roman gods are sometimes shown on ancient gems and other objects wearing a hat and there are examples of the two-headed sky-god, Janus, wearing a hat with a domical centre and a broad flat brim. A. B. Cook refers to R. Eisler's insistence that 'throughout the Levant the sky was often symbolized as a hat: witness the tiara of Zeus Oromásdes, the starry pîlos of Men or Attis or Mithras etc.' 'The same conception', according to Cook, 'prevailed among the nations of northern Europe, as may be seen from Odhin's broad hat, though hardly from the umbrella like head-gear of Rugiwit. And the Greeks, themselves, were capable of equally crude ideas; for Anaximenes of Miletos, who speaks of his aér as condensed by a process of 'felting' (pílesis) declares that the stars move round the earth horizontally 'as the felt hat (pilión) turns about on our head.' 'We need not,' adds Cook, 'therefore, hesitate to interpret the pétasos of Hermes or Argos or Janus as an unsophisticated symbol for the sky overhead.'[1]

It is possible that when the headdress of the cardinal was changed from the mitre to the hat at the Council of Lyons of 1245 that a shape symbolical of the heavens was a deciding factor.

Numerous varieties of hat have developed conforming to the basic shape indicated, and many have become associative symbols, as when particular hats are worn by professions, trades, schools and sportsmen, and the hats are used in design to symbolize these. They are also used to symbolize countries or localities as when the bullfighter's hat symbolizes Spain. The bowler hat could be taken as the symbol of an Englishman, particularly the City business man. Indeed if a picture were shown of a bowler hat, rolled umbrella and gloves its symbolism of the Englishman would be apparent in many countries.

1. A. B. COOK, *Zeus*, Vol. II, God of the Dark Sky, p. 386.

HAT, CARDINAL'S—The cardinal's hat often appears as a symbol in relief sculpture and in ecclesiastical plate and vestments indicating association with a cardinal or with the purpose of a cardinal's office. The representations vary with the decorative context while other symbols are sometimes used with it. Cardinals originally wore mitres but at the Council of Lyons in 1245 they were enjoined to wear hats of a shape which suggested symbolism of the heavens (*see* Hat). The traditional shape is flat, broad brimmed with fifteen tassels, although the number varies with different representations. In the tomb of Cardinal Cristoforo della Rovere (d. 1483) in the Church of Santa Maria del Popolo at Rome, the cardinal's hat is shown in a panel on the plinth with eleven tassels falling on each side of a shield, and two on the hat itself. In the cardinal's hat similarly placed in the tomb of Cardinal Ascanco Sforza (d. 1507) six tassels fall on either side of the shield with two on the hat itself. An equilateral cross appears between the hat and the shield. An interesting circumstance is that in the recumbent effigy of Cardinal Cristofore della Rovere he wears the mitre. In vestments the hat is shown red which is the general colour of the Cardinal's dress, showing that he should be ready to shed his blood for the Holy See.

HAWK—The sparrow-hawk or falcon was sacred to and a symbol of several Egyptian sun-gods: Horus, Ra and Seker, and was thus a symbol of the sun. Horus was variously represented as a hawk, as a hawk-headed man, or as a solar disk with hawks' wings (*see* Winged Disk). Ra was often represented as a man with a hawk's head surmounted by the solar disk and the uraeus-serpent, while Seker was sometimes represented as a hawk and sometimes as a man with a hawk's head. It was also associated with Apollo, the Greek sun-god.

The reason for the hawk being selected as a sun symbol was that it was thought to be the only bird that could look with unflinching gaze at the sun, and was thus regarded as being filled with sunlight and as a bird of fire.[1]

1. *See* A. B. COOK, *Zeus*, Vol. 1, pp. 240–1 (Cambridge, 1919).

HAWTHORN (*Genus crataequs*)—The blossom of the red or white hawthorn is the state flower of Missouri and was adopted in 1923.

HEADDRESS—One of the purposes of a symbol is to enhance the importance of what is symbolized[1] and the headdress has been a particularly significant example of this. From remote ancient times until the present day one of the principal purposes of the numerous headdresses that have been worn has been to enhance the dignity or signify the importance of the wearer. A very large number of different forms have evolved: the crown, diadem, tiara, turban, the many varied headdresses used in religious and civic ceremonies, and for military purposes, while it acquired a symbolism in the fashions of everyday dress. A few of the more significant will be mentioned.

The earliest known examples of headdress are the pre-dynastic crowns of upper and lower Egypt which were combined as the double crown when the kingdoms became united (about 3500 B.C.). The white crown of upper Egypt was a tall cone and was placed on the red crown of lower Egypt and together they formed a tall headdress which must have increased the height of the wearer and given him added dignity. Another ancient form was the tiara worn by the ancient Assyrian and Persian kings. It was a tall conical shape as can be seen from ancient Assyrian reliefs of Khorsabad. Again it was obviously the purpose to enhance, by its height, the dignity and importance of the king, a circumstance confirmed by the evidence that although the tiara was also worn by the ancient nobles and priests they had to wear it turned down or depressed. The tiara of similar shape to the ancient Assyrian was adopted as the crown of the pope to signify his temporal dominion (*see* Tiara). Other forms of ecclesiastical headdress are the bishop's mitre and the cardinal's hat. An example of a distinguishing professional headdress, are the wigs worn by judges and counsel in courts of law (*see* Wig). Military headdress like helmets are largely protective but they have often been ornamented with symbolic devices, sometimes for purposes of identification and sometimes to express power and ferocity, with the intention of impressing an enemy and giving confidence to the defended. The helmet or other military headdress has been used alone to signify a particular war. The shrapnel helmet was used in design in this way, a good example being the design of a French postage stamp of 1958 marking the fortieth anniversary of the First World War Armistice, depicting a soldier's helmet on a tombstone seen behind growing wheat. (*See* Chapter XI.)

1. A. N. WHITEHEAD in *Symbolism–its Meaning and Effect* (Cambridge, 1928), says 'The object of symbolism is the enhancement of what is symbolised', p. 14.

HEART—Symbol of affection, love and devotion.

What is known as the *Sacred Heart* originates from a vision of Margarite Mary Alacoque (1647–90) of Christ with the heart entreating her to further the cause of religion. Christ is recorded as saying in the vision: 'Behold this Heart that has such great love for men.'

The common practice in the Middle Ages of separating the heart from the body at death and according it especial reverence was due to its association with the soul of man.

Representations of two hearts often occur in commemorative designs with the object, doubtless, of suggesting conjugal affection. Fortunately for such representations the old Hebrew signification of two hearts is now obsolete. The Hebrews spoke of 'double-hearted' in the same way that we should say 'double-faced'. For instance, in Psalm xii, 2 we read: 'They speak vanity every one with his neighbour: with flattering lips and with a double heart do they speak.'[1] But even if this were current now it is doubtful that pictorially it would be so understood.

1. Also in I Chronicles xii. 33.

HELMET—*See* Headdress.

HEMLOCK—The hemlock (*Tsuga canadensis*) is the state tree of Pennsylvania, having been adopted in 1931. It is a kind of spruce, indigenous to the country, with dark evergreen foliage. It became a state emblem according to the Act because 'it was of old the tree most typical of the forests of Pennsylvania', it yielded to the pioneers 'the wood from which they wrought their cabin homes' while 'the lighted hemlock at Christmas time dazzles the bright eyes of the child with an unguessed hope, and bears to the aged, in its leaves of evergreen, a sign and symbol of faith in immortality.'

HÊRAKLES—*See* Gods, Goddesses and Heroes of Antiquity.

HEXAGRAM—A symbol of Judaism formed of two equilateral triangles and known among the Jews as David's shield (*magen Dawid*). The meaning that is associated with it is explained by its name which, to the Jew, implies divine protection.

There is no evidence that David's shield had any ancient Hebrew origin. According to a tradition of the Cabbala it was a combination of the alchemists signs for fire and water, which were equilateral triangles, the former with the point upwards and the latter with it downwards. Also, according to the Cabbala, the principal consonants of the Hebrew words for fire and water gave the word for heaven, which was the equivalent of God. Thus, the hexagram was not only the synthesis of fire and water, but the logical symbol of heaven and of God.

The geometric form was common, as in Roman geometric patterns. The hexagram appears, for example, on a fragment of Roman silver plate found at Coleraine in Ireland, and now in the British Museum, which probably dates from the fourth century A.D.

David's shield is first mentioned in Jewish literature during the twelfth century in the *Eshkol ha-Kofer* of the Karaite Judah Hadassi, though its use appears to be much earlier, as an example occurs on a Jewish tombstone at Tarentum which is

255

thought to be of the third century A.D. It was employed to some extent as an architectural ornament of synagogues, and it may have occasionally taken the place of the mezuzah.

In modern times David's shield is used as a device by many important Jewish institutions. (Fig. 43 (*b*).)

HOLLY—The foliage and bright red berries of holly provide the time-honoured Christmas decoration. It was used at the pagan Saturnalia festival in Rome, held from 17th to 23rd December, and signified health and well being.

Holly state tree (*Ilex opaca Aiton*) of Delaware, having been adopted in 1939. One of the conspicuous forest trees of the district, it grows to a considerable size, and its timber is one of the important natural resources of the state.

HORNS—Symbol of power and of associated ideas like strength and dignity. Also symbol of protection and defence, and a common attribute of the devil.

The horns of various animals, but particularly those of the bull and cow, have appeared extensively on the headdress, helmets and crowns of deities, leaders, kings and warriors of various primitive and ancient peoples, denoting power, dignity and strength. The Egyptian god Ammon was represented with a ram's head, or ram's horns. In the identification of Zeus and Jupiter with Ammon, they were also shown with rams' horns. Moses is referred to in Deuteronomy (xxxiii. 17) as wearing horns and he is generally so represented; Michelangelo's sculpture on the tomb of Julius II in Rome being the most famous example. Horns appeared on the helmets of Greek and Roman soldiers, and later on the helmets of warriors of the Middle Ages. Historians of the modern royal crown consider that its form derives partly from the helmet, and it is possible that its arches derived from the horns of the helmet, because several curve inwards in the form of a crescent. Horns as symbols of power and strength were placed on the walls of tombs in guardianship of the dead,[1] and thus became symbols of protection.

The reason for the extensive use of horns as symbols of power and strength is obviously derived from man's observation of the tremendous strength of animals when using their horns, especially bulls. They doubtless observed that these powerful horned animals could toss men and other animals and rip open their bodies.[2]

In many traditional representations of the devil or Satan he is shown with horns. This is probably derived from an early Christian identification of the devil with Greek or Roman gods of a particularly animal nature, who were represented with horns like Pan and Bacchus; or from the custom of representing the devil, or the principle of evil, as a dreadful monster like a serpent or dragon, when some of the features of this monster, like the horns and tail, were given to the human figure of the devil.

1. Some interesting information of the use and significance of horns among various peoples appears in F. T. ELWORTHY's *Horns of Honour* (London, 1900).
2. Modern man has not the same opportunity for making these observations, but anyone who has witnessed a bull fight in Spain, before the horses were provided with protective devices, will have been impressed with the tremendous power of the bulls when using their horns. I well remember in 1928 seeing several horses and riders lifted in the air and literally carried on the horns of the bull.

HORSE—The horse at different times has been variously regarded as a symbol of strength, of courage, of death and the swiftness of life. The horse is associated with Poseidon, who was anciently regarded as its creator and tamer. In the contest for the deityship of Athens represented on the west pediment of the Parthenon, Poseidon offers a horse, symbol of strength, while Athena offers an olive tree, symbol of peace. In ancient Etruria the horse was sometimes regarded as symbolic of the passage from one state of existence to another, or of the passage from this life to the next, for the horse is often represented as carrying the deceased, or the soul of the deceased, to the next life. In Etruscan sepulchral stelae of the fifth and fourth centuries B.C. the deceased is shown on a horse or in a chariot drawn by horses.[1] The horse thus became symbolic of the last journey, and thus of death, and in this sense it also appears in the Christian catacombs. In Christianity, however, it is more often regarded as symbolic of courage because of its association with St. Martin, St. Maurice, St. Victor and St. George.

1. *See* GEORGE DENNIS, *The Cities and Cemeteries of Etruria* (London, 1848; 2nd revised edition, 1878). See also ARNOLD WHITTICK, *History of Cemetery Sculpture*, p. 33 (London, 1938).

HORSESHOE—A symbol of protection, and widely current in modern times as a symbol of good luck.

As a symbol of protection the horseshoe has been placed over the doors of houses, inns, stables, shops, mosques and churches since the early Middle Ages. It was possibly used in this manner in earlier times among ancient civilizations, but no records exist. It was also worn or carried as an amulet. From its wide use as a symbol of protection it has become a universal symbol of good luck.

Many explanations have been given in the course of history of its origin as a symbol of protection and good luck. It is possible that the shape as a symbol is older than the actual horseshoe and that they later became associated. One explanation of its origin is that it is derived from the crescent symbol of Byzantium and of the Ottoman Turks. This would explain why it appears at the entrances to Mosques, because it can be appreciated that the crescent was a protection against evil similar to the cross in Christianity. The sign has also been associated with the nimbus, and it has been suggested that in some representations of heads with nimbi the former had worn away, leaving the gold nimbus in the shape of a horseshoe. Another suggestion is that the horseshoe became a symbol of protection and luck because iron, of which it is made, was habitually regarded as giving protection from harm.[1]

A. H. Keane[2] refers to a belief in Korea that the evil spirits come with the north wind, and the good spirits with the south wind, and he remarks that 'the family vaults of the better classes are sheltered from the evil spirits by horseshoe shaped mounds turned northwards, that is towards the quarter whence come the demons riding on the icy blasts'. He remarks that as originally there were no horseshoes 'it was not the shoe itself, but its peculiar shape that was regarded as propitious, because the entrances so constructed may have been thought favourable to the good and adverse to the evil genii'.

Another writer[3] says that because it was made of iron and because of its supposed resemblance to the form of the female sex organs, it was regarded as an effective

257

door charm. Sex organs are regarded by many primitive peoples as symbols of life and regeneration. It is an easy transition from a symbol of life to a symbol of protection and luck. I have heard, although I cannot remember the source of information, that the Arabs sometimes put the genital organs of the camel on their tent doors, thus using a symbol of life as a symbol of protection. Other explanations have been given, and it may be that all play a part, like the many tributaries of a river, in the creation of this universal symbol of good luck.

1. *See* PLINY, *Natural History.*
2. A. H. KEANE, 'Air and Gods of the Air' in Hastings' *Encyclopaedia of Religion and Ethics.*
3. J. A. MacCULLOCK, 'Door' in Hastings' *Encyclopaedia of Religion and Ethics.*

HOUR-GLASS—Symbol of time. When used in connection with funerary art it is a warning that time passes rapidly and that our life quickly reaches its end.

It was a common symbol in the eighteenth century and was frequently introduced on tablets and gravestones, but it is rarely seen on stones after the early years of the nineteenth century.

Its use in the eighteenth century is a reflection of the philosophical tendency of the age, in which culture, having its source mainly in classic learning, implanted much of Greek philosophical thought regarding life and death.

INDIAN PAINT BRUSH—This flower (*Castillya Pinariaefolia*) was adopted as the emblem of Wyoming in 1917.

IRIS—State flower of Tennessee, officially adopted in 1933. Also (*Iris versicolor*) used as symbolic of the fleur-de-lis for the province of Quebec. It is probable that the iris was the original form of the fleur-de-lis. (*See* Fleur-de-lis.)

IVY—Symbol of friendship or fidelity, and immortality. It has little traditional importance as a symbol of friendship. It is obviously so from the clinging character of its creeping growth.

Shakespeare in *A Midsummer Night's Dream* refers to it somewhat in this sense when Titania says to Bottom:

> Sleep thou, and I will wind thee in my arms.
> Fairies, be gone, and be all ways away.
> So doth the woodbine the sweet honeysuckle
> Gently entwist; the female ivy so
> Enrings the barky fingers of the elm.   (Act IV, sc. i)

It is a symbol of immortality merely in common with other evergreens.

Although references are sometimes made to ivy as a parasite, as when Prospero, in *The Tempest*, speaking of his brother, says:

> He was
> The ivy which had hid my princely trunk
> And sucked my verdure out on 't.

and G. F. Watts calls it a parasite in a well-known picture, it is not, however, a parasite because it receives its nourishment from the ground.

In ancient Greece ivy was, with the vine, sacred to Dionysius, and was prominent

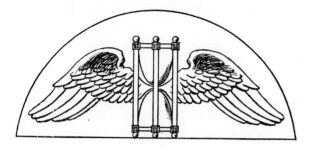

(*a*) Hour-glass, with wings from the tomb of the Hon. Basil Cochran, d. 1826, in the cemetery of Père Lachaise, Paris. Similar designs appear on many other tombs and on the gate piers of the cemetery.

(*b*) Scythes with hour-glass, from a headstone dated 1763 in the parish churchyard, Folkestone. The shapes of the scythes were probably made subservient to the lines of the design.

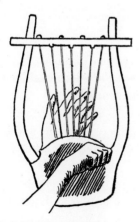

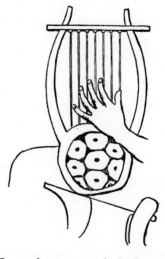

(*c*) Lyre—from a bas-relief on a Greek altar, 464 B.C.

(*d*) Lyre—from a south Italian (Greek colonial) volute cup of the fifth century B.C.

Fig. 45. Hour-glass, scythe and lyre.

as an accessory in Dionysian rites. A tavern sign in ancient Rome was a bush of ivy and vine leaves, which gave rise to the proverb: 'Good wine seeks no bush.'

JESSAMINE—The yellow jessamine, also called carolina jessamine (*Gelsemium semper-virens*) is the state flower of South Carolina, being adopted in 1923.

KANGAROO—Symbol of Australia, being one of the commonest and most spectacular indigenous animals. It appears as the dexter supporter (with the Emu as the sinister supporter) of the Australian coat of arms granted by George V on 19th September, 1912.

KANGAROO PAW—(*Anigozanthus Flavida*)—Often regarded as the emblematic flower of Western Australia. It is a native of the country and a familiar and vivid spectacle, with its scarlet woolly stems with emerald green terminations spread like a cockatoo's crest.

KEY AND KEYS—In Christianity symbol of spiritual power and authority, and the emblem of St. Peter to whom Christ gave the keys of the kingdom of heaven (Matthew xvi. 19), and this 'power of the keys' was transmitted through St. Peter to the Holy See and the Popes as the successors of St. Peter. Keys have thus become a symbol of the spiritual authority of the Pope. The key or keys frequently appear in designs on a wide variety of objects linked with the Basilica of St. Peter. They appear as the principal subject in Vatican postage stamps of 1929, 1958 and 1963, the first issued in recognition of the independent sovereignty of the Holy See of the Vatican and the two others to mark the vacant Holy See.

Signifying as it does the means of opening or closing anything key has a wide use in figurative language.

KIWI—Symbol of New Zealand, the Kiwi is an indigenous flightless bird of the genus *Apteryx* (of which three species exist). It is unknown elsewhere, and by association with the country it has gradually become one of its symbols.

LABYRINTH—In ancient times a labyrinth was a large building with many and intricate passages. It was also an open space with winding passages, and the latter has been interpreted as a solar symbol.

Pliny[1] refers to four great labyrinths of the former type, one of remote antiquity in Egypt, a building of the eleventh dynasty, one in Crete, one in Lemnos and a fourth in Italy. The Egyptian labyrinth was the work of Amenemhe III and was described by Herodotus[2] and Strabo,[3] the ruins having been revealed by the Egyptologists Lepsius and Petrie, which show it to have been an immense building. Pliny speculates on its purpose and cites opinions that it was a palace, a tomb, but adds that 'many others assert that it was a building consecrated to the Sun, an opinion which mostly prevails'. Recent evidence suggests that it was a large building for sepulchral purposes. Pliny's mention that it was consecrated to the Sun gives some clue to its symbolical significance. Of the other open type of labyrinth A. B.

Cook suggests that it was once the orchestra of a solar dance and that by a process of degradation it has become the modern maze.[4]

As noted in Chapters XVI and XVII the dance is an early form of prayer, and primitive and ancient dances are often, therefore, propitiatory in character and take the form of imitation by bodily gesture of the desired occurrence such as leaping in the air to make crops grow. One ancient form of dance among the Egyptians and other eastern Mediterranean peoples was the solar dance in which the dancers followed the course of the sun, moon and stars. A circular space—a logical provision—was allocated for this with an altar in the centre and here the ὀρχήστρα (orchestra: the Greek name for dance) took place and it was in this circular space that the singing and dancing of the chorus in Greek plays occurred between the later additions of the stage and auditorium.[5] The marking of the course of a set solar dance in the circular space becomes the labyrinth which thus becomes a solar symbol.

1. PLINY, *Natural History*, XXXVI, 19.
2. HERODOTUS.
3. STRABO.
4. A. B. COOK, *Zeus*, Vol. 1, p. 490 (Cambridge, 1914).
5. WILLIAM BELL DINSMOOR in *The Architecture of Ancient Greece*, 3rd edition (London, 1950), pp. 119–20. refers to the earliest dancing places in Athens. He speaks of the performance of choral dances associated with the worship of Dionysus, which, when they were introduced from the rural districts into the city, 'were given in the open circular area of stamped earth known as the "Orchestra" (dancing place) in the Agora'. The first remaining actual theatre construction in the precinct of Dionysus, either of the late sixth or early fifth century B.C., had an orchestral space of a perfect circle 83½ feet in diameter with the altar of Dionysus in the centre.

LADYBIRD—Symbol of the Pestalozzi children's villages. It was chosen by the children of the Pestalozzi village in Switzerland because they believe that the ladybird is considered to be lucky in every country of the world. Ladybird badges are issued and worn by those who support the work of the Pestalozzi Children's Village Trust. The ladybird is sometimes used as an ornamental motif in association with other symbols of luck.

LADY'S SLIPPER—*See* Orchid.

LAMB—Symbol of Christ. The lamb, as it was used for sacrifice by the early Hebrews, and had gentle qualities also attributable to Christ, became a symbol of Christ's sacrifice in redeeming the world from sin.

In a more general sense the lamb is symbolic of innocence, gentleness and meekness.

From earliest Christian times the paschal or, more descriptively, the sacrificial lamb has been one of the favourite symbols for Christ. There are numerous examples in the catacombs. Its use was probably suggested by such passages as that in John i. 29: 'The next day John seeth Jesus coming unto him, and saith, "Behold the Lamb of God which taketh away the sin of the world".'[1]

The nimbus was not introduced in the earliest examples, but it was added later, often with the sacred monogram. In still later examples the lamb carries, usually by a fore foot, either a cross or staff, with the banner of victory at the end. (Fig. 46 (*a*).) It was used in this form as the badge of the Templars, and became the device of the Middle Temple. It is well known as the badge of the 4th Queen's Surrey Regiment.

(*a*) Paschal Lamb, from the silver-gilt monstrance in the treasury of Aix-la-Chapelle Cathedral.

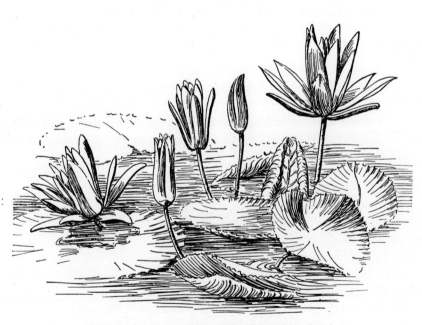

(*b*) Egyptian Lotus Water-lilies (*Nymphaea lotus*).

Fig. 46. Lamb and Lotus.

The lamb became so popular as a symbol that it was represented on the cross with nimbus and monogram, being thus a substitute for the crucifix. In A.D. 692 a council of the Church found it necessary to decree against this substitution. A notion of its importance may be obtained from Van Eyck's famous altar piece of the 'Adoration of the Lamb,' where the Lamb stands upon an altar in a bright flood of light radiating from the Holy Ghost above, and surrounded by adoring angels, saints and fathers.

Less importantly, the lamb symbolizes the young and innocent of the Christian flock, an idea supported by Christ's exhortation to Simon Peter: 'Feed My Lambs.'[2]

1. *See also* Revelation xvii. 14.
2. John xxi. 15.

LAMP—Symbol of guidance, knowledge, enlightenment, and immortality.

The lamp superseded the torch in Greece during the sixth century B.C. They have similar symbolic meanings, though the torch is more exclusively pagan in association by reason of torch races, from which its significance as a symbol is principally derived. It is the lamp rather than the torch that is the Christian symbol.

As a symbol of Christian guidance and enlightenment it is strengthened by Christ's words to His disciples: 'Let your light so shine before men, that they may see your good works, and glorify your Father which is in heaven' (Matthew v. 16); and also by the passage in Psalm cxix. 105: 'Thy word is a lamp to my feet and a light to my path.'

As a symbol of immortality in a religious sense, it was probably derived by the early Christians from its pagan use as a symbol of immortality in a secular sense: that others shall receive and keep aglow the light of their forerunners' work. It was used as a symbol of immortal life in the catacombs, where it was often kept burning near a tomb. The ever-burning lamp by the altar in Roman Catholic churches indicates that the source of all spiritual enlightenment will for ever be found in Christ, and that we live in the blessed light of Christ's salvation of the world by His work of atonement. It is a similar idea that prompted the suggestion of an ever-burning lamp to surmount the Cenotaph. We could call it the lamp of remembrance, but it more exactly suggests that those who died fighting in the European War helped to keep burning the lamp of life of the British Empire. Used in both senses it has a pagan origin which is more appropriately explained under the heading 'Torch'

The lamp is an important Jewish symbol. It is customary amongst Jewish people to keep a light burning directly after a death. In the case of the death of a parent a lamp is kept burning for eleven months, and on every anniversary of the date it is lit for twenty-four hours. In the case of brothers and sisters the lamp is kept alight for one month after their death. This light is known amongst Jewish people as 'Yartzeit'. The usual form that this lamp takes is a glass half-filled with water and then completely filled with oil, on which floats a cork with a special wick which is lit.[1]

This is no doubt chiefly done in remembrance, but its deeper significance is probably akin to that of the perpetual lamp that hangs before the Ark in Synagogues, which is variously interpreted as symbolizing the presence of God in Israel: the spiritual light which went forth from the sanctuary; and God's Law which Israel is to keep alive in the world. The prominent use of the lamp in Jewish ceremony is a survival of old Hebrew customs to which there are many Biblical allusions (I Kings xi. 36; Psalm xviii. 28; Proverbs xx. 27; Job xviii. 6). The Sabbath lamp, lighted on Sabbath eve, is another Jewish use of the lamp.

1. I am indebted to J. Samuel & Son, the monumental sculptors, for this information.

LARK BUNTING—The lark bunting (*Calamospiza melanocorys Stejmeger*) is the state bird of Colorado, having been officially adopted in 1931. It is a native of the region east of the Rocky Mountains from Kansas to Utah.

LARK, MEADOW—The Western meadow lark (*Sturnella neglecta* of the family *Icteridae*) is the state bird of Oregon, officially adopted in 1927; of Wyoming, 1927; of Nebraska, 1929; of Montana, 1931; of North Dakota, 1947. It was also selected by the school children of Kansas in 1925, although not officially adopted. It is extremely common and greatly liked in all these states, which is the obvious reason for its selection.

LAUREL (*Laurus nobilis*)—Symbol of victory, and in ancient Greece of achievement in poetry and song, but now of achievement in the arts generally.

Originating in ancient Greece, and universally employed down to our own times, it has, however, never had any particular significance as a Christian symbol except, with other crowns, as a symbol of martyrdom. It is employed now mainly in the Greek sense.

The laurel crown was awarded to the victors in the Pythian[1] games at Delphi. These festivals were held in honour of Apollo, god of poetry and song, and the nature of the contests was influenced by this circumstance. The laurel is best known in Greek mythology by its association with the sun-god's love of Daphne (the dawn), who, as she fled from Apollo's embraces, was turned into the tree that afterwards bore her name. Daphne, δαφνη, is the Greek name for the laurel tree.

In Rome the laurel was especially consecrated to victory, and according to Pliny[2] it was the sign of tidings of victory, accompanying the dispatches of a general and decorating the lances and javelins of the soldiers, while branches were placed in the lap of Jupiter. Pliny gives sundry reasons for this last custom, the strongest being that it was regarded as the most beautiful tree on Mount Parnassus, and this appealed to Apollo. His reason that it is never struck by lightning may have influenced the Romans in its use. When Augustus celebrated a triumph he wore a laurel wreath on his head and carried a branch in his hand,[3] a custom that was followed by succeeding emperors.

Pliny mentions it as a symbol of peace, and that it was used to signify a truce between enemies; but he admits that in this sense the olive takes precedence over it. The laurel with this significance is now unfamiliar, the olive fulfilling the purpose.

1. Apollo was purified by the blood of the python in the laurel groves of Tempe, and by virtue of that he became the means of purification to penitents.
2. *Natural History*, Book XV, chap. xxx.
3. PLINY explains the origin of this. (Book XV, Chap. xxx.)

LAUREL, MOUNTAIN—The mountain laurel (*Kalmia latifolia*) is the state flower of Connecticut and of Pennsylvania, having been adopted by the former in 1907 and by the latter in 1933. According to George S. Godard[1] it was adopted by the former because of its popularity due to the fine appearance of its beautiful blossom and glossy evergreen foliage.

1. Quoted by SHANKLE, *op. cit.*, p. 334.

LEEK—A Welsh national emblem, and thus symbolic of Wales. (*See* also Daffodil.)

The tradition of the leek as a Welsh emblem appears to be due to an association with St. David. A popular account is that St. David told the Britons when they were fighting the Saxons to wear leeks in their hats, so that they should be distinguished from the enemy. In celebration of the victory obtained by the Britons, St. David directed them to adopt the leek as the national emblem. This may be apocryphal, as there does not appear to be a reliable source for the account.

The only reliable source of information about St. David appears to be his life, by Recimer, who was Bishop of St. David's in the eleventh century. S. Baring-Gould bases his account[1] on this life. It states that when St. David, after his education was completed, retired to the Vale of Ewias for prayer and study, the water from the River Honddhu and the meadow-leek of the fields furnished him with sustenance. The circumstance that the leek was for a period the sole food of St. David probably has something to do with its adoption as the emblem of Wales.

1. *Lives of the Saints* (London, 1874), 1st March, St. David's Day.

LILAC—The purple lilac (*Syringa vulgaris*) is the state flower of New Hampshire, adopted in 1919. Although it was imported from England by the early settlers it now grows in abundance throughout the state, and can be regarded as a typical and representative flower of the country.

LILY, WHITE OR MADONNA (*Lilium candidum*)—Symbol of purity, chastity and virginity, because of its vivid white and therefore pure appearance. (Fig. 47 (*a*).)

For this reason it was the flower, above all others, associated with the Virgin Mother; and in representations of the Annunciation from Byzantine times to the Pre-Raphaelites it is always carried by the angel Gabriel. It denoted purity also in Ancient Greece, where it was fabled to have sprung from the milk of Hera. Poets have made frequent use of this symbol. Chaucer, for example, speaking of St. Cecile in the *Second Nonne's Tale* (line 87), says:

> It is to saye in English 'hevenes lilie,'
> For pure chastenesse of virginitee:

and in Shakespeare's *Henry VIII*, Act V, sc. iv. 60, Archbishop Cranmer, prophesying about the infant Elizabeth, says:

> She must die,
> She must, the saints must have her; yet a virgin,
> A most unspotted lily shall she pass
> To the ground, and all the world shall mourn her.

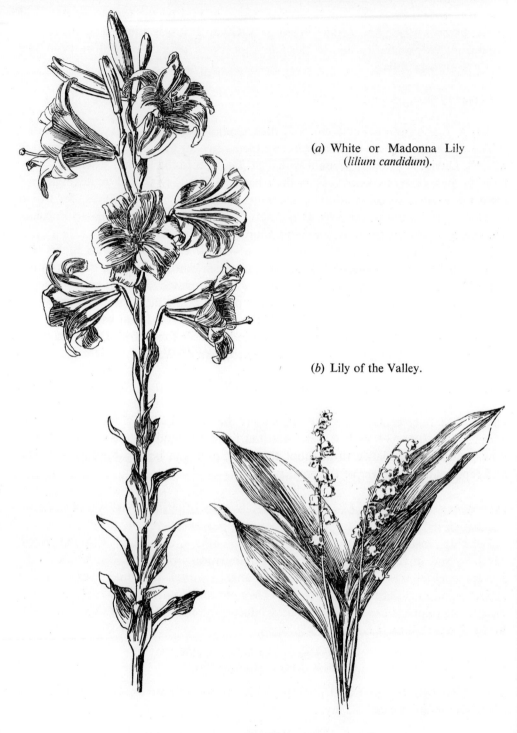

(*a*) White or Madonna Lily
(*lilium candidum*).

(*b*) Lily of the Valley.

Fig. 47.

It is thought by many botanical students that 'the lily among thorns' of the Song of Solomon (II–2) was the *Lilium candidum*.[1]

1. *See* A. W. ANDERSON, *Plants of the Bible* (London, 1956) who gives his reasons for so thinking. From the later allusion to lilies in the Song of Solomon—'his lips like lilies dropping sweet smelling myrrh' (v. 13)—WINIFRED WALTER, *All Plants of the Bible* (London, 1957), suggests the *Lilium chalcedonicum*, the blossoms of which have a drooping character.

LILY OF THE VALLEY—The symbolic purpose of its use in design is probably, like that of the Madonna lily and the snowdrop, to signify purity, while it possesses the additional significance of humility. Its employment has not a very strong traditional support. In the sense of humility it is occasionally mentioned by poets. Wordsworth, *Excursion*, 9, for example, speaks of it as:

> That shy plant the lily of the vale,
> That loves the ground.

As the Madonna lily is better known as a symbol of purity, and the violet as a symbol of humility, it is better to employ either of these flowers in such capacities rather than the lily of the valley. Yet if the desire is to express the combination of purity and humility in one individual, as is often found in youth, then no more suitable symbol could be employed.

LILY, SEGO—The Sego lily (*Calochortus mittallii*) was adopted as the state flower of Utah in 1911.

LION—In a general sense symbol of strength, courage, fortitude, and majesty. Among the early Christians it was a symbol of Christ and, to a less extent, of the resurrection. (Fig. 48 (*c*).)

The analogy of the two meanings is obvious. That it was regarded in the first sense from ancient times is testified by numerous Greek myths and allusions in the Old Testament. Because of the traditional strength and courage of the lion, derived in the Greek mind mainly from their legends, symbolic representations of the lion were often employed on the stelae of Greeks who died in battle. Percy Gardner cites an example where the purpose of the lion shown in bas-relief is suggested by the name of the departed being Leon.[1] A representation of a lion on another stelae is accompanied by an epitaph written by Simonides, which alludes to the 'lion nature' of Leon, whom the stelae commemorates.

As a symbol of Christ it probably arose from the passage in Revelation where the writer laments that there is no man found worthy to open the book sealed with seven seals, when one of the elders says to him: 'Weep not; behold, the Lion of the tribe of Juda, the Root of David, hath prevailed to open the book.' (Revelation v. 5.) The lion symbolizes the majesty and power of Christ; and the way in which the lion is here used, as typifying that almighty power which achieves what none other can, emphasizes the idea of strength and majesty in thinking of the lion. It is no doubt with this association that lions were so often used in the Middle Ages as architectural ornaments, especially as bases to pillars. Those of Nicola Pisano's pulpit in the baptistry at Pisa are a classic example.

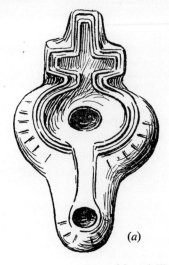

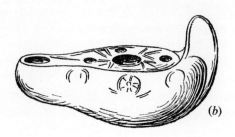

(a) and (b) Terra cotta lamps from the San
Giovanni catacombs at Syracuse, which
are typical of the lamps kept burning near
the tombs.

(c) Pottery lamp of the fifth century A.D.,
with representation of lion. From Carthage,
now in the British Museum.

(d) Symbols of the palm and sacred monogram on a terra cotta lamp, from the San
Giovanni catacombs at Syracuse.

Fig. 48.

As a symbol of the resurrection it arose from the ancient fable that the lion's cub was born dead, and, according to some,[2] was licked into life in three days by its parent; and according to others,[3] was awakened to life in three days by its parent's roaring. An example of its use with this significance occurs in a window of Bourges Cathedral.

Among the ancient peoples of Asia Minor it was, in common with various other animals, symbolic of the sun.[4]

The lion is commonly associated with St. Jerome, and the winged lion is widely known as a symbol of St. Mark. (*See* Lion, winged.)

As a symbol of Christ, or the resurrection, the lion would not now be readily understood and would probably be confused with its more generally understood meaning.

It is used as a symbol of British character and strength, but it is probable that it first came to be so used as a British symbol because of its place in the Royal Arms. It first appeared on the shield in the reign of Henry II or Richard I, and became a dexter supporter in the reign of Henry V. (*See* Chapter III.)

The lion has sometimes been regarded as an emblem of Spain because it figures in the coat of arms of the Kingdom of Leon—meaning lion—and modern Spain is formed of the kingdoms of Castille, Leon, Aragon and Navarre. The lion has also been regarded as a symbol of Belgium, and it appears as the sole charge on the Belgian coat of arms.

1. *Sculptured Tombs of Hellas*, p. 130 (London, 1897).
2. Anna Jameson, for example, *Sacred and Legendary Art*, 2nd edition, Vol. I, p. 27. (London, 1885).
3. Louisa Twining, for example, *Symbols of Early Christian Art*, 3rd edition, p. 31 (London, 1857).
4. *See* Goblet D'Alviella, *Migration of Symbols*, p. 180.

LION, WINGED—Symbol of St. Mark as one of the four evangelists. The symbols of the evangelists—the man for St. Matthew, the lion for St. Mark, the ox for St. Luke and the eagle for St. John, are generally thought to be derived by the early Christians from Ezekiel's vision on the banks of the river Chebor: 'As for the likeness of their faces, they four had the face of a man, and the face of a lion, on the right side: and they four had the face of an ox on the left side; they four also had the face of an eagle' (i. 10), which also corresponds to the four beasts which stood around the throne of the Lamb in Revelation (iv. 7)—'And the first beast was like a lion, and the second beast like a calf, and the third beast had a face as a man, and the fourth beast was like a flying eagle.' Sir A. H. Layard had suggested that Ezekiel's vision may have been prompted by a previous contemplation of the fabulous winged animals of Assyrian art.[1]

St. Augustine chose the lion for St. Matthew and the man for St. Mark, but the significance stated above and now universally accepted is that given by St. Jerome: 'The first face, that of a man signifies Matthew, who begins to write, as of a man, the book of the generation of Jesus Christ, the son of David, the son of Abraham; the second, Mark, in which is heard the voice of the Lion roaring in the Desert, 'Prepare ye the way of the Lord.'[2] This was later put more expressively thus: St. Matthew is represented as a man because he chiefly dwells in his Gospel on the human nature of our Lord, and St. Mark, a lion because he proclaims the royal dignity of Christ, the lion being the king of beasts.[3] (*See also* Eagle and Winged ox.)

These symbols of the evangelists have appeared in all forms of ecclesiastical art of all periods from the fifth century.

1. Sir A. H. Layard, *Nineveh*, Vol. II, p. 465.
2. *See* Louisa Twining, *Symbols and Emblems of Christian Art*, 2nd edition, pp. 95–114 (London, 1885); also Anna Jameson, *Sacred and Legendary Art*, Vol. I, 3rd edition, pp. 132–43 (London, 1857).
3. *See* P. H. Ditchfield, *Symbolism of the Saints*, p. 49 (London, 1910).

LOTUS-FLOWER—This water-lily, a familiar subject of Egyptian architectural ornament, was originally adopted in ancient Egypt as a symbol of the sun, and later as a symbol of the continual renewal of life. From Egypt it migrated to India, where it was employed with similar significance; and from thence it was introduced into China and Japan, where it now appears as ornamentation on pottery and other objects.

The symbolism of the lotus-flower arises from one of the most beautiful analogies in the history of art. The lotus was a water-lily of Egypt which, according to Herodotus, sprang up profusely in the time of flood. The flower opened at dawn and closed in the evening. Opening and closing with the rising and setting of the sun, it thus became a symbol of the sun. The Egyptians, believing that the world originated as a liquid, subsequently discovered in the lotus, expanding from the water as the light came, and closing with darkness, a typification of the very essence of life. From a solar symbol it therefore became a symbol of human life. 'Hence a fresh enlargement given to the figurative meaning of the lotus,' says Goblet D'Alviella, 'the symbol of solar renascence, it became, with the Egyptians, the symbol of human renascence, and generally of life in its eternal and unceasingly renewed essence.'[1] It was accepted mainly in these senses by the religions of India. Both Brahma and Buddha are often represented seated on a Lotus. With the disciples of the former the lotus was the typification of the whole of existence. It was with the different parts of this flower that Brahma was supposed to have created the world. Many of the Indian gods were conceived as being born of the lotus, and the Egyptians, long before, had represented Horus as springing from the lotus held by Hathor.

Can such a symbol, oriental in association as it is, be used for a Christian purpose? If so, in what sense? As a symbol of the renewal of life after death?—though we sleep it is but to awake. A parallel can be found to it in our own English water-lilies, which, closing and opening with the setting and rising sun, symbolize the Christian conception of death as a passing into darkness, but to awake to the morning of a new life.

1. Goblet D'Alviella, *Migration of Symbols*, p. 29.

LUPIN (*Lupin subcamorus*)—State flower of Texas, officially adopted in 1901. It is also called Texas Bluebonnet and Buffalo clover.

LYRE—An ancient Greek musical instrument of the harp type, an emblem of Apollo and Orpheus—the one, god of poetry and song; the other, by sweet music charmer of all created beings—it is often used as symbolic of distinction in music and song. Its decorative character makes it a pleasing subject for design. (Fig. 45 (*c*) and (*d*).)

LYRE-BIRD—Sometimes used as a symbol of New South Wales, of which it is an indigenous bird. It appeared in New South Wales postage stamps in 1888 and 1892. The lyre-bird is so called because its large tail has a shape similar to a Greek lyre.

MACE—Symbol of royal or state authority. It derives from the mace as a military weapon which expresses power, victory and thus authority.

The use of the mace as a symbol of royal or state authority dates from the thirteenth century. It rests in front of the Lord Chancellor and the Speaker while the House of Lords and House of Commons are sitting, as the symbol of deputed authority. It is carried by the Serjeants-at-Arms before the Lord Chancellor and the Speaker. Similarly, it is carried by the mace-bearer before the mayors of city and town, and rests in the chamber during the sitting of the council.

Controversy has arisen as to whether the mace of the House of Commons should be regarded as the symbol of royal authority, of the authority of the House, of that of the Speaker, or that of the Serjeant-at-Arms.[1] Logically it would seem to be the symbol of the royal authority conferred on the Speaker. When the sovereign is present the mace is covered with a cloth, which indicates that this symbol of royal authority is not necessary when the sovereign is present. Lord Campion speaks of the Mace as the symbol of the authority of the House, and, through the House, of the Speaker, and he remarks that 'the authority of the Speaker and the House are indivisible. No Speaker, no House'. The controversy has, however, made a simple subject involved. The mace, whether in Parliament or a local council meeting, is the symbol of the deputed authority; it is the token by which proceedings are given the royal or state sanction, and with the mace present, authority can be exercised.

To signify royal authority the mace has the royal arms engraved on the button at the end of the handle.

For some towns situated on the coast, or on a river, an oar serves the purpose of the mace (see Oar). Saltash has an oar-mace, dating from 1623, which is an oar with a mace head, the latter being engraved with the Stuart royal arms.

1. See The Times, 1st, 4th, 8th, 10th and 11th February, 1954.

MAGNOLIA—The magnolia (Magnolia foetida or Magnolia grandiflora) is the state flower of Louisiana and Mississippi, having been adopted in both states in 1900. Its popular choice is due to its beauty and abundant growth in these states.

MANDALA—The Hindu word for circle, mandala is a widespread oriental symbol of order, unity, wholeness. The term was also employed by Jung to express the inner contemplative self.[1]

Mandalas are of many forms and designs, but they all approximate to or include the circle. As a ritual geometric form it is designed for contemplation whereby man endeavours to resolve order from disorder, or to comprehend variety in a unity. The process of thought is partly on the lines of the mental evolution from the organic or biological to the geometric, mathematical and thus spiritual, and it is possible that it has some connection with early Greek philosophical thinking that gives divinity to mathematical order. In many oriental religions contemplation of the

271

mandala is thought to induce the mental state whereby the sense of order, and with it peace, can be realized. The lotus of Buddha and of Brahma is associated with the mandala. One well known geometric form is the yantra composed of nine linked triangles within a circle, edged with lotus petals, the whole within a square. The symbolism of the mandala has been extended to architectural forms,[2] and it has sometimes been suggested that some, like the stupa and the Borobudur temple, have arisen as an image of the universe and thus as a mandala symbol.[3] It has also been associated with Christian symbols such as the nimbus and with forms in Christian architecture such as the rose window.[4]

1. C. G. JUNG, *Psychology and Alchemy* (London, 1953). *See also Man and his Symbols* (London, 1964). The first and longest essay in this work is by Jung. There are several references to mandala in the essay on 'The process of individuation' by M.-L. VON FRANZ and 'Symbolism in the Visual Arts' by ANIELA JAFFÉ.
2. DIETRICH SECKEL, *The Art of Buddhism* (London, 1964), p. 281.
3. J. E. CIRLOT, *Diccionario de Simbolos Tradicionales* (English translation, London, 1964), pp. 190–4.
4. ANIELA JAFFÉ, *op. cit.*, p. 241.

MANDORLA—The Italian term for almond used to describe the shape of an ecclesiastical panel or aureole summarily representing a fish: symbol of the Christian faith (*see* Fish). It is often termed vesica-piscis. The geometric shape consists of two circles intersecting: ⟨ with the radius of each circle forming the width. The shape is common in church decoration of the middle ages, especially for panels with a representation of the seated figure of Christ, and ecclesiastical seals are generally of this shape.

MAPLE—A national emblem of Canada. As such it largely superseded the beaver about the middle of the nineteenth century. The species so adopted is the sugar or hard maple (*acer saccharum Marsh*) and was referred to as the emblem of the French speaking Canadian in the *Quebec Gazette* in 1805. An early example of its use was at a banquet of the Saint-Jean Baptiste Society held in Montreal in 1836 when the banqueting hall was profusely decorated with branches and leaves of the sugar maple.[1] The reason for its adoption is that it is one of the commonest and most beautiful of the indigenous trees.

In 1867 it received official recognition as a Canadian emblem when it was incorporated in the coats of arms of the provinces of Quebec and Ontario. In 1869 it was worn as a badge in the procession in Toronto which welcomed the Prince of Wales, and in that year was incorporated in the badge of the 100th Regiment (Royal Canadians). Three maple leaves appear at the bottom of the coat of arms of Canada, granted in 1921, and in the crest the lion holds a maple leaf in its right paw.

The sugar maple is also the official state tree of New York, and of West Virginia, having been adopted by the former in 1909. It is a large handsome tree which grows abundantly in each state and provides an excellent furniture wood.

1. *See* THERESA EMILY THOMSON, 'By Law this Bouquet', *Canadian Geographical Journal*, October, 1942.

MARIGOLD—*See* Sunflower.

MAYFLOWER—The mayflower, also known as the trailing arbutus and the ground laurel (*Epigaea ripens*) is the symbolic flower of Nova Scotia and Massachusetts. It was adopted by the former in 1901 and by the latter in 1918.

MENORAH—The seven branched candelabrum or candlestick known as the menorah (Hebrew for candelabrum) has been a well-known symbol of Judaism since the first century A.D. As such it has appeared on coins, on monuments and in synagogues. The earliest surviving representation is a sculptured relief on one of the inner sides of the Arch of Titus, erected in Rome in 82 A.D., which shows the seven branched candelabrum together with other trophies, including the table for shewbread, and the trumpets, from the second Temple in Jerusalem carried in triumphal procession.

In the biblical description (Exodus xxv. 31–40) on which the design of the ancient menorah was based, reference is made to six branches, three on either side, and to seven lamps, so that the centre upright functions as one. In the authorized English version of the Bible of 1611 it is translated as a candlestick—'And thou shalt make a candlestick of pure gold: of beaten work shall the candlestick be made: his shaft, and his branches, his bowls, his knops, and his flowers, shall be of the same.'

The specification for the design with which the representation on the Arch of Titus appears roughly to conform, is that 'six branches shall come out of the sides of it; three branches of the candlestick out of the one side, and three branches of the candlestick out of the other side: Three bowls made like unto almonds, with a knop and a flower in one branch'; and the same on the other side. As it is first lighted at the beginning of the Sabbath, which is a day of rest, the menorah sometimes appears on Jewish memorials to symbolize rest.

The symbolism of the actual seven branches was variously interpreted in Kabbalah. The menorah is associated with the tree of life, the seven as a representation of the planets, and also of the days of creation.

In Jewish ritual there is a special eight branched menorah (a ninth serves as a pilot light) used at the feast of Hanukkah, later termed Hanukkiyyah.

MINERVA—*See* Gods and Goddesses and Heroes of Antiquity.

MIRROR—In various periods of history the mirror has symbolized many things,[1] but that which probably has the strongest tradition is as a feminine symbol. This was probably derived from its being a symbol of Aphrodite and Venus, the Greek and Latin goddesses of love and beauty. The term mirror is derived from Latin miro, meaning to behold and from miror meaning to wonder at. Greek, Etruscan and Roman mirrors were made of copper, bronze or other metal that gives a good reflection when polished. That the mirror was a common item of equipment for Venus meant that the metal of which the mirror was commonly made, copper, was associated with her, and a conventional rendering of the copper mirror became her symbol (*see* Geometric figures). This sign has been used as a feminine symbol in many connections, recent examples being Femina Books, and in an ingenious adaptation by the Women's National Cancer Control Campaign: ♀.

The mirror has also been regarded as a moon symbol because the moon reflects the light of the sun. Mirror has been so extensively used in figurative language that such expressions as the 'mirror of life' and 'art the mirror of life' and many others have become commonplaces.

1. J. E. CIRLOT in *Diccionario de Simbolos Tradicionales* gives a brief account of many of the symbolical associations of mirror (English translation, London, 1962).

MISTLETOE—Ancient symbol of life and protection.

The mistletoe was sacred to the Druids, who regarded it with veneration and as having protective and healing powers.

As recorded by Pliny,[1] the Druids venerated the oak tree and conducted their religious ceremonies in groves of oak. They regarded the mistletoe which grew upon the oak as having been sent by God. They doubtless observed that the oak withered in the winter, and mistletoe when growing upon it alone appeared to have life.

In one of their religious ceremonies the Druids dressed in white robes, cut the mistletoe with a golden sickle and placed it in a white cloak. This ceremony was accompanied by the sacrifice of two white bulls. There is obviously a close connection between this and the ancient beliefs connected with the mistletoe in Scandinavia and Italy, recorded by Sir James Frazer.

The Golden Bough plucked by Aeneas from the oak at the entrance to the underworld is regarded by Frazer as the mistletoe. This theory, which derives from Balder[2] in Scandinavian legend, and from the priest of Diana, the King of the Wood in the sacred grove of Nemi in Italy, which are very similar, is the theme of Frazer's *Golden Bough*. In the legend of Balder he is invulnerable to all harm except from the mistletoe, by which he is killed, the blind god Hothr under the direction of Loki having thrown a twig at Balder, which pierced him. The interpretation is that Balder is the tree spirit of the oak, whose life or heart resides in the parasitic mistletoe growing upon it, which is green in the winter when the oak has withered. The belief was that while the mistletoe was intact the oak, and consequently the tree spirit or god, was alive. When the spirit was anthropomorphized, his life depended on the life of the mistletoe growing upon the oak, and it was only by the mistletoe that he could be killed.

The priest guarding the mystic bough in the sacred groves of Nemi is a variation of the same theme, but here the mistletoe bough growing on the oak is the symbol of the life of the Priest, and the King of the Wood. The priest is the embodiment of the divine presence infused into the oak.

The mistletoe as a symbol of life in this connection is clearly interpreted by Robert Graves.[3] He refers to the annual supplanting of the old oak-king by his successor. 'Zeus', he says, 'was at one time the name of a herdsman's oracular hero connected with the oak-tree cult of Dodona in Epirius, which was presided over by the dove-priestesses of Dione, a woodland Great Goddess, otherwise known as Diana.' He goes on to say 'that the cutting of the mistletoe from the oak by the Druids typified the emasculation of the old king by his successor—the mistletoe being a prime phallic emblem'. He adds that 'the king himself was eucharistically eaten after the castration, as several legends of the Pelopia dynasty testify'.

This interpretation certainly brings the rite of the Druids close to the myths of

Balder and the Priest of Nemi, but whether it is justified by the Druidical ceremonies is open to question. As Pliny records, after the Druids had cut the mistletoe with a golden sickle it was placed in a white cloak as if to preserve in this way the life of the god. Or it may be that this ceremony of the Druids was the choice of a new priest or king and that the cutting of the mistletoe was a symbolic act, but this suggests a mature stage of thought away from the primitive belief in tree spirits. There is inevitably some uncertainty of the true significance and symbolic use of the mistletoe in ancient myths and Druidical rites, but that it was a great symbol of life admits of little doubt, and also of protection because of its supposed healing qualities. In Scandinavian countries it was often hung like the horseshoe over the entrance of buildings.

The origin of the use of mistletoe at Christmas is its use at pagan religious festivals. The use of pagan emblems for Christian festivals is not uncommon. The origin of the custom of kissing under the mistletoe is thought to be a survival of the Saturnalia festival, which in Rome occurred in December, from the 17th to the 23rd. It was a period of licence when things not customary, like kissing between comparative strangers or mere acquaintances, were permitted. It has become so much a custom that if a young woman stands under the mistletoe at Christmas and smiles at a young man, she is asking to be kissed.

The mistletoe is the emblem of the Swedish province of Västmanland, and also of Oklahoma, where it was adopted in 1893. It was the first plant to be adopted as a state symbol in America.

1. PLINY, *Natural History*, XVI, 95.
2. Scandinavian god. SIR JAMES FRAZER, *The Golden Bough*, Part I (Vols. 1 and 2), *The Magic Art and the Evolution of Kings*; and Part VII (Vols. 10 and 11).
3. ROBERT GRAVES, *The White Goddess*, p. 60 (London, 1948).

MITRE—The headdress of a bishop, abbot and other high dignitaries of the church, that often appears alone in ecclesiastical design as a symbol of a bishop, and more rarely of an abbot.

In ancient times the tall conical headdress formed the double crown of Egypt which was similar in character to the turban. A form of turban was worn by the Jewish high priest and this may have suggested it as a headdress for high dignitaries of the church. Before 1245 it was the headdress of a cardinal (*see* Hat, cardinal's), but in more recent times the mitre is generally regarded as the particular headdress of a bishop. It is first mentioned in a bull of Pope Leo X of 1049, and was granted to Abbot Aethelsig of St. Augustine's Abbey, Canterbury, by Pope Alexander II in 1063. Its appearance front and back is somewhat like a tall Gothic arch, and seen at the sides it is deeply cleft at the top. The earlier form during the middle ages was lower and it has gradually grown in height.

The origin and meaning of this shape are uncertain. It has been explained as symbolizing the horns of light shining on the head of Moses, a reflection of the Majesty of God, and also as a symbol of the two testaments of which the bishop is the keeper.[1] Another interpretation is that it symbolizes the cloven tongues of fire which descended on the apostles on the day of Pentecost.[2] It is possible, however, that these are fanciful interpretations long after the form had evolved.

The episcopal mitre is generally of linen or satin often richly embroidered and jewelled. It appears in heraldry as a crest in the arms of episcopal sees.

1. M. C. NIEUWBARN, *Church Symbolism*, English translation by John Waterreus (London, 1910), p. 135.
2. E. COBHAM BREWER, *Dictionary of Phrase and Fable*, 20th edition.

MOCKING BIRD (*Mimus polyglottus* or *Orpheus polyglottus*)—State bird of Florida, Texas, Arkansas and Tennessee, having been adopted in the years 1907, 1927, 1929 and 1933 respectively.

MONOGRAM, SACRED—The two principal forms, XP and IHS, and their many varieties, are universally regarded as signs of the Christian faith.

The former is an abbreviation of the Greek word for Christ, χριστός, being a combination of the two initial letters, X (chi) and P (rho). Another form shows the monogram as in illustration *d*, which is probably an abbreviation of Jesus Christ: ᾽Ιησοῦς χριστός by means of the two initial letters. These abbreviations, principally the former, occur in several inscriptions of the second and third centuries, but they are not used as monogrammatic signs of the Christian faith until after the supposed vision of Constantine. Walter Lowrie[1] has suggested that the monogram owes 'its origin in part to the pagan religious symbol, the sun-wheel'. As the Mithraic cult was at that time the most formidable rival of Christianity, and a religion of sun worship, with a wheel as a principal symbol, the association of the XP and IX with the wheel may have been responsible for some of the forms of the monogram. Many of the early representations of the monogram were surrounded with a circle or wreath, so that the general appearance with the exception of the loop of the P is similar to the sun-wheel. When the cross is added, the likeness is stronger, making a combination of Figs 50 (*b*) and (*c*); and it is stronger still when, as in some examples, the Greek cross and circle are added to the IX abbreviation, so that it appears as in Fig. 50 (*e*) in a circle.[2]

The XP monogram probably became the universal sign of Christianity because it appealed more naturally and logically than any other sign as standing for the founder of the religion. Its use was probably partially suggested by its appearance as an abbreviation in earlier inscriptions. That the general use of the monogram dates from about the time of Constantine's conversion is supported by ample evidence, but that it originated with the supposed vision of Constantine is doubtful.

Eusebius's account, which he professes to have had from Constantine himself, of the appearance before Constantine and his army of the cross, or monogram, above the mid-day sun, inscribed with the words, 'By this sign conquer,' and of Constantine's subsequent dream in which Christ appears with the sign, and other less famous accounts of the vision, although mysterious, are obviously important in Christian history.[3]

After the supposed vision, and after Christianity was formally accepted (A.D. 330), the monogram was introduced on the Labarum: the imperial standard of Constantine. It appeared on coins, tombs, lamps, and seals and was universally adopted for about a century succeeding Constantine. Its use then died out almost completely in Rome, but in the East it continued to be widely employed for many centuries, and it appeared on military standards until the eighth century. There have been many variations in its form, the commonest and most generally adopted being the combination of X and P. (Fig. 50 (*b*).) Another common form was arranged by turning the X from diagonals to vertical and horizontal, so that it became the cross with the P loop at the top. (Fig. 50 (*a*).) A or *α* (alpha) and Ω or *ω* (omega) were sometimes placed on either side, signifying the beginning and end, and suggested, no doubt, by the passage in Revelation: 'I am Alpha and Omega, the beginning and the ending, saith the Lord, which is, and which was, and which is to come, the Almighty.'[4]

The gradual superseding of this monogram by the more familiar IHS commenced during the twelfth century. The latter owes its origin to an abbreviation of the Greek name for Jesus: 'Ιησοῦς (or in capitals, ΙΗΣΟΥΣ) by the two initial and last letters forming ΙΗΣ, the omitted letters being signified by a dash over the space between the H and Σ. This dash was later continued through the upper strokes of the H and, by the addition of a centre stroke, there evolved the common form with the cross. The earliest known example occurs on a cold coin of Basilius I, A.D. 867.

Another form was IHC, which appears in manuscripts as early as A.D. 600, the C being the lunar form of sigma.

The origin of ΙΗΣ or IHC seems to have been forgotten in the Middle Ages. The correct Latin version would be IES, but H (eta), the Greek E, was taken to be the Latin H. The IHS must, therefore, have appeared as mystical letters used to express Christ. Their meaning, it was supposed, was revealed in a vision to St. Bernardine of Siena, as 'Jesus Hominum Salvator'—Jesus, Saviour of Men. Other meanings given to it were, 'Iesu Humilis Societas'—Humble Society of Jesus and 'In Hoc Signo'—In this Sign (thou shalt conquer).

It is now a universal sign of Christianity and is employed on numerous ecclesiastical objects. Though the IHS has, to a large extent, superseded the XP, the latter is still occasionally employed and is sometimes used in panels in ecclesiastical furnishing. The frequent use of the IHS is apparent in most Catholic and Protestant churches.

1. *Monuments of the Early Church*, p. 239 (1906).
2. A sculpture of the fourth century in the Church of St. Demetrius at Salonica shows this form of monogram (illustrated in L. TWINING's *Symbols*, p. 11). It appears almost identical with the Mithraic sun-wheel.
3. *See* GIBBON, *Decline and Fall of the Roman Empire*, Chap. xx.
4. Revelation i. 8. Also Revelation xxi. 6, and xxii. 13.

MOUND—*See* Orb.

MOUNTAIN, ARTIFICIAL—Symbol of the heavens and of the abode of gods.

Among many ancient and primitive peoples mountains have been regarded as the abodes of gods, and mountains have thus been imitated in the form of moundlike structures some of the best known being the ziggurats of Mesopotamian peoples, the stupas or topes of Buddhist India and China and the pyramids of Egypt.

In common with other impressive natural phenomena, where spirits were thought to dwell, mountains were worshipped among many peoples. This prompted imitation when religious structures or large tombs were built. When a people like the Summerians migrated from a mountainous country, which they had conceived as the abode

(*a*) Bay Laurel (*Laurus nobilis*), which is generally regarded as the symbolical laurel (the Daphne) of the Greeks.

(*b*) Olive (*Olen eoropaga*).

(*c*) Myrtle (*Myrtus communis*).

Fig. 49.

of the gods, to flat country there was the natural impulse to build mountains for worship, which they did in the form of ziggurats in the cities of the plains.

According to Sir Leonard Woolley 'ziggurat' could be translated as 'the hill of heaven' or 'the mountain of God'[1] (*see* Ziggurat).

The most familiar sacred mountains in western civilization are Mount Sinai which is traditionally thought to be the mountain which Moses ascended to receive the Commandments of God (Exodus xix. 20) and Mount Olympus of the Greeks. In the ancient Greek religious hierarchy of Zeus, the gods are conceived as dwelling on Mount Olympus, a range of mountains with a summit of 9,700 feet, separating Macedonia and Thessaly. Zeus was conceived as having his throne on the summit of Olympus which was believed as being in perpetual sunshine. A belt of clouds often wreathed the summit which added to the sense of mystery, and within these clouds were the gates of heaven.

Most Greek cities were built with the acropolis as a central feature—$\check{\alpha}\varkappa\rho\sigma\varsigma$, highest, topmost $+$ $\pi\delta\lambda\iota\varsigma$ city—which is either a natural hill utilized or an artificial one. On the summit of the acropolis were the temples each of which held the throne of a god, which is thus an imitation of the throne of Zeus on Mount Olympus. It is a reasonable hypothesis that the acropolis was built in imitation of the sacred mountain (*see* Acropolis).

1. C. LEONARD WOOLLEY, *Ur of the Chaldees—a Record of Seven Years Excavation* (London, 1929). The author describes the ziggurat in Chapter IV, 'The Great Days of the Third Dynasty'.

MOUNTAIN BLUEBIRD (*Sialia arcticia*)—*See* Bluebird.

MYRTLE—Symbol of love, of victory, of an amicable and humane nature; and of constancy and immortality in common with other evergreens.

The Myrtle was regarded by the ancients as sacred to Venus as mother of love, and this association has survived to modern times. Thus, in Elizabethan days there are allusions to it as a symbol of love.

Though given in Rome as a reward to military victors, the fact that it was sacred to Venus required that the victory should not be too inharmonious with the spirit of love. Pliny[1] tells us, for example, that Posthumius Tubertus, having achieved a victory over the Sabines in which none were slain, received an ovation and was crowned with the myrtle of Venus Victrix. The sacred tree of Venus consequently found favour even in the eyes of the enemy. The myrtle, therefore, could never be the highest reward of victory; it always took second place to the laurel. Crassus, for instance, turned from the proffered myrtle crown and persuaded the Roman senate to award him the crown of laurel.

It is a logical derivation from its ancient symbolic use to regard the myrtle as a symbol of victory for love and friendship. This makes its significance unique, apart from the religious victory of martyrdom. But in either of its meanings of love or victory taken separately it has less traditional support than many other symbols. If it were the custom among modern nations to bestow wreaths for public service, the myrtle crown would be appropriately given, say, to a Foreign Minister who by his actions has strengthened the friendship of peoples. And thus, for the personal memorial, what better symbol than a myrtle wreath for those who have succeeded to an eminent degree in increasing love among fellow-beings? (Fig. 49 (c).)

1. *Natural History*, Book XV, Chap. xxix.

NARCISSUS—The significance of this flower is derived from Greek mythology, and it may be regarded as symbolic of self-love, but more importantly, of the death of beautiful youth.

The stories of Narcissus of different Greek writers vary slightly; that of Ovid is generally considered to be the nearest to the original myth. Narcissus was a beautiful youth who fell in love with his own reflection in the River Cephissus, and not knowing it to be his own image (one version says that he thought it to be that of his beloved dead sister) he sorrowed for love of the beautiful face in the water, pined away and died of his grief. In his place there sprang the flower that bears his name.

The myth, as Sir James Frazer has suggested,[1] probably originated in the ancient Greek belief that a man's soul resided in his reflection, and that if he looked at his reflection in the water, the water spirits would drag his soul away and he would die. It was regarded as an omen of death to dream of seeing one's reflection in the water.

To gaze at one's reflection, then, means death. The temptation to do so is stronger in the young and beautiful who are therefore in greater peril of such death, and thus the narcissus may symbolize sad acquiescence in the fate of death of youth and beauty. The life of the flower itself was, among the Greeks, a symbol of youthful death. It blooms naturally near the water's edge, its beauty is mirrored in the water for a brief space, and then it fades.

Pausanias mentions the verses of Pamphos wherein Persephone is described as gathering narcissi just before she was carried off to Hades.[2] Perhaps it was because of this that the narcissus became sacred to Demeter.

Narcissi would fittingly appear in a design commemorating one who died young, the memory of whom stirs thoughts of beauty either of appearance or character. By analogy the narcissus might be regarded as symbolizing the death of one whose life and being are reflected in beautiful work, as, for example, the death of a young poet, artist, or musician, whose work is a beautiful reflection of his life.

These flowers are susceptible of effective, decorative treatment in bas-relief; they thus provide, in meaning and form, a valuable subject for the designer. (Fig. 58 (a).)

1. *Tabor and the Perils of the Soul*, p. 94 (London, 1911).
2. PAUSANIAS, 9, 31.

NIMBUS—(Synonymous in Christianity with the terms glory and halo and aureole.)

A Christian attribute denoting religious sanctity and holiness and given to those who are conceived as having been divinely inspired and privileged in the work of propagating the Christian faith by example and teaching.

This attribute is much older than Christianity. In ancient times among the religions of the East in which sun worship was prominent, a circle, wheel, or disk was employed as a symbol of the sun, and became an attribute of many mythical characters identified with the sun. The disk is a common representation in early sculptures of

(a)

(b)

(c)

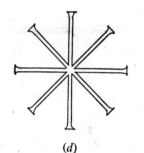

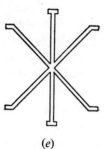

(d)

(e)

(a)–(e) Principal forms of the Constantinian Monogram, the second example being the commonest.

(f) Sacred Monogram with alpha and omega, circle of eternity, and S, probably denoting Saviour. From a slab in the cloisters of the old Augustan convent at Toulouse. The old chapel, destroyed in the fifteenth-century, from which this was probably taken, was a thirteenth-century work.

Fig. 50.

India. It was a symbol of the sun in the Buddhist and Mithraic religions,[1] and occasionally figured, usually with radiations of light, surrounding the head of Apollo.

The attribute appears to have been adopted by the Christian Church during the early fourth century in the reign of Constantine.[2] It retained essentially the same significance, being used to indicate light—the divine radiance which emanates from the blessed. The chief scriptural support comes from St. Matthew who tells us (xvii. 2) that Christ's face at the Transfiguration 'did shine as the sun'. Therefore in the early representations of the nimbus in mosaics and paintings the utmost brightness was the aim, resulting in those bright disks of gold surrounding the heads of Christ, the Virgin, and saints. (Plate LXXI.) A good example is Orcagna's 'Coronation of the Virgin' in the National Gallery.

The representation of the nimbus has varied in the course of artistic development. Until about the twelfth century the most popular type was like a plate of gold. Later an ornamental border was introduced; and during the latter part of the fourteenth century the name of the wearer was often substituted for the ornamental border. These forms were generally superseded during the latter part of the fifteenth century by the thin golden circle represented according to the pose of the head. From the seventeenth century to the early nineteenth the nimbus was less used. In more recent times, however, its use has been revived. It appears in the works of the Pre-Raphaelites and also in modern ecclesiastical mural painting. Eric Gill makes free use of it in his religious sculpture.

Not only does the artistic treatment of the nimbus change at various times, but also its form varies according to the person with whom it is associated. The nimbus of Christ is usually marked with a cross; that of the Almighty, after the twelfth century, is an equilateral triangle; and that of a living saint is a square. The first-named distinction was, however, more generally observed than the others. The nimbus is sometimes represented with beams of light radiating from it.

The light surrounding the whole body, generally in the form of the vesica piscis, is usually regarded as the aureole. It is most commonly employed for the Almighty, and in depictures of Christ's Resurrection and the Transfiguration. Fra Angelico's conception is a good example. Some, among them Didron,[3] Twining,[4] and Hulme,[5] observe a distinction between the aureole and the nimbus, considering the former only in E. Venable's[6] sense of the nimbus of the body.[7] Although it is true that nimbus is now understood to apply exclusively to that which surrounds the head, aureole is not, as these writers state, exclusively applied to that which surrounds the body. The aureole surrounds both the head and body and is thus in the former case synonymous with nimbus. Poets usually prefer the term aureole in alluding to this cincture of the head. Rossetti, for example, frequently alludes to it. Thus in *Jenny* he says:

> Fair shines the gilded aureole
> In which our highest painter's place
> Some living woman's simple face.

The representation of Christ in a panel of the vesica piscis form is a conventionalized derivation from the aureole surrounding Christ at the resurrection.

1. *See* GOBLET D'ALVIELLA, *Migration of Symbols*, pp. 51, 66 and 243.
2. F. E. HULME (*Symbolism in Christian Art*) says that 'the Christian nimbus is not met with on

282

any monument prior to the sixth century' (p. 55), yet it occurs in numerous earlier mosaics. It appears, for example, in the fourth-century apse mosaic in the Basilica of S. Pudenziana at Rome and in the fifth-century mosaic of the Good Shepherd in the Mausoleum of Galla Placidia at Ravenna.

3. *Iconographie Chrétienne*, p. 109. English translation, p. 107, 1851.
4. *Symbols and Emblems of Christian Art*, pp. 203–6.
5. *Symbolism in Christian Art*, pp. 68–72.
6. *Smith's Dictionary of Christian Antiquities*, 1880: 'Nimbus.'
7. The distinction is not observed by ANNA JAMESON, *Sacred and Legendary Art*, Vol. i, pp. 22–3.

NUMBER SYMBOLISM—Since ancient times in Egypt and Greece certain numbers have frequently been given a symbolic or sacred significance, partly for mathematical and partly for associational reasons. The latter is the case with symbolic numbers in Christianity. The most important numbers symbolically have been three, seven, ten and twelve. Three was regarded by Pythagoras as the number of completion, as it represents the beginning, middle and end. It figures largely in Greek mythology, thus, the three Graces, the three Fates, the three magi and the three-headed Cerberus; and in Christianity as the Trinity. This has been responsible for numerous triple arrangements in ecclesiastical design.

Seven was regarded by the Greeks, Jews and Etruscans as the number of perfection, and was a particular favourite with them. The world was created in seven days; there are the seven wonders of the world; the seven wise men; the seven ages of man; while Job says that Wisdom hath hewn seven pillars. The Sabbath lamp of the Jews consists of the lamp with seven branches, or seven lamps or candles. As the Sabbath is a day of rest, the Sabbath lamp is thus a symbol of rest and with this significance is often introduced on Jewish memorials. The number seven was held sacred by the early Christians, being applied to the gifts of the spirit, derived either from Isaiah, as 'the Spirit of Wisdom and Understanding, the Spirit of Counsel and Might, the Spirit of Knowledge and of the Fear of the Lord', or from St. John as 'power, and riches, and wisdom, and strength, and honour, and glory and blessing'. They are generally represented in Christian art as seven doves or seven lamps, and no attempts, as far as is known, have been made to give symbolic representation to each gift according to its nature.

The reason for ten being so important is that it is the basis of our numerical system. It is thus regarded as the symbol of order; it is the number of the commandments, of the persecutions and the plagues of Egypt.

Twelve is chiefly the number of the Apostles and the tribes of Israel. Both ten and twelve are favourite numbers when selecting a certain number of anything, such as the ten or twelve pre-eminent in any field, or the ten or twelve greatest men, or writers.

The symbolism that attached to other numbers is of a very obvious character, while in some cases the symbolism attaches less to the number than to other factors. It is number symbolism if the selection of seven of anything is due to some symbolic significance in the number, but it is hardly so if there is no selection of a number for its significance. It is seven wonders of the world, rather than six or eight, because seven is a sacred number or the number of perfection, but there is no particular significance in five wise and five foolish virgins rather than four or six. Numbers generally acquire their significance either because of some association, such as God creating the world in seven days, or because of some mathematical circumstance connected with the number. An example showing the ancient significance attached to some mathematical phenomena is provided by the Golden section represented in two propositions of Euclid (2 XI and 6 XXX), which cannot be expressed accurately but only approximately in numbers, which has given it a mystical significance and makes it for some a divine rule of proportion.

The superstition attaching to thirteen is supposed to derive from the Last Supper.

OAK—Symbol of strength, glory, and honour.

A wreath of oak leaves was the supreme honour awarded in pagan times for military valour.

The characteristics of the oak-tree at once suggest a symbol of strength and durability. That it has long been so regarded is testified by the phrase in Amos ii. 9, 'strong as the oaks'.

In ancient Rome the civic crown, composed of oak leaves, was awarded to the Roman who saved a fellow citizen's life in battle. According to Pliny,[1] before a citizen was deemed worthy to receive the wreath of oak leaves it was necessary that, in saving the fellow-citizen's life, one of the enemy should be slain and that the enemy should have retreated from the spot where the deed was accomplished. Though of no material value, it was the highest of all honours, superior to the mural crown, the vallor and the rostrate, which were all of gold. A citizen who had won this high honour was privileged to wear it for the rest of his life, and he, his father, and his father's father were exempt from civic duties. It was held in such esteem that on the appearance at the games of a citizen wearing this crown the people, including the senators, rose from their seats, and he was allowed to take a seat by the senators. Augustus received this civic crown, and garlands of oak were thenceforth hung from his palace gates. The Roman significance of the oak wreath, however, has not survived to modern times. When an oak wreath is used for a memorial, either public or personal, it is doubtful whether it is remotely connected, by those responsible for its introduction, with the old pagan oak wreaths. Oak, olive, laurel and myrtle wreaths are too often used indiscriminately, without attention to the finer points of appropriateness.

The oak might be used for a Christian purpose, by virtue of its quality of durability, as a symbol of steadfastness—the steadfastness of those whose faith in Christ endures the storms of life.

The oak was officially adopted as the state tree of Illinois in 1907. The white oak (*Quercus Alba*) is the state tree of Connecticut, as this was the species of tree in which the charter of 1662 granted by Charles II was hidden from Sir Edmund Andros, who was sent by James II in 1678 to recover it. In that year the tree was about fifty years old. It blew down in a storm in 1856.

1. *Natural History*, Book XVI, Chap. iii.

OAR—Some towns situated on the coast, or on a river, which enjoys Admiralty jurisdiction have a mace in the form of an oar, as a symbol of deputed royal authority. Among these towns are Dover, Chester, Beaumaris, Boston, Rochester and Lostwithiel. The mayors of these towns hold titles conferred by the Admiralty; thus the

Mayor of Chester holds the title of the Admiral of the River Dee, the Mayor of Rochester, Admiral of the Medway. Saltash has an oar-mace, which consists of a shaft in the form of an oar terminating with a mace head.

OBELISK—From the available knowledge of the best known and most widely distributed ancient form of the obelisk, the Egyptian, which has been the prototype of modern examples, it may be regarded as symbolizing eternal life, fertility and regeneration. This symbolism is derived from its undoubted connection with Egyptian sun worship. The Egyptian obelisk, together with Semitic and other obelisks, has been thought by some students to have a phallic significance. There is far less evidence for this in the case of the Egyptian than for its connection with sun worship; nevertheless, as a phallic[1] symbol it would have much the same significance as a sun symbol.

The earliest remaining Egyptian obelisks are of the fourth dynasty (c. 3000 B.C.). They are of a small type, and were called ben stones in the hieroglyphics, which means sun stones. It was a common belief among primitive peoples that good or evil spirits resided in stones, and, if none were available of a sufficiently striking natural formation, they were hewn into the requisite shape. Similarly, a belief was held among the earliest Egyptians that the spirit of the sun-god abode in the ben stone, and at the creation emerged from the pyramidion (the pyramid top) in the form of a bird which was called benu. This is thought by some to be the origin of the Phoenix myth.[2]

The most important part of this obelisk was the pyramidion from which the sun spirit emerged. Various interpretations of the significance of this have been given, one being that it represented heaven where the gods dwelt, as heaven was conceived as being composed of a layer of indeterminate material somewhere above the sky and supported on four columns. Sir E. A. Wallis Budge suggests[3] that this may be the reason why tombs were built in the pyramid form, although there is evidence that the pyramid was a structure which evolved from the large platforms over graves, which became a series of platforms in the general form of the pyramid, as at Sakkarah, and ultimately evolved as the great pyramids of the fourth dynasty.[4]

The large granite obelisks of a later time, generally between fifty feet and one-hundred feet high, and erected in pairs at the entrances of the temples, do not appear to have been connected by the Egyptians with the small early obelisks, as the former are called in the hieroglyphics by the totally different name of tekhen. But the tall obelisks may have been a development of the early examples, for the pyramidion, which is really the symbolic part, seems to have had the same significance in each. In the tall obelisks the pyramidion was plated with a bright metal so as to shine in the sun, and it is thought that its shape is a representation of the sun's rays, the sun being the apex and the rays spreading to earth being the slope of the pyramidion to the shaft. Pliny[5] noted its likeness to the sun's rays. Although there is no connection in the names ben and tekhen, names are generally poor evidence compared with symbolic shapes, and thus the strongest evidence indicates that representation of the sun's rays determined the shape of the ben stone pyramidion.

The earliest remaining of the greater obelisks is that of Senworsi I, of the eleventh dynasty, at Heliopolis. It was to these that the Greeks gave the name obelisk, ὀβελίσκος, which means a pointed pillar. They were erected in greatest numbers during the eighteenth and nineteenth dynasties. Thotmes III, of the eighteenth dynasty, erected many of the largest at Karnak and Heliopolis. One was transported to Rome (approximately 105 feet high), and two were transported from Heliopolis to Alexandria by the Romans, while from thence one (approximately 69 feet high) was transported to London in 1877, and the other (approximately 70 feet high) to New York in 1879; these are known as Cleopatra's Needles. The obelisk (75 feet high) in the Place de la Concorde, in Paris, is one of a pair of Rameses II of the nineteenth dynasty at Luxor; the other is still *in situ*.

The hieroglyphics inscribed on these obelisks, standing in pairs on either side of the entrance to sun temples, state in most cases that they were erected by the kings in honour of the sun-god Ra in order to obtain the gift of eternal life. The Egyptian obelisk, therefore, with its top designed in imitation of the sun's rays and dedicated to Ra, symbolized the sun, which, in the Egyptian mind, was the force of creation, or regeneration, and the giver of eternal life.

The reason why the two obelisks of Thotmes III are called Cleopatra's Needles is still a mystery. Sir Wallis Budge suggests one explanation which seems feasible.[6] The Arabs appear to have called the Egyptian obelisks *masâlla Fir'ûn*, which means Pharaoh's big needles. In Arabic, *misâllah* means a big needle used by packers in sewing up bales. Now, the obelisks of Thotmes III were in Alexandria at the time of the residence of Cleopatra, and the Arabs may have thought that 'big needle' was as appropriate to Cleopatra—or even more so, as she was a woman—as to the Pharaohs. It is possible that if these obelisks were regarded as phallic symbols, the more vulgar Arabs took an obscene delight in associating them with Cleopatra.

The best-proportioned ancient examples have a height of between eight and ten times the width at the base. They generally have a slight entasis, and the pyramidion is constructed usually at an angle of about sixty degrees. When erected in the various cities to which they have been transported they are usually placed on pedestals and bases which are of sufficiently modern proportions to be entirely subordinate to the obelisk.

The Egyptian obelisk has been the model for most subsequent European obelisks. In modern times they are often erected as public monuments. The immense obelisk erected on Bodmin Beacon in 1856 to the memory of the soldier, Sir Walter R. Gilbert, and the obelisk over the grave of Daniel Defoe in Bunhill Fields, are well-known examples. The largest obelisk ever erected is that which forms the monument to Washington on the Mall in the American capital. This immense obelisk of white marble is 555 feet high and 55 feet square at its base. Its impressiveness is enhanced by its spacious setting and by the adjacent reflecting pool. Some of the most pleasing of recent examples are those designed by Sir Edwin Lutyens, such as the obelisk fountain of the R.N.V.R. memorial in the Horse Guards' Parade and one of similar design at Delhi.

Should an Egyptian symbol expressing ancient religious thought be used as a modern Christian memorial? As the thought that it expressed—eternal life and regeneration, thus resurrection—is also a part of Christian doctrine, though arrived at by a different approach, there is surely no objection to the symbol, and if well proportioned it is certainly not without beauty. It is not effective on a small scale.

1. Phallus, from the Greek φαλλός, the name for the male organ.
2. *See* Phoenix.
3. *Cleopatra's Needles and Other Egyptian Obelisks*, p. 11 (London, 1926).
4. This development is traced by PROFESSOR J. GARSTANG in *The Burial Customs of Ancient Egypt*, pp. 3 *et seq.* (London, 1907).
5. *Natural History*, Book XXXVI, Chap. xiv.
6. SIR E. A. WALLIS BUDGE, *op. cit.*, pp. 18 and 19.

OCTAGON—As the number eight is mentioned by some early Christian writers as being symbolic of regeneration, the octagon is sometimes regarded as having this significance. The reason for this symbolism, as given by St. Augustine, is that as seven was the number of the old creation, eight is the number of the new creation through Christ, and was thus, to St. Augustine, the number of perfection.

It is unlikely that the early Christian octagonal baptisteries[1] and the octagonal font which, after the Romanesque or normal circular font, became, in the Gothic period, the commonest form, originated from this symbolism of eight, with baptism signifying a new creation by admission into the Church of Christ. More probably reasons of structure and design accounted for the octagonal form. The octagonal shape appears in early Christian and Gothic architecture in a variety of features such as domes, pulpits, and columns. Its use for the dome was due partly to the ribbed structure that it made possible. Brunelleschi's dome of the Duomo in Florence is the most famous example. It is also a common form in Gothic churchyard crosses, remains of which are plentiful.

1. The oldest remaining baptistery, that of the Lateran Palace at Rome, is octagonal in shape. The font in its centre, like a pool, is also octagonal.

OLIVE—The chief symbol of peace. The crown of olives signifies honour and victory. (Fig. 49 (*b*).)

As a symbol of peace it is associated by many with the return of the dove to the ark with an olive branch in its beak, indicating deliverance from anxiety. (q.v.) This, no doubt, was the chief Christian reason for its adoption in modern times; but the symbol probably owes its origin to the Greek myth that tells of the choice of Athênê as deity of the city that bears her name. The Athenians chose Athênê, who offered an olive-tree, symbolizing peace and plenty, as the first gift of man, in preference to Poseidon, who offered a horse, symbolizing strength and courage.

The olive being sacred to Athênê (the Roman Minerva), an olive crown was the reward of victors in games held in her honour. At the Olympian games the highest award was the crown of wild olive. In Greece and Rome it was a reward of military valour, though less often used than the oak and laurel. The early Christians sometimes used this crown as the reward of martyrdom.

For commemorative design it can signify one who has worked with some success in achieving peace among men, such as a recipient of the Nobel Peace Prize, or in the Christian religious sense the peace that faith can bring.

OMEGA—The last letter of the Greek alphabet sometimes used to signify the last, generally used in conjunction with alpha to signify the first and last, or the beginning and end (*see* Alpha).

ORANGE BLOSSOM—An ancient Saracenic symbol of fertility and worn by Saracen brides at weddings. The reason for this symbolism is because the flowers and fruit frequently appear on the tree at the same time. The fruit takes a long time to ripen, and is often only fully ripe when the next flowers begin to appear in the Spring.

Sheridan in *The Rivals* (Act III, Scene 3) refers to this phenomenon. Captain Absolute says to Mrs. Malaprop that 'our ladies . . . think our admiration of beauty so great, that knowledge in them would be superfluous. Thus, like garden trees, they seldom show fruit, till time has robbed them of the more specious blossom. Few, like Mrs. Malaprop and the orange-tree, are rich in both at once.'

Modern European brides wear orange blossom, or some substitute, at weddings, and it is often thought that they are worn as symbols of purity. If that were the case any white flowers would obviously do as well.

Orange blossom (*Citrus trifoliata* or *Citrus sinensis*) is the state flower of Florida, U.S.A., officially adopted in 1909, the reason given being that the state is widely known as the 'Land of Flowers'.

ORB—Signifies the world. Surmounted by a cross it signifies Christian dominion over the world. It thus figures at the top of church steeples and cupolas, an example being the golden ball and cross above the dome of St. Paul's Cathedral. It is obviously with this significance that it appears in the hand of God the Father as represented in many early religious pictures, such as Fra Angelico's 'Adoration of the Magi'.

The orb[1] as an emblem of monarchy, held in the left hand of the monarch, originally signified dominion over the world. It was first employed by the Emperor Augustus, and for him and succeeding Roman emperors its use was not merely empty symbolism, as they were monarchs of the greater part of the civilized world. The orb surmounted by the cross was first used by Constantine, as an indication, doubtless, of the faith by which he ruled the world. The orb of English kings since Edward the Confessor, and of most European kings, is surmounted by the cross. In the minds of mediaeval monarchs it must have changed its significance, if they thought about it at all; for it obviously could not mean to them what it meant to Constantine, as none of them approached the position of ruler of the world, and many were subordinate to the pope.

If a meaning be given to its use in the regalia of modern times it obviously cannot be, as implied by Shipley,[2] that the orb signifies the king's dominion; nor that he rules by the Christian faith that has dominion over the world; for neither is true. It may be given the meaning, however, that the monarch rules in the belief that the Christian God, being the true God, has dominion over the world and over all things. Its employment surmounting a church steeple or dome or on a public or personal monument would also be an expression of this belief.

1. It is sometimes called 'the mound', from the French *le monde*, meaning the world.
2. O. SHIPLEY, *Glossary of Ecclesiastical Terms*, 1872.

ORCHID—The flower known variously as moccasin flower, lady's slipper, Indian shoe and wild orchid *Cyprepedium reginae* is the state flower of Minnesota. Originally, the orchid *Cyprepedium calcarlus*, was adopted in 1893, but it was discovered that this species was not found in the state, so it was changed to the first mentioned in

1903. The orchid *Cyprepedium hirsutum,* also known as lady's slipper, is the floral emblem of Prince Edward Island, being selected because it is the most beautiful of the native orchids.

ORIOLE—The Baltimore oriole is the state bird of Maryland, officially adopted in 1947. It is protected throughout the state.

ORPHEUS—An early Christian symbol of Christ. (*See* Shepherd and Sheep.)

OWL—Symbol of wisdom.

It is traditionally a symbol of wisdom because it was sacred to Athênê and also to the Roman goddess Minerva when she became identified with Athênê. The Greek goddess, it will be remembered, was goddess of peace, learning and the arts, and thus logically of wisdom.

There are various accounts of the gifts brought by Athênê in her contest with Poseidon for the deityship of Attica. One account mentions the olive-tree, the serpent, cock, and owl, and all figure as symbols of Athênê. The owl occurs chiefly on the reverse of coins, on the obverse of which is usually a head of Athênê.

I have not been able to discover why the owl was sacred to Athênê. The common notion that it was because of the rather wise look of the owl is unlikely to be correct as such a notion was probably subsequent to the bird being known as a symbol of wisdom, and is thus merely the suggestion emanating from the association of the Goddess of Wisdom with the owl, and not from anything in the bird's physiognomy.

The owl is widely used as a symbol of wisdom. It has even so figured in mediaeval Christian symbolism. For example, there is a mediaeval figure of Moses in the museum at York in which he is represented holding a rod at the top of which is an owl. The figure was taken from the nave of York Minster in 1828.

OX—An ancient symbol of wealth, probably derived from its being, in common with other cattle, a medium of exchange, prior to metal and coins. Thus, as a depiction of coins might be regarded as indicative of wealth, so in ancient countries, where an ox was used as a medium of exchange, its depiction would similarly be indicative of wealth. The ox was in ancient times an animal of sacrifice and was often so used symbolically. (*See* Winged Ox.)

OX, WINGED—Symbol and emblem of St. Luke as one of the four evangelists. As mentioned under Winged Lion, the symbols of the four evangelists are thought to be derived from Ezekiel's vision on the banks of the river Chebar (i, 10), and from the four beasts in Revelation (iv. 7) who stood round the throne of the Lamb. The traditional identification of the four beasts with the four evangelists derives from St. Jerome's attributions in which he gives the ox or calf to St. Luke. The application is logical, for the ox or calf was an animal of sacrifice, and St. Luke in his gospel wrote chiefly of the sacrifice of Christ and the atonement.

PAGODA—A Buddhist symbol of divinity, of the absolute and of the nirvana.

The pagoda originally had a significance similar to that of the Indian stupa from which it was derived, but in its many migrations this original significance has occasionally been lost while a very large number of different forms have evolved. The name 'pagoda' by which the structure is known in the west originated as a seventeenth century Portuguese corruption of the Persian term 'butkadah', a compound of 'but', an idol or image, and 'kadah', a habitation—thus idol-house or idol-temple.

Judging from the earliest surviving examples of stupa (*see* Stupa) it was surmounted by a series of umbrellas which signified divine authority. In one historical sequence of designs the spire gradually became larger in relation to the dome, the umbrellas became more numerous and it ultimately became a tower-like structure. In most of its various forms it contains the essential features of the stupa. The true Buddhist pagoda has the central column, pole or mast, with a series of umbrellas, erected on a hemispherical base. The whole is often enclosed in a tower-like structure with the umbrellas projecting and sometimes forming floors. Windows were added and stairways introduced, and often the base becomes square or polygonal. The column being the core of the structure, as Buddha is the centre of the universe, was often identified with Buddha in the state of nirvana.

The pagoda in various forms appear over the whole of south-east Asia and in its migrations it was associated with other structures like Hindu towers and was variously elaborated. Some very large pagodas were erected in China such as that at Ling-yen-sse, Shantung, built in the eighth century A.D., which is 169 feet high and has windows and stairways; and that at T'ien-ning-sse, Peking, built in the eleventh century A.D., which is 190 feet high, is windowless with elaborate relief carvings on its octagonal base.

In many of the later large Japanese pagodas constructed of timber each umbrella has become a wide projecting roof forming a storey, the whole being built round a central timber post. The sacred shrine is generally on the ground floor. Sometimes the pagoda is surmounted by a spire with a series of umbrellas. That at Yasaka is a handsome seventeenth century example.

Like the stupa, the pagoda was frequently made in miniature form as a reliquary, and for devotional purposes and as a sepulchral monument.[1]

1. In *The Art of Buddhism* (Baden-Baden, 1964), DIETRICH SECKEL devotes a chapter to the development from the stupa to the pagoda (English translation, 1964), pp. 103–32.

PALM—A symbol of victory. It has been employed in Christianity as symbolic of victory by martyrdom over death and over the enemies and persecutors of the religion.

In pagan times a military victory was signified by the soldiers carrying palm branches.

The people of Jerusalem, when hearing that Jesus was coming to the city, spontaneously 'took branches of palm-trees, and went forth to meet Him, and cried, Hosanna' (John xii. 13). Representations of palm are numerous on the tombs, lamps, and other objects in the catacombs. During the Middle Ages it was borne by Christian pilgrims; and in early representations on mosaics and wall paintings it was placed in the hands, not only of martyrs, but of those who were supposed to have won entrance into heaven: representations probably partly prompted by the passage in Revelation (vii. 9) which refers to a multitude standing 'before the throne, and before the Lamb, clothed with white robes, and palms in their hands'.

The date-palm, being a prominent tree in the East, became among ancient Eastern peoples, by reason of its periodic renewal of fruit, a symbol, like the pomegranate, of the generative force of nature, of constant renewal of life and thus of immortality.[1]

During the Middle Ages the palm was referred to, from the character of its growth, as the upright Christian superior to all adversity. St. Ambrose and the Venerable Bede refer to it as symbolic of the Church of Christ, rugged and suffering hardships below, but spreading its branches fair and fruitful above.

In its modern application it can express victory for a cause, especially for the Christian religion—the hard and effectual work of a minister or missionary of the Church, for instance. Its decorative quality makes it a pleasing subject for artistic treatment.

The Sabol Palm is the state tree of Florida, because, according to an official statement, it possesses a majesty in the country which sets it apart from all other trees.

1. *See* COUNT GOBLET D'ALVIELLA, *Migration of Symbols*, pp. 145–51.

PALMETTO—The Palmetto tree (*Inodes Palmetto*) was adopted as the state tree of South Carolina in 1939. This tree has appeared on the state flag since 1777. South Carolina is often called the Palmetto State.

PALO VERDE—The Palo Verde or Green Pole (*Genera Cercidum*) is the state tree of Arizona, adopted in 1949. It is regarded as 'one of the beautiful trees of the desert and desert foothill regions'.

PANSY—Significant of thought.

This arose from pansy and thought being in French the same word: *pensée*, so that their meanings were associated. Thought in old French was sometimes also spelt *pansé* and *pansée*, which may also have suggested to the English a connection with pansy. In Elizabethan days the meaning appears to have been familiar. Thus Ophelia says to Laertes: ' . . . there is pansies, that's for thoughts.'[1] and it is from that saying that the association is largely known in England today. A symbol that has come into being by an etymological coincidence is of a very crude type. Yet that Shakespeare used it and that the symbol has a certain currency may be sufficient justification, in some minds, for its use.

1. *Hamlet*, Act IV, scene v, 176.

PAPAL TIARA—*See* tiara.

PARSLEY—A crown of parsley was sometimes awarded at athletic and musical festivals in ancient Greece and Rome.

PASQUE FLOWER (*Pulsatilla Tudoviciana* or *Anemone patens*)—State flower of South Dakota, officially adopted in 1903 and of the Canadian Province of Manitoba which adopted it in 1906, the school children having chosen it. The reason for its choice as a symbol is that it is largely distributed in the province, and is one of the earliest of spring flowers to gladden the heart. Its name, Pasque Flower, or Easter Flower, expresses the idea of early blooming. It is also popularly known as wild crocus.

PASSION FLOWER—Symbolic of Christ's Passion: of the sacrifice and suffering in His final act of redemption.

Spanish friars of the sixteenth century first gave the name *flos passionis* (latinized by Linnaeus into *passiflora*) to the flower, seeing in its formation a resemblance to the instruments of Christ's Passion. They interpreted the five sepals and five petals as the ten faithful disciples, excluding Peter who denied his Master, and Judas who

Fig. 51. Passion flower (*Passiflora*).

betrayed Him: the corona as the crown of thorns; the five stamens as the five wounds; and the three styles with rounded heads as the three nails. (Fig. 51.)

The passion flower is common in ecclesiastical design during the last hundred years. It was selected as the state flower of Tennessee by a vote of the school children in 1919, because it is one of the most beautiful flowers of the country and grows abundantly. In 1933, however, the Iris was officially adopted.

PEACH BLOSSOM (*Primus persica* or *Amygdalus persica*)—By association it has become the state flower of Delaware because of the successful and extensive peach growing in the state. It was officially adopted in 1895.

PEACOCK—A pagan symbol of immortality, and an early Christian symbol of immortality and the resurrection.

The peacock was sacred to Juno, and was associated with empresses, doubtless because of its handsome appearance. It thus appears on the reverse of some ancient Roman coins and medals. By reason of the supposed incorruptibility of its flesh it symbolized the apotheosis of an empress.

The early Christians, in adopting it, applied its meaning in accordance with their faith. It retained its significance of immortality, but it also became symbolic of the resurrection by the analogy of the periodic renewal of its beautiful plumage. It was used in wall paintings and on tombs of the catacombs, often being shown with a nimbus.

Goblet D'Alviella thinks that the belief held among the ancients that the peacock killed serpents prompted the Christian adoption of it in this sense, as the serpent is a Christian symbol of evil.[1] There is nothing, however, in Christian representations of it to indicate this.

It is only in later times that the peacock is regarded as symbolic of pride, although in this there is a common line of thought with that which, in pagan times, associated the peacock with Juno and empresses, for it obviously arises in both cases from the bird's appearance and its love of display. Although this significance is now more familiar than its Christian symbolism, there is little possibility that the peacock's appearance in designs with a commemorative purpose would be interpreted in the former sense, for its inappropriateness for this purpose as symbolic of pride would be at once apparent, and intelligent apprehension would inevitably seek for a deeper and less blatant meaning.

1. GOBLET D'ALVIELLA, *Migration of Symbols*, p. 115.

PECAN TREE—The pecan tree was adopted as the state tree of Texas in 1919, having long been popular in the country because of its stately character. Governor James Stephen requested that a pecan tree should be planted by his grave, and this probably influenced the decision to adopt it.

PELICAN AND ITS YOUNG—Symbol of Christ's work of redemption and sacrifice, and of the resurrection.

The most generally accepted version of the analogy originating the symbol is that the pelican was once thought to nourish its young with its own blood, doing so by making a wound in its own breast. Another version, given by Epiphanius, Bishop of Constantia, in his *Physiologus* (1588), is that the mother kills her young with the very fervour of her love, but the male bird, coming after three days and finding the young dead, smites his side, pours his blood upon them, and brings them back to life. The latter version is the better analogy of Christ's work of redemption and sacrifice, and of the resurrection.

A biologist[1] has suggested that the notion probably originated with the secretion of blood that the flamingo ejects from its mouth, the flamingo being anciently confused with the pelican.

There are many allusions to the symbol. Dante, for example, refers to Christ as 'Nostro Pelicano,' and Shakespeare, in *Hamlet*, says:

> To his good friends thus wide I ope my arms,
> And like the kind life-rending pelican,
> Refresh them with my blood.

The symbol was first employed during the thirteenth century and has continually appeared since. It is found in mediaeval manuscripts, on seals, and in ecclesiastical and memorial sculpture. In 1516 it was adopted by Bishop Fox as a device for the new college of Corpus Christi, at Oxford; and by Corpus Christi College, Cambridge, in 1570. It continues to be employed as a symbolic and decorative motif and provides a good subject for design. The memorial designs of the Scottish architect, Sir Robert Lorimer, provide some good examples.

The pelican is the state bird of Louisiana, and the pelican and its young are represented on the Louisiana state seal and flag, the former being adopted in 1902 and the latter in 1912.

1. A. D. BARTLETT, *Proceedings of the Zoological Society*, p. 146 (1869).

PHALLUS—Symbol of life and regeneration.

The phallus is a representation of the male generative organ, and was employed as a symbol of the generative force in nature in many ancient religions. Phallic worship was connected, for example, with the cult of Osiris in ancient Egypt, with the worship of Siva in India, while phallic symbols were carried in processions in the Dionysiac festivals in ancient Greece.

According to Freud's theory of psychoanalysis, phallic symbols figure in instinctive and unconscious symbolism, and are common in dreams (*see* Chapter XII).

PHEASANT—The Chinese ring-necked pheasant (*Phasianus Colchicus Torquatus*) is the state bird of South Dakota. The prairies of the state abound in this bird. The male of the species is richly coloured.

PHOENIX—Adopted by the early Christians as a symbol of the resurrection and of immortality. Also in ancient times a symbol of the sun and of imperial apotheosis.

The phoenix legend varies in the accounts given by different writers: Herodotus, Pliny, Tacitus, and several others. The version of the legend most familiar today is that derived from Epiphanius in his *Physiologus*. The phoenix was an Indian bird that lived for five hundred years. After its long life it flies to the temple of Heliopolis, laden with spices, and, settling on the altar, burns to ashes. A young phoenix rises from the ashes, and on the third day flies away to live for another five hundred years.

In ancient Egypt the phoenix was, in a similar way to the lotus flower, a symbol of the sun, every morning rising from its ashes. The hieroglyphic called the benu, which was sacred to Heliopolis, and which represented the stork, heron, or egret, was probably the prototype of the phoenix.[1] Pliny, however, derives his notion of its appearance from Manilius' description of a bird he brought to Rome under the name and character of phoenix. Pliny's record indicates the golden pheasant.[2] In Rome the phoenix became symbolical of the imperial apotheosis, and shortly afterwards was adopted by the Christians as a symbol of resurrection and immortality. It appears in the catacombs and later in mosaics and manuscripts. It is rarely used as a religious device in modern times, though employed in other connections. A noted example is its use by the assurance company that bears its name. The Company's history, published in 1915, states that: 'It was inevitable that this story (of the

(*a*) Representation of the Phoenix, derived from the design used by the Phoenix Assurance Company. The designs of this company afford some of the best decorative renderings of the subject.

(*b*) Conventional rendering of the Pelican and its young, derived from Hamilton's design for the policy heading of the Old Pelican Assurance Company.

Fig. 52.

Phoenix) should be remembered when Fire Insurance was introduced into this country, though the actual similarity would appear to be rather in the insured houses than in the Insurance Company. In one respect, however, the name was particularly appropriate, for the first Phoenix Insurance Office rose amid the ruins of a burnt city, and apparently expired in its own ashes shortly before the appearance of the present Company.'

Its significance is so widely understood, and it lends itself to such pleasing adaptation for decorative purposes that it provides a good subject for the designer.

1. *See Encyclopaedia Britannica*, 'Phoenix'.
2. *Natural History*, Book X, Chap. iii.

PINE—The pine tree is the state tree of Arkansas, officially adopted in 1939, while the white pine was adopted by Michigan in 1955. The white pine cone (*Pinias Strobus*) was adopted as the state 'floral emblem' of Maine in 1895. Maine is called the Pine Tree State and has a pine tree in the centre of its coat of arms.

PINE-CONE—An ancient symbol of fertility and regeneration, and from this becoming a sepulchral and architectural ornament. To a less extent it was a symbol of healing and of conviviality.

In the worship of tree spirits, as typifying regeneration and the annual renewal of life, ancient peoples usually selected trees according to their value or impressiveness. (*See* Sacred tree.) In Asia Minor and Egypt the seed of the stone-pine was used as food and as an ingredient of medicine. Among the manifold manifestations of Osiris, by which he was worshipped, was the spirit of the pine-tree, typifying the annual renewal of life; and the spirit was so anthropomorphized that an image of Osiris was carved and placed in an excavated hollow in the trunk. In a similar manner, Attis, a god of Phrygia, was regarded as the spirit of the pine-tree, and the worship of the god spread to Rome in the third and second centuries B.C. In Rome the important ceremony attending the worship of Attis, which occurred in the spring, consisted of his image being fixed to the trunk of a pine-tree around which priests and worshippers danced and made offerings of blood by mutilations.[1]

The earliest known representation of the pine-cone in art is in the hall of Osiris at Denderah. On one coffin here Osiris is shown enclosed in a pine-tree, and correspondingly on the monuments pine-cones are represented, symbolizing, of course, the regeneration that Osiris typified. It never became a prominent feature of Egyptian funerary art, as this form of the worship of Osiris was probably not extensive or of long duration. The pine-cone appears in Assyrian ornamentation, a famous example being the border pattern of pine-cones alternating with lotus flowers. Whether the Assyrians obtained it from Egypt or from Phrygia, or employed it for directly religious or aesthetic reasons, it is impossible to say.

In ancient Greece the pine-cone was associated with Dionysus and is usually represented at the top of the Thyrsus, the wand carried by Dionysus and his train. It probably thus figures because a wine was brewed from pine-cones and turpentine. Because of its prophylactic qualities, enumerated by Pliny, it was associated with healing by the Greeks and Romans, and Aesculapius is sometimes represented with a pine-cone. Pausanias mentions a gold and ivory statue of Aesculapius at Corinth, in which he is shown holding a sceptre in one hand and the fruit of a cultivated pine-tree in the other.[2]

It is, however, as a symbol of regeneration, from the ancestry of tree-worship, that the pine-cone figures in architecture and in the commemorative arts. G. Dennis mentions that the pine-cone figures in Etruscan tombs, at the top of urns, and on the summit of pillars.[3] The Mausoleum of Hadrian at Rome, at present surmounted by a statue of the Archangel Michael, was originally surmounted by a gilt bronze pine-cone; and its prominence on the arms and coins of Augsburg is supposed to be a survival of the Roman occupation. The pine-cone figures occasionally in Renaissance architecture, Sir Christopher Wren being especially fond of it. Students of his work will doubtless remember that he removed the heraldic animals from the buttress summits of the Royal Chapel at Windsor, on the plea of insufficient weight, and substituted pine-cones. He also used them on the summits of the western towers of St. Paul's Cathedral. They are sometimes called pineapples, but they are not like pineapples, which have leaves at the top, and further, this fruit of the *ananas sativus* was probably not familiar in England until the eighteenth century, having probably been introduced from America only in the reign of Charles II, when it was first recorded.[4] The pine-cone, on the other hand, has an extensive architectural history, and its symbolical significance of regeneration supplies a fitting motif for the designer.

1. A full account of this worship of Osiris and Attis is given in SIR JAMES FRAZER'S *Adonis, Attis and Osiris*, Vols. v and vi of *The Golden Bough* (London, 1912).
2. Pausanias Book II, chap. x, SIR JAMES FRAZER'S translation.
3. *The Cities and Cemeteries of Etruria*, Vol. ii, pp. 157, 103 and 492 (London, 1848).
4 Evelyn's Diary.

PINON—The pinon, a species of pine, is the state tree of New Mexico.

POINSETTA—Also known as Mexican Flame-leaf, the poinsetta has been adopted by Queensland (Australia) as its floral emblem. It was imported from Mexico, but is very much at home in Queensland, growing profusely along the north coast. The flower is a small pinkish yellow cluster in the centre of a flare or star of scarlet leaves.

POMEGRANATE—Symbol of fertility and regeneration.

It can be traced as a symbol to ancient Semitic peoples.[1] Pomegranates have figured in architectural decoration from Solomon's Temple[2] to modern Georgian fruit and flower mouldings, and are occasionally seen in more modern enrichments. The pomegranate may have been introduced occasionally in Christian sepulchral art as symbolizing immortal life. Mrs. Jameson speaks of it in that connection, referring to it as an emblem of the future—of hope in immortality.[3] There is not, however, a strong Christian traditional support for this.

1. GOBLET D'ALVIELLA, *Migration of Symbols*, p. 154.
2. I Kings vii. 18–20.
3. *Sacred and Legendary Art*, Vol. i, p. 35.

POPPY—Symbol of sleep, and all that it means: rest, peace.

It has been used more often in literature than in art, and refers to the sleep-inducing effects of the opium poppy (*Papaver somniferum*). Poets often allude to it when writing of sleep. Thus Thomas Warton in his *Ode to Sleep*, says:

> On this, my pensive pillow, gentle sleep!
> Descend, in all thy downy plumage drest;
> Wipe with thy wing these eyes that wake to weep,
> And place thy crown of poppies on my breast.

And Keats, in his sonnet to sleep, says:

> O soothest sleep! If so it please thee, close,
> In midst of this thine hymn, my willing eyes,
> Or wait the amen, ere thy poppy throws
> Around my bed its lulling charities.

It expresses rather a Greek than a Christian sentiment, for it stirs no thought of future life, but confines thought just to sleep. Yet that may express the desires of some, who may even feel the weariness expressed in Swinburne's *Garden of Proserpine*.

The golden poppy (*Eschscholtzia californica*) is the state flower of California, having been adopted in 1903. There are several legends explaining its adoption, but it was probably adopted because it is a common and beautiful flower of the Californian landscape.

PORTCULLIS—As the portcullis was a grating which was raised and let down in the gateway of a mediaeval fortress or fortified town, a representation of it has become a symbol of defence, protection and security. A portcullis appeared on coins, crown, half-crown, shilling and sixpence, used by the East India Company in the reign of Elizabeth I, and also on the threepenny piece of Elizabeth II, the idea probably being that thrift, represented by the saving of small coins, is a way to security. The chained portcullis, surmounted by a crown, which appears on much of the furniture of the Houses of Parliament, is symbolic of royal residence.

POWERS—In the angelic hierarchy of the pseudo-Dionysius (*see* Angel) Powers form the third rank of the second order of angels and they signify unflinching virility in the exercise of God's power. Their function is watchfulness.

PRINCIPALITIES—The third order of angels performs the function of revelation to, and guardianship of man, and the principalities are the highest rank or princes of this order.

PROTEA—The national flower of South Africa. There are a large number of species indigenous to Cape Province, and they vary in colour from bright red to orange and yellow. It was no doubt the association of this flower with the familiar landscape that prompted its adoption as a national emblem.

PURPLE—With blue, purple appears to have been a royal colour. It was associated with the Roman monarchy because the Emperor's State robes were of purple. The colour became almost a synonym for the throne, and Gibbon constantly used the expression 'the Imperial purple', or 'the purple' to signify the Roman sovereignty.

The reason for purple being the colour of the Roman monarchy was probably that purple, or scarlet, or violet was the most costly dye, and was used only for the dress of the ruling classes. In some societies the wearing of this colour is the exclusive prerogative of the royal family.

Purple or violet is a liturgical colour which is appropriated to Advent. Purple or violet vestments are worn on days of intercession, and for several ecclesiastical functions, especially those concerned with the Passion.

PYRAMID—There is evidence to support the conjecture that the large Egyptian pyramid was conceived and designed in imitation of a mountain where the gods dwelt, and which fittingly became the tomb of a great Egyptian king. If this is the case it is thus, like the Babylonian ziggurat, a symbol of a sacred mountain where the gods dwelt. The earliest pyramid, that of the third dynasty at Sakkara, is stepped and has a distinct similarity to the earliest ziggurats. A. B. Cook remarks that 'the significance of the pyramid is uncertain', but he is 'disposed to think that like the Babylonian zikkurat or "high place" it was the conventionalized form of a mountain, originally viewed as the dwelling place of the deity'.[1] (*See also* Mountain and Ziggurat.)

1. A. B. COOK, *Zeus God of the Bright Sky* (Cambridge, 1914), p. 603.

QUAIL—The valley quail (*Sophortyx californica*) is the state bird of California, having been officially adopted in 1931.

QUADRIGA—A sculptured four-horse chariot, symbol of victory, often employed as a crowning feature of a triumphal arch.

The earliest known example is the group at the summit of the immense tomb of Mausolus at Halicarnassus (fourth century B.C.). Quadriga occupied the summits of the Arch of Titus (first century A.D.) and the arch of Septimus Severus (third century A.D.). Modern examples are the two quadriga in the Vittorio Emmanuelo Monument in Rome surmounting the flanking structures (1885–1911); and that surmounting the Wellington Arch at the top of Constitution Hill in London. This, a work by Captain Adrian Jones, was added to the arch in 1912. In the chariot a woman holds in one hand a wreath or crown and in the other a sprig of laurel.

QUINCE—Ancient Greek symbol of fertility. It was eaten by the bride at weddings.

RAM—Ancient Egyptian, Greek and Roman symbol of procreation and fertility.

In ancient Egypt it was customary from predynastic time for gods to be associated with animals whose particular powers and attributes they were supposed to possess. About the twelfth dynasty the god Amen, the local god of Thebes, superseded the older gods and became the chief Egyptian god. He was regarded as a great creative god who signified the hidden force and principle of creation, and the generation of all living things. The ram, which because of its prolific procreative powers had been associated with the predynastic god Khnemu, was now associated with Amen, and both were often represented with a ram's head, the latter becoming known under the name of Ammon.

299

Most of the ancient nations had their hierarchy of gods, and it was not unusual for the gods of one nation to assimilate those of another. It can readily be understood that the early Greeks, thinking that Zeus and his hierarchy were the only gods, and finding other gods in other countries, assumed that these were Zeus and his company under other names. Herodotus refers to Amen-Ra as the Theban Zeus. Thus, the attributes of Amen including those of the Ram were given to Zeus, and in many of the representations of Zeus he acquired among other attributes the horns of a ram. Thus, to the Greeks the ram became a religious symbol, and was significant of pro-creative powers and fertility. This significance was perpetuated in Rome, and the use of the ram's head for fountain jets as a common architectural ornament is an expression of the idea.[1]

Being sacred to Zeus and Jupiter, the ram was often an animal of sacrifice, and it was thought that baptism in the blood of the ram imparted the vital force of the animal. Being an animal of sacrifice it often appears as decoration on Greek and Roman sacrificial altars and also on sepulchral altars generally shown at the corners and connected by festoons. The ram's head on the sepulchral altar may also have been expressive of eternal life by an extension of the idea of vital life force. A. B. Cook cites an inscription on a Roman altar of the fourth century, with a ram among the decorations, which speaks of re-birth to life eternal.[2]

1. A. B. Cook deals at length with the Greek religious cult of the ram in his *A Study in Ancient Religion, Zeus: God of the Bright Sky*. Vol. I, pp. 346–428 (Cambridge, 1914).
2. A. B. Cook, *A Study in Ancient Religion, Zeus: God of the Dark Sky*. Vol. 2, p. 306 (Cambridge, 1925).

RATTLESNAKE—At one time the rattlesnake (*genera sisturus* and *crotalus*), indigenous to America, was regarded as a symbol of vigilance, magnanimity and courage, and in these senses was used as a symbol by the American colonial forces during the American War of Independence. It was employed as a symbol on their flag with the words 'don't tread on me'.

The character and habits of the rattlesnake which suggest the symbolic meaning mentioned are that its eyes are very bright, suggesting perhaps vigilance, it is never aggressive, it will try to avoid an encounter and employs instead the noisy rattle in its tail to frighten off an aggressor; yet when once attacked it never surrenders but fights to the bitter end. During the War of Independence many people saw in these qualities those of the American nation and thought of the rattlesnake as an appropriate national symbol.[1] The impressive traditional associations with the eagle, however, prevailed, while there is an element of strangeness in a poisonous snake being a national symbol.

1. *See* Roger Butterfield's introduction to Ernst Lehner's *American Symbols*.

RED—The symbolic significances of the colour red are various. It is the colour of love, of danger, of combat, of anarchy and the Left Wing in politics, and among the liturgical colours it is significant of the sufferings and passion of Christ, and is used at Whitsuntide. These significances are derived from its appearance in nature, chiefly as the colour of blood, fire, and of ripe fruits.

As the colour of love it is derived from fire, which suggests the idea of warmth or heat. In the Celestial Hierarchy of the pseudo-Dionysius seraphim are the highest rank of angels, nearest to the throne of God, having their being in the divine heat and fervour of adoration, and they are usually shown red. They are significant of divine love. (*See* Angel.) The red rose is commonly regarded as symbolic of human love because of its colour.

Red as significant of danger and anarchy is derived from its use as a sign of combat, which seems to have been its use for military purposes for many centuries. The red flag was used as a sign of battle, and there is a reference to it in this sense in the *London Gazette* of 1666. This significance is clearly derived from blood, and its modern political meaning of anarchy and Left Wing tendencies derived from these, being a challenge, violent and bloody if need be, to the established order.

REDBUD—The redbud (*Cercis canadensis* or *reniformis*) is the official state tree of Oklahoma, adopted by the sixteenth legislature in 1937. This tree grows in profusion in the fields, hills and valleys of Oklahoma.

RHODODENDRON—The kind known in America as the Western rhododendron (*Rhododendron californicum* or *machrophyllum*) is the state flower of Washington. Although it has not been officially adopted, references to it as the state flower are common since the early days of the century. There is a tradition that it was selected by the people because it blooms profusely throughout the state.[1]

The kind known as the Eastern rhododendron (*Rhododendron maximum*) is the symbolic flower of West Virginia; it was officially adopted in 1903 following its selection by the school children.

1. *See* G. E. SHANKLE, *State Names, Flags, Seals, Rings, Birds, Flowers and other Symbols*, p. 351 (New York, 1934).

RING—The significance of a ring is, in a general way, the same as that of a circle (*q.v.*) A special symbolism, however, attaches to the finger ring, which is variously a symbol of the delegation of authority, contract, union, and thus of betrothal and marriage.

The impulse of self decoration is probably one reason for wearing finger rings. They were common among many primitive peoples and in most ancient civilizations. Scarab rings found in ancient Egyptian tombs had some religious significance as the scarab was the sacred beetle. Signet rings were common in ancient Greece, being used especially in the absence of an ability to write, to seal letters and contracts; and it is probably from the association of the signet with the ring that the latter became a symbol of contract. Authority was often deputed by the giving of a signet ring, so that contracts could be sealed by the deputy. By this association the ring became a symbol of deputed authority or power, which is generally the significance of ecclesiastical rings such as those conferred on newly-made bishops. The fisherman's ring of the Pope, on which is engraved a representation of St. Peter in a boat pulling a net from the water, signifies that supreme Christian authority is deputed to the Pope on his election.

The origin of the association of the ring with betrothal and marriage is uncertain. The betrothal ring was used in Roman times during the second century A.D., and

301

it is thought by some[1] that it was given as a pledge of contract, being derived in its use from the signet ring. Another view[2] is that as a ring was often given as a token delegating authority, so a wedding ring was given by a husband as a sign that his rights and privileges were given to his wife.

Betrothal and wedding rings, however, have been used by primitive peoples who cannot have known of civilized customs. E. Westermarck, in *The History of Human Marriage*, gives several instances of the use of betrothal and wedding rings which appear to symbolize, in common with numerous other customs, the union of the two parties. Westermarck quotes instances of the use of such rings among the natives of Portuguese Zambesi, the Mikirs and Ahoms of Assam, the Fors of Central Africa, and others.[3] Why they were so used among these peoples there is not sufficient evidence for us to determine, but it may be the same reason as prompted their use in Rome.

Various forms of betrothal rings have been used at different times, one worthy of note being the gimmal (meaning a twin), which was common in the sixteenth and seventeenth centuries. It consisted of two hoops that could be fastened together, which could thus be worn singly or together, and it often had a bezel with a representation of clasped hands. From time to time rings have been used for numerous purposes in addition to their purely decorative function. Thus we hear of memorial and poesy rings in the seventh century. The former were often of a gruesome character.

Though a common social symbol, the ring is rarely used in symbolic design. However, as a symbol of union there is no reason why it should not be so employed; and the gimmal ring with the clasped hands forming the bezel is a more expressive symbol in the case of a married couple than the clasped hands alone.

1. J. H. MIDDLETON and A. H. SMITH in the *Encyclopaedia Britannica*.
2. *See Chambers' Encyclopaedia.*
3. E. WESTERMARCK, *The History of Human Marriage*, Vol. ii, pp. 443–4 (London, 1925).

ROAD RUNNER—The road runner (*Geococcyx californianus*) is the state bird of New Mexico, officially adopted in 1949. It was so named because it ran in the middle of the road a little ahead of early prairie schooners.

ROBIN (*Merula migrataria*)—State bird of Michigan, officially adopted in 1931 because it was the most familiar and best-loved bird in the state. Preferences in a correspondence in *The Times* in October 1960 for a national bird for Britain showed a majority for the robin.

ROSE—Symbol of beauty, often in a superlative sense; hence of perfection. Employed by early and mediaeval Christians to symbolize the Virgin Mary, and also Paradise. It is also the national flower of England, and emblem of many states of America.

In studying the various symbolic significances attached to the rose it will be observed that they are mostly the outcome of associating the rose with the superlatively beautiful and with the perfection of a kind. Thus we say of the loveliest girl of a certain place that she is the rose of ——, and when we speak of a garden of roses or place where roses bloom we think of a spot of the earth blessed with particular beauty. It is in the former connection that the rose became a symbol and emblem of the Virgin Mary, as, perhaps, the rose of womanhood. In Italian paintings, from the eleventh century, she is often depicted carrying roses and lilies in her hand, and many Italian pictures of the Virgin bear the title of Santa Maria della Rosa. The plant rosemary may owe its name in English to this association.

It was as signifying Paradise that early Christians used roses on the tombs in the catacombs. Fra Angelico, in his conception of the subject, depicted roses as the chief flowers that bloom in Paradise.

What is regarded as the rose of England originated with the Wars of the Roses, and is composed of the red rose of Lancaster and the white rose of York, the latter being placed on the former. Each five-petalled rose is the common wild rose, or dog rose (*Rosa canina* or *Rosa arvensis*) of country hedgerows. (Fig. 53 (*b*).) The new town in central Lancashire which was designated in 1970 has been given the name of Redrose.

Many varieties of rose have been adopted as state emblems in North America. The wild rose (*Rosa virginiana* or *Rosa acicularis*), the state flower of Iowa, was adopted in 1897, as it grows profusely in the state. It was also adopted as the flower of the Province of Alberta in Canada in 1930. The school children of New York chose the rose as their state flower in 1891, and tradition associates it with this state, although no variety has been specified. The American beauty rose was adopted by the District of Columbia in 1925. The cherokee rose (*Rosa sinica*) was adopted as the state flower of Georgia in 1916, but there is some doubt whether this flower is indigenous to the country as stated in the enactment, for it may have been introduced from China by way of England. The wild prairie rose (*Rosa blanda* or *Rosa Arkansana*) was adopted as the flower of North Dakota in 1907.

ROSEMARY—Symbol of remembrance.

The Latin name *Rosmarinus* suggests a plant growing near the sea. The English name may have evolved in part from that, but was probably influenced in its present form by the words Rose and Mary, as mentioned under Rose.

Rosemary became the symbol of remembrance because of its lingering scent; and scent, as is well known, is one of the greatest preservers and awakeners of memory. In England, from the fifteenth to the eighteenth century, it was widely familiar in this symbolical character. Numerous allusions to it occur in writers of the period. Sir Thomas More writes of rosemary, or rosemarine, as he calls it: 'I let it run all over my garden wall, not only because my bees love it, but because it is the herb sacred to remembrance, and therefore to friendship.' Shakespeare often refers to it, his most famous allusion being when Ophelia says to Laertes: 'There's rosemary, that's for remembrance; pray, love, remember.' And Perdita says to the disguised Polixenes and Camillo:

> Reverend sirs,
> For you there's rosemary and rue; these keep
> Seeming and savour all the winter long;
> Grace and remembrance be to you both,
> And welcome to our shearing.

Rosemary was for long associated with Christmas, like holly and laurel, but since the beginning of last century it has rarely been seen as Christmas decoration.[1]

(*a*) Rosemary (*Rosmarinus*).

(*b*) The Dog Rose, which was probably the kind visualized
when the symbol of the rose first became familiar in
England.

Fig. 53.

Being the plant of remembrance, it was associated with the dead and introduced at funerals. Friar Lawrence, by the side of dead Juliet, says to Capulet:

> Dry up your tears, and stick your rosemary
> On this fair corse; and, as the custom is
> In all her best array bear her to church.

And Sir Thomas More wrote that 'a sprig of it hath a dumb language that maketh it the chosen emblem at our funeral wakes in our burial ground.' At funerals it served also as a symbol of immortality.

The use of rosemary at funerals has almost died out, though the custom still lingers in a few remote country places of England. In our own day rosemary is often planted on the grave, and this appears now to be its chief association with the dead. A symbol of remembrance is one of the most appropriate devices for a memorial, and none has had such a strong English tradition and enjoyed such wide familiarity at one period as rosemary, which can be utilized for decoration in a variety of ways. (Fig. 53 (*a*).)

1. G. CLARKE NUTTALL, in an article entitled 'Rosemary at Christmas' in the *Nineteenth Century* for December 1925, gives some interesting information on the symbolic use of rosemary.

RUDBECKIA—The variety known as black-eyed-Susan because of the dark centres in the yellow flowers (*Rudbeckia perta* or *serotina*) is the symbol of Maryland, adopted in 1918.

SALT—The main figurative uses of salt are derived from its qualities. It is used to sharpen flavour and is a preservative, and thus it is applied to indicate wit, smartness, piquancy. It is in the last sense that St. Paul says 'Let your speech be always with grace, seasoned with salt' (Colossians iv. 6), and when Christ says in the Sermon on the Mount, 'Ye are the salt of the earth', it is rather as a symbol of worth (Matthew v. 13). As a preservative it carries the meaning of incorruptibility and thus has sometimes been thought of as a symbol of life and of friendship.

SCALES—Symbol of justice. The origin of the symbol is fairly obvious, being the weighing of conduct, or of good and evil, virtue and vice. There are biblical references to the weighing of conduct which have probably given support to the symbol. One occurs in the first book of Samuel (ii. 3) when Hannah prayed and said 'for the Lord is a God of knowledge, and by Him actions are weighed'. Another in Daniel (v. 27) 'Tekel: Thou art weighed in the balances and found wanting.'

Scales were a symbol of justice in ancient Greece, and possibly Egypt. In a Greek vase painting (now in the Louvre) Hermes is depicted weighing the souls of Achilles and Memnon in the presence of Zeus. There are frequent references in Greek literature to Zeus holding the scales and weighing the souls of men.[1] The symbolic figure of a woman representing justice or equity is depicted with scales, an example being the figure on the reverse of the medal of Doge Leonardo Loredano of the early sixteenth century. Sometimes the figure of Justice, with scales, is shown blindfolded, as in the sinister supporter of the arms of New York. In her right hand she holds a sword. (The dexter supporter is the figure of liberty.)

1. *See* A. B. COOK, *Zeus*, Vol. II, pp. 733–4 (London, 1925).

SCAPEGOAT—Symbol of imposed responsibility for guilt.

The symbol derives from the Jewish ritual of atonement when one of two goats was sent into the wilderness with the sins of the people laid upon its head, while the other was sacrificed as a sin offering, as recorded in Leviticus (xvi). Aaron, brother of Moses, 'shall cast lots upon the two goats; one lot for the Lord, and the other lot for the scapegoat (verse 8) . . . which shall be presented alive before the Lord, to make an atonement with him, and to let him go for a scapegoat into the wilderness (verse 10). And Aaron shall lay both his hands upon the head of the live goat, and confess over him all the iniquities of the children of Israel, and all their transgressions in all their sins, putting them upon the head of the goat, and shall send him away by the hand of a fit man into the wilderness.' (verse 21.)

The origin and meaning of the prefix 'scape' is obscure, being a rendering of Azazel in the English translation of the Bible.

The scapegoat has sometimes been regarded as a symbol of the Christian Church, expressing submission and patience under affliction, a symbolism which is apt when applied to the Christian Church in the early days of its history. It was partly with this symbolism in mind that Holman Hunt painted his famous picture of the 'Scapegoat', originally giving it the name of 'Azazel'. In this picture the goat wears a scarlet fillet round his head, apparently as a symbol of the sins with which his head is loaded, for the High Priest kept a portion of this fillet in the belief that it would become white, if that on the goat's head had done so, signifying that the Lord had forgiven their sins.

Scapegoat is frequently employed to express the imposition of guilt on a person or group to excuse failure. Hitler made a scapegoat of the Jews for many of the German misfortunes between the wars.

SCARAB—Symbol of life, especially in the sense of creation and revival.

The scarab, familiar as an amulet or seal, was an Egyptian image of the species of beetle named *Scarabaeus sacer* by Linnaeus. It was held sacred and worshipped by the Egyptians, because of its supposed powers of propagation.

The observations made by the French naturalist, J. H. Fabre, have formed the basis of most modern accounts. When obtaining its food of dung, the scarab beetle procures a sufficient quantity for its needs and rolls this into a ball by propelling it with its hind legs up a sandy slope and occasionally allowing it to roll down. It then makes a hole in the ground, and there deposits the ball and feeds on it. The female pursues a similar operation, but often as an instinctive provision for her young. When she retires to a hole with the ball she removes a portion from the side, leaving a saucer shape with a flange at the edge. She there lays her egg and covers it by bringing over the flanged edges. When the egg is hatched the young beetle feeds on the inside of the ball and gradually makes its way out.[1]

The ancient Egyptian observation of this was obviously only partial. It is probable that they observed the ball in process of being made, saw the beetle deposit it in a hole, noted that the beetle left it, and observed later a new beetle emerge from the ball. They thus probably concluded that the beetle created a new beetle out of the earth. To the Egyptians, therefore, this beetle had mysterious powers, which made it divine. The meaning of the hieroglyph scarab, in Egyptian *kheperer*, was 'become' or 'create', which confirms this explanation as the most probable. It should be mentioned that as the central object of Egyptian religious worship was the sun, it was inevitable that one form of the sun-god should be the scarab. Thus Kheperer is the sun-god in the form of a scarab.

Another explanation of the worship of the beetle is that the Egyptians compared the ball to the globe of the sun.[2] This does not appear to be such a strong or feasible reason for the worship as the foregoing; but apart from this there is no evidence that the early Egyptians conceived the sun as a globe. To them it was always a disk. This objection applies to another explanation: that the beetles 'rolling their balls were typical of the planetary and lunar revolutions'. The same writer[3] adds, in expressing what was apparently once a popular notion, that to the Egyptians 'the sudden appearance of the beetles after a period of complete absence was emblematic of a future life'. This apparently means the reappearance of the same beetle after he has devoured the ball underground. But this is not so impressive as the seeming creation of a new beetle out of the ball of earth. The subject of such widespread worship was probably observed fairly closely; sufficiently, at least, to note that the old beetle had departed, and then to experience the wonder of seeing a new beetle emerge from the ball.

The worship of the beetle arose at a very early period, probably in pre-dynastic times, for images of it are plentiful from the early to the late dynasties. These images were mostly small, and were used as amulets and seals, made in stone, usually steatite, faience, and a kind of porcelain.[4] A large kind was the heart scarab, which was placed on the heart of the deceased as protection and to propitiate Osiris at the time of Judgment. The base was usually inscribed with extracts from the *Book of the Dead*.[5] A number of large stone scarabs have been found which appear to have been erected in temples and worshipped, in the same way as statues of saints are placed in Roman Catholic churches for the purposes of prayer. One, of the eighteenth dynasty, is still *in situ* on its original stone pedestal in the temple of Karnak. Two later examples are in the British Museum. (Fig. 54 (*b*).)

Although scarabs were made in large numbers during most of the dynasties from the fifth to the twenty-sixth, it is improbable that, in the later dynasties, their early religious significance was a general motive for their use. As amulets they became tokens of good fortune and good luck, and their significance made them particularly appropriate for use as seals which would be employed largely for contracts. They spread with such significance throughout the ancient world as far as Italy and Mesopotamia. The scarab has not, however, like the swastika, survived as a symbol of good fortune to modern times. It is now chiefly valued for its decorative use as jewellery.

1. An excellent description is given in *The Fauna of British India*, by G. J. Arrow, pp. 6 *et seq.* (London, 1931).
2. H. L. Griffith and H. R. Hall in the *Encyclopaedia Britannica*, p. 196, 1929.
3. David Sharp in *The Cambridge Natural History*, Part II, p. 196 (London, 1918).
4. H. R. Hall gives an excellent account of the material of which scarabs were made in a little book on scarabs published by the British Museum in 1928.
5. Generally Chap. xxx B.

(*a*) From a bas relief of the figure of Time with the scythe, skull, and hour-glass in the canopy lunette of the tomb of William Cotton, Bishop of Exeter, 1598–1621, in the south aisle of Exeter Cathedral. The collection of symbols redundantly expresses the idea of mortality, and is indicative of the kind of sepulchral representation popular in the seventeenth and eighteenth centuries.

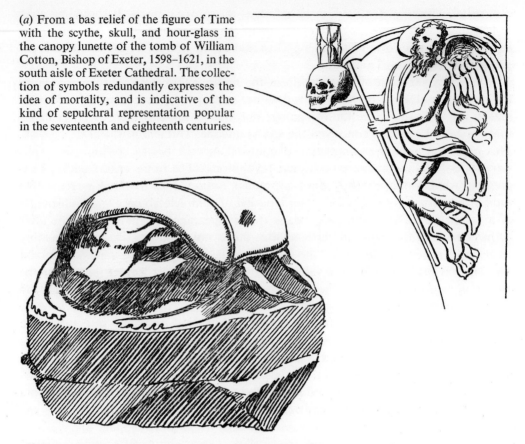

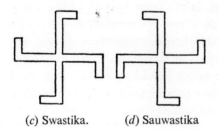

(*b*) Large green granite scarab of the sixteenth Egyptian dynasty. Now in the British Museum.

(*c*) Swastika.   (*d*) Sauwastika

(*e*) The Nazi form of Swastika.

Fig. 54. Scarab, scythe, skull and swastika.

SCEPTRE—Symbol of royal authority.

The sceptre has been an attribute of kings since ancient times. There are many Biblical references to the sceptre held by monarchs in oriental countries, and the gods of ancient Greece, especially Zeus, were frequently represented holding a sceptre surmounted by a variety of objects, such as an eagle, dove, pine-cone, and lotus. In Psalm xlv. 6 there is a figurative reference to the sceptre of God—'Thy throne, O God, is for ever and ever: the sceptre of Thy kingdom is a right sceptre.' In modern times part of the regalia of most monarchs includes one or more sceptres. In the obverse of many of the great seals of England, which usually show the monarch enthroned, a sword or a sceptre is held in the right hand. In the seal of Edward the Confessor, the first of the great seals of English kings, the king is represented seated on his throne in both the obverse and reverse. In the former he holds the sceptre in his right hand, and the orb in his left; and in the reverse he holds the sceptre surmounted by the dove in his right hand and a sword in his left. The general design from William I showed the monarch enthroned on the obverse, and mounted on a horse on the reverse. In many of the earlier seals the monarch holds a sword in the right hand, but after Henry III it is usually a sceptre. (*See* Chapter IV.)

In the monarch's regalia kept in the Wakefield Tower at the Tower of London there are four sceptres. Two are known as the royal sceptres, and one of these is surmounted by the orb and cross, regarded as the 'ensign of kingly power and justice'; the other by the dove, and referred to as the 'rod of equity and mercy'. The former was enriched in the reign of Edward VII with the largest diamond in the world.[1] The other sceptres are that known as St. Edward's Staff, the function of which may have been to guide and support the new king on his way to be crowned, and the Queen's Ivory sceptre.

The sceptre may have originated as a military weapon, like the spear, or as a shepherd's rod or staff, or as a branch of a sacred tree. The first suggestion has perhaps most evidence to support it. Herbert Spencer has pointed out that among ancient and primitive peoples the captured weapon or trophy becomes a badge which is carried or worn as a sign of authority or power. The badge was generally by custom reserved for those in authority. Thus, the captured spear was gradually transformed into the badge of authority and power, and was often given decorative and symbolic embellishments. After citing evidence for this Spencer says that 'we cannot doubt that the sceptre is simply a modified spear—a spear which, ceasing to be used as a weapon, lost its fitness for destructive purposes while becoming enriched with gold and precious stones. That only by degrees did its character as a weapon disappear, is implied by the fact that the prelate who consecrated Otho in 937, said: 'By this sceptre you shall paternally chastise your subjects.'[2]

The view that it is derived from the shepherd's rod or staff is mainly due to the Biblical references. W. Ewing and J. E. H. Thomson[3] state that 'the use of shébet (Heb.) for the symbol of royal authority is clearly a development from its use for the "rod" of the shepherd. The significance of "rod" as mentioned in Leviticus (xxvii. 32) is not very clear, and the famous allusion in the 23rd Psalm—"Thy rod and Thy staff, they comfort me" is part of the figurative allusion to the Lord as a shepherd.'

With regard to its origin as a branch of the sacred tree held in the hand of a god or king, A. B. Cook suggests that the sceptre may be derived from the Roman lituos which is also the ancestor of the pastoral staff. Cook says that the Roman lituos, which appears to have been a kind of crooked stick, may have been, according to Servius, a royal sceptre. Cook then ventures one step further and suggests 'that the lituos is ultimately the conventionalized branch of a sacred tree'. 'If Zeus Lykaios', he continued, 'bears a lituos, it is because his sceptre, so to speak was an oak branch, His priest took an oak branch in hand when he acted as rainmaker on Mount Lykaion.'

It is possible that various factors contributed to the origin of the sceptre, but the strongest evidence suggests its derivation from the spear, which became an attribute of authority and power.

1. *See* MARTIN HOLMES, *The Crown Jewels,* A guide issued by the Ministry of Works.
2. HERBERT SPENCER, *Principles of Sociology,* Part V, Ceremonial Institutions, para. 409 (London, 1879).
3. W. EWING and J. E. H. THOMSON, *The Temple Dictionary of the Bible,* p. 206 (London, 1910).

SCROLL—In memorial art the commemorative inscription is often placed on a scroll which is employed as a symbol of life or time. The scroll is usually represented partly rolled at both ends. The part of the scroll below the inscription represents the past, and the part above, the future. To the determinist the whole scroll is written on, and life is merely the unfolding of the scroll.

It is a motif that has been employed in monumental and memorial design since the days of ancient Rome. The Renaissance provided many fine examples, among which may be mentioned a memorial tablet by Brunelleschi in the Abbey at Fiesole, erected in 1466.

SCYTHE or SICKLE—Symbol of time and of death; familiar as an attribute of figures of Time and Death.

Like the skull and hour-glass, the scythe was often employed on memorials of the eighteenth century, acting, like those symbols, as a warning that life passes rapidly, to end but in the grave.

It is inappropriate on the Christian memorial as, beyond ignoring the fundamental Christian consideration of a future life, it implies that life ends with its material manifestation, and would express a warning consequent on this belief. It is appropriate, however, for those who believe that the death of the mind or soul occurs with the death of the body.

For further comment see notes on the kindred symbols: the hour-glass and skull.

SEAGULL—The California seagull (*Larus californicus*) is the state bird of Utah. Although it does not appear to have been officially adopted by state legislation, it is commonly so regarded. The reason is that in 1848 the seagulls from the lake islands saved the state from a serious plague of crickets, by devouring the insects. The bird is thus honoured in gratitude.

SEASONS—Representations of the seasons, which are often in themselves symbols by association, have often been employed as symbols of the life of man. This has frequently been done in memorial art. A simple and beautiful example is a carved memorial headstone by Gilbert Ledward, consisting of a cross in a square panel, in the corners of which are carved in relief a lamb, sunflower, grapes and falling leaves —the four seasons, expressing the cycle of man's life. It is simple but effective and eloquent.

SERAPHIM—An angel, usually represented in accordance with the description in Isaiah (vi. 2) with a head and six wings. In the Celestial Hierarchy of the pseudo-Dionysius the Areopagite, seraphim is the first rank of the first order and is nearest to God, existing in the immediate illumination that surrounds the throne of God. They are conceived of as of fiery character, having their being in the divine heat and fervour of adoration, and in harmony with this character they are usually coloured red by artists. (*See* Angel.)

SERPENT—The serpent is most commonly used as a symbol of evil and the evil spirit. It has, however, other meanings, of which, the principal are wisdom and healing.

In the numerous allegorical representations of the eternal conflict between the forces of good and evil, from the earliest Oriental and Greek myths to Christian times, an ugly and vicious monster known as a serpent or a dragon has continually served to represent the force of evil. The serpent was probably originally typified as a force of evil because the snakes among the ancient Oriental peoples were large and deadly; and from an Oriental tradition thus formed the Greeks conceived the serpent as an embodiment of evil. It so figures, for example, in the myth of Perseus and Andromeda; and a Greek symbol of victory was the eagle carrying the serpent in its talons. In Indian sculptures Brahma arises from the vanquished serpent; and it similarly lies prostrate at the feet of Christ, as in the Archbishop's cross in Addington churchyard (Fig. 56(*c*)) and in representations of many a Christian saint; while in some mediaeval representations of the cross the serpent lies at its foot as sin overthrown. The serpents or dragons, which figure in mediaeval Christian legends and mystery plays, are usually supposed to typify heresy, which was then considered by the Church to be the worst of all evils.

Coiled round the tree of knowledge, the serpent typifies the Christian notion of temptation by the evil spirit. This image of the serpent and the tree of knowledge, or of life, was familiar among Eastern peoples prior to Hebraism and Christianity, but with a different significance. The serpent was regarded as possessing the secrets of life, and was thus worshipped for its wisdom and shown encircling the tree of life. This corresponds in meaning to the Talmud myth that makes Lilith, the former wife of Adam, change into a serpent and impart to Eve the secret of the propagation of human life.

Serpent worship, with which is closely connected the serpent symbolizing wisdom, probably arose from its significance as a force of evil. It was thought by the early Eastern peoples that immunity from the venomous attacks of their great snakes would be achieved by propitiating the evil power behind them. This in due time led to serpent worship among many peoples, which was ultimately attended by many various customs and forms of ritual. That the notion of the serpent as a symbol of wisdom was widely current is supported by various testimonies. In Genesis iii. 1,[1] the serpent is spoken of as 'more subtle than any beast of the field'; and Christ exhorts His disciples to be 'wise as serpents and harmless as doves'. (Matthew x. 16.)

(*a*) An old shop sign with representation of the sunflower (marigold) turning towards the sun. The inscription 'ainsi mon ame' might be rendered: 'Thus, my soul'.

(*b*) Common marigold, probably the sunflower of the Greek myth.

Fig. 55. Sunflower.

Various legends exist which suggest the origin of the serpent as a symbol of healing. The traditional association of wisdom with the serpent may have contributed to this, for it was an old and widespread belief that the power to heal could be acquired by eating a part of the serpent, thereby assimilating the qualities deemed essential to medical skill—prudence and foresight and suchlike attributes of wisdom. There is a greater probability, however, that its association with the healing art arose, as the Greeks themselves claimed, from the analogy of the periodic sloughing of its skin, which suggested renovation.[2] Whatever the cause, the serpent was widely venerated in this capacity, and thus employed as a symbol of medicine. This, no doubt, explains Moses' brazen serpent which healed the snake-bitten Israelites who beheld it (Numbers xxi. 8 and 9), not unlike a custom observed in parts of India of making an image of a serpent in metal or clay and offering sacrifices on behalf of those requiring medical aid.

There is considerable evidence to support the theory that the serpent which was venerated in early Greece for its healing powers was gradually anthropomorphized, by the natural Greek tendency, into their god of medicine (called Asklêpius, Aesculapius[3] by the Romans). In Greek and Roman mythology, it will be remembered, Asklêpius often performed his functions in the form of a serpent, as, for example, in travelling from Epidaurus, his supposed home and place of birth, to the shrine of Sicyon; and again in journeying to Rome to stay a pestilence, where a temple was afterwards erected in his honour. Asklêpius is usually represented in art as an old man with a staff, round which coils a serpent. This staff and serpent became a device widely adopted by physicians from Roman times to the Middle Ages. It is still occasionally seen, the most noteworthy example being the regimental badge of the Royal Army Medical Corps.

Among many ancient peoples and among many African tribes of the present day, there is a belief that the soul of the dead exists in the form of a serpent, and in this form the old home is often visited. The relatives and friends of the departed usually feed the serpent, mostly with milk, and various customs have attended its reception. In early Greek civilization, where the belief existed, the serpent became a popular symbol of the dead. The not uncommon subject in Greek art of a woman feeding a snake from a kylix of milk probably originated with the idea of ministering to the soul of the dead embodied in the serpent. Sir James Frazer cites the instances of two tombstones found at Tegea, where 'a man and a woman are respectively represented holding out to a serpent a cup which may be supposed to contain milk'.[4] Is there not a similarity of spirit in these tombstones to the ancestor worship of the Spartan stelae? Both depict the living making offerings to propitiate the spirits of their ancestors.

The serpent finds a place in modern ecclesiastical design[5] as the traditional Christian typification of the force of evil. It is shown in opposition to, and vanquished by, the force of good in the sense of Christianity triumphing over the forces of evil. The expression of the idea that most readily comes to the English mind is St. George and the dragon (to the Irish mind St. Patrick and the serpent, and so on), a subject employed considerably for memorials of the First World War, the most famous being the Cavalry Memorial in Hyde Park. The staff and serpent of Aesculapius might fittingly appear in a design connected with medical or surgical interests.

1. And II Corinthians xi. 3.
2. 'The Myth of Tylon', given in SIR JAMES FRAZER's *Adonis, Attis and Osiris*, Vol. i, pp. 186 *et seq.*, may have had something to do with the origin of the idea.
3. *See* SIR J. G. FRAZER's *Pausanias*, Vol. iii, p. 65 (1898).
4. *Adonis, Attis and Osiris*, Vol. i, p. 87 (1914).
5. In Kensal Green Cemetery there is a headstone to Mrs. Sarah Ride, d. 2nd April, 1851, and other members of the family, which shows a large snake curled round the headstone. That is the only subject. It would be interesting to know what idea determined it.

SEVEN—*See* Number Symbolism.

SHAMROCK—A national emblem and symbol of Ireland.

The association of the shamrock with Ireland is due to the legend that St. Patrick employed it to illustrate the doctrine of the Trinity. The legend is not, however, derived from the earliest lives of St. Patrick. One account, made popular by S. Baring-Gould,[1] is that at Easter-time one year St. Patrick was at Slane, where the native king and nobles were preparing for the festival in honour of their sun-god. The preparation consisted of fires being extinguished for a period, to be rekindled at an appointed time from the fire in the temple of Temora. All fires were extinguished in the neighbourhood with the exception of St. Patrick's. The king and nobles rode indignantly towards it, and the king demanded that St. Patrick should be brought before him. He commanded that on the following day, which was Easter Day, St. Patrick should, in his presence, contend with the priests and wise men. It was while thus preaching on that day that St. Patrick plucked a shamrock to demonstrate the doctrine of the Trinity and the triple personality of God.

The particular plant usually regarded as the Irish shamrock is the lesser yellow-trefoil (*Trifolium mimus*).

1. *Lives of the Saints*, pp. 296 *et seq.*, 17th March (London, 1897).

SHELL—In Christianity the scallop-shell is symbolic of pilgrimage, due originally to its association with St. James major, patron saint of Spain.

One of the numerous legends concerned with St. James is that, after the ascension, the apostle travelled to Spain and preached there. After his death in Judea, as recorded in Acts xii. 2, his body was brought to Spain by Hermogenes and Philetus. It appears to have been lost for several centuries owing to the invasions of the barbarians, to be discovered during the eighth century and transported to Compostella, where it became the object of pilgrimage. The pilgrims wore scallop-shells in their hats because of its association with St. James. This habit of pilgrims to Compostella seems to have been followed by other pilgrims, and so the scallop-shell became a general symbol of pilgrimage. Thus Sir Walter Raleigh, in his unfinished poem, *The Passionate Man's Pilgrimage*, says:

> Give me my scallop-shell of quiet,
> My staff of faith to walk upon
> My scrip of joy (immortal diet!)
> My bottle of salvation,
> My gown of glory, hope's true gage;
> And thus I'll make my pilgrimage.

And Thomas Parnell says of *The Hermit* that he travels

> . . . to know the world by sight,
> To find if books or swains report it right,
> He quits his cell; the pilgrim-staff he bore,
> And fixed the scallop in his hat before

Why the scallop-shell is associated with St. James is difficult to discover. That it is an old and familiar association dating from at least the beginning of the Compostella pilgrimage there is little doubt. So familiar is the association that it is responsible for the naming of a species of scallop, the *Pecten Jacobaeus*. One legend seemingly accounts for it, but this affords such a poor reason that it is only repeated in the absence of a better; and it cannot be regarded as supplying the probable reason for the association.

When the body of St. James was being conveyed in a boat from Joppa to Galicia, it was passing near the shore where a marriage party was riding, when the bridegroom's horse took fright and plunged into the sea. The horse and rider miraculously rose above the waves near the boat that carried the body of St. James, the horse and rider's dress being covered with scallop-shells. The disciples of St. James explained to the bridegroom that he was saved by the agency of St. James. So impressed was the bridegroom that he was immediately baptized in the Christian faith; and then rode back over the waves to his astonished friends. On hearing his story they were all baptized and became Christians.

The scallop-shell occasionally appears on various early Christian objects, such as lamps, a few examples being in the British Museum. It also appears on Roman lead coffins, which may or may not have been Christian. Whether, in early Christian art, the shell was used as a symbol or merely as an ornament is uncertain for it is not known when it became a symbol. The pilgrimage to Compostella did not begin until the latter part of the eighth century, but the association of the scallop-shell with St. James may have existed before that.

SHEPHERD AND SHEEP—Symbol of Christ's care for His followers.

In the first four centuries of Christianity the Good Shepherd with a single sheep or with his flock was one of the most important symbols. It probably originated with Christ's interpretation of His own parable of the Shepherd and Sheep, when He says: 'I am the good shepherd.'[1] The symbol is found in the catacomb paintings, sarcophagi, lamps and seals. In these early representations Christ is merely a young shepherd, there is no attempt at representing the image of Christ. Thus it is purely a symbol, unlike conceptions of the subject in modern art where the shepherd is the traditional image of Christ. There are two principal variations of the symbol in the catacombs: one depicts the shepherd carrying the strayed or injured sheep on his shoulders, the other depicts him seated among his flock, sometimes playing a lyre.[2] The former obviously signifies one strayed from the flock into sin being saved and brought back to the flock by Christ; while the other shows Christ tending the faithful who are secure in His keeping. The former subject is responsible for one of the finest statues in early Christian art, namely, that found in the catacomb of St. Callistus and now in the Lateran. The lyre is probably an interfusion of the Orpheus myth,

315

for Orpheus was also a shepherd who enchanted all beings with his music. Christ's teaching was thus symbolized by the enchanting music of Orpheus, and the Good Shepherd symbol was thereby considerably enriched. Thus Christ was sometimes symbolized by Orpheus himself.

This subject did not survive long after the time of the catacombs, and is rarely seen much after the sixth century. It occurs occasionally in mosaics, the most famous representation being that in the mausoleum of Galla Placidia at Ravenna of the fifth century. But in this mosaic, though Christ is still shown as a beardless young man, a representation derived from Classical art, the portrayal is no longer of the simple shepherd, but of Christ enthroned, with the nimbus, and staff terminated with a cross. The subject was sometimes adopted for church west windows, signifying that at the entrance of the church Christ gathers His flock. Christ's words, 'I am the door of the sheep' (John x. 7), may also have suggested this.

The subject was revived in painting in the latter part of the sixteenth century, but, as already mentioned, it is no longer the youthful shepherd with his flock, but the image of Christ. In this change much of the poetry of the symbolism is lost.

It was common in early Christian art to represent the apostles as sheep standing six on either side of the Good Shepherd; but after the fifth century the latter was supplanted by the lamb of the Apocalypse.

The use in ecclesiastical design of the symbol of the Good Shepherd, depicted not as Christ but simply as a shepherd, would be a revival of one of the most important early Christian symbols, which has rarely been employed for fourteen centuries. It is one of the most beautiful of religious symbols.

The image of the shepherd carrying the strayed and wounded sheep on his shoulders is expressive symbolism denoting the humble faith of those who have strayed in life from Christ and true religious conduct, but, having repented of their errors, will, by God's mercy and the Shepherd's tender solicitude, be carried back to the fold and to salvation. The symbol used sepulchrally may be interpreted as an invocation that Christ should treat the departed sinner as a shepherd treats a lost sheep: in the words of the Greek liturgy: 'I am the lost sheep; call me, O Lord, and save me.'

1. St. John x. 11 and 14. In this chapter of St. John, Christ explains at length the meaning of His parable. See also St. John xxi. 15–17; St. Luke xv. 4 and 5; and Hebrews xiii. 20.
2. See excellent account of the Good Shepherd symbols in LOWRIE'S *Monuments of the Early Church*, pp. 214–21. Also TWINING, *Symbols of Early Christian Art*, pp. 35–8, 115 and 116.

SHIP—Symbol of the Christian Church.

This appears in the catacombs and dates a little later than the ark symbol of which it seems to have been a development. The ark symbolizes the Church of Christ and is meant to suggest that in the midst of the vast wickedness of the world the faithful are saved; while the ship symbolizes the Church as carrying the faithful safely over the perilous seas of life. To suggest its significance the ship was usually depicted with symbolic attributes, such as the mast, in the form of the cross and the dove perched on the sails. In some representations the ship is carried on the back of the fish, indicating that members of the Church are piloted through the seas of life by Christ. To be understood in modern design in its religious significance the ship must of necessity have these symbolic accessories; it is otherwise bound to be confused with the ship as a symbol of a maritime life.

SIRENS—the sirens, the sea nymphs of Greek mythology, who lured men by their beautiful yet fatal songs, have often been employed as symbols of empty or deceptive attraction. In the Odyssey they probably signified the beauties of a calm sea luring men to destruction.

Representations of sirens and harpies have appeared on Greek sepulchral monuments, probably as symbols of death.

SKULL (sometimes with crossbones)—Symbol of mortality.

This symbol seems first to have been used in England during the early sixteenth century. At this time effigies of half-decomposed bodies and skeletons were sometimes represented on tombs, as may be seen in Exeter and Salisbury cathedrals.

Its use was unpopular during the Puritan régime, but was revived and became one of the commonest symbols on eighteenth-century memorials. Like its kindred the hour-glass and scythe, it reflects the somewhat pagan philosophic tendency and pessimistic religious spirit of that period. It is not surprising that an age extending from Swift to Hume and Gibbon, an age rich in satire of life, and in its religious writings concentrating overmuch on the vanity of earthly things and the corrupt nature of man, should place such symbols on its tombstones.

The skull with the hour-glass and scythe (Fig. 54(a)) is obviously intended as a reminder that time passes rapidly, that death fast approaches, that life is not endless; a reminder that is often supported by the epitaphs which accompany the representations. F. E. Hulme[1] speaks of a poignant depicture on a tombstone at Basel in which the figure of Death in the form of a skeleton has seized with his bony hands the shield of the family armorial bearings, 'with all its testimony of earthly rank and dignity, and rent it from top to bottom'.

1. F. E. HULME. *The History, Principles, and Practice of Symbolism in Christian Art* (London, 1891).

SNAKE—*See* Serpent and Rattlesnake.

SPACE—In architecture and painting a sense of space is sometimes created as an expression of the infinite and of associated religious emotion, and thus space could be said in such work to have symbolical purpose. The most conspicuous examples in architecture are the great cathedrals where a feeling of space is stimulated by a vast enclosure such as the interior of St. Peter's at Rome. In many of the interiors of very high Gothic cathedrals like Amiens, Chartres, Milan and Liverpool (to give a modern example), the lofty vaults, sometimes half lost in shadow, combine the feeling of space with a sense of mystery and aspiration all expressive of religious emotion. (*See* Chapter XVIII—Architecture.)

The sense of space is created also in some painting, such as the religious pictures of Perugino and Raphael where Christ, the Virgin, saints and devotional figures are seen against a landscape with almost illimitable distance, which suggests the infinite. This feeling of limitless space is sometimes created by landscapes which are known to promote a pantheistic emotion, landscapes such as Rubens' 'Chateau Steen' and Turner's 'Crossing the Brook'. (*See* Chapter XX—Painting.)

Space is often an important element in design in the visual arts, as silence is in music. It has been used as an element in sculpture, in the work of Constructivists like Naum Gabo, in which personal symbolic expression is sometimes apparent.

SPEAR—*See* Sceptre.

SPHINX—Ancient Egyptian symbol of power. Popular in modern time as a symbol of Egypt.

The earliest and most important Egyptian sphinxes were composed of a recumbent body of a lion with a bearded man's head, which Egyptologists regard as the head of the reigning monarch. The purpose of this sphinx seems to have been to express the power of the reigning monarch by associating his image with the utmost of physical power symbolized by the body of the lion. The most famous, largest, and probably the oldest remaining, is the Great Sphinx at Gizeh, carved out of a large rocky protuberance in the sand.[1] From its situation near the Pyramid it is probably a work of the same period—that is, of the third or fourth dynasty. Numerous sphinxes of a similar type remain, although of a more modest size. The two granite sphinxes of Thotmes III and Amenem-Het III in the Cairo Museum, casts of which are in the British Museum, give an idea of a common size—that is, from five to eight feet in length. Small sphinxes about one foot six inches in length were common. They were probably placed on pedestals in the temples.

There were three main types of Egyptian sphinx, each with a lion's recumbent body: the androsphinx, with a man's head; the criosphinx, with a ram's head; and the hieracosphinx, with a falcon's head, so named by the Greeks. The meaning of the ram-headed and falcon-headed sphinxes would appear to be that both the ram and falcon were sacred, the ram being a form of the god Khnemu, and the falcon a form of the god Horus. Their association with the body of a lion was an expression of their power.

Sphinxes appear in Assyrian art in the ninth century B.C., in ivory carvings, sculptures, and bronze and terracotta vessels. From their character it is obvious that they were derived from Egypt. They have the lion's body with the man's, falcon's, or ram's head. The differences are that the lion is walking and wings are added. But the closest Assyrian parallel to the Egyptian sphinxes are the two large human-headed winged lions which were placed at the entrance of the palace of Sargon.[2] It is not improbable that these were suggested as symbols of power by the Egyptian sphinx.

The Greek sphinx was probably derived from the Egyptian and Assyrian, but by the time it appeared in classical Greece it had been changed to sitting posture, and had a female head and breasts. To the Greeks it was a symbol of enigmatic wisdom, exemplified by the famous riddle ultimately solved by Oedipus. This meaning has been wrongly extended in modern times to the Egyptian sphinx.

So prominent and distinctive an object among Egyptian antiquities has not unnaturally become a popular symbol of Egypt—indicating at once some association with that country. It thus figures on numerous crests or badges of British regiments which have fought important engagements in Egypt. The Lincolnshire, Gloucestershire, and East Lancashire regiments, the South Wales Borderers and Royal Welch Fusiliers, all have crests in which the sphinx figures. It also appears on monuments of those whose life's work has been in or connected with Egypt; a few being in St. Paul's Cathedral and Westminster Abbey.

1. The face of this sphinx appears without a beard, but it is thought that this crumbled away centuries ago.
2. The two lions are from Nimrod and are now in the British Museum. Four bulls of a similar character are from Khorsabad, two of which are now in the British Museum and two in the Louvre.

SPIRAL—The spiral has sometimes been regarded as a symbol of movement and progressive development. As a symbol of growth it obviously derives from the spiral growth of numerous climbing plants. The other meanings indicated are an easy transition from this.

The lituus of the Roman augur was shaped at the end in spiral form. It was the staff used to mark out the sacred area (*see* Temple), and by association was sometimes used as a symbol of a sacred place.

The spiral figures widely as an architectural ornament, particularly in Greek and Celtic designs. The best known device is the volute of the Ionic and Corinthian capitals. It is conjectural that in ancient Greece there was a staff with a spiral terminal like the Roman lituus to mark out a sacred space, and as the Ionic capital was first used in temples, the volute may have been derived from this spiral terminal and used as an associational symbol.

SPIRE—The church spire symbolises religious aspiration. It has been referred to as 'a finger pointing heavenwards', and Goethe in his autobiography speaks of it as aspiring to heaven without as the dome encloses heaven within.

The spire first appears as a tall pyramidal termination to a tower in Romanesque architecture of the eleventh century; but in Gothic architecture it is greatly increased in height to such lofty examples as that of Ulm Cathedral (529 feet high) and Salisbury Cathedral (404 feet high).

SPRINGBOK—National emblem of South Africa, the springbok figures as the dexter supporter of the South Africa coat of arms, the sinister supporter being the oryx or gemsbok, a large antelope.

The springbok is a small gazelle native to South Africa. It was once common over the whole area of the country, but with the spread of civilization it is now seen in its wild state chiefly in the regions south of the Zambesi. Representations of the springbok are widely used on objects associated with South Africa.

SPURS—Symbol of knighthood.

When a person was knighted in the Middle Ages, he was often presented with a pair of spurs; thus the saying 'win his spurs', which has come also to mean endeavour or ambition to obtain eminence or high merit. Spurs figure in the English Coronation ceremony. After the anointing, the king's heels are touched with the golden spurs, which are then returned to the altar. At the Coronation of Elizabeth II, she touched them with her right hand.

STAG—*See* Hart.

STAR—Figuratively and symbolically the star expresses supremacy in a particular sphere. Thus in ancient times in the East a star was a symbol of the Deity. Christ is referred to in Revelation xxii. 16 as the 'bright and morning star'; but the chief association of the symbol with Christianity arises from the star that led the Magi to Bethlehem. This was supposed to be the morning star, and as the morning star heralds the dawn, it symbolized Christ, as Christ's birth heralded the passing of the world from night to day—from the darkness of sin to the light of salvation. This analogy may have suggested the passage in Revelation.

Colonel Mackinlay[1] has endeavoured to show that in the figurative language of the Gospels St. John the Baptist regarded himself and was thought of as the morning star that heralded the rising sun (Christ) in such passages as: 'He must increase, but I must decrease,'[2] and 'He was the lamp that burneth and shineth'.[3] The analogy is apt and beautiful, but there is no tradition to support its employment in this sense.

The star is often associated with the Virgin Mary; an association which probably originated from the Roman Catholic interpretation of her Jewish name Miriam as 'Stella Maris', star of the sea. In the Old Testament there are allusions which, to some minds, make the starry host symbols of the angels of heaven. Such a thought doubtless prompted designs of the starry sky on the apse roof of some churches. But these meanings are wholly subordinate in Christianity to the morning star symbolizing Christ, and it is chiefly in this sense that it can appear in ecclesiastical design.

1. *The Magi: How they Recognized Christ's Star*, pp. 56 *et seq.*, 1907.
2. John iii. 30.
3. John v. 35.

STONE AND STONES—Symbols of durability, of permanence and indestructibility. Stones of various kinds have been the objects of worship among numerous peoples from earliest times until the middle ages, and in some instances, even among civilized peoples, as late as the nineteenth century. Among primitive peoples stones, especially those that are large and impressive in appearance, were often conceived as the abode of a spirit or god and were thus worshipped, as trees were worshipped. Also, in ancient times, meteorites when they were not dissipated as dust and reached the earth as large and impressive boulders, were venerated as having been sent by the sky- or sun-god, and were sometimes thought of as the abode of a spirit. In ancient Greece large meteorites were often regarded as having been despatched by Zeus. The fifth-century Greek philosopher Anaxagoras mentions a stone that fell in Thrace as having been sent by Zeus and there are many other examples.[1]

Why other stones were conceived as the abode of gods or spirits it is more difficult to say, but it is probably partly connected with their indestructibility and partly with their impressive appearance and partly, in the case of some stones, the ability to read into them an approximation to a human shape, an ability that has existed among sculptors of all ages.

The allusions in Greek mythology to persons being turned into stone are open to various interpretations. The account in the Iliad of Niobe, after the death of her children, being turned into stone may have been no more than the figurative use of language—that she became petrified with grief. This view is supported by the Greek fourth-century poet, Philemon, who suggested that Niobe, because of her calamities, became speechless and so, from her silence, was called a stone.

When stones came to be used for various purposes they often acquired associational symbolism. Among primitive and ancient societies stones were used to mark spots and among familiar uses were as memorial boundaries and witness stones. Their use for all these purposes was because of their durability and indestructibility. For commemorative purposes they have been used, judging by remains, for at least six thousand years, and are still used in very large numbers as the cemeteries of the world will testify. The widespread use of granite for such a purpose is obviously because it is regarded as the most indestructible of stones.

When in primitive times a sacred place for devotion was defined, stones were often used for marking the boundary, which is the explanation of stone circles. Such stones acquired by association a sacred character. Boundary stones were also used to define the extent of properties, but in ancient Babylon, which provides the most famous examples, the boundary stone for a property was set up in a temple, inscribed with the title deeds. This inscription appears to have been a copy of the deeds inscribed on a clay tablet. Carved emblems of gods appear on many of these stones, probably to invite their protection of the title deeds.

Witness stones used in various countries have a similar purpose. Some have been found among Celtic stones in which holes have been carved, notable examples existing in Ireland. One interpretation of these is that the holes were carved to enable persons making a contract to clasp hands through the stone and declare the appropriate oath.

A large number of special stones are recorded in all times. Pliny[2] and later writers mention several. Many have acquired some associational symbolism. The most interesting for a British public, an account of which will be given as an example, is the Coronation Stone, sometimes called the 'Stone of Scone' and sometimes the 'Stone of Destiny'. It has rested beneath the Coronation Chair in Westminster Abbey since the thirteenth century, except for a brief period when Scottish Nationalists stole the stone on Christmas Day, 1950. It was returned in April, 1951. This incident prompted a debate in the House of Lords in the following month on the right place for the stone.[3] The debate was initiated by Lord Brabazon of Tara who gave a very interesting history of the stone, a history which is obviously partly speculative and probably partly apocryphal.

Lord Brabazon imagined that 'it must have been about 1900 B.C.—nearly 4,000 years ago—that Jacob, afterwards to be called Isaac, had his great dream. He had this Stone as the pillow upon which he slept when he had the dream; and in the dream he received from Jehovah a promise that his descendants would be a great people and populate the whole world, and that all the nations of the world would thereby be blessed. Jacob was so impressed that he turned the Stone on end and anointed it, saying: "This Stone which I have set up for a pillow shall be God's House." And that Stone became for them an enduring witness of the great divine promise, and on his deathbed Jacob instructed Joseph to guard it well.

'That Stone was looked upon as sacred by the Israelites, and was their greatest possession. Through all the wilderness and the wanderings it was taken with them. You can see on it today how it has been worn by the many journeys that it took on those days. At long last it found its true home in Jerusalem, in the Temple, alongside the Ark of the Covenant. Those two things were to the Israelites the two most sacred things in the world. All the Kings of the Royal House of David were crowned upon the Stone, until we come to the last King of Judea, Hezekiah. Hezekiah's history concerns us a little—for this reason. He conspired with the Egyptians to overcome Nebuchadnezzar. They were defeated, and Hezekiah was brought up before Nebuchadnezzar; both his sons were killed before him, and he had his eyes put out. That was meant to be the end of the Royal House of David. Well, Jeremiah, a prophet of those days, had always prophesied disaster for Judea if the policy of Hezekiah was continued.

'It is very odd that, when one looks in the Bible and sees a catalogue of the remarkable things that were taken from the Temple and Jerusalem, there is no mention of what must have been the most valuable thing of all—namely, the Ark of the Covenant. I can quite see that Nebuchadnezzar, not knowing the history, did not think the Stone valuable; but he must have thought that the Ark of the Covenant was valuable. The Ark of the Covenant disappeared. It was obviously taken by somebody who had, first of all, a privileged position, such as Jeremiah had, and was hidden away. Whether it is hidden today in Palestine, or whether he took it with him and it is buried today on the hill of Tara, nobody knows. But it was certainly taken by Jeremiah, who also took the Stone. He left Palestine and went into Egypt, and he took with him the two daughters of Hezekiah, Tamar and Scota—and this is a most important point. Jeremiah dwelt in Egypt for some time, and then there is evidence to show that he went as far west as he could, and stopped on the way in Spain, where the younger daughter, Scota, was married. But he ended up in Ireland with the elder daughter, Tamar, and she was married to the King of Ireland of the day.

'It is interesting to notice in Irish records how Jeremiah was proclaimed on arrival as the great prophet, known in Irish language as Ollam Fodla; and wrapped up with the great prophet are all the stories and legends: the "Stone wonderful" as it was referred to—"lia fail". As I have said, Princess Tamar married the King of Ireland. The king's name was Hereman, and the date was 600 B.C. All the kings of Ireland from that date were crowned upon the Stone on Tara Hill for a thousand years, and it was not until later, in the fifth century, that Fergus, who was King of Ireland, moved into Scotland. Whether he conquered it, or just occupied it, I cannot find out, but he became the first King of Argyll. Knowing the value of having the respect and desire to be crowned King of Scotland upon that Stone, he sent for it from Ireland, and brought it from Tara to a place called Dunstaffnage, which was his capital. There he was crowned upon it, and became King Fergus the Great.

'So it went on; and in the reign of Conran, in 563 A.D., he, being the third King of Argyll, at the request of St. Colomba, sent the Stone to the island which was then called Hy, and is now known as Iona. St. Colomba took a very prominent part in the early development of Christianity, and the island of Iona is always remembered and held sacred through the activities of St. Colomba in those days. Colomba died with his head upon the Stone. It remained there for 300 years. The kings of Argyll were crowned on it until we come to MacAlpin, who became King of Scotland in the ninth century. He moved his capital from Perth, and the Stone was taken from Iona to Scone. It was therefore in Scotland for no fewer than 700 years. Finally, we come to what we might call modern days—that is, Edward I, 1296. He took the Stone to London after the Battle of Bannockburn. He should have restored it to Scotland. Whether it was in the Treaty or not is a little difficult to say, but certainly all the other regalia was restored to Scotland, though the Stone remained in England. It was not until James VI became King of England that, so to speak, it found its rightful place.'

Lord Brabazon, continuing, mentioned, 'that in the Coronation Service no mention is ever made of the King of England; it is always to the King of Great Britain and Ireland. It is of no interest to anybody to be crowned upon this Stone unless whoever is crowned is a descendant of David, and the Kings of Scotland claim to be descended—and rightly, I maintain—from the royal line of the House of David. I draw the attention of those of your Lordships who are interested in the very mystical ceremony of the Coronation, so very analogous to the ancient Israel's coronation. I just want to put those years in their right order: 1,300 years with Israel; 1,000 years at Tara; 900 years in Scotland, and 600 years here. Your Lordships will admit that it is a Stone with a tremendous history.'

Lord Brabazon concluded his speech with a plea that the Stone should be returned to Scotland, and brought to Westminster Abbey for the Coronation ceremony. Lord Brabazon was followed by the Duke of Montrose who said that 'there is a sort of mist about its past and no one seems to have the correct facts about its history'. Many peers joined in the debate and the majority spoke in favour of its return to Scotland. If it were returned, which seems unlikely, the ceremonial of its journey to Westminster Abbey for future coronations would call attention to it and to its symbolism more so than if it remained in Westminster Abbey.

What is that symbolism? It is implied in Lord Brabazon's speech that it signifies that whoever is crowned on this stone is a descendant from the royal line of David, a claim that is made for the royal family of Great Britain. And that claim has obvious Christian significance, and it could be said that it is a symbol of the Judaic kings and their Christian successors.

1. E. A. WALLIS BUDGE, *Guide to the Babylonian and Assyrian Antiquities in the British Museum* (London, 1922)
2. PLINY, *Natural History.*
3. *Parliamentary Debates (Hansard) House of Lords*, 9th May, 1951—columns 830–2.

STORK—Symbol of parental and, to a less extent, of filial piety and affection, derived from the habits of the bird.

The Hebrew name for stork, hǎsīdāh, meaning pious, indicates the ancient prominence of this characteristic of the bird. The Romans regarded it likewise, and it was engraved on the medals of princes who earned the title 'Pius'. With regard to its symbolism of filial affection, Dr. Stanley[1] cites a law among the Greeks, obliging children to support their parents, that employs a reference to these birds: *Πελασγικὸς νόμος*.

It was once erroneously thought that the stork pecked its young with its beak until they bled, and then healed them by licking them with its tongue. This fable occasionally served Elizabethan writers[2] as a simile for a lady's treatment of her lover.

In modern times the stork, as a symbol of parental and filial affection, is most popular in Mohammedan countries,[3] but it is still familiar in many Christian countries. A stork with a cradle hanging from its beak is often a decorative feature of a christening cake. In a design it would symbolize the idea of good parenthood, and the beautiful lines of the bird provide a good subject for effective decorative treatment.

1. *History of Birds*, p. 312 (1892).
2. LYLY, for instance, in *Euphues and his England*.
3. *See* DR. STANLEY's *History of Birds*, pp. 310–11.

STUPA—Buddhist symbol of the universe, of the absolute and of the nirvana. The term is a Sanscrit word and is sometimes in Western countries referred to by the prākrit word 'tope'.

The earliest surviving stupas are at Sanchi, in India, and date from the third century B.C. They are solid domical mounds containing sacred relics, the largest of which is of solid brickwork, 54 feet high, and 106 feet in diameter; at the top forming a small pinnacle is a sequence of three flat umbrellas symbolizing suzerainty and divine authority (*see* Umbrella). Most stupas contained sacred remains, and between the first century B.C. and the twelfth century A.D. very large numbers of all sizes were erected in a variety of designs wherever Buddhism spread—Ceylon, the Malay Islands, China, Korea and Japan, but whatever the design it always retains its domical shape. The stupa was also made in miniature form for the purpose of devotion and as a votive offering, and it sometimes formed the grave memorial.

The larger stupas became centres of devotion and as such were erected inside Buddhist temples and Caitya halls, an early famous example being that inside the Chaitya at Karli of the first century A.D. A stupa generally occupied a central position in earliest Buddhist monasteries such as the centre of a square or circular courtyard surrounded by monks' cells.

The stupa may have originally been erected as an artificial hill symbolical of the sacred hill where the god dwelt, but it is more probable that it was shaped in imitation of the dome of the sky—the vault of the heaven—as a symbol of the universe.[1]

An interesting example of sacred remains contained in a stupa is provided by one of the large stupas at Sanchi or at Satdhara (6 miles west of Sanchi) as there is some uncertainty about the actual one. It contained, it is thought, the ashes in small caskets, of Sariputta and Mahamoggallana, the two principal disciples of Buddha. These were taken by General Cunningham in 1851 and brought to England and deposited in the Victoria and Albert Museum. After Indian Home Rule in 1947 there was a request for their return, which was done in 1949 and a special temple was built to receive them.[2]

1. DIETRICH SECKEL, *The Art of Buddhism* (Baden-Baden and London, 1964). English translation by Ann E. Keep, p. 103.
2. *Pilgrimage to Sanchi, Story of Enshrinement of Buddhist Relics*, Current Affairs Publications (New Delhi, 1951).

SUN—In earlier periods of ancient sun-worship the sun was identified monotheistically with *the* deity, or polytheistically with *a* deity, and thus representations of the sun were conventional imitations of divine manifestation. The various symbols of the sun as a deity are treated under their separate headings. When, in religious development, the sun was no longer regarded as a deity, but merely as an instrument of the deity, representations of the sun, expressing God, became more completely symbolic.

The Hebrews, as is well known, regarded the sun only as the instrument of the Deity and as conforming to His will.[1] The Old Testament affords many examples of the enmity of the prophets of God towards sun-worshippers.

Considering the extensive traditions of sun-worship, and the regard paid to the sun as a principal instrument of God, it was perhaps inevitable that Christianity should use it as a metaphor. Thus Christ is termed the 'Sun of Righteousness'.

For commemorative purposes the symbol is most appropriate as a sunset. Sunset of life is so familiar a metaphor that the meaning of a sunset in commemorative design would be obvious. That the sun always sets to rise again makes it acceptable to Christian feeling, though the symbol of the lotus or similar flower is more beautiful, because here the sun corresponds to the deity, and the flower, dependent for its life on the sun, corresponds to human life.

1. Isaiah xxxviii. 8, and Joshua x. 12 and 13.

SUNDIAL—Although once an instrument for measuring the hours, it is now used as a symbol of time in the same sense as the scythe and hour-glass. Such impersonal symbols are suitable for general rather than personal application. They are employed in many English churchyards where one sundial appears in the midst of the grave-stones, or as an ornamental feature in gardens, to remind us that life is brief.

SUNFLOWER—Symbol of gratitude and affectionate remembrance.

The name is applied vaguely to many flowers of the large daisy type which turn in their growth towards the sun.

The symbol originates with the Greek myth in which Clytie, first beloved of Apollo, was forsaken for Leucothoë, and Clytie in jealousy informed her rival's father of the amours of his daughter with Apollo. As punishment Apollo transformed Clytie into a sunflower and she ever afterwards, in remembrance of their love, turns her face in gratitude towards the sun.

In sculptures Clytie is usually shown surrounded by sunflower petals. The bust by Watts in the Tate Gallery is a beautiful example. It is improbable, however, that the large flower commonly known in this country as the sunflower (*Helianthus annus*), which appears to be that employed by modern sculptors in their conceptions of Clytie, is the flower of the Greek myth. This large sunflower was introduced into this country from America after the name sunflower was used in English. Many think that the flower of the Greek myth was the common single marigold (*Calendula officinalis*). As records of this flower, or a flower very similar, have existed in Europe for centuries, and as the character of the marigold and its habit of turning towards the light make the designation of sunflower very appropriate, it is not improbable that the marigold was the sunflower of the Greeks.

The interesting old shop sign (probably late sixteenth century), shown in the illustration, which used to hang over Child's Bank,[1] depicts the marigold turning towards the sun. It is evidently an illustration of the Greek myth. The words under the sign—'Ainsi, mon âme,'—Thus, my soul—doubtless express Clytie's love and gratitude for the sun. (Fig. 55(*a*).)

The myth has been fancifully translated into Christian terms, the sun becoming God, and Clytie becoming the penitent Christian. This may have suggested to Robertson the idea of speaking, in one of his sermons, of the Christian life as 'the turning of the sunflower to the sun'.

Symbolizing gratitude and affectionate remembrance, it could be used in commemorative design in two ways: from the standpoint of the deceased as thanks for a happy life,[2] and from the standpoint of the mourners who express their affectionate remembrance. Both are gracious thoughts, and though the symbol is perhaps a little remote from us, its symbolic beauty makes it worth reviving.

The sunflower (*Helianthus*) is the state flower of Kansas, having been officially adopted in 1903. In the state enactment by which the flower was adopted, it is stated that it 'has to all Kansas a historic symbolism which speaks of frontier days, winding trails, pathless prairies, and is full of the life and glory of the past, the pride of the present, and richly emblematic of the majesty of a golden future, and is a flower which has given Kansas the world-wide name "The Sunflower State".'

1. It now hangs inside the Bank building over the main door.
2. Both Hazlitt and Millais expressed thanks for a happy life.

SWAN—The white swan was probably at one time a symbol of the Virgin Mary, and generally of beautiful virgins, because of the suggestion of purity and grace. An Order of the Swan was formed in 1440 in the Electorate of Brandenburg, composed of thirty gentlemen and seven ladies, in honour of the Blessed Virgin, and the badge of membership consisted of a medal of the Virgin to which was attached the effigy of a swan, obviously used as a symbol of the Virgin.

Spenser in his poem *Prothalamion* uses the symbolism of the swan for two young brides. . . . He dwells on the extreme whiteness of the birds:

> Two fairer birds I yet did never see;
> The snow which doth the top of Pindus strew
> Did never whiter shew
> Nor Jove himselfe, when he a Swan would be,
> For love of Leda, whiter did appeare;
> Yet Leda was (they say) as white as he,
> Yet not so white as these, nor nothing neare;
> So purely white they were
> That even the gentle streame, the which them bore
> Seem'd foule to them.

Five swans symbolize the five Scandinavian countries, Denmark, Finland, Iceland, Norway and Sweden, and this symbolism is increasingly used as the co-ordination between the five countries becomes closer. A postage stamp was issued in 1956 in each of the five countries, representing five swans in flight.

SWASTIKA—Considered by most archaeologists as having originated as a diagrammatic representation of the sun's course in the heavens, it became an ancient symbol of revival and prosperity (Fig.54 (*c*)).

(a) Wheel cross. Small wheel crosses similar to this are in the churchyards of Millport and St. Blane, Buteshire, Scotland.

(b) Ring cross. This particular shape is taken from the famous cross at Gosforth, Cumberland.

(c) Upper part of archbishop's cross in Addington church-yard, erected in 1911. Christ, as the Good Shepherd, is shown with his right foot on the head of a serpent, thus signifying the triumph of Christianity over evil.

Fig. 56.

327

Swastika is the commonest name given to this widely distributed ancient symbol, formed approximately like four gammas joined together at their bases. Swastika is a Sanscrit word composed of *su* ('well'), and *asti* ('being') with the suffix *ka*, thus meaning 'well-being'. In India it is called swastika when the arms turn clock-wise, and sauwastika when they turn anti-clockwise. In England it received the name fylfot. Goblet D'Alviella explains the derivation of fylfot as 'from the Norse as *fiol* (full, *viel*—'numerous') and *fot* (foot).[1] The Oxford Dictionary, however, says that the origin of the term is found in a mediaeval (1500) manuscript containing instructions for the decoration of a memorial window. The context implies that the term alludes to a pattern to fill the foot of the window: thus 'fill foot'. It may in this case have meant any convenient pattern, but, as the swastika was probably the commonest of all known patterns, it gradually became associated with fylfot. It is also sometimes called Thor's hammer, and gammadion, but the sign is much older than any of its names.

The importance of the swastika in the history of symbolism is second to none. In ancient times it was employed in most countries and in various religions from Western Europe to India and China. The only countries in which it never seems to have appeared are Egypt, Babylon, and Assyria. It occurs on coins of Crete; on Mycenaeian ornaments; on ancient pottery and coins of Greece, Cyprus, Rhodes, and Etruria; in representations of the feet of Buddha and on numerous ornaments connected with Indian religions; on ancient coins of Gaul; in Roman mosaics; and in the catacombs it is associated or identified with the cross, which also doubtless explains its presence on Christian tombstones in Ireland and Scotland.

Many different opinions have been expressed as to its original meaning;[2] it will suffice here to note the meaning which is supported by the greatest evidence and which has received the widest support from archaeologists.[3]

The chief deity, or chief instrument of the deity, amongst many ancient religions was naturally held to be the sun. The sun was conceived of as being the great force of good whence was derived light and warmth without which there is no life. All religions had numerous symbols and myths expressing veneration for the sun. Many of the heroes of the Greek myths were but fanciful allegories of the sun's journey in the heavens where dangers were overcome for the good of mankind. Even the beautiful Greek love stories are based on the symbolism of the sun. The myths of Apollo and Daphne, and Orpheus and Eurydice express the sad but inevitable death of the dawn at the gradual approach of the sun.

The other symbols that seem to have gained a similarly wide currency among ancient peoples, namely, the disk and equilateral cross, and more especially the former, are often represented with the swastika. The likeness of the disk to the sun, and its association with the gammadion implies a similar meaning in the two symbols. Often, as on some Cretan coins, the sun is shown in the centre of the swastika, which suggests its association with the sun. D'Alviella has shown how a representation of the sun in three or four positions of its course would indicate the sun's course in the heavens, as is done in modern astronomical diagrams. The sun in three or four positions is distinctly shown in some ancient Hindu representations. Similarly the swastika depicts the sun's various positions on its course, and also gives a distinct impression of rotary movement by means of its arms.

The sun among ancient peoples being a principal source of life, the swastika became associated with prosperity, fecundity, and propitious events. It thus came to be regarded as a charm by many peoples, especially in India. Its chief interest to the student of Christian symbolism is that it was often used as a variety of the cross. It was particularly acceptable in this capacity as it was universally considered a portent of good faith. By reason of its similarity to the cross, its pre-Christian universality was thought by some Christians—with a faith not unnatural in ardent religious believers—to be a sign of Christ's coming.

As the subject of this diagrammatic figure is the course of the sun, whence we derive light and means of life, typifying the idea of regeneration, which on certain occasions inevitably finds expression, the revival of its use is always a possibility. An illustration of this in recent times is provided by its use as the German Nazi emblem.

In what sense was it employed by Hitler? Some have contended that he employed it because of some anti-Semitic significance, but there is no evidence to support this. Hitler in his speeches, however, referred to the swastika as that symbol of resurrection, of the revival of national life. He thus uses it in what is probably its ancient traditional significance of regeneration and the revival of life. It will be noted that as the Nazi emblem it was shown black on a white disk, and thus repeats the ancient association of these two sun symbols.

1. *The Migration of Symbols*, p. 39.
2. Hoffman sees it as a phallic emblem, Schwartz as a symbol of lightning, Waring as a symbol of water, etc.
3. Percy Gardner, Goblet D'Alviella, Edward Thomas, and many others.

SWORD—Symbol of power, authority, protection, justice, and knighthood.

As a symbol of power and authority it probably originated as a trophy, which thus became a badge with these significations. Often, as in Japan, two swords are worn as an indication of rank or power, one of which derives from the captured sword of the enemy. It is thus worn as a trophy or badge to denote authority over the conquered enemy.[1]

The sword has been used as a symbol of power and authority in many European states since the Middle Ages and has figured in the coronation of monarchs. In the British regalia there are five swords. The sword of state is a large two-handed sword, which being too large to be handled by the sovereign is customarily exchanged for the smaller personal sword in a jewelled scabbard. The sovereign is girded with this sword (although in the case of Queen Elizabeth II it was placed in her hands), while the Archbishop says: 'With this sword do justice, stop the growth of iniquity, protect the holy Church of God, help and defend widows and orphans, restore the things that are gone to decay, maintain the things that are restored, punish and reform what is amiss and confirm what is in good order.' The sovereign then carries it to the altar, where it is offered for the protection of the Church of God. But as this is the personal sword of the sovereign, it is redeemed for one hundred shillings. It is then drawn and carried naked for the rest of the service. It is interesting to note that the personal sword is itself a symbol of the sword of state.

The three other swords are borne before the monarch as symbols of his power.

One is the blunt, short Curtana Sword of Mercy, the latinized form of Courtain, the short sword of Ogier the Dane who was, according to a legend, a peer of Charlemagne and once King of England. In revenge for the murder of his son he was supposed to have drawn his sword against the son of Charlemagne, but was warned by a voice from heaven to show mercy instead of vengeance. Known as the Sword of Mercy, it appears to have descended to Edward the Confessor. The other two swords signify Justice and the defence and protection of the Church.

The sword is a common attribute of the figure of Justice, who is often shown as a woman blindfolded, with scales in her left hand and a sword in her right hand. A well-known example is the figure that forms the sinister supporter of the New York Coat of Arms.

The sword is an emblem of St. Paul, derived from his reference in Ephesians (vi. 17) to the armour of the Christian, wherein he exhorts the Christian to 'take the helmet of salvation and the sword of the Spirit, which is the word of God'.

1. *See* HERBERT SPENCER's *Principles of Sociology*, Part 4, 'Ceremonial Institutions', p. 409.

TABERNACLE—The name of the sacred tent of the Israelites which held the Ark of the Covenant and other sacred objects and which was regarded by the Israelites as the dwelling of Jehovah. The Israelites being a nomad people made a tent their sacred temple. Thus, 'Moses took the tabernacle and pitched it without the camp, afar off from the camp, and called it the Tabernacle of the congregation' (Exodus xxxiii. 7), and it was here that Moses spoke with God.

No clear idea can be formed of the shape of the sacred tent. We can deduce from ancient Assyrian reliefs that the tents of the Assyrians were similar to the bell tents of modern times, with a pole in the centre, and it is possible that the tents of the Israelites were similar. There were probably larger and more elaborate tents for special purposes where several poles were used, and judging from the description of the tabernacle in Exodus xxxv and xxxvi, with its ten curtains each 28 cubits high by 4 cubits wide (42 feet by 6 feet) which were joined together in fives, it must have been fairly large. There was also apparently a slightly larger outer tent.

The tabernacle on the altar of the Roman Catholic Church, which contains the consecrated host or sacramental bread, could be interpreted as the sacred tent of the Israelites in miniature, although its significance is perhaps more akin to the Ark of the Covenant, but all (tent, ark and tabernacle) imply the presence of the divine spirit. The earliest form of this tabernacle was that of a dove, and the miniature tent or temple structure was first used in the sixteenth century.

TEMPLE—Originally the term temple meant a sacred place marked off for the god or spirit to dwell in, derived from the Greek τέμενος meaning a sacred enclosure, and from Latin templum meaning a part cut off. The earliest temples were thus sacred enclosures, like stone circles, and it was not until later that buildings were erected to house the god. In ancient Rome it was the function of the augur to mark out the boundaries of the sacred place with the lituus.

Among ancient religions the gods were often conceived as dwelling on the summit of a mountain (*see* Mountain) and the temple was often erected at the summit to secure communion between the gods and mortals, between heaven and earth. In ancient Greece the principal temples of a city were often built at the summit of a hill known as the acropolis, which was often built up and levelled for the purpose. Artificial hills, like the ziggurats of Babylon and the teocalli of Mexico, were built with the temples at the summit.

Thus the temple is the symbol of the union of, or link between God and man, and heaven and earth, and it has this significance in all religions from the ziggurats of Babylon to the church of Christianity. It is the house of God, the dwelling of a Deity, the place where man can have communion with Him. A particular temple is also by association a symbol of the particular divinity, and is often in its forms symbolical of the emotions associated with the religion, as the Greek temple symbolizes repose and acceptance and the Gothic forms of a Christian church symbolize aspiration.

Miniature temples have been employed as symbols for devotional purposes. Among some African tribes small temples or huts are provided in which the spirit could dwell, and in Buddhist India and China and elsewhere, miniature stupas, temples and pagodas have been similarly used for devotional purposes.

TENT—The sacred tent of the nomad Israelites was the abode of Jehovah, it was thus the House of God, and this together with the crusaders tent, has prompted symbolic tent-like structures in the Christian church. There is some evidence that the sacred ancient oriental tents were circular, either conical or domed. Modern examples of this symbolic form are the Roman Catholic cathedrals at Brasilia and Liverpool and the Anglican Chapel of Unity at Coventry Cathedral.

In ancient military campaigns the royal tent was often one of some magnificence, and the association of the monarch with divine power, which was not uncommon, often gave such tents a sacred character. In the tent there was often a throne room, and it is probable that the tent covering was the origin of the large inverted ciborium or the baldachino over the throne.[1]

1. *See* E. BALDWIN SMITH, *Architectural Symbolism of Imperial Rome and the Middle Ages* (Princeton 1956). The Chapter on 'The Imperial Ciborium' pp. 107–112.

THISTLE—A national emblem and symbol of Scotland.

The first reliable record of the association of the thistle with Scotland occurs in the reign of James III (1460–88), who adopted it as an emblem, although the reason for this is obscure. It has been suggested that it illustrated the motto of James: 'In defence.' Since the time of James III it has been widely used as a Scottish emblem. It appeared on coins of James IV, James V, Mary, and James VI.

The adoption of the thistle as the Scottish national emblem has been traced to an incident in the war with the Norwegians in the thirteenth century, but this incident is probably legendary. The story is that during a night attack at Largs by Hakos' army on Alexander III and his men, one of the Norwegian soldiers trod with his bare foot on a thistle and cried out in pain, thus betraying the army's position and revealing the attack. The Scots, thus warned, secured a decisive victory, and in honour of this the thistle was chosen as the Scottish national emblem.

331

TIARA—A tall headdress of conical shape, known as the tiara, was worn by ancient Persian and Assyrian kings (*see* Headdress). A similarly shaped headdress was adopted in the early period of Christianity as the tiara or crown of the pope to signify his temporal power. The Emperor Constantine is believed to have given a tiara to Sylvester (314–35) and there is mention of it in association with Pope Constantius I (708–15). In the twelfth century the tiara was encircled by a diadem at its base. Innocent III (1198–1216) was depicted wearing a tiara with two diadems, and a third is thought to have been added by Urban V (1362–70).

In its final form the papal tiara consists of a high beehive-shaped cap surmounted by a small cross and orb, encircled by three diadems, and with two lappets hanging down the back. The three diadems symbolize the papal power of order, of spiritual jurisdiction and of temporal jurisdiction, expressing the triple dignity of teacher, lawgiver and judge. The tiara is placed on the pope's head at his coronation by the second cardinal deacon with the words: 'Receive the tiara adorned with three crowns, and know that thou art Father of princes and kings, Ruler of the World, and Vicar of our Saviour Jesus Christ.' Strictly speaking, the second cardinal deacon really assists the pope to crown himself.

The papal tiara shown alone symbolizes the Holy See.

THREE GOLDEN BALLS—A sign indicating a money lender or pawnbroker. The origin is obscure. A popular belief is that it is derived from the Medici coat of arms, as the early bankers came from the Medici states and Lombardy. The Medici coat bore roundels varying from eleven to six, but never three, and they were not gold. The earlier sign of pawnbrokers was three bowls, which have thus changed to balls and to gold. A possible origin is the legend of St. Nicholas, who gave three bag-shaped purses to the three daughters of a nobleman. (*See* Chapter VIII.)

THRONE—The term is derived from the Greek θρονός meaning a chair, which was the seat of a monarch or chief priest, and the throne was thus a symbol of authority and sovereign power. The throne appears to have originated the chair. It is often used in the sense of sovereign power in figurative language, but less frequently in visual design. By transition from earthly to heavenly regions it is the imagined seat of a deity—the throne of Zeus, or the throne of God.

Since ancient times thrones are generally very elaborate and sometimes magnificent chairs of precious materials, such as gold or marble, inlaid with jewels and ornamented with symbols of power or of the dominion ruled. They are usually elevated on a platform above the general level of the floor, thus giving an added impression of dignity and power. In Persia and other oriental countries the throne was often set beneath a canopy, or domical ciborium or baldachino which signified dominion over the world.

THRONES—In the Celestial Hierarchy of the pseudo-Dionysius the Areopagite, which is very largely the textbook on angels for theologians (*see* Angel), thrones constitute the third rank of the first order and signify exaltation, loftiness and the kingly virtues. They are sometimes distinguished from cherubim in representations by a little more of the human figure being shown, but just as often their form is depicted as being the same, that is, a head and six wings. They are sometimes depicted with a throne.

THUNDERBOLT—In ancient times the weapon thought to be discharged by Zeus. It manifested itself as lightning, which, it was believed, indicated the wrath of Zeus. A. B. Cook[1] refers to 'keraunos' as a name for lightning, meaning the destroyer. 'This', he says, 'is usually translated by the word thunderbolt, but must not be taken to denote a solid missile of any sort. It means nothing more than the bright white flash in its destructive capacity.' The earliest signs for the thunderbolt are clearly conventionalized representations of lightning, and usually take the form of a zigzag two-pronged or three-pronged fork, the former probably being earlier, as examples can be seen on Mesopotamian seal cylinders and boundary stones of the twelfth century B.C. In Assyria in the ninth century B.C. the three-pronged fork is duplicated by representing it at either end, as in the famous bas-relief from the palace of Ashur-nasir-pal in the British Museum. In the migration of the representation to Greece the forks of the thunderbolt were often given a stylized rendering like the lotus, which may have been because the decorative character of the latter appealed to artists; but it also may have been a conscious association of the symbolism of the lotus with the thunderbolt. The lotus was a symbol of the sun both in Egypt and India, and the early Greeks, conceiving Zeus as the god of the sky, thought of lightning and the sun as associated—lightning the flash of the fire of Zeus which is also the sun—thus a common form of thunderbolt results from a combination of the lotus and lightning. Another development seems to be the association of the thunderbolt with weapons like dagger blades and arrow heads.[2]

The thunderbolt was thus an early emblem of Zeus, and it is possible that many ancient peoples believed that a bolt of some kind similar to the representations was hurled down from heaven during a storm. Indeed, the belief has survived to modern times, the transformation of metal struck by lightning giving support to the belief.

Thunderbolt is sometimes used figuratively to denote some dreadful occurrence or something very threatening expressed by the phrase 'a thunderbolt from heaven'.

1. *Zeus, op. cit.*, Vol. I, p. 11.
2. A. B. COOK has adduced much evidence for this in the section on 'Modifications in the shape of the Thunderbolt' in *Zeus*, Vol. II, pp. 764–85 (Cambridge, 1925).

THYRSUS—A staff, surmounted by a pine cone and sometimes entwined with vine, is a common emblem of Dionysus (or Bacchus). If represented alone it would logically be a symbol of Dionysus and his votaries, and the ideas and life for which they stand.

TOOLS AND INSTRUMENTS OF PROFESSIONS, CRAFTS AND TRADES—These are common associational symbols, appearing especially in personal commemoration such as medals and stone monuments. Familiar examples are palette and brushes for a painter, compass or dividers, scrolls of paper and set squares for an architect, a harp for a musician and a quill pen for a writer. Chalices, patens, croziers and books often appear on the monuments to priests and ecclesiastical persons in Church monuments. Craft and trade symbols are common on churchyard memorials from the seventeenth century. Examples are a hammer, pincers and anvil for a blacksmith, scissors and glove for a glover, axe for a mason, and a mallet and chisel for a joiner. On a tombstone in Girthon Churchyard, Kirkcudbright, of Robert Glover a gardener who died in 1776, are carved a rake and spade. Another memorial in the form of a chest tomb at Darley Dale in Derbyshire, commemorating a weaver who died in 1640, a shuttle, tenter, loom, spinning wheel and warping-mill are carved on the faces of the tomb.[1] Of a similar kind are the kitchen utensils carved on the walls of an ancient Etruscan tomb of the fifth century B.C., at Cerveteri, which I studied during a recent visit. They are of considerable variety.

1. FREDERICK BURGESS, *English Churchyard Memorials*, p. 132 (London, 1963).

TOPE—*See* Stupa

TORCH—Symbol of immortality in a secular sense.

Of Greek origin, the torch symbol has largely been superseded in intelligent modern Christian symbolism by the lamp. The lamp has a wider significance, and includes, in its modern use, the meanings given to torch by the Greeks as explained under the heading of Lamp, while the early Christians made of the lamp a symbol of eternal life, a significance which in ancient Greece the torch never had. The Greek symbol, by the nature of its origin, has a limited meaning, and was derived from the torch races held at certain festivals where the runners passed the torch one to another in relays. This may roughly be translated into the generally accepted symbolic meaning that the light to humanity of great work is of such intensity that its glow is caught by others and carried onwards. So the title 'Torch Bearers' is given by Alfred Noyes to his epic of the men who have contributed most to civilization.

The inverted torch was employed by the Greeks and Romans as a symbol of death. It was sometimes carried by Eros, thus adding the pleasing sentiment that departure from the world is attended by love. But to be strictly logical the inverted torch means something more than the indefiniteness of death; it must mean the negation of all that the lamp and torch express.

TOTEM—Primitive tribal badge of identification, generally taking the form of an animal, more rarely of a plant or inanimate object. The reason for, and origin of, the totem appears to be connected with exogamy, with the prohibition of marriage or sexual intercourse within a tribe or group, thus among members of the same totem. Theories of the origin of totemism are discussed in Chapter II.

THE SACRED TREE—From the many and varied forms and meanings of tree worship and symbolism among widely distributed peoples, it is deduced that the sacred tree symbolizes, principally, life, mainly in the sense of regeneration and immortality; knowledge and wisdom; and the world or universe.

The tree is the most widespread of symbols, and in considering Christian architecture it can be regarded as second only to the cross. Its importance is apparent in ecclesiastical decoration, in the designs of processional crosses and of memorials where the decorative character has a decided resemblance to the growth of a tree.

The character of much ecclesiastical design has evolved from ancient tree worship and symbolism.

Tree worship was prominent among numerous primitive communities.[1] It has been noted among the primitive and early historic peoples of India, China, Egypt, and Greece; the Semitic nations of Asia Minor; and the Northern Celtic, Teutonic, and Scandinavian peoples. A tree was either worshipped as the abode of a beneficent deity or feared as the abode of demons and evil spirits.[2] With the advance to some form of civilization, the former idea usually prevailed over the latter. It was usual in a tribe or locality for one tree to be venerated as the abode of the god or as the god himself.[3] Herein exists a fine distinction which it is well to observe. With regard to the former, Robertson Smith says: 'The god inhabited the tree or sacred stone, not in the sense in which a man inhabits a house, but in the sense in which his soul inhabits his body.'[4] This distinction is made because the god is conceived of as being inseparable from his abode of tree or stone. But where the tree is conceived of as being the god himself, it implies that there is no distinction between soul and body: they are interfused, are one, and are never thought of separately.

Offerings were made to the tree deity, and the tree served as an oracle. The oak of Dodona is perhaps the most famous of these oracles: biblical testimony affords important Semitic examples;[5] and Prussian tree oracles were noted for their number and frequency.

The sacred tree was usually of the species that was considered to be of the greatest value, or the most imposing. Thus with the Semitic peoples it varied among the date-palm, cedar, pomegranate, cypress, and vine; while with northern peoples the ash, elm, oak, and alder were so venerated.

The stages of development of tree worship are, in some measure, defined by Thomas Barns,[6] who says that from this earliest stage there evolves the sacred grove wherein the sacred tree is planted, which becomes the abode of the god. The best examples of the sacred grove are afforded by ancient Greece, such as the oak grove of Zeus and the laurel grove of Apollo. At a later period, instead of associating the god with one particular tree, he was associated with all trees of the kind. Thus the oak was sacred to Zeus, the laurel to Apollo, the myrtle to Venus, and the olive to Athena.[7]

In the final stage of development the tree was gradually supplanted by its image, which thus became a symbol. In this stage the symbol only was venerated, the tree apparently existing in some mysterious, unapproachable region. The image changed in some instances beyond all recognition; and so the tree was ultimately symbolized by an object such as a stump, spear, or post, which was usually placed on an altar, or similar sacred spot, and worshipped. This is the subject of those numerous representations of acolytes or animals worshipping on either side of an object which have figured in art from early Babylon and Assyria to the present day, the most famous example being the lion gate at Mycenae. The distinction between the symbol of the tree and the tree as a symbol is important.

The anthropomorphizing tendency of the Greeks was responsible for marked developments from their original forms of tree worship. In these earliest forms, as with other peoples, the god dwelt in the tree. The desire to give the god human shape, however, prompted them to give the tree a human semblance, or carve part of it into a human image of the god. From this it was an easy stage to carve an image of the god in the wood of the tree and place it in a sanctuary for worship. The earliest Greek images of the gods were of wood, and as civilization advanced the natural preference for more durable and finer materials was better satisfied by stone, marble, bronze, ivory, and gold. Thus the early carved images of the gods on the sacred tree ultimately developed into the gold and ivory statues by Phidias.

Among the Semitic nations of Asia Minor the tree was widely venerated as a symbol of life. That it was the greatest manifestation of the vegetable world and thus selected to typify the periodic reviviscence in vegetation would appear to supply the main reason for its adoption. It will be observed that the trees selected for this veneration among the different nations—the date-palm, pomegranate, and vine— yield to the people a valuable sustenance. This consideration probably determined the kind of tree employed for the symbol, and was probably responsible, to some extent, for another consideration that seems to have prompted the use of the tree as a symbol of life, of fecundity, of fertility, and other kindred meanings. Goblet D'Alviella, following E. B. Tylor, suggests, in speaking of the Semitic representation by a tree of the female personification of nature, that the 'fertilization of the date-palm by means of the artificial transference of the pollen to the clusters of the female or date-bearing tree', a process known to these ancient peoples,[8] 'might have supplied a symbol of fertilization in general, a symbolic representation of the mysterious operation everywhere performed, under the most different forms, by the fertilizing forces of Nature.'[9]

With the Hindus the tree does not typify life in the same sense as with the Semitic nations. The Hindus, in accordance with their beliefs, see the tree rather as a symbol of divine wisdom, of the Nirvana with which, in their conception of paradise, they are ultimately identified. It is a belief that makes the ultimate end of life a merging of individual identity into the spirit of life conceived in terms of ideal perfection. One sacred tree symbolizing this in the universe is thus one form of the universe or world tree.

W. R. Lethaby wrote at length[10] to show a cosmogonical origin for the sacred tree. He cites Tylor's outline of the primitive man's conception of the earth as a flat plain, covered by the arch of the sky which joined the earth at the horizon. How natural must it have then been to conceive a central tree stretching upwards and supporting the sky: 'and we can understand the thought of some Paraguayans that at death their souls would go up to heaven by the tree which joins earth and sky.'[11]

The conceptions of this universe, or world tree, vary considerably. Most agree, however, in placing it in the centre of the earth, sometimes on a mountain, sometimes at the north pole. The most famous tree of this kind is perhaps the Yggdrasil, the mystical ash in Scandinavian mythology, which by its roots, stem, and branches symbolizes hell, earth, and heaven. Some conceptions make the tree of gold, or of some other precious metal, with fruit of jewels, or fruit identified with the stars.[12] And herein exists a connection between the universe tree and the tree of wisdom and knowledge. The fruit of precious stones or fruit identified with stars were sources of light. They were regarded as the lights of wisdom and of knowledge. Thus fruits, especially bright fruits, are associated with the tree of wisdom and knowledge. This probably explains why, among northern countries, the crimson berries of the mountain ash are held sacred, and why, according to some suggestions, 'it is the original counsel-tree of the northern races'.[13] In Celtic folk-lore the scarlet berries of the rowan-tree are the source of wisdom,[14] and many other instances might be mentioned. It is no doubt this association that has resulted in the choice of holly with its bright red berries as a Christmas decoration, and originated the custom of burning candles on the Christmas tree. The old candelabra and chandeliers bear the stamp of their origin in the jewel-bearing tree, or the tree of the light of wisdom and knowledge.[15]

Enough has been said to demonstrate the wide prevalence of tree worship and symbolism and the inevitable strength of their traditions at the beginning of Christianity. That the tree symbolized immortal life, wisdom, and knowledge, and the universe, was sufficient to suggest to the early Christians that they might adopt it as significant of their beliefs. There is little evidence that the early Christians used the tree alone, unassociated with any more exclusively Christian symbol. The many forms of the sacred tree that came to Christianity from the East, principally Persia, by means of Oriental draperies and ornaments, particularly lavish in the Justinian era, came mainly as decoration for Byzantine churches in Constantinople without much regard to their significance. In the church of St. Maria Antiqua in Rome there is, however, a fresco of the date-palm which shows the dates falling from the tree. It is a veritable image of fecundity, and it would be interesting to know with what Christian intention it was represented. Being a palm, it may have been the object to associate it with martyrdom, implying that from such acts of sacrifice there springs life. The presence of the vine-tree in the catacombs is more easily explained in another connection. The Christmas tree, it may be added, does not date as a custom farther back than the early seventeenth century, and probably arose partly from the mediaeval legend of Christmas flowering trees,[16] and partly from the mediaeval Paradise plays, performed at Christmas, which introduced the Tree of Knowledge.

But though in Christian symbolism the tree figures but little alone, it figures largely in association with other symbols. The tree being so important a symbol, it was natural that some effort should be made to associate it with the cross, the principal Christian symbol, so that the significance of the cross should embrace eternal life, knowledge and wisdom, which Christ's teaching bestows, and the universe of which He is the Creator and Saviour. Mediaeval legend makes the cross on which Christ was crucified of the wood of a tree which sprung from a slip of the Tree of Knowledge, thus connecting the fall and salvation of man, which is the story of Christianity. But whatever legend or superstition was the cause, it is clear that the association was widely adopted. Thus in the earliest memorial crosses we find ornament of such a character that it can without difficulty be interpreted as the representation of the tree. W. R. Lethaby sees in the scrolls of foliage following tree growth on the shaft sides of the Ruthwell and Bewcastle crosses an 'association of ideas between the Cross and the "World Tree" of our Anglican forefathers'.[17] Representations such as this, suggesting the tree, occur in crosses of all periods from the early Middle Ages (Fig. 57(a) and (b)). In some instances the introduction of the tree is very marked, as, for example, in a marble cross in Crystal Palace cemetery which shows a representation of the tree where the roots, trunk, and foliage are clearly defined. Altar crosses afford numerous examples.

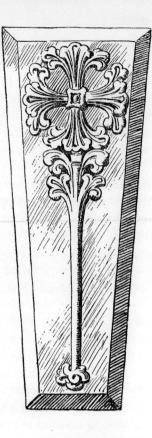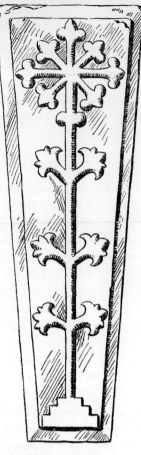

Two mediaeval sepulchral slabs, the designs of which probably
emanate from the association of the cross with the sacred tree.

(a) In Westbourne church, Lincolnshire.
Early thirteenth century.

(b) In Wells Cathedral. Late thirteenth
century.

(c) Unicorn resting its head on a virgin's lap. From a thirteenth-
century bestiary, formerly in Rochester Priory, now in the British
Museum.

Fig. 57.

The representation of a tree-stump, mostly oak, with foliage and branches, is a survival of the pre-Christian tree symbolism of immortal life. The growth of flowers and foliage represented on memorials is no doubt partly prompted in some instances by the vague idea of suggesting life; a hardly-conscious survival of the custom of looking to the vegetable world, and principally the tree as its most imposing creation, as a typification of life.

1. *See* SIR JAMES FRAZER, *The Magic Art*, Vol. ii, pp. 7 *et seq.*, and others mentioned in subsequent footnotes.
2. *See* MRS. J. H. PHILPOT, *The Sacred Tree*, p. 22 (1897).
3. S. A. COOKE cites an example of this from the Gauchos of South America in his article on 'Tree Worship' in the *Encyclopaedia Britannica*.
4. *Religion of the Semites*, p. 84 (1889).
5. Exodus iii. 1–4 and II Samuel v. 24.
6. *Encyclopaedia of Religion and Ethics*, 'Trees and Plants', Vol. xii, p. 448.
7. *See* MRS. PHILPOT, *op. cit.*, pp. 26 *et seq.*
8. Herodotus I, 193, and others cited by SIR JAMES FRAZER, *op. cit.*, p. 24.
9. *Migration of Symbols*, pp. 145–9.
10. *Architecture, Mysticism and Myth*, 1892, pp. 94 *et seq.*
11. *Architecture, Mysticism and Myth*, p. 11.
12. LETHABY deals with this in his chapter on the 'Jewel Bearing Tree', *op. cit.*, pp. 94 *et seq.*, wherein he traces the origin of candelabra and chandeliers to the jewel bearing tree.
13. Barns, *op. cit.*, p. 456.
14. *Ibid.*
15. Some are figured in LETHABY's *Architecture, Mysticism, and Myth*.
16. *See* MRS. PHILPOT, *op. cit.*, pp. 164 *et seq.*
17. *The Builder*, p. 237, 5th February, 1926.

TRIANGLE (EQUILATERAL)—Christian symbol of the Trinity.

It was frequently used by the early Christians, some examples being found in the catacombs. Sometimes it is depicted enclosing the sacred monogram. Later, in mediaeval times, it appears in various church ornamentations, employed especially in painted glass. Two triangles were sometimes worked together, forming a six-point star. This star was one of the less important emblems of the Templars, but is more famous as David's shield, described under the heading of Hexagram. On the coins of Edward I the king's head was placed within an equilateral triangle, doubtless signifying that the monarchy invokes divine protection. In the note on the nimbus, allusion is made to the triangular form of nimbus which is occasionally seen in portrayals of the First and Third Persons of the Trinity. Christ is rarely depicted with this form, as the cross circular form is naturally preferred for its richer significance.

The triangle could be used as a panel enclosing another harmonious symbol. The symbol of the eye of God, or of Providence, is often enclosed in the equilateral triangle (*see* Eye). The bare representation of the equilateral triangle, however, has little to recommend it, as it is an elementary symbol too commonplace to evoke reflection.

TRIDENT—Symbol of the sea. When held by an ancient god such as the Hindu god Siva, the Greek Poseidon, or the Roman Neptune, or by a modern symbolic figure like Britannia, it symbolizes dominion over the sea.

The origin of the trident and of its association with the sea is unknown; but the nature of ancient symbolism and mythology suggest a possible explanation.

Among ancient peoples it was customary to typify natural phenomena by symbolism or by anthropomorphizing myths, or more generally by both. The origin of their religions is often discovered in the anthropomorphizing of natural forces. Often when a natural phenomenon was symbolized by an object, the same object was associated with the phenomenon, when anthropomorphized, in the person of a god. Now storms, thunder, and lightning are powerful and impressive phenomena, and they inevitably deeply stirred the imaginations of ancient peoples. Both thunder and lightning appear to have been symbolized by weapons.[1] The weapon symbolizing lightning in many cases resembles a three-pronged fork, sometimes with zigzag prongs to represent the lightning. Greek myths recount that Poseidon employed this weapon to stir up the seas in storm. It is, therefore, more strictly a symbol of lightning and storm, but it has become associated with the sea, presumably because the most vivid manifestations of storms take place at sea.

The Buddhist trisula is doubtless derived from the trident, although it developed very far in its form and meaning from its prototype, being changed in its meaning by religious influence, and elaborated and changed in form by association with numerous other symbols. Various interpretations of its meaning have been made by archaeologists, but with little general agreement.[2]

1. D'Alviella says that 'Almost all nations have represented the lightning by a weapon'. *Migration of Symbols*, p. 97.
2. D'Alviella has given an erudite account of the transformation of the trisule, *Migration of Symbols*, pp. 237–69.

TRIPOD—Ancient Greek symbol of achievement in dance and song. The tripod was awarded to the master of the chorus in Greek religious festivals and drama.

It was the task of a wealthy citizen, called 'choragus', to collect a chorus for Greek festivals and drama. Prizes of crowns and tripods were awarded to those choruses, and the tripods were often set up on a monument or small temple to commemorate the achievement. These monuments were grouped round the sanctuary of Dionysus in Athens or along the street leading to it, which came to be known as the Street of Tripods. The most famous of these monuments is the Choragic Monument of Lysicrates erected in 335 B.C. This monument is of circular form, consisting of six Corinthian engaged columns rising from a square base and supporting a dome on which a central finial held the tripod.[1] There is an inscription on the architrave which records that 'Lysicrates son of Lysitheides of Cicynna was choragus when the boys of the tribe of Acamantis conquered, when Theon played the flute, when Lysiades wrote the piece, and when Evaenetus was archon'.

The tripod was probably selected as a prize because it was an early form of altar, on which offerings were made. In the early form of Greek theatre an altar, possibly of the tripod form, stood in the centre of the orchestra (the theatre of Epidaurus built in 330 B.C. being an example). The chorus occupied the orchestra, and it would thus be logical that the tripod in its centre, or rather a replica of it, should form the prize for the victorious choragus.

The tripod was also employed in the rites of the pythean priestess of Apollo, who delivered her oracles whilst seated on a slab surmounting the tripod. A bronze bowl was usually placed under the slab to give the utterances resonance.

1. Detailed descriptions are given in BANISTER FLETCHER's *History of Architecture* p. 114 (15th edition, London, 1950). Also in W. B. DINSMOOR's *The Architecture of Ancient Greece*, pp. 236–8 (London, 1950).

TRIQUETRA—*See* Triscele.

TRISCELE, or TRISKELE (also called TRISKELION and TRIQUETRA)—Symbol of the sun, of the revival of life and of prosperity. Badge of Sicily and of the Isle of Man.

This figure of three bent legs joined together at the thighs appears to have an origin similar to that of the swastika. It has been noted that the most widely accepted theory of the meaning of the swastika is that it is a diagrammatic representation of the sun's course in the heavens, the arms being indications of directions. Its proximity on ancient remains to the disk, an undoubted image of the sun, strengthens the theory.

The earliest form of the Triscele was composed of three curves in a circle radiating from a centre, which is a definite expression of rotary motion. This and the three legs are found in large numbers on ancient monuments and coins of Asia Minor, frequently in association with the disk. In some representations the curves, or legs, radiate from a disk[1] in a manner to suggest rotary motion. On another Lycian coin three legs similarly radiate from a disk,[2] and on a Celtiberian coin the disk from which the legs radiate is marked with a face in the manner of many modern representations of the sun.[3]

The swastika and triscele being expressions of the sun's motion round the earth, and the sun being either worshipped or venerated as an agent of the deity, or conceived as a force of good, the expression of its motion would come to be regarded as a portent for good and a symbol of prosperity and good fortune. That this is the case with the swastika there is little doubt, but in the case of the triscele the three legs have somewhat obscured its original diagrammatic expression.

The question arises, why have the three curves, expressing rotary motion, become three legs? One theory is that the sun with many ancient peoples being symbolized by animals such as the lion, bull, and falcon, it is possible that these personifications of the sun were associated with the triscele, and that the curves became animals' legs. On some coins of Syria heads of animals are shown in a similar manner to the legs. And it must be remembered that among ancient peoples the sun was symbolized by the hero working for the good of the people. In Greece was not the sun anthropomorphized into Apollo, Hercules, Orpheus, and others? This may account for the human legs in the triscele.

The triscele figures in Greek art from the sixth century B.C. (Plate IX). It appeared a little later in Sicily, then a Greek colony, being found on coins of Syracuse and other remains. It became an emblem of Sicily, the reason being, according to one suggestion,[4] that it symbolized the shape of the island with its three promontories. A similar reason has been suggested for its adoption as an emblem of the Isle of Man, suggested probably by its use in Sicily. According to John Newton, the triscele was introduced into the Isle of Man by Alexander III of Scotland when he took possession of the island from the Norwegians in 1266.[5] In this account Alexander III took it from the court of Henry III, who was, at the jurisdiction of Pope Innocent III, King of Sicily for a short period. The triscele appears on monuments and regalia of the Isle of Man from the fourteenth century.[6] One appears on a carved cross of the fourteenth century, which stands near the entrance of Kirk Maughold churchyard.

If the triscele is used in a design with the intention of symbolizing the sun or the revival of life, it would no doubt be popularly construed as symbolizing some association with the Isle of Man, or perhaps Sicily.

1. Illustrated in FELLOWS' *Coins of Ancient Lycia*, Plate 10 (London, 1855).
2. Illustrated in PERCY GARDNER'S *Numismatic Chronicle*, Vol. vii, Plate 5.
3. Illustrated in LUDWIG MÜLLER'S *Detåsaakaldte Hagekors*. Fig. 46 (Copenhagen, 1877).
4. GOBLET D'ALVIELLA, *Migration of Symbols*, p. 20.
5. Letter in *The Athenaeum*, 10th September 1892.
6. W. RALPH HALL CAINE (*Isle of Man*, pp. 56 *et seq.*, London, 1909) says that it appears on the Isle of Man sword of state, which is attributed to the thirteenth century. This may have been the sword of Alexander III, but as the legs are clad in armour it is probably of a later date.

TRISKELION—*See* Triscele.

TRISULA—*See* Triscele.

TROUT—The South Fork Golden Trout (*Salmo aquabonita*), a species which belongs to the rainbow series of trout, was officially adopted as the state fish of California in 1947. It is natural only to the upper waters of the Kern River tributaries in the High Sierra country.

TULIP TREE—The tulip tree (*Liriodendron Tulipifera*), was officially adopted as the state tree of Indiana in 1931. It was a prominent tree in the forests that once covered Indiana, and is now extensively used in the state for ornamental planting.

UMBRELLA—Oriental symbol of royal dignity. It was used as a protection from the sun by princes, and was generally, especially on ceremonial occasions, carried by attendants. On such occasions the umbrella was often so elaborate as to become a canopy. Thus the umbrella became by association a symbol of royal dignity. Sir Richard Burton records that from India to Abyssinia the umbrella is the sign of royalty,[1] while Sir John Bowring records that in Siam, at the coronation, the king is presented with a seven-starred umbrella as the primary symbol of royalty,[2] and other countries in the east attach a similar symbolism to the umbrella. An image of the umbrella usually surmounted the Buddhist stupa (*q.v.*). These were generally of a dedicatory character, and the umbrella at the top symbolized the royal dignity of the saint to whom the monument was dedicated. The baldachino, or canopy over the Christian altar, is probably derived from the umbrella, and as Herbert Spencer remarks, covers the Host as it covered the oriental monarch.[3]

1. SIR RICHARD BURTON, *Lake Regions of Central Africa*, p. 141 (London, 1860).
2. SIR JOHN BOWRING, *Kingdom and People of Siam*, p. 425 (London, 1857).
3. HERBERT SPENCER, *Ceremonial Institutions*, *op. cit.*, p. 419.

UNICORN—In early and mediaeval Christian times this mythical animal was a symbol of purity, and, to a less extent, from the supposed habits of the animal, a symbol of solitude and the monastic life.

In ancient Egypt and Persia the unicorn figures as a type of purity, and it was this that probably first suggested its use to early Christians. The early explanation of the symbol is that the unicorn, naturally a fierce animal, is instantly subdued to gentleness by a virgin. This notion was further explained[1] as being derived from the unicorn becoming at mating time very gentle and tender towards its mate.

The unicorn was often represented in manuscripts and church decorations resting its feet and head on a young woman's lap, the former being interpreted as Christ and the latter as the Virgin Mary. A similar representation was sometimes applied personally, as, for instance, on the reverse of Pisanello's medal of Cecilia Gonzaga, where a young girl is shown with a unicorn lying by her side. (Plate XVI(*a*) and Fig. 57(*c*).)

Since mediaeval times the unicorn has been a common device in heraldry, its most famous use being in the Royal Coat of Arms. James IV of Scotland first employed it, and when James VI of Scotland became James I of England, he substituted the white unicorn of Scotland for the red dragon of Wales as the sinister supporter, and it has remained there ever since. (*See* Chapter III.)

1. Aelian XVI, 20.

URN—Used symbolically the urn signifies death, and it is sometimes employed as a symbol of mourning. It has the same significance as a cenotaph, which is an empty tomb or sarcophagus. It has been frequently so used on monuments in churches and cemeteries from the Renaissance until the present day. It is derived from the cinerary urn of the ancient Greeks and Romans, the word urn, from the Latin *urna*, from uro, meaning to burn.

Being used in ancient Rome also as a receptacle for voting tablets, the urn thus became a symbol of fate—of the lottery of life; but it is doubtful whether it has been used in this sense in modern times.

In ancient Greece cremation and body burial existed together to an almost equal extent until about the third century B.C., when the former prevailed. In Roman times cremation continued to prevail until the state adoption of Christianity in the early part of the fourth century A.D., when, owing to Christian doctrine, body burial became the custom. In Greece the ashes seem to have been placed in any kind of vessel and generally buried. More rarely the vessel was placed in the house or on a monument. The choice of the vessel seems to have been determined by some association with the deceased, so that the cinerary urn might be an amphora[1] (vessel for storing liquids), a krater (a vessel for mixing liquids), an oenochoë (a wine jug), a hydria (a water jug), or any similar type of vase, or perhaps a stone or wooden chest. Sometimes a large stone or marble urn was used with a smaller bronze urn inside. One such was discovered in a tumulus on the road from Piraeus to Eleusis, and is now in the British Museum. Inscribed on the rim of the bronze urn are the words, 'I am a prize from the games of Hera of Argos', which indicated the kind of association that determined the choice of a vessel as the cinerary urn. When these cinerary urns were to be buried they were usually of a simple type, but when placed in the house or on a monument they were of a more ornamental character. Evidence of the urn being placed on the top of a monument is provided by Pausanias. When speaking of the death of Orpheus, he says that on the right of the road that leads from Dium to Mount Pieria, in Boeotia, there stands 'a pillar surmounted by a stone urn; and the urn, according to the natives, contains the bones of Orpheus'.[2]

The urn was similarly employed by the Romans. Glass vessels, both round and square, were also much used, and sometimes these were placed in leaden canisters.[3] The custom of placing the urn in the house or on monuments was common in Roman times. The type of Roman marble urn illustrated (Plate LXXVII) was probably placed in houses or on monuments, and it is that used in the latter case, derived doubtless from the Greek, which forms the prototype of the urns placed on modern monuments. It may be, therefore, that the modern ensemble is really a direct descendant from the Greek and Roman cinerary urns surmounting monuments; although no complete ancient example has been found; yet judging by the evidence of Pausanias and of the Roman remains, this is probable.

The use of an urn as a symbol is appropriate, like that of a cenotaph, as a public monument when the body or ashes are elsewhere.

Many architectural and monumental urns since the Renaissance show flames emerging from the top. This is symbolic of life, like the torch, and indicates that a new life is associated with death.

1. LIDDELL and SCOTT'S Greek Lexicon states that the ἀμφιφορεύς, a two-handled pitcher, was also a cinerary urn, hence the shortened form ἀμφορεύς, but it is difficult to know whence this is derived. There is no evidence that a special vase was used for cinerary urns in Greece. Glass amphoras, however, were plentifully used in Rome.
2. PAUSANIAS, IX, xxx. 7. SIR JAMES G. FRAZER'S translation (London, 1898).
3. Numerous examples are in the British Museum. The best examples of the leaden canisters were discovered in 1881 in Warwick Square.

VASE—This has sometimes been used symbolically, as in ancient Greece, and its significance is usually due to some association of the particular vase. It has no definite symbolic significance merely as a vase.

The vase, or similar vessel, has played an important part in burial and memorial art. In the custom in ancient civilizations of making provision for the dead in the tomb, or of making offerings at the tomb, vessels were often placed to contain the supposed requirements of the deceased. In some Greek vase paintings the tomb is shown with vases arranged round it. These vases were usually lekythi, long-necked, single-handled vessels, commonly used for oil and perfumes, and either they were employed in the burial ceremony, or perfumes constituted part of the offering. The sepulchral lekythi were generally decorated with paintings of funeral scenes in a few colours, principally red, on a white ground.

This sepulchral use of the lekythos prompted its use as a symbol either in bas-relief on the stele[1] or as a large stone or marble imitation forming the memorial. Many examples exist, some being in the British Museum. Some vases so employed are more like the amphora or hydria, and it may be that another reason for their symbolic use was the association of the vase with water, which was held sacred by many of the Greeks as being one of the valuable elements of life, just as a tree, yielding a valuable sustenance, was similarly held sacred by many ancient peoples. It will thus be seen that the vase symbolism of ancient Greece was wholly due to the association with that which the particular vessel contained.

The vase continues to occupy a place in the memorial, mainly as a receptacle for flowers. It is thus a parallel to the ancient custom of placing on the monument the vases containing the offerings to the deceased.

1. Stele, στήλη, meaning standing block or stone, similar to the modern headstone.

VEERY—This bird (*Hylocichla fuscescens*) was chosen by the Federation of Women's Clubs of Massachusetts, as a state emblem and an attempt was made to get it officially adopted, but without success. In 1941, Massachusetts adopted the Chickadee[1] instead.

1. *See Shankle, op. cit.*, p. 380.

VESICA-PISCIS—*See* Mandorla and Fish

VINE—Symbol of Christ and His followers; therefore a general symbol of the Christian faith. When represented with wheat it symbolizes the Eucharist.

The parable of the vine, (John xv. 1–8) wherein Christ likens Himself to the vine and His disciples to the branches, prompted its representation as a symbol of the Christian faith. It was frequently used by the early Christians and was a common subject in the catacombs, in wall paintings, and as ornament on sarcophagi and lamps; and was a favourite subject of early Christian mosaics. It appears on the sarcophagi of the Empress Constantia,[1] sister of Constantine, and of Theodore, Bishop of Ravenna.

The vine is frequently mentioned in the Old Testament, and in the eighteenth Psalm it symbolizes the chosen people. The analogous use of the vine both by the Psalmist and Christ was probably because in Assyria it served as the sacred tree of life, for, like the date-palm in Chaldea and the fig-tree in India, it was held in particular esteem by the inhabitants.[2]

As a symbol of the Eucharist the vine has the well-known authority of the Gospels.[3]

As the leaves and fruit of vine are highly decorative it affords an excellent subject for the designer. It is understood in modern times chiefly as signifying the blood of Christ, and if this significance is intended it should be accompanied by wheat, or barley, or rye, or other principal ingredient of bread, the symbol of the body of Christ.

1. Now in the Vatican Museum.
2. See GOBLET D'ALVIELLA, *The Migration of Symbols*, pp. 134, 141, 153, 173. The author states that in Assyria the vine was called 'karanu', and he cites Terrien de la Couperie's interpretation of this as 'The Tree of the Drink of Life', p. 153. He also cites Lenormont's statement that the Chaldean name for vine was 'ges-tin', which is interpreted 'wood of life', p. 173.
3. Matthew xxvi. 29; Mark xiv. 25; and Luke xxii. 18.

VIOLET—Symbol of humility and secrecy.

So regarded because the flower grows in sequestered places beneath hedges, and in woods in the shadows of larger plants.

Appearing symbolically in literature rather than in art, poetical allusions to it are not uncommon. Keats says: 'that flower of secrecy the violet,'[1] and Wordsworth likens the lonely and unknown Lucy[2] to this flower.

(*a*) Narcissus. This species, known as the poet's or pheasant's narcissus (*Narcissus poeticus*), is commonly regarded as the flower of the Greek myth.

(*b*) Dog violet.

Fig. 58.

The violet is the state flower of Illinois, New Jersey and Rhode Island. In the case of Illinois the violet (*viola pedate*) was officially adopted in 1908, having been chosen by vote of the school children. It was officially adopted by New Jersey in 1913. In Rhode Island it was chosen by the school children in 1897, although it has not been officially adopted. The violet was adopted by these states because of the profusion in which many kinds grow in the countryside.

The violet (*viola cucollata*) is also the flower of the Canadian province of New Brunswick, having been adopted by Order in Council in 1936. In this province it is one of the early wild flowers of spring to gladden the heart, and is among the best-loved.

1. Sonnet on the colour blue.
2. 'She dwelt among the untrodden ways', etc.

VIRTUES—In the angelic hierarchy of the pseudo-Dionysius virtues are the angels which occupy the second rank of the second order. They signify exaltation and lofti-ness and, like the other members of the order, they are usually represented with a complete figure, as distinct from angels of the first order, who are shown just with heads and wings.

WALSEROBIN—The large flowered walserobin (*Trillium grandiflorum*) was adopted as the flower of Ontario in 1937. This beautiful plant with white flowers which later turn pink, grows in woodlands from Ontario to Minnesota and South to North Carolina.[1]

1. *See* HAROLD NORMAN MOLDENKE, *American Wild Flowers*, p. 338 (New York, 1949).

WATER—Symbol of purification, regeneration and birth.

Among ancient peoples in the Near and Middle East, where there are many desert areas and periods of drought, the life-giving properties of water were often intensely appreciated. Rain and flood water made the crops grow, water quenched thirst, and cool water washed, and was a solace to, tired and heated bodies. The sense of revival by means of water was thus particularly strong, and it was therefore logical that in many ancient religious rites water was a purifying and regenerating agent. It was regarded as a symbol of birth by the Egyptians, and later the Arabs, who thought of life as springing from water. The Egyptians regarded the lotus water-lily as a symbol of life partly because it rose from the water. The symbolism has some kinship with the utterance of Christ: 'Except a man be born of water and of the Spirit, he cannot enter into the kingdom of God.' (John iii. 5); and the Arabs believed that God created man from water. It was thought, not unnaturally, by some ancient peoples that the sun rose in the morning out of the sea, and sunk into it in the evening.

Cleansing by water appears to have been a purification rite with many religions before Christianity, as it was with the Jews. We read in Ezekiel (xxxvi. 25) that the Lord God will sprinkle 'clean water upon you, and ye shall be clean: from all your filthiness, and from all your idols, will I cleanse you'.

In Christianity the symbolism of water has survived chiefly in the rite of baptism. Its significance appears to cover purification, regeneration or re-birth. In accordance with the doctrine of original sin, baptism by water performs the function of 'the washing away of sin' as stated in the Ministration of Baptism. This also means a re-birth to life in Christ's Church.

Water has also been considered symbolically with the significance of separation, because rivers and seas are natural barriers. This idea of separation has been associated with the crossing of the Red Sea by the Israelites when they returned to their own land and were safe and separated from the Egyptians. Baptism has likewise been regarded as a separation from sin. The passage through the Red Sea has sometimes been regarded as a prophetic symbol of baptism and of entry to the promised land. The subject appears as a relief on a sarcophagus in the catacombs.[1]

In a study of the origins of the rite of baptism the various symbolic significances of water are all involved, that is—of purification, of regeneration, and as that from which life itself has sprung. This last significance, which is deeply set in very ancient traditions, may be the real reason for water being the main agent of initiation into religion and thus into life.[2]

1. See LOUISA TWINING, *Symbols and Emblems of Early and Mediaeval Christian Art*, 2nd Edition, p. 140 (London, 1885).
2. The origin and symbolic significance of baptism is considered in some detail by F. W. DILLISTONE in *Christianity and Symbolism*, Chap. 7, 'Water Symbolism and Christian Baptism', pp. 183–220 (London, 1955).

WHEAT—As bread is the symbol of the body of Christ[1] at the celebration of the Eucharist, but is unsuitable for artistic representation, wheat,[2] standing in similar relationship to bread as the vine to wine, most appropriately serves the purpose. It has no tradition in Christian art having been employed only in recent times. Nevertheless, wheat and the vine, typifying as they do two of the main foods of life, and being Christ's choice as the symbols of his body and blood, are living and impressive symbols of remembrance of Christ's sacrifice, and of gratitude for the life that He gave by redemption. They are good subjects for design.

A wheat sheaf is a common symbol of agriculture, and also figures much as a charge in heraldry, being called 'garb' (from the French for sheaf—gerbe).

1. Matthew xxvi. 26; Mark xiv. 22; Luke xxii. 19.
2. The same can be said of rye, barley, oats, maize, and other vegetable products that are employed to make bread. The principal vegetable ingredient of the bread peculiar to a country would naturally be selected as the Christian symbol. Thus, as in England wheat is principally used, this is selected as the symbol. In Germany rye is perhaps more readily thought of, and so on.

WHEEL—Symbol of fortune, of mutability, of the vicissitudes of life, and of time, and an ancient Oriental and Greek symbol of the sun. Fortune is often personified as a goddess who is recognized by her emblem, the wheel. Sometimes the goddess is represented as blind.

The wheel, like the disk, anciently symbolized the sun by reason of its circular shape. Its spokes indicated the sun's rays,[1] and in addition its suggestion of motion symbolized the sun's course in the heavens. It thus became an effective and popular solar symbol. In the Greek myth of Ixion, Zeus in anger, because of Ixion's amours with Hêrê, sent Ixion spinning through space bound to a winged wheel. Ixion was then really the sun-god.[2] The Buddhists first used a disk to symbolize the sun (as mentioned in the note on nimbus), which they later transformed into a wheel, giving it numerous spokes or rays, and calling it the 'wheel of Law'.[3] In Mithraism the wheel symbolized the sun, which may have been partly responsible for the sacred monogram as mentioned under that heading.

In Christian times the wheel has been blended in design with the cross, which is enclosed within the circle, the cross forming the spokes of the wheel. It is often confused with the ring cross, but the latter shows the circle between the arms of the cross and not enclosing them. It was no doubt an intention of early Christians in designing this, to associate the symbol of the sun with the cross, thereby to convey the idea that He who redeemed the world on the Cross was the source of all spiritual light. The combination thus forms a significant design for ecclesiastical purposes. (Fig. 56(a).)

The wheel is a symbol in more modern times mainly because it suggests the idea of motion—and so change, vicissitudes and fortune. There are numerous allusions in literature to the wheel in these senses and its symbolism has supplied a popular subject for painters, Burne-Jones' conception of 'The Wheel of Fortune' being one of the best known.

1. GOBLET D'ALVIELLA, *op. cit.*, pp. 67, 179.
2. *See* A. B. COOK, *Zeus*, Vol. I, pp. 199 *et seq.*
3. D'ALVIELLA, *op. cit.*, p. 143.

WHITE—Symbol of purity, chastity, innocence, spotlessness, and, to a less extent, of peace.

White, more than any other colour, has been associated with religious devotion since the days of ancient Egypt. The priests of Osiris, the Greek priests of Zeus and the initiated Druids performed their ceremonies robed in white as, to the present day, do the ministers of numerous religions as widely separated as Brahmanism and Christianity. During the Middle Ages it was the custom at Lent to cover the altar, reredos, reading lectern, and pulpit with white cloth, thus expressing the period of restraint by chastity in colour.

The prevailing notion prompting this wide employment of white in devotion is that of spiritual purity and chastity of thought. Its Christian use may be influenced a little by the description of Christ's raiment as 'white as the light'[1] or 'as white as snow'[2] in St. Matthew's and St. Mark's accounts of the transfiguration, and by St. Matthew's description of an angel of the resurrection (xxviii. 3).

In Ecclesiastes (ix. 8) white garments are expressive of joy; in Isaiah (i. 18) white is employed to suggest cleansing of sin; while in Revelation (iii. 4) those of Sardis who have not defiled their garments shall walk in white.

The whiteness of the lily, known now by the name of Madonna, made it a symbol of purity and emblematic of the Virgin Mary.

Religious literature abounds in sacred metaphorical uses of white. Nesse affords an interesting example in his *Church History*[3] when he says that God chequered His providence with the Black of Misery and with the White of Mercy.

White, as the colour of peace, is derived from its typification of innocence, thus harmlessness and so peace. Consequently a white flag signifies peaceful and friendly intentions, and has become in warfare the flag of truce.

It is well known that it was customary among the Romans to mark with a white stone any propitious event worthy of remembrance. It thus became a token of a happy memory, and was often so alluded to in their writings.[4]

Where it is desired that chastity, purity, innocence, peace, and their kindred meanings are to be expressed, then white or a white material is particularly appropriate.

White is a liturgical colour, and vestments of this colour are worn at certain prescribed times, such as Christmas and Easter festivals, at the consecration of bishops and dedication of churches.

1. Matthew xvii. 2.
2. Mark ix. 3.
3. 1680, p. 110.
4. LYTTON, in *The Last Days of Pompeii*, in introducing this symbol thus shows its significance:
   'We shall see you both at my father's villa soon' said Julia, turning to Claudius.
   'We will mark the day in which we visit you with a white stone,' answered the gamester.

WIG—An artificial head of hair called a periwig (contracted to wig) has since the beginning of history been made to rectify natural deficiency, for adornment, for disguise and as a symbol of office or profession. At various times wigs became fashionable adornments, the most recent period being the early seventeenth century to the late eighteenth. When the fashion had waned wigs continued to be worn by some professions, by some state, parliamentary and legal dignitaries and by members of the legal profession, by the Lord Chancellor, by judges and barristers, and also by the Speaker of the House of Commons and the Clerks of Parliament.

In commemorative art a lawyer is sometimes symbolized by a wig. A quill and book occasionally complete the design.

WILLOW—The species, *Salix babylonica*, commonly known as the weeping willow, is a symbol of sadness and mourning.

Its name implies an early association with Babylon, but it was originally a native of China, from which it has widely spread. In ancient Babylon it was mingled with the palm as symbolic of joy and triumph. During the Babylonian captivity, however, the Jews in their lament for Zion (Psalm 137) sat down by the rivers of Babylon and wept and hung their 'harps upon the willows'; and the willow was thenceforth associated with mourning, the graceful hanging forms of its foliage, by reason of which it is called the weeping willow, having probably had much to do with its association with sadness and mourning.

Both the tree itself, like the cypress and yew, and sepulchral artistic representation of it, have often been employed in this symbolic capacity. An example of the former use is the willow-tree which was planted near the grave of Napoleon in St. Helena; though the grave is no longer there, the spot is still overshadowed by the tree. Between the years 1850 and 1890 it was a popular subject on English grave monuments, its forms being arranged mostly hanging over the tops of headstones, numerous examples appearing in the Protestant cemetery at Kensal Green. Its graceful hanging foliage affords a good subject for design, while its drooping forms themselves convey the sentiment of mourning. It is, however, effective rather as a general symbol of the dead, than for permanent, personal commemoration.

WINGS—*See* Angel.

WOODTHRUSH—The woodthrush (*Hylocichla mustelina*) is regarded unofficially as the emblematic bird of the District of Columbia, having been selected by the District Federation of Women's Clubs.

WOOLSACK—The traditional seat of the Lord Chancellor in the House of Lords could be regarded as a symbol of wealth, because a woolsack was originally used for this purpose after the passing of the Act in the reign of Elizabeth I prohibiting the export of wool. It was used as a seat for the Lord Chancellor as a reminder of this source of our national wealth.

WREATH—*See* Crown.

WREN—The cactus wren (*Heleodytes brunneicapillus covesi*) is the state bird of Arizona, having been officially adopted in 1931. The Carolina wren (*Thryothorus ludovicianus*) was selected in 1931 as the state bird of South Carolina by the Federated Women's Clubs, and was officially adopted in 1948.

YALE—The Yale, one of the Queen's beasts, seems to have had an imaginary existence in Roman and mediaeval times. Pliny,[1] who called it eale, described it as being about the size of an hippopotamus with the tail of an elephant and the mouth of a boar, with horns that could move forward or backward according to their usefulness in combat. This description seems to have been partly responsible for the fashioning of the beast in mediaeval heraldry, when it was associated with or regarded as a species of antelope. It figured in the arms of Mary Bohun, wife of Henry IV, and her son, the Duke of Bedford and Earl of Kendal, may have adopted the Yale partly because of this and partly as a pun on his name, Kend-eale. It was later adopted by John Beaufort, Duke of Somerset and Earl of Kendal, from whom it descended to Margaret Beaufort, mother of Henry VII, and thus to the present monarch. Margaret had two yales as her supporters.

1. *Natural History*, VIII, 30.

YELLOWHAMMER—The state bird of Alabama, having been officially adopted in 1927. The bird (*Colaptes auratus lateus*) belongs to the woodpecker family and is also known as the flicker, and by several other names. The reason for its adoption as the state bird of Alabama, nicknamed the Yellowhammer State, is that during the war between the states, a company of cavalry soldiers from Huntsville in new uniforms with bright yellow on their sleeves, collars, and coat-tails, rode into Hopkinsville past the soldiers in faded and worn uniforms who had long been on the battlefields of the Confederacy. At sight of these bright new uniforms one of the latter shouted 'Yellowhammer, yellowhammer, flicker, flicker'. After that the Huntsville soldiers were called the 'Yellowhammer Company', and later all Alabama troops were called the Yellowhammers. Such nicknames are common in military history, and are greatly prized by those to whom they are given. Thus the veteran soldiers of Alabama took pride in being called Yellowhammers, and wore a yellowhammer's feather in their caps or lapels during reunions. It was thus a matter of satisfaction when the yellowhammer was adopted as the state bird.

YEW—Symbol of sadness and mourning, like the cypress and willow. Also, in common with other evergreens, symbol of immortality.

As a symbol of mourning it fulfils its function in the English churchyard as the cypress does in the graveyards of the Mediterranean countries. The reason for the presence in some English churchyards of very old trees is suggested by Hulme[1] to be that the priests of the old Celtic religion regarded the yew as a symbol of immortality, and planted it in their sacred groves—sites which ultimately served for Christian churches and burial grounds. During the Middle Ages and Renaissance sprigs of yew were employed at funerals to signify immortality. Wreaths were sometimes made of it. We read in Dryden,[2] for example, that:

> Sad cypress, vervain, yew, compose the wreath;
> And every baleful green denoting death.

1. *Symbolism in Christian Art*, p. 201.
2. Aeneid, 1, 731. It should be mentioned that Virgil does not make any allusion to yew.

YUCCA PLANT—The state flower of New Mexico, officially adopted in 1927. It was chosen both by the Federation of Women's Clubs and by the school children of the state.

ZINNIA—State flower (*Zinnia Elegans*) of Indiana, officially adopted in 1931 in succession to the carnation, the first flower to be adopted, in 1913, by an Act that was repealed in 1923 when the blossom of the tulip tree was officially chosen. This Act was in turn repealed when the Zinnia was chosen and the tulip tree then became the state tree.

ZIGGURAT—The ancient Babylonian and Assyrian structures like stepped pyramids, known as ziggurats, were probably built in imitation of sacred mountains. The form appears to have originated with the Summerians, who originally dwelt among the mountains at the summits of which they conceived their gods to have dwelt and where possibly they built temples for communion with them. When they migrated to the plains of the Euphrates the habits of religious worship prompted them to rectify the absence of mountains by building artificial ones, and this appears to be the origin of the ziggurat. Each was provided with a temple at its summit. Sir Leonard Woolley says the Summerians built a ziggurat 'whose name might be called "the Hill of Heaven" or "the Mountain of God". In every important city there was at least one such tower crowned by a sanctuary, the tower itself forming part of a large temple complex.'[1]

Remains of ziggurats date from as early as about 3500 B.C. and judging from these they appear to be at first fairly simple two or three tiered structures, but later they became much larger and more complex. The best preserved of the ancient, more elaborate ziggurats is that of Urnammu at Ur of about 2100 B.C. which has four storeys diminishing in size towards the top, with broad terraces at each stage.[2] The later ziggurat at Tchoga-Zanbil, near Susa, Elam, of about 1200 B.C., has five storeys, while the still later somewhat legendary ziggurat of Babylon is conjectured to have been larger and more complex with seven diminishing storeys dedicated to the gods of the seven planets and surmounted by a temple.[3] This ziggurat is supposed to have been the Tower of Babel whose top reached unto heaven (Genesis xi. 4).

The ziggurat is essentially either the symbol of the Mountain of God, or is actually so, as the temple is the House of God. Diminutive representations of ziggurats for devotional purposes have this symbolical significance.

The romantic notion of building ziggurats has sometimes occurred to modern architects—one thought of suggesting building a ziggurat in a new town. If, in this, something of the original significance of the ziggurat is also intended, it is not difficult to conceive that in a high place with a vast panorama some identification of the self with the universe might be prompted. The temple on the mountain top still persists in many partly disguised forms.

1. SIR LEONARD WOOLLEY, *Ur of the Chaldees*, pp. 83 *et seq.* (London, 1929).
2. SIR BANISTER FLETCHER, revised by R. A. Cordingley, *A History of Architecture on the Comparative Method*, 17th edition, pp. 66–75 (London, 1961).
3. J. E. CIRLOT, *A Dictionary of Symbols*, p. 316 (London, 1962).

ZODIAC—The signs representing the twelve constellations of the Zodiac have sometimes been employed as a collective symbol of the universe, of the heavens, or separately, as twelve significant periods of the year, or as the seasons. From ancient times the signs have been fancifully associated with various objects and ideas where a total of twelve can be conveniently, ingeniously or clumsily made.

The names were given to the twelve constellations of the sun's ecliptic by the ancient Greeks—who derived them in some cases from more ancient sources—because of the supposed resemblance in shape of these constellations to sacred beings or animals. The constellations are: Aries the Ram (21st March); Taurus the Bull (20th April); Gemini the Twins (21st May); Cancer the Crab (21st June); Leo the Lion (23rd July); Virgo the Virgin (23rd August); Libra the Balance (23rd September); Scorpio the Scorpion (23rd October); Sagittarius the Archer (22nd November); Capricornus the Goat (22nd December); Aquarius the Water-carrier (20th January); Pisces the Fishes (19th February).

Zeus was sometimes represented surrounded by the signs of the Zodiac, to indicate his functions as the god of the heavens and of the universe.[1] In Christianity the signs have sometimes been associated with the twelve apostles and the twelve tribes; and frequently been used in architectural decorations, in manuscripts, and to decorate various objects. However, the reason for the use of the signs is necessarily a little vague. They have appeared on fonts—an example in England being in Brookland Church, Kent, around doorways, on tiles, and in various other ways. The purpose of their use was probably to suggest the universe and Christian dominion.

The disposition of the constellations of the Zodiac in relation to the planets at certain moments or periods of the year, known as a horoscope, is supposed in astrology to have an influence on human events and to determine character or temperament at birth. This was widely believed in ancient and mediaeval times, but is now largely discredited. It has given rise to a good deal of superstition, but now more often figures as a game—'Know your Horoscope' in popular newspapers and magazines.

As in ancient times a logical and reasonable use of the signs of the Zodiac is as a collective symbol, as an expression or indication of the idea of the universe.

1. A. B. COOK gives the examples of some later coins of A.D. 138–235 in which the figure of Zeus is surrounded by signs of the Zodiac. *Op. cit.*, Vol. I, pp. 751–4.

Bibliographical Note

To GIVE a detailed and lengthy bibliography would be supererogatory, for it would for the most part merely be repeating what has been given in the references, all items of which are completely indexed. As there are not a large number of books devoted entirely to symbolism, or to particular symbols, most of the books to which reference has been made deal mainly with other subjects and symbolism is incidental. Thus in the chapters on Seals, Coins, Medals, Trade Marks and Pictorial Advertising several books on these subjects which provide background information to a study of symbolism and which make references to it are mentioned in the references. In the more speculative chapters in Part III, such as those on Instinctive and Unconscious Symbolism, religion and the different forms of art, several books are referred to in which various aspects of symbolism are discussed.

As the purpose of a bibliography is to assist the reader in pursuing study of a subject further it might be helpful, at the risk of too much repetition, to underline here certain important works that deal mainly or to a good extent with symbolism.

For primitive and ancient symbols, Pliny's *Natural History*, available in several English translations, is a valuable source of information bearing on the symbolism of animals, birds and flowers. One of the best modern books on the early uses of symbols is Eugène Goblet Count D'Alviella's *La Migration des Symboles* (Paris, 1891)—English translation with an introduction by Sir G. Birdwood (London, 1894).

There are numerous and illuminating references to primitive symbolism in Sir James G. Frazer's work, especially *The Golden Bough*, third edition, 12 volumes (London 1910–15), *The Worship of Nature* (London, 1926) and *Belief in Immortality and the Worship of the Dead* (London, Vol. I 1913, Vol. II 1922, Vol. III 1924). Edward Westermarck's *History of Human Marriage*, fifth edition, 3 volumes (London, 1921) and his *The Origin and Development of the Moral Ideas*, second edition, 2 volumes (London, 1912) also contain many references bearing on primitive symbolism.

For symbols and symbolism in ancient Greece the most exhaustive work is A. B. Cook's scholarly *Zeus, A Study in Ancient Religion*, Vol. I, *Zeus, God of the Bright Sky* (Cambridge, 1914) and Vol. II, *Zeus, God of the Dark Sky* (*Thunder and Lightning*) (Cambridge, 1925).

355

Important books dealing with particular symbols of ancient origin are G. Elliot Smith's *The Evolution of the Dragon* (Manchester, 1919), Mrs. J. H. Philpot's *The Sacred Tree or the Tree in Religion and Myth* (London, 1897) and Odell Shepard's *The Lore of the Unicorn* (London, 1930).

Books on Christian symbolism are more numerous than on other forms, although good books in this field are not plentiful. Among those which deal mainly or at some length with it are A. H. Didron's *Iconographie Chretienne, Histoire de Dieu* (Paris, 1843)—English translation by E. J. Millington with additions and appendices by Margaret Stokes, entitled *Christian Iconography* or the *History of Christian Art in the Middle Ages*, 2 volumes (London, 1849, 1851 and 1886); and G. B. De Rossi, *La Roma Sotteranea* (Rome, 1864–77). An English work based mainly on De Rossi's work is Northcote and Brownlow's *Roma Sotteranea* (London, first edition 1869; second and enlarged edition 1897). Other important works that deal with Christian symbolism are Anna Jameson's *Sacred and Legendary Art* (London, first edition 1848; third and revised edition 1857) and Louisa Twining's *Symbols and Emblems of Early and Mediaeval Christian Art* (London, 1852, second edition 1885), and various encyclopaedias, but especially James Hastings' *Encyclopaedia of Religion and Ethics* (Edinburgh, 1908). A recent useful book on Christian Iconography is Louis Réau's *Iconographie de l'Art Chrétien*, 3 volumes, Vol. I, *Introduction Générale* (Paris, 1955), which includes a section on 'Le Symbolisme Universel'; Vol. II, *Iconographie de la Bible*, 1, Ancien Testament, 2, Nouveau Testament (1956); Vol. III, *Iconographie des Saints*.

For the philosophical, sociological and psychological aspects of symbolism, among the best books are Herbert Spencer's *Principles of Sociology* in eight parts (3 volumes), part I, 'The Data of Sociology', part 2, 'The Inductions of Sociology', part 3, 'Domestic Institutions', part 4, 'Ceremonial Institutions', part 5, 'Political Institutions', part 6, 'Ecclesiastical Institutions', part 7, 'Professional Institutions', part 8, 'Industrial Institutions'. Most parts give useful information on the place of symbolism in society and the origin of many symbols is discussed. Particularly valuable in this connection is part 4, which includes chapters on Ceremony in General, Trophies, Presents, Badges and Costumes, and further Class Distinctions. Much that Spencer wrote in this work has been superseded by later writers, but not the sections dealing with symbols and their origins. J. E. Cirlot's *Diccionario de Simbols Traditionales*, English translation by Jack Sage (London, 1962), is a learned work which gives much information of an esoteric character mingled with some rather fanciful psychological interpretations.

A. N. Whitehead's *Symbolism—Its Meaning and Effect* (Cambridge, 1928), is one of the best books from the philosophical standpoint on the function of symbolism in perception, and the uses of symbolism in society and the state. Linked with this are Lewis Mumford's many references to the importance of symbolism in his four major books *Technics and Civilisation* (1934), *The Culture of Cities* (1938), *The Condition of Man* (1944), and *The Conduct of Life* (1951), especially the last. Mumford also deals with symbolism and art in *Art and Technics* (1952), in a manner a little different from Sir Herbert Read's *Art Now* (London, 1933), which gives a narrower yet significant interpretation of symbolism in art.

For psychological symbolism the chief work is Sigmund Freud's *The Interpretation of Dreams*, authorized English translation of third edition by A. A. Brill (London, 1913, revised edition 1915). A good essay on the subject is Ernest Jones' 'The Theory of Symbolism' in *Papers on Psychoanalysis* (London, first edition 1912, fifth edition 1948). Another view of instinctive and unconscious symbolism is given by C. G. Jung in *Psychology of the Unconscious—a Study of the Transformation and Symbolism of the Libido*, authorized English translation by Beatrice M. Hinkle (New York, 1916). Another interesting and speculative work by C. G. Jung is the first and principal essay, 'Approaching the unconscious', in *Man and his Symbols* (London, 1964). Other essays in this book are by Joseph L. Henderson, 'Ancient myths and modern man'; M-L von Franz 'The process of individuation'; Aniela Jaffé 'Symbolism in the visual arts'; and Jolande Jacobi 'Symbols in an individual analysis'.

Index

Numbers in italics refer to illustrations.

Aaron, 306
Aaron's Rod, 38, 194
Abacus, 96
Abyssinia, 342
Acacia (*Acacia seyal*), 193
Acanthus, 193, 227
Accrington, arms of, 64, 66
Achievement, 248; symbol of, 159, 220, 264; in dance and song, symbol of, 340
Achilles, 210, 305
Acropolis, 193, 194
Activities, symbol of, 148
Acton, H. B., *Philosophy*, 190
Adam, Sir Ronald F., 29
Addison, Joseph, 97, 98
Adler, Alfred, *Individual Psychology*, 125
Admetus, 215
Adonis, 197, 248
Adoration, 180, 301, 311
Advertisements, pictorial, 105–11
Advertising, 7, 16, 104; pictorial, 104–11, *Plates XXVII, XXVIII, XXIX, XXX*
Adze, 96
Aegina island, coins of, 74
Aeneas, 274
Aeschylus, 150; *Agamemnon*, 75
Aesculapius, God of Medicine, *see* Asklêpius
Aeternitas, 58
Æetes, King, 243
Affection, 252, 255, 323; symbol of, 266
Afghanistan, 27
Africa, tribes of, 313
Agriculture, symbol of, 348
Agrigentum, coin of, 75

Airborne Division, badge of, 33
Air Survey Co. Ltd., trade mark, *90*, 95
Akheselshrap, O. Kavli, trade mark, *90*
Akrages, coins of, 75
Alabama, seal of, *50*; state flower of, 249; state bird of, 351
Alacoque, Margarite Mary, 255
Alanbrooke, Field-Marshal Viscount, 29
Alaska, seal of, 57
Alberta, flower of, 303
Alcestis, 215
Aldeburgh (Suffolk), seal of, 41
Alexander the Great, on coins, 75, 76
Alexander III (of Scotland), 331, 341
Alfonso V of Aragon, medal of, 81–2
Allied Land Forces, South-East Asia, 29; badge of, *30*
Allsop, Bruce, 169
Almond (*Amygdalus communis*), 194
Alpha, 194, *Plates LXVIII, LXXII*
Altar, 134, 194–5, 209, 239, 263, 294, 300, 320, 329, 334, 340, 342, 349
Altar crosses, 337
Altar piece by Van Eyck, 263
Amaranth, 195–6
Ambition, symbol of, 319
Amen, God of Thebes, 299–300; Amen-Ra, 299–300
Amenem-Het III, sphinx of, 318
America, Pre-Columbian, 224, 235; United States of, Great Seal of, 42, *43*; flag of, 20, 239; Military badges of, 31, 35; Seals of the States, 42–58; State flowers of, *Plates XXXIX, XL*; Symbols of, 236, 300

American Air Force Badges, *34*, 35
Amiens, cathedral, *Plate XLIII*
Ammon, 256, 299
Amphora, symbol of Dionysus, 75
Ampula, 196
Amstuts, André, 106
Amulets, 238
Anarchy, colour denoting, 300–1
Anchor, 58, 76, 97, 102, 196–7, *205*; and ball, 73; with scallop-shell, 315
Anderson, A. W., *Plants of the Bible*, 267
Andromeda, 84, 311
Anemone (*Anemone coronaria*), 197
Angel, 197–202, *Plates LVIII, LIX*
Angelico, Fra, 200, 201, 282, 303; *Adoration of the Magi*, 288
Animism, 130–2
Ankh, 203–4, *205*
Anne, Queen, 19; Royal Coat of Arms, 23, *24*; seals of, 39, 40
Anrep, Boris, 206
Ant, 204
Antef-Ager-Ankh-Khu, 238
Antelope, 27, 319, 351
Antoninus Pius, 221; coins of, 77, 78
Antonius, coins of, 76
Anu, Assyrian Sky-God, 224
Anubis, 239
Anxiety, symbol of deliverance from, 287
Apelles, 75
Aphroditê (Venus), 74, 197, 234, 246, 248, 273, 279, 335
Apollo, Sun God, 6, 175; dolphin as symbol of, 37; god of flocks and herds, symbol of, 37, 75; riding on a man, 37; disk as symbol of, 75; ram's head as symbol of, 75; symbol of, 270
Apostles, symbolized, 316
Apple, 204, *Plate LIX*; blossom (*Pyrus cornaria*), 204, *Plate XXXIX*; blossom (*Pyrus malus*), 204; golden, 236
Appleby (Westmorland), seal of, 41
Aquascutum, trade mark, 92
Aquinas, St. Thomas, 209
Arabia, 77, 217; people of, 347
Aragon, Alfonso V of, 81–2; Maria of, 81
Arch, triumphal, 204–7, *Plate LXI*; ceremonial, 204–7
Archangel, *Plates LVIII, LXVIII*
Archangel Chamuel, 208
Archangel Gabriel, 207, 208, *Plate LXVIII*
Archangel Jophiel, 146, 208
Archangel Michael, 207, 208, *Plate LXVIII*
Archangel Raguel, 208

Archangel Raphael, 207, 208, *Plate LXVIII*
Archangel Remiel, 208
Archangel Saraqâêl, 208
Archangel Uriel, 207, 208, *Plate LXVIII*
Archangel Zadkiel, 208
Archer, Sagittarius the, 353
Architecture, symbolism in, 140*f*, *Plates XLI, XLII, XLIII, XLIV, XLV*
Arês (Mars), God of War, 27, 246–7; god of fertility, 247
Aristotle, 134
Arizona, flag of, 20; seal of, *57*; state flower, 215; state tree of, 291; state bird of, 351
Ark, 83, 208–9, 287, 316; Noah's, 208, 235; of the Covenant, 208, 209, 263
Arkansas, state flower of, 204; seal of, *51*; state bird of, 276; state tree of, 296
Armada, medals of, 83
Armistice of the First World War, Memorial, *Plate XLVI*
Arms, Coats of, 21*f*; Royal Coat of, 23*f*; Civic Coats of, 60*f*; Municipal Coats of, 60*f*
Arondeaux, R., 83
Arrow, 209–10
Arrow, G. J., *The Fauna of British India*, 307
Artemis (Diana), 75, 209, 211, 248; temple of, 215, priest of, 274
Artists' Rifles, 27
Arts, The, symbolism in, 140*f*
Aruntas, 150
Ascension, symbol of, 236
Ash, 335*f*
Ashanti Medal, 85
Ashburton (Devon), seal of, 41
Asklêpius (Aesculapius), God of Medicine, 216, 248, 296–7, 313, *Plate LXXIV*; staff of, 27, 73, 313
Asphodel, 210
Aspiration, symbol of, 148, 170
Assyria, 197, 198, 199, 249; military standards of, 18; winged lion of, 35, 199, 269; ancient palaces of, 35; seals of, 36; winged genii of, 198, 199; art of, 318
Astarte, 234
Astollea, Giulia, medal of, 82
Athena, (Minerva), 18, 74, 75, 76, 77, 175, 335; helmet of, 75; shield of, 77; birth of, 175
Athens, 257, 340; coins of, 74; standard of, 18; age of Pericles in, 249; Parthenon, *Plate XLII*

Attraction, symbol of, 317
Augsburg, 297
Augustus, 284, 288
Aureola (*see* Nimbus), 284, 288
Australia, 17, 238; blue ensign of, 19; products of, 238; coat of arms, 238; symbol of, 238, 260
Austria, 238; emblem of, 237
Austria–Hungary, 212
Authority, fasces as symbol of, 84, 240; eagle as symbol of, 41, 236; arrow as symbol of, 209; royal or state, symbol of, 271; deputed, symbol of, 271, 284, 309; delegation of, symbol of, 301–2; symbol of, 159, 329
Avebury, Lord, *Origin of Civilization*, 164
Avignon, Painter of *Pietà*, 181, *Plate LVI*
Axe, 210–11
Aylesbury, arms of, 212

Baal Hamman, Phoenician Sun-God, 216
Babylon, 36, 197, 199, 224, 235, 328, 335, 350
Bacchus (Dionysus), 77, 96, 100, 101, 247, 256, 333; symbol of, 333
Bacup, arms of, 64, 68, 212
Badges, Military, 60*f*
Bagehot, Walter, 138
Baker, Sir Herbert, 143, 206, *Plate LXII*
Baldachino, 211
Balder, 274
Balkan States, emblem of, 237
Ball, Katherine M., *Decorative Motives of Oriental Art*, 218, 236
Bank signs, *Plate XXIII*
Bank of England, 206, 217; coins, 78
Baptism, 41, 135
Barclay's Bank, 98
Baring, Maurice, *Cat's Cradle*, 210
Baring-Gould, S., *Lives of the Saints*, 179, 265, 314
Barker, E. R., *Burlington Magazine*, 231, 243
Barns, Thomas, *Encylopaedia of Religion and Ethics*, 335, 339
Barnsley, arms of, *65*
Barrie, J. M., 185
Barrington, George, *History of New South Wales*, 164
Barron, Oswald, Article on Heraldry, *Encyclopaedia Britannica*, 35
Barrow-in-Furness, arms of, 64, 212
Bartlett, A. D., *Proceedings of the Zoological Society*, 294

Basildon, arms of, 71
Basilisk, 203, 239
Basilius I, coin of, 277
Basoldella, Mirko, 178
Basse, Henry, 82
Bastet, Sun-Goddess, 218
Bavaria, 161
Bayer, Herbert, 95
Bay Leaves (*see* Laurel)
Beaconsfield, Lord, 101
Bear, 17, 43, 211–12; polar, *33*, 35; California Grizzly Bear (*Ursus horribilis californicus*), 211
Beauforts, Margaret, mother of Henry VII, 25, 351; silver yale of, 25, 351; John, Duke of Somerset and Earl of Kendal, 351
Beauty, goddess of, 234, 246; symbol of, 302
Beauvoir, Simone de, *Pour une Morale de l'Ambiguité*, 190
Beaver, 61, 98, 212, 272
Beckenham, arms of, 66, *68*
Beckett, Samuel, *Waiting for Godot*, 188–90
Bede, Venerable, 64, 209, 291
Bedford, Duke of, and Earl of Kendal, arms of, 351
Bee, 66*f*; symbol of industry, 63, 212–13
'Beefsteak Club', badge of, 6
Beehive, 213
Belgium, symbol of, 269; coat of arms of, 269
Bellew, Sir George, Garter King of Arms, 25, 203
Beneventum, 206
Berensen, Bernhard, *The Italian Painters of the Renaissance*, 173, 184
Betrothal, symbol of, 301–2
Bevan, Edwyn, *Symbolism and Belief*, 134, 136
Birch (*Betula papyreifera*), 213; birch rods, 240
Birch, Walter de Gray, *Seals*, 59
Bird, of prey, 83; divine, 237; of fire, 254
Birth, symbol of, 347–8; symbolized in dreams, 128
Bison, 105, 124
Bitteroot (*Lewisia medeviva*), 213, *Plate XXXIX*
Black, 213
Blackburn, arms of, 72, 151
Black-eyed Susan, *Plate XL*
Black Prince, the, emblem of, 240

Bless, Henri de (Ciretta), 87

Bloom, J. Harvey, *English Seals*, 59

Blue, 213

Bluebird (*Sialia sialis*), 213; (*Sialia arctica*), 213

Bluebonnet, *Plate XXXIX*

Blunstone, F. V., 201

Blyth, arms of, 64, 68

Bobwhite (*Colinus virginianus*), 213

Boeotia, 344; cities of, 75

Bohun, Mary, arms of, 351

Boleyn, Anne, 61

Bonacolsi, Pier Jacapo Alari, 82

Bone, Phyllis M., memorial designed by, *Plate LXXVII*

Book, 213–14

Boskan, Jan, 84

Boston, coat of arms, 61, *62*

Botticelli, 181, 183; *Nativity*, 181; Primavera, *Plate LVI*

Botticini, *Assumption of the Virgin, Plate LVIII*

Bourdelle, Antoine, 174

Boutell, *English Heraldry*, 240

Bovril, trade mark, 91, 92, 94

Bower, George, 84

Bowring, Sir John, *Kingdom and People of Siam*, 342

Bracknell, arms of, *71*

Brahma, 270, 311; Brahmanism, 349

Brancusi, C., 177

Brandenburg, Electorate of, 326

Braque, 145, 147

Bravery, symbol of, 159

Brazil, flag of, 20

Breton, André, *What is Surrealism*, 184

Brewer, *Dictionary of Phrase and Fable*, 250

Bristol, 41; Castle; 41; coat of arms, 61, *62*

Britain, invasion of, 77; North, 82, 102; symbol of, 269; regalia of, 329; Constitution of, 138; coins of, *Plates X, XI, XII*

Britannia, 39, 77, 78, 79, 84, 85, 340, *Plates X, XII*

British Columbia, emblem, 231

British Empire Exhibition, 1925, medals of, 86

British Lubricating Research Organization Ltd.; trade mark, *90*

British Rail, 106, 108; posters, *Plates XXVII, XXIX*

British War Medals 1914–18, 85, 86

Bromley, arms of *67, 73*

Brooke, George C., *English Coins from the Seventeenth Century to the Present Day*, 80

Broom of Plantagenista, 38, 73

Broomstick, witch's, 31, *32*

Brown, A. V. V. and Rankin, W., *A Short History of Italian Painting*, 181, 182

Brown Thrasher (*Toxustoma rufum*), 214

Brunelleschi, memorial tablet by, 310

Brutus, coins of, 76

Buckeye (*Aesulus Ohioensis* or *Gobra*), 214

Buddha, 270, 324, 328

Buddhist symbol 229; symbol of the universe, 324; monument,' 334, 342; religion, 282; wheel of the law, 349; trisula, 340

Budge, E. A. Wallis, *The Gods of the Egyptians*, 203, 231; *Cleopatra's Needles and Other Egyptian Obelisks*, 285–7

Buffalo (*Bos* or *Bison americanus*), 214

Bull, 215, 319, 341, 353; of Clarence, *Plate III*; horns of, 256; sacrifice of; 274; Taurus the, 353

Burgh, Elizabeth de, 215

Burgon, J. W., *The Life and Times of Sir Thomas Gresham*, 250

Burman and Greenwood Ltd., trade mark of, *88*

Burne-Jones, *The Wheel of Fortune*, 349

Burnley, arms of, 212

Burtin, Will, 95

Burton, Decimus, 207

Burton, Sir Richard, *Lake Regions of Central Africa*, 342

Bury, arms of, 64, *65*; shield of, 66

Butler, Reg, 177

Buxton, arms of, *69*, 73

Byzantium, 223, 224, 257, 337

Cabbala, 255

Cactus, 58; Hepal, 215; Saguara (*Cereus Giganticus*), 215, *Plate XXXIX*

Caduceus, 27, 36, 76, 215–16, *Plates LXII, LXIII*

Caine, W. Ralph Hall, *Isle of Man*, 342

Calcutta, Government of, 85

California, 43, 247; seal of, 43, *52*, 247; state animal, 212; state flower of, 298; state bird of, 299; state fish of, 342

Calik, Nehmet Sadi, 178

Camel, 77, 217, 235; genital organs of, 258

Canada, symbol of, 86, 212; emblem of, 272; coat of arms of, 272

Canopy, 217, 342

Canterbury, Archbishop of, 41; Cathedral, 225, 240

Cap, winged, 76; of liberty, 76

Câpek, Karel and Josef, *Insect Play*, 188

Capstan, trade mark, 92, 111, *Plate XXIX*

Cardiff, arms of, *68*

Cardinal bird (*Cardinalis cardinalis*), 217

Caribou, 109

Carlyle, *Sartor Resartus*, 3, 139

Carnation, 217, 352, *Plate XL*

Carp, 217–18

Carpenter's square, 5

Carthage, 216

Castor and Pollux, 76

Cat, 82, 98, 108, 218; black, 31; civet, 98

Caterpillar, 218

Catherine of Braganza, 27

Celtic people, 335; folk-lore, 337; religion, 352

Cenotaph, 218, 263, 343, 344, *Plate LXIV*

Centaur, 37, 239, 247; chiron, 27

Ceremonial, 316

Ceremonies, of everyday life, 149*f*; state and religious, 138, 151; of Christian Church, 18, 135

Ceres (Demeter), 58, 76, 247

Cézanne, 140, 144, 147, 183

Chaldea, 345

Chaldee–Babylonian Empire, 249

Chalice and Host, *205*, 218–19, 348

Chancellor, the Lord, traditional seat in the House of Lords, 351

Change, symbol of, 247, 348, 349

Chardin, 144–5

Charlemagne, 330

Charles I, 101; coins of 78; medals of, 83

Charles II, 27, 101, 284, 297; coins of, 78; medals of, 83

Charles V, reign of, 249

Charoux, Siegried, *Man 1957*, 178

Chartered Insurance Institute, arms of, 197

Chastity, symbol of, 82, 265, 267, 349, 350

Chatwood Steel Partitioning Ltd., Rigid Flexibility advertisement, *110*

Chaucer, *Second Nonne's Tale*, 265

Cheltenham, crest of, 73

Chequers (Checkers), 96, 103

Chéret, Jules, 105

Cherub, *see* Angel

Chester, 284, 285

Chickadee (*Penthestes artricapillus*), 219. Carolina Chickadee (*Parus carolinensis*), 219

Chimera, 239

China, 36, 217, 219, 229, 235, 270, 303, 328, 335, 350; early photography of, 4, 5, 6, 7; coins of, 74; dragon of, 235; flag of, 20; postage stamps of, 219; stupa erected in, 324; Tang dynasty, 249

Chirico, Giorgio de, 184

Chosen People, symbol of, 345

Christ, sacrifice of, 132, 133; symbols of, 195, 224, 237, 261, 267, 276, 290, 293, 345; symbol of resurrection, 293, 294; symbol of care for His followers, 315–16; teaching of, symbolized, 315; paintings of, *Plates LV, LVI, LX. See also* Christian Symbols

Christian, altar, 195; symbols, 220, 224, 231, 232, 234, 235, 236, 237, 238, 241, 243, 251, 252, 255, 260, 261, 263, 265, 267, 269, 272, 276, 280, 282, 284, 287, 288, 289, 290, 291, 293, 294, 302, 311, 314, 315, 316, 317, 319, 323, 326, 329, 330, 331, 332, 334, 337, 339, 342, 345, 349; pilgrims, 291; legends, 311, 326; prayer, 151; ceremonies, 160; civilization, 174; religion, 180

Christian worship and teaching in relation to religious symbolism, 132–5

Christianity, its doctrines, 132–5

Christmas, 303, 337, 350; tree, 337; use of mistletoe at, 275; flowering trees, 337

Chrysanthemum, 219; Order of the, 219

Churchill, Sir Winston S., 203

Ciborium, 219

Cinema, 187*f*

Cinquefoil, ermine, 72

Circle, 220, 277, 280, 301, 302, 341, 349

Ciretta (Henri de Bless), 87

Clare, Elizabeth de, 215

Clarence, Duke of, bull of, 25, 215

Clasped hands, *Plate LXVI*

Claudius, 77; coins of, 77

Clement of Alexandria, 241

Cleopatra, 286; needles of, 286

Clothes, 154–65; clothing as protection, 155–6; for sexual attraction, 156–7; for self-elation and admiration, 157–8; as trophies and badges, 158–60

Clover, Red (*Tritolium pratense*), 220, *Plate XXXIX*

Clovis, 245

Clytie, 325, 326

Coach and Horses, 102

Cock, 82, 95, 96, 100, 102, 220, 289; Black, 73; French, 84, 151, 220

Coenwulf, King of Mercia, lead seal of, 38

Coins, 74*f*; Greek, 74*f*; Roman, 76*f*; British, 77*f*, *Plates X, XI, XII, XIII, XIV, XV*

Cole, Lt.-Col. Howard H., *Heraldry in War—Formation Badges, 1939–45*, 35

Coleridge, *Work without Hope*, 196

Colman's mustard, 106

Colorado, seal of, *54*; state flower of, 220; state bird of, 264

Colour symbolism, 220; *see* black, blue, green, red, purple and white

Columbia, District of, seal of, *57*; flower of, 303; emblematic bird of, 351

Columbine, Blue (*Aquilegia caerulea*), 220, *Plate XL*

Column, 220–2, *Plate LXV*; broken, 222

Combat, colour denoting, 300–1

Comines, P. de, *History of Louis XI*, 153

Commencina, M., *Coins of the Modern World, 1870–1936*, 80

Commando flag, 29

Commerce, symbol of, 215–17, 247

Commercial Bank of Scotland, 98

Commissioners of Customs, flag of, 20

Commonwealth, flags of, 19; seals of, 39, *Plate VII*; symbol of, 138

Communications, symbol of, 247

Compasses, 222–3

Compostella, 314, 315

Cone, sacred, 216

Connecticut, seal of, *45*; state flower of, 265; state tree of, 284

Conquest, symbol of, 159, 249

Constancy, symbol of, 82, 234, 279

Constantine, 18, 77, 206, 211, 221, 224, 276, 277, 282, 288; standard of, 276; monogram of, 276, 277; Constantia, sister of, 345

Constantinople, 377

Contract, symbol of, 301

Conviviality, symbol of, 247, 296

Cook, A. B., 133, 206, 207, 211, 215, 221, 223, 227, 254, 300, 305, 333, 349, 354, 355

Cooke, S. A., *Tree Worship*, 339

Copenhagen, the Church of the Advent, *Plate XLV*

Copinger, W. A., *Heraldry Simplified*, 226

Copknit, trade mark, 92

Corby, arms of, *72*

Corinth, 75; coins of, 75

Cormorant, 64

Cornhill Insurance Company, 99

Cornflower, 223

Cornucopia, 223

Coronation, ceremony of, 160, 319, 320, 329; in Siam, 342; ceremonial of, 138; medals, *Plates XVII, XVIII*

Correggio, 87, 200

Cottonwood tree, 223

Coty, trade mark, 92

Courage, symbol of, 217, 257, 267, 287

Cow, 68, 223; horns of, 256

Crab, the, 75, 353; Cancer, 353

Cranach, Lucas, 87

Crane, Walter, 99

Crawley, arms of, *70*

Creation, symbol of, 237, 238, 287, 299, 306, 307

Crescent, 223; symbol of Crusade, 38; as symbol of Artemis, 75

Crete, swastika on coins of, 328

Croker, John, 84

Cromwell, Oliver, 19, 39, 83; seals of, 39; medals of, 83

Cromwell, Richard, 83

Cross, 224–6, *Plates LX, LXII*; of St. Andrew, 19, 39, *225*; of St. George, 19, 31, 39; of St. Patrick, 19; patée, *225*; celtic, 220, 229; equilateral, *225*; tau, *225*; Latin, *225*; Double Latin, *225*; Maltese, *225*; saltire, *225*; wheel, *327*; ring, *327*; with sacred tree, 338

Crown, 226–7; of grass (*Corona graminea*), 249; myrtle, 279; laurel, 264; of oak leaves, 284; of olives, 287; of thorns, 292

Crozier, 227–8

Crucifix, 228, *Plate LX*

Crucifixion by Velasquez, *Plate LX*

Crux Ansata, 203

Cumberland, Duke of, 85

Cupid (Eros), God of Love, 228

Cuprinol Ltd., trade mark, *94*

Cupola, *see* Dome

Cwmbran, badge of, *72*

Cylinder seals, 36, 37, 235, 333

Cyme, 231

Cypress, 228, 335, 350

Cyprus, swastika on coins and pottery of, 328

Dadaism, 183

Daffodil, 86, 228

Daisy, Ox-eye, *Plate XL*

Dali, Salvador, 184; *Christ of St. John of the Cross, Plate LX*

D'Alviella, Count Goblet, *The Migration of Symbols*, 216, 217, 224, 229, 234, 237,

251, 269, 270, 282, 291, 293, 297, 328, 329, 336, 340, 342, 345, 349, 355

Damareteion of Syracuse, 75

Damascus, 77

Dance, 149–53; achievement in, 340; primitive, 135; agricultural, 149; religious, 149, 150; totem, 150; war, 150; of courtship, 150; country, 150; folk, 150; ballet, 150–1

Danger, colour of, 300

'Danneborg', national flag of Denmark, 19

Dante, 293; *Divine Comedy*, 181

Daphne, 264, 328

Darwin, Charles, 156, 157; *Descent of Man*, 1855; *Journal of Researches: Voyage of the Beagle*, 164

David, shield of, *242*, 246, 255, 339

Davidson, A. B., *Angels*, 198, 202

Death, symbol of, 85, 197, 210, 222, 228, 248, 257, 280, 310, 317, 334, 343, 344; figure of, 310, 317; symbolized in dreams, 128

de Feltre, Vittorino, medal of, 81

Defence, symbol of, 256, 298

Defoe, Daniel, memorial to, 229

Deity, symbol of, 132, 220, 221, 238, 239, 320, 325; sun as agent of, 341

De la Ryver, family coat of arms, 7

Delaware, seal of, *44*; state tree of, 256; state flower of, 292

Delitizch, 202

Delphi, coins of, 75

Demeter (Ceres), 6, 175, 248, 280

Denmark, national flag, 19; symbol of, 328; postage stamps of, 328

Dennis, George, *The Cities and Cemeteries of Etruria*, 257, 297

d'Este, Isabella, Marchesa of Mantua, medal of, 82

d'Este, Marquess Leonello, medals depicting, 81

Destruction, symbol of, 230

Devil, attribute of, 256

Devotion, symbol of, 151, 255

Diadem, 227

Diana (Artemis), *see* Artemis

Didron, A. H., *Iconographie Chrétienne*, 282, 356

Dignity, symbol of, 142, 256; royal, symbol of, 342

Dillistone, F. W., *Christianity and Symbolism*, 348

Dinsmoor, W. B., *The Architecture of Ancient Greece*, 341

Diocletian, 221

Dionysius the Areopagite, 199; pseudo-Dionysius, 197–200, 208

Dionysus (Bacchus), 75, 247, 258, 296, 333, 340; amphora as symbol of, 75; festivals of, 294; symbol of, 333

Disk, 223, 229–30, 245, 248, 280, 307*ff*, 341, 348, 349; symbol of Apollo, 75; winged, 197, 216, 229–30, *230*, 251; solar, 251, 253

Ditchfield, P. H., *Symbolism of the Saints*, 179, 270

Divisional and formation signs, *30, 32, 33*

Dogwood (*Cornus florida*) (*Cornus nuttalli*), 231, 249, *Plate XXXIX*

Dolphin (*Delphinus*), *230*, 231–2

Dome, 232–4

Dominations, angelic rank, 234

Doner, H. Creston, 95

Dormy, trade mark, 95

Dove, 234–5, *Plate LXXI*; with olive branch, 235, 287; turtle, 234

Dover, 284; seal of, 41; castle, 42

Dragon, 7, 18, 23, 25, 27, 42, 61, 78, 82, 85, 87, 101, 203, 235–7

Drake, Sir Francis, 101

Drake, P. C. Ltd., 92

Drama, symbolism in, 185–90

Dreams, 129, 144, 183, 184; unconscious symbols in, 127, 148, 294; day-, 183

Drene, trade mark, 92

Dress, symbolism of 154–65

Dri-brite, trade mark, 92

Droitwich, coat of arms, *62*

Drummond, John & Sons Ltd., trade mark, *88*

Dryden, *Translation of Virgil's Aeneid*, 352

Duccio, 181, 200

Ducksback Ltd., trade mark, *93*

Dugas, *La Pudeur, Review Philosophique*, 158

Durability, symbol of, 284

Dürer, Albrecht, 87, 200; *Virgin and Child*, 180, *Plate LIV*

Durkheim, Emile, *Les Formes Elémentaires de la Vie Religieuse*, 16

Eagle, 236–7; double-headed, 237

Earth, symbol of, 336; powers of, 178

Easter, symbol of creation, 237, 238; eggs, 237; flower, 292

Ebbe, Alex, *The Sun Worshipper, Plate XLVIII*

Ecclesiastical seals, 41

Eddington, Sir Arthur, 9, 10, 11

Edward the Confessor, 23, 38, 288, 330; wax seal of, 38, *Plate V*

Edward I, 18, 101; seal of, 39; coins of, 339

Edward III, 18, 23, 25, 101, 152, 215, 240; seal of, 39; coats of arms, *22*; coins of, 78

Edward IV, coat of arms, 24, *24*, 25; coins of, 78

Edward VI, coins of, 78, 79; medals of, 83

Edward VII, 309; seal of, 40; coins of, 79; medals of, 84

Egg, 238–9; Easter, 238–9

Egypt, flags of, 19; seals of, 37; sphinx of, 174, 239, 318–19; symbol of, 318, 319; festivals of, 149; drama of, 150

Egyptian hieroglyphs, 5, 203, 246; military standards, 17, 18

Einstein tower, 169

Elastica Ltd., trade mark, *93*

Eldorado Ice Cream Co. Ltd., trade mark, *94*

Electoral bonnet, 23

Elephant, 77, 98, 203, 235, 351; charging, 29, *30*; ermined, 61

El Greco, 147, 181

Eliot-Smith, G., *The Evolution of the Dragon*, 236, 245, 355

Elizabeth I, Queen, 23, 25, 236, 298, 351; seals of, 39, *Plate VI*; coins of, 78, 79; medals of, 83; reign of, 249

Elizabeth II, Queen, 298, 329; seal of, 40, *Plate VIII*; coins of, 76, 79; medal of, 84; postage stamps of, 115–19; coronation of, 320

Elliott, Equipment Ltd., trade mark, *90*

Ellis, Havelock, 156; *The Dance of Life*, 141, 150, 171; *Psychology of Sex*, 158

Elm (*Ulmus Americana*), 238

Elworthy, F. T., *Horns of Honour*, 252, 256

Ely, isle of, coat of arms, 64

Emu, 238, 260

Endeavour, symbol of, 319

England, arms of, 39; seals of state, 38–40; shield of, 40; medals of, 82–86; lion of, 203; national flower of, 302

Enlightenment, symbol of, 263

Enoch, Ethiopic book of, 208; Slavonic book of, 199

Epiphanius, Bishop of Constantia *Physiologus*, 293, 294

Epstein, Jacob, *Let There be Sculpture*, 179; *Night and Day, Plate XLIX*

Equality, symbol of, 152

Ernst, Max, 183, 184

Eros (Cupid), God of Love, 209, 247, 334; sexual instincts, 126

Eternity, symbol of, 220

Etruria, seals of, 37; swastika on coins of, 328

Eucharist, symbol of, 345

Euclid, Books II and VI, golden section, 249, 284

Eurydice, 328

Eusebius, 276

Evangelists, symbols of, 198, 237, 269, 289, *Plate LXVIII*

Evelyn, John, *Diary*, 297

Evil, protection from, 229; symbol of, 311, 313

Evolution, theory of biological evolution, 4

Ewing, W. and Thomson, J. E. H., *The Temple Dictionary of the Bible*, 310

Exaltation, symbol of, 332, 347

Excaveyor, trade mark, 92

Exeter Cathedral, 317

Existentialism, 189, 190

Expressionism, 183

Eye, 238–9, *242*; of God, 58, 339; of Providence, 84

Fabre, J. H., 306

Fabulous beasts, 239–40, 251

Falcons, 240; of the Plantagenets, *Plate IV*

Fallow, F. M., *Cross*, 228

Falstaff, Sir John, 101

Farmers' Union Insurance Co., 6

Farming Society of Ireland, 6

Fasces, 240, *244*; Roman, 44, 87

Fate, symbol of, 343

Father, totem as symbol of, 17; symbolized, 128

Fauconer, family coat of arms, 7

Feathers, 240

Fecundity, symbol of, 224, 329, 336

Fehlinger, H., *Sexual Life of Primitive People*, 156, 158

Fellows, Sir Charles, *Coins of Ancient Lycia*, 342

Fern (*Cyanthea dealbata*), 240–1

Fertility, symbol of, 223, 285–6, 296, 297, 299, 300, 336; god of, 247

Fertilization, symbol of, 336

Fidelity, symbol of, 258

Fig, leaf, *30*, 31; tree, 97, 345

Finland, symbol of, 326; postage stamps of, 326

Fire, 241; bird of, 254; of Zeus, 333

Firestone, trade mark, 92

Fish, 241–2, *242*; Pisces the Fishes, 353

Fitzneale, Richard, Bishop of London, 41

Flags, 17–20

Flames, of avenging justice, 29, *30*

Flamininus, 76

Flannath, trade mark, 92

Flax, 243

Fleece, golden, 243

Fletcher, Sir Banister, *History of Architecture on the Comparative Method*, 222, 341

Fleur-de-lis, 243–5, *244*

Flexwelt, trade mark, 92

Florence, 147, 175, 176; painters of, 180; Duomo at, 181; Santa Maria Maddalen Pazzi, 181; paintings of, 182, 183

Florida, seal of, *51*; state bird of, 276; state flower of, 288; state tree of, 291

Flowers, American State, *Plates XXXIX, XL*

Flügel, Dr. J. C., 12; *Introduction to Psychoanalysis*, 129; *The Psychology of Clothes*, 162, 163

Flycatcher (*Muscivora forticata*), 245

Ford Motor Co. Ltd., trade mark of, *89*, 92

Forget-me-not, *Plate XL*

Fortitude, symbol of, 82, 217, 267, 269

Fortune, good, tokens of, 307; symbols of, 307, 348–9

Fountains, 245–6, *Plate LXIV*

Fox, Bishop, 294

Fox-Davies, A. C., *A Complete Guide to Heraldry*, 35, 237; *Heraldic Badges*, 210

France, symbol of, 220; emblem of monarchy, 243–4

Francesca, Piero Della, 147, 181; *The Resurrection, Plate LV*

Frankfort, Dr. H., cylinder seals, 36, 59

Frazer, James, 150, 274; *Totemism and Exogamy*, 16, 17, 153; *The Belief in Immortality and the Worship of the Dead*, 194, 355; *Golden Bough*, 131, 141, 153, 274, 275, 355; *The Magic Art and the Evolution of Kings*, 275, 339; *Tabor and the Perils of the Soul*, 280; *Adonis, Atlis and Osiris*, 313, 314; *Pausanaias*, 314; *Worship of Nature*, 355

Frederick the Great, reign of, 249

Freud, Sigmund, 16, 17, 125, 126, 127, 129, 183; *Totem and Taboo*, 16, 17; *The Interpretation of Dreams*, 356

Friendship, symbol of, 151, 252, 258, 303, 305

Frith, *The New Frock*, 105

Frothingham, A. L., 206

Fry, trade mark, 92

Fry, Roger, *The Artist and Psychoanalysis*, 140, 144, 145, 146, 183

Functionalism, theory of, 167

Fylfot, 328

Gabo, Naum, 177

Galeotti, Pier Paolo, 82

Gambello, Vector, 82

Gammadion, 328

Gardiner, A. H., *Egyptian Grammar*, 11

Gardner, E. A., *Handbook of Greek Sculpture*, 179

Gardner, Percy, 329; *Sculptured Tombs of Hellas*, 252, 267; *Numismatic Chronicle*, 342

Garstang, J., *The Burial Customs of Ancient Egypt*, 287

Gauguin, 146

Gaul, swastika on coins of, 328; cassocks of, 160

Gentleness, symbol of, 261

Geometric figures, 246

George I, 23; medals of, 84

George II, seal of, 39, 247; medals of, 84

George III, seals of, 39, 40, 247, *Plate VII*; coins of, 78; medals of, 84

George IV, seal of, 39; coins of, 78, 79; medals of, 84; as Prince Regent, 85

George V, 40, 238, 260; Great Seal of, 40, *Plate VII*; coins of, 79; medals of, 84

George VI, seal of, 40; coins of 79; medals of, 84; postage stamps of, 113, 114, 115, 228

Georgia, seal of, 45; state emblem, 214; state flower of, 303

Germany, 29; eagle of, 29, 174, 236, 237; flag of, 20; national flower of, 223; reign of Charles V, 249

Gestures, 151–2

Gibberd, Sir Frederick, 169

Gibbon, Edward, *Decline and Fall of the Roman Empire*, 18, 224, 277, 298

Gilbert, Sir Walter, R., memorial to, 286

Gill, Eric, 282

Gillett & Johnston Ltd., trade mark of, *89*

Gillingham, arms of, 73

Ginizburg, Louis, 202

Giorgio, Francesco di, *Nativity*, 180

Giorgione, 143

Giotto, 147, 180, 200

Giovanni da Bologna, Statue of Mercury, *Plate LXIII*

Giovanni, Matteo di, *Madonna of the Girdle*, 200

Giralt, Xavier, Ltd., trade mark, *94*

Glenrothes, arms of, *72*

Glory, symbol of, 4, 220, 226, 227, 284

Gloucester and Hereford, Earl of, seal of, 40

Gloucestershire Regiment, badge of, *26*

Glover, Edward, *Social Aspects of Psychoanalysis*, 129

Goat, Capricornus the, 353

Gods, symbolic significance of, 246–8

Gold, 248–9; golden age, 248; golden mean, 248; golden section, 249; tree of, 336

Golden bough (mistletoe), 274

Golden Fleece, Spanish Order of, 243. *See also* Fleece

Golden Rod (*Genus solidago*), (*Solidago serotina*), (*Solidago patula*), 249, *Plate XL*

Goldfinch (*Spinies trestis trestia*), 249

Gonzago, Cecilia, 81; medal of, 243

Gonzago, Cardinal Francesco, medal of, 82

Goode, Samuel, 92

Good luck, scarab as symbol of, 37, 307; symbol of, 257–8, 261

Goodness, symbol of, 133

Good will, symbol of, 151

Gordon, Charles George, General, 101

Gordon, W. J., *A Manual of Flags* (revised by V. Wheeler-Holsashan), 20

Gorgon, head of, 190, *Plate LXVI*

Goulden, Richard, 201

Grace, symbol of, 326

Graef, P., 206

Grapes, 311; bunch of, 96, 100; Oregon, *Plate XL*

Grass, 249–50; crown of, 227, 249

Grasshopper, 250

Gratitude, symbol of, 325, 326

Graves, Robert, *The White Goddess*, 274, 275

Grays Inn, Society of, insignia of, 251

Great Britain, national flag of, 19

Greece, coins of, 74, 75, 76, 85; medals of, 81; religion of, 133; seals of, 37; symbols of, 339

Green, 250–1

Gresham, family coat of arms, 250; Sir Thomas, 250; James, seal of, 250

Grey, Lord, 221

Gridiron, 251

Griffin, 251, *Plates IV, LXVI*

Griffith, H. L., 307

Grocer, sign of, 250

Gropius, Walter, 172

Grosse, Dr. Ernst, *Die Anfange der Kunst*, 155, 156

Grouse (*Bonasa embellus*), 251

Guhl and Koner, *Life of the Greeks and Romans*, 159

Guidance, symbol of, 263

Guillim, John, *Display of Heraldry*, 250

Guilt, responsibility for, symbol of, 306; imposition of, 306

Guinness, advertisements for, 106

Gunpowder Plot, 83

Gutenberg, Johannes, 86

Hadassi, Judah, *Eshkol ha-Kofer*, 255

Hadrian, coins of, 77, 78

Hall, H. R., 307

Hall-mark, 87

Halo, *see* Nimbus

Hals, Franz, 87

Hamburg, Church of the Trinity, *Plate XLI*

Hamiltonian Functions, 9

Hammer, Thor's, 328

Hand, raised, 76; joined, 76; of St. Paul, 83; emerging from clouds, 251–2, *Plate LXVI*, shaking, 152; kissing, 151

Hands clasped, 252

Hannibal, Ehrenreich, 84

Hanover, arms of, 23, 24, 25; shield of, 23; horse of, 27

Happiness, symbol of, 187

Harlow, arms of, 70

Harp, 96; crowned, 39; of Ireland, 19, 23

Harrison, Jane E., *Ancient Art and Ritual*, 150

Hart, 252

Harrogate, shield of, 73

Hartlepool, seal of, 41

Hassall, John, 106

Hastings, Baron Loughborough, arms of, 64

Hastings, James, *Encyclopaedia of Religion and Ethics*, 356

Hat, 252–3

Hat, Cardinal's, 253

Hathor (or Isis), 223, 245, 270

Hawaii, state seal of, *57*

Hawk, 240, 253–4; head of, 240

Hawthorn (*Genus crataeous*), 254, *Plate XXXIX*

Hazlewood & Company (Products) Ltd., 92

Hazlitt, 326

Head, Barclay V., *Greek Coins*, 75

Headdress, 254

Headquarters of the Supreme Allied Command, South-East Asia, badge of, 29, *30*

Heal, Sir Ambrose, *Signboards of Old London*, 99; *The London Goldsmiths, 1200–1800*, 103

Healing, symbol of, 248, 296, 297, 311, 313

Health, symbol of, 256

Heart, 255

Heat, symbolized, 106

Hebrew, customs, 263; religion, 133, 311

Height, symbol of, 133

Heinz, trade mark, 92

Hell, symbol of, 336

Helmet, plumed, 79; soveriegn's, 58; of Athena Parthenos, 251

Hemel Hempstead, arms of, *70*

Hemlock (*Tsuga canadensis*), 255

Hendon, arms of, 73

Henry II, coat of arms, 269

Henry III, seal of, 38, 40, 61, 309; coins of, 77

Henry IV, 24, 25, 351

Henry V, 23, 24; coat of arms, *22*, 269; coins of, 78

Henry VI, 24; coins of, 78

Henry VII, *24*, 25, 351; coat of arms, *24*, 236; coins of, 78

Henry VIII, 25, 101, 236; seals of, 39; coins of, 78; medals of, 82

Hêphaestus (Vulcan), 248

Hepner, H. W., 109

Hepworth, Barbara, 177

Hêrakles (Hercules), 248, 341

Herculaneum, 96

Hercules, *see* Hêrakles

Hêrê (Juno) or Hera, 248, 265

Heresy, symbol of, 311

Hereward the Wake, knot of, 64

Hermes (Mercury), Messenger of the Gods, 197, 215, 216, 217, 247, 305

Herodotus, 74, 270, 294, 300, 339

Hesiod, 247

Hesperides, 236

Hexagram, *242*, 255–6

Hill, Brian, *Inn-Signia*, 103

Hill, G. F., *A Handbook of Greek and Roman Coins*, 80

Hindle Smart & Co. Limited, trade mark, 95

Hindu, representations, 328; people, 336; gods, 339

Hitler, Adolf, 306, 329

Hoffman, 329

Hogarth, 103

Holiness, symbol of, 280

Holland, 83, 161

Holly (*Ilex opaca Aiton*), 256

Holmes, Martin, *The Crown Jewels*, 310

Holmes, Oliver Wendell, *The Autocrat of the Breakfast Table*, 210

Holub, Dr. Emil, 156

Home, symbol of, 86

Homer, 97, 133, 215; *Odyssey*, 210, 317; *Iliad*, 226

Honour, 284, 287; mark of, 154, 159

Hope, symbol of, 196, 250

Hope, Sir W. H. St. John, 228, *Heraldry for Craftsmen and Designers*, 35

Horace, 97

Horns, 256

Hornsey Town Hall, *Plate XLIV*

Horse, 257; of Hanover, *Plate III*

Horseshoe, 257–8, 274

Horus, 197, 223, 229, 240, 245, 253, 270, 318

Hothr, blind God, 274

Hotton, John Camden, *History of Signboards*, 97

Hound, symbol of constancy, 82

Hour-glass, 258, *259*

Hulme, F. E., *The History, Principles and Practice of Symbolism in Christian Art*, 231, 252, 282, 317, 352

Humboldt, A. von, and Bonpland, A., *Personal Narrative*, 158

Hume, David, 8, 129, *Natural History of Religion*, 131

Humility, symbol of, 267, 345

Hunt, Holman, 363; *Scapegoat*, 181, 306; *The Light of the World*, 181

Hussars, 3rd Kings Own, badge of, *26*

Hyde, arms of, 68

Hydra, 84, 86

Ibsen, *A Doll's House*, 185; *The Wild Duck*, 186

Iceland, symbol of, 326; postage stamps of, 326

Idaho, seal of, *55*; state bird, 213

Illinois, seal of, *50*; emblem of, 217; state tree of, 284; state flower of, 347

Immortality, symbol of, 193, 195, 203, 250, 255, 258, 263, 279, 292, 294, 334, 352

Imperial Chemical Industries (Pharmaceuticals Division) Ltd., First time does it series of advertisements, *107*, Shrink Fit and Cuckoo in the Nest advertisements, *Plate XXX*

Incorruptibility, symbol of, 293, 305

Indiana, seal of, 49; emblem of, 217; state tree of, 342; state flower of, 252

Indian Paint Brush (*Castillya pinariaefolia*), 258, *Plate XXXIX*

Indra, Hindu God, 224

Industry, symbols of, 61, 64, 78, 86, 204, 212

Ingram, O. H. & Sons Ltd., 92

Inn signs, 96*f*, *Plates XXIV, XXV, XXVI*; classification of, 99–103, of drink and food, 100; religious; 100, heraldic, 101; national and patriotic, 101; historical and mythological, 101; trade, 101; transport, 102; geographical, 102; humorous, 103

Innocence, symbol of, 261, 349

Innocent III, Pope, 213, 341

Innoxa, trade mark, 92

Instincts, symbol of, 125*f*

Insurance signs, *Plate XXIII*

International Fisheries Exhibition 1883, medal of, *Plate XIX*

Iô, 223

Iodent trade mark, 92

Iona, coins of, 74, 76

Iowa, seal of, *52*; state bird of, 249; state flower, 303

Iraq, 31

Ireland, symbol of, 314; Irish harp, 23; Celtic Cross of, 229

Iris (*Iris versicolor*), 258

Isis (or Hathor), 223

Israel, tribes of, Children of, 306

Italy, Nationalist Movement of, 240

Ivy, 258–60

Ixion, 348, 349

Jacobson, Egbert, *Seven Designers look at Trademark Designs*, 91, 95

James I (VI of Scotland), 19, 23, 236, 331, 343; medals of, 83; coins of, 331

James II, 284; coins of, 78; oak tree as symbol of, 83

James III (of Scotland), 331

James IV (of Scotland), 343; coins of, 331

James V (of Scotland), coins of, 331

James, Henry, *A Little Tour in France*, 172, 173

Jameson, Mrs, Anna, 202, 208; *Sacred and Legendary Art*, 179, 227, 252, 269, 270, 283, 297, 356

Janus, 76, 133, 204, 205, 206, 239

Japan, flag of, 20; national flower, 219; postage stamps, 219; paintings of, 181, 183

Jasmine, Yellow, *Plate XXXIX*

Jeans, Sir James, 9

Jennings, Sir Ivor, *The British Constitution*, 138, 139

Jessamine, Carolina (*Gelsemium sempervirens*), 260

Jews, symbol, of, 255, 263

John VIII Palaeologus, Byzantine emperor, commemorative medal of, 81

John, King, seal of, 38

John, Prince, arms of, 61

John of Thessalonica, 200

Johnstone, Sir Harry H., *The River Congo*, 164

Johore, flat of, 19

Jones, Dr. Ernest, 10, 11; *Psycho-analysis and the Instincts*, 129; *The Theory of Symbolism*, 129, 357

Jonson, Ben, 101

Joy, symbol of, 349

Judaism, symbol of, 255

Julius Caesar, 76, 221; coins of, 76

Jung, C. G., 183; *Psychology of the Unconscious*, 129, 183, 357

Junker, Dr. Wilhelm, *Travels in Africa during the Years 1879–1883*, 164

Juno, *see* Hêrê

Jupiter, Sky God, *see* Zeus

Justice, with broken sword and balance, 39; symbol of, 61, 208, 305, 329, 330

Justinian, 221; era, 337

Kandinsky, 147

Kangaroo, 260; totem, 17, 150

Kangaroo Paw (*Antigozanthus flavida*), 260

Kansas, 264; seal of, *53*; state animal, 214; state tree, 223; state flower of, 326

Kaschaur, Jacob, 204

Keane, A. H., *Air and Gods of the Air*, 258

Keats, John, 298, 345

Kelantan, flag of, 19

Kendal, John, medal of, 82

Kent, white horse of, 73

Kentucky, seal of, *48*; emblem of, 217; state flower of, 249

Kerly, *Law of Trade marks and Trade Names*, 91

Key, 7, 97, 101, 174, 260

Khensu, 239

Kheperer, Sun God, 307

Khnemu, 239, 299, 318

Kierkegaard, Söven, 189

Kilbride, East, arms of, *72*

King, Elizabeth W., *Seals of our Nation, States and Territories*, 59

King, George W., 92

King's Own Hussars, badge of, *26, 27*

King, Wallace Ltd., 92

Kissing, 151, 152

Kitchener, Lord, coat of arms, 217

Kiwi (Aphteryx), 260

Klee, Paul, 145, 183, 184; *Spring*, 183; *Gay Breakfast Table*, 183; *Gay Mountain Landscape*, 183; *Comedy, Plate LVII*

Knighthood, symbol of, 319, 329

Knowledge, tree of, 204, 311, 336, 337; symbol of, 263, 335, 336; lights of, 336

Kodak, trade mark, 91, 92, 95

Korda, Sir Alexander, *Rembrandt*, 187

Korea, 86, 257

Kraus, Minoan Sky God, 211

Labyrinth, 260–1

Lady's slipper, *see* Orchid

Ladybird, 261

Lamb, 261–3, *262*, 269, 289, 311, *Plate LXXIII*; of the Apocalypse, 316

Lambourn, E. A. Greening, *The Armorial Glass of the Oxford Diocese, 1250–1850*, 35

Lamp, 263–4, 268, 276, 283, 334; miner's lamp on coat of arms, 68

Lang, Andrew, *Social Origins* and *The Secret of the Totem*, 17

Large, Dr., 86

Lark Bunting (*Calamospiza melanocorys Stejmeger*), 264

Lark, Meadow (*Sturnella neglecta*), 264

Larwood, Jacob, 100, 101, 103; *History of Signboards*, 97

Laurel, 264, *278*, 335; wreath, 75, 76, 77, 85, 287; crown, 81, 279, 284; grove, 335; Bay (*Laurus nobilis*), *278*; Mountain (*Kalmia latifolia*), 265, *Plate XL*

Laver, branch of, 64; loin band of, 64

Laver, James, *Taste and Fashion from the French Revolution to the Present Day*, 161, 162, 165

Lawler, Ray, *Summer of the Seventeenth Doll*, 186, 187

Lawrence, D. H., *Twilight in Italy*, 143

Layard, Sir A. H., 198; *Nineveh*, 270

Leamington, crest of, 73

Le Corbusier, 172, 249

Ledward, Gilbert, 40, 310

Lee, Samuel, *London Directory*, 98

Lee, Vernon, *Beauty and Ugliness and other Studies in Psychological Aesthetics*, 173

Leeds, coat of arms, *62*, 243

Leek, 27, 228, 265

Leicester, Earl of, family arms, 64

Leicester, War Memorial, *Plate LXI*

Leicestershire, 64; coat of arms, 64, *65*

Leicestershire Regiment, badge of, *26*

Leighton, Lord, 27

Leonardo da Vinci, 147, 180

Lethaby, W. R., 337; *Architecture, Mysticism and Myth*, 336

Leucothoë, 325

Lewis, M. and Clarke, W., *Travels to the Source of the Missouri*, 165

Libertas, 58

Liberty, cap of, 76; figure of, 58, 305

Libya, 234

Lichfield, seal of, 41

Liddell and Scott, *Greek Lexicon*, 344

Life, symbols of, Ankh, 203, 204, 235, 245, 274, 294, 334, 348; symbols of eternal, 263, 267, 274, 292; renewal of, symbol of, 270, 293, 294, 296, 297, 326, 334, 341, 347; symbols of protection of, 229, 238

Light, gods of, 133

Lightning, symbol of, 210, 211, 230

Lilac, Purple (*Syringa vulgaris*), 265, *Plate XXXIX*

Lily, 265–7, *266*; White or Madonna (*Lilium candidum*), 267, 349

Lily of the Valley, *266*, 267

Lily, Sego (*Calochortus mittallii*), 267, *Plate XXXIX*

Lincoln, 96

Lincolnshire Regiment, 26, 27, 319

Linnaeus, 306

Lion, 267–9, *268*; British, 85, 86, 212; of England, *Plates II, IV*; as guardian, *Plate LXIX*; Leo the, 353

Lion Gate of Mycenae, *Plate LXV*

Lion, winged, 269–70; Assyrian, with human head, 31

Lippi, Fra Filippo, 143, 181

Lippold, Richard, American sculptor, 177

Lipps, Theodor, *Archiv für die Gesamte Psychologie*, 142, 173

Listowel, Lord, *A Critical History of Modern Aesthetics*, 173

Littlewoods, Mail Order Stores Ltd., trade mark of, *88*

Lituos, Roman, 309

Liver bird, 64

Liverpool Cathedral (Roman Catholic), *Plate XLV*

Liverpool, coat of arms, 60, *63*, 64; Mersey tunnel, 230

Livingstone, David, *Missionary Travels and Researches in South Africa*, 155, 164

Lloyd's Bank, 98

Llyewelyn ab Gruffydd, 25

Loftiness, symbol of, 332, 347

Loki, 274

Lombardy, 99, 332

London, H. Stanford, 215

London, 97, 285; City seal, 41; City arms, *63*, 236; County Council Exhibitions, 178

London Transport Advertising, 108, *Plate XXVIII*; sculptures on building, 176, *Plate XLIX*

Loredana, Leonardo, Doge of Venice, medal of, 82

Lotus-flower, 37, 270; Egyptian (*Nymphaen lotus*), *262*

Louis XIV, 207; reign of, 249

Louis XV, reign of, 249

Louisiana, seal of, *49*; state flower of, 271; state bird of, 294; flag of, 294

Louis le Jeune, 245

Love, goddess of, 247; symbols of, 247, 252, 255, 279; self, symbol of, 280; colour of, 300, 301

Lowrie, Walter, *Monuments of the Early Church*, 276, 316

Luck, symbol of, 257, 261, 306; tokens of, 307

Luder, Jan, 84, 86

Lupin (*Lupin subcamorus*), 270

Lustig, Alvin, 95

Lutyens, Sir Edwin, 143, 207, 218, 286

Lux, trade mark, 91, 92

Lycia, coins of, 76

Lydd (Kent), arms of, 69; seal of, 42

Lydia, coins of, 74, 75

Lyly, *Euphues and his England*, 324

Lyme Regis, seal of, 42

Lyre, *259*, 270, 316

Lyre-bird, 271

Lys, Jan Van Der, 81

Lysicrates, monument of, 340

Lysippus, 75

Lytham St. Anne's, 108; arms of, 69

Lytton, *Last Days of Pompeii*, 350

Mabuse, *Adoration of the Kings*, 180, *Plate LIV*

MacCullock, J. A., *Door*, 258

MacDonald, Margaret, memorial to, 175, *Plate XLVI*

Mace, 159, 236, 271, 284, 285

Macedonia, 75, 76

Mackinlay, Colonel, *The Magi: How they Recognized Christ's Star*, 320

Magnanimity, eagle a symbol of, 82

Magnolia (*Magnolia foetida* or *Magnolia grandiflora*), 271, *Plate XXXIX*

Maine, seal of, *50*; state bird of, 219; state floral emblem, 296

Malac Baal, 216

Malay States, flags of, 19

Malden, arms of, 69

Malipiero, Vincenzo, medal of, 82

Malta, cross of, 225 *225*; knights of, 225

Man, Isle of, badge of, 341, 342

Mandala, 271–2

Mandorla, 272

Manchester, arms of, 64, 66, 212

Manitoba, floral emblem of, 291

Manners, symbol of, 161

Maple (*acer saccharum Marsh*), 272; leaves, 86, 212, 272

Marcel, Gabriel, 189

Marcus Aurelius, 221, 222

Marett, R. R., *Hastings Encyclopaedia of Religion and Ethics*, 131

Marigold (*Calendula officinalis*), 98, *312*, 325

Maritime symbols, 61, 69, 73, 196, 197, 231, 232, 247, 317

Marley Tiles Limited, trade mark, 95, 220

Marriage, symbol of, 301–2

Mars, God of war, *see* Arês

Martin, Albert V., trade mark, *93*

Martin, flying, 92

Martineau's Ltd., trade mark of, *88*

Martini, Simone, 181

Martin's Bank, coat of arms of, 250

Martyrdom, symbol of, 287, 290, 337

Marvell, 101

Mary, the Virgin, symbol of, 265, 302, 303, 326, 349; medal of, 326

Mary Stuart, coins of, 331

Mary I, Queen, 25; coins of, 78; medals of, 82

Maryland, seal of, *46*; state bird, 289; state flower of, 305

Masaccio, 147

Massachusetts, seal of, *45*; state bird of, 219; state tree of, 238; state flower of, 273

Matisse, 147

Mattingly, Harold, *Coins of the Roman Empire in the British Museum*, 80

Mayflower (*Epigaea ripens*), 273, *Plate XXXIX*

Mazawattee, trade mark, 91

McDougall, William, *Outline of Social Psychology*, 125, 126

McMillan, W., 85

Medals, 81–6; English, 82f, *Plates XVI, XVII, XVIII, XIX, XX, XXI*

Medical Corps, Royal Army, badge of, *28*

Medici, coat of arms, 99, 332; tombs, 176, *Plate XLVII*

Medicine, symbol of, 247, 311, 312

Medusa, head of, 77, *Plate LXVI*

Meekness, symbol of, 261

Melos, coins of, 77

Mendelsohn, Eric, 171, 173

Menorah, 273

Mercia, Coenwulf, King of, 38

Mercury, Messenger of the Gods, *see* Hermes

Mercy, sword of, 330

Mermaids, 239; wearing crowns, 61

Mesopotamia, 87, 216, 309; seals of, 333

Metaphor, 10, 11

Metcalf, Percy, 79, 86

Mexico, national flower, 215

Meyer, Franz Sales, *A Handbook of Ornament*, 237

Michelangelo, 145, 176, 178, 180, 200, 256; Medici tombs, *Plate XLVII*

Michigan, state flower of, 204; seal of, *51*; state tree of, 296; state bird of, 302

Middleton, arms of, 64, 68

Millais, John, 87, 105, 181, 326

Milton, John, *Paradise Lost*, 195

Minerva, Goddess of the Arts, *see* Athênê

Mining, symbol of, 72

Minnesota, seal of, *52*; state flower of, 288

Minquizza, Luciano, 177

Mirror, 273–4

Mississippi, seal of, *49*; state flower of, 271

Missouri, seal of, *50*; state bird, 213; state flower, 254

Mistletoe, 274–5, *Plate XL*

Mithras, Persian Sun God, 209, 276; religion of, 282, 349

Mitre, bishop's, 275–6, *Plate LXVII*

Mnevis, sacred bull, 215

Moccasin Flower, *Plate XXXIX*

Mocking Bird (*Mimus polyglottus* or *Orpheus polyglottus*), 276

Moldenke, Harold Norman, *American Wild Flowers*, 347

Monarchy, symbol of, 160f, 213, 288

Mond, Dr. Ludwig, 86

Money, symbolism of, 16; lender (symbol of), 332

Monmouthshire Regiment, badge of, *26*

Monograms, sacred, 263, 276–7, *281*, 339, 349, *Plates LXXI, LXXII*

Monson-Fitzjohn, C. J., *Quaint Signs of Olde Inns*, 103

Montana, seal of, *48*, 55; state flower of, 213; state bird of, 264

Moore, Henry, 177; *Warrior with Shield*, 178, *Plate XLVIII*

More, Sir Thomas, 305

Morecambe, arms of, 69

Moretti, 143

Morley, arms of, *65*

Mortality, symbol of, 143, 174, 317

Mortimer, silver lion, 25

Moses, 256, 289, 306, 313

Mother, symbolized, 128

Motion, symbol of, 293

Mound, *see Orb*

Mountain, artificial, 277, 279

Mountain Bluebird (*Sialia arcticia*), *see* Bluebird

Mourning, symbol of, 175, 213, 218, 228, 343, 344, 350

Müller, Ludwig, *Detasaakaldte Hagekors*, 242

Müller, Max, *The Science of Thought*, 4

Mumford, Lewis, *The Conduct of Life*, 3, 147, 148, 356; *Art and Technics*, 147, 148, 170, 356; *The Condition of Man*, 356; *From the Ground Up*, 170, 173; *Culture of Cities*, 173, 356; *Technics and Civilization*, 356

Munch, Edward, *Girls on the Bridge*, *Plate LVII*

Municipal coats of arms, 60f

Municipal seals, 41

Murillo, 200
Music, symbol of, 270
Muss-Arnolt, 202
Mussolini, 240
Mutability, symbol of, 348–9
Mycenae, lion gate of, 335; ornaments of, 328
Myrtle (*Myrtus communis*), 279–80, *278*
Mysore, 85

Napoleon, 161, 207, 213, 221, 222, 236, 350
Narcissus, 280, *346*
Narmer, 226
Nash, Paul, 184; *Landscape from a Dream, Plate LVII*
National symbolism, 137*f*
Nature, generative force of, symbol of, 291, 294; female personification of, 336; worship of, 132, 149
Nazi, flag, 20; oppression, darkness of, 29; emblem, 329
Nebraska, seal of, *54*; state tree of, 238; state flower of, 249; state bird of, 264
Nekhebit, 229
Nelson (Lancs), 243
Nelson, Lord, 101, 221
Neptune, God of the Sea, *see* Poseidon
Nereids, 231
Nesse, *Church History*, 349
Netherlands, medals of, 83
Nevada, seal of, *54*, 58; state bird, 213
New Brunswick, provincial flower of, 347
New Hampshire, seal of, *46*; state tree, 213; state flower of, 265
New Jersey, seal of, *44*; shield of, 58; state flower of, 347
New Mexico, seal of, *56*; state tree of, 296; state bird of, 302; state flower of, 352
New South Wales, coat of arms, 243
Newton Aycliffe, arms of, *71*
New York, arms of, 305, 330
New York, State, 213; seal of, *47*; state tree of, 272; state flower of, 303
New Zealand, blue ensign of, 19; symbol of, 240, 260
Niebuhr, M., *Travels through Arabia*, 152, 153
Nietzsche, 129
Night, figure of, 175, 176, 177; spirit of, 176
Nimbus, 280–3, *Plate LXXI*
Nirvana, 278
Nobility, symbol of, 250
Nordral, trade mark, 92

Norris, Herbert, *Church Vestments, their Origin and Development*, 228
North Carolina, seal of, *47*; state bird of, 219; state flower of, 231
Northcote (and Brownlow), *Roma Sottervanea*, 232, 356
North Dakota, seal of, *54*; state tree of, 238; state bird of, 264; state flower of, 303
Norway, symbol of, 326; postage stamps of, 326; soldiers of, 331, 341
Norwich, associative trademark, 92
Nova Scotia, symbolic flower of, 272
Noyes, Alfred, 334
Number symbolism, 283–4
Nuttall, G. Clarke, *Rosemary at Christmas*, 305

Oak, 284; British, 40; crown or wreath of, 81, 226, 284, 287; of Dodona, 335
Oar, 284–5
Obelisk, 285–7, *Plate LXIX*
Observer Corps Medal, 86
Octagon, 287
Odo, Bishop of Bayeux, 66
Oedipus, complex, 17, 126, 127; riddle solved by, 318
Oenochoë, wine jug, 343
Ogier the Dane, King of England, 330
Ohio, seal of, *49*; state tree, 214; *Ohio Historical Publications*, 214; emblem of, 217; state flower, 217
Oklahoma, seal of, 56; state bird of, 245; emblem of, 275; state tree of, 301
Old Roundhegians Association, trade mark of, *89*
Olive (*Olen eoropaga*), *278*, 287; crown or wreath of, 75, 81; tree, 83, 257, 289
Olive Branch, 235
Olivieri, Maffeo, 82
Olympia, coins of, 75
Olympic Games, founder of, 247
Oman, Sir Charles, *The Coinage of England*, 80
Omega, 287, *Plates LXVIII, LXXI, LXXII*
Ontario, coat of arms, 272; flower of, 347
Orange (France), Arch of Tiberius at, 207
Orange, blossom (*Citrus trifoliata* or *Citrus sinensis*), 288, *Plate XL*
Orb, 309
Orcagna, *Coronation of the Virgin*, 282
Orchid (*Cyprepedium reginae*), 288, (*Cyprepedium calcarlus*), 289; (*Cyprepedium hersutum*), 288

Order, symbol of, 283
Oregon, seal of, *53*; state bird of, 264
Orient, symbol of, 85
Oriole, Baltimore, 289
Orion, 210
Orpheus, 289; symbol of, 270; symbol of Christ, 315
Osiris, 149, 215, 294, 296, 307, 349
Ostrich feather, 240
Ovid, 280
Owl, 289; crowned, 61; in a window, 87
Ox, 289; winged, 289
Oxford, shield of, 61
Oxo, trade mark of, 91

Padua, 82
Pagoda, 289–90
Painting, symbolism in, 180*f*, *Plates LIV, LV, LVI, LVII*
Palm, 229, 290–91, 335, 336, 337; sabol, 291
Palmetto (*Inodes palmetto*), 291
Palmolive soap, 106
Palo Verde (*Genera cercidum*), 291
Pan, 256
Panda, Giant, 31
Pansy, 291
Panther, 77, 109, 247
'Panzer' Division, 31
Papyrus plant, 66
Parachute Regiment, badge of, *28*
Paradise, symbol of, 302
Paraguay, people of, 336
Parazonium, 58
Parenthood, symbol of, 323
Parker, J., 202
Parnell, Thomas, *The Hermit*, 315
Parsley, 291
Parthenon, 257; *Plate XLIII*
Paschal Lamb, 27, 261, *262*, *Plate LXVIII*
Pasque Flower (*Pulsatilla Tudoviciana* or *Anemone patens*), 291–2, *Plate XL*
Passion, Flower (*Passiflora*), 292, *292*, *Plate XL*
Pater, Walter, *The School of Giogione*, 145; *The Renaissance, Studies in Art and Poetry*, 176
Pausanias, 280, 297, 344
Pawnbroker, symbol of, 332
Peace, symbol of, 264, 287, 297, 349, 350
Peach blossom (*Primus persica*) (*Amygdalus persica*), 292, *Plate XL*
Peacock, 77, 97, 99, 292–3, *Plates LXX, LXXI*

Pears soap, 105, 106
Pecan tree, 293
Pedrick, Gale, *Monastic Seals of the XIIIth Century*, 59; *Borough Seals of the Gothic Period*, 59
Pegasus, the winged horse, 74, 239
Pelican and its young, 23, 58, 81, 82, 293–4, 295, *Plate LXXII*
Penguin, trade mark, 92
Pennsylvania, seal of, *44*; state bird of, 251; state tree of, 255; state flower of, 265
Perfection, symbol of, 248, 302; number of, 287
Pericles, age of, 249
Permanence, symbol of, 250
Perrin, W. G., *British Flags, their Early History and their development at Sea*, 20
Persephone, 175, 210, 220, 280
Perseus, rescuing Andromeda, 311
Perseverance, symbol of, 217
Persia, 224, 236, 237, 337, 342; standards of, 17
Personality, symbol of, 142, 147; expression of, 143
Perugino, 87, 145, 181; *Crucifixion*, 181; *Virgin and Child with an Angel*, *Plate LV*
Pestalozzi Children's Villages, symbol of, 261
Pestrucci, 78
Peterlee, arms of, 71
Peter the Great, reign of, 249
Pevsner, Antoine, 177
Phallus, 294; phallic emblem, 149, 274; phallic symbol, 128, 163, 285, 286, 329
Pheasant, Chinese ring neck (*Phosianus colchicus*), 294; Golden, 97
Pheon, 210
Phidias, 336
Philip of Macedon, 75
Philip of Spain, 83
Philip the Good, Duke of Burgundy, 243
Phillips, J. A., & Co. Ltd., trade mark of, *89*
Philo, 133
Philpot, Mrs. J. H., *The Sacred Tree*, 339, 355
Phoenicia, 234
Phoenicians, 216
Phoenix, 294–6, *295*
Phrixus, 243
Phrygia, 296; God of, 296
Picasso, 142, 145, 147, 183, 184
Pickering, Dr. Charles, *The Races of Man*, 156, 164

Pictorial Advertising, 104f
Piety, symbol of, 323
Pilgrimage, symbol of, 314–15
Pineapple, 97, 297
Pine cone, 296–7, 309, 333, *Plate XXXIX*; White (*Pinias strobus*), 296
Pinon, 297
Piquancy, symbol of, 305
Pisanello, medals of, 81, 82, 343
Pissarro, 143
Pitt, William, 101
Planché, J. R., *The Pursuivant of Arms*, 35
Plantagenets, 38, 73; silver falcon of, 25
Plantagenista or Broom, 38, 73
Plato, *Republic*, 9, 15, 16, 134
Player, John & Co. Ltd., trade mark, 92
Plenty, figure with a cornucopia, 39
Pliny, *Natural History*, 227, 239, 249, 250, 251, 258, 264, 274, 275, 279, 280, 284, 286, 287, 294, 296, 351, 355
Poinsetta, 297
Poland, emblem of, 237
Pollajuolo, Antonio, 147
Pomegranate, 291, 297, 335, 336
Pompeii, 96, 104
Pont du Gard, *Plate XLIV*
Poole, arms of, 73
Pope, Alexander, 97
Pope, 252, 288; with eyes bandaged, 83; fisherman's ring of, 301
Poppy, opium (*Papaver somniferum*), 297–298; Golden (*Eschscholtzia californica*), 297–8, *Plate XXXIX*
Portcullis, 298; crowned, 25
Port of London Authority, flag of, 20
Poseidon (Neptune), God of the Sea, 101, 175, 231, 247, 257, 287, 289, 339; with gold crown, 64
Postage stamps, 112f, *Plates XXXI, XXXII, XXXIII, XXXIV, XXXV, XXXVI, XXXVII, XXXVIII;* British Commemoratives, 114–19; United Nations, 119–120; U.S.A., 113, 121
Posters, British Railway, *Plates XXVII, XXIX;* London Transport, *Plate XXVIII; The Times, Plate XXIX*
Potter, ancient Egyptian, in arms of Stoke on Trent, 66
Pottery, industry, 66
Powell, James & Sons (Whitefriars) Ltd., trade mark, *90*, 92
Power, eagle as symbol of, 42, 178; symbol of, 159, 223, 256, 267, 271, 318, 329

Powers, angelic rank, 298
Prayer, symbol of, 132
Pre-Raphaelites, 200
Price, F. G. H., *The Signs of Old Lombard Street*, 103
Pride, symbol of, 293
Priest, symbol of, 219
Prince Edward Island, floral emblem of, 289
Principalities, angelic rank, 298
Procreation, symbol of, 223, 299, 300
Propaganda, symbolism of, 16
Propitiation, 130, 131, 132
Prosperity, symbol of, 326, 327, 341
Protea, 298
Protection, symbol of, 256, 257–8, 274–5, 329–30
Providence, eye of, 339
Prudential Assurance Company, war memorial, 201
Prussia, tree oracles of, 335
Psychoanalysis, 10, 11, 125–9, 163, 183–4
Psychology, 3, 145, 183; of expression, 141; documents of, 184
Ptah, Egyptian god of creation, 237
Punch, 212
Punishment, symbol of administration of, 240
Purification, symbol of, 347–8
Purity, symbols of, 265, 267, 342–3, 349–50
Purple, 298–9
Puttenham, G., *Arte of English Poesie*, 223
Pyramid, 42, 43, 239, 299
Pyrgoteles, 75
Pythagoras, 283

Quadriga, 299
Quail Valley (*Sophortyx californica*), 299
Qualities, symbols of, 247–8
Quatrepomme, Isabella, 87
Quebec, symbol of, 258; coat of arms of, 272
Quebec Gazette, 272
Queen's Beasts, 25, *Plates II, III, IV*
Queensland, floral emblem of, 297
Queen's West Surrey Regiment, 27; badge of, *26*
Quiescence, symbol of, 170
Quince, 299
Quink, trade mark, 92

Ra, Egyptian God, 133, 197, 229, 230, 238, 245, 253, 254, 286

Rainmaker, 254

Raleigh, Sir Walter, 92; *The Passionate Man's Pilgrimage*, 314

Ram, 299–300; head of, 23, 37, 66, 75, 256, 318; horns of, 256; Aries the, 353

Rameses II, obelisks of, 286

Ramsey, family armorial bearings of, 23

Ramsgate, arms of, 69

Rand, Paul, 95

Rank, symbol of, 156, 159, 161, 329

Raphael, 181, 200; *The Crucifixion, Plate LV*

Rattlesnake, 300

Raven, 78

Ravensbourne, River, 73

Rawlins, Thomas, 83

Rawtenstall, 69; arms of, 64, *67*, 68

Read, Sir Herbert, 177, 179; *Art Now*, 146, 147, 148, 182, 184; *The Philosophy of Modern Art*, 182; *Art and Society*, 184

Reality, symbol of, 147

Réaus, Louis, *Iconographie de l'Art Chrétien*, 356

Rebus, 61, 98–9, 250

Red, 300–1

Redbud (*Cercis canadensis* or *reniformis*), 301

Redcar, arms of, 69

Regalia, 5, 309, 329; Isle of Man, 341–2

Regeneration, lotus lily as symbol of, 37; rising sun as symbol of, 42; symbols of, 257, 270, 285, 286, 293, 294, 296, 297, 328, 329, 335, 347–8

Regent, Prince, 85

Regimental badges, *26*, 27, *28*, 29

Regimental Colours, 29

Religious aspiration, symbol of, 134, 252

Religious symbolism, 130–6

Rembrandt, 140, 144, 145, 147, 200; *Crucifixion*, 144; *Night Watch*, 145

Remembrance, symbol of, 194, 263, 303, 325–6, 348; lamp of, 263

Renewal, symbol of, 83, 237–8, 291, 293, 294, 296

Resignation, symbol of, 170

Respect, symbol of, 151

Responsibility, symbol of, for guilt, 306

Rest, symbol of, 283, 297

Resurrection, symbol of, 267, 292, 293, 294, 328–9

Reverence, symbol of, 151

Revival, symbols of, 5, 203–4, 238, 293, 294, 306–7, 326–8

Rhinoceros, charging, 31

Rhode Island, 213; seal of, *48*; state flower of, 347

Rhodes, swastika on coins of, 328

Rhododendron, *Plate XL*; Western (*Rhododendron californicum* or *machrophyllum*), 301; Eastern (*Rhododendron maximum*), 301

Richard I, *22*, 23; seals of, 38, 61, *Plate VI*; coat of arms, *22*, 269

Richard II, 24

Richard III, 25; coins of, 71

Richardson, Jonathan, 87

Riemerschmid, Reinhard, *Plate XLI*

Ring, 301–2; signet, 37

River, symbols of, 61

Road Runner (*Geococcyx californianus*), 302

Roberts, Lord, 100

Robertson, Frederick William, 326

Robin (*Mercula migrataria*), 302

Rochester, 284, 285; See of, 73

Rohe, Miës van der, 172

Roma, head of, 76

Romana, Geancrisoforo, 82

Rome, coins of, 76–7; gods of, 246–8, 313; fasces of, 39, 240; medals of, 81, 293; seals of, 37, 38; standards of, 18, 236

Ronchamp, Notre-Dame de Hautpilgrim chapel, *Plate XLIV*

Rose, 302–3, *304, Plate XL*; red Lancastrian, 69, 303; white Yorkist, 303; wild or dog (*Rosa canina* or *rosa arvensis*), 303; wild (*Rosa virginiana* or *Rosa acicularis*), 303, *Plate XXXIX*; cherokee (*Rosa sinica*), 303, *Plate XL*; wild prairie (*Rosa blanda* or *Rosa arkansana*), 303; beauty, 302

Rose, crowned, Tudor, 25

Rose, Tudor, *see* Tudor Rose

Rose en soleil, 25

Rosemary (*Rosmarinus*), 303, 305, *304*

Rossendale, forest of, 69

Rossetti, Dante Gabriel, 181; *Jenny*, 282; *Dante's Dream*, 181

Rossi, G. B. de, *La Roma Sotteranea*, 356

Rothery, G. G., *Decorators' Symbols, Emblems and Devices*, 232

Round, J. H., 35

Rovere, Guiliano Della, medal of, 82

Rowntree, trade mark, 92

Rowse, Herbert J., 230

Royal Arms, *see* Arms

Rubens, 143, 145, 147, 200; *Rape of the Sabine Women*, 145

Rudbeckia (*Rudbeckia perta* or *serotina*), 305
Rudofsky, Bernard, 95
Russell, Bertrand, 6
Russia, 138, 212; Golden Age of, 249; postage stamp of, 122; emblem of, 237
Rye, as ingredient of bread, 345, 348

Sacrifice, symbol of, 194–5, 224–5, 228, 292; animal of, 261, 300
Sadness, symbol of, 350, 352
Safety, symbol of, 79, 83
Sagebrush, *Plate XL*
St. Ambrose, 291
St. Andrew, 101; cross of, 39, 225, *225*
St. Anthony, 224; falls of, 43
St. Augustine, 135, 158, 238, 269, 287
St. Bernadine of Siena, 277
St. Blazie, 100
St. Christopher, 100
St. Crispin, 100
St. David, 265
St. Ethelreda, arms of, 64
St. George, 20, 31, 40, 42, 85, 257, 313; cross of, 39, 61; with Dragon, 78, 100, 174
St. Gregory, 238
St. James, Major, 314–15
Saint-Jean Baptiste Society, 272
St. Jerome, 135, 269, 289
St. John the Baptist, 135, 283, 320
St. John the Evangelist, 133, 236–7; symbol of, 269
St. Julian, 100
St. Lawrence, 251
St. Leonard, 103
St. Luke, 234; symbol of, 269, 289
St. Mark, 349; symbol of, 269–70
St. Martin, 41, 257
St. Matthew, 282, 349; symbol of, 269
St. Maurice, 257
St. Michael, winged figure with sword, 40
St. Nicholas, 269, 332
St. Patrick, 101, 314
St. Paul, 20, 41, 101, 174, 196, 305; Cathedral, 171, 181, 288, 297, 319; dome of, *Plate XLIII*
St. Peter, 101, 174, 220, 231, 263, 292, 301; Cathedral of, 171
St. Thomas of Canterbury, 41
St. Victor, 257
Salford, arms of, 64, 66
Salisbury cathedral, *Plate XLIII*
Salmon, leaping, 29, *30*

Salt, 305; wicker moulds for, 61
Saltash, 92, 271, 285; Bridge, 92
Sanctity, religious symbol of, 280
Sanguaro, *Plate XL*
Sarcophagus, 345, 348, *Plate LXXI*
Sargent, 142
Sartre, Jean-Paul, 189, 190
Sauwastika, *308*, 328
Saville, family crest, 61
Savonarola, medals of, 82
Savory, H. L., & Co. Ltd., trade mark, *94*
Saxone of Scotland, 106
Scales, 305; pair of, 39, 40, 61, 82, 174, 207, 330
Scallop shell (*Pecten jacobeus*), 314–5
Scapegoat, 306
Scarab (*Scarabaeus sacer*), 306–7, *308*; rings, 301; seal, 37; as symbol of life, 37, 238, 306–7; as symbol of good luck, 37, 306–7
Scaraboid, 37
Sceptre, 309–10; surmounted by dove, 38, 309; surmounted by orb and cross, 309
Schwartz, 329
Scone, Stone of, 321–3
'Scopel' Cream, 109
Scorpion, Scorpio, the, 353
Scotland, 328, 331, 343; arms of, 23, 25, 39, 84; emblem of, 331; flag of, 19; symbol of, 331
Scots Greys, Royal, badge of, *26*
Scott, Geoffrey, *The Architecture of Humanism*, 173
Scott, S. M., stained-glass window designed by, *Plate LXVIII*
Scott-Giles, C. Wilfred, *Civic Heraldry of England and Wales*, 61, 73, 213, 236
Scottish Co-operative Wholesale Society, 92
Scottish Widows' Fund and Life Assurance Society, 99
Scourge, 58
Scroll, 310; unrolled, 81
Sculpture, 174–9; symbolical, *Plates XLVI, XLVII, XLVIII, XLIX, L, LI, LII, LIII*
Scythe, 99, *259*, *308*, 310
Seaby, Peter, *The Story of the English Coinage*, 80
Seagull, Californian (*Larus californicus*), 310
Sea-horses, 69, 108
Seals, 36–59, *Plates V, VI, VII, VIII*; Egyptian, 37; Greek, 37–38; English seals of State, 38–40; Ecclesiastical, 41; Municipal, 41–42; U.S.A., Great Seal of, 42; American State Seals, 42–59

Seas, dominion of, 353

Seasons, 175, 181, 310; symbol of, 353

Secrecy, symbol of, 345

Security, symbol of, 298

Seeon, Church of (Bavaria), 204

Sekhmet, Egyptian Fire Goddess, 203

Sekhovet, 218

Sekker, Sun God, 254

Selangor, flag of, 19

Selinus, coins of, 75

Seltman, Charles, *Masterpieces of Greek Coinage*, 75

Senworsi I, obelisk of, 285

Separation, symbol of, 348

Sepoy, 85

Seraph (and Seraphim), 311

Seringapatam, 85

Serpent, 215–17, 220, 230, 235–6, 239, 256, 289, 293, 311, 313–14; in eagle's beak, 75; Moses' serpent of brass, 220

Sérusier, Paul, 146

Servius, 310

Set square, 86

Severus, Alexander, 221; Septimus, coins of, 77; arch of, 206

Sex, organs, female, 156–7, 163–4, 257–8; male, 156–7, 163–4, 294; instinct, 125–8; organs symbolized in dreams, 128; act, 150; allurement or attraction, 156–7, 163–4; symbols of, 162–4

Shaftesbury, Lord, memorial fountain, 246

Shakespeare, William, 10, 97, 101; *A Midsummer Night's Dream*, 258; *The Tempest*, 258; *Henry VIII*, 265; *Hamlet*, 291, 293, 303; *Winter's Tale*, 303; *Romeo and Juliet*, 305

Shamrock, 314; Irish, or lesser yellow trefoil (*Trifolium mimus*), 314

Shankle, George Earlie, *State Names, Flags, Seals, Rings, Birds, Flowers and other Symbols*, 42, 59, 204, 215, 265, 301, 345

Sharp, David, *The Cambridge Natural History*, 307

Sheep, 227; and shepherd, 315–16

Sheffield, arms of, 64, 66

Shell, scallop, 73, 314–15

Shell Company, 175; memorial, *Plate XLVI*

Shelley, P. B., 11; armorial bearings of family, 23

Shepard, Odell, *The Lore of the Unicorn*, 356

Shepherd, with goat, 38; and sheep, 227, 315–16; Good, statue of, *Plate LXXIII*

Shield, heraldic, 40, 58; of Athena, 77; of David, *242*, 246, 255; of England, 40; of Hanover, 23; of Hêrakles, 75; of Minerva, 43; of Oxford, 61

Ship, 316–17

Shipley, O., *Glossary of Ecclesiastical Terms*, 288

Shop signs, 96–103, 104, 105, *Plate XXII*

Siam, 342

Sicily, coins of, 75; badge of, 341–2

Sickle, *310*

Sidon, 76

Siena, 147; painters of, 180

Sierra Nevada, 43

Signals, Royal Corps of, badge of, *28*

Signet ring, 37

Simon, Thomas, 83

Simpson & Bodman, trade mark, 95

Sirens, 317

Siva, Hindu god, 339; worship of, 294

Skipton (Yorkshire), 243

Skull, 308, 317

Sky, arch of, 168, 205–6

Sky god, 168, 204

Sleep, symbol of, 297

Slumberland, trade mark, 92

Smartness, symbol of, 305

Smeltzing, John, 84

Smith, G. Eliot, *The Evolution of the Dragon*, 236

Smith, Robertson, *Religion of the Semites*, 335

Snake, 215, 300, 311, 313–14; symbol of wisdom, 311, 313

Snowdrop, 267

Solitude, symbol of, 252, 342

Somellini, Francesco, medal of, 82

Somerset, arms of County Council, 236

Song, achievement in, 340

South Africa, national flower of, 298; national emblem of, 319

South Carolina, seal of, *46*; state flower of, 260; state tree of, 291; state bird of, 351

South Dakota, seal of, *55*; state flower of, 291; state bird of, 294

South Wales Borderers, 27, 319; badge of, *26*

Sovereignty, symbol of, 76, 77, 226–7

Space, sense of, 181, 317–8; representation of, *Plate LV*

Spain, 83, 257; Imperial Eagle of, 25; Philip of, 83; emblem of, 269; patron saint of, 314–15

Speedway, trade mark, 92
Spencer, Herbert, 152, 159; *Principles of Psychology*, 16; *Principles of Sociology, Ceremonial Institutions*, 132, 150, 152, 155, 159, 194, 195, 309, 310, 330, 342, 356
Spenser, Edmund, *Prothalamion*, 326
Sperandio, 82
Sphinx, 27, *30*, 174, 198, 239, 318–19
Spiral, 319
Spire, 319
Sports trophies, 5
Spring, symbol of, 194, 250
Springbok, 319
Spurs, 319–20
Square nimbus, 282
Squirrel, 68, 69
Stability, symbol of, 142
Stäel, Madame de, on angels, 202
Stag, 68
Stamps, *see* Postage stamps
Standard, 17, 18; Roman, 224, 235–6; Royal, 19, 79
Stanley, Dr., *History of Birds*, 324
Stanley, Dr. H. M., 157; *Through the Dark Continent*, 164
Starfish, 108
Starkey, Frank, Ltd., trade mark, of, 88
Stars, 320; on flag of U.S.A., 20
State, symbolism of the, 137–9
Status, symbol of, 154
Steadfastness, symbol of, 284
Stevenage, arms of, *70*
Stock Exchange, 212
Stocks, Humphrey, 98
Stoke-on-Trent, arms of, 64, 66, *69*
Stone, 320–3; boundary, 333; sacred, 335; white, 350
Stork, 323–4
Stourbridge, 243
Strength, symbol of, 247, 256, 257, 267, 284
Strong, Mrs. Eugenie, 179
Stuart, family standard, 23; coinage, 79
Stupa, 324, *Plate LXXV*
Submission, symbol of, 150, 151, 152
Suffering, symbol of, 292
Suffolk, Duchess of, Princess Mary, 61
Suffolk Regiment, 27
Sun, 325; on flags, 20; God, 239, 253–4, 285, 307; symbol of, 248, 253–4, 269, 270, 280, 282, 285, 294, 326, 328, 341, 348–9; worship, 280, 285–6, 325
Sundial, 325

Sunflower (*Helianthus annus*), *312*, 325–6, Plate XL
Sunlight, trade mark, 105
Super-ego, 127–8, 183
Supremacy, symbol of, 160, 220, 320
Surrealism, 177, 183, 184
Surrender, symbol of, 151, 250
Susa, 235
Swallow, 203
Swan, 24, 97, 101; trade mark, 92; white, 326; Order of the, 326
Swastika, *308*, 326, 328–9
Sweden, 275; postage stamps of, 326; symbol of, 326
Swift, wings of, 217
Swinburne, 23; *Garden of Proserpine*, 298
Swindon, arms of, 64, 66, *67*
Switzerland, Pestalozzi village in, 261
Sword, 329–30; Crusaders', of liberation, 29, 31; broken, 39; and scales, 61; of St. Paul, 174
Sydney, family coat of arms, 209
Symbolism, Types of, 5
Syracuse, Damareteion of, 75; coins of, 341
Syria, cylinder seals of, 36; coins of, 341
Syringa, *Plate XXXIX*

Tabernacle, 330
Tacitus, 294
Talmud, account of Adam and Eve in the, 158
Tammiz, God of Corn, 36
Tanen, Egyptian god, 237
Taverna, Francesco, Count of Sandriano, medal of, 82
Tchekhov, *The Seagull*, 185–6, 190
Teacher, symbol of, 81
Templars, badge of, 261; emblem of, 339
Temple, 330–1
Tennessee, seal of, *48*; state flower of, 258; state bird of, 276
Tenniel, Sir John, 212
Tennyson, Alfred Lord, *Enoch Arden*, 197
Tent, 331
Tertullian, 134, 135; *De Baptismo*, 209, 243
Texas, seal of, *51*; state flower of, 270; state bird of, 276; state tree of, 293
Thaloc, Weather God, symbol of, 224
Thanatos, winged figure of, 216
Thanksgiving, symbol of, 194
Theatre, symbolism in the, 185*f*
Thebes, coins of, 75; god of, 299

Thermocontrol Installations Co. Ltd., trade mark, *93*

Thistle, 331–2; with crown, 39; Scottish, 99, 331

Thomas, Edward, 329; *Numismatic Chronicle*, 229

Thomas, N. W., article on animals in Hastings' *Encyclopaedia of Religion and Ethics*, 203

Thomson, J. E. H., *see* Ewing W.

Thomson, Theresa Emily, *By Law this Bouquet*, 272

Thor, 66; Hammer of, 328

Thorns, crown of, 292

Thoth, 230

Thotmes III, obelisks of, 286; sphinx of, 318

Three golden balls, 332

Thrift, 298; clump of, 79

Throne, 332

Thrones, 199, 200, 332–3

Thunder, symbol of, 210, 211, 230, 235, 245, 340

Thunderbolt, symbol of Zeus, 75, 84

Thwaites Engineering Co. Ltd., trade mark, *94*

Thyrsus, 333

Tiara, 332

Tiberius, 204, 221

Tiepolo, 87

Time, symbol of, 4, 99, 258, *259*, *308*, 310, 325, 348–9; figure of, 174, 175, *308*, 310

Times, The, 6, 106, 108, 271; posters, *Plate XXIX*; *Times Literary Supplement*, 190

Tipu Sahib, 85

Titian, 143, 200

Titus, arch of, 204

Tools and instruments of professions, crafts and trades, 333–4

Tope, 324

Torch, 334; inverted, 334

Torquay, arms of, 69

Tortoise, 203; symbol of Aphrodite, 74

Totem, 16, 17, 334; theories of origin, 16, 17; dances, 334; poles, *Plate I*

Toulouse-Lautrec, 105

Trade marks, 87–95

Trade Marks Act, 1938, 91

Trajan, 207, 221–2

Treasure, Guardian of, 236, 251

Tree, 334–7, 339, *338*, *Plate LXXVI*; of Knowledge, 204; of Life, 311, 345; Worship, 296, 334–7

Trescele, *see* Triscele

Trezzo, Jacopo da, 82

Triangle, 239, 243, 246; equilateral, 255, 282, 339

Tribe, symbol of, 17

Trident, 339–40; as symbol of Poseidon, 75, 247

Tripod, 340–1

Triscele (or Triskele), 95, 229, 341–2

Triskelion, *see* Triscele

Trisula, *see* Triscele

Triton, 64

Triumph, symbol of, 264

Trophies, 77, 154, 158–61, 309, 329

Trout, South Fork Golden (*Salmo aquabonita*), 342

Truce, symbol of, 350

Trumpington, family coat of arms, 7

Truth, symbol of, 133

Ts'in, Shihuang-ti, Emperor, 5

Tudor, coins, 78

Tudor Rose, 27, 61, 78, 83; crowned, 25

Tulip tree (*Liriodendron tulipifera*), 342

Tumble-Togs, trade mark, 92

Tunbridge Wells, shield of, 73

Tunnicliffe, C. F., 111

Turkey, 212, 223; flag of, 19, 223

Turks, Ottoman, symbol of, 223, 257

Turner, Reginald, *The Spotted Dog*, 103

Twining, Louise, *Symbols and Emblems of Early and Medieval Christian Art*, 196, 197, 234, 269, 277, 282, 283, 316, 348, 356

Twins, The, Gemini, 353

Tylor, E. B., 131, 336, *The Winged Figures of the Assyrian and other Ancient Monuments*, 198, 202; *Primitive Culture*, 130

Uazit, 230

Uccello, Paolo, 147

Ulysses, 210

Umbrella, 161, 342

Unconscious symbolism, 125*f*

Unicorn, 39, 61, 84, 98, 101, 239, 250 *338*, 342–3; of Scotland, 25; as symbol of virginity, 81

Union, symbol of, 252, 301–2

Union 'Jack', 19, 78, 79

Union of Soviet Socialist Republics, flag of, 20

United Kingdom, arms of, 39

United States of America, 42–59, 137–8, 204, 214, 217, 236, 249; badges of, 35, 34–5; flags of, 20; seals of, 42–59; state

United States of America (*contd.*)
flowers of, *Plates XXXIX, XL. See also*
under separate state names
Universe, symbol of, 334–6, 353–4; tree,
336
Ur, ancient dynasty of, 36
Uraeus-Serpent, 254
Urn, 343–4, *Plate LXXVII*
Utah, seal of, *56*; state flower of, 267;
state bird of, 310
Utchat, 238

Vajra, 224
Valentine, 247
Valentinian, 221
Value, symbol of, 248
Van Dyck, 87, 200
Van Eyck, 200; *Adoration of the Lamb*,
263
Vase, 344–5
Vastmanland, Sweden, emblem of, 275
Veery Bird (*Hylocichla fuscescens*), 345
Velasquez, 200; *Crucifixion*, 228, *Plate LX*
Venable, E., *Smith's Dictionary of
Christian Antiquities*, 282–3
Venus, *see* Aphroditê
Veralli, Girolamo, Papal Nuncio, medal of,
82
Vermont, seal of, *48*; state flower of, 220
Veronese, Paolo, *Adoration of the Magi*,
180, *Plate LIV*
Verulam family, coat of arms of, 251
Vesica Piscis, *see* Mandorla and Fish
Vestments, 41, 154, 160–1
Veterinary Corps, Royal Army, badge of,
28
Vicissitudes of life, symbol of, 348
Victoria, Queen, 23, 85; seals of, 40; coins
of, 79; medals of, 84
Victory, 39, 175, 229, 279, 287; banner of,
261; symbols of, 75, 226–7, 236–7, 249,
264, 279, 311; sun of, 85; winged figure
of, 75, 77, 85, 221
Vigilance, symbol of, 220
Vine, 345, *Plates LXXI, LXXVII*; of
Maronea, 75; leaves, 96, 258, 345; tree,
337
Vine Products Ltd., trade mark, *89*
Violet, 345, *346*, 347, *Plate XL*; *viola
pedate*, 345; *viola cucollata*, 345
Virgil, 97; *Aeneid*, 352
Virginia, seal of, *47*, 58; state flower of, 231
Virginity, symbol of, 81, 227, 265–6
Virgins, symbol of, 326

Virgo the Virgin, 353
Virtues, angelic rank, 347; kingly, symbol
of, 332
Virtus, 58
Volkelt, J., *System der Asthetik*, 173
Vulcan (Hêphaestus), 66, 101, 248

Wagner, Anthony, *Heraldry in England*, 11
Wakefulness, symbol of, 194
Waldemar, King of Denmark, 19
Wales, symbol of, 86, 228, 236, 240, 265,
343; Prince of, 240; Princess of, 25
Walserobin (*Trillium grandiflorum*), 347
Walter, Winifred, *All Plants of the Bible*,
267
Wang Fu, 235
War, God of, 246, 247; dance, 150;
trophies of, 159
Waring, 329
Warton, Thomas, *Ode to Sleep*, 298
Warwickshire Regiment, Royal, badge of,
28
Washington, seal of, *55*; state flower of, 301
Watchfulness, symbol of, 194
Water, 347–8; symbol of, 329; carrier,
Aquarius the, 353
Waterloo, battle of, 85
Watteau, *Fêtes Galantes*, 143
Watts, G. F., 181, 258, 325; *Life's Illusion*,
181; *Love and Life*, 181; *Love and Death*,
181; *The Angel of Death*, 181; *Time,
Death and Judgement*, 181; *Hope*, 181
Wealth, symbol of, 160, 248, 289, 351
Weaving, symbol of, 64, 66
Webster & Co. (Fernbank) Ltd., trade
mark of, *88*
Wellbeing, symbol of, 256
Welles, Orson, *Citizen Kane*, 188, 190
Wellington, Duke of, 85, 101, 207, 221
Westermark, Edward, *The History of
Human Marriage*, 156, 158, 302, 355;
*The Origin and Development of the
Moral Ideas*, 355
West Virginia, seal of, *53*; state tree of,
272; state flower of, 301
Western Australia, emblem of, 260
Westminster Abbey, 23, 319
Wheat, 348
Wheatsheaf, 58, 66, 86, 348
Wheel, 348–9; potter's, 66; sun symbol of,
276, 348–9; winged, 66, 349
Wheel cross, *327*
Wheel of the Doctrine, *Plate LXXVII*
Whitbread, advertisements, 109

White, 349–50
Whitehead, A. N., 7, 8, 11, 91, 129, 130; *Symbolism: its Meaning and Effect*, 3; *Uses of symbolism*, 8
Whittick, Arnold, *History of Cemetery Sculpture*, 229, 257; *Eric Mendelsohn*, 173; *European Architecture in the Twentieth Century*, 173; *War Memorials*, 179
Whittington, Dick, and cat, 35, 101
Widnes, arms of, *67*
Wiedemann, A., *Religion of the Ancient Egyptians*, 230
Wig, 350
Willement, Thomas, *Regal Heraldry, the armorial Insignia of the Kings and Queens of England from Coeval Authorities*, 35
William the Conqueror, 23, 40, 64, 66, 77; seal of, 38, 40, *Plate* V; coins, of, 77
William II (Rufus), Great Seal of, 38, 40
William III (and Mary), 83, 84; coins of, 78; medals of, 83
William IV, seal of, 40; medals of, 84
Willow (*Salix babylonica*), 350–1
Willows Francis Pharmaceutical Products Ltd., 92
Willow tree, trade mark, 92
Wilson, Sir Henry Maitland, 29
Windsor, House of, 25; royal chapel at, 297
Wine, symbol of, 247
Wisconsin, seal of, *52*
Wisdom, snake as symbol of, 61, 311, 313; of God, 200; symbol of, 133; symbol of enigmatic wisdom, 289, 334, 337; divine symbol of, 337
Wit, symbol of, 305
Witch, on broomstick, 31, *32*
Woodford, James, 25
Woodthrush, 351
Woollen industry, 61, 68, 69; symbol of, 64, 66
Woolley, C. Leonard, *The Development of Sumerian Art*, 59
Woolsack, 351

Wordsworth, William, 9, 267, 345
World, symbol of, 288, 334; symbol of Christian domination over the world, 288; tree, 336–7
Wormalds & Walker Ltd., trade mark, 95
Worship, symbol of, 150, 194–5
Worth, symbol of, 305
Wren, Cactus (*Heleodytes brunneicapillus covesi*), 351; Carolina (*Thryothorus ludovicianus*), 351
Wren, Christopher, 221, 297
Wymer, Norman, *English Town Crafts*, 96
Wyoming, seal of, *56*; emblem of, 258; state bird of, 264
Wyon, A., *The Great Seals of England*, 59
Wyon, Thomas, 85
Wyon, W., 85

Xavier Giralt Ltd., trade mark, of, *94*

Yale, 351
Yellowhammer (*Colaptes auratus lateus*), 351–2
Yemen, 152
Yeo, Richard, 85
Yew Tree, 102, 350, 352
Yggdrasil, 336
York, White Rose of, 78; Duke of, 221; House of, 25; Minster, 289
York and Lancaster Regiment, 27; badge of, *26*
Yucca plant, 352, *Plate XL*

Zancle-Messina, coins of, 75
Zeus (Jupiter), Sky God, 37, 42, 75, 84, 133, 205–6, 210–11, 215, 217, 221–2, 223, 236, 239, 248, 264, 274, 300, 305, 309–10, 333, 335, 348, 349, 353; symbols of, 75, 236, 333
Ziggurat, 352–3
Zinnia (*Zinnia elegans*), 352, *Plate XXXIX*
Zion, 350
Zodiac, signs of, 353–4, *Plate LXXVIII*